The Child's World

of related interest

Quality Matters in Children's Services
Messages from Research
Mike Stein
Foreword by Baroness Delyth Morgan
ISBN 978 1 84310 926 6
Quality Matters in Children's Services series

Safeguarding Children Living with Trauma and Family Violence
Evidence-Based Assessment, Analysis and Planning Interventions
Arnon Bentovim, Antony Cox, Liza Bingley Miller and Stephen Pizzey
Foreword by Brigid Daniel
ISBN 978 1 84310 938 9
Best Practice in Working with Children series

Safeguarding Children in Primary Health Care
Edited by Julie Taylor and Markus Themessl-Huber
Foreword by Brigid Daniel
ISBN 978 1 84310 652 4
Best Practice in Working with Childen series

The Survival Guide for Newly Qualified Child and Family Social Workers
Hitting the Ground Running
Helen Donnellan and Gordon Jack
ISBN 978 1 84310 989 1

Learning Through Child Observation
2nd edition
Mary Fawcett
ISBN 978 1 84310 676 0

Good Practice in Safeguarding Children
Working Effectively in Child Protection
Edited by Liz Hughes and Hilary Owen
ISBN 978 1 84310 945 7
Good Practice in Health, Social Care and Criminal Justice series

A Multidisciplinary Handbook of Child and Adolescent Mental Health for Front-line Professionals
2nd edition
Nisha Dogra, Andrew Parkin, Fiona Gale and Clay Frake
ISBN 978 1 84310 644 9

Supporting Children and Families
Lessons from Sure Start for Evidence-Based Practice in Health, Social Care and Education
Edited by Justine Schneider, Mark Avis and Paul Leighton
ISBN 978 1 84310 506 0

The Social Workers Guide to Children and Families Law
Lynn Davis
ISBN 978 1 84310 653 1

The Developing World of the Child
Edited by Jane Aldgate, David Jones, Wendy Rose and Carole Jeffery
Foreword by Maria Eagle MP
ISBN 978 1 84310 244 1

The Child's World

The Comprehensive Guide to Assessing Children in Need

Second Edition

Edited by Jan Horwath

Jessica Kingsley Publishers
London and Philadelphia

First published in 2001 by Jessica Kingsley Publishers. This edition published in 2010
by Jessica Kingsley Publishers
116 Pentonville Road
London N1 9JB, UK
and
400 Market Street, Suite 400
Philadelphia, PA 19106, USA

www.jkp.com

Copyright © NSPCC and the University of Sheffield 2001
Copyright © Jessica Kingsley Publishers 2010

Library of Congress Cataloging in Publication Data
The child's world : the comprehensive guide to assessing children in need / edited by Jan Horwath. -- 2nd ed.
    p. cm.
  Rev. ed. of: The child's world : assessing children in need. 2001.
  Includes bibliographical references and index.
  ISBN 978-1-84310-568-8 (pbk. : alk. paper) 1. Children with social disabilities--Services for--Great Britain. 2.
Abused children--Services for--Great Britain. 3. Needs assessment--Great Britain. 4. Family assessment--Great Britain. 5.
Social work with children--Great Britain. 6. Family social work--Great Britain. I. Basarab-Horwath, Janet Anne, 1952-
  HV751.A6C62 2009
  362.710941--dc22
                            2009013036

British Library Cataloguing in Publication Data
A CIP catalogue record for this book is available from the British Library

ISBN 978 1 84310 568 8

Printed and bound in Great Britain by
MPG Books Limited

Contents

PART III ASSESSING PARENTING CAPACITY AND PARENTING ISSUES

PART IV ASSESSING CULTURAL AND SOCIO-ECONOMIC FACTORS

Acknowledgements

I am indebted to the many people who gave generously of their time and expertise in order to produce this book. First, I would like to acknowledge the contribution of all the authors who produced timely and well-researched chapters. Their patience and willingness to meet deadlines and respond to the comments of the reviewers and myself as editor made editing this book a pleasurable task.

Particular thanks go to those who gave up their time to act as reviewers. As the book is aimed at practitioners and students it seemed appropriate that it was front-line staff and educators who reviewed the chapters. My thanks, therefore, go to the following: my colleagues at the University of Sheffield, Nora McClelland, Joe Smeeton and Peter Castleton. I would also like to thank Fiona Addison for the part she played in recruiting and briefing the following reviewers within Sheffield local authority: Gary Wilson, Christine Bennett, Amy Mathews, Lisa O'Keefe, Anna Gale, Sarah Hazlehurst, Donna Taylor, Karen Barden, Kathleen Paessler, Allie Buckingham, Donna Taylor, Phil Vyse, Denise Bentley, Phil Jones, Jennifer Jessop, Bev Jowett, Sue Wallbridge, Brian Cranswick, Dominic Batten, Liz Sinclair, Vicky Horsefield, Jane Laing, Mohammed Afzaal, Rachel Hope and Bea Kay.

Without the support of the Department for Children, Schools and Families this book would not have been written. Particular thanks goes to Jenny Gray, professional adviser, who provided the contributing authors and myself with invaluable guidance on both policy and practice issues.

Finally, I would like to thank Sue Plummer for providing an efficient administrative service and Stephen Jones at Jessica Kingsley Publishers who has always been encouraging, positive and accommodating.

Introduction

Jan Horwath

Fundamental to establishing the extent of a child's need is a child-centred, sensitive and comprehensive assessment... Assessment processes should build up an increasingly clear understanding of a child's situation over time.

(Lord Laming 2009, pp.28–29, 3.9)

Lord Laming (2009), in *The Protection of Children in England: A Progress Report*, goes on to identify the key components of a high quality assessment for a child in need. These include gathering information in order to have a full understanding of what is happening to the child within the context of both the family and their particular circumstances and the wider community. He also stresses the importance of engaging both the family and the professionals who know the child and their family in gathering and making sense of the information. Assessments of children in need and their families, in both England and Wales, are completed using the *Framework for the Assessment of Children in Need and their Families* (Department of Health *et al.* 2000; National Assembly for Wales and Home Office 2001). The Assessment Framework, as it is commonly referred to, provides statutory guidance to assist practitioners in assessing and planning actions to meet the needs of children and their families where the children are defined as 'children in need' under section 17 of the Children Act 1989. The Assessment Framework is not a procedural manual; rather it is a conceptual framework that takes an ecological approach to identifying the needs of a child and their family.

Since the Assessment Framework was introduced there have been significant research, policy and practice developments that have had a positive impact on practitioners' ability to complete high quality assessments. For example, government polices aimed at both early and sensitive identification of any concerns and timely, appropriate and well co-ordinated provision of services (Cm 5860 2003; Children's Workforce Development Council 2009). There have also been some challenges which have been described in Government reports, for example, about ways in which agencies worked together when children have died or suffered serious injuries as a result of abuse and maltreatment (Brandon *et al.* 2008, 2009; Cm 5730 2003; Cm 7589 2009; Rose and Barnes 2008). Moreover, as practitioners have built up a body of experience of using the Assessment Framework it has become apparent that they require knowledge of a wide range of topics in order to ensure that the assessments remain child focused and meet the needs of the child and their family. Furthermore, professionals with specific knowledge of relevant areas, such as domestic violence and mental health issues, should be involved in the assessments.

In response to the significant policy and practice developments that have taken place since the Assessment Framework was originally introduced and in light of practitioners' experiences of using the Assessment Framework, a new, fully revised version of *The Child's World: Assessing Children in Need* (Horwath 2001) has been produced. This edition is called *The Child's World: The Comprehensive Guide to Assessing Children in Need*. The title reflects the wide range of topics that are considered in this book. Topics have been included to reflect the current assessment challenges encountered by practitioners, as well as recent research, policy and practice developments. All of the authors who have contributed to *The Child's World: The Comprehensive Guide to Assessing Children in Need* are experts in their field and have a thorough understanding of the recent research, policy and practice developments that impact on their particular assessment area. They combine this recent knowledge with research, theory and best practice that has stood the test of time. The contributors also recognise that practitioners frequently assess children and families in complex and challenging circumstances and the task can be, on occasion, both stressful and anxiety provoking. This has been taken into account in the practical guidance that is offered to the reader.

The book is divided into four parts:

- The Assessment Task and Process
- Assessing the Developmental Needs of Children
- Assessing Parenting Capacity and Parenting Issues
- Assessing Cultural and Socio-economic Factors.

The Assessment Task and Process

The first part of the book includes an introductory chapter (Chapter 1) which provides the reader with a brief history of assessment guidance and practice and the policy and practice context that led to the development of the Assessment Framework and its introduction in 2000. Consideration is also given to the policy and practice developments that have taken place since its introduction, including the Children Act 2004. In Chapter 2 Wendy Rose, who was involved in the development of the Assessment Framework, describes the different domains and dimensions of the Framework, the principles underpinning it and the questionnaires and tools that have been introduced to support the assessment of children in need and their families using the Assessment Framework. She also explores the connections between the Assessment Framework, the Common Assessment Framework (HM Government 2008), the Integrated Children's System and other practice developments. Her chapter concludes with a brief description of ways in which the English framework has been adopted and adapted in other countries. In Chapters 3 and 4 the reader is taken through the assessment process. Chapter 3 focuses on ways in which practitioners can prepare for core assessment completion and ways in which information can be gathered. Practical guidance is provided to help social workers, responsible for leading the assessments, to engage not only children and families, but also the diverse range of professionals who have contact with the child and their family. In Chapter 4 attention is given to the critical tasks of analysis, planning and reviewing interventions. Particular consideration is given to ways of making sense of information to inform analysis and decision-making at different stages of the assessment process. The nature of professional judgement and the different types of judgements that practitioners make during an assessment are explored. In Chapter 5 Peter Sidebotham and Mary Weeks take up the theme of inter-agency practice and consider the various ways in which professionals working with children and their families can contribute to the assessment. They outline the different components of a successful inter-agency approach to assessment and discuss some of the barriers to effective inter-agency working and ways in which they can be overcome. In Chapter 6 Sally Holland considers how professionals can engage children and families in the assessment process effectively. She explores the importance of establishing an effective assessment relationship with family members and discusses some of the barriers to achieving this. She also considers the importance and value of engaging fathers as well as mothers in the assessment process. In Chapter 7 Norma Howes continues to explore the importance of engagement, looking at it from a child's perspective. She highlights the factors practitioners should consider when preparing themselves and children for inclusion in the assessment process and identifies methods and resources available for communicating with children. The final chapter in this part, Chapter 8, centres on the role of the supervisor in supervising assessments. Rosemary Gordon and Enid Hendry discuss the important contribution that supervisors can make to ensuring that assessments remain child focused. They consider the key issues and challenges that should be explored in supervision at different stages of the assessment process.

Assessing the Developmental Needs of Children

The developmental needs of children are the focus of the second part of this book. In Chapter 9 Harriet Ward and Danya Glaser begin by considering which children are defined as 'in need' under section 17 of the Children Act 1989. They go on to provide a comprehensive overview of the seven dimensions of children's needs that practitioners should consider as part of the assessment. To assist practitioners assessing a child's needs the authors draw on recent research on brain development to identify factors that can impact adversely on the health and development of a child. In Chapter 10 Robbie Gilligan explores aspects of children's lives that can promote positive outcomes, highlighting the potential that exists in everyday relationships and experiences. He considers ways in which these relationships and experiences can act as protective influences assisting children in dealing with adversity. He concludes with suggestions as to how practitioners can identify these protective factors. David Howe, in Chapter 11, considers why attachments are so important for the wellbeing of the child and the impact the quality of attachment has on the health and development of children. He discusses ways in which practitioners can assess both the caregiver as the attachment figure and the quality of the attachment.

The final five chapters in this part consider the developmental needs of five particular groups. In Chapter 12 Ruth Marchant explores good practice in relation to assessing children with complex needs. She begins by considering what complexity means in this context. She then discusses the circumstances under which assessments are likely to take place for this group of children and explores the value base that should inform the assessment. She identifies how lead person models and integrated working can contribute to effective assessments for children with complex needs. She then moves from the general to the specific exploring the domains of the Assessment Framework: safeguarding issues for children with complex needs and ways of involving children in the assessment process. Chris Dearden and Jo Aldridge discuss the nature of caregiving by young carers in Chapter 13. They consider ways in which practitioners can identify the needs of young carers using the Assessment Framework, specific assessment issues and ways of engaging young carers and their families in the assessment process. The next chapter, Chapter 14, is written by Di Hart about pre-birth assessments. She discusses the purpose and content of an assessment before birth, taking account of the current law and policy regarding unborn children and the ethical and practice dilemmas practitioners encounter. In Chapter 15 Arnon Bentovim considers assessing the needs of children and young people who have been sexually abused. Whilst the focus of this chapter is on sexual abuse, it is also useful for practitioners assessing children who have suffered other forms of abuse and neglect. For example, this chapter includes a section on making sense of information gathered using the domains and dimensions of the Assessment Framework, using cycles of positive and harmful parenting. He begins by defining child sexual abuse, and identifying harm from possible sexual abuse, factors associated with the risk of re-abuse and the prognosis for intervention. Finally Chapter 16 explores another aspect of sexual abuse: young people who sexually abuse. In this chapter Bobbie Print, Helen Bradshaw, James Bickley and Marcus Erooga provide a way of understanding a young person's motivation to sexually abuse, outline the importance of a strengths-based assessment approach and review the newly designed AIM2 assessment model. They conclude by considering how an assessment using AIM2 can contribute to a core assessment using the *Framework for the Assessment of Children in Need and their Families* (Department of Health *et al.* 2000).

Assessing Parenting Capacity and Parenting Issues

The third part of the book is about parenting capacity and the parenting issues that may impact on parenting capacity. David Jones begins in Chapter 17 by considering the assessment of parenting. This includes exploring contemporary perspectives on parenting and what children need from their caregivers. He goes on to consider in detail how to assess parenting, making use of observation, assessment tools and interviews with parents and children. Jones also pays attention to assessing parenting in cases of suspected abuse and neglect. He argues that a crucial aspect when assessing parenting capacity is the assessment of a parent's motivation to change if their care is not meeting the needs of their child. This is the focus of Chapter 18 which has been written by Tony Morrison, in which he discusses the concept of motivation and its fit with constructs of parenting, and outlines a model of change and the seven stages of contemplation. He also describes the concept of motivational dialogue and the impact of the assessor's interviewing style on the assessment of parental motivation. The final chapter in this part, Chapter 19, written by Nicky Stanley, Hedy Cleaver and Di Hart, is divided into four parts with each part focusing on a different parenting issue: drug and alcohol misuse; learning disabilities; mental health issues; and domestic violence. The authors consider the commonalities and differences in relation to assessing the impact of these issues on a carer's ability to meet the needs of their child.

Assessing Cultural and Socio-economic Factors

The final part of this book takes the reader beyond the family to consider the interface between the child, the family and the environment. In Chapter 20 Ratna Dutt and Melanie Phillips discuss assessing the needs of children and their families, taking diversity into account. Particular attention is given to assessing children in families from minority ethnic groups and where religion is significant to the family. In Chapters 21 and 22 Gordon Jack and Owen Gill consider the socio-economic factors that practitioners should take into account when assessing children in need and their families. In Chapter 21 they consider the subjective meaning of poverty and income equality for children and families and identify those at greatest risk of poverty, describing the impact it has on their lives. They also think about the influence of other factors such as housing and geographical location. In Chapter 22 they discuss the importance of informal social support for parents or caregivers and children, and support from community organisations and faith communities. They consider the role of wider family networks and caregivers' relationships with friends and neighbours and the social world of the child outside of the family.

Target readership

This new edition has been written specifically for a multidisciplinary audience. As can be seen from the description of the contents of this book, it is a comprehensive and valuable guide to assessing children in need. It also provides a helpful and important resource for practitioners who are responsible for co-ordinating the assessment, such as social workers, and for practitioners who are likely to be involved in contributing to an assessment of a child's needs because of their knowledge of the child, the parent or carer or the family and community network. Assessments of children in need require contributions from practitioners working in both children's and adult services: the authors have therefore considered the topics they cover from both perspectives. Thus the book should prove valuable for practitioners in terms of increasing their understanding not only of their own roles and responsibilities, but also those of others who are likely to be involved in an assessment using the *Framework for the Assessment of Children in Need and their Families* (Department of Health *et al.* 2000).

As described above, this book has been written primarily to support practitioners using the *Framework for the Assessment of Children in Need and their Families* (Department of Health *et al.* 2000). However, the chapters have been written to take into account the needs of practitioners undertaking assessments in all jurisdictions. Therefore, irrespective of the policy, procedures and frameworks utilised by practitioners and their managers, this book should assist those practitioners and their managers who wish to complete high quality child focused assessments.

Professional practice builds on knowledge from theory and research gained during professional training. With this in mind, the material in this book is of significant relevance to students completing social work, health, social care and education qualifying and post-qualifying training. Not only will it help students in terms of their academic studies, but will also provide valuable guidance to assist students completing practice placements. Students should find the recommended reading at the end of each chapter particularly useful in directing them towards texts for more in-depth study.

The Child's World: The Comprehensive Guide to Assessing Children in Need has also been written to inform training and staff development on assessment using the Assessment Framework. Trainers and educators will find the book useful for accessing the underpinning knowledge required for knowledge and skills development on particular assessment topics. The chapters provide valuable material that can also be used to prepare handouts. As the book has been written for a multidisciplinary audience the content will prove invaluable to inter-agency as well as in-house trainers.

Lord Laming made clear (Cm 5730 2003; Lord Laming 2009) that senior and middle managers must have an understanding of quality front-line practice in order to satisfy themselves that members of their organisations are working effectively to meet the needs of children and their families. This book provides managers with a very clear overview of high quality practice related to assessing children in need and their families. It is anticipated that managers will use this knowledge to provide the resources, operational context, supervision and support to practitioners to enable them to complete high quality, child focused assessments.

To summarise, the authors hope that this book will be a useful resource to practitioners when assessing children in need in what can be difficult, complex and stressful circumstances; to managers responsible for providing an environment conducive to producing high quality child focused assessments; and to educators and staff development officers who are tasked with developing the knowledge and skills of those in contact with children and families. We trust that readers not only find the book a useful resource, but also enjoy reading it.

References

Brandon, M., Belderson, P., Warren, C., Howe, D. *et al.* (2007) *Analysing Child Deaths and Serious Injury through Abuse and Neglect: What Can We Learn? A Biennial Analysis of Serious Case Reviews 2003–2005.* London: Department for Education and Skills.

Brandon, M., Bailey, S., Belderson, P., Gardner, R. *et al.* (2009) *Understanding Serious Case Reviews and their Impact. A Biennial Analysis of Serious Case Reviews 2005–7.* DCSF-RB129. London: Department for Children, Schools and Families. Available at www.dcsf.gov.uk/research/programmeofresearch/projectinformation.cfm?project id=15743&resultspage=1, accessed 19 August 2009.

Children's Workforce Development Council (2009) *The Common Assessment Framework for Children and Young People: A Guide for Practitioners.* Available at www.dcsf.gov.uk/everychildmatters/strategy/deliveringservices/caf, accessed on 9 August 2009.

Cm 5730 (2003) *The Victoria Climbié Inquiry Report.* London: The Stationery Office.

Cm 5860 (2003) *Every Child Matters.* Green Paper. London: The Stationery Office.

Cm 7589 (2009) *The Protection of Children in England: Action Plan. The Government's Response to Lord Laming.* London: Department for Children, Schools and Families.

Department of Health, Department for Education and Employment and Home Office (2000) *Framework for the Assessment of Children in Need and their Families.* London: The Stationery Office.

Horwath, J. (ed) (2001) *The Child's World: Assessing Children in Need.* London: Jessica Kingsley Publishers.

Lord Laming (2009) *The Protection of Children in England: A Progress Report.* London: The Stationery Office.

National Assembly of Wales and Home Office (2001) *The Framework for Assessing Children in Need and their Families.* London: The Stationery Office.

Rose, W. and Barnes, J. (2008) *Improving Safeguarding Practice: Study of Serious Case Reviews 2001–2003.* London: Department for Children, Schools and Families.

PART I
The Assessment Task
and Process

CHAPTER 1

Assessing Children in Need: Background and Context

Jan Horwath

In this chapter the following are considered:

- the Children Act 1989 in practice

- policy developments shaping assessment practice

- the implementation of the *Framework for the Assessment of Children in Need and their Families*

- *Every Child Matters* and the Children Act 2004: broadening the assessment focus.

Introduction

Lord Laming concluded in his Inquiry Report into the death of Victoria Climbié that none of the professionals who had come into contact with the eight-year-old understood what a day in Victoria's life was like (Cm 5730 2003, p.3, 1.16). Yet, understanding what daily life is like for a child is crucial in order to identify and meet his or her needs. Victoria died in February 2000. Later the same year the Government published, in England, its assessment guidance, the *Framework for the Assessment of Children in Need and their Families* (the Assessment Framework) (Department of Health *et al.* 2000), with an implementation date of 1 April 2001. The guidance is based on an ecological model, which emphasises the importance of understanding the world of the child. That is, knowing what is happening to the child within their family and the community in which they live. This chapter begins by considering the policy, research and practice which informed the development of the Assessment Framework. The second part of the chapter explores recent policy developments which set the current context for assessment practice.

The Children Act 1989 in practice

Underpinning current child welfare practice in England are two key Acts: the Children Act 1989 and the Children Act 2004. The former is considered here; the latter will be considered in more detail later in the chapter. The Children Act 1989 includes the concept of a 'child in need' in Part III, section 17. This part of the Act emphasises the importance of family support services designed to both safeguard and promote the welfare of the child and assist parents in bringing up their children. Parts IV and V of the Act relate to the local authority's duty to protect a particular group of children in need: those suffering from, or likely to suffer from, significant harm. Part V provides the legal steps which may be taken to protect a child at risk of, or suffering, significant harm. One of the principles underpinning the 1989 Act is that for the majority of children their family is the most appropriate place for them to be brought up, and that parents should retain responsibility for the upbringing of their children. Despite the legislation, providing support to families whilst safeguarding children from harm proved to be a challenge for service providers and practitioners in the 1990s.

Providing support to families and safeguarding children

Through the Children Act 1989, local authorities are required to support and work with parents and carers to meet the needs of their children; that is, promoting their welfare whilst at the same time safeguarding children from harm. However, research studies and reports completed in the 1990s indicated that local authorities struggled to achieve both at the same time. For example, Aldgate and Tunstill (1996) found priority given to children perceived to be at risk of significant harm. This study reinforced the findings of the *Children Act Report 1993* (Department of Health 1994) that section 17 was not being fully implemented according to the spirit of the 1989 Act. The *Children Act Report* recommended a shift to a more positive partnership between families and service providers, with the provision of services aimed at preventing family breakdown. The Audit Commission (1994) supported this, recommending the emphasis should be not only on assisting children whose health and development may be *significantly* impaired without the provision of services, but also assisting those children whose health and development *may be* impaired without the provision of services designed to support carers in meeting the needs of these children and young people.

Whilst local authorities tended to focus on children suffering or likely to suffer significant harm, an overview report summarising the key findings from 20 research studies commissioned by the Department of Health – *Child Protection: Messages from Research* (Department of Health 1995) – indicated that services provided to this group of children did not always meet their needs. Key findings from the studies indicated:

- emphasis within the child protection system on section 47 enquiries rather than planning and carrying out interventions to meet the needs of these children (section 47 enquiries are undertaken when there are concerns a child is suffering, or at risk of suffering, significant harm) (Farmer and Owen 1995; Hallett 1995)

- enquiries tended to be incident focused (Gibbons *et al.* 1995a); yet, a negative environment, particularly one of low warmth and high criticism, was found to be far more damaging than an isolated incident of physical abuse (Gibbons *et al.* 1995b)

- more than half of the families who are filtered out of the system prior to the child's name being placed on the then child protection register[1] received no services (Gibbons *et al.* 1995a)

- the section 47 process can alienate and anger parents (Farmer and Owen 1995; Thoburn *et al.* 1995).

Other studies and inspections, completed in the 1990s, supported these findings (see for example Calder and Horwath 1999; Social Services Inspectorate 1997a; 1997b). Additional studies also highlighted that disabled children are more vulnerable to child maltreatment and yet formed a disproportionately small number of children placed on the child protection register (Westcott 1993). Researchers also found an under-representation of children from Asian communities (Luthera 1997), compared to over-representation of African-Caribbean children, on both child protection registers and in the numbers of children looked after by the local authority (Armstrong 1995; Luthera 1997).

Assessment practice in the 1980s and 1990s

Until the late 1970s assessment was generally perceived to be a task that was undertaken when children were received into the care of the local authority. However, in 1981 a working party on observation and assessment recommended that a broader approach should be taken incorporating assessments for all children who required 'special help' (Department of Health and Social Security 1981, p.2, cited in Gray 2002). Despite the responsible government department advocating a broader approach in the early 1980s, the first government practice guidance on assessment was not produced until 1988. The guidance – *Protecting Children: A Guide for Social Workers Undertaking a Comprehensive Assessment* (Department of Health 1988) – was designed to standardise assessment practice for one group of children who needed special help: children on the child protection register who required comprehensive assessments to inform long-term plans. This guidance became known as the 'Orange Book'. It was produced in response to concerns about the lack of structured social work assessment and planning, which was an issue raised consistently in social services inspections and inquiry reports following the deaths of children from maltreatment (Department of Health 1991; Department of Health and Social Security 1982, 1985).

---

1   A register held by local authorities of those children who are believed to be suffering, or likely to suffer, significant harm and therefore require a multidisciplinary child protection plan (Home Office *et al.* 1991).

The Orange Book provided a much needed, structured assessment framework, and continues to offer a helpful resource to inform assessments. Despite this useful material, concerns arose in the 1990s about the way in which the Orange Book was being used. Some practitioners used it as a checklist, which was not the original intention. Others, although completing comprehensive assessments, did not use the findings from these assessments as a basis for planning and assessment. In sum, assessment practice varied considerably amongst social workers (Katz 1997; Social Services Inspectorate 1997b).

Whilst the Orange Book was available as a guide for assessing and planning interventions in cases of child maltreatment, there was no standardised framework available for gathering information and assessing children in need. This resulted in a lack of standardisation and consistency within and between local authority social services departments (Department of Health 2001; Social Services Inspectorate 1997a). Moreover, when assessments of need were completed these were often perfunctory leading to inadequate responses (Department of Health 2001; Social Services Inspectorate 1997a). Having identified these issues the Social Services Inspectorate recommended that services should be provided on the basis of an assessment of need and the information gathered should inform planning. In addition, assessments should include the views of children and their families as well as information from agencies in contact with the family. With regard to process, the Inspectors recommended identified timescales for completing assessments. They also highlighted the importance of clear and accurate recording and regular supervision, monitoring and training (Department of Health 2001).

The family and the community

It was not only the process of assessment that was criticised in the 1990s but also the focus of assessments. A narrow focus on child abuse incidents, and immediate protection and safety, meant that insufficient attention was given to assessing parents' ability to meet the child's specific needs in the longer term.

In order to assess parenting capacity one has to understand the carer's situation. During the 1990s there was a growing awareness amongst practitioners that a diverse range of factors influence a carer's ability and motivation to meet the needs of their child. For example, Falkov (1996) completed a study of child deaths which highlighted the importance of both child welfare workers, and other professionals who work with carers, being aware of ways in which mental health issues can have an impact on parenting capacity. Other researchers noted a high level of domestic violence in families referred to local authority social work services (Farmer and Owen 1995; Thoburn et al. 1995). Cleaver et al. (1999), in their overview of the research findings on parenting issues, concluded that not only mental health issues and domestic violence but other parenting issues, such as drug and alcohol misuse and learning disabilities, could impact on parenting capacity.

A narrow focus of assessment and intervention was also found to reinforce an individualistic model of understanding maltreatment (Stevenson 1998). This individualistic approach meant that assessment was concentrated on the family with the positive and negative influences of the family network and the community being marginal to the core business of child protection practice (Jack 1997). Yet, as with parenting issues, there was a growing awareness, during the latter part of the 1990s, of the impact of factors such as social isolation, poverty, unemployment and racism on family life and the parents' ability to meet the needs of their child (Goodman *et al.* 1997; Gregg *et al.* 1999; HM Treasury 1999; Quinton 2004). For further information see Chapters 21 and 22.

Inter-agency child welfare practice

The needs of children and their families are multifaceted, hence one professional cannot be expected to identify all their needs as well as the particular issues that may impact on parenting or family functioning. With this in mind, it is not surprising that since 1945 there have been 'rumblings' about the importance of co-ordination (Stevenson 2000). Statutory guidance to assist practitioners was issued in 1988 in *Working Together: A Guide to Arrangements for Inter-agency Co-operation for the Protection of Children from Abuse* (Department of Health and Social Security 1988). Updated guidance – *Working Together under the Children Act 1989: A Guide to Arrangements for Inter-agency Cooperation for the Protection of Children from Abuse* (Home Office *et al.* 1991) – was subsequently issued to accompany the introduction of the Children Act 1989. (This guidance has since been revised in 1999 and 2006, and at the time of writing this book is in the process of being revised again (Department of Health *et al.* 1999; HM Government 2006b).)

Working Together provided a framework to enable a co-ordinated response from professionals to identify and meet the needs of those children who are suffering or likely to suffer significant harm. However, whilst subsequent guidance increasingly emphasised the importance of inter-agency working, it has proved hard to achieve. A poor understanding by practitioners of their own role and that of others, and a lack of commitment to inter-agency working, have been highlighted, consistently, in research studies, inspections and inquiry reports as barriers to effective practice (Armstrong 1996, 1997; Department of Health 1995; Department of Health and Social Security 1982; Hallett and Birchall 1992; Joint Chief Inspectors 2002; Rose and Barnes 2008). In relation to multidisciplinary assessment practice, common issues identified in the 1990s included: variations in the quality of information that is selected and shared amongst practitioners; conflicting perspectives on harm; and variations in threshold criteria informing decisions regarding significant harm or children in need (Department of Health 2001; Reder *et al.* 1993; Scott 1997).

To summarise, by the mid to late 1990s there was a growing concern that assessments of children in need tended to be incident-driven and focused on immediate safety. This narrow focus resulted in children and families, who would have benefited from services, being filtered out of the welfare system without having received any help. The narrow focus also meant that wider issues, such as drug misuse, parental mental health issues or socio-economic factors, which can affect a parent or carer's ability to meet the needs of a child, were marginalised. Finally, whilst there was an expectation that identifying the needs of children would be a multidisciplinary task, there was a lack of clarity amongst professionals as to how they should contribute to assessments. The net result was significant variations in practice across the country.

Assessing children in need: policy developments in the late 1990s

When the Labour Government came into power in 1997 it was keen to improve the quality of life for children and their families, most particularly vulnerable children. The Green Paper *Supporting Families* (Home Office 1998) demonstrated this commitment by outlining funding schemes for new initiatives, such as Sure Start, designed to help and support parents to care for their children. There was also recognition, by the new Government, of the negative effects of poverty on children's health and wellbeing and that a lack of socio-economic resources can impact on the ability of a carer to meet the needs of a child (see Chapter 21). The Government made a commitment to improving the quality of life for vulnerable children and families by various means: in particular reducing child poverty, strengthening communities and reducing social isolation and unemployment through schemes such as the National Childcare Strategy, a New Deal for Communities and Neighbourhood Renewal (Jordan and Jordan 2000; Pugh 2005).

The Government also committed to modernising statutory children's social services. Cumulative recommendations from the reports into child deaths, inspections and findings from research studies informed government thinking about the ways in which services should be altered and modernised. Up to the mid-1990s work with children and families tended to be service-led, rather than based on the needs of the child (NCH Action for Children 1996). In addition, as identified above, initial enquiries and assessments tended to focus on the incident of abuse rather than the developmental needs of the child. This was to change. The introduction of Children's Service Plans in 1996 meant that knowledge of the aggregated developmental needs of children was to determine the services provided by local authorities. The message was clear: do not ignore issues of maltreatment; rather, be mindful that a more integrated approach is required that identifies and meets the needs of all vulnerable children. Moreover, the children's service planning guidance stressed the importance of consulting locally with those requiring and providing services in order to inform service provision. Finally, all plans should be published. The emphasis on consultation with children and families during the planning process addressed earlier concerns identified in *Child Protection: Messages from Research* (Department of Health 1995) and by the Association of Directors of Social Services and the NCH (NCH Action for Children 1996) about organisations failing to identify the wishes and feelings of children and families with regard to which services to provide.

The development of a national assessment framework was announced in September 1998 as part of the Government's broad aim to modernise services and improve outcomes for children in need. The Assessment Framework was regarded as a key element of the Government's *Quality Protects* programme, which aimed to deliver better life chances for vulnerable and disadvantaged children. This five-year programme had a focus on transforming the management and delivery of children's social services. In support of the *Quality Protects* programme, the Government published objectives for children's social services (Department of Health 1999). Improved and timely assessment and ensuring that referral and assessment processes discriminate effectively between different types and levels of need were identified as objectives.

The Framework for the Assessment of Children in Need and their Families

The Assessment Framework, published in 2000, provides national guidance to assist in assessing and planning actions to meet the needs of children defined as 'children in need' under section 17 of the Children Act 1989 and their families. '[It] is not written as a procedure manual setting out step-by-step procedures to be followed, rather, it offers a conceptual framework which can be adapted and used to suit individual circumstances' (Gray 2002, p.172). The Assessment Framework is based on identifying the developmental needs of the child and takes an ecological perspective.

The conceptual framework itself and the principles underpinning the guidance are discussed in detail in Chapter 2. By focusing on the developmental needs of the child, and taking an ecological perspective, the Assessment Framework addressed many of the concerns raised about assessment practice in relation to children in need. The Framework was introduced with a range of materials designed to assist practitioners and their managers in its use. These included practice guidance (Department of Health 2000a), training materials (NSPCC *et al.* 2000), including the first edition of this book (Horwath 2001), assessment recording forms (Department of Health and Cleaver 2000), tools to assist in assessing particular domains and dimensions (Department of Health and Cox and Bentovim 2000) and a book about the studies that had informed the development of the Framework (Department of Health 2001).

In 1999, the Government commissioned a two-year study into the implementation of the Assessment Framework, the assessment records, the costs of assessments and the experiences of children and families (Cleaver *et al.* 2004). Although this study was completed in the early days of implementation, the findings indicated that the use of the Assessment Framework resulted in a more transparent and accountable relationship with the family, and a more focused approach to assessment with increased consultation with the family and other professionals. However, whilst the Framework assisted practitioners in gathering information in a much more coherent manner than previously, the researchers found that many social workers felt anxious and ill-prepared for analysing this information. In order to support analysis the then Department for Education and Skills commissioned the National Children's Bureau to write *Putting Analysis into Assessment* (Dalzell and Sawyer 2007) to assist practitioners in this aspect of their practice.

Policy and practice developments in the early twenty-first century: implications for assessment practice

Since the implementation of the Assessment Framework in 2001, there have been a number of significant policy developments in child welfare which have influenced approaches towards children and families who require assessments to identify their needs. These are considered below.

The Integrated Children's System

As described above, the Assessment Framework provides a standardised approach to assessment. When the Assessment Framework was first introduced assessment records were produced to assist practitioners in gathering, analysing and making sense of information to inform planning and interventions. Whilst these forms assisted practitioners to gather valuable information about the child and family there was no electronic system in place enabling practitioners to systematically retrieve this information to inform future work if, for example, the family was re-referred or children were looked after by the local authority. Moreover, a lack of consistency was noted in terms of the quality of information gathered and the amount of detail included on the assessment records and in case files (Cleaver *et al.* 2004; Horwath 2002). The failure of practitioners to systematically record, retrieve and understand the significance of information on children's files had been an ongoing criticism in inspections and inquiries into child deaths (Cm 5730 2003; Social Services Inspectorate 1997a). The Integrated Children's System (ICS), as part of improving outcomes for children, is designed to improve and standardise recording practice and assist practitioners to collect and record information systematically about the child and their family. This information is stored on an electronic social care record, which is readily accessible to relevant professionals if required for future work with the child and their family.

ICS brings together the Assessment Framework and the Looked After Children System by creating a coherent framework and set of principles to underpin work with all children in need and their families. The development of the system was announced in the Government's response to the Waterhouse Inquiry, *Learning the Lessons* (Department of Health 2000b). The Waterhouse Inquiry had highlighted serious concerns about the care received by looked after children in children's homes and in its response the Government set out ways of improving the quality of care and standardising practice. One of these was to improve the quality of assessment and care planning for looked after children. This can only happen effectively if practitioners are aware of and use salient information from the child's past history (Cleaver *et al.* 2008).

ICS means that irrespective of where children are living and irrespective of the circumstances which bring them and their families into contact with children's social care services, there should be a consistent approach to the processes followed. In addition, the use of ICS should support the development of uniform data sets which can be used for management and strategic planning of children's social care services at local, regional and national levels (Department of Health 2002).

More recently, the Government had written to all local authorities setting out the actions it will take to facilitate immediate improvement in local systems and to support local authorities in making them (Baroness Morgan of Drefelin 2009).

Every Child Matters and the Children Act 2004

The Green Paper *Every Child Matters* (Cm 5860 2003) and the Children Act 2004, which followed it, have had a significant impact on assessment practice. The emphasis is on prevention and identifying early concerns, and broadening the focus of assessment to include children with additional needs. (These are defined as those requiring services over and above universal services (Children's Workforce Development Council 2009).) In addition, the 2004 Children Act and associated guidance have brought about significant changes to the organisational and practice contexts in which assessments of children's needs take place.

The Green Paper *Every Child Matters* was informed by Lord Laming's Inquiry Report into the death of Victoria Climbié (Cm 5730 2003). Victoria was an eight-year-old girl from the Ivory Coast who came to live in England with her aunt. The aunt and her newly acquired boyfriend physically ill-treated and neglected Victoria for months before her death in February 2000. The Green Paper, however, went beyond a focus on children such as Victoria, who were at risk of suffering significant harm, to 'build on existing plans to strengthen preventative services' (Cm 5860 2003, p.4). This was to be achieved by focusing on four themes: increasing the focus on supporting families; ensuring appropriate interventions before a child reaches crisis point and also when they require protection; addressing weak accountability and poor integration of services; and finally ensuring the workforce are valued, rewarded and trained. The *Every Child Matters* programme (HM Government 2004) has resulted in significant changes in the way in which services are planned and delivered at both government and local level. The focus on children and families has been more specific with the creation of a new government post: Minister of State for Children, Young People and Families; a Children's Commissioner for England; a Director for Children's Services; and a lead member for children being required in each of the 152 local authorities in England. In addition, machinery of government changes meant that, in 2007, the Department for Children, Schools and Families was created within which the ministerial post is located.

System changes in line with the four themes of *Every Child Matters* are continuing to have implications for assessment practice, which are explored below. However, before doing so it is helpful to consider the key aim of the Green Paper: to promote better outcomes for all children.

An outcome approach

The incident-driven practice of the 1980s and 1990s, as described earlier in this chapter, led to short-term interventions, with children's social care cases being closed when concerns about the immediate safety of the child were allayed. Little consideration was given as to whether the intervention had positively affected the health and development of the child. However, the introduction of the Assessment Framework shifted the focus of assessment to identifying the developmental needs of the child. In addition, as more attention was being given to prevention and early intervention, meaningful systems were required to measure the effectiveness of these services in relation to meeting the needs of children and their families. Work undertaken in the USA (see, for example, Hogan and Murphy 2002) and in England (Utting *et al.* 2001) focused on identifying what specific outcomes are desired by a community for their children and then identifying how services will both contribute to and be measured on how they are achieving these outcomes. This work informed the Green Paper, which introduced five key national outcomes or goals that 'really matter for children and young people's well-being' (Cm 5860 2003, p.14). The outcomes are:

- being healthy

- staying safe

- enjoying and achieving

- making a positive contribution

- achieving economic wellbeing.

These have recently been reiterated in *The Children's Plan* (Cm 7280 2007; Department for Children, Schools and Families 2008a).

The emphasis on outcomes for children marks a major shift from focusing on processes and outputs to demonstrating how interventions for children contribute to and improve their health, development and quality of life. The five outcomes are relevant from prevention and early interventions through to services for families with complex problems and children at risk of suffering significant harm. These goals for children are compatible with the domains and dimensions of the Assessment Framework. Children will achieve the five outcomes if the developmental needs of each child are met, parents/carers have the capacity to meet their needs and the wider family and environment support both the child and family.

Every Child Matters

Identifying prevention, early intervention and support services for families

In order to identify and meet the additional needs of children who require a level of support over and above universal services, from health, education and the independent sector, the Government introduced a Common Assessment Framework (CAF) (HM Government 2006a) and, currently, an information-sharing system called ContactPoint is being implemented for all children (Department for Children, Schools and Families 2009). The aim is to identify prevention, early intervention and support services for families. ContactPoint will hold core demographic data on every child in England and contact details of practitioners providing most services to the child. (The exceptions are sensitive services, such as sexual health, where contact details are only held with consent.) The information held on ContactPoint will be available to those authorised staff who require it for their work. By identifying, through ContactPoint, who else is working with a child, it is anticipated that practitioners will be able to offer more co-ordinated support to the child and their family.

The Common Assessment Framework for children and young people is a voluntary, shared assessment tool used across agencies in England which draws on the domains and dimensions of the Assessment Framework. It is designed to facilitate assessment of children with additional needs: for example, children displaying disruptive or anti-social behaviour; lack of parental support or boundaries; disabilities; and poor nutrition. These are children who need additional targeted support from health, education and social services or other services over and above that provided by universal services. The aims of the CAF are to develop a shared language of need in order to promote a common understanding of children's needs and for practitioners to agree a process for working together to meet the identified needs early and effectively. The process should be assisted through the appointment of a lead professional who is responsible for co-ordinating the actions identified in the assessment process, and is to be a single point of contact for children with additional needs who are being supported by more than one practitioner (Children's Workforce Development Council 2009).

More recent government initiatives, following the introduction of the Children Act 2004, demonstrate the Government's continuing commitment to identifying and meeting needs of children beyond those eligible for help under section 17 of the Children Act 1989. For example, the Department for Children, Schools and Families (DCSF) published *The Children's Plan: Building Brighter Futures* which sets out the Government's plans for children for the next ten years. It is aimed at 'making this the best place in the world for our children and young people to grow up' (Cm 7280 2007, p.3). This intention is reflected in one of the principles underpinning the Plan and in the progress report: 'children and young people need to enjoy their childhood as well as grow up prepared for adult life' (Cm 7280 2007, p.5; Department for Children, Schools and Families 2008a). The six strategic objectives 'to improve children and young people's lives' include securing the health and wellbeing of children and young people and safeguarding the young and vulnerable; achieving world-class standards; closing the gap in educational achievement for children from disadvantaged backgrounds; ensuring young people are participating and achieving their potential to 18 and beyond; and keeping children and young people on the path to success (Cm 7280 2007, p.15). The *Staying Safe: Action Plan* (HM Government 2008) introduces specific initiatives designed to ensure children are safe to enjoy life, learn and explore within the family and wider community.

Shared assessment processes and service integration

In the few months Victoria Climbié lived in England she was known to three housing authorities, four social services departments, two child protection teams of the Metropolitan Police Service, a NSPCC centre and two different hospitals because of suspected deliberate harm (Cm 5730 2003, p.3, 1.16). Yet, staff working for these services failed to provide a co-ordinated response to identifying and meeting Victoria's needs. Many of the same concerns identified in the 1980s and 1990s about poor inter-agency practice were echoed in the Inquiry Report. For example, these were poor communication, lack of understanding of professional roles, misinterpretation of information shared between professionals and organisational systems that did not facilitate multidisciplinary practice. The Inquiry Report, therefore, recommended better service integration in order to improve multidisciplinary working and highlighted the importance of increased professional accountability at all levels within organisations working with children and families. This issue was addressed in the *Every Child Matters* Green Paper and the subsequent Children Act 2004.

Following the enactment of the Children Act 2004, the Government launched the *Every Child Matters: Change for Children* programme (HM Government 2004), which was designed to enhance inter-agency co-operation to improve the wellbeing of children. It set out a model for change in which integrated services are core at every level. The section 10 statutory guidance, which accompanies the Children Act 2004, sets out how services for children and young people should be both built around their needs and co-ordinated (Department for Children, Schools and Families 2008b). Service integration, in the form of children's trusts, is a key feature of the reforms. The trust brings together local services which work with children and families, such as children's social care services, education, early years and child care provision, with the aim of promoting co-operation to improve wellbeing for children from 0 to 19 years. Local authorities must take the lead and relevant partners (key statutory bodies such as primary care and National Health Service trusts) must co-operate with the authority in making these arrangements. Within the guidance there is also recognition of the importance of engaging a wide group of partners in working with children and young people (Department for Children, Schools and Families 2008c; HM Government 2005).

The children's trust should be outcome and child and family focused. Integration is key to achieving this, requiring integrated front-line services, integrated practice processes and integrated strategies for planning, commissioning and pooling budgets. ContactPoint and the CAF are crucial for having 'the potential to drive multi-agency working by embedding a shared process, developing a shared language of need and improving the information flow between agencies' (HM Government 2005, p.15, 2.23).

Safeguarding children: clarifying roles and responsibilities

A consistent theme in inspections and reports, following the deaths of children from maltreatment, has been weaknesses in inter-agency working to safeguard and promote the welfare of children (Brandon *et al.* 2008, 2009; Ofsted *et al.* 2008). Although, on a more positive note, the Second and Third Joint Chief Inspectors' Reports on *Safeguarding Children* (Joint Chief Inspectors 2005, 2008) have noted improvements in collaborative practice, such as identifying and acting on welfare concerns, and listening and consulting with children. Both the Joint Chief Inspectors' Reports did question, however, the priority given to safeguarding particular groups of children, such as disabled children, young offenders and asylum-seeking children and families.

Guidance on inter-agency working to safeguard and promote the welfare of children has been in existence since 1988 (Department of Health and Social Security 1988) and has been updated in line with policy developments. The most recent guidance (currently being updated) – *Working Together to Safeguard Children* (HM Government 2006b) – outlines how agencies will meet their statutory duties as outlined in the Children Acts of 1989 and 2004, with regard to safeguarding and promoting the welfare of children. In relation to assessment practice, one of the most significant changes is that under section 11 of the 2004 Act many organisations, such as NHS health bodies, Connexions, and probation and prison services, have a statutory duty to make arrangements to ensure their functions are discharged with regard to the need to safeguard and promote the welfare of children. Education services have this duty under section 175 of the Education Act 2002. To fulfil this commitment all organisations are expected to make arrangements to work effectively with other organisations to safeguard and promote the welfare of children. This includes actively contributing to the assessment, planning and intervention processes, which is discussed in detail in Chapters 3 and 4, and having arrangements in place for sharing information (Department for Children, Schools and Families 2008b). Moreover, the Joint Area Review that took place in Haringey following the death of Baby Peter from physical abuse (Ofsted *et al.* 2008) reinforced what is in *Working Together*

(HM Government 2006b), i.e. that staff from front-line practitioners through to senior managers should have the necessary knowledge and skills to ensure they are able to work with children, families and other professionals to safeguard and promote the welfare of children. This was further emphasised in Lord Laming's progress report, *The Protection of Children in England: A Progress Report* (2009).

Summary

The assessment task, in relation to children in need, is to identify which developmental needs are not being met in order to plan and deliver services to meet these needs. What has changed over the last 50 years is the group of children who are the focus of the assessment. As described above, in the 1970s child welfare assessments focused primarily on children in the care of the local authority. During the 1980s and early 1990s the focus widened, and although it should have included all children in need, practitioner attention was concentrated on children suffering, or at risk of suffering, significant harm. By the late 1990s and early 2000s practice was improving and more attention was directed towards all children in need. More recently, the Government has been keen to improve the quality of life for all children and has introduced initiatives designed to target children and families in need of support through prevention and early intervention services, as well as those defined as children in need, including those at risk of harm. The *Every Child Matters* Green Paper (Cm 5860 2003), the Children Act 2004 and the subsequent *Every Child Matters: Change for Children* programme (HM Government 2004), and more recently *The Children's Plan* (Cm 7280 2007) and the *Staying Safe: Action Plan* (HM Government 2008) consolidated much of the earlier work. First, by identifying five outcomes children should achieve to ensure their wellbeing and, second, by modernising services designed to improve outcomes for all children. In order to achieve these outcomes practitioners have to be able to assess and meet the needs of children 'to ensure we properly protect children at risk of neglect and harm within a framework of universal services which aims to prevent negative outcomes and support every child to develop their full potential' (Cm 5860 2003, p.13).

Recommended reading

Cm 5730 (2003) *The Victoria Climbié Inquiry Report*. London: The Stationery Office.
Cm 5860 (2003) *Every Child Matters*. Green Paper. London: The Stationery Office.
Scott, J. and Ward, H. (eds) (2005) *Safeguarding and Promoting the Well-being of Children, Families and Communities*. London: Jessica Kingsley Publishers.
See also the Department for Children, Schools and Families *Every Child Matters* website (www.everychildmatters. gov.uk) for up-to-date information on recent Government policies and their implications for practice.

References

Aldgate, J. and Tunstill, J. (1996) *Making Sense of Section 17*. London: HMSO.
Armstrong, H. (1995) *Annual Reports of Area Child Protection Committees 1994–5*. London: HMSO.
Armstrong, H. (1996) *Annual Reports of Area Child Protection Committees* (No. 2). London: Department of Health ACPC Series.
Armstrong, H. (1997) *Annual Reports of Area Child Protection Committees 1995–6*. London: HMSO.

Audit Commission (1994) *Seen But Not Heard: Co-ordinating Community Child Health and Social Services for Children in Need. Detailed Evidence and Guidelines for Managers and Practitioners.* London: HMSO.

Baroness Morgan of Drefelin (2009) *Letter Dated 22 June 2009 to Directors of Children's Services, Integrated Children's System: Responding to the Recommendations of the Social Work Taskforce.* Available at www.dcsf.gov.uk/everychild-matters/safeguardingandsocialcare/integratedchildrenssystem/ics, accessed on 14 August 2009.

Brandon, M., Belderson, P., Warren, C., Howe, D. *et al.* (2008) *Analysing Child Deaths and Serious Injury through Abuse and Neglect: What Can We Learn? A Biennial Analysis of Serious Case Reviews 2003–2005.* Research Report DCSF-RR023. London: DCSF.

Brandon, M., Bailey, S., Belderson, P., Gardner, R. *et al.* (2009) *Understanding Serious Case Reviews and their Impact. A Biennial Analysis of Serious Case Reviews 2005–7.* DCSF-RB129. London: Department for Children, Schools and Families. Available at www.dcsf.gov.uk/research/programmeofresearch/projectinformation.cfm?project id=15743&resultspage=1, accessed 19 August 2009.

Calder, M.C. and Horwath, J. (eds) (1999) *Working for Children on the Child Protection Register: An Inter-agency Guide.* Aldershot: Arena.

Children's Workforce Development Council (2009) *The Common Assessment Framework for Children and Young People: A Guide for Practitioners.* Available at www.dcsf.gov.uk/everychildmatters/deliveringservices1/caf, accessed on 9 August 2009.

Cleaver, H., Unell, I. and Aldgate, J. (1999) *Children's Needs – Parenting Capacity. The Impact of Parental Mental Illness, Problem Alcohol and Drug Use, and Domestic Violence on Children's Development.* London: The Stationery Office.

Cleaver, H. and Walker, S. with Meadows, P. (2004) *Assessing Children's Needs and Circumstances.* London: Jessica Kingsley Publishers.

Cleaver, H., Walker, S., Scott, J., Cleaver, D. *et al.* (2008) *The Integrated Children's System. Enhancing Social Work and Inter-agency Practice.* London: Jessica Kingsley Publishers.

Cm 5730 (2003) *The Victoria Climbié Inquiry Report.* London: The Stationery Office.

Cm 5860 (2003) *Every Child Matters.* Green Paper. London: The Stationery Office.

Cm 7280 (2007) *The Children's Plan: Building Brighter Futures.* London: Department for Children, Schools and Families.

Dalzell, R. and Sawyer, E. (2007) *Putting Analysis into Assessment: Undertaking Assessments of Need.* London: National Children's Bureau.

Department for Children, Schools and Families (2008a) *The Children's Plan One Year On: A Progress Report.*London: DCSF.

Department for Children, Schools and Families (2008b) *Children's Trusts: Statutory Guidance on Inter-agency Cooperation to Improve Well-being of Children, Young People and their Families.* London: DCSF.

Department for Children, Schools and Families (2009) *ContactPoint.* Available at www.dcsf.gov.uk/everychildmat-ters/strategy/deliveringservices1/contactpoint/contactpoint, accessed on 9 August 2009.

Department of Health (1988) *Protecting Children: A Guide for Social Workers Undertaking a Comprehensive Assessment.* London: HMSO.

Department of Health (1991) *Child Abuse: A Study of Inquiry Reports 1980–9.* London: HMSO.

Department of Health (1994) *Children Act Report 1993.* London: HMSO.

Department of Health (1995) *Child Protection: Messages from Research.* London: HMSO.

Department of Health (1999) *The Government's Objectives for Children's Social Services.* London: Department of Health.

Department of Health (2000a) *Assessing Children in Need and their Families: Practice Guidance.* London: The Stationery Office.

Department of Health (2000b) *The Government's Response to Lost in Care: The Report of the Tribunal of Inquiry into the Abuse of Children in Care in the Former County Council Areas of Gwynedd and Clwyd since 1974.* London: The Stationery Office.

Department of Health (2001) *Studies Informing the Framework for the Assessment of Children in Need and their Families.* London: The Stationery Office.

Department of Health (2002) *The Integrated Children's System.* London: Department of Health.

Department of Health and Cleaver, H. (2000) *Assessment Recording Forms.* London: The Stationery Office.

Department of Health and Cox, A. and Bentovim, A. (2000) *The Family Pack of Questionnaires and Scales.* London. The Stationery Office.

Department of Health and Social Security (1981) *Observation and Assessment: Reporting of a Working Party.* London: The Stationery Office.

Department of Health and Social Security (1982) *Child Abuse: A Study of Inquiry Reports 1973–81.* London: HMSO.

Department of Health and Social Security (1985) *Social Work Decisions in Child Care: Recent Research Findings and their Implications*. London: HMSO.

Department of Health and Social Security (1988) *Working Together: A Guide to Arrangements for Inter-agency Co-operation for the Protection of Children from Abuse*. London: HMSO.

Department of Health, Department for Education and Employment and Home Office (2000) *Framework for the Assessment of Children in Need and their Families*. London: The Stationery Office.

Department of Health, Home Office and Department for Education and Employment (1999) *Working Together to Safeguard Children: A Guide to Inter-agency Working to Safeguard and Promote the Welfare of Children*. London: The Stationery Office.

Falkov, A. (1996) *Study of Working Together 'Part 8' Reports: Fatal Child Abuse and Parental Psychiatric Disorder: An Analysis of 100 Area Child Protection Committee Case Reviews Conducted under the Terms of Part 8 of Working Together Under the Children Act 1989*. London: Department of Health.

Farmer, E. and Owen, M. (1995) *Child Protection Practice Private Risks and Public Remedies*. London: HMSO.

Gibbons, J., Conroy, S. and Bell, C. (1995a) *Operating the Child Protection System*. London: HMSO.

Gibbons, J., Gallagher, B., Bell, C. and Gordon, D. (1995b) *Development After Physical Abuse in Early Childhood*. London: HMSO.

Goodman, A., Johnson, P. and Webb, S. (1997) *Inequality in the UK*. Oxford: Oxford University Press.

Gray, J. (2002) 'National Policy on the Assessment of Children in Need and their Families.' In H. Ward and W. Rose (eds) *Approaches to Needs Assessment in Children's Services*. London: Jessica Kingsley Publishers.

Gregg, P., Harkness, S. and Machin, S. (1999) *Child Development and Family Income*. York: York Publishing Services.

Hallett, C. (1995) *Interagency Coordination in Child Protection*. London: HMSO.

Hallett, C. and Birchall, E. (1992) *Coordination in Child Protection*. London: HMSO.

HM Government (2004) *Every Child Matters: Change for Children*. London: Department for Education and Skills.

HM Government (2005) *Statutory Guidance on Inter-agency Co-operation to Improve the Wellbeing of Children: Children's Trusts*. Nottingham: DfES Publications.

HM Government (2006a) *The Common Assessment Framework for Children and Young People: Practitioners' Guide*. London: Department for Education and Skills.

HM Government (2006b) *Working Together to Safeguard Children. A Guide to Inter-agency Working to Safeguard and Promote the Welfare of Children*. London: The Stationery Office.

HM Government (2008) *Staying Safe: Action Plan*. Available at www.everychildmatters.gov.uk/staying safe, accessed on 21 April 2009.

HM Treasury (1999) *Tackling Poverty and Extending Opportunity*. London: The Stationery Office.

Hogan, C. and Murphy, D. (2002) *Outcomes: Reframing Responsibility for Well-being*. Baltimore, MD: The Annie Casey Foundation.

Home Office (1998) *Supporting Families*. Green Paper. London: HMSO.

Home Office, Department of Health and Department for Education (1991) *Working Together under the Children Act 1989: A Guide to Arrangements for Inter-agency Cooperation for the Protection of Children from Abuse*. London: HMSO.

Horwath, J. (ed.) (2001) *The Child's World: Assessing Children in Need*. London: Jessica Kingsley Publishers.

Horwath, J. (2002) 'Maintaining a focus on the child? First impressions of the "Framework for the Assessment of Children in Need and their Families" in cases of child neglect.' *Child Abuse Review 11*, 4, 195–213.

Jack, G. (1997) 'Discourses of child protection and child welfare.' *British Journal of Social Work 27*, 659–678.

Joint Chief Inspectors (2002) *Safeguarding Children. A Joint Chief Inspectors' Report on Arrangements to Safeguard Children*. London: Department of Health.

Joint Chief Inspectors (2005) *The Second Joint Chief Inspectors' Report on Arrangements to Safeguard Children*. London: Ofsted.

Joint Chief Inspectors (2008) *The Third Joint Chief Inspectors' Report on Arrangements to Safeguard Children*. London: Ofsted.

Jordan, B. and Jordan, C. (2000) *Social Work and the Third Way*. London: Sage.

Katz, I. (1997) *Current Issues in Comprehensive Assessment*. London: NSPCC.

Lord Laming (2009) *The Protection of Children in England: A Progress Report*. London: The Stationery Office.

Luthera, M. (1997) *Britain's Black Population: Social Change, Public Policy and Agenda*. Aldershot: Arena.

NCH Action for Children (1996) *Children Still in Need: Refocusing Child Protection in the Context of Children in Need*. London: Association of Directors of Social Services and NCH.

NSPCC, University of Sheffield and Department of Health (2000) *The Child's World: Assessing the Needs of Children. A Training and Development Pack.* London: NSPCC.

Ofsted, Healthcare Commission and HM Inspectorate of Constabulary (2008) *Joint Area Review. Haringey Children's Services Authority Area.* Available at www.ofsted.gov.uk/oxcare_providers/la_download/(id)/4657/(as)/JAR/jar_2008_309_fr.pdf, accessed on 13 July 2009.

Pugh, G. (2005) 'Policies in the UK to Promote the Well-being of Children.' In J. Scott and H. Ward (eds) *Safeguarding and Promoting the Well-being of Children, Families and Communities.* London: Jessica Kingsley Publishers.

Quinton, D. (2004) *Supporting Parents: Messages from Research.* London: Jessica Kingsley Publishers.

Reder, P., Duncan, S. and Gray, M. (1993) *Beyond Blame – Child Abuse Tragedies Revisited* (1st edn). London: Routledge.

Rose, W. and Barnes, J. (2008) *Improving Safeguarding Practice: Study of Serious Case Reviews 2001–2003.* Nottingham: Department for Children, Schools and Families.

Scott, D. (1997) 'Inter-agency conflict: an ethnographic study.' *Child and Family Social Work 2, 2,* 73–80.

Social Services Inspectorate (1997a) *Assessment, Planning and Decision-making in Family Support Services.* London: Department of Health.

Social Services Inspectorate (1997b) *Messages from Inspections: Child Protection Inspections 1992–6.* London: HMSO.

Stevenson, O. (ed.) (1998) *Child Welfare in the UK.* Oxford: Blackwell Science.

Stevenson, O. (2000) 'The Mandate for Inter-agency and Inter-professional Work and Training: Legal, Practical, Professional and Social Factors.' In M. Charles and E. Hendry (eds) *Training Together to Safeguard Children: Guidance on Inter-agency Training.* London: NSPCC.

Thoburn, J., Lewis, A. and Shemmings, D. (1995) *Paternalism or Partnership? Family Involvement in the Child Protection Process* (1st edn). London: HMSO.

Utting, D., Rose, W. and Pugh, G. (2001) *Better Results for Children and Families: Involving Communities in Planning Services Based on Outcomes.* London: The National Council of Voluntary Child Care Organisations.

Westcott, H. (1993) *Abuse of Children and Adults with Disabilities.* London: NSPCC.

CHAPTER 2

The Assessment Framework

Wendy Rose

A framework has been developed which provides a systematic way of analysing, understanding and recording what is happening to children and young people within their families and the wider context of the community in which they live. From such an understanding of what are inevitably complex issues and inter-relationships, clear professional judgements can be made.

(Preface to the Framework for the Assessment of Children in Need and their Families, p.viii)

In this chapter the following are considered:

- improving outcomes for children
- the Assessment Framework – the legislative and policy context
- exploring the Assessment Framework, its domains and dimensions
- underpinning principles of the Framework and their use in practice
- relating the Assessment Framework to the Common Assessment Framework, the Integrated Children's System and other practice developments
- using questionnaires, scales and recording tools
- implementing the Assessment Framework – findings from research
- assessment frameworks in England and other countries.

Introduction

The four nations of the United Kingdom have all expressed their commitment to improving children's outcomes. However, in order to achieve this ambition, it means that special attention has to be given to helping those children who, for whatever reason, are likely to experience difficulties in doing well (HM Government 2004). A critical part of the contemporary improvement agenda in England includes a range of government policies directed, for example, at reducing child poverty, promoting social inclusion and increasing the provision of early years and out-of-school services. These policies aim to enhance opportunities for groups of children growing up in circumstances of deprivation and disadvantage. At the same time, just as important are the government policies aimed at ensuring improved services are available to individual children and their families when children have additional needs. This requires early and sensitive identification of any difficulties and timely, proportionate and well co-ordinated provision of services.

As a result, in England, the Government has placed increasing emphasis on the responsibility of the children's workforce, when there are concerns about a child, to assess what may be happening and its impact, and then to take appropriate action. In order to assess, make decisions and plans, and deliver services, it has been recognised that all practitioners working with children require a common core of knowledge and skills (HM Government 2005). Most importantly, this common core has to be underpinned by a set of common values, a common language and consistency of approach, which make sense to children and family members and enables them to have confidence in the practitioners they meet. Equally, shared knowledge and skills are essential in facilitating good communication and joint working between practitioners across different agencies.

It is for these reasons that the *Framework for the Assessment of Children in Need and their Families* (the Assessment Framework), a practice approach for assessing children's needs developed for national use, has gained increasing prominence in child welfare policy and practice since its introduction in England and Wales (Department of Health *et al.* 2000; National Assembly for Wales and Home Office 2001). This chapter describes the Assessment Framework and its use, set within the context of developments in child welfare legislation and policy. It is mostly focused on England but includes reference to developments in other nations of the UK and internationally.

Focusing on assessment to improve outcomes

> Assessment is a continuous process whereby problems are identified and appropriate responses decided upon.
>
> *(Department of Health and Social Security 1981, p.2)*

A prevailing theme, found in current government guidance across the UK, is that improving outcomes for children and enabling all children to achieve their full potential requires effective intervention. This in turn must be based on a sound understanding of what is happening to a child. This is not a new theme. The quality of professional and clinical 'diagnosis' of problems has long been acknowledged as fundamental to the effectiveness of interventions by those agencies with responsibility for working with children and families, whether in health, education, children's social care or youth justice services. It is a continuous thread that can be found running through policy and professional discussions since the reforming post-war legislation of the 1940s. For example, in the early 1980s the Department of Health and Social Security (1981) commissioned a report on what were called 'observation and assessment services', because of concerns about their effectiveness. It was echoed again in the Department of Health's statement of national objectives for children's social services, one of which was headed 'Better Assessment Leading to Better Services' (Department of Health 1999a, p.3).

A second thread has been the importance of early identification of any likely impairment to development. In this respect, early identification has been associated with prevention. This means either dealing with a likely problem through early intervention to prevent it occurring or taking action to prevent the development of more complex or intractable difficulties at a later stage. This theme was reflected in a 1970s monograph on child development, where the caption of a photograph of a child having a hearing test reinforces the message, 'Early detection means early treatment' (Kellmer Pringle and Naidoo 1975, p.56). A scheme to tackle antisocial behaviour by ten-year-olds in the 1980s was called Catch 'em Young (see Cleaver 1991). Research findings on the effectiveness of interventions have continued to emphasise how important it is to identify the onset of difficulties as early as possible in a child's life and to take action quickly, in order to increase the potential for making a difference (see, for example, Hagell's 2003 research and practice briefing about understanding and challenging youth offending).

Horwath has described in the first chapter how the Government has responded to the reports of working parties (Department of Health and Social Security 1981), national inspections (Social Services Inspectorate 1986) and child abuse inquiries (Department of Health 1991; Department of Heath and Social Security 1982) that commented critically on the quality of assessment practice in children's residential and community settings in the 1980s. An area of particular concern to policymakers was how child protection issues were identified and assessed. Despite successive governments issuing and updating guidance on the processes and procedures which should be adopted in circumstances of child abuse and neglect, there was increasing evidence that some social services practitioners were experiencing difficulties in assessing and forming professional judgements about serious child abuse concerns. Findings from different sources suggested over-preoccupation with meeting the requirements of procedures and formal systems, insufficient skilled direct work with children and families, and an absence of structure and focus in undertaking complex assessments. In response, as discussed in Chapter 1, policymakers in the Department of Health took the unusual step, at the time, of producing practice guidance to assist social workers undertaking comprehensive assessments when child abuse had been identified (Department of Health 1988). However, despite this guidance, assessment practice remained variable and, too often, child protection plans were not informed by comprehensive assessments (Katz 1997).

At the same time, findings from research, inspections and the audit commission, following the implementation of the Children Act 1989, suggested that practice in children's social services was too narrowly focused on child protection and incidents of abuse at the expense of a wider group of children in need in the community and their families. When problems were identified by other agencies, referrals were too often funnelled through the child protection system, although only 15 per cent of those referrals to children's social services were subsequently registered as requiring a child protection plan (Department of Health 1995). Children whose health and development was at risk of being impaired without the provision of services were being excluded from appropriate assessment, planning and services.

By the mid 1990s researchers were drawing attention to the impact that parental problems can have on children as well as the increased vulnerability of children growing up in conditions of poverty, social exclusion and poor community resources (for example, Bradshaw 1990; Holman 1998; Utting 1995). Moreover, it was being recognised that disabled children were particularly vulnerable to socio-economic disadvantage (Gordon *et al.* 2000; Lawton 1998). These families were not getting access to the services they needed (Aldgate and Tunstill 1995; Cleaver *et al.* 1999). As part of a strategy to refocus children's services so that they would be more broadly based to meet the needs of vulnerable children and their families and deliver improved services, the Government decided that in England and Wales a national assessment framework should be developed to assist practitioners in meeting one of the key children's social services objectives: 'To ensure that referral and assessment processes discriminate effectively between different types and levels of need and produce a timely service response' (Department of Health 1999b, p.20).

Legislation underpinning the assessment of children in need

The primary legislation in England and Wales which defines the state's responsibilities towards children in need and their families remains the Children Act 1989, although there have been subsequent amendments and extensions. More recent major legislation, the Children Act 2004, does not repeal or replace the Children Act 1989 but strengthens the earlier provisions in a number of ways as outlined in Chapter 1.

Local authorities have been given general powers in the Local Government Act 2000 to promote the economic, social and environmental wellbeing of their area and improve the quality of life of local residents. To this end, they have a duty to develop community strategies together with other local bodies. However, in the Children Act 1989 there is a specific duty laid on every local authority to identify the extent to which there are children in need in their area (Schedule 2.1). Assessing need is therefore emphasised within the legislation in two respects: at a population level for planning purposes by the local authority (Schedule 2.1) and, equally important, at an individual level (Schedules 2.3 and 2.4, and section 47) (see discussion by authors in Ward and Rose 2002). Local authorities have a duty to safeguard and promote the welfare of children in need and, in so far as is consistent with that duty, promote the upbringing of such children by their families by providing a range and level of services appropriate to their needs (section 17(1)). Relevant partner agencies have a duty to co-operate with the local authority's children's services in the exercise of these responsibilities (section 27, strengthened by section 10 of the Children Act 2004).

But who are children in need? The Children Act 1989 marks a change from previous child welfare legislation by defining need broadly and in developmental terms and, furthermore, links need to the provision of services (Department of Health 2001). Children in need are defined as children unlikely to achieve or maintain a reasonable standard of health and development without services, or whose health and development will be significantly impaired without services, or children who are disabled (section 17(10)). Children in need, therefore, include those children suffering, or likely to suffer, significant harm. Local authorities made aware of children in such circumstances have a duty to make enquiries, that is to assess what is happening to them, in order to enable them to decide whether they should take any action (section 47(1)). The concept of need thus encompasses a wide spectrum, from children who may have relatively straightforward or short-term needs through to those whose needs are urgent, serious, complex and possibly life-threatening, including those at risk of significant harm. Critical to this definition is that their development will be impaired without the provision of services. Disabled children are included in their own right in recognition of the special developmental needs they may have. The duty to safeguard and promote their welfare applies to all the children within this wide spectrum. Aldgate and Statham discuss the significance for practice of the twin aims of safeguarding and promoting children's welfare in their report, *The Children Act Now: Messages from Research* (Department of Health 2001). They note that, within the legislation, safeguarding children has two elements (p.41):

- a duty to protect children from maltreatment
- a duty to prevent impairment of development.

Thus the legislation requires practitioners when assessing concerns about maltreatment to take account of the needs of a child rather than focusing only on the presenting problem.

Identification of need requires skilled assessment by practitioners who will be in a position to help a child and family gain access to appropriate advice or services. Here, the Children Act 1989 marks two further important changes. First, the appropriate response may require services to be provided not just for the child but for the whole family, or for particular members of the family or any other person with whom a child has been living. Second, services may be provided by a single agency or by a number of agencies working co-operatively together.

The extent of need

At the last full Children in Need Census (CIN), based on a sample week in February 2005, 385,300 children in England were reported as receiving support from children's social care services (Department for Education and Skills 2005). An estimate in 2008 suggested that the figure had fallen by 13 per cent to 335,600 children (Mahon 2008). Government statistics recorded 34,000 of those children as being the subject of a child protection plan (Department for Children, Schools and Families 2008). However, these children are part of a far larger group of children who are vulnerable either because of intrinsic reasons, such as some aspect of their health, or because of issues in their wider world, such as family conflict, bullying or poverty, which may have an impact on the progress they can make. There are over 3.6 million children calculated to be in this group of vulnerable children, as represented in Figure 2.1, who may be at risk of difficulties or have additional needs that may prevent their achieving the five priority outcomes identified for all children (Cm 5860 2003). These outcomes are listed in Chapter 1.

In circumstances where children may be vulnerable, parents need access to good information about services and sources of support. Vigilance is also required by agencies, such as health, early years and education services that have daily or regular contact with almost all children. This is necessary in order to identify children with any difficulties and additional needs as early as possible and consider what additional support may be required.

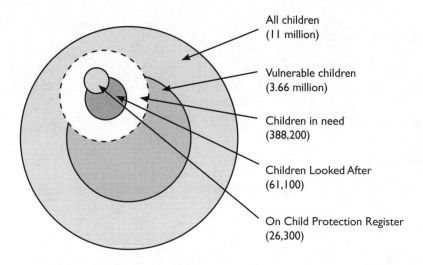

All children
(11 million)

Vulnerable children
(3.66 million)

Children in need
(388,200)

Children Looked After
(61,100)

On Child Protection Register
(26,300)

From Department for Education and Skills (2005)

Figure 2.1: Representation of the extent of children in need in England at year ending 31 March 2004

A framework for assessing children's needs

The Assessment Framework has been constructed as a guide or map to help practitioners across all disciplines organise their thinking about what is happening to a child when there are concerns or a family is asking for help. It also assists practitioners to make sense of the information they gather. It gives expression to the emphasis in the Children Act 1989 on the importance of children's development, and promoting and safeguarding their welfare by preventing development from being impaired. It is designed to capture those aspects of the inner and outer world of children that may influence their development and their current wellbeing as well as their future well-becoming in adulthood (Ben-Arieh 2002). Its purpose is to enable practitioners to explore these aspects with a child, family members or others who may be involved and come to an agreement about what is happening and what help is needed.

The Assessment Framework has been conceptualised as a triangle made up of three domains representing the key aspects of a child's inner and outer world:

- a child's developmental needs

- the capacity of parents or carers to support their child's development and respond appropriately to his or her needs

- wider family and environmental factors that may have an impact on a child's development and on the capacity of their parents or carers to support the child's development and respond to the child's needs. (See Figure 2.2)

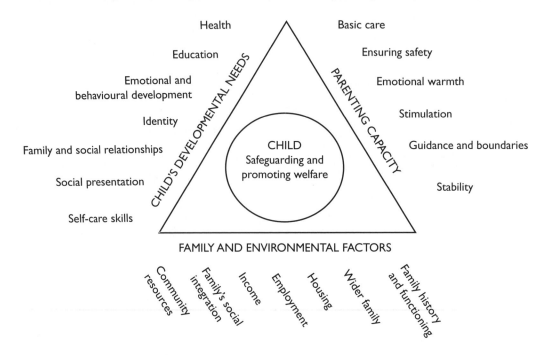

From Department of Health *et al.* (2000)

Figure 2.2*: The Assessment Framework*

In emphasising the importance of all three domains, the Framework is recognising that, alongside a developmental perspective to children's progress, there is also an ecological perspective to their development (see discussion in Part 1 of *The Developing World of the Child*, Aldgate *et al.* 2006). Many writers have argued that, to understand and help children and families, practitioners need to focus not just on what is happening within the family but also take account of 'the outer world of the environment, both in terms of relationships and in terms of practicalities, such as housing' (Schofield 1998, p.57; see also Jack 1997; Jones and Ramchandani 1999; Prilleltensky and Nelson 2000; Stevenson 1998). They suggest a systems approach to the child's world is required that involves systems beyond the immediate family and includes wider networks of relatives, friends and neighbours, the local community, resources and culture, and policies and structures at a societal level. The relationships between these systems and their impact on a child and family can then be explored. Families do not exist in a vacuum and such an approach allows the family's own perceptions and interpretations of their experiences and difficulties to be given appropriate prominence.

Jones and Ramchandani (1999) explain why the 'developmental ecological' perspective is particularly useful. The developmental perspective

> stresses that the child becomes increasingly organised, integrated, yet more complex as an individual as he or she grows up. There are many influences on this process, amongst them genetic, physical, psychological, and family influences as well as wider neighbourhood and cultural influences. (p.2)

The ecological perspective, Jones and Ramchandani suggest, is important because it

> considers the child within their environment surrounded by layers of successively larger and more complex social groupings, which have an influence on him or her... As well as this, both the child and their parent influence the outcome of events via their personalities and social functioning. (Jones and Ramchandani 1999, p.2)

This approach builds on work by Bronfenbrenner (1979) and others, and has been successfully applied in understanding, for example, the interplay of factors in child maltreatment (see Belsky and Vondra 1989) and in the development of antisocial behaviour (see Capaldi and Eddy 2000). It recognises that, in each domain, there is a range of factors that may influence a child's development or the parents' or carers' capacity to be appropriately receptive, attentive and responsive (Simmonds 1998). Child development is seen as a process which involves interactions between a growing child and his or her social environment (Jones and Ramchandani 1999). The same factors may have a positive or negative impact, depending on the child and circumstances. That is why the interactions and transactions between internal and external factors, between factors within one domain or in relation to another, always need to be carefully explored and understood.

Such interactions are vividly described in accounts by Easterhouse residents bringing up their children on the Glasgow estate in Scotland (Holman 1998). Anita, a widow with seven children, writes:

> I dread to think what the future holds for my kids if I don't get away from Easterhouse soon while they are still young, I know in my heart that they will either turn to drugs or end up in prison. My kids keep asking to move. They are lovely kids and intelligent and I would dearly love to see them making something of themselves. Maureen is very clever for her age, eight, and I don't want her growing up in this environment. But what can I do with no money? My children don't stand a chance. (Quoted in Holman 1998, p.96)

As Utting (1995) in his report on family and parenthood concludes: 'Living on low income in a rundown neighbourhood does not make it impossible to be the affectionate, authoritative parent of healthy, sociable children. But it does, undeniably, make it more difficult' (Utting 1995, p.40). Jax, aged 11, from another part of Scotland, illustrates below how play areas can become dangerous and unusable wastelands for children:

'I live near this football court. It's got lots of spray paint swears, trolleys, lots of glass.'

(Jax, aged 11 years)

The dimensions in each domain are derived from knowledge based on theory, research and professional experience in which practitioners may have confidence (Rose and Aldgate in Department of Health 2000; Seden 2000). They are defined in government guidance and explored in detail in the following chapters of this book and in *The Developing World of the Child* (Aldgate *et al.* 2006).

The Framework as a triangle

There are many ways in which systems and their inter-relationships can be represented diagrammatically, each emphasising different features. Some writers such as Bronfenbrenner (1979) and Stevenson (1998) have used circles; others such as Belsky and Vondra (1989) and Jones and Ramchandani (1999) have used squares and flow diagrams. A triangle was chosen as a symbolic way of capturing the key domains, helping the practitioner to keep them in mind and think broadly about a child's world, but always with the child firmly at the centre. Furthermore, as Jack and Gill (2003) remind practitioners, it is a way of ensuring that the influence of wider family and environmental factors on families' lives is not neglected in the equation but given equal weight. Buckley and colleagues also reinforce this view: 'a visual representation of the process that is easy to recall [helps] to ensure comprehensive gathering of data on all relevant aspects of assessment' (Buckley *et al.* 2007, p.46).

Using the Framework in principle and practice

Assessing, planning, taking action and reviewing progress are processes at the foundation of practitioners' work with children in need and families. These activities are underpinned by a set of principles (Figure 2.3) and a set of expectations which are subject to regular monitoring. The principles are important in helping practitioners to understand the key features of the Framework and to consider how they will approach assessment with a child and family. These principles apply equally to all practitioners who may be working with children in need and families, irrespective of agency and specific roles and responsibilities. They are set out more fully in the *Framework for the Assessment of Children*

Each process:

- is child-centred, ensuring the child is always kept in focus
- is rooted in child development, which includes recognition of the significance of timing in a child's life
- is ecological in approach, locating children within their family and wider community
- ensures equality of opportunity for all, working sensitively with the diversity of children's circumstances
- involves working actively with families, children and young people
- builds on strengths in each of the three domains, as well as identifying difficulties
- is inter-agency in approach, recognising the contribution of multi-agency working to helping children and families
- is a continuing process and not just a single event
- involves action and services being provided in parallel with assessment, according to the needs of a child and family
- is informed by evidence.

Figure 2.3: *Principles underpinning processes of assessing, planning, intervening and reviewing*

in *Need and their Families* (Department of Health *et al.* 2000, pp.10–16). In order to ensure that, in practice, work with children in need and families is proportionate and timely, the assessment process has been divided into two stages – an *initial assessment* to be completed within seven working days of referral which may be followed by a *core assessment*, if a more in-depth, detailed assessment is required, for completion within 35 working days.

The social worker's contribution to assessment

Putting these principles into practice immediately highlights some important features of assessment activity. Most obviously, they emphasise that assessment is not a paper exercise. It cannot simply be done by gathering information and views from sources such as agency records or other professional staff. To understand how well a child in need is doing and what may be the strengths and pressures faced by the family requires the social worker (the lead professional) to see and know the child and family. This involves speaking to and communicating with children, as explored in Chapter 7, as well as with adult family members and other practitioners who have contact with the child and their family.

Assessment in this sense is a relational activity. The social worker who wants to understand what is happening becomes a critical part of the equation and influences the outcome of the process (see discussion by Jones 1998, pp.109–110). The development of trust and confidence between the social worker and family members is essential, so that a clear understanding is achieved by all concerned about the purpose of the social worker and other practitioners' involvement, why information is being sought, with whom it will be shared and what will happen next. (This is discussed in more detail in Chapter 6.) This may take time. Sometimes, the severity or immediacy of a child's situation will accelerate the pace, scope and formality of the way the contact proceeds. However, even in difficult circumstances of severe child maltreatment including sexual abuse, Jones and Ramchandani (1999) and others have observed that the sensitivity and quality of early or initial contact can influence later working relationships positively. Thus, the way the social worker uses him or herself in working with the family is a significant factor in the effectiveness of assessment activities and can influence the effectiveness of help subsequently provided.

As discussed in Chapter 8, the corollary of being involved in direct work with children and families is that it has an emotional impact on practitioners, to which agencies, through their managers and supervisors, are required to be alert. Situations may be stressful or cause anxiety or fear, especially in circumstances where resistance, hostility and violence are exhibited by a child's adult carers. Writers such as Reder *et al.* (1993), Ferguson (2004) and Cooper (2005) have explored the way such experiences may influence practitioners' perceptions of what is happening to a child and how the focus can move away from the child who may even become 'seen but unseen' (Cooper 2005, p.8).

Sharing information in the best interests of children

A critical feature of assessment, expressed in the principles, is that it is likely to be in a child and family's best interests if information is gathered and shared on a multi-agency basis. Individual staff in contact with a child and family will not necessarily know about every relevant aspect of their lives. When there has been a request for help or concerns about a child's welfare have been registered, gathering sufficient information may be a cumulative process, piecing together with the family what is happening and involving other practitioners. Assessment is very often an inter-agency activity. A child and family are likely to have contact with a number of different agencies in the normal course of their lives, as considered in Chapter 5.

Different practitioners will have their own professional perspective of a child and family, for instance as the result of providing day care to a toddler at a nursery or developing a relationship with a young person attending a youth club, but they will also have an important contribution to make to understanding other aspects of a child's world. They may have observed, heard or had matters reported to them that have wider implications concerning a child's welfare. A youth justice worker, for instance, undertaking a programme on offending behaviour, may learn about the difficult living arrangements of a young person, or that a child is regularly avoiding school, which may be important to share with school staff or other practitioners involved.

It is essential in this respect that all practitioners hold the whole child in mind, think about what is happening in the child's world, record it and identify other agencies that may already be or need to be involved. Avoiding what is often called 'a silo approach' is imperative. Sharing information in the best interests of the child, however, requires that the family is fully informed, understands and, unless a child's safety would be compromised, has given appropriate consent.

The importance of family history and functioning

In making sense of complex circumstances or where there are concerns about the likelihood of harm, a critical task of social workers and other practitioners is learning about a family's history and what has happened in the parents' lives, previous patterns of family behaviour and response, and the continuities and discontinuities experienced by the family. The exploration of family history and functioning is often given too little attention in training and in practice. Such exploration can provide insights and make connections for both family members and practitioners, and its contribution to understanding the child's world and the potential for change is underestimated. As Munro observes, 'the best predictor of future behaviour is past behaviour' (2002, p.105). The scales and questionnaires accompanying the Assessment Framework materials may be useful for practitioners in this work, such as the *Recent Life Events Questionnaire* or *The Family Activity Scale* (Department of Health and Cox and Bentovim 2000), as well as using the *Family Assessment* (Bentovim and Bingley Miller 2001) to understand more complex family situations. These evidence-based tools are referred to again later in this and other chapters.

Analysing information and making decisions

As discussed earlier, a principle of assessment is ensuring that proportionate and timely help is provided when it is needed. Between the points of gathering information and delivering effective help, social workers and their managers need to make sense of information, form judgements about what is happening, make a series of decisions and agree a child's plan on which they and others act (see Chapters 3 and 4, and discussion by Hollows 2003; Jones *et al.* 2006). In reality, much of this work is happening in parallel. These are perhaps the most important activities in the assessment process. Sometimes assessment is only understood as gathering information. Analysing information, and all that is entailed in that process, is seen as a separate activity. Assessment requires both activities to take place so that judgements can be formed and decisions made. Horwath, in the opening chapter, has already noted the difficulties that practitioners continue to experience in analysing information and she explores the analysis of information in detail in Chapter 4.

In order to be clear about what is involved, Hollows (2003) advocates separating out professional judgement from decision-making, even though in reality the two activities often become intertwined. She quotes a useful distinction made by Goldstein and Hogarth (1997): judgement being the way people 'integrate multiple, probabilistic, potentially conflicting cues to arrive at an understanding of the situation' and decision-making as the way people 'choose what to do next in the face of uncertain consequences and conflicting goals' (Hollows 2003, p.61). Increasingly, different approaches and tools are being developed to assist practitioners with this difficult part of assessment, for example the National Children's Bureau toolkit *Putting Analysis into Assessment* (Dalzell and Sawyer 2007) and the workbooks on *Assessing and Promoting Resilience in Vulnerable Children* (Daniel and Wassell 2002). Writers stress that practitioners should be helped to develop 'a critical and reflective mindset' (Dalzell and Sawyer 2007, p.11). Emphasis is also placed on the importance of available, quality supervision for practitioners at the front-line who are making difficult and complex decisions about children (Hughes and Pengelly 1997; Jones *et al.* 2006).

As detailed in Chapter 4, once decisions have been made about what to do next, a plan can be developed with the child and family. The process follows the same pattern even if the situation is straightforward and only a single agency is involved. However, planning is likely to become more elaborate and formal according to the complexity and severity of the circumstances and the level of inter-agency involvement. The completion of an assessment will form a baseline for the subsequent review of the child's plan and how well the child is progressing in order to determine whether the desired changes are being achieved.

The Assessment Framework and current practice developments

The Assessment Framework has underpinned the practice outlined in a range of government guidance on different aspects of children's welfare since it was introduced in England. The inter-agency government guidance on safeguarding, *Working Together to Safeguard Children* (HM Government 2006), has a key chapter on 'Managing Individual Cases' which sets out how the Assessment Framework should be followed when undertaking assessments on children where there are safeguarding concerns. At the same time, development work has continued in line with the Government's overarching policy of *Every Child Matters* to provide a coherent approach to work with children in need through the Integrated Children's System (Cleaver *et al.* 2008) and to ensure early identification and early intervention where there are concerns about children through the *Common Assessment Framework* (Children's Workforce Development Council 2009). The Assessment Framework provides the underlying model for both these practice developments. This means that practitioners from different disciplines and different agencies are now sharing a common language and a common approach in identifying when children may be experiencing difficulties, and this continues throughout work with a child and family. When a child is in need, the Integrated Children's System provides practitioners with a more structured and systematic approach by integrating the processes of working with the child and family from the first point of contact through to the final review. This is referred to as 'guided practice' in Australia (Scarf Australia 2001). The Assessment Framework is now a core element in translating *Every Child Matters* into changes in practice.

Using questionnaires, scales, recording and other tools to improve practice

The implementation of the Assessment Framework has been accompanied by an unprecedented range of resources commissioned by the Government to ensure widespread understanding and familiarity with the approach and to help managers and practitioners integrate its use into front-line practice. As discussed earlier in the chapter, effective assessment requires direct work with children and families. In some situations, practitioners and families are finding it helpful to use a more structured and systematic approach to talking about particular aspects of families' lives, such as the hassles parents may be experiencing or an adolescent's feelings about his wellbeing. Well-tested questionnaires and scales can offer a positive way of practitioners and family members working together on these issues and provide a baseline of information against which to measure change (see, for example, the use by community-based projects of standardised tests in their practice, described in Aldgate *et al.* 2007). Some of the tools that have been developed are listed in Table 2.1.

These resources allow detailed and practical exploration of different aspects of a child and family's world and to do so in circumstances that may be more comfortable and even fun for children, such as when a computer is used to assist a child to tell the practitioner his or her story, as *In My Shoes* (Calam *et al.* 2000). In addition, Barnardo's has produced a guide and resources, *Say It Your Own Way*, to help practitioners facilitate children's participation in assessment (Hutton and Partridge 2006).

It has to be remembered that there is a third domain of the Assessment Framework, concerned with wider family and environmental factors. A model has been developed for analysing the impact of the local community on parents and on children in *The Missing Side of the Triangle* by Jack and Gill (2003). It ensures that very specific and practical questions are asked about both community strengths and pressures from the perspectives of children and of parents or carers, and the cumulative impact of these experiences is carefully assessed.

Findings about how the Assessment Framework is working in practice

Since the Assessment Framework was introduced in 2000, it has been subject to considerable scrutiny. There have been a number of critiques of the conceptual framework examining whether it is fit for purpose and whether it will help to improve practice (for example, Calder and Hackett 2003; Garrett 2003). They have also looked at the context in which the Government intended it to be used, including the distinction made between initial and core assessments, the timescales laid down for their completion, the exemplars issued for recording assessments electronically and the effect on social work practice in different circumstances (see Booth *et al.* 2006; Holland 2004; Millar and Corby 2006). Challenging questions have been asked, such as by Millar and Corby:

> Does the *Framework for the Assessment of Children in Need and their Families*...embody an ethos of bureaucratic regulation with stultifying effects on social work, or is there evidence, as was anticipated in the guidance accompanying the Framework's introduction, that it has potential for therapeutic social work? (Millar and Corby 2006, p.887)

Inevitably, most published studies so far are based on fieldwork undertaken in the first year or so of the introduction of the Assessment Framework, and reflect what might be called the 'settling in' period. The messages drawn from recent research findings, some more positive than others, must therefore be regarded as tentative.

Table 2.1: Evidence-based assessment tools for use with children and families

Tool	Purpose
The HOME Inventory: A Guide for Practitioners – the UK Approach (Cox 2008)	Assesses a child's experiences in the home environment which influence their development, including the quality of parenting. It covers all children up to early adolescence, including those who are looked after or disabled.
The Family Assessment Assessment of family competence, strengths and difficulties (Bentovim and Bingley-Miller 2001)	Enables professionals to develop a systematic and evidence-based approach to observing, describing and assessing family life and relationships, parenting and the impact of family history.
The Family Pack of Questionnaires and Scales (Department of Health and Cox and Bentovim 2000) • Home Conditions Scale • The Family Activity Scale • The Parental Daily Hassles Scale • The Recent Life Events Questionnaire • The Adult Wellbeing Scale • The Alcohol Scale • The Strengths and Difficulties Questionnaire • The Adolescent Wellbeing Scale	Provide an economical and effective way of gathering information about children's emotional and behavioural strengths and difficulties, parenting, adult mental health and alcohol difficulties, life events and family activities.
The Attachment Style Interview (Bifulco *et al.* 2003)	Provides an assessment of the attachment style of adults, the quality of a couple's marital/partner relationship and their patterns of support and relating.
In My Shoes (Calam *et al.* 2000)	This is a computer-assisted interview for communicating with children and vulnerable adults about their experiences, thoughts, feelings and wishes, including traumatic or abusive experiences. It is particularly helpful to support participation of younger children, disabled children and those with communication difficulties.

Reproduced with permission of A. Bentovim and L. Bingley Miller, Child and Family Training, 2007.

In parallel, several studies have also been undertaken specifically to find out how the Assessment Framework has been implemented, as well as its impact on practice (for example, Cleaver *et al.* 2004; Horwath 2002; Platt 2001, 2006; Rose *et al.* 2007). It was recognised, from the development stage, that the introduction of the Assessment Framework, together with the principles underpinning it, was part of a much more fundamental change in working with children and families. It would require a major review and revision of local policies, procedures and practices, as well as protocols for inter-agency working (Department of Health *et al.* 2000). A study of early implementation was undertaken by Cleaver and colleagues in 24 local authorities (Cleaver and Walker 2004). In a summary, Cleaver acknowledged the challenge of bedding in the new approach and identified 16 essential features from the study which contributed to successful implementation (Department of Health and Cleaver 2003). A detailed case study in one authority for a period of over two years (Rose *et al.* 2007) confirmed the complexity of integrating the approach into front-line practice in the real world of children's services and highlighted the management commitment required.

Inspections of children's services are an additional source of information about how the Assessment Framework is working in practice. Some inspections have focused on how effectively assessments are being carried out by practitioners in agencies with safeguarding responsibilities for children. A Joint Chief Inspectors' report (*Safeguarding Children: A Joint Chief Inspectors' Report on Arrangements to Safeguard Children*, 2002, pp.46–58), undertaken shortly after the Assessment Framework was introduced, commented on how demanding agencies had found implementation. Whilst practice varied, it recorded a number of concerns about the quality of assessments: 'Too few [core] assessments demonstrated an engagement with the social history of the family, a reflection on the evidence, synthesis and analysis, and a concluding assessment of need and risk of significant harm' (Joint Chief Inspectors 2002, p.51).

Three years later, a second Joint Chief Inspectors' report on safeguarding children (Commission for Social Care Inspection 2005) found evidence that the use of the Assessment Framework was improving and making a difference. For example, when used to inform care plans for new placements, the higher quality information was found to lead to better outcomes for the children (p.62). The third Joint Chief Inspectors' report in this series (Ofsted *et al.* 2008) recorded increasing numbers of referrals leading to initial assessments, further improvement in timescales for completion but still considerable variation in the quality of assessment practice (p.69). Government statistics for the year ending 31 March 2008 showed continued improvement in completion rates of initial and core assessments within the timescales, 71 per cent and 80 per cent respectively for 2007/8 (Department for Children, Schools and Families 2008) compared with 65 per cent and 74 per cent respectively two years earlier in 2005/6 (Department for Education and Skills 2006).

Horwath (2002) and Platt (2006) have continued to be interested in how the Assessment Framework is being used when concerns about children are identified, particularly where there is risk of child maltreatment and neglect. Neglect is the most common category of abuse, constituting 45 per cent of all children registered as requiring a multi-agency, co-ordinated child protection plan (Department for Children, Schools and Families 2008). This is important because some commentators have interpreted the Framework as leading to 'the splitting of assessment from protection' and have suggested the Assessment Framework model is 'not an appropriate tool for [child protection] investigative work' (Davies 2008, p.33). Whilst in the early stages of its introduction Horwath (2002) found there were indeed tensions to be resolved, for instance about information-sharing in circumstances of neglect, Platt (2006) was able to conclude in his study that: 'initial assessments…provide a form of practice that offers benefits in terms of balancing child protection and child welfare approaches, and in terms of relationships with parents' (Platt 2006, p.267).

Implementation has highlighted practice issues where practitioner confidence has often been lacking, particularly applying knowledge of child development, incorporating analysis into assessment and undertaking direct work with children. This has led to subsequent government initiatives to support the development of effective practice, some of which have been referenced in this chapter and which also include addressing the support and training needs of supervisors of practitioners. Further studies are now required to evaluate how assessment practice is changing and whether it is improving as the Assessment Framework becomes embedded.

Use of the Assessment Framework in the UK and internationally

An unexpected feature of the Assessment Framework has been the widespread interest shown by other countries and the use that has been made of it by organisations such as the Council of Europe and the World Health Organisation (WHO) Europe. It has been found to have relevance for practice in work with children and families that transcends differences in systems and culture. A recent report by the Council of Europe on parenting in contemporary European societies develops the concept of *positive parenting* and uses the Assessment Framework to demonstrate how the content and context of parenting can be combined in the one model, thus moving away from emphasis on a particular parenting style (Daly 2007). The Council of Europe report notes that the Assessment Framework is being used effectively in many countries, including Australia, Canada, Romania, the Russian Federation, Slovakia, Sweden, Ukraine and the United States of America (Daly 2007, p.19). To these countries can also be added Malta, Croatia and the Republic of Ireland as well as the other nations of the UK: Wales, Scotland and Northern Ireland.

Scotland, in parallel with England and Wales, has developed the *My World Triangle* for use in assessing a child and family's circumstances as an integral part of its practice model within the Scottish Government's overarching policy, *Getting it Right for Every Child* (Scottish Government 2008). The *My World Triangle* has drawn on the domains of the English triangle but has framed them from the point of view of a child:

- how I grow and develop
- what I need from people who look after me
- my wider world.

This gives a different perspective on the same set of factors, reminding practitioners of the importance of understanding a child's experience and perceptions, and the wide range of influences that contribute to how well a child is developing.

In Northern Ireland, the Department of Health and Social Services and Public Safety (DHSSPS) has introduced a new standardised assessment process for children in need within all Health and Social Services Trusts based on the Assessment Framework. This followed a careful review of existing systems and practice (Bunting 2004). The new Assessment Framework, UNOCINI (*Understanding the Needs of Children in Northern Ireland*), was prepared from an extensive consultation process, including front-line staff in trusts and other agencies. It has been designed to help practitioners achieve a sufficient under-standing of the needs of children in Northern Ireland to ensure that effective and safe decisions are made about their needs and how these needs might be addressed (UNOCINI 2008). The Framework uses the same language for assessing and understanding children's needs and aims to improve communication between different disciplines and agencies. It is underpinned by similar policy intentions to those of other UK nations of earlier identification of needs, so that children receive services that make a positive difference to the quality of their lives.

Development work since 2002 in the Republic of Ireland has resulted in a model for assessment, designed and developed by Buckley and Whelan at Trinity College Dublin and Horwath at the University of Sheffield with Irish practitioners, that is now being widely used (Buckley *et al.* 2007). The assessment tool uses the same three areas of a child's life as in England as the focus for gathering information and analysis but also makes explicit 'additional considerations' as part of the tool, such as adult problems of domestic violence and substance misuse that may affect children's needs and parental capacity. Buckley and her fellow authors comment positively on the standardisation of practice that such a framework can bring, the promotion of transparent, evidence-based practice which is child-centred and reinforces multidisciplinary co-operation and col-laboration (Buckley *et al.* 2007, p.46).

Barnardo's in Australia has incorporated the Assessment Framework into its family casework model (*SCARF – Supporting Children and Responding to Families*) and this was evaluated by Fernandez and Romeo (2003) and Tolley (2005). Tolley recorded two major benefits to service delivery:

> Firstly, workers became confident in using a common language, that is, they mean the same thing when they speak about such notions as strengths, needs, risk of harm, or good enough parenting. Establishing a common language has had the effect of improving communication and reducing the chance of erroneous decisions in case management. Secondly workers using SCARF reported that they paid more attention to the effect their work had on the needs of the children rather than looking at its impact on the parent or carer. (Tolley 2005, pp.16–17)

The Assessment Framework has thus begun to provide a much needed international lan-guage about the challenge of improving children's outcomes and a common, standardised approach that can be used to develop child focused practice.

Conclusions

The Assessment Framework was introduced in 2000 and since then has become part of the children's services policy and practice landscape in England. It is underpinned by theory and research about children's development in the context of family and community, together with an explicit set of principles. The Framework as a model to assist practice is proving to be robust and to have widespread relevance across disciplines and agencies concerned with children and families. Moreover, it has been found to have relevance cross-nationally as well, with numerous examples of the Assessment Framework being incorporated into other countries' child welfare systems. There are encouraging signs, albeit more on a reported basis from service managers and less as yet from recent research findings, that assessment practice is improving and that a common language used by practitioners in different settings is resulting in better inter-agency communication. There are still challenges to be addressed, such as improving analysis for making decisions and planning, increasing direct work with children and providing sufficient expert supervision for practitioners. And Horwath (2002) reminds us that the Assessment Framework requires knowledgeable, confident and competent practitioners, committed to its underpinning principles, to achieve the desired improvements in work with children and families.

Acknowledgements

The drawing and commentary by Jax is part of a response by children and young people to consultation with them about their experiences of services in Highland (Highland Children's Forum 2006). I am grateful for Jax's permission and that of Highland Children's Forum to use it in this chapter.

Recommended reading

Aldgate, J., Jones, D.P.H., Rose, W. and Jeffery, C. (eds) (2006) *The Developing World of the Child*. London: Jessica Kingsley Publishers.

Children's Workforce Development Council (2009) *The Common Assessment Framework for Children and Young People: A Guide for Practitioners*. Leeds: Children's Workforce Development Council.

Department of Health (2000) *Assessing Children in Need and their Families: Practice Guidance*. London: The Stationery Office.

Jack, G. and Gill, O. (2003) *The Missing Side of the Triangle: Assessing the Importance of Family and Environmental Factors in the Lives of Children*. Barkingside: Barnardo's.

References

Aldgate, J. and Tunstill, J. (1995) *Making Sense of Section 17: Implementing Services for Children in Need within the Children Act 1989*. London: Her Majesty's Stationery Office.

Aldgate, J., Jones, D.P.H., Rose, W. and Jeffery, C. (eds) (2006) *The Developing World of the Child*. London: Jessica Kingsley Publishers.

Aldgate, J., Rose, W. and McIntosh, M. (2007) *Changing Directions for Children with Challenging Behaviour and their Families: Evaluation of Children 1st Directions Projects*. Edinburgh: Children 1st. Available at www.children1st. org.uk/shop/product/37/0/changing-directions--full-report-, accessed on 25 April 2009.

Belsky, J. and Vondra, J. (1989) 'Lessons from Child Abuse: The Determinants of Parenting.' In D. Cicchetti and V. Carlson (eds) *Child Maltreatment*. Cambridge: Cambridge University Press.

Ben-Arieh, A. (2002) 'Evaluating the Outcomes of Programs versus Monitoring Well-being: A Child-centred Perspective.' In T. Vecchiato, A.M. Maluccio and C. Canali (eds) *Evaluation in Child and Family Services.* New York, NY: Aldine de Gruyter.

Bentovim, A. and Bingley Miller, L. (2001) *The Family Assessment: Assessment of Family Competence, Strengths and Difficulties.* York: Child and Family Training.

Bifulco, A., Mahon, J., Kwon, J., Moran, P. and Jacobs, C. (2003) 'The Vulnerable Attachment Style Questionnaire (VASQ): An interview-based measure of attachment styles that predict depressure disorder.' *Psychological Medicine 33,* 6, 1099–1110.

Booth, T., McConnell, D. and Booth, W. (2006) 'Temporal discrimination and parents with learning difficulties in the child protection system.' *British Journal of Social Work 36,* 997–1015.

Bradshaw, J. (1990) *Child Poverty and Deprivation in the UK.* London: National Children's Bureau.

Bronfenbrenner, U. (1979) *The Ecology of Human Development: Experiments by Nature and Design.* Cambridge, MA: Harvard University Press.

Buckley, H., Whelan, S., Murphy, C. and Horwath, J. (2007) 'Using an assessment framework: outcomes from a pilot study.' *Journal of Children's Services 2,* 1, 37–47.

Bunting, L. (2004) *Assessment of Children in Need in Northern Ireland.* Belfast: National Society for the Prevention of Cruelty to Children, NSPCC Northern Ireland Policy and Research Unit.

Calam, R.M., Cox, A.D., Glasgow, D.V., Jimmieson, P. and Groth Larsen, S. (2000) 'In my shoes. Assessment and therapy with children: can computers help?' *Child Clinical Psychology and Psychiatry 5,* 3, 329–343.

Calder, M.C. and Hackett, S. (2003) 'The Assessment Framework: A Critique and Reformulation.' In M.C. Calder and S. Hackett (eds) *Assessment in Child Care: Using and Developing Frameworks for Practice.* Lyme Regis: Russell House Publishing.

Capaldi, D.M. and Eddy, J.M. (2000) 'Improving Children's Long-term Well-being by Preventing Antisocial Behaviour.' In A. Buchanan and B.L. Hudson (eds) *Promoting Children's Emotional Well-being.* Oxford: Oxford University Press.

Children Act (2004) *Explanatory Notes.* London: The Stationery Office.

Children's Workforce Development Council (2009) *The Common Assessment Framework for Children and Young People: A Guide for Practitioners.* Leeds: Children's Workforce Development Council.

Cleaver, H. (1991) *Vulnerable Children in Schools.* Aldershot: Dartmouth.

Cleaver, H., Unell, I. and Aldgate, J. (1999) *Children's Needs – Parenting Capacity: The Impact of Parental Mental Illness, Problem Alcohol and Drug Use, and Domestic Violence on Children's Behaviour.* London: The Stationery Office.

Cleaver, H. and Walker, S., with Meadows, P. (2004) *Assessing Children's Needs and Circumstances: The Impact of the Assessment Framework.* London: Jessica Kingsley Publishers.

Cleaver, H., Walker, S., Scott, J., Cleaver, D. *et al.* (2008) *The Integrated Children's System: Enhancing Social Work and Inter-agency Practice.* London: Jessica Kingsley Publishers.

Cm 5860 (2003) *Every Child Matters.* Green Paper. London: The Stationery Office.

Commission for Social Care Inspection (2005) *Safeguarding Children – The Second Joint Chief Inspectors' Report on Arrangements to Safeguard Children.* Newcastle: Commission for Social Care Inspection.

Cooper, A. (2005) 'Surface and depth in the Victoria Climbié Inquiry Report'. *Child and Family Social Work 10,* 1, 1–9.

Cox, A. (2008) *The HOME Inventory: A Guide for Practitioners – The UK Approach.* York: Child and Family Training.

Daly, M. (ed.) (2007) *Parenting in Contemporary Europe: A Positive Approach.* Strasbourg: Council of Europe.

Dalzell, R. and Sawyer, E. (2007) *Putting Analysis into Assessment. Undertaking Assessments of Need – A Toolkit for Practitioners.* London: National Children's Bureau.

Daniel, B. and Wassell, S. (2002) *Assessing and Promoting Resilience in Vulnerable Children: 1. The Early Years; 2. The School Years; 3. Adolescence.* London: Jessica Kingsley Publishers.

Davies, L. (2008) 'Reclaiming the Language of Child Protection. Mind the Gap Family Support versus Child Protection: Exposing the Myth.' In M. Calder (ed.) *Contemporary Risk Assessment in Safeguarding Children.* Lyme Regis: Russell House Publishing.

Department for Children, Schools and Families (2008) *Referrals, Assessments and Children and Young People Who Are the Subject of a Child Protection Plan, England: Year Ending 31 March 2008.* Available at www.dcsf.gov.uk/rsgateway/DB/SFR/s000811/index.shtml, accessed on 13 July 2009.

Department for Education and Skills (2005) *Statistics of Education – Referrals, Assessments, and Children and Young People on Child Protection Registers: Year Ending 31 March 2004.* London: The Stationery Office.

Department for Education and Skills (2006) *Statistics of Education: Referrals, Assessments and Children and Young People on Child Protection Registers: Year Ending 31 March 2005.* London: Department for Education and Skills.

Department of Health (1988) *Protecting Children: A Guide for Social Workers Undertaking a Comprehensive Assessment.* London: Her Majesty's Stationery Office.

Department of Health (1991) *Child Abuse: A Study of Inquiry Reports 1980–1989.* London: Her Majesty's Stationery Office.

Department of Health (1995) *Child Protection: Messages from Research.* London: Her Majesty's Stationery Office.

Department of Health (1999a) *The Government's Objectives for Children's Social Services: Summary.* London: Department of Health.

Department of Health (1999b) *The Government's Objectives for Children's Social Services.* London: Department of Health.

Department of Health (2000) *Assessing Children in Need and their Families: Practice Guidance.* London: The Stationery Office.

Department of Health (2001) *The Children Act Now: Messages from Research.* London: The Stationery Office.

Department of Health and Cleaver, H. (2003) *Assessing Children's Needs and Circumstances: The Impact of the Assessment Framework. Summary and Recommendations.* London: Department of Health.

Department of Health and Cox, A. and Bentovim, A. (2000) *The Family Pack of Questionnaires and Scales.* London: The Stationery Office.

Department of Health and Social Security (1981) *Observation and Assessment: Report of a Working Party.* London: Department of Health and Social Security.

Department of Health and Social Security (1982) *Child Abuse: A Study of Inquiry Reports 1973–1981.* London: The Stationery Office.

Department of Health, Department for Education and Employment and Home Office (2000) *Framework for the Assessment of Children in Need and their Families.* London: The Stationery Office.

Ferguson, H. (2004) *Protecting Children in Time.* London: Palgrave.

Fernandez, E. and Romeo, R. (2003) *Supporting Children and Responding to Families. Implementation of the Framework for the Assessment of Children in Need and their Families: The Experience of Barnardos Australia.* Sydney: University of New South Wales, School of Social Work.

Garrett, P.M. (2003) 'Swimming with dolphins: the new Assessment Framework, New Labour and new tools for social work with children and families.' *British Journal of Social Work 33,* 3, 441–463.

Goldstein, W.M. and Hogarth, R.M. (1997) 'Judgement and Decision Research: Some Historical Context.' In R.M. (ed.) *Research on Judgement and Decision Making: Currents, Connections and Controversies.* Cambridge: Cambridge University Press.

Gordon, D., Parker, R.A. and Loughran, F. (2000) *Disabled Children in Britain.* London: The Stationery Office.

Hagell, A. (2003) *Understanding and Challenging Youth Offending. Quality Protects Research Briefings, 8.* London: Department of Health.

Highland Children's Forum (2006) *Are We There Yet? Highland Children's Forum Consultation on For Highland's Children 2 Service Plan 2005–2008. Interim Report 2006.* Highland: Highland Children's Forum.

HM Government (2004) *Every Child Matters: Change for Children.* London: Department for Education and Skills.

HM Government (2005) *Common Core. Skills and Knowledge for the Children's Workforce.* London: Department for Education and Skills.

HM Government (2006) *Working Together to Safeguard Children: A Guide to Inter-agency Working to Safeguard and Promote the Welfare of Children.* London: The Stationery Office.

Holland, S. (2004) *Child and Family Assessment in Social Work Practice.* London: Sage.

Hollows, A. (2003) 'Making Professional Judgements in the Framework for the Assessment of Children in Need and their Families.' In M.C. Calder and S. Hackett (eds) *Assessment in Child Care: Using and Developing Frameworks for Practice.* Lyme Regis: Russell House Publishing.

Holman, B. (1998) *Faith in the Poor.* Oxford: Lion Publishing.

Horwath, J. (2002) 'Maintaining a focus on the child? First impressions of the *Framework for the Assessment of Children in Need and their Families* in cases of child neglect.' *Child Abuse Review 11,* 4, 195–213.

Hughes, L. and Pengelly, P. (1997) *Staff Supervision in a Turbulent Environment.* London: Jessica Kingsley Publishers.

Hutton, A. and Partridge, K. (2006) *Say It Your Own Way'. Children's Participation in Assessment: A Guide and Resources.* London: Department for Education and Skills/Barnardo's.

Jack, G. (1997) 'An ecological approach to social work with children and families.' *Child and Family Social Work 2,* 109–120.

Jack, G. and Gill, O. (2003) *The Missing Side of the Triangle: Assessing the Importance of Family and Environmental Factors in the Lives of Children.* Barkingside: Barnardo's.

Joint Chief Inspectors (2002) *Safeguarding Children. A Joint Chief Inspectors' Report on Arrangements to Safeguard Children.* London: Department of Health.

Jones, D.P.H. (1998) 'The Effectiveness of Intervention.' In M. Adcock and R. White (eds) *Significant Harm: Its Management and Outcome.* Croydon: Significant Publications.

Jones, D.P.H. and Ramchandani, P. (1999) *Child Sexual Abuse: Informing Practice from Research.* Oxford: Radcliffe Medical Press.

Jones, D.P.H., Hindley, N. and Ramchandani, P. (2006) 'Making Plans: Assessment, Intervention and Evaluating Outcomes.' In J. Aldgate, D.P.H. Jones, W. Rose and C. Jeffery (eds) *The Developing World of the Child.* London: Jessica Kingsley Publishers.

Katz, I. (1997) *Current Issues in Comprehensive Assessment.* London: National Society for the Prevention of Cruelty to Children (NSPCC).

Kellmer Pringle, M. and Naidoo, S. (1975) *Early Child Care in Britain.* London: Gordon and Breach.

Lawton, D. (1998) *The Numbers and Characteristics of Families with More than One Disabled Child.* York: University of York, Social Policy Research Unit.

Mahon, J. (2008) *Towards the New Children in Need Census. Research Report DCSF-RW039.* London: Department for Children, Schools and Families.

Millar, M. and Corby, B. (2006) 'The *Framework for the Assessment of Children in Need and their Families* – A Basis for "Therapeutic" Encounter?' *British Journal of Social Work 36*, 6, 887–899.

Munro, E. (2002) *Effective Child Protection.* London: Sage Publications.

National Assembly for Wales and Home Office (2001) *Framework for the Assessment of Children in Need and their Families.* London: The Stationery Office.

Ofsted, Healthcare Commission, Commission for Social Care Inspection, HM Inspectorate of Constabulary *et al.* (2008) *Safeguarding Children: The Third Joint Chief Inspectors' Report on Arrangements to Safeguard Children.* London: Ofsted.

Platt, D. (2001) 'Refocusing children's services: evaluation of an initial assessment process.' *Child and Family Social Work 6*, 2, 139–148.

Platt, D. (2006) 'Investigation or initial assessment of child concerns? The impact of the refocusing initiative on social work practice.' *British Journal of Social Work 36*, 2, 267–281.

Prilleltensky, I. and Nelson, G. (2000) 'Promoting child and family wellness: priorities for psychological and social interventions.' *Journal of Community and Applied Social Psychology 10*, 2, 85–105.

Reder, P., Duncan, S. and Gray, M. (1993) *Beyond Blame: Child Abuse Tragedies Revisited.* London: Routledge.

Rose, W., Aldgate, J. and Barnes, J. (2007) 'From Policy Visions to Practice Realities: The Pivotal Role of Service Managers in Implementation.' In J. Aldgate, L. Healy, B. Malcolm, B.A. Pine, W. Rose and J. Seden (eds) *Enhancing Social Work Management: Theory and Best Practice from the UK and USA.* London: Jessica Kingsley Publishers.

Scarf Australia (2001) *The Supporting Children and Responding to Families (SCARF) Case Management System.* Available at www.scarf.org.au/toolkit.html, accessed on 13 July 2009.

Schofield, G. (1998) 'Inner and outer worlds: a psychosocial framework for child and family social work.' *Child and Family Social Work 3*, 1, 57–67.

Scottish Government (2008) *A Guide to Getting it Right for Every Child.* Edinburgh: Scottish Government.

Seden, J. (2000) 'Assessment of children in need and their families: a literature review.' In Department of Health, *Studies Informing the Framework for the Assessment of Children in Need and their Families.* London: The Stationery Office.

Simmonds, J. (1998) 'Making Decisions in Social Work – Persecuting, Rescuing or Being a Victim.' In M. Adcock and R. White (eds) *Significant Harm: Its Management and Outcome.* Croydon: Significant Publications.

Social Services Inspectorate (1986) *Inspection of the Supervision of Social Workers in the Assessment and Monitoring of Cases of Child Abuse.* London: Department of Health and Social Security.

Stevenson, O. (1998) *Neglected Children: Issues and Dilemmas.* Oxford: Blackwell.

Tolley, S. (2005) 'A family casework model with client and worker friendly assessment, planning and review tools.' *Australian Institute of Family Studies NCPC Newsletter 13*, 2, 16–19.

Understanding the Needs of Children in Northern Ireland (UNOCINI) (2008) *Guidance and Forms.* Available at www.dhsspsni.gov.uk/index/ssi/oss-childrens-services.htm, accessed on 13 July 2009.

Utting, D. (1995) *Family and Parenthood: Supporting Families and Preventing Breakdown.* York: Joseph Rowntree Foundation.

Ward, H. and Rose, W. (eds) (2002) *Approaches to Needs Assessment in Children's Services.* London: Jessica Kingsley Publishers.

CHAPTER 3

The Assessment Process: Practitioner Preparation and Gathering Information for a Core Assessment

Jan Horwath

Gathering information requires careful planning. However difficult the circumstances the *purpose* of assessing the particular child and the family should always be kept in mind.

(From the Framework for the Assessment of Children in Need and their Families, p.40, 3.37)

In this chapter consideration is given to:

- assessment as a phase within the assessment, planning, intervention and review (APIR) process
- assessment as an ongoing activity
- preparing for a core assessment
- gathering information: task and process.

Introduction

A road map contains a great deal of useful information. It can assist us in planning journeys; help us make judgements about the quickest route and decisions about where to stop en route. In addition, whilst on the journey, the map can be of assistance if one gets lost or the intended route is closed. However, to gather information from a map one needs to be able to understand the signs and symbols. But gathering information alone is insufficient. The skill lies in making sense of the information to plan the journey and manage any unanticipated changes required en route. In exactly the same way, the *Framework for the Assessment of Children in Need and their Families* (Assessment Framework) provides a 'conceptual Assessment Framework map' (Department of Health *et al.* 2000, p.17, 2.1). It is designed to enable practitioners to gather and make sense of information about a vulnerable child, within the context of their family and community, in order to meet their needs. However, as with a road map, circumstances can change, so practitioners should be able to use the Assessment Framework to identify and re-evaluate the child's changing circumstances and decide whether the original planned interventions continue to meet the needs of the child.

In Chapter 2 the information practitioners should gather using the Assessment Framework was discussed. In this chapter and Chapter 4, consideration is given to the process that practitioners should follow to complete an effective assessment. Although this process is explored in relation to an in-depth or 'core' assessment, it is still necessary to follow a similar process irrespective of the type of assessment.

The assessment process

Assessment is the crucial first phase of a process often referred to as 'APIR', standing for Assessment, Planning, Intervention and Review. Detailed assessment is the only way of ensuring we recognise the 'uniqueness of individual cases, that we maximise our chances of coming to a good understanding of what is going on and what it might therefore be logical or rational to do by way of response' (Macdonald 2001, p.230).

As the first phase of the APIR process, it is easy to assume that assessment is a discrete activity. However, it is only the beginning. This is clear if one considers two of the principles that underpin the Assessment Framework. First:

> Assessment should run in parallel with actions and interventions. In other words, as the needs of the child and family are identified, these needs should be met and reviewed. (Department of Health *et al.* 2000, p.1, 1.1)

A frequent criticism, made of assessment practice in the past, was that practitioners did not offer services until the assessment was completed (Department of Health *et al.* 2000). Thus, when a need for services is identified, as part of initial or core assessment activity, these services should be provided as soon as possible rather than necessarily waiting for the assessment to be completed. The second principle of the Assessment Framework recognises that:

Assessment is an ongoing process, not a single, one-off event. This means that practitioners should not only assess the immediate needs of the child in relation to safeguarding their welfare but also the longer-term needs of the child and their family. In addition, the effectiveness of actions and interventions designed to meet these needs should be revisited to ensure the changing needs of the child and family are met. (Department of Health *et al.* 2000, p.1, 1.1)

By following this principle practitioners will avoid the negative consequences of focusing solely on current incidents, described in Chapter 1.

Assessment consists of four interconnected phases (Adcock 2001; Buckley *et al.* 2005; Horwath 2007):

- preparing for the assessment
- gathering information
- analysing and making sense of the information
- action planning.

The first two phases – preparing for the assessment and gathering information – are discussed in this chapter and the final two phases are considered in Chapter 4.

Preparing for the assessment

Before an assessment begins it is important to clarify the purpose of the particular assessment and the anticipated outputs. The overall aim of an assessment, using the Assessment Framework, is to safeguard and promote the welfare of the child so that he or she can go on to achieve their full potential. In order to achieve this aim, practitioners should assess the child's developmental needs, parenting capacity to meet these needs and family and environmental factors that impact on the child and family. It is only by gathering and making sense of this information that practitioners are in a position to make judgements as to whether the child is a 'child in need' under section 17 of the Children Act 1989. These judgements should then inform decisions about the actions to be taken and services provided to meet the needs of the child and their family.

The *Framework for the Assessment of Children in Need and their Families* defines the core assessment (the focus of this chapter) as:

An in-depth assessment which addresses the central or most important aspects of the needs of a child and the capacity of his or her parents or caregivers to respond appropriately to these needs within the wider family and community context. (Department of Health *et al.* 2000, p.32, 3.11)

The core assessment usually begins at the point where an initial assessment ends, or those involved in a strategy discussion decide to initiate enquiries under section 47 of the Children Act 1989. However, new information on an open case may indicate that a core assessment should be undertaken. When making a decision whether to progress with a core assessment it is worth noting that both Cleaver and Walker (2004) and Rose and Barnes (2008) found that multiple-problem families, that is, families where concerns have been identified about two or three dimensions in all domains of the Assessment Framework, had not, as anticipated by the researchers, been the subject of a core assessment. One of the reasons for this may be that practitioners are overwhelmed by the complexity of a family's situation and may anticipate that resources are not available to meet the family's needs (Cleaver and Walker 2004; Horwath 2007). By pre-empting the outcome of the assessment in this way, practitioners can lose focus on the child and leave him or her in a very vulnerable situation.

Social workers, together with colleagues from other disciplines, have 35 working days to complete a core assessment. A qualified and experienced social worker, from the local authority children's social care services, should be responsible for leading the assessment. In order to be effective and child focused, it is important that consideration is given to answering the following questions:

- What were the reasons for referral?

- What preceded the core assessment and how can this influence the assessment?

- Is the child currently at risk of suffering significant harm?

- What information is, and should be, available and which professionals should be involved in the assessment process?

- How will the child and their family be engaged in the assessment process?

- Does the child and family have any particular requirements taking account of their race, faith, ethnicity and learning or physical disability?

- What methods will be used for gathering information?

- Are any specialist assessments required?

- What are the timescales?

- With whom and how will information be shared?

These questions are considered in detail below.

What were the reasons for referral, what preceded the core assessment and how can this influence the assessment?

The process of assessment usually begins with a referral. The way in which children's social care staff respond to this referral can lay the foundation for future work, affecting later working relationships with the family and other professionals (Department of Health *et al.* 2000, p.29, 3.3, 3.9). For example, a teacher may continue to feel aggrieved with a social worker who did not appear to take her concerns seriously until the police became involved with the family. Thus, when planning the core assessment it is important to know what the reason was for the referral, the source of the referral and how the child, family and other professionals responded to this referral. It is also useful to establish the nature of any involvement of professionals before the core assessment. For example, who was involved in the initial assessment, however brief, before section 47 enquiries were initiated? If, however, a core assessment is being undertaken on a family well known to an agency or agencies, it is important to establish how the child, family and professionals have worked together in the past.

Is the child suffering or likely to suffer significant harm?

> The core assessment should begin by focusing primarily on the information identi-
> fied during the initial assessment as being most important when considering whether
> the child is suffering, or is likely to suffer, significant harm.

> *(HM Government 2006, p.118, 5.60)*

When planning a core assessment, and in particular as part of section 47 enquiries, prac-titioners should draw on the available evidence of harm or likelihood of possible harm to the child and what, if any, actions are required immediately, or in the short term, to safeguard the child's welfare. When making these decisions it is important that practitio-ners take proper account of historical concerns and information from agencies about risks to the safety of the child (Ofsted *et al.* 2008). Consideration should continue to be given throughout the APIR process as to whether immediate, short-term or longer-term actions are required to safeguard and promote the welfare of the child.

What information should be available and which professionals should be involved in the assessment process?

No one professional has the knowledge and skills to complete a core assessment in isola-tion. Thus, multidisciplinary collaboration is essential, most particularly where a police investigation is being undertaken at the same time. A joined-up approach to assessment can lead to earlier and more efficient identification of a child's needs (Boddy *et al.* 2006). It can also avoid duplication and, as noted by one of the respondents in the study by Cleaver and Walker, ensures 'we are all working from the same hymn sheet' (Cleaver and Walker 2004, p.139).

The professionals who should contribute to the assessment are those who have contact with the child and their carers. This could mean health visitors, school nurses, community paediatricians, early years' and family centre workers, teachers and children's social care workers depending on the age and circumstances of the child. The contributions specific professionals can make are discussed in detail in Chapter 5. These practitioners are likely to hold existing information about the child and family that can inform an assessment and are well placed to gather further information in relation to the domains and dimensions of the Assessment Framework. However, if the child has additional needs and there are specific parenting issues, the contribution of other professionals such as those working in adult services may be required. For example, Rose and Barnes (2008, p.12) note that an assessment of the needs of a disabled child may require the involvement of practitioners from both adult and children's universal and specialist services. This can make an assess-ment 'more complex to co-ordinate and manage'.

Some professionals may have a limited understanding of their role and responsibilities. For example, Pithouse (2006) in a study of the implementation of the Common Assessment Framework (CAF)[1] in Wales found that practitioners in some occupational groups demonstrated a limited capacity to engage with particular assessment domains, such as identity and social presentation. Pithouse could not ascertain whether this was because the professionals considered this was beyond their area of expertise or they considered it not to be relevant. This study demonstrates the importance of clarifying roles and responsibilities in relation to gathering information and is relevant irrespective of the type of assessment that is being completed. At the planning stage of a core assessment clarification can be achieved if the lead social worker explains to each contributing professional:

- the purpose and anticipated outputs from the assessment

- what information the professional is expected to gather and from whom

- how they should record this information

- how information obtained should be shared with the child, their family, as well as across professional boundaries and within agencies

- ways in which the professional is expected to contribute to decision-making and action planning

- the roles and responsibilities of the worker who is co-ordinating the assessment and the respective roles of each professional involved.

(Adapted from Department of Health et al. 2000, p.7, 1.23)

How will the child and their family be engaged in the assessment process? Does the child and family have any particular requirements taking account of race, faith, ethnicity and learning or physical disability?

The quality of an assessment can be significantly affected by the way in which a child and family are engaged in the assessment process (Holland 2000). Dale *et al.* (2005) found that parents involved in section 47 enquiries sometimes felt they were treated unfairly and their interactions with practitioners tended to be negative. Engagement is likely to be poor if the child and family feel that practitioners are only interested in gaining information without trying to understand their point of view. Thus, ascertaining the wishes and feelings of the child and each family member is not only important in terms of gathering information but also in relation to positively engaging them in the assessment process. Platt (2007), in his study of social workers, commented that the extent to which they understood the family's situation affects the degree of co-operation shown by the parents. Brandon *et al.* (2000) (cited in Morrison 2007) found that the quality of the relationship between worker and carer influenced the comprehensiveness of the information collected. If the worker was perceived by the carer to be non-judgemental and empathetic, families were more likely to share emotionally and morally laden information. Subsequently, Cleaver and Walker (2004) reported that carers, who had been involved in assessments using the *Framework*

---

1   A standardised approach to conducting an assessment of a child's additional needs.

for the Assessment of Children in Need and their Families (Department of Health *et al.* 2000), considered they had been consulted and involved in the assessment and that workers had not only listened to them but obtained and recorded their views.

Lord Laming in his Inquiry Report (Cm 5730 2003) stressed the importance of understanding what a day in the life of a child is really like. If practitioners are to achieve this understanding then attention has to be given to engaging children in the assessment process. However, this is an area where practitioners experience difficulty (Cleaver and Walker 2004). Practitioners are most likely to achieve effective engagement if they have opportunities to: build up relationships with children that are dependable and based on honesty and trust; communicate and consult with children and young people about assessment methods; include children and allow them control as to how to express themselves (for example, through verbal or written communication); and decide whether to have others representing their views (Curtis *et al.* 2006; Holland 2004).

Crucial to effective engagement is helping both the child and the family understand: the purpose of the assessment; who will be contributing to the assessment; the focus of meetings and who will attend; and ways in which the child and family can participate in the process. At the planning stage, professionals should also consider who is best placed to ensure that the child and family understand the purpose of the assessment, the anticipated outputs and that they are able to participate in the process. It is particularly important that children and their carers are made aware of what to expect during the assessment process, in particular the possible emotional impact of attending meetings or reviews and hearing the content of assessment reports (Buckley *et al.* 2005). Preparing family members for an assessment can, therefore, be time consuming, as each member of the family should be prepared individually, taking account of their particular needs and concerns.

As discussed in Chapters 6 and 7, there are a range of factors which may act as barriers to effectively engaging the child and family in the assessment process. These should be considered when planning an assessment. For example, if working with an Orthodox Jewish family, will their religious beliefs and practices influence their availability and their expectations of professionals? If working with a family in which English is a second language, is an interpreter required and who would be appropriate? If the child or carer has a learning disability, to what extent will this influence the time required to actively engage them in the assessment process?

In certain situations, family members may not wish to co-operate with statutory agencies. This may be the result of fear, previous negative experiences or parenting problems and difficulties. In these situations practitioners should make every effort to keep the family informed about the assessment and recognise that this level of resistance may alter. When families are resistant, consideration should be given as to how to keep the door open for future engagement. Practitioners may also find it difficult engaging with young people. The joint area review into Haringey's Children's Services Authority Area, following the death of Baby Peter in Haringey, found that engagement with children and young people was not consistently demonstrated in assessments. The Inspectors concluded that the reasons for not seeing a child alone should be noted and addressed by managers and if it is considered appropriate for the child not to be seen alone other methods should be used to enable the voice of the child to be heard (Ofsted *et al.* 2008). Engaging the child and family in the assessment process is discussed in detail in Chapters 6 and 7 and in the overview of Serious Case Reviews completed by Brandon and her colleagues (Brandon *et al.* 2008).

What methods will be used for gathering information? Are any specialist assessments required?

The Assessment Framework provides practitioners with guidance as to *what* information should be gathered as part of the assessment process; it does not direct the practitioner as to *how* this information should be gathered. It is for this reason that a range of assessment tools, such as *The Family Pack of Questionnaires and Scales* (Department of Health and Cox and Bentovim 2000), have been published to accompany the Assessment Framework. In addition, consideration should be given to the nature of concerns about the child, parenting capacity and any specific areas where specialist assessments and assessment tools may assist in gathering information. Specialist assessments are discussed in detail below.

What are the timescales?

Social workers have 35 working days in which to complete the core assessment. At the planning stage consideration should be given to ways in which this process will be managed. For example, when will information be gathered; how, with whom, and when will it be shared?

The process will be influenced by the nature of the concerns about each child. For example, if concerns are substantiated but the child is not judged to be at continuing risk of significant harm, a child protection conference may not be required. However, if concerns are substantiated and the child is judged to be at continuing risk of significant harm, then an initial child protection conference should take place within 15 working days of the last strategy discussion (HM Government 2006, p.122, 5.76, 5.79). In these cases, a social worker from the local authority children's social care services is expected to provide a written report to the conference summarising and analysing the information obtained to date as part of the core assessment. Bell (2007) notes that social workers often lack confidence in selecting the information that is key to the conference. The appropriate information is more likely to be selected if social workers keep the conference objectives in mind. At the planning stage social workers should consider the objectives of the conference: that is, to share and analyse information, and make judgements about the likelihood of a child suffering significant harm and to decide on appropriate actions. It is also important to remember that other professionals are likely to have information about the child and family and should, therefore, contribute to the report.

The conference serves a number of useful purposes. First, it provides a vehicle for taking stock of the information gathered and analysed. Second, it offers an opportunity to identify gaps in information gathered to date. Third, the conference forum provides an opportunity to consider, based on the information gathered so far, what interventions should be made available to the family and when. In addition, it provides an opportunity to clarify the roles and responsibilities of the family and professionals in relation to ongoing assessment and meeting the needs of the child and their family.

At the planning stage, those undertaking a core assessment should consider what specific features of this case could influence the quality of the information they are likely to gather, such as:

- an ability to access and engage family members and professionals in gathering information: for example, school holidays may affect the availability of school staff

- the time required to establish a relationship with a child

- particular issues, such as a carer having a learning disability or requiring an interpreter which may lengthen the process of engagement.

With whom and how will information be shared?

An effective holistic assessment can only be undertaken if professionals are prepared to not only gather but also to share information. Knowing when and what information to share has historically been an area that practitioners have found difficult. Tensions lie between sharing personal information about service users across agency boundaries and respecting the family's right to confidentiality. Furthermore, Cleaver and Walker (2004) found that some professionals were more reluctant than others to share information and practitioners interpreted 'personal information' in different ways. Richardson and Asthana (2006) argue that professional ethos, levels of trust between professional groups and professional attitudes are likely to influence the approach to information sharing. Recognising these challenges, the Government has produced guidance for practitioners who work with children and families about information sharing (HM Government 2008a). This guidance contains seven golden rules for information sharing designed to enable practitioners to share information to deliver better services.

A common anxiety amongst practitioners is deciding what information can be shared without the consent of the child and family. Where there are concerns about significant harm, professionals should consider, at this planning stage, whether discussion and seeking agreement to share information will place the child at increased risk of significant harm or lead to interference with any potential criminal investigation. This is particularly important in suspected cases of fabricated and induced illness by a carer (HM Government 2008b). In principle, professionals should discuss the information they intend to share with the family unless it could place the child at increased risk of significant harm. If children and families are informed when they first engage with a service about the service's approach to sharing information, experience shows they are more likely to give consent to information being shared (HM Government 2008a).

Gathering information

The *Framework for the Assessment of Children in Need and their Families* (Department of Health et al. 2000) is an *aide-mémoire* designed to provide guidance to practitioners regarding information that should be gathered about a vulnerable child and their family (Macdonald 2001). If practitioners are to get a real sense of what life is like for the child who is subject to an assessment, then it is necessary that information is gathered, ideally with the child and family, in relation to all three domains of the Assessment Framework. This information should enable practitioners and the family to reflect not only on whether the needs of the child are being met but also how they are being met. It is, however, all too easy for an assessment to become distorted if particular domains and dimensions are ignored or over-emphasised (Horwath 2002). For example, the social worker co-ordinating an assessment may be unable to actively engage carers or professionals who are working with parents. In this situation, child care professionals may be the main source of information. The focus of an assessment could, therefore, become the developmental needs of the child with little consideration being given to factors that influence parenting capacity.

It is unusual for a core assessment to be the only assessment that a child and family have experienced. Previous assessments are likely to have left an impression on the family and may influence the way in which they approach this current assessment. It is useful, therefore, to begin an assessment by asking the child and their family what they understand to be the purpose of this assessment, what their previous experiences of assessment have been and how they think this assessment will compare. Based on this information, professionals should be able to clarify with the family the purpose of the core assessment and compare and contrast it with the aims of previous assessments. They can use this information to assess what impact these previous assessments are likely to have on the family's willingness and ability to engage in the assessment process.

Methods for gathering information

Gathering information both from, and about, a child and their family can be assisted through the use of a variety of tools such as questionnaires and scales. A range of tools and the way in which they can assist assessment have been summarised in Chapter 2.

Although the tools and scales have been designed for use in the UK it is important to ensure that they are relevant to members of ethnic minority and faith groups living in the UK (Murphy-Berman 1994). It is also important that they are not used in isolation. For example, carers and children may respond over-optimistically or over-pessimistically to questionnaires depending on their desired outcome. They are designed to act as aids and can only give part of the picture. It is therefore important to gather information from a range of other sources.

Further methods of gathering information are considered in detail below.

CHRONOLOGIES

Police and social workers in children's social care were criticised, in the Joint Area Review that followed the serious case review into the death of Baby Peter in Haringey in London, for not always having chronologies on individual case files. The inspectors felt that without chronologies it is difficult to establish the key points at which decisions are made about a child and their family (Ofsted et al. 2008). A chronology should always be included as part of a core assessment. It provides a readily accessible summary of the key life events of a child. From this, practitioners are able to obtain an overview of the child's life. A chronology can bring to the fore significant patterns and experiences which are often buried in the case records held by different agencies. Chronology templates are provided as part of the Integrated Children's System. The areas that should be considered as part of the chronology include: involvement of services, most particularly children's social care; health history such as immunisations and significant health events such as hospital admissions; education, training and employment history including results of school tests of attainment and significant educational events, such as school exclusion; records of changes in the legal status of the child and placement history; and offence records and significant events and changes in the young person's birth family and wider social networks.

FAMILY HISTORIES

Current behaviours are usually influenced by past experiences. Thus, it can be very useful, when undertaking an assessment, to gain information from the parents about their family histories. As Brandon *et al.* (2008) state:

> Carers' experiences of being parented themselves and the history of their own relationships with family, peers, partners and professionals influence their representational models of self and others. These emotional histories, cognitive models and current life stresses will affect the way parents understand and interpret the needs and behaviour of their own children. (Brandon *et al.* 2008, p.59)

In their analysis of serious case reviews into child deaths and serious injuries through abuse and neglect between 2003 and 2005, Brandon *et al.* (2008) found that little attention was given to the background and history of the carers. Brandon *et al.* point out that obtaining a family history is particularly important so that patterns of behaviour, responses to past experiences and help provided to the family inform the current assessment. Without this information practitioners may fall subject to the 'start-again syndrome' discussed in further detail in Chapter 4.

The areas to consider when preparing such a family history are:

- parents' memories of their own parenting experiences and relationships with their carers
- the family history in relation to significant events, such as deaths, unemployment, etc.
- their parents' perceptions of the pregnancy, birth of the child and achievement of developmental milestones
- past difficulties experienced by the child, such as bullying
- history of the child's successes and achievements
- past parenting difficulties and their causes, for example drug and alcohol misuse
- history of coping mechanisms in relation to previous stressful events
- factors that have triggered reduction in parenting capacity in the past
- support systems used in the past and now; their strengths and weaknesses
- environmental factors that have affected family functioning in the past and present, such as racial harassment. (Adcock 2001; Department of Health *et al.* 2000; Glaser 1995)

OBSERVATIONS

Observation is an assessment activity which can provide a wealth of information about the caregiving environment and the quality of the relationships within that environment (Howe *et al.* 1999). Yet, this is an activity which is not used to its maximum potential. For example, in a recent study of child neglect, it was noted that practitioners commented in case records that they had 'seen' the child but went no further in describing the physical circumstances, demeanour of the child or interactions between the child and their carer (Horwath 2007).

Observation activity, in relation to a core assessment, can be both formal and informal. Informal observation takes place throughout the assessment. For example, when recording a home visit, practitioners should comment on the condition of the home, as they observed it, the parents' approach both to the child and to professionals, the moods of family members, the tone in which they respond to questions, as well as what they actually say. Family members may be unaware that these informal observations are recorded and used to gather information. It is, therefore, important that families are informed of this at the start of the assessment process and that any observations, and their interpretation by the practitioner, are validated by information from the family and other sources. This is particularly important if factors such as cultural or religious diversity may influence what is being observed and its possible interpretation.

Practitioners may wish to complete more formal observations as part of the assessment process. For example, if there are concerns that a baby is failing to thrive, practitioners may want to observe a parent or carer feeding the baby. When formal observations take place, Holland (2004) suggests that practitioners should adhere to three principles. The first is ensuring family members have a clear understanding as to why the observation is taking place. Second, they should agree to the observation. Third, the context in which the assessment is taking place should be recognised and ways in which this can influence what is being observed taken into account. For example, a carer may feel embarrassed and inhibited if they know they are being watched while feeding their baby and may well not talk or sing to the child as they would under normal circumstances. With this in mind, ideally, observations should take place on a number of occasions and in different settings so that family members feel comfortable. In addition, children and carers should have an opportunity to comment on ways in which they consider their behaviours were influenced by observation. Jones, in his chapter on parenting capacity (Chapter 17), provides additional advice on the part that observation can play in parenting assessments.

SPECIALIST ASSESSMENTS

Specialist assessments may be commissioned as part of the core assessment 'to provide specific understanding about an aspect of the child's development, parental strengths and difficulties or the family functioning' (Department of Health *et al.* 2000, p.42). The timing and the particular contribution to analysis and planning interventions should be carefully considered as these assessments may take longer than 35 working days to complete. Adult psychiatric assessments may be commissioned if there are concerns about the way in which a carer's mental health issues are influencing parenting capacity. Psychological assessments can be used to assess factors relevant to understanding parenting capacity and can be particularly useful in assessing a learning disabled parent's ability to care for a child. Residential assessments can provide a wealth of information about the relationship between a child and their carer and have been used very effectively in suspected cases of fabricated and induced illness by the carer. Family centre assessments assist in assessing parenting skills and the ability of the carers to relate to children (Dale *et al.* 2005).

Gathering information: subjective influences

Irrespective of the methods used to gather information, the information can be interpreted in different ways depending on the perceptions and beliefs of the practitioner and their view of acceptable standards. It is therefore important, when gathering information, that practitioners record specific examples. This enables both the family and other professionals to be clear about the evidence informing decisions. For example, the description 'the mother did not maintain eye contact with the baby whilst feeding her, although the baby kept looking at the mother's face. She placed the bottle brusquely into the child's mouth causing the child to cry. She then shouted at the baby when she began crying' provides much clearer evidence of the mother/baby interaction than, for example, 'the mother does not seem to be interacting with the child and was irritated by her, which was evident when she was feeding her'.

Brandon *et al.* (2008) found that in approximately one third of the serious case reviews analysed, assessments were considered to be inadequate because insufficient evidence and information had been collected. This may occur because practitioners feel rushed as they try to complete the assessment within the prescribed timescales. This pressure can be exacerbated by heavy caseloads which place conflicting demands on a practitioner's time. In a study in the Irish Republic, social workers often had problems accessing information from other professionals because of school holidays, staff sickness and leave. Moreover, reluctance to share information about a child and their family because of concerns about the way in which the family would perceive the professional sharing the information also affected the quality of information gathered (Horwath 2007). Brandon *et al.* (2008, p.65) also found 'many assessments amounted to little more than the accumulation and presentation of disparate facts and information'. This may occur for a number of reasons. For example, practitioners may be unsure of the relevance of information they hold and therefore record it all, indiscriminately. This is most likely to occur if practitioners are anxious about a particular situation and do not feel confident selecting the relevant information (Horwath 2007). Other assessments, according to Brandon *et al.* (2008), were weak because, whilst the information was available, practitioners failed to examine the evidence and try to understand what it meant in relation to meeting the needs of the child and their family. In Chapter 4, consideration is given to ways in which practitioners can begin to make sense of the information they gather to inform their decisions and the plans they make for children in need and their families.

Summary

This chapter has described the complex process of undertaking a core assessment to assess the in-depth needs of children in need and their families. Contributing to this complexity is the fact that assessment is not an isolated phase of activity: it is an ongoing process that occurs throughout the assessment, planning, intervention and review (APIR) cycle. In addition, it runs parallel to the provision of services to meet the identified needs of children and families.

If an assessment is to be effective, in terms of identifying ways in which the needs of a child can be met, then it has to be a collaborative activity, actively involving practitioners who have knowledge of and are in contact with the child and the family themselves. No one practitioner holds the knowledge necessary to complete a core assessment. For this reason, planning and preparing how the core assessment will be completed is crucial. A key part of this preparation is clarifying the roles and responsibilities of the different professionals who will be contributing to the assessment. As important is identifying how the child and their family will be actively engaged in the assessment process. This engagement is crucial if practitioners are to really understand a day in the life of the particular child.

There is a range of tools available to enable practitioners to gather information in relation to the three domains of the Assessment Framework. These tools should be used to gather information in particular areas. A range of different methods should be used for gathering information and information should be gathered from a variety of sources.

By the end of this stage of the assessment process practitioners should have identified whether the child is at risk of harm and, if so, ensured the child is protected; established the developmental needs of the child; have a comprehensive overview of the family's past history and carers' patterns of behaviour with regard to meeting the needs of the child and other children in the family; and information about family strengths and relevant family and environmental factors. In the following chapter consideration is given to making sense of this information to inform planning and interventions.

Recommended reading

Horwath, J. (2007) *The Neglected Child: Identification and Assessment*. London: Palgrave.

Munro, E. (2008) *Effective Child Protection*. London: Sage.

Wilson, K. and James, A. (eds) (2007) *The Child Protection Handbook: The Practitioner's Guide to Safeguarding Children*. London: Baillière Tindall.

References

Adcock, M. (2001) 'The Core Assessment – How to Synthesise Information and Make Judgements.' In J. Horwath (ed.) *The Child's World: Assessing Children in Need*. London: Jessica Kingsley Publishers.

Bell, M. (2007) 'Safeguarding Children in Case Conferences.' In K. Wilson and A. James (eds) *The Child Protection Handbook: The Practitioner's Guide to Safeguarding Children*. London: Baillière Tindall.

Boddy, J., Potts, P. and Statham, J. (2006) *Models of Good Practice in Joined-up Assessment: Working for Children with Significant and Complex Needs*. London: Thomas Coran Research Unit.

Brandon, M., Belderson, P., Warren, C., Howe, D. *et al.* (2008) *Analysing Child Deaths and Serious Injury through Abuse and Neglect: What Can We Learn? A Biennial Analysis of Serious Case Reviews 2003–2005*. Research Report No. DCSF-RR023. Nottingham: Department for Children, Schools and Families.

Brandon, M., Thoburn, J., Lewis, A. and Way, A. (2000) *Safeguarding Children with the Children Act 1989*. London: The Stationery Office.

Buckley, H., Horwath, J., Whelan, S. and Health Service Authority (2005) *A Framework for Assessing Vulnerable Children and their Families.* Trinity College Dublin and University of Sheffield. Dublin: Children's Research Centre.

Cleaver, H. and Walker, S. (2004) *Assessing Children's Needs and Circumstances. The Impact of the Assessment Framework.* London: Jessica Kingsley Publishers.

Cm 5730 2003. *The Victoria Climbié Inquiry Report.* London: The Stationery Office.

Curtis, D., Shaw, J. and Byrne, A. (2006) 'Children and Young People's Consultations on their Experiences of Social Care.' In National Children's Bureau and Children's Workforce Development Council (eds) *Options for Excellence: Improving and Developing Social Care.* London: National Children's Bureau.

Dale, P., Green, R. and Fellows, R. (2005) *Child Protection Assessment Following Serious Injuries to Infants: Fine Judgements.* Chichester: John Wiley and Sons.

Department of Health and Cox, A. and Bentovim, A. (2000) *The Family Pack of Questionnaires and Scales.* London: The Stationery Office.

Department of Health, Department for Education and Employment and Home Office (2000) *Framework for the Assessment of Children in Need and their Families.* London: The Stationery Office.

Glaser, D. (1995) 'Emotionally Abusive Experiences.' In P. Duncan and C. Lucey (eds) *Assessment of Parenting: Psychiatric and Psychological Contributions.* London: Routledge.

HM Government (2006) *Working Together to Safeguard Children. A Guide to Inter-agency Working to Safeguard and Promote the Welfare of Children.* London: HM Government.

HM Government (2008a) *Information Sharing: Guidance for Practitioners and Managers.* London: Department for Children, Schools and Families.

HM Government (2008b) *Safeguarding Children in whom Illness is Fabricated or Induced. Supplementary Guidance to Working Together to Safeguard Children.* London: Department for Children, Schools and Families.

Holland, S. (2000) 'The assessment relationship: interactions between social workers and parents in child protection assessments.' *British Journal of Social Work 30,* 149–163.

Holland, S. (2004) *Child and Family Assessment in Social Work Practice.* London: Sage.

Horwath, J. (2002) 'Maintaining a focus on the child? First impressions of the "Framework for the Assessment of Children in Need and their Families" in cases of child neglect.' *Child Abuse Review 11,* 4, 195–213.

Horwath, J. (2007) *The Neglected Child: Identification and Assessment.* London: Palgrave.

Howe, D., Brandon, M., Hinings, D. and Schofield, G. (1999) *Attachment Theory, Child Maltreatment and Family Support.* Houndmills: Macmillan.

Macdonald, G. (2001) *Effective Interventions for Child Abuse and Neglect.* Chichester: Wiley.

Morrison, T. (2007) 'Emotional intelligence, emotion and social work: context, characteristics, complications and contribution.' *British Journal of Social Work 37,* 245–263.

Murphy-Berman, V. (1994) 'A conceptual framework for thinking about risk assessment and case management in child protective services.' *Child Abuse and Neglect 18,* 2, 193–201.

Ofsted, Healthcare Commission and HM Inspectorate of Constabulary (2008) *Joint Area Review. Haringey Children's Services Authority Area.* Available at www.ofsted.gov.uk/oxcare_providers/la_download/(id)/4657/(as)/JAR/jar_2008_309_fr.pdf, accessed on 13 July 2009.

Pithouse, A. (2006) 'A common assessment for children in need? Mixed messages from a pilot study in Wales.' *Child Care in Practice 12,* 3, 199–217.

Platt, D. (2007) 'Congruence and co-operation in social workers' assessments of children in need.' *Child and Family Social Work 12,* 4, 326–335.

Richardson, S. and Asthana, S. (2006) 'Inter-agency information sharing in health and social care services: the role of professional culture.' *British Journal of Social Work 36,* 657–669.

Rose, W. and Barnes, J. (2008) *Improving Safeguarding Practice: Study of Serious Case Reviews 2001–2003.* Nottingham: Department for Children, Schools and Families.

CHAPTER 4

The Assessment Process: Making Sense of Information, Planning Interventions and Reviewing Progress

Jan Horwath

The purpose of an assessment is to identify the child's needs within their family context and to use this understanding to decide how best to address these needs. It is essential that the plan is constructed on the basis of the findings from the assessment and that this plan is reviewed and refined over time to ensure the agreed case objectives are achieved.

(From the Framework for the Assessment of Children in Need and their Families, p.62, 4.37)

In this chapter the following are considered:

- analysing and making sense of information gathered as part of a core assessment
- making judgements and decisions about the needs of children
- action planning
- evaluating progress
- recording
- subjective factors that influence the assessment process.

Introduction

In Chapter 3 consideration was given to ways in which practitioners should prepare for an in-depth or 'core' assessment and ways in which information can be gathered using the *Framework for the Assessment of Children in Need and their Families* – the Assessment Framework (Department of Health *et al.* 2000). Emphasis was placed on assessment being part of an ongoing process. Preparing for an assessment and gathering information is of little use if practitioners do not go on to make sense of what this information tells them about the life of a child in a particular family, and the impact that this is having on the child's health and development. Only by understanding this impact can practitioners begin to consider how to work together with the child and family to meet the child's needs. In this chapter consideration is given to 'case formulation' (Brandon *et al.* 2008, p.66), that is the process whereby practitioners, and where appropriate families, 'summarise, integrate and synthesise the knowledge brought together by the assessment process' in order to make judgements about the nature of current concerns, their development, and family strengths. This understanding will in turn inform decisions about appropriate interventions.

Crucial to effective assessment is high quality recording. Ways in which practitioners should record information and decisions made as part of the assessment process will be explored, drawing on the Integrated Children's System (ICS) exemplars (Department of Health 2003) which are available to enable practitioners to record at each stage of the assessment process.

As indicated in Chapter 3 a variety of subjective factors may influence practitioners' approaches to gathering information. Subjective factors, such as fear of violence from a carer, continue to influence the assessment process. Hence, the chapter ends by discussing the types of factors that may distort assessments, and strategies practitioners and their supervisors can put in place to avoid this occurring.

Analysing information

As soon as practitioners start the assessment process they begin, consciously or unconsciously, hypothesising about what they know and observe in order to try to understand the child and family's situation. Some hypotheses will be confirmed, others discarded and replaced by new ones as the process of gathering information continues (Dalzell and Sawyer 2007; Holland 2004). What is important is that, whilst gathering information, practitioners keep an open mind and revise their hypotheses in light of new information, rather than ignoring information which does not fit with their original hypotheses (Munro 2000). For example, in the case of Victoria Climbié, practitioners focused on her carer's housing application, ignoring evidence that Victoria was potentially suffering significant harm (Cm 5730 2003).

Although hypothesising takes place throughout the information-gathering phase, at some point this information has to be collated and analysed to inform the action plan to safeguard and promote the welfare of the child. Practitioners may be overwhelmed by the amount of information obtained, as well as the accuracy, detail, value and the significance of this information. Indeed, Cleaver and Walker (2004) found social workers expressed anxiety about analysing information collected as part of an assessment. There is a danger that under these circumstances an assessment becomes little more than a summary of data collected (Brandon *et al.* 2008; Crisp *et al.* 2006). Summarising information obtained under each of the three domain headings of the Assessment Framework is a useful way of beginning the process of making sense of it. The different perspectives of practitioners, family members and the child should be compared and contrasted in order to ensure a balanced analysis. For example, carers may consider they provide an appropriate environment for the child to do their homework, whereas the child may disagree. A summary should include identified strengths as well as difficulties (Department of Health *et al.* 2000).

Gambrill (2005), who draws on the work of Paul (1992), and Buckley *et al.* (2005) provide useful lists of questions to assist practitioners to begin to analyse information. The questions below are adapted from their work:

- Is the meaning of what is being reported clear?

- Are assumptions being made, unsupported opinions formed or is the analysis based on fact and/or observation?

- Are the views and feelings of the child and each family member made explicit?

- What is being implied by the available evidence and what are the possible consequences in relation to safeguarding and promoting the welfare of the child?

- What evidence is there from practice experience, guidance, inspection reports, research findings and the literature to draw these conclusions?

- Are there other viewpoints and perspectives which mean particular information could be interpreted differently?

- Are there other questions that practitioners should be asking?

Making sense of information

Having analysed the information, the next step is to consider what this says about the child and their situation. In order to answer this question it is necessary to make what Hollows (2003, p.69) refers to as 'issues' judgements. That is, to establish the issues or concerns in relation to the needs of the child, the carer's ability to meet these needs, and family and environmental factors that may impact on these. As part of this process consideration should be given to both child and family vulnerabilities and strengths.

Judgement-making has been described as a magical quality (Eraut 1994). It involves making deductions from the information gathered to inform decisions about appropriate interventions. Practitioners should use research, theory and practice experiences to make judgements but judgement-making is still vulnerable to human error. Organisational context, personal and professional beliefs and values, fears and anxieties may all affect the judgements made, as may over-dependence on past experiences of what appear to be similar situations (Munro 1999; Reder *et al.* 1993; Taylor and White 2001). (This is discussed in detail below.) When making issues judgements, practitioners should remain child focused, drawing on knowledge about stages of child development and reasonable standards of care. The answers to the following questions may assist:

- What has been happening to this child? Do practitioners have a sense of what a day in his or her life is like?

- Which of the developmental needs of the child are being met and which are not?

- Why has this been happening?

- What are the implications of the needs not being met?

- How does the child and the carers perceive concerns about needs not being met?

- What aspects of parenting capacity and family and environmental factors are contributing to these needs not being met?

- Are the concerns about the child's needs, parenting capacity and family and environmental factors pre-existing or recent?

- What is there about the current situation that increases or decreases the likelihood that the needs of the child will not be met?

- What are the pre-existing and current strengths that safeguard and promote the welfare of the child?

- What do practitioners know about past patterns of parent and child behaviour which may inform judgements about the vulnerability of the child?

- What is the likelihood of change?

There are two areas where it is particularly difficult to make sense of information: first, in relation to assessing likelihood of harm and, second, assessing the potential for change amongst carers. The second is covered in detail by Morrison in Chapter 18. The first is considered below.

Significant harm and identifying protective as well as risk factors

A criticism that has been levelled at the *Framework for the Assessment of Children in Need and their Families* (Department of Health *et al.* 2000) is that a focus on needs means that risk of harm and dangerousness are marginalised, leaving children vulnerable to incidents of maltreatment and significant harm (Calder 2003). However, as described in Chapter 1, a focus primarily on risk and dangerousness rather than need has, in the past, resulted in an incident-driven system that centred on the actual incident of abuse and paid little attention to the impact of the abuse on children. What is required is for practitioners to assess whether children are suffering or are likely to suffer significant harm, in terms of their development needs.

Little *et al.* (2004) explore the concept of risk of harm and make a number of helpful suggestions about the use of the term and its application to children in need. First, risk should be used to describe the factors that may impair a child's development, rather than using the term to describe the risk of the child needing a service, for example 'risk of coming into care'. Hence, as defined by Hagell (1998), 'risk' is the possibility of a serious negative outcome for a child. The way in which practitioners assess possible negative outcomes for a child is to consider the health and development of the child. This is explicit in the definition of significant harm in section 31 of the Children Act 1989 which is re-produced in *Working Together* (HM Government 2006, p.35, 1.23). Thus, risk of harm and a child's developmental needs are inextricably linked both in our primary legislation and in practice. Therefore, the task for practitioners is to specify, by drawing on the domains of the Assessment Framework, what, in relation to their health and development, the child is at risk of and how significant they consider this risk to be.

Little *et al.*'s (2004) second point is that assessing the significance of risk of harm also requires consideration of the protective factors that can reduce risk to the child's health and development. This is explicit in the Assessment Framework (Department of Health *et al.* 2000), which emphasises the importance of analysing strengths as well as difficulties. Turnell and Edwards (1999) describe these protective factors as 'signs of safety'. They argue that family members are more likely to engage with professionals if they are not labelled as problematic, but professionals acknowledge resources within the family to provide increased safety, however small and seemingly insignificant. These signs of safety can be used to identify possible small, specific and achievable changes that the family can make, which in turn can build the family's confidence and motivation. Little *et al.* (p.114) conclude that: 'need provides a language for summarising risk and protective factors in a statement of what is required if the child is not to suffer further impairment to their health or development'. This reinforces what is in the Assessment Framework (Department of Health *et al.* 2000, p.8, 1.27).

When assessing protective and risk factors related to harm, practitioners frequently ask 'How do we know if this is harmful?' Jones, in his chapter on parenting capacity (Chapter 17), describes some of the factors that have been identified to be risk factors for recurrence of child maltreatment. (See also Bentovim 1998 and Brandon *et al.* 2008.) However, there are a number of points that should be considered when evaluating risk and protective factors in relation to significant harm to a child. These are summarised by Little *et al.* (2004) as:

- A risk factor increases the chance of a specified outcome: it does not mean it is inevitable.

- Rarely does one risk factor impact on a child's development; it is more likely to be an interaction of several risk factors.

- The same risks may produce different outcomes depending on the stage of development of the child and the context.

- Risk factors may not have an immediate effect; rather they may set off a longer-term 'chain re-action' (*ibid.*, p.107).

- Different children may respond differently to the same risk factor/s.

- Risk factors may have a direct impact on development through, for example, poor parenting, or they may have an indirect impact through, for example, poverty or poor housing.

- Risk factors may be *mediator* variables, such as genetic factors which are likely to lead to a specific outcome, or *moderator* variables, such as motivation which can change the strength of relationship with the outcome.

Action planning

Having made judgements about the vulnerability of the child, those engaged in the core assessment have to make decisions about appropriate interventions to safeguard and meet the identified needs of the child, and those of parents or carers and other family members. This process can be difficult and, on occasion, demoralising for practitioners and families as they realise that there are often no perfect solutions (Munro 2000). Rather, they are weighing up the advantages and disadvantages of different available options or courses of action, drawing on the most up-to-date evidence base. It can also be tempting, when completing an assessment on a family well known to the child welfare agencies, to want to start with a clean sheet. This is referred to by Brandon *et al.* (2008, p.72) as the 'start again syndrome'. This can be dangerous as the past history and cumulative effects of poor parenting, described by Jones in Chapter 17, are not used to inform current planning. The temptation to start again can occur when workers are overwhelmed by the amount of information on case files and feel helpless trying to make sense of all this information. Alternatively, a practitioner new to the case may have decided to 'start afresh' to form an 'unprejudiced view of the case' (p.73). In either case practitioners are ignoring an important dimension of the Assessment Framework: family history and family functioning.

Decision-making

By this stage of the core assessment practitioners should have an understanding of the wishes and views of each child and family member, how the family is functioning and how the needs of the child are being responded to. However, bearing in mind that a core assessment should be completed in 35 working days, it is all too easy for practitioners to feel that there is more they want to know, particularly if they had problems engaging with family members. Some of the practitioners who participated in the work by Dalzell and Sawyer (2007), for example, felt that they were not in a position to draw conclusions about the child and their family. It is important that this is recognised and that any limitations, in terms of knowledge and understanding about the child and their situation, are acknowledged. Conversely, practitioners should make the best use of the known information and recognise that there will always be 'more to know' (Department of Health *et al.* 2000).

Ideally, by the time practitioners begin to develop an in-depth plan, they should have an understanding of:

- the issues regarding safeguarding the welfare of the child
- family strengths, sources of protection and resilience and what can be built on
- previous responses to interventions
- motivation and insight of the carers in relation to meeting the needs of the child

- the child's wishes and feelings and what they want to happen

- the carers' ideas as to what will assist them in meeting the needs of the child

- the influence of culture, language, religious beliefs and practices on this family's life

- how the carers have or have not begun to meet the needs of the child as the assessment has progressed

- patterns of behaviour that are emerging.

Decision-making in relation to children in need, and in particular those subject to section 47 enquiries, has been criticised in the past for lacking clarity and focusing on short-term interventions (Calder and Horwath 1999; Department of Health 2001; Joint Chief Inspectors 2002). Moreover, practitioner reluctance to make difficult decisions, such as removing children from their carers, has resulted in procrastination and cases drifting (Sinclair and Bullock 2002).

If practitioners are to plan interventions that are timely and best meet the needs of the child and their family they should consider all feasible options and identify which types of intervention are most likely to result in the best outcomes for this child. As part of this process they should take into account (Department of Health *et al.* 2000, p.58, 4.20):

- existing positive relationships and experiences that can be nurtured and developed

- the interventions known to have the best outcomes in these situations

- next-best interventions if identified ones are not available

- providing services that will not overwhelm the child and family

- identifying an optimal hierarchy of interventions, some that are likely to lead to early success and have a beneficial effect, others that will assist in achieving the longer-term goals

- identifying the highest priority from the child's perspective

- establishing a timescale.

An effective way of exploring the options available is to use a decision-making tree (Dalzell and Sawyer 2007; Munro 2000). In brief, the way in which the tree can be used is for practitioners and the family, for example at a case planning meeting or child protection conference, to consider each area of concern and in the light of this ask themselves:

- What decision should be made?

- What are the options or possible actions available?

- What information do we have and do we need additional information to inform the choice?

- What are the possible consequences of each option in both the short and longer term?

- What is the probability of each of these consequences occurring in terms of research, practice experience and our knowledge of the child and their family?

- What are the advantages and disadvantages of each of these consequences?

- Which option offers the most desirable consequences and is most achievable?

The tree can be drawn with various branches as shown in Figure 4.1.

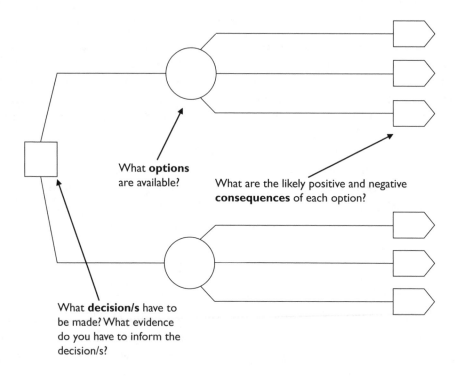

Figure 4.1: *A decision-making tree (adapted from Munro 2000)*

Individual practitioners can place a numerical value on each of the possible options by grading the various anticipated consequences on a scale of 0 to 10, 0 being very undesirable and 10 being very desirable. The option with the highest score is then selected.

It may well be, with certain cases, that there are a significant number of decisions to be taken. In these situations it may not be practical to use the tree to make all decisions. It can, however, be useful in terms of making key decisions, most particularly when professionals and family members hold different views as to how to progress. Exploring the different options and consequences enables practitioners and family members to both articulate and challenge different viewpoints. What is crucial is that these discussions should be evidence-based and child focused. Clearly, this exercise cannot be undertaken without taking into account the resources available. However, by making decisions in this way, practitioners are likely to think more widely (Dalzell and Sawyer 2007) and often more creatively.

For further information on decision-making trees see Dalzell and Sawyer (2007) and Munro (2000).

From needs to outcomes

> The details of the plan are bench marks against which the progress of the family and the commitment of workers are measured, and therefore it is important that they should be realistic and not vague statements of good intent.
>
> *(Department of Health et al. 2000, p.60, 4.32)*

A common problem with planning is that practitioners are not specific when identifying *how* particular interventions are expected to meet the needs of the child and their family. Although, Cleaver and Walker (2004) found that the Assessment Framework did assist practitioners to clarify the aims and objectives of interventions, they also found that where practitioners had not been involved in planning this acted as a barrier to collaboration in the delivery of services. This would indicate that meetings, such as family group conferences, children in need planning meetings, child protection conferences and core group meetings, have a significant part to play in ensuring that both practitioners and family members understand the relevance of the identified interventions in relation to meeting the particular needs of the child and the family.

Effective planning is dependent on practitioners and the family setting specific objectives. In other words, being clear about the needs that should be addressed as part of the plan and the outcomes they hope to achieve through particular interventions. The Integrated Children's System includes different pro-forma that are designed to keep a focus on specific planning objectives and outcomes. However, if the plan is to be completed effectively and used as a vehicle to inform interventions and lead to better outcomes for children, then a number of factors should be considered. First, it is often presumed that there is a common understanding, amongst professionals and the family, as to what they want to achieve and how particular services will meet these needs. As a result of this it is all too easy, particularly when completing a pro-forma such as the child and young person's plan, to use a short-hand presuming that everyone understands what it means. For example, when considering parenting capacity in relation to responding to the identified needs of the child, there may be concerns about a mother's ability to provide guidance and boundaries to her four-year-old. In order to address this concern, attendance at a parenting group is recommended on a weekly basis with the desired outcome being described as 'mother successfully attends all sessions, things improve at home'. Each practitioner, and indeed the mother herself, may have very different ideas about what is an 'improvement'. Practitioners should be clear and have a common understanding about the outcomes they wish to achieve and the steps required to achieve these outcomes and share this with the family. Without this clarity, how are they going to know if the interventions are successful and contributing to improving the health and wellbeing of the child? How are they going to be able to evaluate progress or make difficult decisions as to whether a child should be removed from their carers? A more specific outcome approach to planning can be achieved by considering the following questions when developing a child's plan.

- What specific needs of the child are practitioners and the family meeting?

- What change is required in order to meet these needs?

- What is expected of the carers, child and other family members if this change is to take place?

- What do professionals need to do to assist the carers and support the child?

- What would it look like if the identified needs of the child are met?

- How will we measure improvements?

- What are the timescales?

- Do we need a contingency plan?

- Do professionals and family members engaged in the plan have a shared understanding of the above?

At this planning stage each professional and family member should have an understanding of the aims and objectives of particular actions and be clear as to what is expected of them as individuals and their agency, in relation to achieving these aims and objectives. It is also helpful to ensure that there is a common and realistic understanding of frequency and length of service provision. Dates should be agreed for evaluating progress, with specific measures negotiated for establishing progress.

Whilst it is relatively easy to identify a series of actions that will meet the needs of the child, the assessment task, at this stage, is deciding what is required and what can be achieved realistically. It is all too easy to over-burden carers. For example, the author recently read a multidisciplinary child protection plan where a lone mother with two children under three years of age was expected to use a rather infrequent bus service to attend different services in different parts of the city on the same day and engage with a diverse range of practitioners at different venues during one week. In these situations, it is important to consider whether the expectations placed on carers are realistic or whether they are being set up to fail.

Evaluating progress

As was made clear at the beginning of Chapter 3 assessment is an ongoing process. It does not stop when the core assessment is completed. Rather, the nature of the assessment changes. The focus becomes assessing whether the interventions provided are meeting the needs of the child, whether the needs identified at the beginning of the core assessment have changed and whether new needs are being identified. However, what can occur at this stage is that the focus becomes output measures rather than outcomes. One example would be recording regular attendance at a parenting group as a measure of success. This type of measure tells us more about system throughput than improvements to the health and development of the child. When evaluating progress the focus should be on the needs of the specific child. Hence, the information that is required is about the original concerns, the progress made to date to address those concerns and the final outcome that professionals working with the family hope to achieve. Questions to consider, and supported by the exemplars in the Integrated Children's System, are:

- How are the services provided meeting the needs of the child?

- What evidence do practitioners have to support this?

- What are the wishes and feelings of the child and views of their carers?

- Are the interventions addressing our original and emerging concerns?

- Is progress being made at a pace that will safeguard the child's welfare in both the short and longer term?

- Are any additional services required or changes made to current service provision to achieve the desired outcomes?

When evaluating progress practitioners should consider the carers' commitment and engagement in the change process as discussed in Chapter 17.

Recording

> Practitioners need to make a clear, detailed record of events so that past history is available to be scrutinised. Patterns can be detected only if practitioners have written down a precise account of what happened.
>
> *(Munro 2000, p.148)*

Effective recording not only provides an account of the assessment, which can inform subsequent work with the child and family, but also act as a tool assisting both practitioners and families steer a clear course through the assessment process. In order to assist effective recording of core assessments, the English and Welsh Governments developed assessment exemplars as part of the Integrated Children's System. Cleaver and Walker (2004) studied ways in which these exemplars were used by social workers who co-ordinated core assessments. They found that there was considerable variation in the quality of the recorded information. For example, basic information, such as ethnicity, was missing. In only a third of cases was a clear picture provided as to who was involved in the assessment, the information gathered, the analysis evidenced and the objectives and plans reflecting the assessment findings. They concluded that the social workers in their study, who completed the records, were often confused about how to use them, most particularly the sections left clear for 'free script'. This occurred even though there are instructions on the exemplars as to what should be considered under each section. We should, however, be cautious about the way in which these findings are interpreted as the study was completed when both the Assessment Framework and recording forms were relatively new. The questions and prompts included in both Chapters 3 and 4 should enable practitioners to complete the 'free script' sections of the exemplars.

It is very easy, when completing exemplars such as those designed to support the core assessment, to use professional language and abbreviations. However, these are documents which should be easily understood not only by other practitioners from a range of different disciplines but also the family. Cleaver and Walker (2004) found that practitioners did not necessarily communicate with families about whether they had received assessments and plans, let alone whether they fully understood what was written about them. Yet, if children and families are to actively engage in working together with practitioners to meet the needs of the child, then it is crucial that the plan is discussed with them and that practitioners ensure that the family has a clear understanding of the content of the assessment plan.

Subjective factors that influence the assessment process

Assessing the needs of vulnerable children and their families brings to the fore a diverse range of feelings. The feelings experienced by practitioners – and they are likely to be different with each family – will be influenced by personal and professional experiences and the organisational context in which practitioners work. For example, a practitioner may meet a carer who reminds them of their own parents and this influences their approach towards the carer. Alternatively, a practitioner may have been hit by a service user and may find themselves fearful when meeting someone who reminds them of the violent service user. These feelings and experiences can distort the assessment, resulting in practitioners becoming selective about the information they gather and the way they make sense of the information. For example, if a practitioner is afraid of a carer they may avoid asking questions that may make the carer angry. A failure to gather all relevant information will consequently influence decisions made about the situation (Horwath 2007; Morrison 2001; Reder and Duncan 1999). Moreover, as Brandon *et al.* (2008, p.90) put it, 'workers become paralysed by their own fears and anxieties, which can lead to the assessment process remaining incomplete'. Ultimately, this can lead to a loss of focus on the child. The common ways in which feelings and experiences can distort assessments are described in Figure 4.2.

It is not only the way in which practitioners perceive families that can distort assessments; the perceptions they have of each other will also influence decision-making. Ways in which professionals interpret the information they receive from each other will be informed by factors, such as their past experiences of working together; the perceptions of the agency; stereotypes held about different professionals; and expectations of roles and responsibilities. What is easily forgotten is that each professional's practice will be influenced in this way. Thus, when two or more practitioners come together all these influences will be affecting their approach towards each other and the way in which they select information. The way in which the information is conveyed is also significant. For example, when professionals meet face-to-face or communicate by telephone, the tone of voice, the language used and facial expressions will all influence the way in which the information is shared and how that information is interpreted. This is described very graphically by Reder and Duncan (2003).

Munro (2000) found that irrespective of the subjective influences affecting the assessment certain types of information are remembered more readily than others. The features of a case that are remembered most easily are: vivid, emotionally ladened, recent and concrete. This means that information gathered verbally, most particularly when the

SUBJECTIVE RESPONSE	IMPACT ON ASSESSMENT
Over-optimism: a misguided positive belief in the carer's ability to meet the needs of the child. For example, 'Now that Dad knows what he has done wrong I'm sure the family will be OK. You know they are really nice people.'	This results in an over-emphasis on assessing strengths and minimising concerns. The practitioner may accept the carer's perception that all is well without an evidence-base.
Over-pessimism: a belief that the carer is unable to meet the needs of the child. For example, 'She's a hopeless case, the child is best out of there.'	This can lead to an assessment that focuses on concerns and parenting deficits, ignoring or minimising any strengths.
Collusion: choosing to believe what carers say despite evidence to the contrary. For example, 'Mum is trying so hard, she's a lovely person; she says she's learnt her lesson and I believe her.'	In these situations workers focus on the carer's perspective and do not seek evidence to confirm or refute these beliefs, either through the current assessment or by identifying past patterns of behaviour.
Fixed idea: holding a specific idea about the nature of the case, often pre-judging a situation. For example, 'I know the problem is Dad's drinking; why bother with an assessment, it will just confirm this'.	The fixed idea is often formed early on. Indeed it may be the practitioners first hypothesis and they stick to it. In these situations practitioner's tend to gather information that confirms their ideas and they ignore information that contradicts this.
Overriding beliefs: having a fixed idea about the needs of the family and ways in which they can be met. For example, 'If only we could clean the house out the neglect would cease.'	In these situations practitioners make an early decision about appropriate interventions and ignore information which may indicate that these are not appropriate. A common overriding belief is that the family will eventually be able to meet the needs of the child when there is no evidence to indicate this and the child should be placed out of home.
Ignoring difference: treating all families as the same. For example, 'another dirty, smelly family.'	The practitioner tends to categorise families and make judgements about them without considering differences. This can be particularly common when working with families from different ethnic and religious backgrounds.
Avoidance: failing to ask difficult questions or challenging what the carer says. For example, 'I did not ask about his drinking. I did not want to annoy him.'	This response is most likely to occur if the practitioner is intimidated by the carer. In this situation selected information is gathered. This is likely to be non-controversial or positive and can mean that areas of concern are not explored.

Figure 4.2: *Ways in which feelings and experiences can distort assessments*

informant uses strikingly descriptive adjectives, will overshadow information that is presented by others in factual reports. This can have a significant influence in planning or core group meetings if some members present verbally whilst others, who may not be able to attend the meeting, present written reports. Bias towards remembering recent events highlights the importance of completing chronologies and family histories as part of the core assessment. If these are not used, patterns of behaviours, past triggers that increase vulnerability and strengths that have averted problems in the past will become marginalised when making decisions about current concerns.

Whether through family group conferences, child protection conferences, core groups or children in need (including looked after children) planning and review meetings, practitioners are likely to come together to make decisions and plan to meet the needs of the child. Distortion and bias can play a part in these meetings, meaning that children can be left in vulnerable situations. Describing case conferences, Gambrill (2005, p.467) says they 'represent a complex social situation in which participants have different goals, skills, values, styles of interaction, practice theories, prejudices and biases'. The impact that these can have on interactions have been well documented (Farmer and Owen 1995; Reder *et al.* 1993).

Practitioners may be reluctant to disagree with others, particularly if they perceive they are of higher status and authority (Cm 5730 2003). Different thresholds may operate depending on knowledge and experience. Gambrill goes on to describe how both task and setting influence the process. For example, anxiety levels are likely to be high if professionals are concerned that the child is suffering significant harm; members of the conference may feel compromised in terms of what they are prepared to say knowing aggressive family members are present. Some of these distortions and biases can be managed if the chair of the meeting is not only aware of what can occur but ensures that the members of the meeting are clear about the purpose of the meeting, the decisions that need to be taken and checks out continually whether statements made are fact or opinion and the evidence-base to support these views. The Integrated Children's System format for recording child protection conferences provides a vehicle to assist with this.

What has been described above are feelings that practitioners may only be partly aware of. What they are more likely to be aware of, but minimise or try to ignore, are feelings in relation to what is perceived to be in the interests of the practitioner and the agency. Whether practitioners like to admit it or not the decisions made about cases are going to be influenced by the way in which the decisions impact on the practitioner. For example, if practitioners have heavy workloads and are expected to make space for complex and time-consuming work with the family, then they may resist this option, as opposed to one which means less work for themselves. Likewise, ongoing contact with aggressive carers may appear less appealing than sub-contracting this work to another worker, even though the former may be in the best interests of the child. It is not only practitioners' interests that are likely to influence decision-making in this way but those of the agency. The allocation of precious resources will inevitably influence decision-making and workloads will impact on the ability of practitioners to 'action all cases effectively' (Ofsted *et al.* 2008, p.7, 15). Moreover, the agency and the worker's caution will also affect their approach to planning. This is graphically illustrated by what has been called the 'Baby P effect'. Cafcass (2008) noted a sudden increase in applications for care proceedings following the publicity surrounding the death of Baby Peter and criticism of Haringey Local Authority for failing to remove the child from his mother's care.

The feelings of practitioners do not inevitably distort assessments. What is important is that practitioners and managers are able to be honest about ways in which feelings and agency demands are influencing practice. Continually evaluate the evidence used to inform decision-making in supervision, core groups and other planning fora. But what is most important is to keep a child focus throughout the assessment.

Summary

This chapter, and the preceding one, have explored the complex process of assessing the needs of vulnerable children and their families using the core assessment as an example of this process. Arguably the most challenging aspect of the assessment process is making sense of the information gathered in order to make professional judgements about the health and development of the child and whether they are suffering or are likely to suffer significant harm. Judgements about immediate safety, and short- and long-term needs, should be made. These judgements should take account of both strengths and difficulties. This stage of the process informs decision-making and action planning about the interventions that are required in order to meet the identified needs of the child and their family. Clarity in terms of planning ensures each family member and practitioner understands the aims and objectives of the plan and the way in which they are expected to contribute towards implementing the plan. It is important when constructing a plan to be clear about what outcomes professionals and family members intend to achieve through different activities and actions. It is all too easy to consider this in terms of completing activities rather than considering the impact of the various activities and actions on improving the health and development of the child. Assessment does not finish with intervention; rather the process of assessment continues as practitioners re-assess the effectiveness of the plan in terms of it achieving the specific objectives and desired outcomes: ultimately safeguarding and promoting the welfare of the child.

Assessment records, plans and case records serve two purposes. First, they provide the official record of information on what work has been undertaken with a vulnerable child and their family. It is therefore important that this is accurate, with clear evidence provided to support the judgements made and the decisions about interventions. Second, they constitute a part of the child's history. This can be used in future assessments to identify patterns of behaviour, family strengths and effective interventions. The Integrated Children's System is specifically designed to ensure that past information and interventions related to a child and their family are available to inform subsequent assessments and interventions.

The quality of any assessment will be significantly influenced by the approach of the practitioners undertaking the assessment. A diverse range of factors will influence this approach. These include the organisational context, for example workloads, timescales and resources; the professional influences, such as professional values and attitudes towards child welfare; personal factors, for example previous experiences, fears and anxieties; and what is perceived by the worker to be in their best interest. Effective assessment practice depends on practitioners and their managers accepting these are all part of the reality of practice and should recognise ways in which these can influence and distort assessments.

Recommended reading

Cleaver, H. and Walker, S. (2004) *Assessing Children's Needs and Circumstances.* London: Jessica Kingsley Publishers.

Cleaver, H., Walker, S., Scott, J., Cleaver, P. *et al.* (2008) *The Integrated Children's System: Enhancing Social Work and Inter-agency Practice.* London: Jessica Kingsley Publishers.

Dalzell, R. and Sawyer, E. (2007) *Putting Analysis into Assessment: Undertaking Assessments of Need.* London: National Children's Bureau.

Hollows, A. (2003) 'Making Professional Judgements in the Framework for the Assessment of Children in Need and their Families.' In M.C. Calder and S. Hackett (eds) *Assessment in Child Care.* Lyme Regis: Russell House Publishing.

References

Bentovim, A. (1998) 'Significant Harm in Context.' In M. Adcock and R. White (eds) *Significant Harm.* Croydon: Significant Publications.

Brandon, M., Belderson, P., Warren, C., Howe, D. *et al.* (2008) *Analysing Child Deaths and Serious Injury through Abuse and Neglect: What Can We Learn? A Biennial Analysis of Serious Case Reviews 2003–2005.* Research Report DCSF-RR023. Nottingham: Department for Children, Schools and Families.

Buckley, H., Horwath, J., Whelan, S. and Health Service Authority (2005) *A Framework for Assessing Vulnerable Children and their Familes.* Trinity College Dublin and University of Sheffield. Dublin: Children's Research Centre.

Cafcass (2008) *Cafcass Notes Sharp Rise in Care Order Applications.* Available at www.cafcass.gov.uk/news/2008/increase_in_care_cases.aspx, accessed on 26 April 2009.

Calder, M.C. (2003) 'The Assessment Framework: A Critique and Reformulation.' In M.C. Calder and S. Hackett (eds) *Assessment in Child Care: Using and Developing Frameworks for Practice.* Lyme Regis: Russell House Publishing.

Calder, M.C. and Horwath, J. (1999) *Working for Children on the Child Protection Register: An Inter-agency Guide.* Aldershot: Arena.

Cleaver, H. and Walker, S. (2004) *Assessing Children's Needs and Circumstances.* London: Jessica Kingsley Publishers.

Cm 5730 (2003) *The Victoria Climbié Inquiry Report.* London: The Stationery Office.

Crisp, B.R., Anderson, M.R., Orme, J. and Lister, P.G. (2006) 'Assessment frameworks: a critical reflection.' *British Journal of Social Work 37,* 6, 1059–1098.

Dalzell, R. and Sawyer, E. (2007) *Putting Analysis into Assessment: Undertaking Assessments of Need.* London: National Children's Bureau.

Department of Health (2001) *Studies Informing the Framework for the Assessment of Children in Need and their Families.* London: The Stationery Office.

Department of Health (2003) *The Integrated Children's System.* London: Department of Health.

Department of Health, Home Office and Department for Education and Employment (2000) *Framework for the Assessment of Children in Need and their Families.* London: The Stationery Office.

Eraut, M. (1994) *Developing Professional Knowledge and Competence.* London: Falmer Press.

Farmer, E. and Owen, M. (1995) *Child Protection Practice: Private Risks and Public Remedies.* London: HMSO.

Gambrill, E. (2005) *Critical Thinking in Clinical Practice.* Hoboken, NJ: John Wiley.

Hagell, A. (1998) *Dangerous Care: Reviewing the Risks to Children from their Carers.* London: Policy Studies Institute.

HM Government (2006) *Working Together to Safeguard Children. A Guide to Inter-agency Working to Safeguard and Promote the Welfare of Children.* London: The Stationery Office.

Holland, S. (2004) *Child and Family Assessment in Social Work Practice.* London: Sage.

Hollows, A. (2003) 'Making Professional Judgements in the Framework for the Assessment of Children in Need and their Families.' In M.C. Calder and S. Hackett (eds) *Assessment in Child Care.* Lyme Regis: Russell House Publishing.

Horwath, J. (2007) *The Neglected Child: Identification and Assessment.* London: Palgrave.

Joint Chief Inspectors (2002) *Safeguarding Children. A Joint Chief Inspectors' Report on Arrangements to Safeguard Children.* London: Department of Health.

Joint Chief Inspectors (2008) *The Third Joint Chief Inspectors' Report on Arrangements to Safeguard Children.* London: Ofsted.

Jones, D.P.H., Hindley, P. and Ramchandi, A. (2006) 'Making plans, assessment, interventions and evaluating outcomes' in Aldgate, J. and Rose, W. (eds.) *The Developing World of the Child*. London: Jessica Kingsley Publishers.

Little, M., Axford, N. and Morpeth, L. (2004) 'Research review: risk and protection in the context of services for children in need.' *Child and Family Social Work 9*, 1, 105–117.

Morrison, T. (2001) *Staff Supervision in Social Care: Making a Real Difference for Staff and Service Users*. Brighton: Pavilion.

Munro, E. (1999) 'Common errors of reasoning in child protection work.' *Child Abuse and Neglect 23*, 8, 745–758.

Munro, E. (2000) *Effective Child Protection*. London: Sage.

Ofsted, Healthcare Commission and HM Inspectorate of Constabulary (2008) *Joint Area Review. Haringey Children's Services Authority Area*. Available at www.ofsted.gov.uk/oxcare_providers/la_download/(id)/4657/(as)/JAR/jar_2008_309_fr.pdf, accessed on 13 July 2009.

Paul, R. (1992) *Critical Thinking: What Every Person Needs to Survive in a Rapidly Changing World*. Santa Rosa, CA: Foundation for Critical Thinking.

Reder, P. and Duncan, S. (1999) *Lost Innocents? A Follow-up Study of Fatal Child Abuse*. London: Routledge.

Reder, P. and Duncan, S. (2003) 'Understanding communication in child protection networks.' *Child Abuse Review 12*, 2, 82–100.

Reder, P., Duncan, S. and Gray, M. (1993) *Beyond Blame – Child Abuse Tragedies Revisited*. London: Routledge.

Sinclair, R. and Bullock, R. (2002) *Learning from Past Experience: A Review of Serious Case Reviews*. London: Department of Health.

Taylor, C. and White, S. (2001) 'Knowledge, truth and reflexivity: the problem of judgement in social work.' *Journal of Social Work 1*, 1, 37–59.

Turnell, A. and Edwards, S. (1999) *Signs of Safety: A Solution and Safety Orientated Approach to Child Protection*. New York, NY: W. W. Norton and Company.

CHAPTER 5

Multidisciplinary Contributions to Assessment of Children in Need

Peter Sidebotham and Mary Weeks

From birth, all children will become involved with a variety of different agencies in the community, particularly in relation to their health, day care and educational development. A range of professionals, including midwives, health visitors, general practitioners, nursery staff and teachers, will have a role in assessing their general wellbeing and development... An important underlying principle of the approach to assessment...is that it is based on an inter-agency model.

(From the Framework for the Assessment of Children in Need and their Families, p.14, 1.50)

The purpose of this chapter is to:

- examine the role played by different professionals in the assessment, within the context of the *Framework for the Assessment of Children in Need and their Families* (Department of Health *et al.* 2000)

- explore the three different domains of the Assessment Framework, identifying some of the ways in which different professionals may contribute to the overall assessment

- outline different components of an effective inter-agency approach to assessment

- discuss some of the barriers to effective inter-agency working

- highlight ways in which individuals and organisations can promote inter-agency collaboration.

Introduction

Children are complex social actors living in complex social worlds. During the course of their childhood they will interact with a wide range of family members, peers and others, including different professionals. When a child is a child in need, including those subject to abuse or neglect, that world becomes even more complex. In order to assess the nature of any possible needs therefore, as described in Chapters 3 and 4, it will be necessary for professionals from a range of backgrounds to work with the child, their family and others to provide, assimilate and interpret information about the child and family. No one professional will know all there is to know about a child or family, nor will any one professional have all the skills to evaluate these complex situations or to plan and implement appropriate intervention.

Government guidance, including the *Framework for the Assessment of Children in Need and their Families* (Department of Health *et al.* 2000), is clear that the lead responsibility for assessing children in need rests with local authority children's social care services (HM Government 2006, p.43, 2.17). It is also clear that there needs to be a shared responsibility and effective joint working between agencies and professionals that have different roles and expertise in assessing children in need and their families (*ibid.*, p.33, 1.14). As part of the assessment, different professional groups may have very specific responsibilities. For example, the police have the lead for any criminal investigation. Similarly, where there are issues around a child's health or education needs, assessments should be led by practitioners with expertise in these areas. The input of different professionals is crucial not only in relation to adequate assessment, but also for appropriate intervention and support designed to safeguard and promote the welfare of the child. These themes are expanded on in the *Framework for the Assessment of Children in Need and their Families* (Department of Health *et al.* 2000), which emphasises that a range of professionals from different agencies will have a role in assessing children in need in terms of referring to children's social care, in providing information about the child and family, providing more specialist assessments, and in responding to the needs of vulnerable children (p.14, 1.50).

As is discussed in Chapters 3 and 4, the assessment process is not a one-off or static event, but should be seen within the context of the child's life course and the wider ecological framework of the child's world. Moreover, assessment is an ongoing process drawing on past and current experience to inform current and future intervention. Applying this framework to the multi-agency assessment of children in need allows us to expand the scope of the assessment and to see it within the wider context of promoting positive outcomes for all children (Cm 5860 2003; HM Government 2004). Whilst the focus of the assessment is on the present, on identifying the child as a child in need and defining what makes that child a child in need, a full understanding of that child's needs must incorporate an assessment of the past, of those factors that have led to the child's current context; and on the future, and the potential outcomes (both positive and negative) for that child, along with those interventions that may then serve to minimise risk of harm and promote resilience. In the next sections of this chapter, we will explore the three different domains of the Assessment Framework, identifying some of the ways in which different professionals may contribute to the overall assessment.

Multidisciplinary contributions to the assessment of children in need and their families

Table 5.1 provides some examples of the kind of information that may be provided by different professional groups to support the assessment of children in need and the types of services they may provide. This table addresses information within the three domains of the Assessment Framework. Although neither comprehensive nor exclusive, it illustrates areas where different professionals can contribute information to an assessment, and may assist social work practitioners in identifying potential sources of information.

Child's developmental needs

As the child grows, different professionals may contribute significant elements to an understanding of that child's development. In the early stages, health professionals, including health visitors, general practitioners, paediatricians and various therapists, may have a detailed understanding of that child's development, any developmental milestones they have achieved, and any impairments or difficulties affecting their development (Department of Health *et al.* 2000, p.67, 5.25). The programme of universal child health surveillance used to provide a comprehensive review of each child's development at different stages (Hall and Elliman 2006). This health surveillance programme is now being targeted at those children who are assessed to have particular requirements or where parents request a developmental check or have a concern about the development of their child. Nevertheless, the health visitor will know what assessments have been done, and may be able to provide a comprehensive review of that child's developmental progress. Where there are concerns about a child's developmental progress, it may be appropriate to carry out a more detailed developmental assessment, using any one of a number of assessment tools. These specialist developmental assessments may be carried out by paediatricians, psychologists or other therapists (Department of Health *et al.* 2000, p.84, 6.18). An assessment of a child's developmental status may give an important snapshot of their current abilities and limitations. Development, however, is not static but a dynamic process, so in order to gain a full appreciation of a child's development, multiple assessments may be needed, involving both retrospective and prospective reviews of the child's progress. In these early stages, health practitioners may provide important perspectives on the specific needs of the child in relation to her age and developmental stage. They may also, in conjunction with other professionals and agencies involved, be able to anticipate particular needs or potential outcomes for the child and how these may be met, as is illustrated in the example below.

Table 5.1: Contributions of different professionals to the assessment

Professional group	Child's developmental needs	Parenting capacity	Family and environmental context	Service need and provision
Community nursing staff: Midwives Health visitors School nurses	Chronology of child's history – infancy, pre-school, school years; child's development, behaviour and temperament; health needs; growth parameters; feeding; hygiene; specific indicators of abuse or neglect	Mother's obstetric history; observations of parent–child interaction (positive and negative); evaluation of parents' understanding of and capacity to respond to the child's needs at different developmental stages	Information on other family members; growth and development of other children; knowledge of the community and other families; social support structures; housing conditions	Antenatal care; child health surveillance; school health service provision and uptake; engagement and co-operation of parents with health provision; engagement of young person with adolescent health care
General practitioners	Chronology of child's medical history; identified health problems, past and current treatment and referrals; health needs; specific indicators of abuse or neglect	Parents' background medical history; any identified medical or mental health issues; current treatment; mother's obstetric history; observations of parent–child interaction (positive and negative)	Information on other family members; health of other children	Primary and secondary care offered and uptake; engagement and co-operation of parents with health provision
Secondary health care providers: Paediatricians Specialist consultants Hospital staff Therapists	Specific assessments of child's health, growth or development; identified health needs; specific indicators of abuse or neglect	Specific assessments of parents' health; observations of parent–child interaction (positive and negative); evaluation of parents' understanding of and capacity to respond to the child's needs at different developmental stages		A&E attendances; other hospital attendances; secondary care offered and uptake; engagement and co-operation of parents with health provision

Continued over page

Table 5.1: Contributions of different professionals to the assessment (*cont.*)

Professional group	Child's developmental needs	Parenting capacity	Family and environmental context	Service need and provision
CAMHS staff: Child psychiatrists Clinical psychologists Community psychiatric nurses Therapists	Identified emotional or behavioural difficulties; specific assessments of child's behaviour; specific indicators of abuse or neglect, particularly emotional abuse; assessment of attachment and attachment disorders	Observations of parent–child interaction; evaluation of parents' understanding of and capacity to respond to the child's needs at different developmental stages	Information on behaviour issues in other children	CAMHS services needed or offered; engagement and co-operation of parents with health provision; engagement of young person with adolescent mental health care
Adult mental health care: Psychiatrists Psychologists Community psychiatric nurses Drug and alcohol support teams Social workers Therapists Specialist intervention teams	Specific assessments and treatments for young people with specific emotional and psychological difficulties		Identified mental health issues in parents, including learning difficulties, mental illness, alcohol and substance abuse; specific assessments of parental emotional and psychological needs; specific assessments of parents' learning abilities and parenting capacity; assessment for caring responsibilities and support needs of adults subject to 'Care Programme Assessments'	Provision of adult mental health services, including services for alcohol or substance abuse; engagement of parents with professionals

Professional group	Child's developmental needs	Parenting capacity	Family and environmental context	Service need and provision
Police and probation services: Police officers Police child protection units Probation officers Youth offending team	Offending behaviour of young person		Criminal and offending history of parents; incidents of domestic violence; information on others resident at the property; any record of illicit activity; background knowledge of the neighbourhood	
Education staff: Sure Start and early years providers Teachers, head teachers, SENCOs Connexions Educational psychologists	Educational history of child; past and current educational attainment; assessment of any learning disabilities; presentation and behaviour in school or pre-school; interaction with others; aspirations and plans of young person		Educational history of parents; educational history of other children in the family; knowledge of the community; out-of-school activities	Services offered: pre-school, school, and out of school; school attendance; statements of special educational need, or other specialist provision required
Other council services: Housing			Quality of housing and environment; health and safety issues	Provision of council housing or other accommodation
Voluntary and non-statutory agencies: Youth groups Faith groups Community groups	Participation of child or young person in activities; presentation and behaviour of child; interaction with others; specific indicators of abuse or neglect	Participation of parents in activities or groups; observations of parent–child interaction	Social support networks; knowledge of the community	

N.B. This table is illustrative, providing examples of possible contributions from different professional groups. It is in no way intended to be comprehensive or exclusive.

Liam is a six-month-old boy, born to a substance abusing mother. He is being assessed as a child in need and is the subject of a core assessment. Although he was initially placed with his mother, concerns have been raised about his growth and development. As part of the assessment, Liam's health visitor provides information on Liam's development to date, highlighting developmental milestones. She is also able to comment on his growth, his feeding and his interaction with his mother. A paediatrician sees Liam for a thorough medical and developmental assessment and involves a multidisciplinary child development team to provide a comprehensive evaluation of Liam's current developmental status. The team, together with input from an early years worker and the social worker, and drawing on published literature on the outcomes of children of substance abusing mothers, are able to make some tentative judgements about Liam's likely developmental trajectory, and what will be needed to promote his health and development.

As the child grows and enters an early years setting and then school, their needs change. There may continue to be involvement of health services, particularly where the child has chronic illnesses or underlying sensory or motor impairments. Indeed, all children will need access to health services at times of need, including acute illness. Increasingly, however, other aspects of development gain prominence including their cognitive and social development. Many other agencies will become involved with the child and their family and will have information and perspectives to contribute to any assessment. Pre-school services, including nursery and playgroup workers, children's centres and other family services may be involved with the child and family and able to contribute to the assessment. Education services, including teachers, support workers, educational psychologists and educational welfare officers, may be able to contribute information on the child's learning abilities and any specific learning needs and how these are being or may be met (Department of Health *et al.* 2000). Connexions may become involved as the child grows older and begins to plan for leaving school, and may be able to help with assessment of future plans for the young person. The child may have a formal Statement of Special Educational Needs, outlining their needs and how these can be met within the educational services (Department for Education and Skills 2001 DfES/581/2001). These will lead on to annual Statement reviews, providing an up-to-date reassessment of the child's needs. Where there are specific behaviour issues such as concerns about possible Attention Deficit Hyperactivity Disorder (ADHD), Child and Adolescent Mental Health Services (CAMHS) may be involved, or could be approached to undertake focused assessments. In some cases, youth offending services and the police may have important contributions in relation to offending behaviours.

Socialisation takes place in a variety of settings, including the home, extended family, school and extra-curricular activities. The importance of adequate opportunities for socialisation and participation cannot be emphasised enough in relation to promoting resilience in children. This may involve voluntary agencies and faith and cultural groups through different youth programmes.

Parenting capacity

A newborn baby will be entirely dependent on her parents or carers to meet all of her needs, including the aspects of basic nurture, nutrition, health and safety outlined above. In addition, she will have ongoing emotional and social needs which again will primarily be met by her parents or primary carers. As the child grows, these needs change, but do not disappear. The teenager may be able to clothe and feed herself but, being economically dependent, will still require her parents to provide food and shelter. In order to thrive and achieve positive outcomes, she needs emotional warmth, encouragement and increasing opportunities to develop her own identity and independence within the security of stable relationships. To facilitate this, parents or carers need to have some understanding of the child's developmental needs, resources (physical, emotional and social) to meet those needs and an ability to prioritise those needs. Assessing the parents' capacity both to understand and to meet the child's needs again requires the input of a range of professionals working with the parents, as described in the example below.

> Vicky, a three-month-old baby, was referred following multiple attendances at an accident and emergency department with minor injuries. During the assessment, it became clear that both parents had moderate learning disabilities and had attended special schools; in addition, the father had a physical disability affecting his ability to carry his daughter safely, which had been the cause of some of the injuries. As part of the assessment, the GP was able to provide information on the nature of the father's medical condition and its impact on his motor skills. A psychologist carried out a specialist assessment of the parents' cognitive abilities and their parenting capacity. This information was used to consider what support was needed to help the parents to safely bring up their child and enable her to grow and develop to reach her potential.

A parent's capacity to understand the developing child's needs will be influenced by a range of factors in their own background, including their educational input and attainment, their own experiences of being parented and any prior experience of being a parent (Belsky and Vondra 1989). Parents with learning disabilities may experience difficulties in understanding how their child will develop and change over time and what their child's needs are at different stages. Professionals who know the parents, including GPs, social workers and support workers, may be able to provide perspectives on their abilities; education staff, such as previous teachers or educational psychologists, may be able to shed light on their background and ability to learn and their capacity to take in and use information given to them. There may also be the need for more specific assessments of learning ability carried out by trained psychologists. An understanding of the parents' own experiences of being parented may shed light on how they interpret the needs of their child and how to meet those needs. This requires work with the parents, ideally by professionals whom they trust. Health visitors, social workers from adult services or other professionals may undertake such work, although again the full picture is likely to be gleaned from a variety of sources rather than just one professional.

Translating an understanding of the child's needs into practical care of the child brings in a further and far more complex dimension to parenting capacity. Parental physical impairments may affect their capacity to respond to the child's needs. Both acute and chronic or recurrent illness may mean that a parent is not available for the child. As discussed in Chapter 19, some parents with mental illness or personality disorders may, on occasion, pose direct risks of harm to the child. Parents need to be able to prioritise the child's needs above their own. This ability may be affected by physical or mental illness, by substance misuse, or by financial or other stresses. Equally, parents with highly demanding jobs may find it difficult to prioritise their child's needs above their own professional careers or busy social lives. Health professionals may be able to provide information on the parents' backgrounds and health (both physical and mental); police and probation services can contribute information on potential risks of harm posed by any offending history; for substance misusing parents, the substance misuse support teams will be able to assess the patterns of substance use and how that affects the parents' capacity to understand, prioritise and meet their children's needs.

All professionals who have contact with the parents should comment on what they have observed of the parents' behaviour and interaction with the child. This will include examples of positive behaviour – taking the child to a health provider when ill or for routine health services; playing with the child or showing affection; using appropriate discipline and setting boundaries. It may also include examples of negative behaviour or interaction (Glaser 2002) – ignoring the child; spurning or rejecting; putting the child down; threatening or physically harming the child; failing to respond to observed needs; or failing to access appropriate services.

The assessment of parenting capacity in teenage parents brings in further dimensions, as the assessment will be required to consider the ongoing needs of the teenage parent as well as the child. It is crucial then that education services, including the school and Connexions workers, are intimately involved in the assessment. Similarly, in those engaged with probationary services, the requirements of custodial sentences or other restrictions on the parents need to be considered alongside the needs of the child.

Family and environmental factors

As described in Chapters 2 and 9, a full understanding of the child in need also requires an assessment of factors relating to their wider family and environment (see Chapters 21 and 22 for more detail). The degree of social support, including extended family and friends, the quality of housing or of the neighbourhood in which they live, and factors that influence the parents' culture including ethnicity and religious beliefs, will all have an impact on the parents' capacity to respond to their child's needs. Again these factors may be either positive – building resilience – or negative. Social workers and other professionals need to work closely, together with the family and with others in the community, to fully assess the nature and impact of these wider factors. Local authority housing services may provide information on the housing needs and priorities of the family; the health and safety executive may advise on the suitability of any housing; police and community leaders may provide different perspectives of the community and neighbourhood in which the family live. Where a family holds particular religious or social affiliations, liaison with religious leaders, youth workers or voluntary agencies may provide understanding of particular influences on the parents or child, or may identify sources of support and practical or social resources.

> Josie, a six-week-old baby, presented to hospital with a severe head injury having reportedly fallen down a flight of stairs. During the assessment, a police officer undertook a joint home visit with a social worker from children's social care, to review the scene and evaluate the circumstances around the incident, including an appraisal of the safety and suitability of the housing for this family. A paediatrician, together with a radiologist, assessed the injuries and they were able to conclude, in the light of published literature and the information provided by the police officer and social worker, that the injury was consistent with the fall described. Issues around the safety of the stairway and the suitability of the housing were addressed as part of the multidisciplinary child protection plan.

Key pointers for practice

- When carrying out an assessment of a child in need, social workers should consider which other professionals may hold information about the child and family.

- Professionals in all agencies should be prepared to share information about the child, the parents, the family and environment, and service need and provision.

- As well as contributing information, professionals can contribute to the analysis of the information gained, and to considering appropriate plans in the light of this understanding.

Contributing to an effective assessment

The format and content of any professional's contribution to an assessment will, in part, be dictated by the nature of the assessment; however, some general principles will apply in most situations. The key responsibilities of individual agencies and practitioners in the assessment process are outlined in Chapter 5 of the *Framework for the Assessment of Children in Need and their Families* (Department of Health *et al.* 2000) and in Chapter 2 of *Working Together to Safeguard Children* (HM Government 2006).

Gathering information

Both facts (ideally specific, verifiable and documented) and opinion are valid components when gathering and sharing information, but the two need to be separated, and it should be clear in the contribution which is which. As described above, different professionals will be able to contribute a range of background information and observations on the child, parents or wider family and environmental context, along with outlining services provided from within their own agency. It is helpful if each professional includes a chronology of their own agency's involvement with the child and family. This chronology does not need to include every contact or event, but should focus on those events that will be significant in the life of the child. The concept of an 'analytic chronology' has been used in Serious Case Reviews (Brandon *et al.* 2008; Reder and Duncan 1999) and can help in other assessments. This would include a summary of key events and factors within the child, the parents and the environment, matched with any professional or agency involvement at different key stages of the child's life.

The chronology should be supplemented with what is known about the child's developmental needs (including a review of past, current and predicted future needs), parenting capacity, and wider family and environmental factors. In addition, this overview of the ecology of the child's world should be supplemented with details about professional involvement from the agency in the past as well as current input, including the family's engagement with services; what is needed and what could be provided by the agency in the future to promote positive outcomes. It is helpful at all stages to outline any family strengths identified by members of the agency within each of the three domains.

Multidisciplinary contributions to analysis and planning

An assessment involves not just a description of facts relating to the child and family, but also multidisciplinary input to analysis and planning. Professionals contributing to the assessment should not be afraid to offer their own opinion on the child's needs and the parents' ability to meet those needs. An assessment that incorporates both information from and analysis by a range of professionals will be more valuable than one that relies only on one professional or agency evaluating a range of information. This analysis should include:

- identification of any specific concerns, along with any protective or resilience-building factors

- hypotheses about how any background factors may have led to the child's current situation and potential risks of harm for the future

- an outline of what could be anticipated as outcomes for the child without intervention, along with the potential for positive outcomes

- a plan of possible interventions that might help to achieve such positive outcomes.

At all times in the process of the assessment, it is important to keep a focus on the child – their needs, rights and the intended outcomes.

Engaging children and families

As outlined in Chapters 6 and 7, the involvement of children and families is crucial to the success and validity of the assessment. This is not just the role of the social worker, but all professionals should promote engaging the child and their family where possible. This can occur at a number of different levels. For example, an employer asked, with parental consent, to provide an employment history may confirm that consent and provide a copy to the parent so they know what information has been shared; a GP asked to provide information on a parent's mental health history should, wherever possible, discuss this with the parent and agree what details can be shared and how they are interpreted; a health visitor may work with a parent to assess and comment on the child's developmental status; a Connexions worker may sit down with a young person to talk through her hopes for the future and what might be needed to achieve these. There may be situations where a worker will act as an advocate either for the child or the family; this is important but should not be a substitute for a formal advocate where one is required. In some instances the use of an advocate for the child may be necessary to obtain and represent their views, particularly where there are conflicts between the views of the child and carer, the child is reluctant to speak to a new professional, or the child has a learning disability. Where the family or child's first language is not English then an appropriately qualified interpreter should be used who is not a family member or friend.

> Mark, a 12-year-old boy with cerebral palsy and severe learning disabilities, was noted at school to have finger-tip bruising on his trunk. Information provided by Mark's teacher, and a church leader who knew the family, indicated that the mother, who had recently been deserted by her partner, was struggling to cope with Mark's very difficult behaviour and his total dependence for all his self-care needs. The family was not in receipt of any respite care, and although it had been requested, a long delay in occupational therapy assessments meant that no hoist had been provided to help the mother with lifting Mark. An urgent assessment by a social worker and occupational therapist enabled both aspects to be provided.

Engaging with the child and family in the process of the assessment guards against the assessment being biased by the practitioner's own values and perspectives, but runs the risk of being swayed by the parents' opinions, particularly where parents are manipulative or coercive. It is therefore important to maintain one's objectivity and to come away from the family to reflect, prior to completing any report. This reflection may involve formal supervision, or discussion with colleagues to ensure that both facts and opinions are presented accurately.

Recording

Any contribution to an assessment should be carefully documented. When a written contribution is prepared for an initial or core assessment, a copy should be retained in the case notes together with an indication of who it was supplied to and for what purpose. All written contributions should follow best practice for record keeping and be clearly signed and dated. Involvement in meetings and telephone discussions should also be documented, with an indication of what information has been shared and with whom.

As indicated earlier in this chapter, assessment should not be seen as a static event, but rather as an ongoing and often cyclical process. As the child grows, she is an active agent in her own world, influencing and being influenced by events and circumstances. Thus, new information may come to light during the course of or following any assessment and should be shared with others involved. Similarly, the accumulation of further information may alter initial interpretations and the professional should not be afraid to indicate where his opinions have changed.

The process of multi-agency assessments is achieved by the gathering of information and the analysis of those data. As described in Chapter 4, staff are generally good at information gathering but sometimes struggle with the analysis. It is important to stress the positives and strengths of the assessment as well as looking at what else the family needs from others. It is also helpful to look at what, if anything, needs to change in the world of the child. Assessments should be dynamic and need to be regularly updated to ensure that actions are fulfilled, the child is making progress, the family are supported, the child's wishes and feelings and family members' views are taken into account, and partnership working is achieved.

Service need and provision

The assessment will not be complete without decisions being made by professionals and the family with regard to the needs of the child and the degree to which such services are required to meet these needs and those of the family. This may identify gaps in services or difficulties. Any identified gaps should be explored to consider how those services may be provided.

Key pointers for practice

- Any professional contributing to an assessment should prepare a brief, structured chronology of the child and family and their own agency involvement.

- The chronology should be supplemented with what is known about the child within the three domains of the child's developmental needs, parenting capacity, and wider family and environmental factors.

- Professionals should identify what services have been provided by or required of their agency in the past, and make an assessment of likely current or future needs and how their agency may help to meet those.

- Planning should address how to achieve the intended developmental outcomes for the child based on her assessed needs.

- Children and families should be involved in the process of assessment, and their consent to sharing information sought where appropriate.

- All contributions should be carefully documented by the professional providing the information as well as by the receiver.

Inhibitors to working together

A number of barriers to effective joint working have been consistently identified in the literature (Brandon *et al.* 2008; Cm 5730 2003). Hudson *et al.* (1999), drawing on the work of Hardy *et al.* (1992), suggest that these barriers can be categorised as structural;

procedural and financial; professional barriers; and barriers related to status and legitimacy. To these categories can be added a sixth of personal barriers.

Structural barriers

The main structural barriers relate to fragmentation of service responsibilities both between and within agencies, inter-organisational complexity and non-coterminosity of boundaries. It follows that promoting simple structures both within agencies and for inter-agency collaborations, with clear frameworks or flowcharts for such working, and clearly defined roles and responsibilities, may promote better collaboration. Where possible coterminosity between agencies should be promoted. Following the publication of *Every Child Matters* (Cm 5860 2003), considerable progress has been made in this area, through the establishment of Local Safeguarding Children Boards, and the introduction of Children's Trusts. All organisations that work with children and families share a commitment to safeguard and promote the welfare of children and for many organisations this is underpinned by a statutory duty. The duty to cooperate to improve outcomes for children inherent in the Children Act 2004, along with joint inspections, should help to strengthen systems and structures that promote inter-agency working.

Procedural and financial barriers

Procedural barriers include differences in planning, budgetary cycles and procedures themselves. The importance of this is addressed through the development of joint agency procedures in child protection work. Where individual agency procedures are needed, as indeed they are, it is important to ensure that they are consistent with those of other agencies and with any published local or national guidance. Financial barriers such as differences in funding mechanisms, or competing priorities for budgets, can often lead to difficulties in inter-agency working, for example in failures to agree which agency will be responsible for funding a particular support package for a disabled child. Some areas have tackled this through the development of joint budgets for particular services, or through joint commissioning or budget planning.

Professional barriers

Professional barriers may exist because of differences in ideologies and values, through professional self-interest and through conflicting views about user interests and roles. For example, in relation to promoting the welfare of the child, a police officer may see his primary duties to be to preserve and protect life, and to investigate possible crime; a paediatrician may consider his role as being to promote the child's health and wellbeing and to investigate and treat any ill-health; a general practitioner or a health visitor will have responsibilities to the whole family, and will be aware of the need to preserve ongoing working relationships with all family members; and a social worker has a defined duty to safeguard and promote the welfare of children in the family. It is important, therefore, that all practitioners recognise these differing perspectives and are able to acknowledge that all are important in the overall welfare of the child and family and can work in complementary ways. An understanding of different professionals' roles is seen as crucial to safeguarding practice (HM Government 2006, p.39, 2.1).

Professional barriers may also be seen through the language used by different agencies (Reder and Duncan 2003; White and Featherstone 2005). Professional jargon is all too easy to misinterpret and can potentially lead to failures of care: for example, the word 'investigation' will carry very different connotations for health professionals and police officers. Finally, professional barriers may arise through different perceptions of information sharing and of thresholds for intervention. We address some of the issues around information sharing below. Differing understandings of thresholds for intervention may be a source of conflict between agencies (Brandon *et al.* 2008, p.91) and may relate to some of the structural and procedural issues identified above, as demonstrated in the example below.

A 12-year-old girl was referred for a medical assessment following allegations of sexual abuse. These had come to light after a teacher questioned her over repeated sexually inappropriate comments and behaviour in school. The girl was not at all specific in her allegations during a video-interview, carried out in line with *Achieving Best Evidence* guidance (Criminal Justice System 2007), and the medical examination failed to reveal any abnormal physical findings to support the allegations. The case did not meet police thresholds for a criminal charge and the social worker was reluctant to take it forward in the absence of any clear supportive evidence. Nevertheless, the school remained very concerned about her behaviour and a number of professionals remained concerned about ongoing perceived risks of harm to the child.

One of the biggest barriers to involvement in child in need cases is the perceived negative consequences for the professional. These cases can take up considerable professional time, through attending meetings, following up on referrals, carrying out assessments and maintaining documentation. The case that comes to light on a Friday afternoon may well be treated very differently from one occurring earlier in the week when more time is available (Horwath 2007). Fears of litigation or of being reported to their professional body have adversely influenced the willingness of some paediatricians to engage in this type of work (Jenny 2007; Turton and Haines 2007).

Barriers related to status and legitimacy

Issues around status and legitimacy include organisational self-interest, and concerns about threats to autonomy and domain may also affect inter-agency practice. This was dramatically highlighted in the Laming Inquiry into the death of Victoria Climbié in which a failure to challenge others was seen as a direct contributor to the failure of agencies to respond to manifest child protection concerns (Cm 5730 2003). This was also highlighted as an issue in a recent overview of serious case reviews following child deaths and serious injury from maltreatment (Brandon *et al.* 2008, p.93). The authors point out that a failure to challenge others may stem from a lack of confidence, a lack of knowledge or a lack of experience. They emphasise the importance of sustained professional challenge, and highlight that a reliance on electronic information sharing, rather than direct personal challenge, may further limit the effectiveness of inter-agency working (*ibid.*, p.94).

Personal barriers

In a review of the identification and reporting of physical abuse by physicians, Warner and Hansen (1994) identify a number of personal variables which may influence a physician's willingness to identify or report suspected child abuse. These include gender, age, uncertainty over the diagnosis, their own perceptions or history of child discipline and child abuse, and perceived consequences of reporting. Horwath (2007) found these concerns also existed amongst other professionals such as teachers, health visitors and staff from adult services. Uncertainty is a key feature of much child protection practice, and can have a negative influence on professionals' willingness to refer cases or share information. Professionals who have lower tolerance for physical discipline, those who have experienced abuse in their own childhood or those who have come across more cases or more severe cases of abuse may have lower thresholds for reporting, and for sharing information in relation to possible child protection cases (Warner and Hansen 1994). Previous experience of the system may also affect willingness of professionals to engage, with a greater willingness if previous concerns have been appropriately responded to, but hesitation if it is felt that a heavy-handed approach has been used, or if concerns have been raised but seemingly dismissed (Joint Chief Inspectors 2002; Warner and Hansen 1994).

Key pointers for practice

- It is helpful to identify potential barriers to effective inter-agency working, at structural, procedural, professional, status and personal levels.

- Practitioners should examine their own practice and reflect on any potential barriers within any of the above domains.

- Whenever difficulties arise in relation to inter-agency working, the practitioner should discuss these with their supervisor. This can help in addressing these and promoting good practice.

Information sharing

One of the major issues raised by many professionals when asked to contribute to a multi-agency assessment is that of consent and confidentiality in relation to information sharing. This is particularly so when the information may be sensitive, for example related to medical issues or criminal records. Two basic principles need to be considered in relation to sharing information: ensuring that the welfare of the child is paramount; and respecting the rights of the individual to confidentiality. Although professionals may receive conflicting advice and often assume that data protection laws prohibit the sharing of information, the Government's guidance is clear that information, including sensitive personal information, can and indeed should be shared in order to ensure the protection of children (HM

Government 2006a, 2008). It is salutary to remember that no child ever died as a result of information being shared between professionals, whilst repeated Serious Case Reviews have identified failure to share information as a factor contributing to children's deaths.

The question professionals should ask themselves, in relation to the assessment process, is not 'Should I share information?' but rather 'What information should I share, with whom, for what purpose and how?' Essentially, any information about the child, the parents or the wider family and environmental circumstances may contribute to an assessment of the child's needs and therefore could potentially contribute to safeguarding that child and promoting their welfare. This principle holds even when there are no identified child protection concerns, as it is often only when multiple items of information from various sources are compiled that potential risks of harm to the child emerge. Having said that, it is important also to treat information with respect, and to consider who needs to know the information, for what purpose, and how it will be used in a way that will protect the rights of the person to whom it pertains. In most circumstances it will be appropriate to seek the consent of the subject to sharing information, explaining what information you wish to share, with whom, how, and for what purpose. Normally this consent will have been sought by the keyworker or social worker undertaking the assessment, and this should be clarified with the social worker. Generally there should be no surprises for the family about the information that professionals are holding, because in working practice openness with the family is encouraged.

If a person has given their consent to information being shared with other agencies then there is no conflict in sharing that information. It is good practice to back this up by providing individuals with a copy of any written information shared about them. If the individual does not consent to the sharing of information, then a judgement has to be made as to whether the sharing of that information without consent is justified by principles of protecting the child, or of the wider public good. If information is shared without consent, whenever possible, without placing a child at risk of harm, individuals should be informed that information will be shared. There will be some situations, fortunately rare, where it is not appropriate to seek consent to sharing information – for example where to do so may put a child at risk of further harm or may jeopardise a police investigation. Rarely, if consent cannot be obtained, a local authority may apply to the courts for a child assessment order under the Children Act 1989, allowing further assessments to take place without requiring parental consent.

Key pointers for practice

- Information sharing between professionals is crucial to effective safeguarding of children and promoting their welfare.

- Normally consent should be sought from the child and parent before sharing information, unless to do so may put a child at risk of further harm or may jeopardise a police investigation.

- If consent is not given, or there are valid reasons for not seeking consent, the practitioner must make a judgement as to whether sharing information is justified by principles of protecting the child, or of the wider public good.

Promoting inter-agency working

There are a number of steps that practitioners and managers in children's services and other agencies can take to promote inter-agency assessment, both in individual cases, and in promoting a culture of inter-agency co-operation within which assessments can take place. The published literature on what works well in relation to inter-agency working is sadly sparse, but some examples of good practice can be found.

One of the most striking findings in numerous studies of Serious Case Reviews is that, in many cases, information that could have prevented the child's death was readily available to different agencies (Brandon *et al.* 2008; Dent 1998; Reder and Duncan 2003; Rose and Barnes 2008). What was lacking was the collation and evaluation of that information in order to identify and act on known risks of harm to the child (Macdonald 2001). The first stage in any assessment, therefore, must be to ensure that relevant information is shared between agencies and collated in a useful framework. This will require individual practitioners to review their own case files and distil the relevant information in order to share it with others, as 'important facts are often buried in large amounts of text' (Fitzgerald 2001, p.13). In an excellent book on the evidence base for intervention in child abuse and neglect, Geraldine Macdonald points out that 'assessments are not truth finding exercises' but, rather, 'attempts to make sense of what is going on in a particular family, what the risks are to a particular child or children, what factors have brought the situation about, and therefore what it might be possible to do to address identified concerns, or expedient to do to protect a child' (Macdonald 2001, p.260). The next stage in promoting effective working, therefore, is to enable all practitioners to contribute to analysing the information gathered and from there to planning effective intervention. This can be achieved in child protection cases through the involvement of different agencies in section 47 strategy discussions and in child protection conferences. Outside child protection situations, similar involvement can be achieved through their involvement in multi-agency information sharing and planning meetings. Key to effective working in all these situations is good chairing of such meetings, enabling individuals present not only to present information known to them, but also to comment on and help interpret all the information shared, and to give their perspectives on the relevance and feasibility of any plans to help meet the child's needs. Similarly, in relation to planning services, practitioners from different agencies may have access to relevant information to support or challenge the evidence base for different interventions. Again, the chair of any meeting can help create a culture of creative thinking and sensitive critique within the meeting, to facilitate effective planning.

At a wider level, effective inter-agency working can be promoted through organisational commitment, through building a trusting environment, through establishing opportunities for collaboration, through developing systems and processes that support collaboration, and through supporting individual practitioners. In an experimental study of children's services in Tennessee, Glisson and Hemmelgarn (1998) found that organisational climate (including factors such as clarity of roles, low conflict, co-operation and a personalised approach) had a major impact on both service outcomes and on outcomes for children. It is important to recognise that where there is a history of successful inter-agency working in other areas then inter-agency assessments are more likely to be successful and positive for all involved; therefore promotion of other aspects of inter-agency working is as important as a focus on inter-agency assessments.

Organisational commitment to inter-agency working is an essential prerequisite to effective collaboration, but cannot guarantee it. Such commitment can be demonstrated through statements of intent, or joint goals, such as through organisational 'compacts' (Barasi 2006). It will perhaps be most effectively modelled through the commitment of senior practitioners and managers to inter-agency working (White and Featherstone 2005). The importance of strategic bodies such as Local Safeguarding Children Boards (LSCBs) and Children and Young People's Strategic Partnerships should not be underestimated, but it must be recognised that commitment at a strategic level will not necessarily translate to equal commitment at an operational level. Further opportunities may exist, however, through delegated responsibilities, for example through encouraging individual practitioners to sit on sub-committees of the LSCB or to be directly involved in inter-agency working groups. It is important that any demonstrated organisational commitment to inter-agency working does not ignore the very real difficulties and tensions inherent in such working (Horwath and Morrison 2007; Hudson et al. 1999).

Attitudes of trust are often seen as essential to effective inter-agency co-operation, but can be difficult to define (Hudson et al. 1999). They do not develop automatically, nor can they be imposed from above. However, such attitudes can be nurtured and, with commitment, will develop over time. One of the keys to building trust is investing in personal relationships, enabling individuals from different organisations to get to know each other. One of the biggest barriers to information sharing is when a practitioner from one agency is approached by another professional whom they have never met and asked for information which they are then expected to entrust to that professional. Promoting opportunities at a local level for networking and for meeting individuals from other agencies can go a long way towards building up such relationships. Support and supervision of practitioners by seniors who are more directly engaged in inter-agency working may also go a long way to encouraging mutual trust.

Drawing on this emphasis on building trust, opportunities for local networking are important. These may come for example through joint agency training or through specific networking events. Multi-agency training can help to break down barriers of misunderstandings, professional mistrust and role perceptions (HM Government 2006, p.91, 4.2; Joint Chief Inspectors 2002). Agencies can also develop systems and processes for joint working at different levels. Horwath (2009), drawing on the work of Hudson et al. (1999) and others, identifies different levels of collaborative relationship: networks, in which practitioners come together to work on a specific case; one-stop shops, with services delivered from the same building; and multidisciplinary teams – integrated services with practitioners from different disciplines operating as members of one team. Different examples of these may be seen in relation to the assessment of children in need and their families. For example, different agencies may undertake a mapping exercise to identify which agencies or organisations provide particular services within a locality; individual practitioners may work together to develop a joint assessment or action plan, whilst maintaining their individual roles within that; or different agencies may develop actual or virtual teams for responding to families who have unmet needs, potentially even sharing office space, management structures or budgets. Children's Centres and Children's Trusts can be examples of effective integrated services with multidisciplinary teams working in the same geographical location and within shared management structures.

Evidence from a study by Cleaver and Walker (2004) suggests that the introduction of the Assessment Framework has helped to promote inter-agency working, particularly through joint initiatives such as inter-agency referral records, or joint agency protocols. Developing clear local operational protocols based on the Assessment Framework and the core principles in *Working Together to Safeguard Children* is important to facilitating good inter-agency working, and in reducing unfocused or duplicated work (Department of Health *et al.* 2000, p.84, 6.16; HM Government 2006).

Staff contributing to multi-agency assessments require support and regular supervision to ensure that anxieties they may have are identified and supported (Brandon *et al.* 2008; Department of Health *et al.* 2000, p.85, 6.26). To enhance the multi-agency work, staff need to have a clear structure, fully understand each other's roles and responsibilities and feel confident to challenge decisions being made. Supervision at times will need to be directive and not reflective, to ensure that the responsibility for these families is being shared by all the professionals involved. Professional and family collusion needs to be monitored and challenged as necessary. Supervisors will need to understand the full picture, not only of the inter-agency assessment process, but also of the structures involved, and the roles and responsibilities of others. Supervisors can play a vital role as mentors and role models, as well as providing support to their supervisees in what can often be a highly stressful area of work.

Key pointers for practice

- Effective inter-agency working can be promoted through organisational commitment, through building a trusting environment, through establishing opportunities for collaboration, through developing systems and processes that support collaboration, and through supporting individual practitioners.

Summary

The very complexity of the child's world, and the involvement of a range of professionals in different aspects of that world, emphasises the necessity of involving different professionals in any assessment of a child and family's needs. No single professional or agency will have a monopoly of knowledge in relation to a child and family, nor will they have a monopoly of skills in carrying out assessments and in responding to those needs. As emphasised in the Assessment Framework (Department of Health *et al.* 2000), all assessments should be based on an inter-agency model, recognising the contribution of different professionals to referral, collecting, collating and interpreting information, and using that information to develop robust action plans to support children and families and promote their welfare. However, such inter-agency co-operation does not necessarily come easily and it is important to recognise the potential barriers to collaborative working, and the threats this may pose on individual practice or corporate identity. Promoting cultures of co-operation and trust, supported by systems and processes designed to facilitate joint working, can go a long way to achieving these goals, with the ultimate aim of improving services for children and families.

Recommended reading

Cawson, P., Cleaver, H. and Walker S. (eds) (2009) *Safeguarding Children: A Shared Responsibility.* Chichester: Wiley.

HM Government (2008) *Information Sharing: Guidance for Practitioners and Managers.* London: Department for Children, Schools and Families.

Murphy, M. (2004) *Developing Collaborative Relationships in Inter-agency Child Protection Work.* Lyme Regis: Russell House.

Reder, P. and Duncan, S. (2003) 'Understanding communication in child protection networks.' *Child Abuse Review* 12, 2, 82–100.

References

Barasi, P. (2006) *Local Compact Implementation Workbook.* London: National Council for Voluntary Organisations.

Belsky, J. and Vondra, J. (1989) 'Lessons from Child Abuse: The Determinants of Parenting.' In D. Cicchetti and V. Carlson (eds) *Child Maltreatment: Theory and Research on the Causes and Consequences of Child Abuse and Neglect.* Cambridge: Cambridge University Press.

Brandon, M., Belderson, P., Warren, C., Howe, D. *et al.* (2008) *Analysing Child Deaths and Serious Injury through Abuse and Neglect: What Can We Learn? A Biennial Analysis of Serious Case Reviews 2003–2005.* London: Department for Children, Schools and Families.

Cleaver, H. and Walker, S. (2004) 'From policy to practice: the implementation of a new framework for social work assessments of children and families.' *Child and Family Social Work 9,* 1, 81–90.

Cm 5730 (2003) *The Victoria Climbié Inquiry.* London: HMSO.

Cm 5860 (2003) *Every Child Matters.* Green Paper. London: The Stationery Office.

Criminal Justice System (2007) *Achieving Best Evidence in Criminal Proceedings: Guidance on Interviewing Victims and Witnesses and Using Special Measures.* Available at www.cps.gov.uk/publications/docs/achieving_best_evidence_final.pdf, accessed on 27 May 2009.

Dent, R. (ed.) (1998) *Dangerous Care: Working to Protect Children.* London: Bridge Child Care Development Service.

Department for Education and Skills (2001) *Special Educational Needs: Code of Practice.* London: Department for Education and Skills.

Department of Health, Department for Education and Employment and the Home Office (2000) *Framework for the Assessment of Children in Need and their Families.* London: The Stationery Office.

Fitzgerald, J. (2001) 'Policy and Practice in Child Protection: Its Relationship to Dangerousness.' In R. Dent (ed.) *Dangerous Care: Working to Protect Children.* London: Bridge Child Care Development Service.

Glaser, D. (2002) 'Emotional abuse and neglect (psychological maltreatment): a conceptual framework.' *Child Abuse and Neglect 26,* 6–7, 697–714.

Glisson, C. and Hemmelgarn, A. (1998) 'The effects of organizational climate and interorganizational coordination on the quality and outcomes of children's service systems.' *Child Abuse and Neglect 22,* 5, 401–421.

Hall, D.M.B. and Elliman, D. (2006) *Health for All Children.* Oxford: Oxford University Press.

Hardy, B., Turrell, A. and Wistow, G. (1992) *Innovations in Community Care Management.* Aldershot: Avebury.

HM Government (2004) *Executive Summary: National Service Framework for Children, Young People and Maternity Services.* London: Department of Health.

HM Government (2006a) *Working Together to Safeguard Children.* London: The Stationery Office.

HM Government (2006b) *What to Do if You're Worried a Child is being Abused.* London: Department for Education and Skills.

HM Government (2008) *Information Sharing: Guidance for Practitioners and Managers.* London: Department for Children, Schools and Families.

Horwath, J. (2007) *The Neglected Child: Identification and Assessment.* London: Palgrave.

Horwath, J. (2009) 'Managing Difference: Working Effectively in a Multi-Agency Context' In P. Carson, H. Cleaver and S. Walker (eds) *Safeguarding Children: A Shared Responsibility*. Chichester: Wiley.

Horwath, J. and Morrison, T. (2007) 'Collaboration, integration and change in children's services: critical issues and key ingredients.' *Child Abuse and Neglect 31*, 1, 55–69.

Hudson, B., Hardy, B., Henwood, M. and Wistow, G. (1999) 'In pursuit of inter-agency collaboration in the public sector: what is the contribution of theory and research?' *Public Management: An International Journal of Research and Theory 1*, 2, 235–260.

Jenny, C. (2007) 'The intimidation of British pediatricians.' *Pediatrics 119*, 4, 797–799.

Joint Chief Inspectors (2002) *Safeguarding Children: A Joint Chief Inspectors' Report on Arrangements to Safeguard Children*. London: Department of Health.

Macdonald, G. (2001) *Effective Interventions for Child Abuse and Neglect: An Evidence-based Approach to Planning and Evaluating Interventions*. Chichester: Wiley.

Reder, P. and Duncan, S. (1999) *Lost Innocents: A Follow-up Study of Fatal Child Abuse*. London: Routledge.

Reder, P. and Duncan, S. (2003) 'Understanding communication in child protection networks.' *Child Abuse Review 12*, 2, 82–100.

Rose, W. and Barnes, J. (2008) *Improving Safeguarding Practice: Study of Serious Case Reviews 2001–2003*. London: Department for Children, Schools and Families.

Turton, J. and Haines, L. (2007) *An Investigation into the Nature and Impact of Complaints Made against Paediatricians Involved in Child Protection Procedures*. London: Royal College of Paediatrics and Child Health.

Warner, J.E. and Hansen, D.J. (1994) 'The identification and reporting of physical abuse by physicians: a review and implications for research.' *Child Abuse and Neglect 18*, 1, 11–25.

White, S. and Featherstone, B. (2005) 'Communicating misunderstandings: multi-agency work as social practice.' *Child and Family Social Work 10*, 3, 207–216.

CHAPTER 6

Engaging Children and their Parents in the Assessment Process

Sally Holland

In the process of finding out what is happening to a child, it will be critical to develop a co-operative working relationship, so that parents or caregivers feel respected and informed, that staff are being open and honest with them, and that they in turn are confident about providing vital information about their child, themselves and their circumstances.

(From the Framework for the Assessment of Children in Need and their Families, p.13, 1.44)

Chapter contents:

- introduction
- the assessment relationship
- engaging children and young people in assessments
- engaging men and women in assessments
- blocks and barriers to effective engagement.

Introduction

This chapter explores the human engagement at the heart of an assessment. It is argued that the 'assessment relationship' – that is, the relationship between those being assessed (adults and children) and the professionals carrying out the assessment – is central to ensuring an effective and fair process and outcome. Whilst the focus in this chapter is on social workers engaging children and their parents in the assessment process, the content and pointers for practice are relevant to all professionals working with children and families.

The *Framework for the Assessment of Children in Need and their Families* (Assessment Framework) (Department of Health *et al.* 2000) promotes dialogue between assessor and assessed. For example, included in the recording forms used when completing assessment is space for comments, on both the outcomes and the process, by parents/carers and children and young people. And, indeed, some research findings suggest that the Assessment Framework is popular with parents (particularly parents of disabled children) because they feel that the process is transparent and they therefore can understand how decisions about the provision of services are made (Cleaver and Walker 2004). Transparency, alongside empathy, reliability, humour and truthfulness, are all traits valued by children, young people, parents and carers engaged in children's services, as has been repeatedly shown by research and practice (see, for example, Maiter *et al.* 2006; Morgan 2006). This suggests that, despite an increasing emphasis on systems and outcomes, relational aspects remain at the core of successful practice with children in need and their families.

Assessment of children in need involves an intensely human encounter. For example, exploration of areas such as the nature of family relationships, care, the child's needs and sometimes abuse and neglect is not simply an objective, neutral process. It is also an intervention. By asking people to consider such personal aspects of their lives, practitioners may cause them to reflect, acknowledge difficulties they may have faced (or even caused others to face in cases of domestic or child abuse) and even think and act differently about their lives. In the same vein, an in-depth assessment, such as a core assessment, may have therapeutic aspects (Department of Health *et al.* 2000; Holland 2004). De Boer and Coady (2007) argue that a positive relationship is a pre-condition for learning and change where families have had poor experiences of relationships in the past.

There will be no single set of 'facts' to be established during an assessment; indeed often there are many different and contradictory accounts of why a child is in need and how they and their family may best be supported. Ethical issues are to the fore in assessment practice and this means paying attention to making the assessment accessible to those being assessed. This can be achieved by adopting an attitude that individuals have the foremost expertise on their lives, seeking the views of those who are often excluded from such processes (especially men and children), and being clear about why information is being sought, how it will be analysed and what the possible outcomes of an assessment are likely to be.

The assessment relationship

The relationship between family members and practitioners can be influenced by a number of factors, two of which are explored below.

The influence of co-operation

In the late 1990s the Coastal Cities study completed in Wales examined the processes that take place when social workers carry out in-depth assessments in child protection situations (Holland 2004). In these assessments it was notable that a central part of the process was the assessment relationship between social workers carrying out the assessments and the parents who were being assessed. (It was also notable that in these pre-framework assessments children were a rather marginal part of the process.) It could be seen that in some assessments a positive assessment relationship was formed. The central feature of this relationship was that parents were seen by social workers to be co-operative and had come to an agreement with the social worker on the causes for concern about child safety and what needed to be done in the future to keep their child(ren) safe. Social workers who reported only a poor or virtually non-existent assessment relationship suggested that parents did not accept concerns about their level of care, could not agree a plan for moving forward and did not co-operate well with the assessment process. There was another group of parents who were seen as passively accepting of the assessment process but did not actively engage with discussions about their circumstances and plans for the future. In this study it was only the first group of parents, the co-operators, where the children remained or returned home. Other studies, both in the UK and internationally, have also found that practitioners value co-operation and acceptance of concerns by parents when assessing their parenting (see, for example, Atkinson and Butler 1996; Fernandez 1996; Platt 2007; Waterhouse and Carnie 1992).

Whilst in the Coastal Cities study the cases were serious child protection ones and do not represent the full range of children in need situations, the following lessons for practitioners, based on the findings, can be applied to all assessment situations:

- Practitioners should work towards a constructive and positive assessment relationship, as this relationship appears central to outcomes and decision-making in child welfare situations.

- Being constructive and positive does not mean that practitioners cannot be appropriately challenging of unacceptable and harmful parenting practices; it does mean, however, that they are more likely to be able to explore such issues in a meaningful fashion.

- It is crucial that practitioners critically reflect on an assessment relationship and avoid any tendency to simply blame family members for not engaging with children's services.

- A reliance on verbal skills may serve to exclude, from a positive assessment relationship, those who may be less articulate, including those with learning disabilities or experiencing mental health issues.

- Practitioners need to develop a range of assessment methods that will include, but not over-rely on, verbal dialogue for gathering information and exploring needs and strengths. Observations of day-to-day caring and assessment activities, including those developed specifically for people with poor literacy or verbal skills, can be used during assessments and may give a fairer and more thorough assessment to parents who may potentially be excluded by only interviewing.

Power 'over' and power 'with'

Two recent studies from Canada (de Boer and Coady 2007; Dumbrill 2006) have found that the perceived use of power by social workers in the relationship will affect caregivers' attitudes towards the assessment process. De Boer and Coady studied relationships between statutory social workers and service users that had worked well, despite there being difficult or contentious issues to address. They found that a 'soft, judicious and mindful use of power' (2007, p.35) was agreed by service users and workers to be vital. This involved clarity regarding concerns, acknowledgement of the power differences and acceptance that fear, defensiveness and anger on the part of the service user is normal. It also involved listening and not pre-judging according to the referral or case file and not reverting to coercion or counter-hostility even when the service user displays negativity. In an unrelated study of 18 parents involved in child welfare cases, Dumbrill (2006) found that when service users perceived power as being used *over* them (for example, by not listening to the parents' accounts of how concerns had arisen or by presenting plans for children without previous discussion) they either openly opposed them or 'played the game' by feigning co-operation. When workers were seen as using their power *with* them (for example, by acting as advocates or organising additional services) service users and workers were able to work together in co-operative relationships. Dumbrill found that many service users stated that they had experienced both types of power use, at different times, in their relationship with the same social worker, or noticed a change with a new social worker. For example:

> From the grandparent's perspective the case had shifted from one where she and the worker focused their joint energies on meeting her grandson's mental health needs to one where she and the worker expended energy dealing with each other. (Dumbrill 2006, p.32)

Dumbrill found that some social workers were perceived as using power *with* some service users, and using power *over* others. There were also no consistent patterns as to whether the worker was involved on a voluntary or involuntary basis. This suggests that neither the individual worker's personality and attitude, nor the type of case, will necessarily predict the quality of the relationship and that the dynamics are complex. Dumbrill suggests that the worker's task is, therefore, not just to find out what caregivers' perceptions of their needs are, but also their perceptions of the relationship with the worker and how power issues are affecting that relationship, in order to work towards a more constructive relationship.

De Boer and Coady (2007, p.35) also found that a 'humanistic attitude and style' from workers was valued by service users. This included using a down-to-earth manner, (careful) self-disclosure to establish a personal connection, getting to know the whole person (the parent), recognising strengths and being realistic and optimistic about goals. De Boer and Coady's findings echo those found in much research into the social worker–service user relationship. In numerous studies, as described in the Introduction, it has been found that service users value empathy, good listening skills, humour, respect, warmth and honesty in their social workers (see, for example, Drake 1994; Howe 1998; Leigh and Miller 2004). Whilst these studies have focused on the relationships between social workers and families, the lessons learnt are as applicable to any practitioner working with a child and their family.

This section has focused on the assessment relationship. Most of the research cited has concentrated on the relationships between adult caregivers and professionals involved in assessments. Of equal importance in an assessment of children in need is the relationship between the worker and children and young people in the family, and this is discussed in the next section.

Engaging children and young people

Chapter 7 will provide detailed discussion about skills necessary for effective communication with children. This section is therefore devoted to the process of engaging children and young people in an assessment, and research findings on children's views of their relationships with children's services staff.

Research findings, reported in the last section, mainly focused on relationships between adults: practitioners and caregivers. There has been much less attention paid to the views of children and young people who are receiving children's services. Some specific groups have become more regularly involved in consultations on local and national policies and research, particularly looked after children and, to a lesser extent, disabled children. The views of children who are living at home and are in need of support and/ or protection, however, are less well known (Holland and Scourfield 2004). Nonetheless, where children's views of children's services practitioners have become known, their expectations are remarkably similar to those of adult service users. They are looking for reliability, honesty, flexibility and action. Additionally, they want to gain a sense that the practitioner is not always siding with adults' perspectives, but listening to and empathising with the child or young person's experience and opinion (Morgan 2006).

The Coastal Cities study found that children and young people were generally marginal in children in need assessment processes and in the resulting assessment reports. Both focused largely on the actions, motives and statements of parents. (This finding predates the requirement of section 53 of the Children Act 2004, whereby a local authority must ascertain the wishes and feelings of children in relation to services provided and to give due consideration to these before determining what (if any) services to provide to children where the local authority has a duty to safeguard and promote the welfare of children in need by providing suitable services to those children.) Where children and young people's perspectives were reported, there was some unevenness in *how* they were reported, with some children being presented as sensible and trustworthy, and others as whimsical and unreliable (Holland 2004). The best examples of positive engagement presented a full and balanced account of the child's views. This was achieved without attempting to place a value judgement on the child's opinions and acknowledging that children may have complex and sometimes contradictory views about a situation.

We know from research studies that children and young people have views on how they wish to be involved with children's services professionals and other adults, especially in meetings and in court processes. Smart et al. (2001), in their study of 117 children and young people who have experienced parental divorce, note that children in contemporary society *assume* that they will be involved to some extent in decision-making about their lives. This is more complex than simply having a legal right to be consulted (which can be done at a very superficial level) but involves the notion of an ongoing process in a relational context:

> What children seem to want is social recognition, respect and inclusion rather than simply legal rights. They do not appear to want to be free, autonomous individuals, but persons in their own right in the context of a set of relationships. (Smart *et al.* 2001, p.109)

For this type of involvement, children and young people need to be included in the *process* of an assessment, not tokenistically interviewed at one specific point. It can also be tokenistic to invite children to participate in meetings which are adult-centric in the set-up and procedure. Children regard these at best as a chore, or at worst as incomprehensible and alienating (Sanders and Mace 2006; Thomas 2002). Research findings with children and young people also suggest that they will sometimes also wish to make an active decision *not* to participate, but that they also need to know that the opportunity to participate in the future is not then closed to them (O'Quigley 2000).

Children, therefore, expect and require involvement that feels genuine and is centred on relationships that are ongoing and will develop over time. This suggests that priority should be given to maintaining worker continuity throughout the assessment, in order that children are not being asked to talk about intimate and possibly painful subjects to a relative stranger.

In addition to evidence about *how* children and young people wish to be involved in children in need processes, there is also some research evidence regarding *what* children wish to discuss with children's services professionals. First, it should be remembered that whilst adults often focus on the 'bigger picture', such as permanency plans and legal status, for children and young people the priority is as likely to be the everyday. For example, Thomas's research with looked after children aged eight to twelve reminds us that: 'Everyday decisions such as where they go and who their friends are can be as important as long term decisions about their future' (2002, p.137).

It is the perceived lack of action on issues such as permission for sleepovers and funding for school trips that lead some children and young people to complain that their social workers do not listen and act (Morgan 2006). Their social workers in the meantime may be understandably preoccupied with care proceedings and assessment reports, but it is important to listen to a child's priorities rather than always setting the agenda in meetings with children and young people.

O'Quigley (2000) and Smart *et al.* (2001) note that many children wish to have their views listened to and recorded, whilst not necessarily feeling responsible for final decisions. Many are anxious about showing a lack of loyalty to parents and are concerned about how information they have given will be used in reports. It is important, therefore, that clear information is given about how decisions are made, what happens to information, and the nature and limits of confidentiality. Interestingly, in Smart *et al.*'s (2001) study, it was the young people who had the most negative experiences of adult trustworthiness who wanted most direct involvement in decision-making and more explicit rights to be heard.

We have seen, therefore, that children and young people, like adults, value relational aspects of social work intervention, such as having a worker whom they feel listens and understands, who is clear and reliable. Some also have concerns about what happens to information they give, and that adult priorities might dominate processes.

Points for practice when engaging children and young people in assessments

- Aim for early engagement of children and young people in the process.

- Give clear information about what the assessment will involve, what decisions can be made and by whom.

- Consult on assessment methods; for example: 'What do you think are the best ways to find out about and understand you and your family?'

- Children and young people can be included at the stage of analysis: 'This is how I'm beginning to understand what life is like for you and your family. How is that similar or different to how you understand things?'

- Children and young people can be consulted on the most important information to go into a report, and asked to give feedback on the assessment findings.

- Children and young people can usefully advise practitioners on how any cultural, linguistic or religious elements to their lives should be taken into account during the process of assessment. Consider culture in the broadest sense, which might include what language or dialect each person feels most comfortable speaking, the need to remove shoes at the door, or the fact that piano practice is unmissable in their family.

- Disabled children and young people may also be able to advise a practitioner on the impact of their impairment on the assessment, showing how they communicate most effectively (see Chapter 12 for more detail).

Consulting with children and young people, as suggested in these points for practice, acknowledges their expertise about their own lives (Parton and O'Byrne 2000) and may help adjust the power gulf created by age, professional status and (sometimes) class, gender and ethnicity.

Engaging men and women

In the chapter so far, emphasis has been placed on the importance of reliability, clarity of purpose, empathy and warmth to engaging service users of all ages. All service users require clear, accessible information to help them understand what an assessment will involve and what the possible outcomes might be. However, there are some differences between groups of service users, both in how practitioners tend to work with them, and their needs in terms of engagement. One clearly documented area of difference is that of gender. Men and women service users tend to be treated differently according to gender in many aspects of involvement, but particularly when an assessment and intervention includes child protection concerns. Patterns of avoiding or marginalising men and of expecting women to take central responsibility for child care and wider family issues have been highlighted repeatedly in research studies in the UK and internationally (see, for example, Parton *et al.* 1997; Scourfield 2003). Assessments of children's circumstances too often become an assessment of mothering, especially where there are concerns about a child's welfare. For example, Swift's (1995) research into the construction of neglect describes how women come to be more often labelled as neglectful parents than men, as society's, and professionals', expectations are that mothers are more responsible for children's day-to-day care than fathers are.

Scourfield (2003), in an ethnographic study of a child protection team, found that the social workers were informed by feminism and were aware of gender issues in relation to responsibility for caring and domestic violence. They were also aware of the potential for bias in the responses of statutory services. However, because of their emphasis on the centrality of the welfare of the child, they felt the need to accept the 'reality' of women's responsibility for child care and therefore placed responsibility for caring and protection of children onto mothers. As a result, women were expected to protect themselves and their children from violent men, rather than the violent men being challenged and worked with directly. Women who transgressed their perceived roles, for example by putting their own social needs before that of their child, were subject to particular criticism, in a manner that men's prioritisations of self might not be.

Research findings in relation to working with men highlight how fathers (and father figures) are less likely to be engaged in statutory interventions than mothers (see, for example, Kullberg 2005). Quantitative data on this problem can be difficult to find, as 'parental' involvement in interventions is often recorded, which can serve to mask the predominance of mothers' engagement in this work. Scourfield (2003) notes that men are not all treated alike by social workers and he typifies social worker understandings of men in the following ways:

1. *Men as a threat.* This acknowledges that some men whom practitioners come into contact with have been violent towards others, including partners and children. Many workers will find it daunting to engage such men. This issue is discussed further below.

2. *Men as no use, men as irrelevant or men as absent.* These highlight how men are often not involved because they are seen as marginal to family life, perhaps because they are little involved in child care, they do not engage with professional workers, or live elsewhere.

3. *Men as no different from women.* This is either because the two parents are thought to be 'as bad as each other' in a particular household, or because social workers declare it would be discriminatory to have different approaches to men and women.

4. *Men as better than women.* Scourfield also noted a small number of cases where the father was seen as the more capable parent, on whom the worker concentrated most of their efforts.

Findings from the biennial analysis of serious case reviews 2005–7 suggest some similar patterns in cases which have become the subject of serious case reviews (Brandon *et al.* 2008). First, they have found that little is known about men in these cases, even where the male is the suspected perpetrator of harm to the child. Second, they, too, have noted that men often are presenting as a threat in these cases – to their families and to professionals. Third, they suggest that men are being categorised rather rigidly as a risk or protective figure for the child, when the situation may be less straightforward than that.

Whilst there is much evidence about processes of intervention, there is less direct evidence about fathers' views. Ghate *et al.* (2000) found that men were reluctant to take part in interviews and interventions related to child welfare and parenting, seeing staff and premises as women's spaces. Featherstone and White (2006) have more recently analysed interviews with men, which were carried out by the Family Rights Group. These men, too, tended to suggest that children's social care services were focused on women, and that women's accounts were more likely to be believed than men's. Although the men often had positive reports to give of their individual social workers, in general they described social workers as 'predictably unpredictable' (often changing direction of focus or pace of work) and 'going by the book' (p.80) rather than treating the men as individuals. In attempting to engage men, who seem reluctant to engage, practitioners could discuss these views with men, encourage an open dialogue about how they are experiencing the intervention and demonstrate a willingness to listen. This does not mean that practitioners should not challenge perceptions that they believe to be wrong, but in the author's experience all service users, and perhaps particularly men, appreciate a 'down-to-earth', straight-talking approach.

The research findings, therefore, suggest that men and women are worked with differently by children's services staff or social workers. Women can be seen as centrally responsible for children and, when they transgress this role, are subject to criticism. Men are less frequently engaged, due to being seen by some practitioners as marginal or threatening. Men also may exclude themselves because of their perceptions of the service as women-centred or unfair to them. Practitioners need to be aware of these tendencies when planning and carrying out assessments. Critical reflection is needed on the part of the professional to examine expectations of gender roles and why they may have, for example, not attempted to gain the view of an absent father. By perpetuating these patterns practitioners not only do women a disservice, by sometimes placing too high expectations on their mothering role, but they also marginalise men as a potential resource for caring and support within the family. A basic step, at the beginning of any children in need assessment, would be to establish who the significant adult males are within a family (not necessarily within the actual household), and to ask how they may be involved in the assessment. Second, when practitioners find themselves expecting women to manage men's violence, they should ask what the barriers might be to engaging directly with those men themselves. It is potential blocks and barriers to engagement that are considered next.

Blocks and barriers

> Developing a working relationship with children and family members will not always be easy to achieve and can be difficult especially when there have been concerns about significant harm to the child. However resistant the family or difficult the circumstances, it remains important to continue to try to find ways of engaging the family in the assessment process.
>
> *(Department of Health et al. 2000, p.13, 1.47)*

Two of the major barriers to achieving a successful assessment relationship are where carers do not wish to co-operate with the assessment and where there is a fear or threat of violence towards the worker. There is a danger that 'failure to co-operate' is always constructed as the service user's problem, without critical reflection on whether the approach of the agency or worker may be contributing to the lack of engagement. The imposition of an assessment procedure and agenda, without consultation on the family's preferred way of working, and a listing of 'agency concerns' without a genuine attempt to listen to family members' perspectives in a first meeting, can serve to alienate people who are likely to feel defensive or even threatened by the intervention. A shift in initial approach from 'professional-as-expert' to 'service user-as-expert' about their own lives, and, therefore, the professional as 'not knowing', can help emphasise values of respect and empathy which may help engagement (Parton and O'Byrne 2000). This is not meant to suggest that the professional lacks knowledge and expertise in general, only that a vital part of successful engagement is to start with listening and then demonstrating that the person's views have been heard and taken note of. Finding workable solutions to difficulties can only be achieved if the solutions feel acceptable and achievable to those expected to carry them out, often the parents, and therefore it makes sense to develop the solutions.

Nonetheless, some families will not engage, nor co-operate with an assessment. This might manifest itself in a number of ways, including avoiding the worker and threatening violence. If there are concerns about a child's welfare then it is a statutory requirement that a child is seen in person, and occasionally local authorities may need to apply for a court orders or, in emergency situations, involve the police to gain access to a child. In these situations there is a danger that all agencies involved assume that another professional has seen the child. Therefore, information must be carefully cross-checked with other agencies.

Fear or threat of violence is a central barrier to carrying out an assessment. It is often the understandable cause of reluctance to engage men, especially in domestic violence cases, and in a context where the majority of children's services staff are female (although male workers are of course also vulnerable in this context[1]). However, a policy of avoidance or non-engagement with men who may be violent is unconstructive and, indeed, there is evidence that violent, abusive men can be constructively engaged. Such men are often successfully engaged by specialist providers, such as those offering groupwork for

---

1   O'Hagan and Dillenburger (1995) cite research that shows male workers to be at greater risk of violence from service users and female service users to pose greatest risk of assaulting social workers. This is in the context of child welfare settings where the majority of adult service users are female.

men who are sexual offenders or who are violent to their partners. Some approaches to this work have proven successful in reducing re-offending (Featherstone *et al.* 2007). Such specialist providers may be able to offer advice, training or interventions in children in need cases. There is also the possibility that direct engagement with a violent parent (often but not always the male carer) may reduce harm or risk to family members. There may be a long-term emotional benefit for a child who may be placed permanently elsewhere. Even where it is unlikely that a very violent or abusive carer will be able to play any future direct part in unsupervised caregiving, their engagement at some level may still be important to the child's emotional development and identity.

Workers and their supervisors need to acknowledge fear of violence to themselves and to colleagues. Agencies must recognise the stress that workers may be placed under in such situations and the potential risk this might pose to the child's safety (Littlechild 2005). The following measures can be taken:

- Potential risk of harm to other family members (adults and children) and workers should be assessed. Workers must be supported by managers who should encourage the reporting of all threats and violent acts and take direct action against the perpetrator if necessary.

- Issues of risk of harm, and other blocks and barriers to effective engagement, should be central topics in supervision meetings between practitioners and line managers.

- Teams should aim to provide supportive environments where practitioners feel able to share their concerns without feeling inadequate or to blame. Discussions in team meetings can encourage the sharing of concerns.

- All involved agencies should work together to provide a co-ordinated response to situations where workers feel they are being placed at risk of harm. It is essential to ensure that the child continues to be directly engaged with and their welfare monitored. Concerns must be shared across agencies.

- It should be noted that black and ethnic minority staff may experience racial abuse, and again clear action should be taken against perpetrators.

- The use of written agreements can be constructive. They can set out the expectations of both practitioners *and* family members in terms of respectful behaviour, and also clearly outline the aims of the assessment and its possible consequences.

- It can be fruitful to agree to meet in a neutral venue where both parties feel safe and unthreatened. This might be in the premises of an agency that is already familiar to the person being assessed, such as a room in a children's centre.

- A trusted worker, such as a health visitor, probation officer or the child's teacher, or in some circumstances another family member or friend, may be willing to sit in on assessment meetings. For example, as an assessing social worker, several years ago, the author assessed a father with a personality disorder and a history of violence, including towards female professionals. His male mental health social worker, with whom he had a good relationship, sat in on our meetings, helping us both to feel more comfortable and safe.

Understanding personal blocks and barriers: cultural review

As well as difficulties with co-operation and violence, workers sometimes experience personal barriers when attempting to engage family members. This might include a difficulty in empathising with another's world view, or feeling unsure about attitudes towards parenting practices in other cultural groups. Constant critical reflection by the worker, preferably alongside a supervisor, is necessary. Drawing on the work of Taylor and White (2000), reflection in assessment is a process where the aim is to become critically aware of the impact of self and belief systems on the assessment, and of the service user's response to this. The impact of self will include 'categories' such as gender, age, ethnicity, religion and class, and also the employing agency's culture and dominant policies, practices and theories in the profession more widely. Shaw (1996) draws on McCracken's (1988) process of 'cultural review' which McCracken suggested researchers should carry out before interviewing for research. Shaw notes that this could be applied to practice. A 'cultural review' means a systematic questioning of all of our cultural categories relating to the subject at hand:

- What knowledge do we have of the culture, language and religion of the family, and where does this knowledge come from?

- Do we hold positive or negative prejudices relating to this family's cultural group?

- In looking at the age and stage of the children in the family, what might we expect of their lives, abilities and needs?

- What impact might the assessment have on these family members' lives and how might they perceive me as an individual and as a representative of my employer?

- What might they be expecting from the assessment?

- What would surprise us when we visit this family and why would it be a surprise? (See Holland 2004, p.130, for a specific example.)

Such personal and critical reflection can help practitioners understand why they may be having difficulty in engaging with a family member, and also help plan practical ways of working with this.

Overcoming blocks and barriers

There are several ways in which, by adopting positive approaches, we might be able to work with service users who feel alienated, threatened or bewildered by social work assessment processes. An emphasis on identifying and building families' strengths, and solution-based approaches (see Parton and O'Byrne 2000), will help build a positive assessment relationship, which is a necessity in order to be able to discuss and explore safe ways forward where there are concerns about a child's welfare.

One intervention which uses such an approach and which is rapidly gaining ground in the UK is the family group meeting or conference (Holland et al. 2005). For many families, such a meeting, worked towards in conjunction with an assessment and taking place towards the end of a core assessment or following an initial assessment, is an excellent way of mobilising family strengths and resources towards providing a safe and enhancing environment for a child, in a manner that suits the specific style of that family. Even in cases where there are serious child protection concerns, there is evidence that family group meetings can enable workable multi-agency child protection plans to be agreed by key members of the family network and professionals. Whilst this specific intervention will not be suitable for, or desired by, all families, the attitudes prevalent in the approach can be applied in almost all situations.

Summary

This chapter has considered the engagement of adult primary carers, children and young people in the assessment process. It has been emphasised that developing a positive assessment relationship is central to conducting a successful assessment. Research findings from service users' accounts of their engagement with social work services have been noted, and it can be seen that relational aspects such as perceived empathy, listening, humour, reliability and honesty are emphasised by adults and children. Additionally, caregivers respond to how they feel that practitioners are using power over or with them. Understandably, those being assessed want assurance that they are being treated as individuals and that their circumstances and needs are fully understood by those assessing them. Some differences in patterns between men's and women's engagement were noted. Where family members are difficult to engage, practitioners are encouraged to critically reflect on the institutional, cultural and interpersonal reasons for this, to acknowledge why many being assessed may be reluctant to fully engage and to openly discuss with all participants how the process can be made to feel more welcoming and accessible to them. It was noted that adopting a strengths-based and positive attitude does not mean avoiding challenging issues such as child protection concerns, but that by establishing a positive working relationship practitioners are more likely to be able to tackle those issues constructively and work together towards the best plan for the child's welfare.

Recommended reading

Featherstone, B., Rivett, M. and Scourfield, J. (2007) *Working with Men in Health and Social Care.* London: Sage.

Holland, S. (2004) *Child and Family Assessment in Social Work Practice.* London: Sage.

Parton, N. and O'Byrne, P. (2000) *Constructive Social Work.* Basingstoke: Macmillan.

Taylor, C. and White, S. (2000) *Practising Reflexivity in Health and Welfare: Making Knowledge.* Buckingham: Open University Press.

Thomas, N. (2002) *Children, Family and the State.* Bristol: The Policy Press.

References

Atkinson, L. and Butler, S. (1996) 'Court-ordered assessment: impact of maternal noncompliance in child maltreatment cases.' *Child Abuse and Neglect 20,* 3, 185–190.

Brandon, M., Belderson, P., Bailey, S., Gardner, R. *et al.* (2008) *Analysing Child Deaths and Serious Injury through Abuse and Neglect: What Can We Learn? A Biennial Analysis of Serious Case Reviews 2005–2007.* London: Department for Children, Schools and Families.

Cleaver, H. and Walker, S. (2004) 'From policy to practice: the implementation of a new framework for social work assessments of children and families.' *Child and Family Social Work 9,* 1, 81–90.

de Boer, C. and Coady, N. (2007) 'Good helping relationships in child welfare: learning from stories of success.' *Child and Family Social Work 12*, 1, 32–42.

Department of Health, Department for Education and Employment and the Home Office (2000) *Framework for the Assessment of Children in Need and their Families.* London: The Stationery Office.

Drake, B. (1994) 'Relationship competencies in child welfare services.' *Social Work 39*, 5, 595–602.

Dumbrill, G.C. (2006) 'Parental experience of child protection intervention: a qualitative study.' *Child Abuse and Neglect 30*, 1, 27–37.

Featherstone, B. and White, S. (2006) 'Dads Talk about their Lives and Services.' In C. Ashley, B. Featherstone, C. Roskill, M. Ryan and S. White (eds) *Fathers Matter: Research Findings on Fathers and their Involvement with Social Care Services.* London: Family Rights Group.

Featherstone, B., Rivett, M. and Scourfield, J. (2007) *Working with Men in Health and Social Care.* London: Sage.

Fernandez, E. (1996) *Significant Harm: Unravelling Child Protection Decisions and Substitute Care Careers of Children.* Aldershot: Avebury.

Ghate, D., Shaw, C. and Hazel, N. (2000) *Fathers and Family Centres: Engaging Fathers in Preventative Services.* York: York Publishing Services.

Holland, S. (2004) *Child and Family Assessment in Social Work Practice.* London: Sage.

Holland, S. and Scourfield, J. (2004) 'Liberty and respect in child protection.' *British Journal of Social Work 34*, 1, 17–32.

Holland, S., Scourfield, J., O'Neill, S. and Pithouse, A. (2005) 'Democratising the family and the state? The case of family group conferences in child welfare.' *Journal of Social Policy 34*, 1, 59–77.

Howe, D. (1998) 'Relationship-based thinking and practice in social work.' *Journal of Social Work Practice 12*, 1, 45–56.

Kullberg, C. (2005) 'Differences in the seriousness of problems and deservingness of help: Swedish social workers' assessments of single mothers and fathers.' *British Journal of Social Work 35*, 3, 373–386.

Leigh, S. and Miller, C. (2004) 'Is the third way the best way? Social work intervention with children and families.' *Journal of Social Work 4*, 3, 245–267.

Littlechild, B. (2005) 'The nature and effects of violence against child protection social workers: providing effective support.' *British Journal of Social Work 35*, 3, 387–401.

Maiter, S., Palmer, S. and Manji, S. (2006) 'Strengthening social worker–client relationships in child protection services: addressing power imbalances and "ruptured" relationships.' *Qualitative Social Work 5*, 2, 167–186.

McCracken, D.G. (1988) *The Long Interview.* Beverly Hills, CA: Sage.

Morgan, R. (2006) *About Social Workers: A Children's Views Report.* Newcastle Upon Tyne: Office of the Children's Rights Director.

O'Hagan, K. and Dillenburger, K. (1995) *The Abuse of Women within Childcare Work.* Buckingham: Open University Press.

O'Quigley, A. (2000) *Listening to Children's Views: The Findings and Recommendations of Recent Research.* York: Joseph Rowntree Foundation.

Parton, N. and O'Byrne, P. (2000) *Constructive Social Work.* Basingstoke: Macmillan.

Parton, N., Thorpe, D. and Wattam, C. (1997) *Child Protection: Risk and the Moral Order.* Basingstoke: Macmillan.

Platt, D. (2007) 'Congruence and co-operation in social workers' assessments of children in need.' *Child and Family Social Work 12*, 4, 326–335.

Sanders, R. and Mace, S. (2006) 'Agency policy and the participation of children and young people in the child protection process.' *Child Abuse Review 15*, 2, 89–109.

Scourfield, J. (2003) *Gender and Child Protection.* Basingstoke: Palgrave Macmillan.

Shaw, I. (1996) *Evaluating in Practice.* Aldershot: Arena.

Smart, C., Neale, B. and Wade, A. (2001) *The Changing Experience of Childhood: Families and Divorce.* Cambridge: Polity Press.

Swift, K. (1995) *Manufacturing 'Bad Mothers': A Critical Perspective on Child Neglect.* Toronto: University of Toronto Press.

Taylor, C. and White, S. (2000) *Practising Reflexivity in Health and Welfare: Making Knowledge.* Buckingham: Open University Press.

Thomas, N. (2002) *Children, Family and the State.* Bristol: The Policy Press.

Waterhouse, L. and Carnie, J. (1992) 'Assessing child protection risk.' *British Journal of Social Work 22*, 1, 47–60.

CHAPTER 7

Here to Listen! Communicating with Children and Methods for Communicating with Children and Young People as Part of the Assessment Process

Norma Howes

Fundamental to establishing whether a child is in need and how those needs should be best met is that the approach must be child centred. This means that the child is seen and kept in focus throughout the assessment and that account is always taken of the child's perspective.

(From the Framework for the Assessment of Children in Need and their Families, p.10, 1.34)

This chapter will:

- provide an overview of factors to consider when communicating with children of various ages and abilities

- explore factors that practitioners should consider when preparing themselves for engaging children and young people in the assessment process

- identify methods and resources available for communicating with children

- consider ways in which practitioners can utilise these resources taking into account the assessment task, age and ability of the individual child

---

- explore the additional factors that should be considered when using communication tools and resources as a vehicle for communicating with children, such as

  ○ setting

  ○ monitoring the child's emotional, behavioural and somatic (body feeling) responses

  ○ the impact of trauma/abuse on a child and consequences for communicating with children as part of the assessment

  ○ children's assessment skills

  ○ why taking seriously what the child says is so important.

- briefly consider a child's neurobiological responses to any anxiety-making or fear-filled situation, which may include being part of an assessment.

Introduction

Children can contribute much to the assessment process as Holland discusses in Chapter 6. Their powers of observation and their assessment skills are first class. Not many children, however, will be able to 'just tell' practitioners what it is they know or feel. As explored in this chapter there are many reasons why a child cannot 'just tell'. It will be the skill, knowledge, aptitude, tenacity and preparation of the practitioner to find out what the child knows and feels that will enable the child's wishes and feelings to be fully included and valued in any assessment. The way in which the practitioner prepares both themselves and the child or young person for active involvement in the assessment process is crucial. Therefore, the focus of this chapter is on planning for and engaging with children and young people to establish what the child knows or feels.

Preparing to engage children and young people in the assessment

Practitioner preparation

It is so important to be clear about the purpose of communicating with a particular child, to know when the purpose is achieved and when to stop. Children will be asked to contribute to an assessment in any of the following situations: family breakup, family dysfunction, separation, bereavement, loss, assessment of needs, including special needs, disability assessment, illness, pain, or where abuse is suspected. Therefore, children who are involved in an assessment using the *Framework for the Assessment of Children in Need and their Families* (Department of Health *et al.* 2000) may well have experienced a variety of assessments in the past. Being as clear as possible about the reason for the assessment will guide the preparation for and the content of the interview.

It is useful for practitioners to prepare for engaging children and young people in the assessment process by hypothesising or asking 'What if?' This can help practitioners keep an open mind and prepare themselves for a range of different scenarios. For example:

- What if there is nothing to be concerned about?
- What if this is a false report or allegation of maltreatment?
- What if as a consequence of the assessment the child needs to be removed from his/her parents' care?
- What if the child is worried about that or asks if that might happen?
- What if the child is hostile or won't join in?
- What if I am out of my depth or don't know enough or don't get something right?

Discussing the 'what ifs' in supervision and with an experienced colleague will help in confidence building and being better prepared.

Children are very forgiving of errors or what they perceive as stupid questions, as long as the practitioner is genuine, properly curious without being voyeuristic and engages well with them in an age appropriate and respectful way. Marchant makes this point very well in Chapter 12, which focuses on assessing children with complex needs.

Gathering information

Information from as many sources as possible should be obtained about the child. Parents and teachers will be the main sources of information. Care must be taken, however, to assess whether anyone who contributes information has an agenda that would influence what they contribute. For example, a violent father may describe his two children as having no issues or problems with his violence to their mother, to benefit him, and the mother may exaggerate the impact, to benefit her. Neither has their children clearly in mind but is more driven by their own needs and issues. Determining whether either parent is able to put their children's needs before their own forms an important part of the assessment.

It is not enough to just gather the information but to measure and assess it against other children of the same age, background and heritage (Garbarino *et al.* 1992, pp.1–17). Practitioners should consider before the assessment begins how they will explain the purpose of the assessment to the child and how the child's contribution will be used. This will need careful thinking through for each situation. The practitioner needs to wonder how the child will hear the explanation and what questions the child is likely to have in their head or ask. Just thinking about the child's questions is one part: thinking about the answers is more important. The answer given must *never* be a lie or contain misinformation. However, one of the challenges for a practitioner is deciding how much information to impart. For example, how frightening is it for a child to hear that his answers will be shared with, perhaps, the twenty-plus people who will attend the initial child protection conference or perhaps eventually be used in court?

This author made this mistake by 'cleverly' drawing heads, with faces completed by the child, to represent those who would know what the child had said. Twenty-two heads later the child was in tears and withdrawing physically and psychologically from the interview. It may be better to say that only people who need to know will have access to the information. Think ahead to the answer you will give if the child asks who that might be.

Practical preparation of the practitioner

The practitioner who will be gathering information from the child must know about child development, the impact of trauma on development, mind, body and neurobiology, be curious about what is making the child behave in the way they do, and about how children blame themselves for problems in their family, often reinforced by parent, school and possibly others. It is very likely it will have been the child's behaviour that has drawn attention to whatever the problem is in the family (Perry *et al.* 1995). The child may then feel responsible for the assessment and any distress to, or consequences for, his family. It is also important to think about any threats to the child not to tell or not to co-operate. The chapter 'The Abuse Dichotomy' in *Child Abuse Trauma* (Briere 1992) is very helpful further reading on this issue, as is the chapter 'Child Abuse' in *Trauma and Recovery* (Herman 1992).

Threats used to silence children will only work if they are effective. The most effective threats link to what is missing in the child's life and are then tailored to that specific child. For example, a child with a secure attachment would never believe the threat that, if they tell, their mother will not love them any more (Schore 2001). A child with an insecure attachment may believe this.

It is also important to think through how the practitioner will explain to the child their role in the assessment. Choosing the right words to explain their job should be tailored to each child and how much they need to know or already know about the practitioner and the work they do. In choosing the correct words workers should take account of what this child might already know about their role from previous experiences, parents, friends or the media and how this might positively or negatively influence the child's view of the practitioner and the purpose of the assessment.

Emotional preparation of the practitioner

As a practitioner, consider the following questions:

- What are your fears, for example that you might be out of your depth or lack confidence, and what impact might this have on the child?
- What is likely to make you feel embarrassed or uncertain? How might you react?
- Do you know what will happen next?
- Are you clear about your role in the assessment process?
- Do you believe it is your job to listen to children or talk to children?

- What is your belief about whether children lie or not?

- What will you do if this child reminds you of another child or yourself as a child?

- Are you clear about the consequences for you and the child if this interview is successful or not?

- Do you have a tendency to minimise effects of maltreatment or to minimise the nature of maltreatment?

- Are you aware of any financial pressures – budget restrictions – which could influence your approach to engaging this child in the assessment process?

- What might the child say that could affect working in partnership with parents?

- Do you tend to look for easy solutions to complex situations?

- If you believe the child, will your manager or others believe you?

Discussion of any of the above in supervision will help the practitioner prepare for interviewing the child.

Preparation of the child or young person

Before thinking through how to prepare the child for the assessment think through what has been the child's experience of other assessments and interviews, being questioned, and giving information about themselves or their family. Consider, from what you know about this child, what the child's issues might be around attachment, denial, grief, anger, fear, responsibility, health, education. It is also important to gain an understanding of their use of and skill with language, for example use of pronouns, metaphor, imagination. This is particularly important if working with a child with a diagnosis of autistic spectrum disorder (Howe *et al.* 1999; James 1994; Jewett 1982). Preparation for the interview must also take into consideration what age the child is and the child's competencies and history (Dixon and Stein 1992). Although the worker may be respectful of ethnicity, disability and heritage, the child's experiences may not have been respectful and her expectation may well be that you will be yet another adult who is not trustworthy or interested in her as the unique individual she is.

Considerations of family culture: ethnicity

From what you know of this child consider:

- the child's view of you and what you represent

- the belief systems and values of the child's culture, and how these conflict or agree with your own values, status and belief system

- the structures and decision-making in the child's close and extended family and the child's place within this

- the importance or otherwise of the family network

- the traditional solutions to problems

- the sex roles

- if this family are first or second generation immigrants, the likely losses experienced in moving to/living in Britain

- the racial/cultural pressures and the impact on the child of talking with you. (Harris 2006)

The need to consider where the information came from and gathering the information is only one part of the task. Evaluating it and assessing it against the norm is the greater task. Additional considerations in relation to children with complex needs are considered in Chapter 12 and for children from British minority ethnic groups in Chapter 20.

Choosing the correct venue

Children may experience being called to the quiet room behind the head teacher's office as a time of remembering being in trouble in school and then at home. Being taken in a car may bring back thoughts of being taken to a place or house where she was hurt. In addition, sitting opposite an adult who is asking questions can be a scary reminder of getting answers wrong and being punished. As one can see from these examples, what seems like an ideal venue for the practitioner may not be the best place for the child. The practitioner must think where to interview the child, from the individual child's perspective. It is also useful to remember that children talk more freely when they are engaged in a task, for example baking or making a craft item, or when they think the adult is busy with something. The position of the child and the adult in these circumstances is best not face-to-face, but side-by-side. Think through where would be a suitable venue by asking the following questions:

- Is this place a safe place for the child?

- Will what the child has to talk about change how the child experiences this place in the future?

- Is the room quiet and free from interruptions?

- Does the room contain any toys, pictures, etc. which could trigger the child or influence what they might say? (It is of course not possible to create a trigger-free environment but care should be taken to check what is in the room is appropriate and not potentially upsetting.)

- Is the equipment available age-appropriate, working and of good quality? It does nothing for a child's self-esteem to be asked to use pens which do not work or write on paper which has been used on the other side for another purpose. If the child has difficulty reading or writing, asking the child to use pen and paper should be avoided. If the child is disabled or has difficulty with fine motor skills, fat felt tips or other more specialist items can be used.

Preparation of the venue

The ideal is a child-friendly, appropriate venue. The author remembers being offered an interview room with life-size paintings of Snow White and the Seven Dwarfs on one wall with the wicked witch all in black, holding an apple, on the other. Not the best place to interview a black child or indeed any child. On another occasion, in October, the author was offered a room in a family centre full with Halloween paraphernalia, which could be frightening. If it can be avoided, do not use the child's bedroom, or a room in the child's school; both of these may be safe places for some children which may then be 'contaminated' by the interview. Alternatively, for others this may be the best place. Think about who could advise you about the impact on the child or think it through yourself using the 'what if?' technique described earlier.

Public places, like burger bars, are not appropriate places for children to discuss personal experiences. The decision about where to see the child will be made on what you know about them, and indeed the practitioner making some hypothesis about each possible venue and identifying the positives and negatives for this particular child. It is, however, important to remember that the venue and the equipment available will not in themselves make the interview successful. It is the skill, appropriate confidence, attunement, curiosity and genuineness of the practitioner which will make the process successful, often in spite of the venue or equipment.

Preparing for the unexpected

Think ahead to the end of the session and any consequences for the child and his family from the information you have obtained from the child. Again the 'what ifs':

- What if a criminal offence has been disclosed and referrals to children's social care services and the police are needed?

- What if the child indicates he is suicidal or planning to run away?

- What if the child fears being hurt or told off for talking to you in such detail or for not talking to you at all?

- What if the child refuses to return home?

It is important also to think ahead to what support you will need, and from whom. Whether you will need to debrief or plan the next step may help you choose who you need to involve in this process.

Engaging children and young people: first steps

As stated earlier it is the skill, appropriate confidence, attunement, curiosity and genuineness of the practitioner undertaking the interview from the beginning of the session that will influence how well the child engages in the assessment process. Many interviews with children begin with the words 'Do *you* know why *you* are here?' followed by the practitioner explaining, '*I* am here to *talk* to you about what has happened' and then 'I will need to make some notes in case I forget what you have said.'

The risk in starting with 'Do you know why you are here?' is that it implies the child has done something and may make an already self-blaming child feel so shamed, anxious or concerned about what he believes he is responsible for that communication is then limited by normal neurobiological responses to the child's feelings of shame; that is, one of seven 'F' responses – fight, flight, feed, reproduce, freeze, flop and fart (van der Kolk 1996). The second comment, 'I am here to talk to you…', places the emphasis on the practitioner as the person in the session who will do the talking. The third, 'I will need to make some notes…', gives the child the message that what is said is not worth remembering.

How much better if the interview starts with 'Do you know why *we* are here?', sharing the task and creating an important alliance with the child, followed by 'so that *I can listen carefully* to what you can tell me about what has happened', giving the message that the worker will listen and the child will do the talking, and then 'I may have to make some notes because what *you say will be important* and I want to make sure I have got it right.'

Again, it is useful to think through the 'what ifs':

• What if this child is scared off by my saying it is important?

• What if the child looks anxious?

• What if the child won't talk or wants to leave straight away?

Remember to think through solutions to the 'what if' problems before the session so that you do not have to think them all through in the session.

Schore (2007) comments that a child's feelings of shame will be twice as big as the feelings associated with any fear or terror the child feels or felt. The practitioner therefore needs to be aware of any of her behaviour or questions which will increase the child's feelings of shame or sense of responsibility for what has happened or what will happen. To paraphrase Briere (1992), children believe they are as 'bad' as what has happened to them, so if something really 'bad' had happened then the child is a really 'bad' child. (The word 'bad' is in inverted commas because at all costs this word must be avoided in any work being done with children.)

Herman (1992) comments that children often need to take on the responsibility to absolve their parent of blame and by doing so preserve that relationship, and the hope that one day if the child was a more lovable child, the parent would love them more. In other words, to blame their parent means giving up on hope that one day something positive will happen. So, from the child's perspective, it is much better to take the blame themselves and only speak/think/feel positive about their parents.

As part of the beginning, or the end, of the session, children are often asked if they have any questions for the interviewer. Children ask questions to obtain information. What appears to be the most immediate answer may not be the information the child is looking for. It is therefore very important that before answering any question the child has, the practitioner thinks of possible hypotheses about the meaning of the question and clarifies these with the child before answering. For example, the child who asks 'Where did I come from?' may not be asking for sex education but simply wondering which country he was born in. This is important when considering any questions the child has about contact with a parent. It is particularly important when the child has been hurt or harmed by their parent. Knowledge about the form of disorganised attachment, called a trauma bond, will help extend the hypotheses, and an exploration of the purpose of the question with the child will be helpful before the answer is given. (For further information on attachment see Chapter 11.) This point is illustrated in the following case example.

> A six-year-old girl had been physically assaulted by her father, who was serving a prison sentence for the offences he had committed against the child, her mother and siblings. She asked the worker if she could see her dad. The worker then had two options as to how to answer this: 1) follow current practice about the importance of contact and demonstrate she is listening to the child by answering that she will see what she can do to arrange this, or 2) answer that this is a very interesting question and wonder with the child where the idea came from about seeing her dad. The latter opens up the issue and enables, for example, the child to say whether or not this was her idea or was put there by someone else. In this real-life example the child said the idea came to her because she had had a very bad nightmare that her father was able to escape from prison and had come back to her home to hurt her and her mother again. Seeing him in prison would enable her to make sure he was locked up very tightly and could not escape. The type of visit organised, if one was needed at all, would therefore be quite different to one organised for a child who wished to maintain regular contact with the father while he was in prison.

In summary:

- Use simple language.
- Keep sentences short.
- Use familiar words.
- Avoid unnecessary words.
- Use action words.
- Use your usual way of talking.
- Use terms the child can picture.
- Remember the child's experience.
- Speak to express not impress.

Equipment and resources

Concern is often expressed about the lack of resources available to the worker to improve or enhance her communication with a child. The most important resource is the practitioner herself and her capacities to engage with the child. A well-prepared practitioner who is ready to engage with the child in a congruent, respectful and empathic way will enable the child to communicate as effectively as possible. The more competent the practitioner feels, the more competent the child will feel (Garbarino *et al.* 1986).

It should also be remembered that, when stressed, the expressive and receptive language centres of the brain (Broca's and Wernicke's areas) are turned down or even turned off (Gerhardt 2004; Sunderland 2006; van der Kolk 1996). The expression 'speechless with terror' reflects this. The tone, timbre and texture of the practitioner's voice will then be an important resource to assist the child in relaxing enough to allow their language centres to become operational (Perry *et al.* 1995; van der Kolk 1996). Recent developments in neurobiology identify the presence of mirror neurons in the brain of practitioner and child, reinforcing how the practitioner feels about the session, which in turn influences how the child feels about it and the practitioner (van der Hart *et al.* 2006).

One of the tasks frequently undertaken with a child, as part of the assessment process, is to ask the child to complete a genogram or an eco-map. The genogram contains factual information about who is in the family and their relationship with each other; the eco-map centres on the child's opinion of the quality of those relationships. Eco-maps can also include other people in the child's system, such as their best friend, worst enemy and other unrelated but perhaps more emotionally important people, for example a teacher, godparent or youth worker. The suggested inclusion of their worst enemy allows the child to place this person far away from themselves and then compare their negative feelings about other people in relation to this most negative relationship.

Often, completing these can be complex and messy, as the worker tries to construct the genogram from the child's description or the child tries to draw circles in the right places for their eco-map. A very useful way of completing both is to use sticky notes. These are available in a multitude of shapes, colours and sizes up to A3, and even the size of a flip-chart pad. The child begins by writing each person's name on a sticky note. If appropriate the child can be asked to draw that person as an animal, or an imaginary animal, or think of a word to describe that person. (If the worker is going to use the word 'imaginary', or say 'let's pretend', care should be taken to ensure that what the child subsequently says in the session is not pretend or make-believe. This is important if the notes are likely to be used in any future care or criminal proceedings when the 'let's pretend', without checking, could render information inadmissible.)

The wonderful thing about the notes is they can be moved around the paper before drawing any lines. Using sticky notes is so much more effective than using buttons or stones or any other toy to represent family members and their relationships. Their stickiness represents the stickiness of relationships. The movement they allow can also be used to explore with the child, 'What would happen if…?' Asking how the various animals get on together removes some of the tension from asking how those people get on. It can also be useful to ask the child to complete an eco-map three times – one for how things were before the assessment or before the intervention, one for how it is today and one for how she would like it to be if things were perfect.

Other useful equipment includes (remember to choose which is most appropriate for the task and the child):

- magnet, string, glue, sellotape
- finger paints, clay, playdough, sand
- dolls, animals, puppets, doll's house
- cars, trucks, planes, boats

- craft kit
- games
- puzzles
- Lego
- baby equipment
- books, writing stories
- soft toys
- treasure box
- music
- telephone
- hats, masks, candles
- face paints
- finger and hand puppets
- **yourself.**

Communicating with the child

Monitoring the child's emotional, behavioural and somatic (body feeling) responses

Whatever the task engaged in it is the worker's responsibility to monitor the child's emotional and/or physical arousal and distress in the session. This attunement, technically the adult's right brain to child's right brain limbic system, is a wonderful resource enabling the practitioner to maximise the positives and minimise the negatives of the session for the child. It enables the child to experience connection with an adult who is responsive and who offers an external source of explanation, support, comfort, reassurance and soothing, enabling the child to feel calm(er) and increase their curiosity and energy to engage more fully in the interview (Siegal 1995).

Another important reason for modulating the child's arousal is to ensure she does not become so anxious by the content that she disengages by either leaving the room (physical flight), dissociating (psychological flight), breaking pens, toys or the drawings done already (fight), ends the interview by crying for her attachment figure, or feels overwhelmed with distress and collapses (flop). Close observation of the child *and* emotional attunement, in other words not *just* listening to what the child is saying but observing body movements and attuning to the child's emotional state, are key to knowing when to intervene and lowering or increasing the intensity of the session. If the child has an awful experience in the first session, why would they want to attend again (Levine and Kline 1997, 2007; Ogden *et al.* 2006; Rothschild 2000)?

This is demonstrated in the following example:

James was asked a question. 'What do you feel about seeing your dad?' James's memory of Dad is Dad's violence to his mother. James's somatic (body's) response, triggered by this memory, makes his toes twitch (flight response), his fingers clench (fight response) and his tummy turn over (energy needed for fight and flight), but James has learned that when in danger he must not allow himself to move or, if he must, in a way which will not bring any attention to him, i.e. with hardly noticeable micro-movements. His level of anxiety rises and to try to stop the worker from asking him an even more difficult question, which triggers more memories and would add to his distress, he smiles at her to evoke kindness from her and not more harm. With this smile come the words 'I don't mind'. To say 'no' would be too scary, to say 'yes' would be too scary, but why the smile?

When James lived with his dad he needed to be able to do a quick assessment of what Dad wanted in answer to any question in order to ensure his survival. Smiling at his dad would very often lessen his anger. James knows that his dad wants him to behave as if he loves his dad. James's behavioural script, or conditioned response to feeling frightened, is to smile and meet the needs of the person making him frightened. In the interview situation asking him a question which does not have a simple answer, or at least an answer which does not have consequences for himself and his mother, provokes the same automatic response. His experience is that it is not safe to wonder about his own needs and feelings but to meet the other person's.

When James smiles care is needed not to assume this is because he is pleased to be asked about seeing his dad. In general it is considered to be good for children to have contact with parents and it is important that practitioners recognise contact can take many forms. However, by missing the somatic (body's) indicators of James's distress and terror at the thought of only having to think about seeing his dad, there would be a likelihood of coming to the wrong conclusion. The terror provoked by actually seeing his dad would need further coping strategies, resulting in further behavioural difficulties for James because of his somatic and neurobiological responses to his fear.

It is better if the practitioner goes into the session with a completely open mind. James then cannot work out what the worker wants from him as the 'correct' answer to any question. She can observe his somatic micro-movements and comment on these without any judgement about whether they are all right or not. For example, 'James, I just noticed what happened when I asked you that question. Your toes moved and your muscles in your face twitched. I wonder what made that happen. Did your tummy flip at the same time?' She watches James very closely while she describes these movements and with his nod of recognition is then able to say to him, 'I wonder if that question made you feel a bit anxious, because all those movements usually happen when someone is anxious?' Again she watches and attunes to his emotional and somatic response. She is watching to ensure the questions do not make him any more anxious, leading to a hyper (alert) or hypo (collapsed) response to the questions, either of which would make his answers not a true representation of his feelings (Ogden *et al.* 2006).

The interviewer's interest in his responses, and the tone she uses, calms him down and makes him curious about his responses. Evoking his curiosity enables him to wonder about seeing his dad in addition to the question he has just been asked about the impact it has on him. He can then be curious about other things which have the same impact. For example, in the second session with James, he wore his wellington boots and kept his hands in his pockets, telling the interviewer that they (his fingers and toes) were not talking to her today. The worker wondered with them (his fingers and toes) what had made them come to that conclusion and complimented them on being able to think ahead to wearing their wellington boots. The tone used was validating and curious rather than negative or dismissing. It transpired that James had had a card from his dad in the time between sessions. The card had been sent to remind James how much his dad loved him and how his dad knew he would do the right thing.

The impact of trauma/abuse on a child and consequences for engagement in the assessment

It is crucial to know what the child has experienced or is actually experiencing before the assessment begins. It is not enough to just have a chronology or a flow chart or time line but also to have analysed it to determine at what age(s) the child experienced trauma. Lenore Terr (1990) identifies two types of trauma:

Type I trauma
A short-term, unexpected, single blow, isolated, sudden, surprising. For example, this is more likely to lead to typical post-traumatic stress disorder (PTSD) symptoms. There is more likely to be a quicker recovery from natural disaster, car accident, rape.

Type II trauma
A situation which is chronic, long-standing and usually of intentional human design. For example, it may lead to an altered view of self and the world and accompanying feelings of guilt, shame and worthlessness. It is more likely to lead to long-standing interpersonal problems and/or what Herman (1992) calls Complex PTSD Reaction. There is more likely to be a poorer recovery from ongoing physical or sexual abuse or neglect.

Children who are being assessed because they have experienced Type I trauma will come into the session expecting the adult to be caring, friendly and interested in them and their experience of this one-off event. Creating an atmosphere or co-operation in the session is likely to be easy and quick. Children who have experienced Type II trauma are more likely to view the worker with suspicion and distrust. More time is then likely to be needed to build an atmosphere of trust and co-operation.

Frank Putnam's (1997) Abuse Trauma Variables are a useful prompt and guide when thinking through the issues around the impact of trauma on children. His view is that the variables he identifies are interactive and need to be considered together to be able to form a view about the impact on the child of any trauma and the factors which will have lessened that impact. In other words, both the strengths and resilience factors in the child, as well as the negative impacts on their physical and psychological wellbeing and development, need to be noted.

It is well researched and noted that trauma has a major impact on a child's development and that, if the trauma is serious enough or goes on for a long time, the child will, to a lesser or greater degree, miss the developmental tasks for that age (Dixon and Stein 1992; James 1994). (This is discussed in more detail in Chapter 9.)

Children's assessment skills

Children being interviewed as part of an assessment are likely to have well-developed attunement and assessment skills. Their emotional and physical survival may well have depended on them. At the moment their parent or carer walked into the room they would have needed to assess, in an instant, what was the right way to respond to that adult. A mistake could have had catastrophic circumstances. If the practitioner is unclear about their task or is feeling unsure about the purpose or validity of interviewing the child, the child will pick this up and adjust their responses. For example:

A family care worker was asked to interview George about what, if any, of the violence between his parents he had actually witnessed and assess what impact this had had on him. She was not sure at all that this was her job, thinking that it was a task which should be done by the social worker or a psychologist. She had shared this concern with her manager but was told that as she knew George from the summer play scheme she would be the best person to interview him. She was not convinced by this argument when she met George. George immediately attuned to her uncertainty. Just as he had done with his mother, in taking care of her, he closed down his need to tell, to meet the need of the worker not wanting to know what he had witnessed. (James 1994; Schore 2001)

Why is taking seriously what the child says so important?

Lord Clyde in his conclusions, following his chairmanship of the Orkney Inquiry (Orkney Report 1992), said that it was important workers should not just believe what a child says without undertaking further work. He recommended that what the child says should be taken seriously and then, as a consequence of taking the child seriously, make the necessary enquiries about what was said. If, as a result of these enquiries, evidence is found to support what the child alleges, at that point the child can be believed. However, one of the consequences for children, who have been harmed by someone who they should be able to trust and depend on, is a fear or certainty that should they try to tell they will not be believed. This is a very common silencing technique used by those who harm children to stop them from telling.

One of the dangers of following Lord Clyde's advice is that the child is given the message that the child is not believed. This could result in the child withdrawing a tentative attempt to be heard. It is important, however, to follow Lord Clyde's advice to make further enquiries to corroborate what a child has said *but it is even more important that the worker does not give the child any impression that the child is disbelieved*. It is much better that the worker is curious and interested in what the child is saying; for example, when a child says 'My mummy loves me very much', rather than believe or disbelieve this statement, the worker could say, 'Tell me one [or some] of the things your mummy does for you that lets you know she loves you.' In just the same way the child who says 'It was all my fault this happened to me' has the same response of neither belief nor disbelief, but is asked, 'Tell me when you came to that decision' or 'Tell me how you came to that decision.' The tone, timbre and quality of the worker's response must be one of genuine curiosity and empathy whether in response to a negative or positive statement about the child's experience.

Summary

Each child in their own way is unique and each child will require a unique approach, well planned, well executed and well recorded. Communicating with children can be a complex task but one which will always be made easier by knowing as much as possible about the child to be assessed, their history, family, system, the reasons for the assessment and the child's understanding of their part and contribution to what prompted the assessment and the process of the assessment.

There are many practical resources available for use in communicating with children but it will be the competence, skill and attitude of the worker which will be more important than any other thing or other resource available. The relationship created by the worker will have more impact and be remembered for much longer than any piece of equipment used; furthermore, the child will be heard and will feel heard.

Recommended reading

Briere, J. (1992) *Child Abuse Trauma*. London: Sage.

Gerhardt, S. (2004) *Why Love Matters: How Affection Shapes a Baby's Brain*. Hove: Routledge.

Herman, J.L. (1992) *Trauma and Recovery*. New York, NY: Basic Books.

James, B. (1994) *Handbook for the Treatment of Attachment-Trauma Problems in Children*. New York, NY: Free Press.

Jones, D.P.H. (2003) *Communicating with Vulnerable Children: A Guide for Practitioners*. London: Gaskell.

Sunderland, M. (2006) *The Science of Parenting*. London: Dorling Kindersley.

References

Briere, J. (1992) *Child Abuse Trauma*. London: Sage.

Department of Health, Department for Education and Employment and the Home Office (2000) *Framework for the Assessment of Children in Need and their Families*. London: The Stationery Office.

Dixon, S.D. and Stein, M.T. (1992) *Encounters with Children – Paediatric Behaviour and Development*. St Louis: Mosby Year Book.

Garbarino, J., Guttman, E. and Seeley, E.W. (1986) *The Psychologically Battered Child: Strategies for Identification, Assessment and Intervention*. San Francisco, CA: Jossey-Bass.

Garbarino, J., Stott, M. and Faculty of the Erikson Institute (1992) *What Children Can Tell Us*. San Francisco, CA: Jossey-Bass.

Gerhardt, S. (2004) *Why Love Matters: How Affection Shapes a Baby's Brain*. Hove: Routledge.

Harris, P. (2006) *In Search of Belonging: Reflections by Transracially Adopted People*. London: BAAF.

Herman, J.L. (1992) *Trauma and Recovery*. New York, NY: Basic Books.

Howe, D., Brandon, M., Hinings, D. and Schofield, G. (1999) *Attachment Theory, Child Maltreatment and Family Support*. Basingstoke: Palgrave.

James, B. (1994) *Handbook for the Treatment of Attachment-trauma Problems in Children*. New York, NY: Free Press.

Jewett, C.L. (1982) *Helping Children Cope with Separation and Loss*. Harvard, MA: Harvard Common Press.

Levine, P. (1997) *Waking the Tiger*. Berkeley, CA: North Atlantic Books.

Levine, P. and Kline, M. (2007) *Trauma through a Child's Eyes: Infancy through Adolescence.* Berkeley, CA: North Atlantic Books.

Ogden, P., Minton, K. and Pain, C. (2006) *Trauma and the Body.* New York, NY: Norton.

Orkney Report (1992) *The Report of the Inquiry into the Removal of Children from Orkney in February 1991.* Edinburgh: HMSO.

Perry, B.D., Pollard, R., Blakley, T.L., Baker, W.L. and Vigilante, D. (1995) 'Childhood trauma, the neurobiology of adaptation and "use-dependent" development of the brain: how "states" become "traits".' *Infant Mental Health Journal 16*, 4, 271–291.

Putnam, F. (1997) *Dissociation in Children and Adolescents.* New York, NY: Guilford.

Rothschild, B. (2000) *The Body Remembers: The Physiology of Trauma and Trauma Treatment.* New York, NY: Norton.

Schore, A.N. (2001) 'Effects of a secure attachment relationship, on right brain development, affect regulation and infant mental health.' *Infant Mental Health Journal 22*, 7–66.

Schore, A.N. (2007) Handout given out at Confer Conference, September, London.

Siegal, D. (1995) *The Developing Mind.* New York, NY: Wiley.

Sunderland, M. (2006) *The Science of Parenting.* London: Dorling Kindersley.

Terr, L. (1990) *Too Scared to Cry.* New York, NY: Basic Books.

van der Hart, O., Nijenhuis, E. and Steele, K. (2006) *The Haunted Self.* London: Norton.

van der Kolk, B.A. (1996) *Traumatic Stress: The Effects of Overwhelming Experience on Mind, Body and Society.* New York, NY: Guilford.

CHAPTER 8

Supervising Assessments of Children and Families: The Role of the Front-line Manager

Rosemary Gordon and Enid Hendry

Staff who are in the frontline of practice must be well supported by effective supervision.

(From the Framework for the Assessment of Children in Need and their Families, p.85, 6.26)

This chapter focuses on supervision in the context of assessment and considers the following themes:

- the policy and organisational context

- core principles and theoretical models that underpin professional supervision

- functions of supervision as they apply to the assessment of children in need, working to the *Framework for the Assessment of Children in Need and their Families* (Department of Health *et al.* 2000)

- key issues and challenges for supervision at four different stages of the assessment process

- factors that may have an impact on the assessment process

- methods, styles and approaches

- supervisory tasks and prompts at four stages of assessment (see chapter appendix, p.153).

Supervision can be both formal or informal, and although each have their place, in this chapter we focus on the formal supervision of professionals carrying out or contributing to assessments of children in need. The chapter is primarily directed at those supervising social workers but has relevance for the supervision needs of other professionals who contribute to assessments, all of whom should have access to professional advice and support.

Introduction

Just as the assessment process is pivotal to the planning and delivery of improved outcomes for children, so supervision is a key factor in ensuring the quality of assessment, planning, implementation and review.

Professional supervision is defined in *Providing Effective Supervision* (Skills for Care and Children's Workforce Development Council 2007) as: 'an accountable process which supports, assures and develops the knowledge, skills and values of an individual, group or team. The purpose is to improve the quality of their work to achieve agreed outcomes' (p.5).

As explored in detail in previous chapters, the *Framework for the Assessment of Children in Need and their Families* (Department of Health *et al.* 2000) has set out the assessment task and process since its introduction in 2000. A successful assessment requires that relevant information is gathered, systematically collated, recorded and critically analysed by the practitioner, who must then exercise professional judgement in order to decide how best to safeguard and promote the welfare of the child.

Agency inspections and serious case reviews have highlighted some weaknesses in practice that supervision can and should address, as illustrated by the following comment from *Safeguarding Children* (Joint Chief Inspectors 2002, p.51): 'Too few assessments demonstrate an engagement with the social history of the family, a reflection on the evidence, synthesis and analysis and a concluding assessment of need and risk of significant harm.'

All those working with children in need or at risk of significant harm, whatever their agency or role, need someone who is not directly involved in the case to help them deal with the complexities and challenges of the work and to make sense of what they are seeing, hearing and feeling. Supervision can provide a much-needed space for reflection, critical review and for probing, thinking and analysis. *Working Together to Safeguard Children* (HM Government 2006, p.113) emphasises the need for supervision for practitioners from all agencies who are working day to day with children and families.

> Within agencies where supervision is not readily available, at a minimum, a structured process of consultation should exist for child protection concerns. Without supervision or accessible consultation, practitioners working with children and families with early needs may struggle to cope. (Brandon *et al.* 2008, p.105)

The context for supervising assessments of children and families

We begin by considering some of the key policy drivers influencing thinking about the supervision of assessment and then move on to examine aspects of the organisational, multidisciplinary and practice context within which it takes place.

The Victoria Climbié Inquiry (Cm 5730 2003) identified critical weaknesses in the quality of assessment practice and management supervision. Lord Laming considered supervision to be 'the cornerstone of all good social work practice' (Cm 5730 2003, p.12, 1.59) and found it to be woefully inadequate at times with over-reliance on 'corridor conversations' rather than planned formal sessions. Moreover, he noted a failure of the supervisor to read, review and sign case files or to rigorously test the basis on which action was taken or decisions made. Lord Laming described examples of supervision that were irregular, unfocused, superficial and lacking in analysis. He also highlighted poor practice in case allocation, with cases arriving on people's desks with no guidance or discussion, often with very little consideration given to the worker's experience, current commitments or workload. 'Sometimes it needed nothing more than a manager doing their job by asking pertinent questions or taking the trouble to look at the case file' (Cm 5730 2003, p.3, 1.17). He observed the passivity of the supervision process, describing occasions where the manager seemed to be a recipient of information, not playing a proactive role in seeking and probing information. He went on to emphasise the need for supervisors to get a grip of the case, to know key milestones, to read the case file and to be mindful of the ability of some adults to mislead.

Lord Laming's pivotal report was the catalyst for a major programme of reform and a determination to learn the lessons and improve outcomes for children and young people. The resulting *Every Child Matters* programme of change, discussed in Chapter 1, has brought a wealth of new legislation, policy and guidance, including guidance and competences for supervision (Skills for Care and Children's Workforce Development Council 2007). It has also led to extensive structural and organisational changes taking place and included a powerful drive to improve the integration of services. This massive programme of government-led change with increased emphasis on accountability, performance management and on outcomes inevitably affects the management of practice and the provision of services, and impacts on the context and culture in which supervision takes place.

In this context managers can be under considerable pressure to meet performance targets, often working with limited resources. The performance culture can lead to an overemphasis on the managerial aspects of supervision at the expense of professional case-work supervision, for example a focus on the time taken to complete an assessment, rather than the quality of the assessment. The quality of relationships between practitioners and those with whom they work is vital to achieving positive outcomes. This quality of relationship can be influenced by the relationship between the supervisor and supervisee and the content of supervision sessions. It can be enhanced by professional supervision, which addresses not just the task but values, self-awareness and the interpersonal skills and emotional intelligence needed to work with families and children in need.

> People who use social care and children's services say that services are only as good as the person delivering them. They value workers who have a combination of the

right human qualities as well as the necessary knowledge and skills. (Skills for Care and Children's Workforce Development Council 2007, p.4)

Assessments of children and families are carried out in a variety of settings with different professionals having a contribution to make (for more detail see Chapter 5). This means that supervision of those contributing to assessments can be conducted by a range of front-line managers. Agencies each have their own traditions and ways of supervising and quality assuring practice. However, despite different and distinct characteristics there are some core principles, which apply to professional supervision wherever and however it is carried out, and these are considered next.

Core principles of professional supervision

There is now a good deal of consensus about the key features of effective social work supervision. In particular, it is widely recognised that such supervision should be well documented and should include the discussion of individual cases.

(Cm 5730 2003, p.102, 6.630)

Drawing on the work of Morrison (2005) and Myers and Green (2008) the key principles and features of effective supervision are:

- All staff conducting assessments have the right to receive high quality supervision.
- The quality of supervision is critical to the quality of service delivery, the experience of service users and children's outcomes.
- Supervision must ensure the effective management of assessment practice, develop and support staff and promote their engagement with the organisation.
- All staff bear responsibility for the quality of their own work and, to this end, should prepare for and make a positive contribution to the supervisory process.
- Supervision should be recorded, with decisions about individual cases noted on case records. Even if supervision takes place urgently or informally, possibly as a 'corridor conversation', it is essential that any significant issues or decisions are recorded.
- Supervision provides an opportunity to challenge assumptions and judgements about cases and to agree action plans.
- Senior managers have a responsibility to promote good supervision by implementation of a supervision policy and ensuring training is provided for those conducting supervision.
- Supervision should be child-centred, promote the involvement of service users and promote anti-discriminatory practice.

- A mechanism for ensuring quality and compliance should be in place to ensure that relevant policy and guidance is followed and that the standard of service is one that meets the needs of service users.

Supervision policies should outline an agency's interpretation of these principles by addressing three key elements in supervision agreements or contracts:

- administrative: frequency, location and recording
- professional: purposes, focus, principles and accountabilities
- psychological: motivation, commitment, ownership and investment.

Agreements should also clarify how power and difference will be addressed and how this and the supervisory relationship will be regularly reviewed, possibly as part of an annual appraisal or performance review. Examples of policies, standards, agreements and recording methods are included in *Providing Effective Supervision* (Skills for Care and Children's Workforce Development Council 2007).

Theoretical models of supervision

The scope of this chapter only allows limited space to consider theoretical models underpinning supervisory practice. Having a theoretical model or models can help new supervisors to understand and respond to the different approaches taken by their supervisees to assessment practice. The first is adult learning theory (Knowles 1980) which describes how adults as learners characteristically make use of experience; learn from problems; are present orientated – in other words learning has to be relevant now and not at some unknown future point; are activity based; need to share ideas, thoughts and feelings; and experience openness, trust and commitment. Casework supervision in social care is underpinned by this understanding of how adults learn. The concept of the learning cycle introduced by David Kolb (1984) takes this a stage further describing how all adults move through a number of processes systematically in order to learn effectively, despite probably having one preferred mode of learning. An understanding of these stages and of an individual's preferred learning style can assist the supervisor, for example, in exploring with a supervisee an assessment that is causing concern.

The first stage of the learning cycle is **Experiencing** – the actual event: for example, a visit to carry out an assessment; followed by **Reflecting** – thinking about the experience and using feelings and intuition to make sense of the experience; then **Conceptualising** – analysing and creating a meaning; to **Actively Experimenting** – preparing for the next action and trying out ideas or conclusions. Supervision can help in the active experimenting stage by encouraging rehearsal of how to discuss a particularly contentious issue in an assessment, for example explaining to a parent that it is necessary to see the child on their own.

Morrison (2005) has developed this concept of a reflective cycle as it applies to supervision in social care. If this learning process or cycle becomes blocked for whatever reason, then the supervisor requires skills to recognise these processes and help the supervisee to move back to a more positive learning cycle. In carrying out an assessment, for example, a supervisor may see that a practitioner has become blocked in reflecting, gathering and considering more and more information, and has been unable to move on to make sense of this and reach a hypothesis or conclusion. Readers are recommended to refer to Morrison's work for suggestions of how supervisors can help to unblock the process.

Approaches drawn from behavioural psychology and psychotherapeutic theories also provide useful sources for supervisors when considering their practice, and some concepts from these approaches are drawn on later in this chapter, but in the main the chapter takes a functional approach to supervision based on the different roles and tasks to be performed in relation to assessment practice.

The functions of supervision

Four functions of supervision have been identified in the literature, each of which is relevant to ensuring effective assessments and positive outcomes for children. We outline below key areas of assessment practice that supervisors should address in relation to each function. In addition, we highlight some of the issues and challenges faced by supervisors and suggest some pointers for practice.

The management function

The manager is responsible for ensuring that assessments improve outcomes for children and that they are compliant with relevant local or national policies, procedures and standards. Supervision can be used to:

- clarify the purpose of assessment – 'the essential pre-requisite of a good assessment is clearly defined and agreed objectives' (Cm 5730 2003, p.353, 17.33)

- ensure the principles of assessment are addressed and that children and their carers are appropriately involved

- ensure that the information gathered is rigorously analysed, drawing on up-to-date research or enquiries

- ensure that timescales are met

- assist in forming professional judgements and making decisions on plans, interventions and methods, for example by providing expert input

- ensure recording is carried out and information shared and stored appropriately.

KEY ISSUES AND POINTERS FOR PRACTICE

Balancing the pressures and demands of day-to-day operations, and ensuring that all case files are regularly reviewed with the need for in-depth discussion of dilemmas in specific cases, is a continuing challenge for managers. The review of case files can become a time-consuming task and it is essential that this activity is used as an opportunity not solely to check compliance with policies but also to periodically stand back and review all the available information – an even greater challenge and necessity in cases where work with the family has continued over many years, or even generations. When available information is reviewed as part of reviews or inquiries into child deaths it can be glaringly apparent that information about family history and past patterns of behaviour is often on case files and this could have informed the assessment of current risks of harm to the child.

Managers need to plan systematically how they will review all case files, making sure they have time to understand the child or family's circumstances as they have developed over time, not simply checking case records as a bureaucratic process nor focusing purely on the current situation.

In *Putting Analysis into Assessment*, Dalzell and Sawyer (2007) offer a range of tools and activities designed to assist critical reflection, analysis and decision-making. These can be used in one-to-one supervision in relation to specific cases or in team development sessions.

The development function

It is essential that this aspect of supervision is regularly addressed and that assumptions and complacency about knowledge and skills are avoided, even with highly experienced staff. All staff should be given adequate opportunity to reflect critically on their performance and helped to address any deficiencies. 'If you are just learning from practice without suitable training and supervision, you don't have time for reflection. The danger is that you develop bad habits that are unsound and dangerous' (Hendry 2004, p.19).

Supervision can be used to:

- encourage the worker's ability to reflect on their work and interactions with service users and colleagues

- encourage the application of theory, research and developments of best practice in assessment practice

- assess the worker's level of knowledge, for example about child development, their skills and values, and to identify and plan how to meet learning needs

- provide regular and constructive feedback to the worker on aspects of their assessment practice.

KEY ISSUES AND POINTERS FOR PRACTICE

Supervision must be tailored to the particular needs and stage of professional development of individuals, as well as to the different types of assessment being undertaken. While it is obvious that newly qualified practitioners will need more detailed guidance, it should not be assumed that very experienced workers do not need an opportunity to reflect. Over time they may have become so used to seeing children living in very poor conditions that they lose a sense of what is tolerable or consistent with healthy development. This can be a particular issue when working with neglect (see, for example, Brandon *et al.* 2008, pp.70–73; Stein *et al.* 2009). To illustrate with a case example: an experienced practitioner recorded the presence of dog faeces around a child's cot and a ferocious dog, which the owner, a man recently released from serving a prison sentence for violence, was finding hard to control. The child's young mother was described as passive and apparently indifferent to the child whose fingers and toes were blue with cold and who was only wearing a wet nappy. No action, other than recording these observations, had been taken by the practitioner, who saw this as normal for this family. The supervisor's role is to challenge, provide a benchmark for what is acceptable in circumstances such as these and ensure the necessary protective action is taken.

Dalzell and Sawyer (2007) include a scaling exercise, the aim of which is to ascertain individual and team ability to undertake a thorough and balanced analysis. It involves reading and rating oneself against a series of questions and then discussing the learning. This exercise can be used in one-to-one or group supervision sessions.

Hawkins and Shohet (2006) consider that giving and receiving feedback – the process of telling another individual how they are experienced – are key elements of supervision. This can be fraught with difficulty because it may stimulate memories of being rebuked as a child, whereas positive feedback can be clouded by perceptions of being seen as arrogant. It is often only given or experienced when something has gone wrong. However, a few tips can help provide a positive context within which feedback can take place. Feedback should be: clear and accurate, owned, timely, regular, balanced, specific and reciprocal – in other words the supervisor should be prepared to receive feedback too. It should also lead to change, and in this way the assessment task with all its challenges and complexities can be tackled together, making a real difference to the individual worker, the organisation and, importantly, the service users.

The support function

Assessment work can be a source of anxiety and uncertainty, particularly where there are concerns about a child's safety, or about how long support for needy parents should be provided when, despite this supplement to their parenting capacity, a child's developmental and, in particular, emotional needs are still not being met. These types of situations call for the supervisor to provide a 'safe context within supervision to explore the impact of the work and whether it is blocking their ability to offer an effective service' (Noakes *et al.* 1998, p.14).

The support function of supervision can be used to:

- validate the worker as a professional and as a person
- consider the use of self in assessment practice
- provide a safe climate for the worker to consider their assessment practice and its impact on them as a person
- explore emotional blocks or obstacles to practice
- identify common barriers to supervision (for supervisor and supervisee) and to assist in identifying ways of overcoming these
- monitor the overall health and wellbeing of the worker, especially the effects of stress caused by the work.

KEY ISSUES AND POINTERS FOR PRACTICE

The assessment task can involve working with ambiguity, conflict and the threat of violence on a regular basis. It raises strong emotional issues and powerful moral and ethical dilemmas. Work with children and families can only be effective if the worker is able to relate to and feel empathy for those with whom they work. Brandon *et al.* (2008, p.106) argue, based on the cases they reviewed, that practitioners and managers need to be sceptical, to think critically and systematically and at the same time to remain compassionate – a tough balancing act. The supervisor needs to be able to understand the impact of the work on the practitioner, the feelings engendered and how these are being dealt with. Understanding and being able to work with how the practitioner feels, as well as what they think, is a key aspect of good supervision.

The mediation function

Supervisors may be required to mediate between workers, families, agencies and disciplines in order to secure the necessary contributions to an assessment or to secure the supportive services that are required.

Hawkins and Shohet (2006) describe how, at any time in supervision, there are many levels operating. At a minimum there are four elements involved: a supervisor, a supervisee, a client, a work context (organisational). Although only two components are usually physically present (supervisor and supervisee), the client and the context of the work are carried into the session. Thus, the process involves two interlocking systems or matrices:

- the client/supervisee matrix
- the supervisee/supervisor matrix.

Attention will need to be given to these by the supervisor. Hawkins and Shohet go on to state that:

> This is complicated further in a situation of cultural difference. Any one of the three may be culturally different and indeed all three may be culturally different from each other. In the situation where the client comes from a different background it is particularly important that the supervisee and supervisor do not collude to misunderstand factors which are based in culture rather than in personal psychology. (Hawkins and Shohet 2006, p.109)

Additional to this are the dynamics of carrying out assessments in an inter-agency context.

The mediation function of supervision can be used to:

- manage the complexity of children's agencies (statutory and voluntary) and the multidisciplinary relationships
- identify areas of conflict or difference, including those of culture, between workers and other professionals or family members
- work with practitioners and others to develop strategies for managing or overcoming conflict
- champion children's involvement in the process of assessment of their needs
- encourage the principle of working in partnership with parents and carers.

KEY ISSUES AND POINTERS FOR PRACTICE

Throughout the assessment process attention should be paid to the place of power and control in relationships. These can be in the relationship within and between supervisor and supervisee, the practitioner and family members and the practitioner and other agencies. Power dynamics in these inter-related domains can mirror one another and on occasion be played out in supervision. For instance, the practitioner may come away from a meeting with a family feeling powerless and out of control. The practitioner may mirror this sense of hopelessness and helplessness in their assessment and in their behaviour in inter-agency meetings.

Supervising the assessment process

The tasks associated with an assessment of a child in need and their family will be determined by its purpose, scale, breadth and the multidisciplinary setting within which it is conducted. Four key stages of assessment, which are described in detail in Chapters 3 and 4, can be identified as follows:

- planning and preparation

- carrying out the assessment, including gathering information from a range of sources

- analysis and decision-making

- planning and review.

In the appendix to this chapter we have identified some prompt questions to consider at each stage of the assessment process. These may be of particular assistance when working with relatively inexperienced practitioners or for use by those who are new to the role of supervising assessments.

There are a number of factors that impact on the assessment process which supervision can help to mediate. These can be personal, professional, organisational or relational. Many of these have been examined elsewhere in this book (see, for example, Chapter 4) and we have referred to some of these earlier in this chapter. The following are some potential pitfalls for supervisors to be aware of when supervising a practitioner's assessment practice and in the next section we consider some of them in more detail:

- Reactive behaviour – getting drawn into the family dynamics, including over-identification with a family member. This can be linked with failure to see the individual child or focus on their needs.

- Lack of critical reflection – overload of information gathered and description, and little or no analysis.

- Discrimination and lack of cultural competence which can in turn lead to an over-reliance on cultural explanations and cultural relativism. This is discussed in more detail in Chapter 20.

- Thresholds of concern get raised either as practitioners get 'case hardened' or in response to lack of resources and limited availability of support services.

- Reluctance to question parents even when there are discrepant explanations and taking what is said at face value without exercise of due caution and critical thought.

- Staff stress and low morale.

Factors that may have an impact on supervision of the assessment process

Part of conducting effective supervision is recognising potential blocks or pitfalls and finding ways of overcoming them. We look first at factors related to the assessment process and then move on to consider the supervisory process itself.

Reactive behaviour

The supervisor should be alert to reactive behaviour. This is behaviour that is a response by the worker to some of the hidden processes within the work rather than to the actual facts generated. This can cause distortion of judgement, stereotyping of individuals (within the family or the professional network), or a 'fixed idea' about the situation. It can also lead to either over-cynicism or over-optimism about the family. 'Practitioners should be enabled or challenged by supervisors to avoid being steered too readily into what can become a fairly entrenched "agency view" in relation to families over time' (Dalzell and Sawyer 2007, p.131).

Lack of critical reflection

Supervisors can support analysis by probing and 'ensuring that a range of explanations for causes of concern are explored over time, and by encouraging practitioners to seek to disconfirm their original hypotheses' (Dalzell and Sawyer 2007, p.131).

In a study conducted by Eileen Munro (1996) of common errors of reasoning in child protection work she concludes:

> It may be that one-to-one professional supervision is a better context (as opposed to the forum of case conferences) in which to expect a systematic and critical review of a case. This can offer a safe, supportive environment in which it is clearly understood that making mistakes is an inevitable feature of working in such a complex area. Changing your mind should be seen as a sign of good practice and of strength not weakness. (Munro 1996, p.155)

Discrimination and lack of cultural competence

Many perspectives are marginalised through the processes of disability, racism, homophobia, sexism and a failure to understand another's culture or their way of seeing. This will result in a seriously ineffective assessment. It is the supervisor's task to ensure that difference and the possibility of discrimination are constantly on the agenda and that the worker is given every opportunity to explore the impact and relevance of diversity on the process.

Inappropriate thresholds

Unless there are clear, shared and understood thresholds for intervention between agencies working within authority areas, the reasons for a request for an assessment of a child in need and their family, for example from a health visitor or teacher, can be misunderstood and practitioners can either over- or under-represent concerns. Unless this is addressed it will lead to confusion between all those contributing to an assessment. Inappropriate thresholds are particularly important to address at the stage of using the Common Assessment Framework (Children's Workforce Development Council 2009) or undertaking an initial assessment using the Assessment Framework (Department of Health *et al.* 2000). For further discussion of communication issues and inter-professional misunderstandings see Reder and Duncan (2003).

Another difficulty can be when there are insufficient resources to respond to the needs identified by the assessment. This can occur when the commissioned authority or team has greater resources to put into the assessment than the long-term or intervention team can offer as follow-up services. In these instances, recommendations are often not carried out and, if there is no immediate crisis, things are left alone – until the next crisis occurs.

Reluctance to question parents and carers

The death of Baby Peter highlighted again that adults who are abusing children may well set out to deliberately deceive the professionals who are working with them (Haringay Local Safeguarding Children Board 2009). Baby Peter's face was covered in chocolate on one occasion to disguise injuries. His mother's apparent cooperativeness and willingness to bring Peter for medical attention created an effective smoke screen, making professionals less likely to question or doubt. Sustaining an open mind, being willing to doubt and question and retaining healthy scepticism – these qualities are hard to sustain over time while maintaining a working relationship with parents and carers. Supervisors have a key role to play in helping to check out whether the carer's version of events is being taken too much at face value. They can do this by asking probing questions – how do you know, what supporting evidence is there and is there anything that contradicts that view, have you seen the child on their own? More practically an occasional joint visit to bring in another, more objective view and fresh pair of eyes can help.

Staff stress, low morale and organisational change

Account should be taken of levels of staff stress, whether it is personal, team or organisational. If the worker is preoccupied with difficulties, these can distort professional judgement, or the worker can disengage and withdraw from the process. If the team or the organisation has recently faced a critical inspection of their work, or is facing a reorganisation that is unpopular, then this may well have an impact on morale.

The timescales and demands of working with the Assessment Framework can, of itself, prompt anxieties. Dalzell and Sawyer's (2007) study identified how workers experienced difficulty in reaching conclusions at the 35 working day stage of the core assessment and how this should be seen as a line in the sand, rather than an end point, with assessment as a continuing and iterative process.

Methods, style and approach

The focus thus far in this chapter has been on formal one-to-one supervision, drawing largely on the social care literature. However, given the importance of multi-agency assessments and the expectation that different agencies contribute, different approaches to supervision should be recognised. In some health-based settings, for example, professionals are accountable both to an administrative manager – who may not be health trained – and to their professional body for their clinical practice; supervision may, therefore, effectively be split.

Group supervision can be an effective method and has the advantage of economy of time and resources, especially when there is a large number of staff to be supervised. It should not, however, replace individual supervision. An advantage is that the group itself can provide additional expertise and support; a disadvantage is that the detail of an assessment may be missed, as well as a diversion into group dynamics occurring. It relies on every member of the group actively contributing to the process and on being willing to learn from the experience of others. It requires careful management, a clear framework and a level of groupwork skills. Paired supervision can also provide an additional angle but, again, clear boundaries will be necessary with attention to confidentiality.

Whatever the approach and method used, the following questions and interventions adapted from Hawkins and Shohet (2006) can be a useful summary:

1. *Contracting* – starting with the end (of the assessment) in mind and agreeing how you are going to get there together.

2. *Listening* – facilitating the supervisee in generating personal insight into the situation being assessed.

3. *Exploring (i)* – helping the supervisee to understand the personal impact the situation is having on themselves.

4. *Exploring (ii)* – challenging the supervisee to create alternative hypotheses and ways of making sense of the information gathered through the assessment process or new possibilities for action in resolving blocks or difficulties.

5. *Action* – supporting the supervisee in committing to the proposed plan and creating the next step.

6. *Review (i)* – taking stock and reinforcing the ground covered, identifying how the process could be improved.

7. *Review (ii)* – debriefing on the completed assessment and learning from it.

Conclusion

Assessment is a complex and crucial process, providing the basis for decision-making and undertaking relevant interventions. No matter what the experience of the practitioner supervision can enhance or diminish the quality and effectiveness of assessments. A systematic and structured approach to the supervision of assessments has been outlined, based on four key supervisory functions and stages of assessment. Supervision that is both supportive and challenging can help ensure greater objectivity and provide a much needed opportunity for critical reflection. Good quality supervision is not a mechanistic or bureaucratic process, but supports the practitioner to manage the assessment task with all its complexities and challenges. For supervision practice to be truly effective it needs to combine a quality assurance and compliance management approach with a dynamic, flexible and supportive supervisory relationship. It should improve practice, support the development of integrated working, engage with users of services and ensure the continuing professional development of the worker.

However, a clear organisational commitment to good quality supervision must be the starting point and needs to be reflected in a positive supervisory culture within an organisation. In addition, in order to carry out their role effectively senior managers must ensure that front-line managers have the time, the up-to-date knowledge and expertise, as well as the support and backing in their own right, to deliver quality supervision. Their developmental and support needs are just as important as those of practitioners who carry out the assessments.

Appendix

Some prompt questions for selective use in supervision at different stages of the assessment of a child in need.

Stage 1: Setting up, planning and preparation

[This stage should ideally take place during supervision but before the child and family has been seen.]

What is the purpose of the assessment?

Who is requesting the assessment?

What are the issues and the likely consequences for the child's health and development if the present situation continues?

Is the child safe? Is there a risk of significant harm?

Which of the seven developmental outcomes for the child require particular assessment?

Who is most worried about this family? Is anyone else worried and are their concerns the same or different?

Do the family and the child understand the purpose of the meeting? Have they been assessed before and do you know what the result was?

Are they in agreement with carrying out the assessment?

Who needs to be involved in the assessment – family members, workers, agencies, other organisations? Anyone else?

Can the child be seen alone and does the worker have the necessary skills in communication?

Are there special considerations, such as language and understanding, or any disability? Is there a need for an interpreter or any other specialist to assist with the assessment?

Are there any likely barriers to carrying out the assessment? Are the professional agencies in agreement about the need for and purpose of assessment as well as their respective roles and tasks?

Who has lead responsibility? Is everyone aware of this role?

How will information be stored and what information will be shared and with whom?

Are there adequate resources to carry out the assessment?

Is the worker competent and suitably experienced? Are they confident about assessing stages of child development and about seeking the child's wishes and feelings (according to their age, ability and understanding)?

Is the worker adequately prepared for the meeting? Have you explored any anxieties they may have?

Are there any safety issues for the worker?

Stage 2: Carrying out the assessment with the child and family

[This stage may take several meetings between the worker, the child and the family, either at the office or in the home, as well as discussions with others who know the family. Supervision can be used to review how the assessment is being carried out.]

Is there a written agreement for working with the child and family? If not, why not?

Were all family members seen? Are the parents being seen together if appropriate – even if they are separated?

Was/were the child/ren seen alone? Have they participated in the assessment?

What was observed about the child and the family?

Might it be appropriate to set up an observation session?

How did the parent/s or carer/s behave towards the child?

Is there another significant adult or carer in the household or who plays a significant role with the child, such as a grandparent? How did they behave towards the child? How did the child respond?

How did the child describe or talk about their family? How much do they know about the situation? How detailed is the information? If the child has an absent parent, do they know why this is so and what level of contact do they have?

How resilient does the child appear to be? What factors of resilience could be built upon?

How did the worker describe the child and the way the child related to them? For example, was the child attention-seeking, over-familiar, friendly, relaxed or anxious?

What is the quality of the housing and the local community environment?

What other supports are there either within or outside the family, including day care? Are the family excluded, for example, through racism?

What other professionals are involved and in what capacity?

Is the school involved? Is there a Special Educational Needs Statement in relation to the child/ren?

Is the youth offending team involved? Have they prepared an assessment profile (ASSET)?

Is there a recognisable beginning, middle and end to the assessment in sight and will this meet the required assessment timescales?

How does the worker feel about assessing this family? How do they perceive their own family? This might relate to their own value base, their personal experiences, history or levels of anxiety.

How do they think the family perceives them? Are age, gender or identity playing a part?

Is there a place for using specific assessment questionnaires and scales?[1]

[In subsequent meetings] What has changed since the last time? Is anything better or worse?

Have the strengths as well as the difficulties in the family been noted?

Stage 3: Analysis, applying professional judgement and decision-making

[This is possibly the most difficult part of supervising assessment work. It is easy to become mechanistic and to check that tasks are being carried out to timescales, but it is less easy to bring the necessary objectivity, challenge and rigour to this part of the process in a way that is supportive and constructive to the worker.]

Has the assessment provided adequate evidence to be analysed before making judgements leading to decisions about future actions?

Is the worker distinguishing between fact and opinion?

Have any cultural or other assumptions been made?

Is there reasonable cause to suspect that a child is suffering, or is likely to suffer, from significant harm?

Is the worker worried about any physical or emotional care for this child? If so, why, or why not?

Does the worker have a hypothesis about what is going on here?

Have needs relating to the seven developmental outcomes been identified clearly?

Has the assessment revealed significant unmet needs for support and services?

---

1   Bentovim and Bingley Miller (2001); Cox and Walker (2002); Department of Health and Cox and Bentovim (2000).

If the decision is not to provide services, this is itself a decision. What is the next step?

Is the worker able to evaluate the evidence drawing on their understanding of theory, especially child development?

How does the child compare with a similar child? What have they observed about the child and is this consistent with what is known?

Is the worker drawing on knowledge of research?

How has the family made the worker feel? Are they scared, protective, vulnerable or defensive? Why might this be?

What are the family's strengths? How far do any strengths compensate for difficulties or limitations?

Is the worker concerned? What is the evidence for any concerns? What weight should be given to them?

Is there any other information or any other person who needs to be seen?

What would improve this situation for this child? If nothing, why is the worker content with the situation?

Is everything being recorded properly, and has an accurate and effective record been made? Is information stored and/or shared appropriately?

If a report is required, for example for court, is this under way?

Is any immediate action needed? Is the child safe?

Stage 4: Planning

[At this stage of an assessment, the information has been collected, the meetings have been reflected upon and together an analysis has been made. The material needs to be organised and the process of planning the next stages will begin. In terms of supervising the assessment process, the stages are complete; however, assessment does not take place in a vacuum, it is an iterative process and should link seamlessly into the next stage of planning.]

Has the worker communicated effectively with everyone concerned? Have they maintained confidentiality appropriately, bearing in mind that if the child's welfare is at risk of harm, this may be superseded? [Refer to *Information Sharing: Guidance for Practitioners and Managers* (HM Government 2008).]

Does the worker have the child and family's consent to seek or share information with informed written consent?

Should anyone else be consulted?

What immediate support is required and who will provide this? Can the extended family or close friends help with this?

What longer-term support is required and who can provide this? What resources are there?

What changes need to happen to ensure this child's welfare? What types of services might help the child, the family?

Which interventions might support strengths and help meet unmet needs? Which intervention is likely to produce the most immediate and effective benefits and which might take longer?

Has a plan been made and has it been shared with the family? How did they respond? Have any blocks been identified and strategies identified to overcome them?

How does the supervisee feel about the process?

[What comes next for the supervisor is to ensure implementation (of the plan), monitoring and review and evaluation. Depending on the setting this may now be passed to another part of the service or another agency.]

Recommended reading

Children's Workforce Development Council (2009) 'Supervising Assessment Work: Frameworks, Tasks and Tools.' In *Supervision Guide for Social Workers*. Available at www.cvdcouncil.org.uk/assets/0000/469/NQSW_Handbook_ch5_LR.pdf, accessed on 7 August 2009.

Gould, N. and Baldwin, M. (eds) (2004) *Social Work, Critical Reflection and the Learning Organisation*. Farnham: Ashgate.

Hawkins, P. and Shohet, R. (2006) *Supervision in the Helping Professions*. Milton Keynes: Open University Press.

Morrison, T. (2005) *Staff Supervision in Social Care*, 3rd edn. Brighton: Pavilion Publishing.

Noakes, S. and Hearn, B. with Burton, S. and Wonnacott, J. (1998) *Developing Good Child Protection Practice: A Guide for First Line Managers*. London: National Children's Bureau.

Skills for Care and Children's Workforce Development Council (2007) *Providing Effective Supervision*. Leeds: Skills for Care and CWDC.

References

Bentovim, A. and Bingley Miller, L. (2001) *The Family Assessment: Assessment of Family Competence, Strengths and Difficulties*. York: Child and Family Training.

Brandon, M., Belderson, P., Warren, C., Howe, D. *et al.* (2008) *Analysing Child Deaths and Serious Injury through Abuse and Neglect: What Can We Learn? A Biennial Analysis of Serious Case Reviews 2003–2005*. Research Report, DCSF-RR023. London: Department for Education and Skills.

Children's Workforce Development Council (2009) *The Common Assessment Framework for Children and Young People: A Guide for Practitioners*. Leeds: Children's Workforce Development Council.

Cm 5730 (2003) *The Victoria Climbié Inquiry Report*. London: The Stationery Office.

Cox, A. and Walker, S. (2002) *The HOME Inventory: A Training Approach for the UK*. Brighton: Pavilion Publishing.

Dalzell, R. and Sawyer, C. (2007) *Putting Analysis into Assessment*. London: National Children's Bureau.

Department of Health and Cox, A. and Bentovim, A. (2000) *The Family Pack of Questionnaires and Scales*. London: The Stationery Office.

Department of Health, Department for Education and Employment and the Home Office (2000) *Framework for the Assessment of Children in Need and their Families*. London: The Stationery Office.

Hawkins, P. and Shohet, R. (2006) *Supervision in the Helping Professions*. Milton Keynes: Open University Press.

Haringey Local Safeguarding Children Board (2009) *Executive Summary of Baby Peter Serious Case Review*. Available at www.haringeylscb.org/index/news/babypeter_scr.htm, accessed on 6 August 2009.

Hendry, E. (2004) 'Supervision key to learning at work.' *Care and Health Magazine*, October, 19–25.

HM Government (2006) *Working Together to Safeguard Children. A Guide to Inter-agency Working to Safeguard and Promote the Welfare of Children*. London: The Stationery Office.

HM Government (2008) *Information Sharing: Practitioner's Guide*. London. Every Child Matters.

Joint Chief Inspectors (2002) *Safeguarding Children – A Joint Chief Inspectors Report on Arrangements to Safeguard Children*. London: Department of Health.

Knowles, M.S. (1980) *The Modern Practice of Adult Education: Andragogy versus Pedagogy*. Chicago, IL: Follett Publishing.

Kolb, D. (1984) *Experiential Learning: Experience as the Source of Learning and Development.* Englewood Cliffs, NJ: Prentice-Hall.

Morrison, T. (2005) *Staff Supervision in Social Care: Making a Real Difference for Staff and Service Users.* Brighton: Pavilion Publishing.

Munro, E. (1996) 'Common errors of reasoning in child protection work.' *Child Abuse and Neglect 23*, 8, 745–758.

Myers, J. and Green, R. (2008) *Supervision Policy and Standards: Guidance for Northern Ireland Health and Social Care Trusts.* Unpublished.

Noakes, S. and Hearn, B. with Burton, S. and Wonnacott, J. (1998) *Developing Good Child Protection Practice: A Guide for First Line Managers.* London: National Children's Bureau.

Reder, P. and Duncan, S. (2003) 'Understanding communication in child protection networks.' *Child Abuse Review 12*, 2, 82–100.

Skills for Care and Children's Workforce Development Council (2007) *Providing Effective Supervision.* Leeds: Skills for Care and CWDC.

Stein, M., Rees, S., Hicks, L. and Gorin, S. (2009) *Neglected Adolescents – Literature Review.* Research Brief. DCSF-RBX-09-04. Available at www.dcsf.gov.uk/research/programmeofresearch/projectinformation.cfm?projectid=14848&type=5&resultspage=1, accessed 20 August 2009.

PART II
Assessing the Developmental Needs of Children

CHAPTER 9

The Developmental Needs of Children: Implications for Assessment

Harriet Ward and Danya Glaser

Children have a range of different and complex developmental needs which must be met during different stages of childhood if optimal outcomes are to be achieved.

(From the Framework for the Assessment for Children in Need and their Families, p.101, 1.36)

In this chapter consideration is given to the following:

- which children are 'children in need'?
- the seven dimensions of children's developmental needs
- factors that can impact adversely on development: emerging issues
- measuring progress
- resources to assist effective assessment of children in need.

Introduction: which children are 'children in need'?

Children have a range of different and complex developmental needs, which must be met during different stages of childhood if they are to achieve their potential in each of the seven developmental dimensions set out in the Assessment Framework (Department of

Health *et al.* 2000). Section 11 of the Children Act 2004 places a duty on 'key persons and bodies to ensure that in discharging their functions they have regard to the need to safeguard and promote the welfare of children'. This responsibility has to be understood within the context of the earlier Children Act 1989, which places a specific duty on local authorities to 'safeguard and promote the welfare of children within their area who are in need by providing a range and level of services appropriate to those children's needs' (section 17). But which children are 'children in need'? Judged by commonly accepted indicators of deprivation, potentially large numbers of children could fit this category. For instance, about 2.6 million children in the UK are living in poverty; about 3.2 million are living in single-parent families; and about 19 per cent of boys and 17 per cent of girls have a long-standing illness or disability (see Department of Work and Pensions 2008; Office for National Statistics 2004).

As Rose points out in Chapter 2, it is clear from the Children Act 1989 (section 17(10)) that not all children who are disadvantaged are necessarily 'in need': the term applies only to those whose vulnerability is such that they are 'unlikely to reach a satisfactory standard of health or development', or 'their health or development will be significantly impaired' without the provision of services. Children with disabilities are included in this defini-tion. However, many children living in extremely difficult family circumstances receive sufficient support from parents, friends, relatives and the wider community to compensate for potential disadvantage and are not thought to require additional services in order to achieve satisfactory outcomes.

The Government's *Every Child Matters* (Cm 5860 2003) initiative has clearly set out the primary purpose of providing services to support families in responding to children's needs as they grow towards adulthood. At a very basic level, all children have similar developmental needs, such as for food, clothing, shelter, intellectual stimulation and social interaction. We know that children are more likely to achieve satisfactory outcomes if these needs are met, mainly by parents and other family members, but with additional support from universal services such as those provided by health care professionals, teach-ers and so on.

However, some children have *additional needs* at some point in their childhood. Such needs may relate to issues such as bullying, truancy, disruptive or anti-social behaviour, teenage pregnancy, ill-health, disabilities and so on. In addition to universal services, these children require targeted support from a range of children's services, often in a uni-versal setting, if they are to achieve satisfactory outcomes. Their parents also may require targeted support from adult services.

A much smaller group of children have *significant and complex needs* which cannot be adequately met without them and their families receiving support from specialist and/or statutory services. Such needs may relate to issues such as abuse and neglect, severe and complex special educational needs, complex disabilities or health problems, significant mental health problems, offending behaviour and so on. These groups of children can be identified as 'children in need' in that they are unlikely to achieve satisfactory outcomes without the provision of services.

The *Framework for the Assessment of Children in Need and their Families* (Department of Health *et al.* 2000) is designed to provide professionals with a common approach to deciding if a child is in need and how best to respond to the child and family. Professionals will not be able to make such decisions without a thorough understanding of child development. *The Developing World of the Child* (Aldgate *et al.* 2006) was specifically commissioned to help professionals develop appropriate knowledge and skills in this area. Those who seek comprehensive information about children's developmental needs should turn to this resource; this brief chapter can do no more than explain the theories of child development that underpin the Assessment Framework and identify some emerging issues from current research that are of particular relevance to its implementation.

The 'child developmental needs' domain in the *Framework for the Assessment of Children in Need and their Families* identifies the seven dimensions along which children must progress if they are to achieve long-term wellbeing in adulthood; within each of these dimensions, children's needs must be met either by themselves as they grow older, or by parents or parent figures, whose capacity can be separated out into six further dimensions. Domestic violence, mental health issues, drug and alcohol misuse and learning disabilities can inhibit parental capacity, as is demonstrated in Chapter 19. Other factors within the parents' and child's immediate social and physical environment can either enhance or inhibit both parental capacity and children's successful development. These form the third domain which an assessment should consider. The *Framework for the Assessment of Children in Need and their Families*, therefore, offers a structure which should make it easier for professionals to:

- distinguish between those children and families who do, and those who do not, require the provision of services

- identify those areas of developmental need, parental capacity and the environment which can benefit from the provision of specific services to enhance children's health and development

- evaluate the outcomes of such services in terms of their potential or perceived impact on children's developmental progress.

A standardised approach to the assessment of developmental need

The child development domain of the *Framework for the Assessment of Children in Need and their Families* is based on a theoretical model whose relevant features are that:

- all children need to progress across a spectrum of developmental dimensions if they are to achieve satisfactory wellbeing in adulthood

- they will make satisfactory progress only if their developmental needs are met

- attempts to evaluate the outcomes of services should not only take account of children's developmental progress, but also the extent to which they have been offered experiences that are relevant to success. (Ward 2002)

The spectrum of development along which each child progresses can be broken down into the following seven interlocking dimensions which in turn link to the five *Every Child Matters* outcomes to be achieved by all children within our population.

Health: includes growth and development as well as physical and mental wellbeing. Children's health needs are more likely to be met if, for instance, they are taken to the doctor when they are ill; if they receive dental and optical care; if they are given an adequate, nutritious diet; if younger children receive immunisations and developmental checks; and if older children and teenagers are given appropriate advice about issues such as sexual behaviour, smoking, alcohol consumption and substance abuse.

Education: covers all areas of cognitive development from birth onwards. Children's education needs are more likely to be met if, for instance, they have frequent opportunities to play and interact with other children; if they have access to books; if they are given opportunities to acquire a range of skills and interests; if those with special educational needs receive appropriate support at school; and if an adult is interested in the child's educational activities.

Identity: concerns the child's growing sense of self as a separate and valued being. Children make successful progress on this dimension as they become confident about themselves *and* their abilities, if they feel accepted by their family and by the wider society, and if they develop a strong sense of their own individuality. Children's needs on this dimension are more likely to be met if, for instance, they encounter positive role models of their own gender and culture; if they are frequently praised and encouraged; and if parents and parent figures are open about relationships within the family, such as the presence of a step-parent or an adopted child.

Family and social relationships: involve the child's ability to make friends and get on with other people. Although younger children's relationships with parents and parent figures may be central to their development along this dimension, the quality of friendships with peers will become increasingly important. In this dimension children's needs are more likely to be met if they experience a stable family life, with changes of carer kept to the minimum; if they are given opportunities to socialise and are encouraged to bring friends home; and if parents and parent figures show appropriate physical affection.

Social presentation: concerns children's growing understanding of the way in which their appearance and behaviour are perceived by the outside world. This area of development is often undervalued, yet it is of central importance; the primary concern is that children should learn to pick up messages about the impression they are creating, not necessarily that they should feel forced to conform. In this dimension their needs are more likely to be met if parents take an interest in their children's appearance and make sure that they are reasonably clean, pay attention to personal hygiene, and are appropriately dressed, bearing in mind their age, gender, culture and religion; if children have opportunities to learn that behaviour and appearance can be adjusted to different situations; and if teenagers feel able to ask for (though not necessarily accept) advice about appropriate ways of presenting themselves on important occasions such as job interviews.

Emotional and behavioural development: concerns the appropriateness of response in children's feelings and actions, initially to parents and parent figures and increasingly to others beyond the family. It includes children's growing ability to adapt to change, to respond appropriately to stress and to demonstrate self-control. It also covers children's ability to empathise with others and to 'pick up' social signals. Development will be affected by the nature and quality of children's early attachments and also by the temperament of the individual child. Children's needs on this dimension are more likely to be met if they are given the security of consistent boundaries within a context of emotional warmth and approval. Although emotional state is not part of development, children have a need to be (essentially) not unhappy, to be able to modulate their affect or curb their emotional responses rather than 'fly off the handle', and to be able to cope with anxiety.

Self-care skills: are the competencies, both practical and emotional, that all children and young people need to acquire if they are to achieve independence in adulthood. Children's needs on this dimension are more likely to be met if they are encouraged to acquire appropriate self-care skills from a very early age: parents can, for instance, help toddlers to learn how to dress and feed themselves; older children need opportunities to learn how to cross roads safely and to use public transport; and young people approaching independence need to learn how to cook and to manage a budget.

How issues concerning parenting capacity and family and environmental factors impact on the child's developmental needs

The *Framework for the Assessment of Children in Need and their Families* links the capacity of parents or caregivers to perform those tasks necessary to promote children's successful development to those factors within their own or the child's circumstances or the wider family and environment that promote or inhibit their ability to do so. The key factors in the *family and environment domain* – income, employment, housing; the family's history, functioning and integration; the support or lack of it from the wider family; and the resources available within the community – are all considered in depth in Chapters 20 to 22. The key factors in the *parenting capacity domain* – basic care; ensuring safety; emotional warmth; stimulation; guidance and boundaries; and stability – are explored in Chapters 17 to 19. The effect that factors in both these domains have on the extent to which children's developmental needs are met is well documented (see for instance Cleaver and Nicholson 2007; Cleaver *et al.* 2007, forthcoming). It is evident, for instance, that parents who are living in acute poverty have difficulty in providing basic care in the form of nutritious food or adequate housing, and that this has a detrimental effect on children's long-term health chances. Parents who feel themselves isolated may find it difficult to promote children's friendships, and so on. Factors within the environment may also exacerbate parents' difficulties, making them more prone to problems such as alcoholism, domestic violence or mental illness, which further inhibit their capacity to promote children's welfare. Research by Moyers and Mason (1995) was able to demonstrate that the greater the combination of circumstances that served to weaken parenting capacity, the more likely were children to be 'in need'. It is the purpose of the Assessment Framework to provide a structure that will enable practitioners to identify systematically those factors which may obstruct children's successful development, assess whether there are sufficient strengths within the family or the wider community to mitigate the potential effects of adversity, and to decide which services might be required to safeguard and promote the welfare of the child.

Factors that impact adversely on development: emerging issues

In many families protective factors will mitigate the impact of adverse experiences on children's development, and indeed the next chapter explores the concept of resilience and how positive outcomes can be promoted. Nevertheless, practitioners need to be aware of the potential negative impact on outcomes when mitigating factors are inadequate or absent.

Research on child poverty, for instance, shows that insufficient material resources not only impact adversely on children's health and growth rates, but also on their educational attainment and their experiences of social inclusion (Bennett 2005).

All forms of abuse are known to have adverse consequences for children's satisfactory development. Physical abuse most obviously can lead to permanent injury or disability and in extreme circumstances death, while there is a substantial body of evidence relating all forms of abuse in childhood to mental health problems in adulthood (see, for instance, Anda 2008; Edwards *et al.* 2003). There is also increasing evidence of the effects of maternal drug and alcohol abuse in pregnancy on children's long-term life chances. For instance, a sample of children exposed to substance abuse *in utero* who are being tracked in a Norwegian longitudinal study are showing persistent and long-standing educational and behavioural difficulties at entry to primary school and beyond (Moe 2002; Moe and Slinning 2002).

However, perhaps the most significant research findings that have recently emerged concern the impact of adverse experiences on the development of the brain in early child-hood (Gerhardt 2004; Glaser 2000; Lee and Hoaken 2007). These show that there are three ways in which brain development can be affected adversely by experiences which the infant and young child undergoes: in response to extreme neglect, undesirable or distorted experiences, and stress.

Extreme neglect

Certain pathways in the developing brain expect and await input signals before they 'wire' permanently. Serious psychological and emotional neglect, and failure of environmental stimulation during the sensitive periods of development of these pathways, may lead to the lack of development of certain functions, which may not be remediable later.

In the domain of interpersonal development, some children who have lacked at least one constant, responsive caregiving adult by the age of about three years will not develop the capacity for making selective attachments to a limited number of adults and will present as indiscriminately sociable. These children will nevertheless show attachment behaviour – seeking proximity to adults when they feel threatened or frightened, but doing so to any adult. This is an important discovery that underlines the imperative of finding stable placements when children come into care – a point that is emphasised by evidence of the lack of stability experienced by many children before they enter the care system (Ward *et al.* 2006).

There is also likely to be a sensitive period for the development of affect regulation, particularly the regulation of arousal. The primary carer's caregiving response is calming the child when the child is aroused. If the young child does not experience this external calming, and especially if the child's experiences repeatedly lead the child to become angry, frustrated or distressed, then the child may not develop the capacity to regulate his or her own affect and arousal. These children repeatedly 'fly off the handle' and have difficulties in calming down.

Evidence such as the above is of particular importance to practitioners because emotional abuse and neglect are notoriously difficult to identify, as they do not become apparent through a single incident, but through a slowly accumulating pattern of behaviours, and the severity of their consequences is often underestimated.

Undesirable, insensitive (distorted) experiences

Most of the harmful effects of dysfunctional early experiences are due to the distortion of normal development rather than to the complete absence of aspects of experience at particular time points in development. This is because, for much of the brain's developing circuitry, it is the signals that the brain receives by way of the child's experiences which shape and determine which connections will be made.

For instance, in comparison to children with 'normal' experiences, children who have been faced with violence and aggression in early life have been found to have a higher ERP (Evoked Response Potential, a variant form of the Electroencephalogram) when instructed to respond to angry, rather than happy, faces presented to them. Moreover, they have also been found to interpret facial expressions which are ambiguously sad/angry or frightened/angry as angry. The implication is that being presented repeatedly with anger and aggression in early life leads to an altered, measurable, enhanced physiological response when faced even with minor aggression. It is adaptive for children's survival to recognise preferentially possible signals of danger. This predisposition becomes maladaptive when used indiscriminately and outside abusive situations.

The response to stress

Abuse and neglect are both stressful experiences. The body's response to stress is a physiological coping response necessary for survival, and involves several body systems. There are individual variations in the threshold above which an individual perceives an experience to be stressful. These individual differences in stress responsiveness are partly innate (genetically determined) and partly based on prior experience. Although necessary for survival, the stress response carries costs, and children who are or become more reactive to stress are therefore more vulnerable to its consequences.

One aspect of the stress response is the increased secretion of cortisol, and this response commences in early infancy. Cortisol acts in a number of different ways and on most tissues and organs in the body. Its actions include suppressing the immune response, increasing the level of circulating glucose and dampening of fear responses to the stressor, as well as adverse effects on certain parts of the brain including the hippocampus, which is particularly involved in the processing of memory for events. Children who have been abused and neglected have been found to show alterations in the normal cortisol secretion pattern. Children who show raised levels of cortisol during normal days at nursery have greater difficulty in focusing and sustaining attention.

The response of the sympathetic nervous system to stress results in secretion of adrenaline and noradrenaline. The effects of these hormones include raising heart rate and blood pressure, sweating and activation of the fight or flight response. There is also an increase in neurotransmitter secretion in the brain in response to stress which includes serotonin and dopamine. Significantly raised levels of these neurotransmitters in the pre-frontal cortex interfere with its functions, which include the planning and organising of actions using 'working memory' and the inhibiting of inappropriate responses and attention to distractions ('executive functions'), a disturbance not unlike Attention Deficit Hyperactivity Disorder (ADHD). Children who have been abused show a diminished capacity to avoid responses which have negative consequences.

Measuring progress

All children need to progress along all seven of the child development dimensions if they are to achieve long-term wellbeing in adulthood. Even though, for instance, one might be more concerned if a 15-year-old were having difficulty in establishing a strong sense of identity than if the same were true of a three-year-old, if children's needs in this and every dimension are not met from an early age, they will be increasingly likely to experience difficulties as they grow up.

Similarly, progress along all of these dimensions is important for all children, regardless of their race, culture or ability. Children who experience discrimination because, for instance, they come from a minority ethnic group or have an impairment may require additional support to develop a positive sense of self-esteem; those with learning disabilities may have different educational objectives from their peers; and those with physical disabilities may require extra support in the acquisition of self-care skills. Nevertheless, evidence of progress across the complete range of dimensions is inherent to the successful development of all children.

Although each child will progress at a different pace, it is nevertheless possible to group children into six age-bands that mark different stages of psychosocial development. Those used in the templates for recording work with children and families that accompany the Assessment Framework are: under 1 (including the pre-birth stage); 1–2; 3–4; 5–10; 11–15; and 16 and over (Department of Health 2003). The unequal spans demonstrate the unevenness of children's development, which progresses particularly rapidly in all dimensions in the early years. Although the cut-off points mark progression from one stage of development to another, they also reflect socially determined requirements imposed externally on children by, for instance, the education system.

In order to establish whether a child is 'in need' under the Children Act 1989, it is necessary to understand their current functioning in the various dimensions. Based on this information, an assessment of need can be made. Progress across all the developmental dimensions, and particularly in those areas where specific needs have been identified, will then be monitored. Without monitoring progress it is not possible to identify whether or not the services that have been introduced to meet the child's needs have been effective. For instance, if a child has poor literacy skills because they have missed out on school, it is important to find out whether they are now attending school, whether they have accessed any catch-up schemes to improve literacy and if progress has been made. If there is evidence that poor school attendance is linked, for instance, to a child's role in caring for a parent with mental health problems, then it is important to know whether the parent is now receiving appropriate support.

Are the dimensions of the child's developmental needs applicable to all children?

We know that all children are unique both in terms of their genetic or temperamental predispositions and their experiences. Their experiences will be determined by a vast diversity of cultural expectations, family situations and living conditions. How can we be sure that the Assessment Framework will be of use in helping professionals assess the needs of any child?

The seven dimensions of development have been tested out in England with a representative sample of 400 children living at home, in order to find out how far the areas covered and the links made between children's experiences and outcomes represent the preoccupations and needs of ordinary families. The researchers found that the seven dimensions of development are, almost universally, recognised as the key areas in which children need to progress if they are to achieve satisfactory wellbeing in adulthood. Within each dimension almost all parents, from all walks of life, hold similar basic age-related expectations for their children. Moreover, the vast majority of parents are aware of the type of experiences that children require if they are to meet these objectives. The difference lies in parents' ability to make use of this knowledge (Moyers and Mason 1995).

One further question remains: are there some children who have needs that cannot be identified through the Assessment Framework? For instance, does the Framework adequately address issues that are relevant to the culture of children from minority ethnic groups? Is the assumption that all children have similar developmental requirements inappropriate when assessing the needs of those with multiple disabilities?

Children from minority ethnic groups

The Assessment Framework addresses the fundamental needs that all children hold in common. As outlined in the accompanying practice guidance (Department of Health 2000), all children, whatever their ethnic background, have the same inherent developmental needs; however, the effects of racism may mean that black children growing up in a predominantly white society may require different services to counteract additional disadvantage. Different cultural groups may also meet children's developmental needs in different ways: in some cultures, for instance, parents may help children develop their language skills by telling stories rather than by reading to them. The Assessment Framework is, nevertheless, likely to address sufficiently fundamental issues to avoid the charge of cultural specificity: all children need to grow, to learn to communicate, and to develop secure attachments; at this very basic level it is the manner in which these needs are met rather than the specific nature of the needs themselves that may differ from one culture to another. These issues are explored in greater depth in Chapter 20, and in the Assessment Framework Practice Guidance (Dutt and Phillips 2000, pp.37–72).

Children with disabilities

There are also obvious issues to be addressed concerning the extent to which a methodology based on a concept of normative development can be applicable to children with profound disabilities, whose progress may be very different from that of their peers. However, attempts to identify different stages of development or different expectations for some children do not necessarily solve the problem. It would be valuable to develop criteria that would help practitioners identify those children whose disability is so severe that normative measures are inappropriate in every area of development; however, few children would be included in this category. Moreover, the range of disability is so extensive that alternative indicators would only be applicable to very small groups of children; numerous subsets would be necessary, causing further difficulties in determining how children might be grouped. Second, providing a separate methodology for disabled children undermines the now widely accepted principle that such children are 'children first': to regard them as having different needs and expectations from their peers could be regarded as discriminatory in that it would encourage practitioners to collude with the assumption that, because disability prevents children from progressing in some areas of development, it will restrict them in every area. It is, for instance, inappropriate to assess the overall development of children with learning disabilities by using measures designed for children of a much younger age, for, although their cognitive development may be restricted, their physical development may not, and issues such as physical and sexual maturational changes at adolescence will need to be addressed at the appropriate chronological age.

The seven dimensions of development are important for all children, regardless of ability. The challenge is to offer a methodology that allows assessors to identify different expectations for those areas of development that will be *unavoidably* impaired by the disability of a child; to ensure that additional experiences are offered by parents or parent figures in those areas where disability might otherwise impair progress; and to use normative measures in those areas which are unaffected. These issues are explored in greater depth in Chapter 12 and in the Assessment Framework Practice Guidance (see Marchant and Jones 2000, pp.73–112).

Resources to assist effective assessment of children in need

As indicated in the *Framework for the Assessment of Children in Need and their Families* (Department of Health *et al.* 2000), practice materials have been developed to assist practitioners systematically to collect and analyse information in order to make evidence-based decisions regarding children in need. Some of these materials are considered below along with those developed more recently; others are considered in detail elsewhere in this book.

A standardised approach to assessment across agencies

One of the primary aims of the Assessment Framework is to ensure that families are not subject to a barrage of overlapping or unco-ordinated assessments undertaken by a range of professionals, all of whom may reach different conclusions. Central to the Assessment Framework is the concept of assessing how far factors within the domains of parenting capacity and family and environment are impacting on the extent to which children's needs are being met across a broad spectrum of development. This concept also underpins the Common Assessment Framework (CAF), the shared method of assessing children with additional needs introduced across all children's services and across all local areas in England. Completion of a CAF assessment is undertaken by a lead professional from a range of agencies where there are concerns that a child may have additional needs and require additional services. The Common Assessment Framework (Children's Workforce Development Council 2009) offers a basis for early intervention and, for some children, for referral and information sharing between agencies. The practice guidance states that:

> [Local authorities] should agree with Local Safeguarding Children's Board partners, criteria with local services and professionals as to when it is appropriate to make a referral to [local authority] children's social care in respect of a child in need.

It also makes it explicit that:

> If somebody believes that a child may be suffering, or be at risk of suffering, sig-nificant harm, then they should always refer their concerns to LA [local authority] children's social care. (HM Government 2006, p.104, 5.15–5.16)

The Integrated Children's System exemplars

The conceptual model for the *Framework for the Assessment of Children in Need and their Families* underpins the design and use of all exemplars. The processes of assessment, planning, intervention and review for social work with all children in need are integral to the Integrated Children's System. It is intended that social workers undertake this recording electronically rather than on paper. The electronic system should be supported by information technology that can capture and process data which can then be used to determine outcomes of children at both an individual and an aggregate level. The exemplars reflect the requirement to record information about this work at particular stages in the process. The system operates both horizontally, as it models the different processes that social workers and their managers need to undertake in order to identify children's needs, provide services and monitor children's progress, and vertically, as it links with wider management information systems. Practitioners record key information through a range of records that are intended to capture the data necessary to underpin each process. The exemplars published for use by local authorities in developing their IT systems include formats for undertaking core assessments, completed where social care professionals may be required to provide long-term or complex packages of support, and assessment and progress records, designed to monitor the developmental progress of children who spend extensive periods in care and for whom the local authority therefore has specific responsibilities.

Age-related assessment records for children in need

The core assessment records are intended to help social workers make detailed assessments of children's needs and their parents' capacity to respond to them in an age-appropriate way within each of the areas of development. The attention of those completing the records is drawn to relevant research evidence, included in order to help social workers contextualise their observations and to make clear to children and parents some of the evidence on which professional judgements are made. The records require social workers to complete a methodical and detailed assessment procedure that is designed to ensure that identified needs are matched with appropriate provision from both adult and children's services.

Age-appropriate Assessment and Progress Records are completed after the second review of a looked after child, when it has become apparent that children are unlikely to return home in the immediate future. These records are aligned with the Core Assessment Records, but cover a number of issues of particular significance to looked after children, such as attachment and relationships with birth parents and carers. They are also designed to assess both the child's current position and changes since the previous assessment, with the aim of providing detailed indicators of progress within each of the seven developmental dimensions.

Questionnaires and scales

In understanding these assessments more specialist instruments can be used. These are described in detail in Chapter 2. *The Family Pack of Questionnaires and Scales* was published alongside the Assessment Framework and includes eight questionnaires and scales (Department of Health and Cox and Bentovim 2000). The *Strengths and Difficulties Questionnaire*, the *Parenting Daily Hassles Scale*, the *Adult Wellbeing Scale* and the *Home Circumstances Scale* were selected because they screen for particular problems or needs. They have been standardised so that a score above a particular cut-off indicates the strong probability of a significant problem of the type for which the questionnaire is screening. Scores above or below a cut-off do not guarantee the presence or absence of a significant problem in an individual case. Discussion with the child or adult completing the questionnaire is essential and will provide clarification about the responses and an increase in understanding of the child, adult or family's situation.

Summary

The *Framework for the Assessment of Children in Need and their Families* provides a conceptual basis for assessing children's developmental needs and identifying how far factors within their families, the community and their immediate environment promote or inhibit their chances of progressing towards optimal outcomes. Assessing how far children's developmental needs are met requires a holistic approach that covers a wide range of dimensions. Progress across the seven developmental dimensions included in the Assessment Framework is widely recognised as important for all children across a range of cultures and circumstances, and should be monitored if the effectiveness of interventions is to be understood. Recently, research has demonstrated the impact of adverse experiences on the development of the brain in early childhood, with potentially long-term consequences for children's life chances. These are factors which need to be taken into account when assessing strengths and difficulties in the circumstances of children and their families.

Recommended reading

Aldgate, J., Jones, D., Rose, W. and Jeffery, C. (2006) *The Developing World of the Child.* London: Jessica Kingsley Publishers.

Gerhardt, S. (2004) *Why Love Matters: How Affection Shapes a Baby's Brain.* London: Brunner-Routledge.

Lee, V. and Hoaken, P. (2007) 'Cognition, emotion and neurobiological development: mediating the relation between maltreatment and aggression.' *Child Maltreatment 12*, 3, 281–298.

Ward, H. and Rose, W. (2002) *Approaches to Needs Assessment in Children's Services.* London: Jessica Kingsley Publishers.

References

Aldgate, J., Jones, D., Rose, W. and Jeffery, C. (2006) *The Developing World of the Child.* London: Jessica Kingsley Publishers.

Anda, R. (2008) *The Health and Social Impact of Growing Up with Adverse Childhood Experiences.* Available at www.acestudy.org/files, accessed on 30 April 2009.

Bennett, F. (2005) 'Promoting the Health and Well-being of Children: Evidence of Need in the UK'. In J. Scott and H. Ward (eds) *Safeguarding and Promoting the Well-being of Children, Families and Communities.* London: Jessica Kingsley Publishers.

Children's Workforce Development Council (2009) *The Common Assessment Framework for Children and Young People: A Guide for Practitioners.* Leeds: Children's Workforce Development Council.

Cleaver, H., Unell, I. and Aldgate, J. (forthcoming) *Children's Needs – Parenting Capacity. The Impact of Parental Mental Illness, Learning Disability, Problem Alcohol and Drug Use, and Domestic Violence on Children's Safety and Development.* Second Edition.

Cleaver, H. and Nicholson, D. (2007) *Parental Learning Disability and Children's Needs: Family Experiences and Effective Practice.* London: Jessica Kingsley Publishers.

Cleaver, H., Nicholson, D., Tarr, S. and Cleaver, D. (2007) *Child Protection, Domestic Violence and Substance Abuse: Family Experiences and Effective Practice.* London: Jessica Kingsley Publishers.

Cm 5860 (2003) *Every Child Matters.* Green Paper. London: The Stationery Office.

Department of Health (2000) *Assessing Children in Need: Practice Guidance.* London: The Stationery Office.

Department of Health (2003) *Integrated Children's System.* Available at www.everychildmatters.gov.uk/socialcare/integratedchildrenssystem/resources/exemplars, accessed on 13 July 2009.

Department of Health and Cox, A. and Bentovim, A. (2000) *The Family Pack of Questionnaires and Scales.* London: The Stationery Office.

Department of Health, Department for Education and Employment and Home Office (2000) *Framework for the Assessment of Children in Need and their Families.* London: The Stationery Office.

Department of Work and Pensions (2008) *Households Below Average Incomes.* London: Department of Work and Pensions.

Dutt, R. and Phillips, M. (2000) 'Assessing Black Children and their Families.' In Department of Health, *Assessing Children in Need and their Families: Practice Guidance.* London: The Stationery Office.

Edwards, V.J., Holden, G.W., Anda, R.F. and Felitti, V.J. (2003) 'Experiencing multiple forms of childhood maltreatment and adult mental health: results from the adverse childhood experiences (ACE) study.' *American Journal of Psychiatry 160*, 8, 1453–1460.

Gerhardt, S. (2004) *Why Love Matters: How Affection Shapes a Baby's Brain.* London: Brunner-Routledge.

Glaser, D. (2000) 'Child abuse and neglect and the brain: a review.' *Journal of Child Psychology and Psychiatry 41,* 1, 97–116.

HM Government (2006) *Working Together to Safeguard Children: A Guide to Inter-agency Working to Safeguard and Promote the Welfare of Children.* Norwich: The Stationery Office.

Lee, V. and Hoaken, P. (2007) 'Cognition, emotion and neurobiological development: mediating the relation between maltreatment and aggression.' *Child Maltreatment 12,* 3, 281–298.

Marchant, R. and Jones, M. (2000) 'Assessing Needs of Disabled Children and their Families.' In Department of Health, *Assessing Children in Need and their Families: Practice Guidance.* London: The Stationery Office.

Moe, V. (2002) *A Prospective Longitudinal Study of Children Prenatally Exposed to Drugs: Prediction and Developmental Outcomes at Four and a Half Years.* Oslo: Department of Psychology, University of Oslo.

Moe, V. and Slinning, K. (2002) 'Prenatal drug exposure and the conceptualization of long-term effects.' *Scandinavian Journal of Psychology 43,* 1, 41–47.

Moyers, S. and Mason, A. (1995) 'Identifying Standards of Parenting.' In H. Ward (ed.) *Looking After Children: Research into Practice.* London: HMSO.

Office for National Statistics (2004) *Social Trends.* London: ONS.

Ward, H. (2002) 'Current Initiatives in the Development of Outcome-based Evaluation of Children's Services in England and Wales.' In A.N. Maluccio, C. Canali and T. Vecchiato (eds) *Assessing Outcomes in Child and Family Services: Comparative Design and Policy Issues.* New York, NY: Aldine de Gruyter.

Ward, H., Munro, E. and Dearden, C. (2006) *Babies and Young Children in Care: Life Pathways, Decision-making and Practice.* London: Jessica Kingsley Publishers.

CHAPTER 10

Promoting Positive Outcomes for Children in Need – The Importance of Protective Capacity in the Child and their Social Network

Robbie Gilligan

Successful children [who do well despite adversity] remind us that children grow up in multiple contexts – in families, schools, peer groups, baseball teams, religious organisations, and many other groups – and each context is a potential source of protective as well as risk factors. These children demonstrate that children are protected not only by the self-righting nature of development, but also by the actions of adults, by their own actions, by the nurturing of their assets, by opportunities to succeed and by the experience of success.

(Masten and Coatsworth 1998, p.216)

The purpose of this chapter is to:

- highlight the potential value of protective factors in assisting children to deal with adversity in their lives
- highlight the protective potential that lies in everyday relationships and experiences in children's lives

> • help the reader to identify and engage with possible protective factors in relevant cases.

Introduction

In their work with children and families in conditions of stress, professionals may be liable to do two things. First, they may *underestimate* the healing and recovery powers to be found in the child, family and surrounding context; they may thus also underestimate the competence and capacity to be found in the child and surrounding networks. Second, they may *overestimate* the importance of professionals and services in securing resolution to problems. Undoubtedly, professionals may have a part to play in sudden crises or in helping to find fixes for short-term difficulties. But in the case of long-term, more embedded difficulties, longer-term supports are often more likely to be found amongst the local networks of the child, family and surrounding community. In this chapter, the emphasis is on highlighting, for assessment purposes, the positive outcomes that may flow from the protective and restorative powers of everyday opportunities and experiences in children's lives.

Vulnerability and resilience

The impact of a negative experience on a child depends on the precise nature of the experience itself. A number of questions will help to clarify the issues in a given case:

- What was the stage and character of the child's life – and the surrounding contexts of that life – preceding the critical experience?

- How well were things going for the child in the earlier period and what support could the child access?

- What was the immediate context of the critical experience?

- Did the child have access to key supportive adults and how did they respond?

- In the longer term, after the experience, what kind of support did the child enjoy in the key contexts of their life: home, school, neighbourhood, peer group, etc.?

- What was the balance of adversity and protective factors in the different phases – before, during and after the critical experience?

Sexual abuse illustrates this latter point very well. The particular longer-term developmental impact of sexual abuse may be related to a whole range of factors that include the age and gender of the child; the balance of other harmful and protective factors; the child's intelligence; and the child's own appraisal of the abuse experience and of his or her responsibility. In addition, the context of the abuse will be important, including factors such as the frequency, duration and nature of abuse and the child's relationship to the abuser, the level of support the child receives following disclosure, and the level of other stress in the household. For a child who is getting on well at school, who had been doing well otherwise, who is intelligent, who has good social skills and has support from mother and other key adults, the prospects for recovery would seem more promising. The opposite might apply to a child who does not enjoy such advantages.

Therefore, when assessing a child in need using the *Framework for the Assessment of Children in Need and their Families* (Department of Health *et al.* 2000), it is important not to be preoccupied solely with the nature of the problem or adversity. It is also important to give significant weight to the nature of potential strengths and assets that may help to underpin healing and recovery. Ideally, one will find a cluster of positive factors that may help to sustain development in a positive direction. A committed mother, a supportive and available grandmother, thriving friendships and good progress in school may be the crucial ingredients of a sustaining context for one particular child in the aftermath of adversity or in coping with the long-term stress of, for example, a father's alcoholism. In another scenario the web of support may include an engaged father, a committed teacher, a supportive aunt, and so on. Even a single positive factor may be very important for concerned professionals to nurture and support. It may prove important in either of two ways: at a particular point, it may help to tilt the crucial balance between negative and positive factors in a child's life in a favourable direction; or it may prove the first critical element in what proves to be a positive chain of events in a child's life – for example, for a particular child being good at sport may help build self-esteem, which in turn may help to forge friendships with peers and build strong attachment to teachers, which in turn may help motivation, confidence and attainment in school, and so on.

Importance of how we view 'the child'

Many variables may serve to influence outcomes for the child; these may include factors related to:

- the child
- the immediate set of caring relationships surrounding the child
- the social and economic context immediately surrounding the child's daily life
- the wider societal factors that serve to shape the more immediate contexts.

In thinking of what influences outcomes for children or young people, it is important we consider adult views of children and young people and their capacity and competence, as well as their vulnerability. Adults may previously have seen children merely as 'belongings' or 'becomings' rather than as *beings*, who deserve attention now in their own right, not just as the belongings of adults or as an 'investment' in the community's future. Today, adult anxieties may mean that professionals and others view children primarily through the lens of 'risk'. Thus, they may cast children and young people more in the vulnerable role of 'bearers of risk', that is they see children as heavily exposed to, or 'carrying', risk by virtue of their very status as children. Adults, especially professionals, arguably then spend much of their time fretting about such risks. But an alternative view holds that such risks do not or should not define the child – from this perspective, there are many other dimensions to the child beyond the issue of risk. What the United Nations Convention on the Rights of the Child and related thinking emphasises is that children are 'beings' as of right and in their own right, and that they are beings right now, not some time in their future (James and Prout 1990). They are also active agents in their own development and the shaping and seeking of their destiny. In so many ways, the child or young person's own sense of agency and autonomy is crucial to their progress. Their energy, their drive, their autonomy helps them move forward in their development. This agency needs to be valued and recognised. The American social psychologist Peggy Thoits (1994) has advocated the value of seeing the person as a 'psychological activist' in their own life. This seems to be a metaphor that is especially helpful and illuminative in the case of children and young people.

From this perspective, the fate of children does not lie solely in the hands of adults – or the actions of services. The child or young person may adopt different strategies in the face of adversity. They may seek to negotiate their way through, or adapt or respond to, stressful situations in some proactive way, or they may not. Highlighting this point is not to imply that every child *ought* to respond, but arguing instead that adults must not assume that they will not or cannot respond. Children and young people may attempt various strategies in the face of stress:

- resistance (for example, in the face of negative or shaming identities) (Ungar 2004)

- avoidance (for example, by avoiding a problem-drinking parent at home; see Velleman and Orford 1999)

- seeking of a new identity or community (as in the case of displaced youth in East Africa, as reported in Tefferi 2007).

Recognising the importance of the young person's sense of self-efficacy or 'sense of perceived control' is not merely some gesture supportive of children's autonomy rights. There is evidence that this 'sense of perceived control' in the child is associated with more positive adaptation in the face of maltreatment (Bolger and Patterson 2003).

In their study tracking the lives of troubled teenagers, Hauser *et al.* (2006, p.39) found three key ingredients that are 'intricately intertwined' (p.41) and ultimately linked to resilience in the lives of the young people:

1. *reflectiveness*: 'curiosity about one's thoughts, feelings, and motivations, and the willingness to try to make sense of them and handle them responsibly'

2. *agency*: 'conviction that what one does matters, that one can intervene effectively in one's own life'

3. *relatedness*: 'engagement and interaction with others may be highly valued even when there are no helpful others around, and this may predispose youngsters to be able to use supportive connections when they are available'.

The developing child – some important considerations

In considering a given child's circumstances and prospects it is important to bring a number of perspectives to bear:

- Circumstances may change favourably and may have a positive impact on the child's health and development. The early years are influential in terms of longer-term prospects, but it is never too late to aim or hope for change.

- Children may display resilience in the face of adversity, that is they may do better than might be expected for lots of reasons, often in some key part of their life. There is no guarantee that this will happen and science is still trying to understand why and how it operates. Broadly supportive relationships over time seem to be a key ingredient.

- Gender and ethnicity are important variables influencing opportunities and prospects especially in the light of dominant societal norms and expectations.

- Social capital is important for children and families: understanding this as connectedness within a web of relationships based on norms of trust, reciprocity and mutual identification. Children and families lacking this asset are likely to be more isolated and unsupported and therefore more vulnerable to the impact of stress.

- Self-esteem is an important influence for the child. High self-esteem has been found to help neutralise the effects of exposure to childhood adversity (Fergusson and Horwood 2003).

The power of belonging and relationships

As indicated in the dimensions used within the Assessment Framework (Department of Health *et al.* 2000), children need to feel a sense of belonging to people who matter to them and to whom they matter. This sense of belonging gives rise to a feeling of security in the child which promotes growth and exploration. The child can explore the world and new experiences, safe in the knowledge that he or she can retreat to a 'secure base' to be comforted and protected when necessary and prepared for further adventures when ready (Bowlby 1988). The consistent and reliable responsiveness of people who constitute the child's secure base teaches the child that the world is fundamentally a safe place, that people can generally be trusted, and that new experiences are mostly worth trying.

Parents and parent figures

Relations with parents or parent figures are clearly critical for almost all children. But it should not be forgotten that relationships of meaning and quality are important to children with whomever they emerge.

> Stated simply, relationships are the 'active ingredients' of the environment's influence on healthy human development. They incorporate the qualities that best promote competence and well-being – individualised responsiveness, mutual action-and-

interaction, and an emotional connection to another human being, be it a parent, peer, grandparent, aunt, uncle, neighbour, teacher, coach, or any other person who has an important impact on the child's early development. (National Scientific Council on the Developing Child 2004, p.1)

Relationships with parents are undoubtedly the most significant for the vast majority of children and young people. For most, it is to be hoped that these relationships will be a source of protective influences. While mothers are very important, it should not be assumed, in the face of much negative publicity about men in the lives of children, that fathers are necessarily marginal or unhelpful. In a recent major review of evidence on the developmental significance for children of their father's role (Flouri 2005), it is shown that father's involvement in their children's lives is associated (a) with the child's (i) happiness and (ii) academic motivation, (b) with their adult daughters' educational attainment (linked to the father's interest in education) and (c) low risk for delinquency in sons and low risk of homelessness in adult sons. It should be remembered, however, that in the case of maltreated or vulnerable children, relations with parents may sometimes be compromised, requiring the child to rely more on other kinds of relationships.

Non-parental adults

Relationships with non-parental adults with a strong and, ideally, partisan commitment to the child may play a very formative and protective role in the life of the growing child. Grandparents, other relatives, the mothers of friends, and sports coaches are but some examples of the kind of people who may play a special role in the life of a vulnerable child.

Siblings, friends and peers

While relationships with non-parental adults may be a valuable additional resource for many children, it should also be noted that relations with non-adults may prove important, whether with siblings or friends. Recent findings from data from the Avon Longitudinal Study of Parents and Children in Britain suggest that in the context of stressful life events 'sibling affection is protective regardless of the age gap found between siblings and the gender composition of the dyad…and of the quality of the parent–child relationship' (Gass et al. 2007, p.172).

According to the authors, their results taken with others suggest that 'the provision of security and comfort once ascribed mainly to parental figures *may* [emphasis in original also be a role that siblings can fulfil when children experience stress caused by life events' (*ibid.*) While awaiting replication by other researchers, the authors note that their findings underline the value and importance of 'interventions that support the development and strengthening of relationships between siblings' (p.173).

Friends may also be important as a non-adult source of support for vulnerable youngsters. Bolger and Patterson (2003) found in the Virginia Longitudinal Study of Child Maltreatment in the US that, for a maltreated child, 'having a positive, reciprocal friendship was associated with an increase over time in self-esteem' (p.175). The paradox, of course, is that child maltreatment may impair the young person's capacity to engage successfully in peer relationships, but there is further evidence that, if successful peer relationships emerge, they are strongly associated with resilience for the maltreated young person (Collishaw *et al.* 2007).

Bullying or victimisation by peers may be a deeply debilitating form of maltreatment, especially for a vulnerable child, adding to their spiral of descent into a dwindling sense of confidence and esteem. Such bullying may occur within school or its environs. Children already subject to other adversity may be less able to resist and may have fewer supports to call on. While there is rightly much emphasis on adult responsibility in fashioning a climate opposed to bullying, it is also true that there is evidence that peer support may prove important for vulnerable children: peer support at school from friends (Schmidt and Bagwell 2007) or from siblings, as for example in the case of looked after children in care placed together. There is evidence that, in such circumstances, siblings may prove a very important source of support in reducing the risk or occurrence of such instances of bullying (Daly and Gilligan 2005).

Positive school experiences

Schools may serve valuable functions beyond their important specific educational role in the child's life by:

- assisting in the integration of minority ethnic children into new communities (Scourfield *et al.* 2002)

- enabling young people to form friendships with fellow students

- assisting young people (and their parents) in acquiring valued social roles (club member, sports participant, committee member, etc.) that may prove a precious resource in strengthening school engagement, wider social engagement and self-esteem

- offering young people access to relationships with supportive adults (Gilligan 1998)

- offering opportunities to build self-esteem and self-efficacy through competence and attainment in academic and non-academic areas of school life.

Positive spare-time activities

Spare-time activities have considerable power to influence young people's lives. These activities may be in the areas of sport, culture, care of animals or community service or in the area of part-time work. While in some instances such activities may open up risk for the young person, much research evidence supports the case for how involvement in such activities may be protective for young people. There is evidence (Gilligan 2007a, 2007b, 2008) that such engagement may:

- serve as a pathway to ultimate inclusion in the labour force

- open up relationships with adults who play a mentoring or otherwise supportive role in the young person's life

- help to build the self-esteem and self-efficacy of the young person
- help to build social skills and relationships with peers
- enhance academic engagement and attainment.

Planning interventions

At the moment there is too often an expectation that comparatively short bursts of intervention can deliver life-changing impact. In the light of the evidence, this simply seems too ambitious and unrealistic. Entrenched, embedded and often inter-generational difficulties are unlikely to submit to short-term efforts at their resolution. From the evidence available, it seems that early (and later) childhood interventions are more likely to have an impact if they have:

- sufficient *dosage* (frequency, intensity)
- sufficient *breadth* (approaches dealing with parent and child, and perhaps the parent–child relationship)
- sufficient *duration*. To have impact a programme may need to have a number of dimensions: good quality child care, adult education (and not just parenting education) and family support.

We therefore need to remember that:

- low dosage interventions may not prove to have high impact
- where there appears to be short-term impact, this may not endure
- complex multi-factorial issues may require complex multi-factorial responses
- user satisfaction may not be the best indicator of effectiveness. It may be a necessary, but not a sufficient, source of evidence that something will make a difference
- special needs arising, for example, from cultural difference, disability or particular family stresses (for example domestic violence) are likely to require a diverse range of approaches
- early childhood programmes cannot, on their own, compensate for failures in economic or housing or wider educational provision
- in the case of school-age children, school is a source of key experiences (positive or negative) and school life will usually need to be an integral part of any intervention
- social networks (mainly comprised normally of non-professionals) are crucially important in the lives of children and families. Within them may flow support or negativity that has a big bearing on outcomes.

Messages for practice

Promoting positive outcomes for vulnerable children involves harnessing the resources of committed supportive adults in informal networks and professional systems. It also involves tapping into positive resources in peer groups and other contexts in the local community. This message sounds relatively simple, but delivering on it takes skill, sympathy and persistence. It also takes a realisation on the part of professionals that not all help or good outcomes for children come through professional systems alone. Further, it requires active commitment to the notion of a 'therapeutic alliance' (Green 2006) between helpers and the person at whom help is directed. Finally, it requires appreciation of the therapeutic power of everyday opportunities and experiences in children's lives. With this in mind, when completing assessments using the Assessment Framework, the following questions should be considered.

Child's developmental needs

- Does the child have access to supportive non-parental adults?

- Does the child have relationships with supportive siblings or friends?

- Does the child have at least some regular positive age-appropriate experiences at school or in leisure time?

- Are professional services able to find some positive strengths/capacities in the child on which to build further work?

Parenting capacity

- Does this child's parents have access to supportive relations within their social network?

- Does this parent have a record of being able to connect with and use positive resources in their social network and community?

- Does this child's parents have at least some positive perceptions/memories in relation to the parenting role, their relationship with this child, and their own and their child's capacities?

- Have professional services been able to find some positive strengths/capacities in the parent on which to build further work?

Family and environmental factors

- Do family members have positive connections to at least some professional systems or community resources?

- Do family members have opportunities to play valued social roles and make positive contributions in at least some aspect of life in the community, at work or in school/college?

- Are professional services able to find some positive strengths/capacities in the child's family and environment?

Recommended reading

Armstrong, C. and Hill, M. (2001) 'Support services for vulnerable families with young children.' *Child and Family Social Work 6*, 351–358.

Gilligan, R. (2009) *Promoting Resilience* (2nd edn). London: British Agencies for Adoption and Fostering.

Werner, E. and Smith, R. (2001) *Journeys from Childhood to Midlife – Risk, Resilience and Recovery.* Ithaca, NY: Cornell University Press.

References

Bolger, K. and Patterson, C. (2003) 'Sequelae of Child Maltreatment: Vulnerability and Resilience.' In S. Luthar (ed.) *Resilience and Vulnerability – Adaptation in the Context of Childhood Adversities.* Cambridge: Cambridge University Press.

Bowlby, J. (1988) *A Secure Base: Clinical Applications of Attachment Theory.* London: Routledge.

Collishaw, S., Pickles, A., Messer, J., Rutter, M., Shearer, C. and Maughan, B. (2007) 'Resilience to adult psychopathology following childhood maltreatment: evidence from a community sample.' *Child Abuse and Neglect 31*, 3, 211–229.

Daly, F. and Gilligan, R. (2005) *Lives in Foster Care.* Dublin: Children's Research Centre.

Department of Health, Department for Education and Employment and Home Office (2000) *Framework for the Assessment of Children in Need and their Families.* London: The Stationery Office.

Fergusson, D. and Horwood, L.J. (2003) 'Resilience to Childhood Adversity – Results of a 21-Year Study.' In S. Luthar (ed.) *Resilience and Vulnerability – Adaptation in the Context of Childhood Adversities.* Cambridge: Cambridge University Press.

Flouri, E. (2005) *Fathering and Child Outcomes.* Chichester: Wiley.

Gass, K., Jenkins, J. and Dunn, J. (2007) 'Are sibling relationships protective? A longitudinal study.' *Journal of Child Psychology and Psychiatry 48*, 2, 167–175.

Gilligan, R. (1998) 'The importance of schools and teachers in child welfare.' *Child and Family Social Work 3*, 1, 13–25.

Gilligan, R. (2007a) 'Adversity, resilience and the educational progress of young people in public care.' *Emotional and Behavioural Difficulties 12*, 2, 135–145.

Gilligan, R. (2007b) 'Spare time activities for young people in care: what can they contribute to educational progress?' *Adoption and Fostering 31*, 1, 92–99.

Gilligan, R. (2008) 'Promoting resilience in young people in long term care – the relevance of roles and relationships in the domains of recreation and work.' *Journal of Social Work Practice 22*, 1, 37–50.

Green, J. (2006) 'Annotation: the therapeutic alliance as a significant but neglected variable in child mental health treatment studies.' *Journal of Child Psychology and Psychiatry 47*, 5, 425–435.

Hauser, S., Allen, J. and Golden, E. (2006) *Out of the Woods – Tales of Resilient Teens.* Cambridge, MA: Harvard University Press.

James, A. and Prout, A. (eds) (1990) *Contructing and Reconstructing Childhood.* Basingstoke: Falmer.

Masten, A.S. and Coatsworth, J.D. (1998) 'The development of competence in favorable and unfavorable environments: lessons from research on successful children.' *American Psychologist 53*, 2, 205–220.

National Scientific Council on the Developing Child (2004) *Young Children Develop in an Environment of Relationships.* Working Paper No. 1. Available at www.developingchild.net/pubs/wp-abstracts/wp1.html, accessed on 30 April 2009.

Schmidt, M.E. and Bagwell, C.L. (2007) 'The protective role of friendships in overtly and relationally victimized boys and girls.' *Merrill-Palmer Quarterly–Journal of Developmental Psychology 53*, 3, 439–460.

Scourfield, J., Evans, J., Shah, W. and Beynon, H. (2002) 'Responding to the experiences of minority ethnic children in virtually all-white communities.' *Child and Family Social Work 7*, 3, 161–175.

Tefferi, H. (2007) 'Reconstructing adolescence after displacement: experience from eastern Africa.' *Children and Society 21*, 14, 297–308.

Thoits, P.A. (1994) 'Stressors and problem-solving: the individual as psychological activist.' *Journal of Health and Social Behaviour 35*, 2, 143–160.

Ungar, M. (2004) *Nurturing Hidden Resilience in Troubled Youth.* Toronto: University of Toronto Press.

Velleman, R. and Orford, J. (1999) *Risk and Resilience – Adults who were the Children of Problem Drinkers.* Amsterdam: Harwood Academic Publishers.

CHAPTER 11

Attachment: Implications for Assessing Children's Needs and Parenting Capacity

David Howe

Emotional and behavioural development – concerns the appropriateness of response demonstrated in feelings and actions by a child initially to parents and caregivers and, as the child grows older, to others beyond the family. [It] includes the nature and quality of early attachments.

(From the Framework for the Assessment of Children in Need and their Families, p.19)

This chapter considers:

- why attachments are important for the welfare of the child
- the assessment of the caregiver as attachment figure
- attachment and the developmental needs of children
- assessment issues.

Introduction

Under the creative genius of John Bowlby, insights garnered from evolutionary theory, ethology, systems theory and developmental psychology were fashioned over a number of years into what is today known as attachment theory (Bowlby 1973, 1979, 1980). Attachment theory is a theory of affect regulation and personality development in the context of close relationships. If the quality of close relationships has a bearing on children's emotional and social development, attachment theory should be of particular relevance and interest to social workers and other practitioners who work with children and families (Howe *et al.* 1999).

Particular attachment patterns and careseeking behaviours represent different psychological and behavioural strategies developed by children to maximise the care and protection available under particular caregiving regimes. Children increase their chances of survival when they can mentally represent, in the form of an internal working model, the way their interpersonal world appears to work. In particular, they need to sense what increases and reduces the caring and protective responses of their caregivers. Children, including those who are maltreated and neglected, actively seek ways of adapting to their world rather than being victims of it (Crittenden 1996). Understanding children's behaviour as an adaptive strategy, developed in the context of their caregiving environment, offers practitioners a powerful conceptual tool that links knowledge of the caregiving environment, children's behaviour and their psychological development. An understanding of attachment theory, therefore, plays a key role in helping practitioners make judgements about children's welfare.

Attachment behaviour

Human infants remain highly vulnerable and dependent for a number of years. If children are to survive into adulthood, it is important that they receive reliable care and protection. An evolutionary perspective suggests that as a species our origins are those of hunter-gatherers on the open plains of East Africa. This is an environment in which there are dangers including predators. Babies would be easy prey without the protection of adults and the safety of the group. It would therefore be biological folly, said Bowlby (1988), if vulnerable human infants did not come equipped with a range of programmed behaviours to increase their chances of survival under conditions of danger.

Attachment is one of a number of instinctive proximity, careseeking behavioural systems that also include affiliation, sexuality and caregiving. Whenever human infants feel in danger or need they become physiologically and emotionally aroused and dysregulated. This activates the attachment system, triggering attachment behaviour. Attachment behaviour involves the display of a number of distress signals including crying, clinging, eye gazing and following. Such signals typically draw the parent's attention to the child's distress. The goal of attachment behaviour is therefore to recover proximity with an adult (typically a parent) where care, protection and safety lie. Repeated interactions between babies and their primary caregivers establish an attachment bond. Over their first few months, babies begin to have a clear sense of where protection, comfort and regulation lie. By six or seven months, primary caregivers are destined to become children's selective attachment figures. That is, at times of need, these are the people to whom children turn.

In robust fashion, Prior and Glaser (2006) make clear the following distinctions between 'attachments' and 'bonds':

> In the relationship between the child and parent, the term 'attachment' applies to the infant or child and the term 'attachment figure' invariably refers to their primary

caregiver. In terms of attachment theory, it is incorrect to refer to a parent's attachment to their child or attachment *between* parents and children. Attachment, therefore, is *not* synonymous with love or affection; it is not an overall descriptor of the relationship between the parent and child which includes other parent–child interactions such as feeding, stimulation, play or problem solving. The attachment figure's equivalent tie to the child is termed the 'caregiving bond'. (Prior and Glaser 2006, p.15, emphases as in original)

Children can have more than one attachment figure, although they tend to be organised hierarchically. So, for example, when upset a child might seek out her mother, but in her absence, fathers or grandmothers might offer alternative behavioural goals.

It is worth noting that, from an evolutionary perspective, loss, separation or abandonment by primary caregivers represents absolute danger for infants. The young of most mammals experience high levels of physiological and emotional distress whenever they sense the absence of care and protection. This is why neglect (whether physical, emotional or psychological) is such a disturbing experience for young children. Although there may no longer be the predators and dangers associated with the hunter-gatherer life, biologically we are little different from our recent evolutionary ancestors. An unresponsive, neglectful caregiver signals potential exposure to danger inasmuch as their availability at times of need and danger cannot be taken for granted. Neglect, therefore, feels like abandonment, which leads to significant physiological and emotional dysregulation and, if chronically suffered, developmental impairment.

Threats to children's welfare might come from a number of sources, including those that:

- are internal to the child (hunger, illness, pain)
- are external to the child (danger, threat, fear)
- imply the loss of the caregiver, either physically, emotionally or psychologically.

When children's attachment behaviour is not activated, their mental energies can be concentrated on learning about the world and their part in it. This is known as exploratory behaviour and includes play, curiosity, novelty-seeking, conversation and enquiry. Caregiving relationships that fail to help children feel safe and emotionally regulated increase the risk of attachment systems being chronically over-activated and exploratory systems behaviour being under-activated. This is why attachment behaviour, sustained at the expense of exploratory behaviour, has an adverse effect on children's psychosocial development.

Affect regulation

At the point when attachment behaviour has achieved its goal of recovering proximity with the caregiver, the child is in an emotionally aroused, physiologically dysregulated state. The next key task of the primary caregiver, therefore, is to help the child manage and regulate his or her arousal and distress. Attachment theory is often characterised as a theory of affect regulation, a way of controlling anxiety.

As babies are unable to regulate their emotions on their own, they need a relationship with another who can help them contain, manage and make sense of what is happening – physiologically, sensorily, emotionally and cognitively – at times of need. And of course, the people who do most of this containing and regulating are children's attachment figures, particularly their primary caregivers. Babies are born 'pro-social', with an instinct to relate with other people. They begin to develop a relationship with those who interact with them, both at times of need (attachment behaviour) and at times when they are content and relaxed (exploration, play, curiosity). The quality of this relationship is not only important in determining the character of children's attachment behaviour and organisation, but also in influencing the development of their psychological self. Schore (2001) observes that young minds form in the context of close relationships, and so the nature of the burgeoning psychological self, in part, will be affected by the nature of these early caregiving relationships. As the adult mind interacts with the child's emerging mind, we have what Trevarthen and Aitkin (2001) call a condition of 'purposeful' or 'primary intersubjectivity'.

> Researchers found that as early as 2 months, infants and mothers, while they were looking at and listening to each other, were mutually regulating one another's interests and feelings in intricate, rhythmic patterns, exchanging multimodal signals and imitations of vocal, facial, and gestural expressions… Mothers and fathers were behaving in an intensely sympathetic and highly expressive way that absorbed the attention of the infants and led to intricate, mutually regulated interchanges with turns of displaying and attending. The infant was thus proved to possess an active and immediately responsive conscious appreciation of the adult's communicative intentions. This is what was called primary intersubjectivity. (Trevarthen and Aitkin 2001, p.5)

Sensitive, attuned parents give their young children the strong message that emotions happen but they need not overwhelm us. Feelings can be thought about and understood. They can be contained and managed. Emotions also tell us interesting and important things about how we are currently experiencing our relationship with the world, particularly the world of other people. Fonagy *et al.* (2002) refer to this process of thinking about how feelings affect us and other people as 'mentalisation' or 'reflective function'. Meins *et al.* (2001) refer to a similar process as 'mind-mindedness', the idea that 'good enough', attuned parents have in mind their child's mind, including their needs, wants, desires, emotions and beliefs.

It is the caregiver's sensitive perception and acknowledgement of her infant's emotional states that enables her to make sense of her baby's inner feelings. Sensitive and emotionally attuned parents are also very good at reflecting back what they perceive to be their child's emotional and mental states. In these ways, the maturing child begins to develop an understanding of their own psychological make-up and how they work emotionally. They learn to recognise and regulate their own emotional condition because they had carers who recognised and regulated their arousal when they were young.

The parents' capacity to observe the child's mind seems to facilitate the child's general understanding of minds, including his or her own. We are able to think of others in psychological terms because we were thought of in psychological terms (Fonagy *et al.* 2002). To be understood by another promotes self-understanding. 'Feeling felt' conveys a sense of emotional connectedness between mother and child. This is a pleasurable, reassuring, confirming and psychologically constructive experience. Children begin to recognise, understand and reflect on their own and other people's mental states and how these affect behaviour.

The more children are cared for by psychologically attuned, mind-minded, sensitive parents, the more they can begin to make sense of their own and other people's emotional and mental states. All of this marks the beginning of emotional self-regulation and the emergence of various resilience factors including good self-esteem, self-efficacy and social understanding. Possessed of these psychological and emotional skills, children who have enjoyed good enough parenting tend to be socially competent and skilled players. They are at low risk of suffering mental health and behavioural problems. They have carers who recognise, support and respect their autonomy. They have parents who are able to cooperate with their children's needs and accomplishments.

Assessing attachments

Researchers have developed a variety of instruments and ways of measuring attachment in infants, children and adults. Some depend on sound observations of children and their behaviour when their attachment system is aroused. Others attempt to access children's internal working models (mental representations) of attachment, typically in situations of play and story telling.

Perhaps the earliest and best-known assessment is Ainsworth and Wittig's (1969) 'Strange Situation' procedure to measure attachment behaviour in young children aged between 9 and 18 months. It examines the balance between the child's exploratory and attachment behaviours when the attachment figure is present and absent from the room and during the reunion event. Narrative story stem techniques are often used to assess mental representations of attachment in older children aged four to eight years of age. Children are given the beginning (or stem) of an attachment-related story and asked to complete the story using dolls in a play format. Separation Anxiety Tests are also used for children in this age range. The coding, scoring and analysis of these and other procedures requires considerable skill and training. (For a useful review of these and other measures, including the assessment of adult attachments and caregiving, see Goldberg 2000; Prior and Glaser 2006; Solomon and George 1999.)

Secure attachments

Sensitive, psychologically minded, mentalised caregiving and its positive effect on children's psychosocial development predicts a 'secure' attachment. Securely attached children begin to sense that, at times of need, their caregivers are available and sensitively responsive. They develop feelings of trust. When secure children become distressed, more often than not carers are able to soothe and comfort them quickly. Such responses allow children to see themselves as both loved and effective at eliciting care and protection. Children feel understood and emotionally regulated.

Recent work by neuroscientists has shown that emotionally intelligent parents who can 'mentalise' and help children regulate their arousal at times of need also affect young children's early brain development. The more psychologically rich, attuned and mind-minded is the quality of the caregiver's interaction with the child, particularly at times of need and arousal, the more complex and coherent is the child's brain. Secure children have more complex, integrated brains that have the capacity to reflect on their own and other people's mental states, including how thoughts, feelings and behaviour affect each other. Individuals with these capacities have more behavioural options in situations of challenge. They cope better under stress. They are often said to be 'emotionally intelligent' (Howe 2008).

Internal working models

With repeated experiences of relating with primary caregivers, young children begin to develop more conscious, cognitive understandings or models of themselves and other people. For example, secure children who feel loved, valued and praised begin to develop an internal working model of the self as lovable, worthy and effective.

In terms of achieving emotional and social competence, children need to generate mental representations of (i) the self, (ii) other people and (iii) the relationship between self and others. These 'mental representations' refer to the kind of memories, experiences, outcomes, feelings and knowledge about what tends to happen in relationships, particularly with attachment figures, at times of need and stress. With these mental models of how others are likely to behave and how the self is likely to feel, children begin to *organise* their attachment behaviour to increase the availability, proximity and responsivity of their carers and reduce negative affect. They develop strategies to recover their own feelings of security when they feel anxious or frightened. In time, these mental representations begin to guide the child's expectations, beliefs and behaviour in all important relationships. Children begin to enter into a 'goal-corrected partnership' with their carer in which they learn to modify their own behaviour in the light of the parent's plans, intentions, beliefs and personality, still with the ultimate goal of maximising, over the long term, the parent's willingness to provide care and protection. They begin to see how things might appear from the other person's point of view. Discussion, sharing and negotiation become the preferred way of pursuing goals and conducting relationships.

The formation and development of internal working models explains how the quality of external relationships influences the character of children's internal psychology. As attachment relationships become psychologically internalised, the quality of a child's social experiences becomes a mental property of the child. Over time, internal working models begin to organise experience rather than be organised by it. In this sense, mental modelling produces continuity in the way we behave, relate, feel and respond. Our personality begins to acquire a regular, enduring quality. We begin to expect certain things of ourselves and of others, while others feel that we are becoming more familiar and predictable to them.

Insecure attachment organisations

For insecure children, the psychological availability, sensitivity and responsivity of carers at times of need is less straightforward (Howe *et al.* 1999). Caregivers who are less than optimally sensitive, who have impairments in their ability to 'mentalise', will affect their children's attachment organisation and subsequent psychosocial development. The reduced sensitivity and restricted emotional attunement is the result of caregivers dealing defensively with their own needs and anxieties as they are triggered by the child's needs and displays of attachment behaviour. Under these caregiving conditions, children cannot take their carer's availability for granted — hence their attachments are described as 'insecure'. Insecurely attached children will have internal working models of the self and others that are less positive.

Ainsworth *et al.* (1978) recognised two basic patterns of insecure attachment: 'avoidant' and 'ambivalent'. Even when the caregiving is anxious and insecure, the goal of the child's attachment behaviour is the same: to recover the caregiver's proximity and availability at times of need and anxiety. Insecure children therefore develop more defensively organised attachment behaviours to increase carer availability. These adaptive strategies involve downplaying or excluding some types of psychological information from conscious processing. This affects the child's ability to cope in a fully rounded, reflective and flexible way with many of the stresses met in social relationships.

'Avoidant' ('defended') children have carers who become anxious and defensively rejecting of emotional need whenever others place demands on them. Avoidantly attached children cope and adapt to this dismissing type of caregiving by excluding attachment-based feelings and behaviours from conscious processing. They over-regulate feelings of emotional distress. Children sense that strong displays of attachment behaviour actually decrease their caregiver's availability. Signs of need, weakness, dependency and vulnerability in the self or others make avoidant children feel anxious. In order to be acceptable and increase their caregiver's availability, avoidant children become emotionally self-contained yet remain keen observers of other people's feelings and behaviour.

More extreme avoidant strategies are used by children who suffer rejection, abuse and psychological maltreatment. For example, physically and emotionally abused children typically do not seek comfort or safety when upset, ill, vulnerable or frightened. They have learned that care and protection are not unconditionally available, and that being in a state of need only seems to make matters worse and might even make the carer more dangerous. Trust in the availability, care and interest of others at times of need is largely absent. This means that any relationship in which there are attachment-related issues will trigger feelings of anxiety, distress and aggression.

'Ambivalent' ('resistant', 'dependent') children have carers who are anxious about their own acceptance and lovability, whose emotional needs are high, and who are inconsistent and poor at recognising other people's needs and attachment signals. Ambivalently attached children cope and adapt to being cared for by preoccupied, needy parents by maximising their distress and attachment behaviour. This behavioural strategy increases their chances of getting noticed by their anxious, needy parent. The children's greatest anxiety is being ignored, abandoned and left alone with needs unmet and arousal unregulated.

They live in an unpredictable world, in which there is no guarantee that others will be there or respond at times of need and distress.

Ambivalent children have little confidence in their own abilities to bring about change and get the things they need. This results in a fatalistic attitude to events; an anxious preoccupation with other people's inconsistent emotional availability; and an angry, demanding, dissatisfied, needy, pleading and provocative approach to relationships. There is little monitoring of their own behaviour or emotional condition. Their immaturity, impatience and impulsivity mean that they repeatedly 'go too far'. Underpinning all their behaviour is the drive to be noticed, valued, acknowledged and recognised. They act as if always in a crisis (Crittenden 1999). This produces children who are demanding and yet never satisfied or reassured. Pronounced versions of this attachment strategy are typically met in families where there is chaotic neglect. Under stress, children feel helpless. Here, family life is often chaotic, dramatic, crisis-ridden, emotionally competitive and enmeshed (Howe *et al.* 1999).

In Ainsworth *et al.*'s (1978) original tripartite attachment classification, approximately 65 per cent of children were categorised as secure, 20–25 per cent avoidant, and 10–15 per cent ambivalent. To be classified insecure, but with an organised attachment strategy, in itself does not indicate pathology or suggest clinical status. After all, 35–40 per cent of any normal population of children will be classified as either avoidant or ambivalent.

Organised but insecure patterns represent adaptations to particular caregiving environments, which in turn are embedded in particular cultural contexts. Indeed, the proportions of the two insecure patterns have been found to vary across different classes, cultures and geographies, though across all populations secure attachments remain the modal pattern. So, for example, in harsh, demanding physical environments in which life is tough we find more children classified avoidant and fewer ambivalent. From an adaptive perspective, containing need and emphasising independence make sense in terms of survival. Populations who maintain their traditions, even when they have moved to a different part of the world, may continue to show a distribution of attachment patterns typical of their cultural origins. Nevertheless, in spite of these variations in the distribution of insecure attachments, in most cultures secure attachments tend to predominate.

Child factors and attachment

Attachment theory considers that children's patterns of attachment are largely determined by the characteristics of their caregiving, and that child factors play a less significant role in attachment organisation. However, there is research evidence that some child characteristics can influence attachment behaviour. For example, a study by Belsky and Rovine (1987) found that, although caregiver factors determined whether or not an infant developed a secure or insecure attachment, the child's temperament affected the manner in which the security or insecurity was expressed (also see Vaughn and Bost 1999 for a review). Parental sensitivity might be affected by the child's ease of arousability, temperamental difficultness, and ability to self-regulate. Children who are irritable, sensitive and easily aroused might place higher demands and increased levels of stress on their parents. Studies by Susman-Stillman *et al.* (1996) and van den Boom (1994) found that irritable infants in disadvantaged environments were more likely to be classified insecurely attached. This suggests that challenging children cared for by parents under stress act as an additional stressor. Stress reduces caregivers' psychological availability and this increases the risk of children developing insecure attachments.

A more complex picture emerges in the case of disabled children (Howe 2006a, 2006b). It is not the children's disability *per se* that is associated with the increased occurrence of insecure attachments but rather the interaction between the disabled child and the caregiver's state of mind with respect to attachment and any stress or insensitivity that a particular parent might experience caring for a disabled child.

Helpless and hostile caregiving; disorganised and controlling attachments

Caregivers who have suffered relationship histories of abuse, neglect, loss, rejection and trauma are at increased risk of being emotionally and psychologically unavailable to their children at times of need and distress. Reduced availability and the limited capacity to mentalise will be made worse whenever levels of stress increase, for example when poverty, poor housing, discrimination or a relationship with a violent partner are suffered.

It does not mean that, because a parent experienced abuse or neglect as a child, he or she will maltreat their own children if the early traumatic experience is psychologically 'resolved'. Parents who are able to reflect on and mentalise how their own difficult relationship experiences have affected them develop what Main (1995) refers to as 'earned' security. This ability to recognise the nature and origins of one's own psychological strengths and weaknesses is often achieved in the context of a relationship in which the partner was emotionally available, protective and cognitively attuned. A thoughtful teacher, an emotionally responsive foster carer or protective partner in adulthood can help someone with a traumatic history reflect on and make sense of their difficult background and its psychological legacy. The ability to develop the capacity to mentalise predicts increased resilience and good enough parenting.

However, parents with 'unresolved' states of mind with respect to attachment, and who remain psychologically and behaviourally vulnerable, pose significant developmental risks for their children. Children whose caregivers are the direct cause of their distress find it particularly difficult to organise an attachment strategy that increases feelings of safety and reduces feelings of upset.

Hostile attachment figures frighten and menacingly threaten, physically or sexually abuse and emotionally abandon their children when they face the stressful, dysregulating experience of dealing with their child's attachment needs.

Helpless attachment figures behave in a frightened, distressed, neglectful manner when faced with their children's needs and anxieties. Some carers switch unpredictably between hostile and helpless states of mind.

Helpless/hostile caregivers are the source of their children's fear. And, as the children's attachment figure, they are the ostensible solution to that fear. In these out-of-control states of mind, the ability of hostile/helpless caregivers to be emotionally available and mentalise their children's needs goes 'off-line'. Whether the caregiving is hostile or helpless, children experience further anxiety and fear when faced with their parents' agitated state. Children try to 'escape' the source of the fear (the abusive/neglectful attachment figure) at the same time as their activated attachment system triggers an 'approach' response to the attachment figure in the form of attachment behaviour. Behaviourally, the child finds himself or herself in an impossible situation: escape and approach behaviours are simultaneously activated. Under these conditions, children find it difficult to organise an attachment strategy that increases the carer's availability, hence the classification: 'disorganised' attachment (Main and Solomon 1990).

When faced with hostile/helpless (that is, abusive/neglectful, or frightening/frightened) caregiving, disorganised children's attachment systems remain highly activated, their distress escalates, and their emotions catapult into a state of hyperaroused dysregulation. The risk of children developing disorganised attachments is highest in cases of physical abuse; sexual abuse; neglect; parental depression and substance abuse; domestic violence; and multiple placements (Howe 2005).

Much of the mental time and energy of disorganised children is spent trying to increase feelings of safety, security and control. Being the cause of their children's distress, and being caught up in their own anxiety and dysregulation, hostile/helpless parents fail to perceive and emotionally attune with their children's distressed mental states at the very time the children most need to feel safe, recognised, understood, contained and regulated. Children therefore fail to develop coherent models and mental representations of their own and other people's psychological make-up. They find it difficult to regulate their own arousal or deal reflectively with their own needs. It is this group of children who are most at risk of developing behavioural problems (including aggression) and mental health difficulties, and being placed in foster or adoptive care.

With maturation, disorganised children do manage to develop fragile and more coherent representations of themselves as less helpless and less at the mercy of others. With carers who are unavailable and frightening, children begin to take control of their own safety and needs. This results in the development of various 'controlling' behaviours and strategies, including compulsive compliance, compulsive caregiving and compulsive self-reliance. In effect, the child tries to out-manoeuvre the parent and so control their parent's availability by switching between threatening, aggressive, humiliating, disarming, helpless and vulnerable behaviours (Crittenden 1995, 1997; Howe 2005). Controlling strategies represent desperate attempts by abused and neglected children to take charge of their own safety, wellbeing and regulation. It is safer to look after oneself; to control rather than be controlled. They display a range of behaviours that suggest that psychologically they are in frightened 'survival mode' for much of the time. They certainly do not trust primary caregivers to keep them safe or engage with them in an emotionally attuned, sensitive, containing and responsive way.

Disorganised, controlling children experience themselves as people who can generate anger, violence, distress and panic in others. These experiences produce a self that lacks integration and coherence, a self that can feel powerful and bad, invulnerable yet unlovable, alone and frightened. As a result, disturbed mixtures of low self-esteem, recklessness, hypervigilance and aggression can appear (Crittenden 1996). These are children who have difficulty recognising and understanding their own and other people's affective states. They are unpopular with their peers. They easily attribute negative intentions to other people's behaviour. Levels of social understanding and competence are typically low. As a result they show both high levels of aggression and social withdrawal, and behavioural and mental health problems. Many children who attack or sexually abuse other children and animals, who show extreme conduct disorders and perform very poorly educationally, can be understood within the dynamics that define these disorganised/controlling patterns of attachment (Cicchetti 1989; Crittenden 1996, 1997; Howe 2005; Lyons-Ruth 1996).

Nevertheless, it must be remembered that even children whose parents are violent and abusive develop and show attachment behaviour in the presence of their caregivers, albeit of a distinctive, insecure kind. It is the *type* and *quality* of attachment behaviour that is of interest, and not its perceived presence or absence, strength or weakness. Only in extreme, special cases of deprivation (institutional nurseries, profound neglect, multiple serial caregiving) might we expect to find children who show no attachment behaviour under conditions of distress and anxiety. Children who suffer disorders of non-attachment are at elevated risk of behavioural and mental health problems.

Assessing parenting capacity

Whether considering the mentalising capacity of caregivers, cultural contexts, child factors or peer groups, we have to remind ourselves that children's development takes place in and interacts with a continuously changing psychosocial environment. Attachment therefore has to be woven into a dynamic ecological model of children's psychosocial development. However, although an ecological-transactional perspective does not privilege any one factor, developmental outcomes achieved early on in the transactional dynamic, by virtue of being early, will interact with and influence later stages.

> [The] hypothesis is not that only early experience is important, or even that early experience is more important than later experience. Rather, the hypothesis is that early experience, because of its very place in the developmental course, has some special importance for the development of the person. (Sroufe *et al.* 2005, p.10)

A child's attachment with his or her caregiver is one such early stage event. Cicchetti and Valentino (2006) argue that:

> From an ecological-transactional perspective, the primary attachment relationship remains a salient developmental issue across the lifespan, as it lays the foundation for representational models and subsequently shapes an individual's selection, engagement, and interpretation of all future experiences, including the ability to successfully resolve ensuing developmental tasks…including parenting. (Cicchetti and Valentino 2006, p.148)

The quality of care provided by parents is also a product of their own developmental and relationship history. Therefore, the psychological resources and behavioural responses that parents bring to the demands of caregiving can be understood as the product of their own relationship and developmental and environmental experiences. If we are to make sense of parents' capacities to care and protect, we need to consider both their childhood *and* adult relationship histories. This is particularly important when conducting assessments of parenting capacities. Viewing children's development transactionally leads Sroufe *et al.* (2005) to believe that:

> Assessments of the parents' own developmental histories…have notable predictive power…the stresses and other surrounding circumstances (e.g., violent neighbour-hoods, substandard housing, and frequent moves) that impact on parents may also directly impact on the child. (Sroufe *et al.* 2005, p.18)

To the extent that a parent's own caregiving problems are a product of their own history of being cared for, social workers need to be extra thoughtful about placing children with other family members, including their grandparents. This cautionary note is not meant to exclude such practices, but it does demand that the analysis and assessment of parents and their caregiving is conducted in the light of a full and well-understood family psychoso-cial history and should form part of the assessment of family history and functioning.

Intervention

A developmental attachment perspective, supported by a good deal of international and cross-cultural research, can help social workers to make sense of complex and turbu-lent cases in which there are concerns about the developmental wellbeing and safety of children (Howe 1995; Howe *et al.* 1999). The approach also sheds a powerful light on adult psychosocial behaviour, particularly in situations where there are emotional and attachment-related issues (Main 1995). These include relationships with sexual partners, one's own children, social workers and other practitioners. The theory also helps workers to understand their own emotional and psychological behaviours in difficult and demand-ing situations. This is a reminder that, if practitioners are to function sensitively, astutely and safely, they need good-quality supervision and case analysis, as discussed in Chapter 8.

The increasing stability of the internal working model means that an individual's behavioural and relationship style becomes more predictable, self-confirming and dif-ficult to shift. However, change remains possible at any time across the lifespan. New experiences always have the capacity to alter people's representations and expectations of the worthiness and effectiveness of the self and the availability of others. Support and understanding, provided within the context of a confiding relationship, has repeatedly been found to promote psychological wellbeing, esteem, confidence and resilience (for example, Brown and Harris 1978). Improved sensitivity, mentalisation, emotional attune-ment, mind-mindedness and psychological availability form the basis of most attachment-based interventions (Atkinson and Goldberg 2004; Howe *et al.* 1999; Main 1995). By altering people's experiences of close relationships, insecure internal working models, in which the self and others are represented negatively, can be changed. For example, parents might be helped to improve their caregiving behaviour so that they behave with greater sensitivity, attunement and interest.

The survival strategies developed by disorganised/controlling children are very partial, incomplete and brittle. They can easily break down under stress leaving the child once more frightened, angry, sad and highly dysregulated. The therapeutic aim for these children (and their parents) is to help them feel safe enough to recognise, acknowledge and process their emotions, both at the psychological and physiological level. They only feel safe when they are in anxious control, but this strategy denies them experiences designed to help them engage emotionally and psychologically with caregivers, and look at, understand and handle their own and other people's minds.

The ability of child welfare practitioners, such as social workers, to remain available and consistent provides families with a secure professional relationship within which reflection and understanding might increase. Foster carers, teachers and peer groups might also offer relationships in which children and adults develop more secure and positive views of themselves and others (for example, see Schofield and Beek 2006; Wilson *et al.* 2008). An attachment perspective recognises that relationships are where things can go wrong in the first place, but equally relationships are generally the place where things are eventually put right.

Summary

Attachment theory offers a compelling set of ideas about how children develop close relationships with their main caregivers, how they attempt to adapt and survive in their particular caregiving environment, and how their behaviours and coping strategies can be understood as functional within the caregiving settings which gave rise to them. However, to the extent that adaptive behaviours require children to distort, deny and omit information, their ability to develop coherent, integrated and balanced mental representations of themselves and others is frustrated. Behaviours which appear functional within the parent/child relationship, therefore, may be dysfunctional in other social contexts such as the nursery, classroom and peer group.

A lifespan approach is now taken to attachment theory. There is great interest in the continuities and discontinuities that affect attachment organisations and internal working models from childhood to adulthood. In their attempts to promote children's welfare, social workers and other practitioners seek to disconfirm children's insecure working models, either by improving the quality of their close relationships with parents and peers, or by providing them with new caregiving relationships in substitute families.

Attachment behaviour is triggered by feelings of distress, particularly where attachment-related issues are present. It occurs in most emotionally demanding situations, and it occurs in adults as well as children. Day in, day out, child welfare practitioners (and their agencies) practise in emotionally demanding environments which trigger characteristic coping styles, defensive strategies and adaptive behaviours. Underpinning all practice, using a developmental attachment perspective, is the provision of relationships in which the other is experienced as available and responsive, consistent and understanding. If social workers are to offer and promote these kinds of relationships, their capacity to reflect on their own functioning has to be maintained (Fonagy *et al.* 1991). As well as the role of good supervision, agency support is essential to this process.

Recommended reading

Bowlby, J. (1988) *A Secure Base: Clinical Applications of Attachment Theory.* London: Routledge.

Cassidy, J. and Shaver, P. (1999) *Handbook of Attachment.* New York: Guilford Press.

Heard, D. and Lake, B. (1999) *The Challenge of Attachment for Caregiving.* London: Routledge.

Howe, D. (2005) *Child Abuse and Neglect: Attachment, Development and Intervention.* Basingstoke: Palgrave Macmillan.

Howe, D., Brandon, M., Hinings, D. and Schofield, G. (1999) *Attachment Theory, Child Maltreatment and Family Support: A Practice and Assessment Model.* Basingstoke: Macmillan.

References

Ainsworth, M. and Wittig, D. (1969) 'Attachment and Exploratory Behavior of One-year-olds in a Strange Situation.' In B. Foss (ed.) *Determinants of Infant Behavior IV.* London: Methuen.

Ainsworth, M.D.S., Blehar, M., Aters, E. and Wall, S. (1978) *Patterns of Attachment: A Psychological Study of the Strange Situation.* Hillsdale, NJ: Lawrence Erlbaum.

Atkinson, L. and Goldberg, S. (eds) (2004) *Attachment Issues in Psychopathology and Intervention.* Mahweh, NJ: Lawrence Erlbaum Associates.

Belsky, J. and Rovine, M. (1987) 'Temperament and attachment security in the strange situation: an empirical rapprochement.' *Child Development 58,* 3, 787–795.

Bowlby, J. (1973) *Attachment and Loss, Volume II: Separation, Anxiety and Anger.* London: Hogarth.

Bowlby, J. (1979) *The Making and Breaking of Affectional Bonds.* London: Tavistock.

Bowlby, J. (1980) *Attachment and Loss, Volume III: Loss, Sadness and Depression.* London: Hogarth.

Bowlby, J. (1988) *A Secure Base: Clinical Applications of Attachment Theory.* London: Routledge.

Brown, G. and Harris, T. (1978) *Social Origins of Depression.* London: Tavistock.

Cicchetti, D. (1989) 'How Research on Child Maltreatment has Informed the Study of Child Development.' In D. Cicchetti and V. Carlson (eds) *Child Maltreatment.* New York, NY: Cambridge University Press.

Cicchetti, D. and Valentino, K. (2006) 'An Ecological-transactional Perspective on Child Maltreatment: Failure of the Average Expectable Environment and its Influence on Child Development.' In D. Cicchetti and D.J. Cohen (eds) *Developmental Psychopathology,* 2nd edn. Hoboken, NY: John Wiley.

Crittenden, P. (1995) 'Attachment and Psychopathology.' In S. Goldberg, R. Muir and J. Kerr (eds) *Attachment Theory: Social, Developmental and Clinical Perspectives.* Hillsdale, NJ: Analytic Press.

Crittenden, P. (1996) 'Research on Maltreating Families: Implications for Intervention.' In J.N. Briere, L. Berliner, J. Bulkley and C.A. Jenny (eds) *The APSAC Handbook on Child Maltreatment.* Thousand Oaks, CA: Sage.

Crittenden, P. (1997) 'Patterns of Attachment and Sexual Behavior: Risk of Dysfunction versus Opportunity for Creative Integration.' In L. Atkinson and K. Zucker (eds) *Attachment and Psychopathology.* New York, NY: Guilford Press.

Crittenden, P. (1999) 'Danger and Development: The Organization of Self-protective Strategies.' In J. Vondra and D. Barnett (eds) *Atypical Attachment in Infancy and Early Childhood among Children at Developmental Risk.* Monographs of the Society for Research in Child Development, Series No. 258, 64, 3, 145–171.

Fonagy, P., Gergely, G., Jurist, E. and Target, M. (2002) *Affect Regulation, Mentalization and the Development of the Self.* New York, NY: Other Press.

Fonagy, P., Steele, H., Moran, G., Steele, M. and Higgit, A. (1991) 'The capacity for understanding mental states: the reflective self in parent and child and its significance for security of attachment.' *Infant Mental Health Journal 12,* 3, 200–217.

Goldberg, S. (2000) *Attachment and Development.* London: Arnold.

Howe, D. (1995) *Attachment Theory for Social Work Practice.* Basingstoke: Macmillan.

Howe, D. (2005) *Child Abuse and Neglect: Attachment, Development and Intervention.* Basingstoke: Palgrave Macmillan.

Howe, D. (2006a) 'Disabled children, parent–child interaction and attachment.' *Child and Family Social Work 11,* 2, 95–106.

Howe, D. (2006b) 'Disabled children, attachment and maltreatment.' *British Journal of Social Work 36,* 5, 743–760.

Howe, D. (2008) *The Emotionally Intelligent Social Worker.* Basingstoke: Palgrave Macmillan.

Howe, D., Brandon, M., Hinings, D. and Schofield, G. (1999) *Attachment Theory, Child Maltreatment and Family Support: A Practice and Assessment Model.* Basingstoke: Macmillan.

Lyons-Ruth, K. (1996) 'Attachment relationships among children with aggressive behavior problems: the role of disorganised early attachment patterns.' *Journal of Consulting and Clinical Psychology 64,* 1, 64–73.

Main, M. (1995) 'Recent Studies in Attachment: Overview, with Selected Implications for Clinical Work.' In S. Goldberg, R. Muir and J. Kerr (eds) *Attachment Theory: Social, Developmental and Clinical Perspectives.* Hillsdale, NJ: The Analytic Press.

Main, M. and Solomon, J. (1990) 'Procedures for Identifying Infants as Disorganized/Disoriented during the Ainsworth Strange Situation.' In M. Greenberg, D. Cicchetti and E.M. Cummings (eds) *Attachment during the Preschool Years: Theory, Research and Intervention.* Chicago, IL: University of Chicago Press.

Meins, E., Fernyhough, C., Fradley, E. and Tuckey, M. (2001) 'Rethinking maternal sensitivity: mothers' comments on infants' mental processes predict security of attachment.' *Journal of Child Psychology and Psychiatry 42,* 5, 637–648.

Prior, V. and Glaser, D. (2006) *Understanding Attachment and Attachment Disorders.* London: Jessica Kingsley Publishers.

Schofield, G. and Beek, M. (2006) *Attachment Handbook for Foster Care and Adoption.* London: BAAF.

Schore, A. (2001) 'Effects of secure attachment relationships on right brain development, affect regulation, and infant mental health.' *Infant Mental Health Journal 22,* 1–2, 7–66.

Solomon, J. and George, C. (1999) 'The Measurement of Attachment Security in Infancy and Childhood.' In J. Cassidy and P. Shaver (eds) *Handbook of Attachment: Theory, Research and Clinical Applications.* New York, NY: Guilford Press.

Sroufe, L.A., Egeland, B., Carlson, E. and Collins, W.A. (2005) *The Development of the Person.* New York, NY: Guilford Press.

Susman-Stillman, A., Kalkoske, M., Egeland, B. and Waldman, I. (1996) 'Infant temperament and maternal sensitivity as predictors of attachment security.' *Infant Behavior and Development 19,* 1, 33–47.

Trevarthen, C. and Aitkin, K. (2001) 'Infant intersubjectivity: research, theory, and clinical applications.' *Journal of Child Psychology and Psychiatry 42,* 1, 3–48.

van den Boom, D. (1994) 'The influence of temperament and mothering on attachment and exploration: an experimental manipulation of sensitive responsiveness among lower-class mothers with irritable infants.' *Child Development 65,* 5, 1457–1477.

Vaughn, B.E. and Bost, K.K. (1999) 'Attachment and Temperament: Redundant, Independent, or Interacting Influences on Interpersonal Adaptation and Personality Development?' In J. Cassidy and P. Shaver (eds) *Handbook of Attachment.* New York, NY: Guilford Press.

Wilson, K., Ruch, G., Lymbery, M. and Cooper, A. (2008) *Social Work: An Introduction to Contemporary Practice.* Harlow: Pearson.

CHAPTER 12

Making Assessment Work for Children with Complex Needs

Ruth Marchant

Ensuring equality of opportunity does not mean that all children are treated the same. It does mean understanding and working sensitively and knowledgeably with diversity to identify the particular issues for a child and his or her family, taking account of their experiences and their family context.

(From the Framework for the Assessment of Children in Need and their Families, p.12, 1.43)

This chapter considers:

- complexity: what it means
- the context for assessments
- the role of assessment
    - value-based assessments
    - lead person models
    - integrated working
- the domains of the Assessment Framework
- safeguarding issues for children with complex needs
- involving children in the assessment process.

Introduction

This chapter aims to support high quality assessment work with children whose needs are complex, by bringing together recent research, practice examples and current guidance within a clear value base. The following principles underpin the chapter:

- Children with complex needs have the same fundamental rights and basic needs as all children.

- All children have the right to an assessment which is responsive to their individual needs, however unusual or complex these may be.

- Skilled assessment should make things simpler and not more complex: clarifying needs so that they can be met in ways that empower and enable children and families.

- The more complex a child's needs or situation, the more competent and robust the assessment process must be.

- Getting things right for children with complex needs will improve our practice with all children and families, strengthening our ability to respond to children as unique individuals and developing integrated working.

These ideas have been strongly influenced by children, young people and their families, particularly through Triangle's consultative groups. The quotes and examples are from these groups, unless referenced otherwise.

Definitions of complexity are briefly outlined, and models of integrated working are considered, alongside the current legislative and guidance context. Key issues for this group of children across the three domains used in the *Framework for the Assessment of Children in Need and their Families* (Assessment Framework) (Department of Health *et al.* 2000) are then explored: understanding children's developmental needs; assessing parenting capacity; and the crucial importance of considering wider family and environmental factors. Guidance is given on specific safeguarding issues for children with complex needs and strategies outlined for involving them as active partners in the assessment process.

Defining complexity

The dictionary definition of 'complex' has two sources: complicated and compound (made up of many). There are no absolute criteria for deciding which children have 'complex needs': complexity is a measure of the competence of families and services as much as anything inherent in a child. Where a child's needs are skilfully assessed and met they may no longer be seen as complex. As a 13-year-old with multiple impairments and major healthcare needs put it: 'there's nothing complicated about me'.

In general, the threshold for complexity has shifted upwards over the years and is likely to continue to shift as increasing numbers of children live with complex needs, and as services and communities become more competent at meeting these needs.

Currently, government guidance describes a continuum of needs and services, with children who have complex needs located at the top end of this continuum, as a subset of children with additional needs (Cm 5860 2003).[1] The current definition of complexity relates to the multiplicity and chronicity of need and the involvement of multiple agencies:

> Children with complex needs have a number of discrete needs – relating to their health, education, welfare, development, home environment and so on – that require additional support from more than one agency. Their needs are often chronic and may be life-long. Different needs tend to interact, exacerbating their impact on the child's development and well-being. (Department for Education and Skills 2007, p.37)

As currently defined and discussed in Chapter 2, all children whose health and development would be impaired without the provision of services meet the criteria for assessment as children in need under section 17 of the Children Act 1989. This includes children who are the subject of a child protection plan; looked after children; care leavers; children with severe and complex special educational needs; young offenders; children diagnosed with significant mental health problems; and children with complex disabilities or complex health needs.

This chapter focuses primarily on the last group in this list – children with complex disabilities or complex health needs – but has wider relevance for other children who require multi-agency support. Also, there is a high degree of overlap between different groups of children with complex needs. For example, disabled children are significantly over-represented in the populations of looked after children[2] and young offenders[3] and research tells us that a significantly higher proportion of disabled children should have a child protection plan,[4] although it appears that this is rarely the case.[5]

The context for assessments

The policy context for children with complex needs is rapidly evolving. This follows many years of research documenting high levels of unmet need, duplicated assessments, poor information and fragmented, unco-ordinated service provision (Audit Commission 2003;

---

1 Children with additional needs is a broad term used to describe all those children at risk of poor outcomes as defined by the Green Paper, *Every Child Matters*. An estimated 20–30% of children have additional needs at some point in their childhood, including those identified as being 'in need' under the Children Act 1989, those with special educational needs under the Education Act 1996, disabled children, those with mental health difficulties, and others whose needs may not have been formally identified but who may, nonetheless, be at risk of poor outcomes.

2 Disabled children are disproportionately represented within the looked after population, making up 10% of all children in care, and only around 5% of the overall population.

3 See Herrington *et al.* 2007, p.14, for a recent summary of the research.

4 A retrospective US study of 50,000 children found an unequivocal link between childhood maltreatment and disability, with disabled children being 3.4 times more likely to be abused (a 31% prevalence rate against 9% for non-disabled children) (Sullivan and Knutson 2000).

5 Some 2% of disabled children in need are on the child protection registers in comparison with 8% of the general population of children in need (Cooke 2000). Concerns about the abuse of disabled children are 50% less likely to be case conferenced (Cooke and Standen 2002).

Beresford 1994; Birth Defects Foundation 2007; Commission for Social Care Inspection 2007; Marchant *et al.* 2007; Mukherjee *et al.* 1999). We now have some clear standards about what *ought* to be happening for this group of children and their families:

> Co-ordinated, high-quality child and family-centred services which are based on assessed needs, which promote social inclusion and, where possible, which enable them and their families to live ordinary lives. (Department of Health and Department for Education and Skills 2004, National Service Framework Standard 8)

We also have a range of approaches designed to improve practice, particularly through integrated multi-agency working. The Government recently noted that disabled children – because they often need support from a range of services – should be benefiting 'even more than most' from the reforms of the *Every Child Matters* programme (HM Treasury 2007b). The flip side of this is that, in many areas, disabled children and children with complex needs are paving the way for integrated working, and being the first in line is not always easy. Certainly, the Common Assessment Framework, the Integrated Children's System and the Early Support Programme[6] all have the potential to significantly change provision for children with complex needs.

This chapter focuses primarily on assessments undertaken under the Children Act 1989 (which contains a power but no duty to assess unless it is suspected a child is at risk of significant harm) using the *Framework for the Assessment of Children in Need and their Families* (Department of Health *et al.* 2000). However, it is important to remember that disabled children and their families are now entitled to assessment under a baffling array of legislation and guidance: the Chronically Sick and Disabled Persons Act 1970; the Disabled Persons (Services, Consultation and Representation) Act 1986; the NHS and Community Care Act 1990; the Carers (Recognition and Services) Act 1995; and the Carers and Disabled Children's Act 2000. The *Framework for the Assessment of Children in Need and their Families* was one of the first statutory guidance documents to include specific practice guidance on assessing disabled children (Department of Health 2000).

The role of assessment

Assessment is critical in identifying and meeting children's needs. The more complex the child's needs or situation, the more competent and robust the assessment process should be. Assessment quality is particularly important given the complex service system and wider societal values that children with complex needs and families have to navigate. Skilled assessment should make things simpler and not more complicated: this means understanding and clarifying children and families' needs so that these needs can be met.

Children with complex needs have the same fundamental rights and basic needs as all children. When planning an assessment the same principles, the same guidance and the

---

6　The Early Support Programme, set up in 2002, is a partnership between the Government and the voluntary sector to improve the quality, consistency and co-ordination of services for disabled children and their families. Originally piloted from birth to 3, it is being rolled out for disabled children in 2007–8 from birth to 5 across the country.

same laws apply. There is no need to begin from a different place. However, children with complex needs and their families swim against many tides and it is essential to recognise this in the assessment process. Crucially, the assessment must address the child and family's wider situation, as well as the child's individual needs, and consider the interaction between all of these.

When using the Assessment Framework with this group of children, a holistic perspective and a coherent approach over time are crucial. Children with complex needs and their families require properly co-ordinated assessments that enable support to be delivered as soon as they need it, to respond quickly when circumstances change, and to identify needs at key transition points in their lives (Boddy *et al.* 2006).

Assessments do not take place in a value-free context. For children with complex needs and their families, the very word 'assessment' may have difficult connotations. For example, the *Oxford Dictionary* definition of 'assess' is: 'To fix or determine the amount of; to estimate officially the value of.' Some children with complex needs and their families may, therefore, approach assessments with a degree of apprehension, knowing that some children can be seen as 'worth less' than other children.

Most children with complex needs will have had extensive previous experiences of assessment, as will their families. At least some of these experiences are likely to have been within a pathologising, deficit model where the child was 'tested' against some concept of normality. Children can be very clear about the focus of this kind of assessment and its impact:

> It's always about what's wrong with me…they're only interested in the bits of me that don't work. They want to see what I can't do. (11-year-old girl with severe physical impairments)

Families, understandably, can also find assessments difficult and stressful:

> I found assessment meetings a nightmare. I felt I was listening to people talk about somebody other than the child I lived with. After the first assessment at the child development centre I went home and cried for four days… (Murray and Penman 1996, p.11)

Value-based assessment

In this context, values matter. Part of the challenge in assessment work with children with complex needs is the confusing and oppressive context in which such assessments take place. As the Government has recently noted, it has 'traditionally' been the case that disabled children are likely to have poorer outcomes across a range of indicators compared to their non-disabled peers, including lower educational attainment, poorer access to health services and therefore poorer health outcomes, more difficult transitions to adulthood and poorer employment outcomes (HM Treasury and Department for Education and Skills 2007a).

Assessments of children with complex needs cannot be value-free on these issues. Low expectations are dangerous starting points for any assessment. Our perceptions of what it means to be disabled will affect our approach to assessment. It is helpful to actively explore our own attitudes and understanding, and to be aware of our own prejudices, fears and stereotypes. Practitioners working together to complete an assessment using the Assessment Framework need to share core values that are explicit and transparent, particularly about the equality and the rights of all children. Clear guidance, training and skilled supervision are essential in maintaining clarity about these core values. Westcott and Cross list some questions which might be used to trigger a personal review of workers' attitudes (1996, pp.132–136). Part of this exploration needs to be a consideration of our own power with disabled children, both as adults and (often) as part of the non-disabled world.

The absence of explicit values can lead to a dangerous tolerance of poor care and damaging experiences. As Read *et al.* note: 'in almost all aspects of their lives, experiences that would be regarded as too narrow, unsettling, exclusionary or damaging for a non-disabled child have often not even seemed to require justification for their disabled peers' (2006, p.33).

Patterns of care that would generally cause serious concern are not unusual for children with complex needs. For example, Callum at the age of seven sleeps in four different places every month: residential school; home; link family; and respite care unit. He also has frequent hospital admissions. With most seven-year-olds, such a fragmented pattern of care would cause serious concern.

Similarly, in an average week, Shona has more than 25 adults involved in her everyday support and care: her mum and dad, three home care workers, two community nurses, a taxi driver and escort, a teacher and three classroom assistants, two lunchtime helpers, a physiotherapist and assistant and a team of eight day and night staff at a residential respite care unit. There are another 16 professionals involved on an occasional basis. Again, such discontinuity would cause very serious concern for most children, but is often accepted without question for children with complex needs.

'Lead person' models

In recognition of the historical difficulties encountered when assessing children with complex needs, *lead person* models are increasingly being developed for this group of children (Children's Workforce Development Council 2007a, 2007b). The lead person role may be combined with a primary practitioner role, or 'designated', where people are employed specifically to carry out the lead person role. The lead person may be variously known as a keyworker, care manager, lead professional, lead practitioner or care co-ordinator depending on the nature of the assessment. Those in existing roles, such as SENCO (special educational needs co-ordinator) or named clinician, may act as lead professionals in relation to the Common Assessment Framework, whereas social workers take on this role with regard to the Assessment Framework.

The lead role might simply involve accessing information or being a single point of contact as, for example, in relation to ContactPoint[7]. However, it might involve complet-

---

7   ContactPoint is a new database of basic information for all children in England (see www.everychild-matters.gov.org/deliveryingservices/contactpoint/about).

ing a core assessment which includes supporting the child and family in navigating the system and accessing services; ensuring that interventions are well planned, reviewed and delivered; providing co-ordination; and preventing date clashes and duplicated interventions. It may also involve advocacy, monitoring, safeguarding responsibilities and personal support. The competence and confidence of practitioners has a major impact on the success of the role.

Such lead person models represent a significant step forward but are not in themselves enough to ensure that all children's needs are met, particularly where those needs are more complex or where children's situations render them more vulnerable.

Integrated working

The Government is promoting integrated or multi-agency working through the Children Act 2004. However, there is a recognition of the 'immense challenges' presented by the *Every Child Matters* programme in this regard (Siraj-Blatchford *et al.* 2007). These challenges are particularly relevant when working with children with complex needs. Integrated, collaborative multidisciplinary working is designed to address the unco-ordinated support many families have experienced in the past, where 'everyone does their own sweet thing' (parents quoted by Limbrick 2004).

Lead person models are not enough to produce integrated practice, and can just shift the problem one step away from the family, such that everyone continues to do their own sweet thing but someone other than the child and family knows about it. To achieve properly joined-up provision for children and families, attention must be given to the complexity and contested nature of roles in multidisciplinary teams, including issues of location, information sharing and professional identities (Frost and Robinson 2007). New skills must be developed in organising and managing multi-professional teams, supporting professionals as they learn to adapt to new roles and responsibilities, and learning how to share professional knowledge and expertise (Anning *et al.* 2007).

Of the emerging models, *Team around the Child* (TAC) is one of the best established, involving different practitioners collaborating closely to support an individual child. The model does not imply a multi-disciplinary team located together or working together all the time; rather, it suggests a group of professionals working together only when needed to help one particular child. TACs have thus been described as *virtual* teams because practitioners work with a range of different colleagues at different times to support different children (Limbrick 2005).

TACs are typically small (three to five people) and place the emphasis firmly on the needs of the child, rather than on organisations or service providers. A keyworker (or lead professional) facilitates each individual team, and parents are equal members of the team. Interestingly, children are not yet considered members of the team, but this may be because the TAC model has evolved with babies and very young children. Limbrick (2005) notes most parents feel the TAC approach is just common sense.

Common sense is unfortunately not always common, and many children and families continue to experience fragmented and disjointed services and assessment processes. The imbalance of power between different professionals and the vulnerability of children with complex needs has led some to propose an enforced teamwork approach. As Limbrick (2004) puts it:

> The plurality of needs of these children and families, and the influence these needs have on each other, disqualify any single practitioner, no matter how well trained, experienced and motivated, from acting alone in the provision of support. (Limbrick 2004, p.2)

Parents have traditionally been expected to act as advocates for their disabled children, and it is still often felt that parents are likely to be the child's best advocates. For many children this is undoubtedly the case, and most parents will also take into account the child's own views and feelings. However, informal advocacy usually means the adult acting on their perception of the best interests of the child, rather than representing the child's own view. As Russell (1996, p.124) notes, 'parents do not necessarily agree amongst themselves and they certainly do not always agree with their children'.

Children with complex needs who live away from home, like all looked after children, have the right to independent advocacy. Some recent approaches suggest also consulting with disabled adults about what disabled children need both in terms of individual and collective advocacy (see Marchant and Cole forthcoming; Westcott and Cross 1996).

Assessing children with complex needs using the Assessment Framework

High quality assessment work with children with complex needs requires integrated working and clarity of roles. It also requires consideration of key issues for this group of children and their families across the three domains of the *Framework for the Assessment of Children in Need and their Families* (Department of Health *et al.* 2000).

The child's developmental needs

A child's development will be affected not only by their impairment or condition, but also by the life that they lead, including their experience of disabling barriers and social exclusion. When a child has complex needs, understanding concerns about their development can be particularly challenging. There is some guidance within the Assessment Framework in relation to developmental delay and variation:

> Disabled children, including those with learning disabilities, may have a different rate of progress across the various developmental dimensions. Many disabled children will have quite individual patterns of development, for example a child with autism may acquire some skills ahead of the usual milestones but may never develop some communication skills. (Department of Health *et al.* 2000, p.10, 1.36)

One of the functions of assessment is to identify and clarify a child's needs. As a first step towards this, the direct impact of a child's condition or impairment should be clearly described in ways that are accessible and respectful. It is important not to make assumptions about what an impairment means to a child and family. Practitioners should aim to understand the impact from the child's perspective – what it means for this child and family in this situation and at this stage in their development – rather than in the abstract.

Investing time and care to avoid making assumptions at an early stage, in partnership with children and families, will provide a sound foundation for an assessment. These two questions are a useful starting point – what is the child's condition and what does that mean for them? For example:

> Jon has autism and learning disability, which means that he finds communication and social interaction extremely difficult.

> Sula has cerebral palsy affecting all her limbs, which means that her movement is extremely restricted.

Starting points like this give a clear basis from which to explore the impact of disabling barriers and keep these separate from the direct impact of the child's impairment; for example:

> Jon has not attended school for more than a year, which has limited his opportunities to learn and to make friends, and also added to the pressures on his family.

> Sula's family home is unsuitable for her needs, and the family have been waiting seven months for an assessment of their housing needs. This is creating significant risk for the whole family.

This kind of clarity is essential if practitioners are to avoid implying wrongly that all of a family's difficulties are an inevitable result of the child's needs. We know that children with extremely complex needs and their families can live positive lives, if appropriate support is provided. We also know that children and families consistently rate their lives and their health more positively than professionals (Nuffield Council on Bioethics 2006, p.68).

The same clarity is needed when considering specific needs. For example, children with learning disabilities, autism or language delay face an increased risk of developing challenging behaviour. However, this increase is not necessarily a direct result of the impairments; it may be a consequence of the way in which others respond to these impairments. For example, these children often also face disrupted relationships; frequent investigations; repeated rejection; low expectations; and poor social opportunities. The untangling of the impairment and the disability can be very helpful for young people; for example, 'You are up against two things: number one you have autism, number two the world isn't set up very well for people who have autism.' This is an important assessment task.

Almost all parents and carers want what is best for their children, but the more complex a child's needs the less there is likely to be consensus on what is 'best'. Exemplars and pathways can help by giving clear guidance on what ought to be happening at different stages of a child's life. For example, many children with complex needs have developmental programmes in place at home, at school and in other settings. Part of the function of an assessment is to make sure that such approaches are coherent, consistent and compatible so that all those who care for, work with and play with the child work together to meet the child's needs or at least do not work against each other.

Issues around treatment, or the withholding of treatment, may be part of the focus of an assessment. Clarity about who can give consent, assent and dissent becomes crucial. A useful guiding principle for assessment is that children's particular, additional or 'special' needs should always be met in ways that least disrupt their ordinary needs. Sometimes the concerns are not so much about the actual 'treatment' the child receives but the knock-on impact it has on their day-to-day lives, perhaps spending long periods of time away from family and friends or missing out on time to play or relax.

The following are drawn from a list of questions suggested for evaluating treatments for autism, but can be more generally applied to assessments where there is disagreement about appropriate treatment:

- How long has the therapy been used?
- What research is available?
- For whom does this approach work best?
- What alternative interventions might be tried?
- How has the decision been made that this therapy is appropriate for this child?

Particular caution is needed where there are no individual assessments, no evidence base and no formal outcome measures for a treatment (Howlin 1998).

Children's views are essential in setting developmental goals. In wide-ranging consultations with children and young people with complex needs about what matters to them, they consistently give the most attention to people, especially family and friends.[8] This suggests that skills in making and keeping relationships should be high on the developmental agenda, which is rarely the case.

> When I was little I spent hours and days learning to use special equipment to feed myself. It took me four times as long to eat my meals. I would much rather have someone to feed me, then they can talk to me. But it's only now I can say it. (15-year-old with severe physical impairments)

Parenting capacity

The concept of good enough parenting can be particularly challenging to apply with families of children with complex needs. Some children undoubtedly need more parenting or more skilled parenting than others; some children need 'intensive' parenting for much longer than others. Some children are parented in a far less supportive social context than others (see Marchant and Jones 2003 for further discussion). Parenting a child with

---

8   Triangle has consulted with more than 2500 disabled children and young people and there has been amazing consistency across time, area, age and impairment. What matters most is people: friends, family, workers.

complex needs is, by definition, likely to be more complicated, more time-consuming, less familiar, more anxiety provoking, physically harder and emotionally more difficult.

Knowing just what is involved in a child's day-to-day care can operate powerfully on our expectations about what is good enough parenting. One possible consequence of realising the demands is a downward shift in our assessment standards, for example lowering expectations of what constitutes reasonable parenting. The pressures of parenting a child with complex needs can be quite different and very demanding. The more complex the child's needs the higher the risk of skewed expectations and standards. Again, this is where a clear and explicit value base is essential: we should not expect less for certain groups of children.

Considering the support available to the family in meeting their child's needs is an important part of any assessment. Usual sources of support available to most parents are often less available to parents of children with complex needs. The risk of family breakdown is higher, and baby-sitting and other informal supports may be much harder to find (Baldwin and Carlisle 1994; Beresford 1994). Several studies also suggest that the circumstances of black and minority ethnic parents of children with complex needs may be particularly bleak, with higher rates of poverty, reduced access to services, lack of services that are sensitive to cultural issues and lower take-up of financial support (Baxter et al. 1990; Chamba et al. 1999; Flynn 2002). Recent research demonstrates that good practice is possible (Simon 2006).

Family and environmental factors

Assessments that identify the child as the sole source of difficulty can be extremely damaging both for children and their families. This is not to deny the reality of the child's needs, nor the extent to which they disadvantage the child. As Shakespeare (2006, p.43) notes: 'For many, impairment is not neutral, because it involves intrinsic disadvantage. Disabling barriers make impairment more difficult, but even in the absence of barriers impairment can be problematic.' Assessments, and assessors, should focus on the whole situation, aiming to identify the barriers that a child with complex needs faces in accessing their rights, and ways of removing these barriers.

Assessments must start from an understanding that many of the potential problems faced by children with complex needs are not caused by their conditions or impairments, but by societal values and adult behaviour: 'a major problem for disabled children is that they live in a society which views childhood impairment as deeply problematic' (Shakespeare and Watson 1998, p.20). Put another way, some of the most damaging aspects of the lives of children with complex needs and their families are not an inevitable consequence of the child's condition or impairments. The five outcomes in *Every Child Matters* (Cm 5860 2003) are relevant for all children, but are much harder to achieve for some children than others. A knowledge review about children with complex health care needs concludes that although they have the same 'ordinary' wishes and needs as other children, that is to live at home with their families, go to school, spend time with their friends and participate in leisure and community activities with family and peers, they face major barriers on all levels, such that getting 'ordinary' things remains extraordinarily difficult (Marchant et al. 2007).

Safeguarding issues for children with complex needs

Children with complex needs are rendered particularly vulnerable to abuse, in part because of the fragmented approach to service delivery and the conflicted value base described above. Yet children with complex needs are seriously under-represented in UK child protection systems. Given this context, recognising possible indicators of concern about significant harm must be part of the agenda when undertaking an assessment and assessors need to bear in mind that children with complex needs are significantly more likely to have experienced abuse and neglect than most children. Therefore, everyone involved in assessing children with complex needs should know how to respond when a child may be showing or telling about abuse (HM Government 2009).

Practitioners should also be supported to 'think the unthinkable' in order to keep children safe. For example, Nat was three when she was found to have two different sexually transmitted diseases. Nat had autism and severe learning difficulties. All those involved in her day-to-day care were initially adamant that she could not be at risk of abuse. They believed Nat would be safe *because* she presented extremely challenging behaviour and *because* she resisted having her nappy changed with such violence that two adults were required. These behaviours would generally raise serious concern, but were actually perceived as safeguarding Nat from abuse. Possible indicators of concern about children's safety or welfare can thus be denied, ignored, attributed to a child's impairment or condition or even somehow seen as evidence that a child could not be abused. Direct communication with children is essential when there are concerns (Marchant and Page 1993, 1997).

In assessments where there are issues around control of a child's behaviour, clarity about the boundaries between reasonable control and physical and/or emotional abuse become essential. The following are adapted from Lyons (1994):

- The child's welfare must be the paramount consideration.

- Any response to a child's behaviour must be based on a consideration of what is in that child's best interests and what they would recognise themselves as being in their own interests, were they of the age and capacity to make such decisions themselves.

- Restrictive measures should only be adopted to deal with severe challenging behaviour when there is no alternative and should be used in the least detrimental manner and for the shortest possible time.

- Any measures of control should always be part of a plan with long-term strategies to meet the child's needs and encourage other behaviours, and should first have been discussed by the parents, professionals and carers involved.

Involving children in the assessment process

Given this context, it is crucial that children are defined as active partners in the assessment process, and that the function of assessment is presented to children in an accessible, honest and fair way. Giving time and attention to this is important. The explanation needs to be tailored to the child's age and understanding. For example, 'I want to spend some time with you and see how things are for you.' 'It's my job to find out what you think about things; I want to know whether things are OK for you, whether you are safe and whether you have everything you need.' 'I'd like to find out how your life is and what you wish for in the future.'

Children may have particular needs, especially in relation to communication, which must be addressed to make an assessment meaningful. It is the adult's responsibility to ensure the child has the best possible chance of communicating. This might mean learning about the child's communication method, working with interpreters or facilitators or using resources to support communication.

Involving children with complex needs in meaningful ways requires practitioners to broaden their definition of communication and to be willing to try new approaches. Individualised, responsive ways of working are essential. We often act as if speaking is the only valid way to communicate and yet we know that this is rarely the case for any child. Total communication means tuning in on all channels and recognising the two-way nature of communication.[9]

Sometimes 'being alongside' a child is the most potent assessment tool. Often the help of a familiar adult will be required to get communication going.[10] Sometimes communication with a child will need the help of an appropriately skilled third party.[11] Thought needs to be given when selecting this person: independent, objective interpreters are often not available for children with complex needs, whose communication methods may be very idiosyncratic. The ideal is someone who knows the child well, is trusted by the child and yet is relatively neutral in relation to the assessment process. For example: Paul communicates using eye pointing on a personalised communication board of words and symbols. It takes time to understand how he indicates yes and no. He is dependent for all his care and spends his time at residential school and in foster care. At the beginning of his assessment his social worker finds out who can communicate well with him, and offers Paul a choice of three people to help her learn how to communicate with him.

This gives Paul control within safe boundaries. Sometimes establishing direct communication with a child is easier than anticipated. For example: Janice communicates with gestures, signs and some words, although her speech is difficult to understand. Her new social worker spent time with her at home and at school. She and Janice became more confident in each other's presence and by the end of the assessment were able to communicate directly with each other without any help.

Conclusion

Although assessment frameworks and procedures may come and go, the basic core principles of decent, sound assessment remain the same.

(Read et al. 2006, p.55)

---

9   *Two Way Street* is a DVD, made with disabled children and young people, to enable better communication with professionals. Available from www.triangle-services.co.uk.

10   *Three Way Street* is a new DVD, made with children and young people, about communicating with a child with the help of another adult. Available from www.triangle-services.co.uk.

11   The stages of involving children, from making initial contact through to representing children's views, are considered further in Marchant and Jones (2003) and Marchant (2008).

The context for the assessment of children with complex needs is evolving rapidly, giving opportunities for co-ordinated, shared assessments, although truly joined-up assessment requires a substantial cultural shift, which will take time (Boddy *et al.* 2006). It is essential that children and parents are active partners in assessment, and that children's safety and welfare are explicitly considered. A clear value base is crucial, particularly about the equality of all children.

The Government is now advocating integrated assessment, and in many areas children with complex needs and their families are paving the way for integrated assessment processes. Assessment work with children with complex needs will test integrated working to its limits, which will potentially benefit all children and families.

Recommended reading

Anning, A., Cottrell, D., Frost, N., Green, J. and Robinson, M. (2007) *Developing Multiprofessional Teamwork for Integrated Children's Services.* Milton Keynes: Open University Press.

Marchant, R. (2008) 'Working with Disabled Children who Live Away from Home Some or All of the Time.' In M. Lefevre and B. Luckock (eds) *Direct Work with Children in Care.* London: BAAF.

Marchant, R. and Jones, M. (2000) 'Practice Guidance for Assessing Disabled Children and their Families.' In Department of Health, *Framework for the Assessment of Children in Need and their Families.* London: Department of Health.

References

Anning, A., Cottrell, D., Frost, N., Green, J. and Robinson, M. (2007) *Developing Multiprofessional Teamwork for Integrated Children's Services.* Milton Keynes: Open University Press.

Audit Commission (2003) *Services for Disabled Childen and their Families: A Review of Services.* London: Audit Commission.

Baldwin, S. and Carlisle, J. (1994) *Social Support for Disabled Children and their Families: A Review of the Literature.* Edinburgh: HMSO.

Baxter, C., Poonia, K., Ward, L., Nadirshaw, Z. and Martin, A. (1990) *Double Discrimination: Issues and Services for People with Learning Difficulties from Black and Ethnic Minority Communities.* London: Kings Fund Centre.

Beresford, B. (1994) *Positively Parents: Caring for a Severely Disabled Child.* York: Social Policy Research Unit.

Birth Defects Foundation (2007) *It's Not too Much to Ask.* London: Birth Defects Foundation.

Boddy, J., Potts, P. and Statham, J. (2006) *Models of Good Practice in Joined-up Assessment: Working for Children with 'Significant and Complex Needs'.* London: Thomas Coram Research Unit.

Chamba, R., Ahmad, W., Hirst, M., Lawton, P. and Beresford, B. (1999) *On the Edge: Minority Ethnic Families Caring for a Severely Disabled Child.* York: Joseph Rowntree Foundation.

Children's Workforce Development Council (2007a) *The Lead Professional: Practitioners' Guide.* Leeds: CWDC.

Children's Workforce Development Council (2007b) *The Lead Professional: Managers' Guide.* Leeds: CWDC.

Cm 5860 (2003) *Every Child Matters.* Green Paper. London: The Stationery Office.

Commission for Social Care Inspection (2007) *Children's Services CSCI Findings 2004–2007.* London: CSCI.

Cooke, P. (2000) *Final Report on Disabled Children and Abuse.* Nottingham: The Ann Craft Trust.

Cooke, P. and Standen, P. (2002) 'Abused and disabled children: hidden needs?' *Child Abuse Review 11,* 1, 1–18.

Department of Health (2000) *Assessing Children in Need and their Families: Practice Guidance.* London: The Stationery Office.

Department for Education and Skills (2007) *Multi-Agency Working: A Glossary.* London: Department for Education and Skills.

Department of Health and Department for Education and Skills (2004) *National Service Framework for Children, Young People and Maternity Services.* London: HMSO.

Department of Health, Department for Education and Employment and Home Office (2000) *Framework for the Assessment of Children in Need and their Families.* London: The Stationery Office.

Flynn, R. (2002) *Short Breaks: Providing Better Access and More Choice for Black Disabled Children and their Families.* Bristol: The Policy Press.

Frost, N. and Robinson, M. (2007) 'Joining up children's services: safeguarding children in multi-disciplinary teams.' *Child Abuse Review 16*, 3, 184–199.

Herrington, V., Harvey, S., Hunter, G. and Hough, M. (2007) *Assessing the Prevalence of Learning Disability among Young Adult Offenders in Feltham.* London: Institute for Criminal Policy Research, King's College.

HM Government (2009) *Safeguarding Disabled Children. Practice Guidance.* London: Department for Children, Schools and Families.

HM Treasury and Department for Education and Skills (2007a) *Policy Review of Children and Young People – A Discussion Paper.* London: HM Treasury and Department for Education and Skills.

HM Treasury and Department for Education and Skills (2007b) *Aiming High for Children: Better Support for Families.* London: HMSO.

Howlin, P. (1998) *Children with Autism and Asperger Syndrome: A Guide for Practitioners and Carers.* London: Wiley.

Limbrick, P. (2004) *Early Support for Children with Complex Needs: Team around the Child and the Multiagency Keyworker.* Birmingham: Handsel Trust.

Limbrick, P. (2005) *Principles and Practice that Define the Team-Around-the-Child Approach and their Relationship to Accepted Good Practice.* Birmingham: Handsel Trust.

Lyons, C. (1994) *Legal Issues Arising from the Care and Control of Children with Learning Disabilities who also Present Severe Challenging Behaviour: A Guide for Parents and Carers* London: Mental Health Foundation.

Marchant, R. (2008) 'Working with Disabled Children who Live Away from Home Some or All of the Time.' In M. Lefevre and B. Luckock (eds) *Direct Work with Children in Care.* London: BAAF.

Marchant, R. and Cole, M. (forthcoming) *Expert Advocacy: Deaf and Disabled Advocates for Deaf and Disabled Children.* Brighton: Triangle.

Marchant, R. and Jones, M. (2003) *Getting it Right: Involving Disabled Children in their Own Assessments and Reviews.* Brighton: Triangle.

Marchant, R. and Page, M. (1993) *Bridging the Gap: Child Protection Work with Children with Multiple Disabilities.* London: NSPCC.

Marchant, R. and Page, M. (1997) 'Interviewing Disabled Children.' In J. Jones and H. Westcott (eds) *Perspectives on the Memorandum.* London: Arena.

Marchant, R., Lefevre, M., Luckock, B. and Jones, M. (2007) *Necessary Stuff: The Social Care Needs of Children with Complex Health Care Needs.* London: Social Care Institute of Excellence.

Mukherjee, S., Beresford, B. and Sloper, P. (1999) *Unlocking Key Working: An Analysis and Evaluation of Key Worker Services for Families with Disabled Children.* Bristol: The Policy Press.

Murray, P. and Penman, G. (1996) *Let Our Children Be: A Collection of Stories.* Sheffield: Parents with Attitude.

Nuffield Council on Bioethics (2006) *Critical Care Decisions in Fetal and Neonatal Medicine: Ethical Issues.* London: NCBO.

Read, J., Clements, L. and Ruebain, D. (2006) *Disabled Children and the Law,* 2nd edn. London: Jessica Kingsley Publishers.

Russell, P. (1996) 'Listening to Children with Disabilities and Special Needs.' In R. Davie, G. Upton and V. Varma (eds) *The Voice of the Child: A Handbook for Professionals.* Oxford: Routledge.

Shakespeare, T. (2006) *Disability Rights and Wrongs.* London: Routledge.

Shakespeare, T. and Watson, N. (1998) 'Theoretical Perspectives on Research with Disabled Children.' In C. Robinson and K. Stalker (eds) *Growing Up with Disability: Research Highlights in Social Work 34.* London: Jessica Kingsley Publishers.

Simon, J. (2006) *Diversity Matters: Good Practice in Services for Disabled Children from Black and Other Minority Ethnic Communities.* London: National Children's Bureau, Council for Disabled Children.

Siraj-Blatchford, I., Clarke, K. and Needham, M. (2007) *The Team Around the Child: Multi-agency Working in the Early Years.* London: Trentham Books.

Sullivan, P. and Knutson, J. (2000) 'Maltreatment and disabilities: a population-based epidemiological study.' *Child Abuse and Neglect 24*, 10, 1257–1273.

Westcott, H. and Cross, M. (1996) *This Far and No Further: Towards Ending the Abuse of Disabled Children.* Birmingham: Venture Press.

CHAPTER 13

Young Carers: Needs, Rights and Assessments

Chris Dearden and Jo Aldridge

Consideration must be given as to whether a young carer is a child in need under the Children Act 1989. The central issue is whether a child's welfare or development might suffer if support is not provided to the child or family.

(From the Framework for the Assessment of Children in Need and their Families, p.49, 3.63)

In this chapter the following is considered:

- the nature of caregiving by young carers
- identifying the needs of young carers using the Assessment Framework
- a family approach to assessment
- assessment issues
- engaging young carers and their families in the assessment process.

Introduction

Young carers are children and young people, under the age of 18, who provide care or support to a relative in the home. That relative is usually a parent but may be a sibling, grandparent or other family member. Young carers have only relatively recently been recognised as children who may require support and services in their own right. This recognition is largely the result of research which, initially, attempted to ascertain the extent of the 'problem' (O'Neill 1988; Page 1988) and later reported on the identified needs and experiences of young carers (Aldridge and Becker 1993, 2003; Bilsborrow 1992; Dearden and Becker 2000). This early research and campaigning by groups such as the Carers National Association (now Carers UK) resulted in considerable interest in what had previously been a hidden social issue.

As interest and recognition has grown, so estimates as to the extent of the issue have been formulated. The first 'official' Department of Health estimate suggested there were between 19,000 and 50,000 young carers nationally (Walker 1996). These Department of Health figures were based on young people providing, or intending to provide, 'regular and substantial' care; the terminology used in the Carers (Recognition and Services) Act 1995. Researchers and campaigners alike have suggested that a definition must take account not just the *amount* of time children care, but also the *impact* caring has on them as children. In the UK there are almost three million children under the age of 16 (23% of all children) who live in households where a family member is 'hampered in daily activities by any chronic physical or mental health problem, illness or disability' (Becker *et al.* 1998, p.xii). Thus, using an impact definition, the 'official' figure is likely to be an underestimate. More recently, the 2001 census included figures for caring by those under 18. The census relies on self-reporting and asked about caring for family members, friends and neighbours. It pointed to a total of 175,000 young carers in the UK. The majority care for up to 19 hours per week. Across England 16 per cent (22,000 children and young people) are reported to be caring for between 20 and 50 or more hours a week (HM Government 2008a).

Over time, research studies have examined the experiences and needs of young carers and consistent patterns have emerged irrespective of the geographic location of young carers (see Aldridge 2007) or the nature of the illness or disability of those receiving support. This does not mean that all young carers have identical needs, nor that all young people who have an ill or disabled parent will require specialised support, but research does tell us that parental illness or disability should be seen as a potential trigger for the onset of care provision among children.

The research literature on young carers indicates that children undertake a range of caring tasks. Broadly, these tasks include household responsibilities, including domestic chores, such as cooking and cleaning; general care, such as assisting with mobility, giving medication; intimate care, such as bathing and toileting; and emotional support. One in ten young carers provide care to more than one person and many, in addition to caring responsibilities, also provide child care to their siblings (see, for example, Aldridge and Becker 1993, 1994; Bilsborrow 1992; Dearden and Becker 1995, 1996, 1998, 2004; Frank 1995). Caring tasks are influenced, to a large extent, by the nature of the illness or disability of those receiving support. While most young carers undertake domestic responsibilities, intimate care is more likely to be provided for parents with physical health problems or disability, and emotional support is more likely to occur for parents with mental health problems (Aldridge and Becker 2003; Becker *et al.* 1998; Dearden and Becker 1998, 2004). Furthermore, girls are more heavily involved in all aspects of care provision, especially domestic and intimate care, those tasks that are more often gender delineated among adult carer populations (Dearden and Becker 1998, 2004).

The Assessment Framework and young carers

The *Framework for the Assessment of Children in Need and their Families* (Department of Health *et al.* 2000) includes three domains which should be considered in terms of assessing children in need in order to safeguard and promote their welfare: the child's developmental needs; parenting capacity; and family and environmental factors. These will be considered in relation to the needs of young carers.

Young carers' developmental needs

Young carers have needs similar to all children, but many may have additional needs (and rights) related to their caring roles. Meeting their developmental needs may be compromised as a result of taking on tasks which could be considered inappropriate to their age and development. Personal, intimate care provides a good example of this. In most families children would not be expected to bathe or toilet other family members, particularly their parents. In some families, cross-gender personal care may be considered taboo. Moreover, undertaking these types of intimate tasks for parents can be embarrassing for children and parents alike.

> I'm used to it [giving personal care] now…sometimes it's a bit awful when she's [mother] had an accident – a big accident – but apart from that we don't really see it like that. She wears pads and things…I just find it embarrassing when she's had a really big accident. (Marianne, age 14, in Dearden and Becker 1998, p.42)

Young carers may also experience educational difficulties. For example, research indicates that young carers may miss periods of school, have difficulty completing homework, experience persistent lateness, and so on (Aldridge and Becker 1993; Frank 1995; Marsden 1995).

> I missed a lot of school because he [father] wasn't well and I didn't like leaving him in case he fell over and he couldn't reach a phone or pull the cords… I went to it [school] twice a week, that was it…until year 11 and then I just drew the line and told them to give me home tuition or I don't come at all. And I got my home tuition. (Mark, age 16, in Dearden and Becker 2000, p.21)

These findings are supported by larger studies of young carers who receive help and support from specialist young carers' projects (Dearden and Becker 1995, 1998). These studies indicate that a third of young carers of secondary school age are either missing school or experiencing educational difficulties. More recently, however, research that draws on data from young carers' projects indicates that the proportion of young carers experiencing such educational difficulties has fallen to 22 per cent, which, although still high, shows some improvement (Dearden and Becker 2004). This may be the result of young carers' projects supporting children not only with their educational difficulties and offering homework support but also in relation to their social and emotional development. In addition, it may also reflect the increasing recognition of these young carers' needs within schools and the provision of support services to address educational, social and emotional needs. We do not know if this is true for those young carers who do not receive specialist support services, but we do know that educational difficulties make young carers' transitions into adulthood more problematic and can continue to affect them throughout early adult life (Dearden and Becker 2000; Frank *et al.* 1999).

Some young carers may experience isolation and feelings of alienation or 'difference' from their peers if they take on domestic and caring responsibilities from an early age (see, for example, Aldridge and Becker 1993; Becker *et al.* 1998; Bilsborrow 1992; Dearden and Becker 1995, 1996, 1998; Frank 1995; Meredith 1991; Newton and Becker 1996). The adoption of household tasks and caring responsibilities can leave them little free time and so can reduce opportunities associated with a healthy psychosocial development, such as spending time with friends, attending clubs and playing sports (Becker *et al.* 1998).

> Well I didn't get to go out and about…the friends that I had, they were at school and home was home really. Once I got home I didn't really go out. At that time I couldn't, and wouldn't say to my friends, 'After school come round my house', because I thought if they said to me to come round to their house it would be a problem. (Shazia, age 17, in Dearden and Becker 1998, p.47)

The emotional and psychological impacts on children who care can, in some instances, be severe. While adequate support from the wider family and professionals may mitigate the impacts, some children will inevitably suffer negative consequences. For example, those children whose parents have a terminal, progressive or degenerative illness may be uncertain and fearful about the future – both for their parents and for themselves. Some children will inevitably experience the death of a parent. Others may witness a parent in chronic pain and feel powerless to help. Those children whose parents have mental health difficulties may witness unpredictable and sometimes irrational behaviour and can find gauging mood and behaviour and trying to ensure parental safety (particularly in parents who may be suicidal) particularly stressful (see Aldridge and Becker 2003; Dearden and Becker 1995). When children provide intimate care for parents this can be embarrassing for all concerned, but often families feel they have little choice. Aldridge and Becker's (2003) study found that children provide care for a number of reasons: through love and concern, but also because they are available to care (through co-residency) and can offer flexible and consistent support.

However, it is also important to point out that there are positive aspects of caring for children and for parents, as long as support services are in place and that these address adequately the needs of all family members. These positive aspects include enhanced maturity, responsibility and independence, life skills gains, increased understanding about disability issues and stronger family ties. While inappropriate caring can have a detrimental effect on children, positive aspects of caring have been recognised, by children and young people themselves, in a number of research studies. (See, for example, Aldridge and Becker 2003; Dearden and Becker 2000.) However, without appropriate support services, caring may not be the most appropriate way for children and young people to gain such skills and attributes.

> I think I became an adult overnight when that [stroke] happened to mam. I was thrown into being responsible then. I mean, obviously it will vary for different people

and different situations. Some people my age haven't got a care in the world. (Diana, age 23, in Dearden and Becker 2000, p.41)

Parenting capacity

Some commentators have argued that an assessment of parenting capacity inevitably implies parents are not good enough (see Göpfert *et al.* 1996). In the context of parental mental illness this can be particularly the case, given the stigma associated with mental illness and the assumption among some practitioners that children are at inevitable risk of harm when parents are thus affected (see Aldridge 2006). While the parenting capacity of some parents *may* be compromised as a result of illness or disability, this is not necessarily the case. The majority of ill or disabled parents are able to provide basic care, emotional warmth, stability, stimulation and adequate guidelines and boundaries to their children. Parenting capacity must not be confused with the practical tasks associated with parenting, with which some disabled and ill parents may require support and assistance from professionals. However, lack of parenting support services for disabled parents has been identified by the Social Services Inspectorate and others (Social Services Inspectorate 2000; see also Morris and Wates 2006; Wates 2002). Many parents with a physical disability will be healthy and their disability will have no, or little, impact on their parenting capacity; but they may require practical support (and/or parenting support). Others, however, may experience chronic pain, may have exacerbations and remissions of illness and others may be facing death from a progressive, terminal illness. Thus, there are instances where parenting capacity will be compromised as a result of illness or disability. In the case of parental mental illness, Falkov argues:

> The presence of mental illness can reduce and/or change a parent's responsiveness towards their child. For example, a parent may become less emotionally involved, less interested, less decisive or more irritable with the child. This will affect the quality of the parent–child relationship, parenting capacity and the child's well-being. (Falkov 1998, p.64)

However, Falkov also indicates that chronic, unremitting illnesses often have a greater negative impact on children and that many parents, even those who experience acute, intermittent psychotic episodes, are able to adequately parent their children in most cases. Preventive strategies can be adopted to support both parent and child and reduce the likelihood of parental separation: the major personal concern of children living with a depressed parent (Garley *et al.* cited in Falkov 1998, p.155). Mapping and monitoring children's experiences and needs, alongside those of their ill or disabled parents, is a key recommendation from more recent research on children who care for parents with mental health problems (see Aldridge and Becker 2003).

Booth and Booth's (1998) pioneering work with adults who grew up with parents with learning disabilities provides a further example of how support can mitigate some of the negative aspects of parental impairment (see also Cleaver and Nicholson 2007). Booth and Booth's research shows that children of parents with learning disabilities experience many negative external and environmental factors, such as family breakdown, poverty, victimisation, 'stigma by association' and lack of support. However, they also suggest that such families are often resilient and that the emphasis should be on supporting families rather than protecting children. Booth and Booth therefore question common assumptions about 'good enough' parenting, suggesting that factors indicating risk of harm need to be balanced against children's and families' resilience. Indeed, Cleaver and Nicholson's (2007) study emphasised the importance of long-term service provision for families where there is a parent with learning disabilities. They found that more than 80 per cent of children referred to children's services, who were living with a parent with learning disabilities, remained with the parent three years after referral, indicating that statutory support can result in families staying together.

Family and environmental factors

Research on young carers indicates that environmental factors, such as poverty, low income, inadequate housing, a lack of community support and alienation from the wider community as a result of prejudice, discrimination and disabling barriers, can have negative impacts on disabled parents and their children (Becker *et al.* 1998).

Disability and illness are often associated with poverty (Barnes 1992; Black 1980) and many families will be reliant on welfare benefits. In research focusing on young carers' transitions to adulthood, virtually all of the families were reliant on some form of welfare or disability benefits (Dearden and Becker 2000). The majority of young carers who are supported by specialist projects are living in low income families consisting mainly of lone parents who are especially vulnerable to poverty (Dearden and Becker 1998). Fifty-six per cent of young carers in Dearden and Becker's (2004) study were living in lone parent families. Further, where data were available (more than 1000 cases), only 4 per cent of adult care recipients were in paid employment. In lone parent families there is generally no other adult available for support if the parent becomes ill, leaving children to care in the absence of professional help and assistance. Even where there are two parents, one may abdicate responsibility leaving one or more children to take on the caring role. Financial pressures may also mean that children need to provide care while the well parent is out at work (Aldridge and Becker 1993, 1994; Dearden and Becker 1995, 1998).

> [I eat] anything I can lay my hands on, we ain't got the money to eat healthy food.
> (Gill, age 17, in Dearden and Becker 2000, p.29)

Some families living in inadequate housing may also have to rely more on children because the family home is not designed for wheelchair access, or the family does not have a downstairs bathroom or shower facilities. Much of the social housing for disabled people is designed for one or two people rather than for families, resulting in long waits for rehousing or expensive adaptations to existing properties. This situation can be exacerbated for families from minority ethnic groups as community care provision has been criticised for failing to meet the needs of people from minority ethnic communities (Atkin 1991; Dominelli 1989; Local Government Information Unit 1991). These environmental factors can also be accompanied by the absence or lack of support from members of the extended family.

In addition, some families will experience multiple disadvantages and discrimination relating to their health, cultural background, income, and so on, and, when these factors combine, social isolation and exclusion can occur.

Assessing the needs of young carers and their families

Growing recognition of the nature of caregiving by young carers should ensure that practitioners identify and intervene early in providing support services to both the child and their family to prevent young carers becoming children in need. The Common Assessment Framework can be used by those in contact with young carers and their families to identify those children with additional needs and to provide support services to ensure that the young carer's health and development is not impaired. However, if the situation is such that early intervention is not sufficient and young carers may require interventions as children in need, as defined in section 17 of the Children Act 1989, then an assessment should be completed using the *Framework for the Assessment of Children in Need and their Families* (Department of Health *et al.* 2000). The holistic approach underpinning the Assessment Framework should ensure the child's needs are identified and that services are provided to both the child as well as family members, under section 17 of the Act, which enable the child to be supported in the family without having to resort to family separations or care proceedings.

The whole family support approach

The whole family support approach to young carers highlights and promotes the needs and rights of all family members where illness or disability is present. Underpinning this approach is a view that lack of access to adequate, high quality services contributes significantly to some children becoming young carers in the first place and others experiencing the negative consequences of caring. Moreover, their situation can be aggravated by poverty and low family income (Becker *et al.* 1998).

While adequate services (and financial resources) to parents with ill-health or disability will benefit the whole family, many young carers express a need for recognition of their situation and services in their own right. Some young people require additional support for themselves, often in the form of someone to speak to about their experiences, worries and concerns (Aldridge and Becker 1993). Many express satisfaction with young carers' projects (Department of Health 1996a; HM Government 2008a), which provide not only someone to talk to, but also the opportunity for young carers to meet other children in similar situations – something which often validates their own experiences. If practitioners consider the needs of the whole family, rather than the parent or child in isolation, services can be provided or adapted to reduce the negative consequences of young caring.

The aims of assessing young carers should be to prevent children from adopting inappropriate caring roles or to enable children to stop caring, in a practical sense, in order to safeguard and promote their welfare. Recent government policy initiatives give priority to early prevention. For example, the recent Carers' Strategy (HM Government 2008a) has a chapter devoted to young carers and its vision is that: 'Children and young people will be protected from inappropriate caring and have the support they need to learn, develop and thrive, to enjoy positive childhoods and to achieve against all the *Every Child Matters* outcomes' (HM Government 2008a, p.123).

The Government's aim, set out in *Every Child Matters* (Cm 5860 2003), is that all children should have the right to: be healthy; stay safe; enjoy and achieve; make a positive contribution; and achieve economic wellbeing. Early assessment of young carers is one way of preventing inappropriate caring roles from becoming established, by the provision of support to the young carer and her/his family, and so help to ensure that young carers achieve the *Every Child Matters* outcomes. As indicated earlier, research has identified many ways in which some young carers fail to achieve these outcomes.

One way of preventing this failure is through early identification of concerns through, for example, the Family Pathfinder programme. This is currently operating in 15 local authorities. Six of these programmes are Extended Family Pathfinders which will focus specifically on how to support families that are at risk of becoming reliant on children to provide care. The emphasis will be on preventing the onset of young caring in families. It is anticipated that these local authorities will share their knowledge of appropriate support and models of prevention at the end of the pilot period (Cm 5860 2003).

Thus, in line with current government policy, when completing assessments practitioners should aim to prevent intensive and inappropriate caring by children from becoming established wherever possible, or where it has, to lend support which will relieve young carers of levels of responsibility that are clearly inconsistent with enabling them to achieve the *Every Child Matters* outcomes.

Issues of assessment

Local authorities have a duty to safeguard and promote the welfare of children under the Children Act 1989 and to recognise their needs as carers under the Carers (Recognition and Services) Act 1995. For those considered to be children in need the local authority should assess their needs, decide if they are children in need and determine what, if any, services they should be provided with. In the most recent national survey of young carers supported by projects, Dearden and Becker (2004) found that, of more than 6000 young carers, only 18 per cent had received any formal assessment of their needs by children's social care services. Of those who had been assessed, more had been assessed under the Children Act 1989 than the Carers (Recognition and Services) Act 1995, although it is not clear whether they had been assessed as children in need under section 17 of the 1989 Act or as children suffering or at risk of suffering significant harm under section 47 of that Act.

The likelihood of a young carer receiving *any* assessment under the Children Act 1989 or Carers (Recognition and Services) Act 1995 is not always increased by factors which one might have thought would be influential, such as the child's age or the nature of the tasks they perform. So, for example, Dearden and Becker's (2004) data reveal that it does not matter whether a child is very young or whether they are performing intimate care; these factors (age and caring tasks) are not associated with an increased likelihood of an assessment under either Act. Young carers who are most likely to receive an assessment are those from black and minority ethnic communities (25% compared to 17% of white young carers), those caring for a relative with drug or alcohol problems (28% in total) and those living in lone parent families (Dearden and Becker 2004). We have no way of knowing from these data whether assessments completed under child welfare legislation were as a result of concerns regarding their vulnerability as carers or whether there were safeguarding concerns. However, other research (Aldridge and Becker 2003; Dearden and Becker 2000) suggests that concerns over parental drug or alcohol use, especially if accompanied by mental health problems, may lead to section 47 enquiries being instigated due to concerns about significant harm.

There are several factors which may explain why so few young carers are assessed, and it is important to be aware of and acknowledge these factors if children and their families are to be supported. The most important of these are the lack of awareness among children's social care staff about young carers' needs and rights; families' fear of professional interventions; a lack of consensus regarding which department or section should be responsible for assessing need; and whether young carers should be assessed as children in need, children at risk of harm, or as carers. Each of these is discussed in turn.

Professional awareness

Research indicates that professionals from health and social care often overlook the contributions that children make to caring and household management where a parent or other household member has a chronic illness or disability (Aldridge and Becker 1993, 1994, 2003; Dearden and Becker 1995). Children need recognition for what they do as carers (see Aldridge and Wates 2005). A new study that used photographic participation techniques with young carers whose parents had serious mental health problems shows emphatically that children are competent social agents both as carers and in research processes, and that recognition for the roles that they undertake as carers is a vital component in respect of children's coping strategies and resilience (see Aldridge and Sharpe 2007). Such recognition requires professionals to understand the young caring experience and to include children in discussions wherever possible, accepting that they are competent and capable, while also recognising that they may have additional or specific support needs. Ongoing awareness-raising about the needs and rights of young carers, and recognising their contributions, is therefore critical.

Fear of professional interventions

Across the spectrum of literature and research on young carers, evidence underlines the fear among children and parents of professional interventions in their lives (see, for example, Aldridge and Becker 1993, 1994; Dearden and Becker 1995, 1996, 2000; Meredith 1991). This seems to be particularly true of attitudes to social workers, a view reinforced by the Department of Health's report on young carers (1996a, p.28), which suggested that work needs to be done to promote 'a more positive profile for social work, based on performance, recognising families' legitimate concerns about delays and child protection'. Families are unlikely to approach professionals for support if they fear that their children will be removed from their care. However, the most recent carers' strategy states that:

By 2018, our aim is that all areas will be delivering better joined-up, whole-family support to families affected by illness, disability or substance misuse who have young carers. Assessments and support offered will take proper account of the need to protect children from inappropriate caring while families and parents themselves will have a greater say in the shaping of services around them. (HM Government 2008a, p.125)

This should reassure families that support will be appropriate and that interventions will be positive and constructive.

Parental illness was, in the late 1990s, the third most common reason for children becoming looked after (Department of Health 1998). Although the categories of reasons for children becoming looked after have changed since then, by 2008 parental illness accounted for only 5 per cent of children becoming looked after (although it may be a contributory factor in other admissions where reasons cited include 'families in acute stress', 'family dysfunction' and 'absent parenting') (Department for Children, Schools and Families 2008). Thus, only a minority of families' fears of negative professional interventions and having their children removed are borne out in practice. However, many children who become looked after have experienced multiple deprivations (Bebbington and Miles 1989) and indicators such as poverty, poor health, lone parenthood and poor housing are often also associated with young caring.

Whose responsibility?

Because young carers are children first but also fulfil the role of carer, there is often some uncertainty among health and social care practitioners as to who should take responsibility for the assessment and support of young carers (Becker et al. 1998; Dearden and Becker 1998; Department of Health 1996a). This has, in the past, resulted in young carers 'falling through the net' of service provision and their needs not being met fully or appropriately. In order to address these oversights it is crucial that the needs of each member of the family are considered. This means that ill or disabled parents should be assessed under the NHS and Community Care Act 1990 and other disability legislation, while their children (if they are providing care) can be assessed under either the Children Act 1989 or Carers (Recognition and Services) Act 1995, as children in (potential) need and/or as carers. This is most likely to occur if there are clear protocols across social care which promote joint working and encourage close cooperation between staff in adult and children's services.

Children in need, children at risk of harm, or carers?

There is a strong argument that young carers should be categorised as children in need as defined under section 17 of the 1989 Children Act (Children's Rights Development Unit 1994; Department of Health 1996a; Family Rights Group 1991). By doing so it becomes possible to assess the child and provide services to the *family* if these services will promote the health and development of that child. It follows that all children in families where there is chronic illness or disability could be viewed as children in *potential* need and, should specific needs arise, they can be assessed quickly. Section 17 of the Children Act 1989 as amended by section 53 of the Children Act 2004 states that:

> Before determining what (if any) services to provide for a particular child in need in the exercise of functions conferred on them by this section, a local authority shall, so far as is reasonably practicable and consistent with the child's welfare, (a) ascertain the child's wishes and feelings regarding the provision of those services; and (b) give due consideration (having regard to his age and understanding) to such wishes and feelings of the child as they have been able to ascertain.

Thus, it is important that young carers (and their families) are consulted about the provision of services. This may go some way towards ensuring that children and their families obtain services that meet their individual needs, rather than only those needs deemed appropriate by practitioners.

The Carers (Recognition and Services) Act 1995 offers another route to assessment for some young carers, but using this Act currently depends on the young carer's relative also being assessed or reassessed under community care legislation. Use of terms such as 'regular' and 'substantial' may also make it difficult for those young people caring for someone with mental health problems to access an assessment under the Act, since it is difficult to quantify the type of support provided by children and young people in these contexts. Nevertheless, the inclusion of young carers in this Act acknowledges their contribution as carers and allows for their views and perspectives to be included. It also acknowledges implicitly that there is the potential for conflict between the needs of carers and those of care recipients and allows for separate or joint assessments as appropriate. The Practice Guide to the Carers Act (Department of Health 1996b) suggests that the Children Act 1989 is the appropriate framework for service provision *once young carers have had their needs assessed*. A whole-family approach to assessment should ensure that all needs of each family member are taken into account and that service provision meets the needs not only of disabled parents, but also of their children.

Early assessment of young carers' needs and early interventions to address these needs should reduce the likelihood of safeguarding children procedures having to be initiated. However, there are some cases where abuse or neglect may become a concern and may result in section 47 enquiries. Although currently there are no statistics available on the number of young carers who are the subject of care or supervision orders, earlier data, anecdotal evidence and literature on children looked after indicate that parental mental health problems may, in some cases, be a significant factor. Research has highlighted how health care professionals have neglected to include children in discussions about parental mental health issues, and how subsequent social work interventions have sometimes resulted in children becoming looked after by their local authority (Aldridge and Becker 2003; Dearden and Becker 1995; Elliott 1992). Again, early support and recognition of the needs of the *family* may reduce the necessity for such interventions. Talking about her childhood experiences of caring, Marlowe (1996, p.101) argues: 'People tend to protect children and young people. For me, this translated into ignoring my need to be informed and involved.' Thus, an assessment should ensure that the child is able to remain living within the family unit wherever possible unless to do so would place the child at risk of significant harm.

Engaging young carers and their families in the assessment process

The assessment process should be considered a positive means of deciding what services are needed to support families, to recognise their strengths, as well as any difficulties they face. Ill and disabled parents must be confident that their needs will be assessed and their rights taken into account and promoted, and that this information used to decide what services are required and will be helpful to them. Equally, young carers must feel confident that their caring contributions are acknowledged and valued and that they are not patronised or ignored in decision-making processes.

Holistic child and family assessments can identify needs using the three Assessment Framework domains by fully including parents and children. Young carers will be empowered if their competencies and experiences are acknowledged and their views sought. One way of gaining the cooperation and confidence of families is to acknowledge their strengths and ask them where problems lie. The areas covered by the three domains are wide and, during an assessment, young carers' needs in one or more of the Assessment Framework domains may be identified. Ascertaining these needs will require more than one assessment visit and is likely to require the sharing of information between several professionals, from adult health and disability services, social care and education sectors and those responsible for providing community care services. Processes for information sharing should follow the guidance on consent and confidentiality outlined in the Government's information sharing guidance (HM Government 2008b).

Assessments should take place at a time appropriate to the family, when all members will be present. An advocate may help the children involved to participate fully and ensure that their views are adequately represented. It is also important that children are seen and spoken to separately from their parents in a manner appropriate to their age and understanding (see section 53 of the Children Act 2004). Given that many families are fearful of acknowledging the extent of children's caring roles, assumptions should not be made regarding the distribution of tasks within the family. Equally, parents should not feel that they are being unfairly judged when disclosing the nature and extent of their children's caring responsibilities. It is important to acknowledge that this is how an individual family copes with a difficult situation, which may well have arisen because of a lack of adequate formal support.

When assessing young carers, colleagues from education may need to share information if young carers' educational needs are to be addressed. Where there is a local young carers' project, young carers can be referred to these groups for support. Additional needs may be for counselling or bereavement support. Parents may require financial advice from specialist supporters such as the Citizens Advice Bureau or local money advice organisations to ensure they are receiving all of the benefits to which they are entitled.

Effective assessment procedures, leading to positive outcomes for both parents and children, will be beneficial not only to the whole family, but also to the wider community.

The aim should be to acknowledge, value and respect the reciprocal and interdependent nature of caregiving between young carers and their families, and to support and nurture these relationships through a range of policies, services and procedures. Using the *Framework for the Assessment of Children in Need and their Families* should ensure that this is the case for those families where parents are ill or disabled and where children and young people are providing care.

Summary

Three million children in the UK live in families where illness or disability is present and in the majority of these cases an adequate income, appropriate accommodation, effective services and the support of family and friends will ensure that children are not drawn into caring roles. In some cases, however, a lack of resources and support, combined with other factors, which include family structure and the gender of care recipients and potential carers, will mean that some children become more heavily involved in care provision (Becker *et al.* 1998).

The 2001 Census indicated that there are 175,000 young carers under 18 providing some care to family, friends or neighbours, 139,000 of them living in England. The inclusion of young carers in children's and young people's plans and community care plans should assist in the identification of this group of children and can act as a 'trigger' to assessment when required. Families should not be subject to disagreements regarding which department or section is, or should be, responsible for assessing or meeting their needs. Young carers are specifically mentioned in the Department for Children, Schools and Families' *The Children's Plan* (Cm 7280 2007) and the Carers' Strategy (HM Government 2008a), indicating that the Government is taking their needs seriously and has made clear its intention to support them.

A holistic child and family approach will ensure that the needs of all family members are taken into account. Assessment procedures and service provision should reflect all family members' needs and should support parents in their parenting role, while promoting children's rights and their health, welfare and emotional wellbeing. Services provided under children's legislation, as opposed to adult legislation, will usually be free of charge, a factor which is important to those families experiencing poverty and low income or who are subsisting on benefits.

Effective assessment procedures, leading to positive outcomes for parents and children, will be beneficial not only to the whole family, but also to the wider community. The aim should be to acknowledge, value and respect the reciprocal and interdependent nature of caregiving between young carers and their families, and to support and nurture these relationships through a range of policies, services and procedures. Using the *Framework for the Assessment of Children in Need and their Families* (Department of Health *et al.* 2000) should ensure that this is the case for those families where parents are ill or disabled and where children and young people are caring for them.

Recommended reading

Aldridge, J. and Becker, S. (2003) *Children Caring for Parents with Mental Illness: Perspectives of Young Carers, Parents and Professionals.* Bristol: The Policy Press.

Becker, S., Aldridge, J. and Dearden, C. (1998) *Young Carers and their Families.* Oxford: Blackwell Science.

Dearden, C. and Becker, S. (2000) *Growing Up Caring: Vulnerability and Transitions to Adulthood – Young Carers' Experiences.* Leicester: Youth Work Press.

Frank, J. (2002) *Making it Work: Good Practice with Young Carers and their Families.* London: The Children's Society.

HM Government (2008) *Carers at the Heart of 21st Century Families and Communities.* London: The Stationery Office.

References

Aldridge, J. (2006) 'The experiences of children living with and caring for parents with mental illness.' *Child Abuse Review 15,* 79–88.

Aldridge, J. (2007) 'All work and no play? Understanding the needs of children with caring responsibilities.' *Children and Society 22,* 4, 253–264.

Aldridge, J. and Becker, S. (1993) *Children Who Care: Inside the World of Young Carers.* Loughborough: Young Carers Research Group, Loughborough University.

Aldridge, J. and Becker, S. (1994) *My Child, My Carer: The Parents' Perspective.* Loughborough: Young Carers Research Group, Loughborough University.

Aldridge, J. and Becker, S. (2003) *Children Caring for Parents with Mental Illness: Perspectives of Young Carers, Parents and Professionals.* Bristol: The Policy Press.

Aldridge, J. and Sharpe, D. (2007) *Pictures of Young Carers.* Available at www.lboro.ac.uk/department/ss/centres/ YCRG/downloadable_publications.html, accessed on 13 July 2009.

Aldridge, J. and Wates, M. (2005) 'Young Carers and their Disabled Parents: Moving the Debate On.' In T. Newman and M. Wates (eds) *Disabled Parents and their Children: Building a Better Future.* Ilford: Barnardo's.

Atkin, K. (1991) 'Community care in a multi-racial society: incorporating users' views.' *Policy and Politics 19,* 3, 159–166.

Barnes, C. (1992) 'Discrimination, disability benefits and the 1980s.' *Benefits 3,* 3–7.

Bebbington, A. and Miles, J. (1989) 'The background of children who enter local authority care.' *British Journal of Social Work 19,* 349–368.

Becker, S., Aldridge, J. and Dearden, C. (1998) *Young Carers and their Families.* Oxford: Blackwell Science.

Bilsborrow, S. (1992) *'You Grow Up Fast As Well…' Young Carers on Merseyside.* Liverpool: Carers National Association, Personal Services Society and Barnardo's.

Black, D. (1980) *Inequalities in Health: Report of a Research Working Group.* London: Department of Health and Social Security.

Booth, T. and Booth, W. (1998) *Growing Up with Parents who have Learning Difficulties.* London: Routledge.

Children's Rights Development Unit (1994) *UK Agenda for Children.* London: CRDU.

Cleaver, H. and Nicholson, D. (2007) *Parental Learning Disability and Children's Needs: Family Experiences and Effective Practice.* London: Jessica Kingsley Publishers.

Cm 5860 (2003) *Every Child Matters.* Green Paper. London: The Stationery Office.

Cm 7280 (2007) *The Children's Plan: Building Brighter Futures.* London: The Stationery Office.

Dearden, C. and Becker, S. (1995) *Young Carers – The Facts.* Sutton: Reed Business Publishing.

Dearden, C. and Becker, S. (1996) *Young Carers at the Crossroads: An Evaluation of the Nottingham Young Carers Project.* Loughborough: Young Carers Research Group, Loughborough University.

Dearden, C. and Becker, S. (1998) *Young Carers in the United Kingdom: A Profile.* London: Carers National Association.

Dearden, C. and Becker, S. (2000) *Growing Up Caring: Vulnerability and Transitions to Adulthood – Young Carers' Experiences.* Leicester: Youth Work Press.

Dearden, C. and Becker, S. (2004) *Young Carers in the UK: The 2004 Report.* London: Carers UK.

Department for Children, Schools and Families (2008) *Children Looked After in England (Including Adoption and Care Leavers) Year Ending 31 March 2008.* Available at www.dcsf.gov.uk/rsgateway/DB/SFR/s000810/index. shtml, accessed 6 May 2009.

Department of Health (1996a) *Young Carers: Making a Start.* London: Department of Health.

Department of Health (1996b) *Carers (Recognition and Services) Act 1995: Practice Guide.* London: Department of Health.

Department of Health (1998) *Children Looked After by Local Authorities, Year Ending 31 March 1997, England.* London: Department of Health.

Department of Health, Department for Education and Employment and Home Office (2000) *Framework for the Assessment of Children in Need and their Families.* London: The Stationery Office.

Dominelli, L. (1989) 'An uncaring profession? An examination of racism in social work.' *New Community 15,* 3, 391–403.

Elliott, A. (1992) *Hidden Children: A Study of Ex-young Carers of Parents with Mental Health Problems in Leeds.* Leeds: City Council, Mental Health Development Section.

Falkov, A. (ed.) (1998) *Crossing Bridges: Training Resources for Working with Mentally Ill Parents and their Children. Reader – For Managers, Practitioners and Trainers.* Brighton: Department of Health/Pavilion.

Family Rights Group (1991) *The Children Act 1989: Working in Partnership with Families.* London: HMSO.

Frank, J. (1995) *Couldn't Care More: A Study of Young Carers and their Needs.* London: The Children's Society.

Frank, J., Tatum, C. and Tucker, S. (1999) *On Small Shoulders: Learning from the Experiences of Former Young Carers.* London: The Children's Society.

Göpfert, M., Webster, J. and Seeman, M.V. (1996) *Parental Psychiatric Disorder, Distressed Parents and their Families.* Cambridge: Cambridge University Press.

HM Government (2008a) *Carers at the Heart of 21st Century Families and Communities.* London: The Stationery Office.

HM Government (2008b) *Information Sharing: Guidance for Practitioners and Managers.* London: Department for Children, Schools and Families.

Local Government Information Unit (1991) *Community Care Comment 2: The Black Community and Community Care.* London: LGIU.

Marlowe, J. (1996) 'Helpers, Helplessness and Self-help. "Shaping the Silence": A Personal Account.' In M. Göpfert, J. Webster and M.V. Seeman (eds) *Parental Psychiatric Disorder, Distressed Parents and their Families.* Cambridge: Cambridge University Press.

Marsden, R. (1995) *Young Carers and Education.* London: Borough of Enfield, Education Department.

Meredith, H. (1991) 'Young carers: the unacceptable face of community care.' *Social Work and Social Sciences Review 3* (supplement), 47–51.

Morris, J. and Wates, M. (2006) *Supporting Disabled Parents and Parents with Additional Support Needs.* Bristol: Social Care Institute of Excellence, The Policy Press.

Newton, B. and Becker, S. (1996) *Young Carers in Southwark: The Hidden Face of Community Care.* Loughborough: Young Carers Research Group, Loughborough University.

O'Neill, A. (1988) *Young Carers: The Tameside Research.* Tameside: Metropolitan Borough Council.

Page, R. (1988) *Report on the Initial Survey Investigating the Number of Young Carers in Sandwell Secondary Schools.* Sandwell: Metropolitan Borough Council.

Social Services Inspectorate (2000) *A Jigsaw of Services: Inspection of Services to Support Disabled Adults in their Parenting Role.* London: Department of Health.

Walker, A. (1996) *Young Carers and their Families: A Survey Carried Out by the Social Survey Division of the Office for National Statistics on Behalf of the Department of Health.* London: The Stationery Office.

Wates, M. (2002) *Supporting Disabled Adults in their Parenting Role.* York: York Publishing Services.

CHAPTER 14

Assessment before Birth

Di Hart

The midwife and health visitor are uniquely placed to identify risk factors to a child during pregnancy, birth and the child's early care.

(From the Framework for the Assessment of Children in Need and their Families, p.67, 5.25)

This chapter considers:

- the purpose of assessment before birth
- current law and policy regarding unborn children
- ethical and practice dilemmas
- the assessment process
- the content of assessments
- analysis and planning.

Why consider the unborn child?

Pre-birth assessments are not routine and usually reflect a high degree of concern about the risk of significant harm to the unborn child. The first year of life is a uniquely vulnerable time, not only because of the baby's complete physical and emotional dependency but also because studies have shown that children are at most risk of fatal or severe assaults at this age, usually inflicted by their carers (Brandon *et al.* 2008; Creighton 1995; Rose and Barnes 2008; Sinclair and Bullock 2002). Apart from such tangible risks, there is an increasing body of evidence about the effects of early trauma on subsequent brain development (see Chapter 9). If the babies at greatest risk of harm can be identified before they are born, there is an opportunity to prevent them from future harm. A recent government initiative is intended to target unborn babies, through the Family Nurse Partnership Programme, as part of the initiative to reduce criminality and social exclusion. However, the challenge for those providing such early intervention programmes can be the difficulty in accurately predicting which families are unsafe and the potential for stigmatising those who are already disadvantaged (Dingwall 1989; Peters and Barlow 2003). Even where a family present with a number of identified risk factors each family must be individually assessed: there may be strengths that outweigh the difficulties or there may be evidence of capacity for change, as described in Chapter 18.

There is a growing body of evidence about the importance of getting such assessments right: inquiries into a number of child deaths have suggested that such babies may not have died if a protection plan had been formulated before the birth (Lambeth, Southwark and Lewisham Area Review Committee 1989; London Borough of Lambeth 1987), yet practice continues to be variable. For example, a recent inquiry into the death of Caleb Ness in Scotland suggested that the potential risks he faced as the child of a brain-damaged father and drug-misusing mother, with previous children in care, could, and should, have been identified before he was born (Edinburgh and the Lothians Child Protection Committee 2003). Proactive intervention before a child's birth may also improve outcomes in less extreme ways: for instance, a study of mothers with mental health problems referred for assessment in a psychiatric mother and baby unit found that they were more likely to retain care of the baby if there had been adequate antenatal planning (Seneviratne *et al.* 2003). Whatever the potential benefits, undertaking a pre-birth assessment can be a complex and challenging task.

Current law and policy regarding unborn children

Unborn children do not have an independent legal status. Although the *UN Convention on the Rights of the Child* refers to a child's right to 'special safeguards and care, including appropriate legal protection, before as well as after birth' (United Nations 1991, p.1), it is not clear how these rights could be enforced in the case of unborn children. There have, however, been occasional attempts to intervene through the courts to compel a pregnant woman to comply with medical advice in the interests of her baby, such as seeking to order a caesarean birth, but such cases are rare and controversial in the UK (see Dyer 1994). Applications cannot be made under the Human Rights Act 1998, neither can care proceedings nor adoption applications be initiated before a child is born. ContactPoint, the new national database designed to improve information sharing about children in need, will not contain details of unborn children: again because they have no independent identity. Given this lack of a separate legal status, it could be argued that little can be done to safeguard or promote an unborn baby's welfare and that a formal assessment of their needs is therefore of little value.

The policy framework does not support non-intervention and reflects a growing awareness of the need for early intervention to prevent harm to children born into vulnerable families. The *National Service Framework for Children, Young People and Maternity Services* (Department of Health and Department for Education and Skills 2004) placed responsibilities on health professionals for identifying potential harm to children during pregnancy, birth and early care. The Children Act 2004 requires agencies to work in partnership to safeguard and promote the welfare of all children and the latest version of *Working Together to Safeguard Children* (HM Government 2006) reminds agencies that concerns about unborn children should be assessed and managed in the same way as those relating to any child:

> Where a core assessment under s47 of the Children Act 1989 gives rise to concerns that an unborn child may be at future risk of significant harm, LA children's social care may decide to convene an initial child protection conference prior to the child's birth. Such a conference should have the same status, and proceed in the same way, as other initial child protection conferences, including decisions about a child protection plan. (p.138)

Ethical and practice dilemmas

What are the barriers to effective assessment before birth? First, there are ethical difficulties. Practitioners are used to balancing the respective rights of parents and children but there is a sense that the bond between a mother and her unborn baby is particularly sacrosanct. In reality, very few babies are removed at birth but the possibility tends to colour the perceptions of all involved when a pre-birth assessment is suggested. In describing their role in situations where the removal of a baby at birth was being considered, social workers talk about feeling 'cruel', as if they were 'stealing children' (Tredinnick and Fairburn 1980), or 'like playing God', 'against the laws of nature' (Corner 1997). There is also fear about parents' reactions: that they may disappear, avoid antenatal services, deliver the baby at home without medical care or even seek to terminate the pregnancy, rather than have their parenting capacity assessed (Barker 1997).

A further ethical difficulty is the risk of stereotyping. By definition, a pre-birth assessment is triggered by the characteristics of the parents. This could be seen as persecutory, based on prejudices about who is deemed to be a fit parent and who is not. Some parents are particularly vulnerable in this respect and negative assumptions, for example that people with learning disabilities cannot be adequate parents, must be guarded against. The principle that must be followed is that it is the parent's *behaviour* (violent, intoxicated) that presents a risk of harm to a child, not the *label* (schizophrenic, crack user) that has brought them to an agency's attention.

These ethical dilemmas may be compounded by problems in practice. Although *Working Together* (HM Government 2006) states that pre-birth assessments should proceed in the same way as those once a child has been born, there are inevitable differences. Corner (1997) identifies differences in parental attitudes, professional anxiety and working relationships within the network that make the task more complex. In addition there is no specific allegation to consider and the usual timescales are difficult to apply. Practitioners should attempt to follow the same procedures and consider what timescales are possible. Even where the assessment indicates significant concerns, practitioners may struggle to arrive at an effective protection plan. What does it actually mean to make an unborn child the subject of a child protection plan? The child has no name, no gender, no date of birth and no action can be taken to legally ensure her or his safety. This may explain the variation in the extent to which this facility has been used (Barker 1997). Individual local authority data on unborn children is no longer published but the most recent national statistics (Department for Children, Schools and Families 2008) indicate that of 29,200 children subject to a child protection plan at 31 March 2008 only 420 were unborn.

This apparently tentative approach may be reinforced by a judgment of Mr Justice Munby in a judicial review of care proceedings, reflecting the gravity of state interference at this time: 'the removal of a child from his mother at or shortly after birth is a draconian and extremely harsh measure which demands "extraordinarily compelling" justification' (Munby 2003). Perhaps the most fundamental challenge for the assessor, therefore, is in determining what counts as evidence in a pre-birth assessment. With no baby to observe or monitor, the assessment is inevitably speculative: the task being to form a judgement about future-parenting. In what circumstances might it be necessary to embark on such an assessment?

When is pre-birth assessment indicated?

A pre-birth assessment should be considered when there are concerns about:

- abuse or inadequate care of previous children
- parental problems or characteristics that may adversely affect parenting capacity.

A study of activity in one local authority over a 12-month period found considerable over-lap between these categories. Twenty-six families were considered at a child protection conference because of concerns about their ability to care for their expected or new baby. All of the mothers had substance misuse or mental health problems and, of 33 previous children, only two were still in their care (Hart 2002). When the babies were followed up one year after the child protection conference, only a quarter were living with their mother in the community and one baby had died in suspicious circumstances, supporting the view that this vulnerable population is particularly in need of a skilled response.

Although concerns are likely to be particularly evident where there is a history of problematic parenting, it is important to be equally alert to the possibility of harm where this is the first baby. The threshold for undertaking a pre-birth assessment can be a source of conflict between agencies but a number of local authorities have developed specific guidance on pre-birth assessments. The *London Child Protection Procedures* (London Safeguarding Children Board 2007) stress the importance of making an early referral for a pre-birth social work assessment in the following circumstances:

- A parent or other adult in the household, or regular visitor, has been identified as posing a risk of harm to children.
- A sibling in the household is subject of a child protection plan.
- A sibling has previously been removed from the household either temporarily or by court order.
- The parent is a looked after child.

- There are significant domestic violence issues.

- The degree of parental substance misuse is likely to impact significantly on the baby's safety or development.

- The degree of parental mental illness/impairment is likely to impact significantly on the baby's safety or development.

- There are significant concerns about parental ability to self care and/or to care for the child, for example unsupported, young or learning disabled mother.

- Any other concern exists that the baby may be at risk of significant harm including a parent previously suspected of fabricating or inducing illness in a child.

- A child aged under 13 is found to be pregnant. (London Safeguarding Children Board 2007, p.280)

The assessment process

An organisational framework for pre-birth assessment

One of the challenges for practitioners undertaking pre-birth assessments is taking a robust and consistent approach. In the study described above (Hart 2002), assessments were tentative and decisions often postponed until after the child was born in spite of the vulnerability of the babies. Based on the findings of the study, an organisational framework to support practitioners to take a more robust and consistent approach would include:

- the situations where unborn children should be assessed using the Common Assessment Framework

- the situations where unborn children should be referred to children's social care for a specialist pre-birth assessment

- the process for making such referrals

- the nature of the assessment to be undertaken

- the contribution of other professionals towards the assessment

- a system for offering family support

- a system for considering and managing the risk of significant harm

- clarification of the situations where it is appropriate to decide that an unborn child should be the subject of a child protection plan and the process for doing so.

Ensuring that referrals are made

Midwives are in a unique position to identify families where a pre-birth assessment is indicated because they routinely ask questions about substance use, psychiatric conditions or previous pregnancies. The presence of children's social workers within hospitals seems to support the referral process because it improves working relationships (Datta and Hart

2008). Alternative means of communication between health and children's social care services will need to be developed where a social worker is not based within a hospital.

There will always be parents who fail to have antenatal care or do not disclose the extent of their problems because of fears about professional intervention. They are likely to be known to other agencies or local authority departments, however, and *all* practitioners, whatever their role, should be clear about their responsibility to identify and refer both prospective mothers and fathers if they pose a potential risk of harm to the baby (HM Government 2006). The increasing separation of social care services for adults and children has led to a degree of fragmentation and it is important that the duty to consider the needs of the unborn child is made explicit to all workers. Adult-focused agencies may want to protect their service users from the perceived intrusion of children's services but a failure to refer is not only a breach of their statutory responsibility (HM Government 2007) but may do parents a disservice. The *London Child Protection Procedures* (London Safeguarding Children Board 2007) stress the importance of avoiding delay in referral, partly because of the time needed to undertake a thorough assessment, but also in order to allow time for problems to be tackled so that parenting capacity is improved before the baby is born.

Undertaking a multidisciplinary assessment

The task does not end once a referral has been made to children's social care services, although a social worker will be responsible for co-ordinating these assessments. Other agencies have a major contribution to make: a specialist service may be commissioned to assess parenting; midwives and obstetricians will be able to monitor antenatal attendance; substance misuse workers will have important information about ongoing drug or alcohol use; and psychiatric services will know about a parent's mental state. A mechanism for planning the assessment and sharing information will be helpful, for example through strategy discussions or professional planning meetings. (This is considered in more detail in Chapter 3.)

Where parents are not currently receiving help with identified problems, they are entitled to expect that this will be arranged. Access to specialist help will inform the assessment about the extent of a parent's difficulties and its likely impact on their parenting capacity, and will increase their chances of being able to care for the baby. It is helpful if such services can be commissioned or agreed in advance rather than on a case by case basis: for example some NHS Trusts have a designated psychiatrist who will offer an expert opinion on the impact of mental illness on parenting capacity, and local drug clinics may fast-track pregnant women and their partners into treatment.

Strategies for engaging parents

The period before a baby is born is usually a time when both mothers and fathers are well motivated. They want to do their best for their child, often seeing her or him as an opportunity for a 'fresh start' and a way of making up for past losses and deprivation. Substance misusing parents may see the child almost as a cure: the motivating factor to enable them to stop using. Although the unreality of these aspirations may be worrying, they do form the basis for working in partnership with parents. Given parents' fears and the lack of a legal framework, pre-birth assessments can suffer from drift. Ultimately, parents can refuse to cooperate. If a practitioner is feeling uncertain about their mandate they may be tentative about making contact but it will be much more difficult to ensure the safety of a vulnerable new-born without a pre-birth assessment and plan.

What strategies can practitioners adopt to engage a reluctant family?

- Acknowledge and deal openly with the fear that the baby will be removed.

- Be honest with parents about the decision-making process.

- Involve other professionals, such as midwives or drug workers, in the dialogue with parents.

- Explain the format of the assessment, the concerns about parenting, the measures which parents can take to allay these concerns and the support that will be offered, and confirm this in writing.

- Be proactive about involving prospective fathers in the assessment.

The content of the assessment

The nature of the evidence

Having prepared the ground, what is the nature of the evidence on which judgements should be based? Corner (1997) offers a model for pre-birth assessment based on the following information:

- birth parents' relationship and lifestyle

- view and understanding of the past abuse

- acceptance of responsibility for the abuse

- attitude to previous children and the effects of the abuse upon them

- view of past professional intervention

- what has changed since previous child was abused, including support network

- whether the unborn child's needs are given priority

- impact of the baby on parental relationship and plans

- parents' relationship with professionals.

The model does not, however, provide a framework for assessing a first baby. Calder (2003) develops the model further, providing a list of the components that should inform pre-birth assessments and a matrix for determining the level of risk of harm. For example, a lack of antenatal care or concealed pregnancy indicate an elevated risk, whilst babies whose mothers have sought early medical care are said to be at lower risk of harm. The Core Assessment Record for use with unborn babies, provided within the Integrated Children's System (Department of Health 2003), also contains specific questions about the developmental needs of unborn children and parental capacity, focusing particularly on issues that will affect the baby's health and on maternal behaviour.

The first task of a pre-birth assessment will be to consider the baby's basic needs, i.e. will they be fed, kept warm and clean, handled gently and provided with health care? Any special needs of the baby should inform the decision-making: for example, babies affected by opiate withdrawal may be particularly difficult to care for. This is not to say that the baby's other needs, such as the opportunity for a secure attachment, can be ignored: we know that the building blocks for the development of emotional wellbeing are laid in infancy, as outlined in Chapters 9 and 11.

It is important to consider the impact of any parental problems on their parenting capacity. Will a father with a personality disorder be able to tolerate his baby's incessant crying without lashing out, or a mother with severe learning disabilities be capable of changing her baby's nappy? These factors are considered in more detail in Chapter 19. Judgements will be informed by current behaviour towards the unborn baby. For example, a mother's failure to stop using cocaine during pregnancy may raise doubts about her ability to recognise and respond to the needs of the baby once he or she is born. Reder and Duncan (1999) suggest that a failure to seek antenatal care is a significant factor in subsequent fatalities, although it must be borne in mind that there may be reasons for non-attendance, other than indifference to the health of the baby. The meaning ascribed by each parent to the unborn child is a useful source of information: is the child a replacement for a previous child, a means of maintaining the parental relationship, an impediment (Featherstone 2000; Houston and Griffiths 2000)?

The environmental needs of a new-born baby are not complex: the emphasis within a pre-birth assessment will be to ensure that parents have a safe place to live with their baby, basic baby equipment and an income. The inevitable challenge of pregnancy and birth will highlight the support structures available to prospective parents. Extended family may be a significant source of support – or potential alternative carers – if parents are unable to cope.

Analysis and planning

Arriving at a judgement

Those completing the assessment will need to consider not only whether parents have the capacity to meet their child's needs, in the short term, but also whether they are likely to be able to sustain parenting over time. Assessment is not an exact science, however, and there is emerging evidence that true objectivity is difficult to achieve (see Munro 2002; White 1998). A study of 26 assessments of future-parenting found that there were clear themes that social workers presented as evidence for their judgements (Hart 2002). The expectations of a 'safe' mother included compliance with the assessment and an expressed willingness to sacrifice her own needs in order to 'put her child first'. In contrast, fathers were assessed more superficially or not at all. There appeared to be different and less onerous expectations of them as the secondary parent. Fathers' problems and parenting history were seen as less significant and, as long as they were not actively aggressive, their compliance was not seen as essential. Fathers are often marginalised in assessments, in spite of the fact that they pose an equal or greater risk to children (O'Hagan 1997), but it may be that this phenomenon is particularly marked in pre-birth intervention: pregnancy and infancy being seen as a women's issue.

This suggests that judgements are influenced by the beliefs of the assessor about the nature of parenting rather than being the pure, reasoned models of risk assessment offered by Corner (1997) and Calder (2003). For example, one mentally ill mother repeatedly denied she was pregnant and referred to the maternity service as a 'butcher's shop'. When her son was born she talked about wanting to smother him. After a year in a variety of residential mother and baby placements, in which the baby was described as 'quiet', 'pale and depressed', 'dirty', 'emotionally neglected – not stimulated in any way', he was finally removed from her care (Hart 2002). Perhaps this reflects the beliefs described earlier about the seriousness of breaking the bond between a mother and her baby, even where the evidence suggests that the baby's needs are unmet.

Wherever possible, the aim should be to support parents to care for their baby. For example, it may be identified that a mother with learning disabilities will need additional help in making up feeds and a service put into place to help her. There will be other situations where the outcome of the assessment is less optimistic. A mother may be unable to stabilise her use of drugs; a psychiatric opinion may suggest that a father continues to have delusions about his expected baby; where parents have abused previous children, there may be no evidence of change; or parents may have refused to comply with the assessment, leaving grave doubts about the safety of the baby. It might be judged that one parent does not pose a risk of harm but cannot safeguard the baby against a violent partner.

Pre-birth plans

Whatever the conclusion of the assessment, a multidisciplinary meeting, convened either as a child in need meeting or child protection conference, is likely to be helpful in order to establish a plan. A good pre-birth plan should ensure that everyone is clear about what will happen when the baby is born. Where will the baby live and who will care for her or him? It may be that, although the concern is too great to allow the baby to be discharged into the community, a further period of assessment in a supervised setting is indicated. Is such a place available and how are the arrangements going to be made? Are there going to be legal proceedings initiated or a child protection review conference? Is it likely that the mother will go somewhere else for the birth? If so, what needs to happen? What further assessment is required and who should undertake it? What is the timescale for this? The latter is particularly important if the impetus afforded by early intervention is not to be lost by allowing the situation to drift.

Removal at birth?

Despite the wish to 'give parents a chance' there will be situations where the decision is taken to seek the court's agreement to remove the baby at birth. This will be the case where there is concern about the immediate safety of the new-born baby or where there is no realistic prospect of the parents ever being able to meet their child's needs. There will be a high level of anxiety amongst practitioners, as well as parents, when such a decision has been taken and it is helpful if the plan is as detailed as possible and recorded in writing:

- Who should the hospital contact when the mother is admitted?
- Should this contact be when the mother is in labour or after the baby is born?
- What happens if the baby is born out of office hours?
- What level of contact can the parents have with the baby?
- What is the plan in relation to breast-feeding?
- Is there a need to alert other hospitals of the plan?
- What are the arrangements for initiating legal proceedings?
- Are the parents aware of the plan and what is their attitude towards it?

These issues can all provoke a crisis if not clarified in advance and it is important that the contents of the plan is shared with parents as far as possible.

It is also important to ensure that the process is managed in a way that is fair and proportionate to the level of risk of significant harm. The European Court of Human Rights considered that there had been a violation of Article 8 of the European Convention of Human Rights, which is concerned with the right to family life, when a local authority had removed a baby at birth and placed her in a foster family.[1] This judgment was based, not on a view that the emergency protection order itself was unreasonable, but that the manner in which it had been implemented was unnecessarily harsh. The risks of harm to the baby were not deemed to be so overwhelming or immediate that mother and baby could not have spent time together in hospital, under supervision. Immediate separation was said to be 'traumatic for the mother and places her own physical and mental health under a strain, and it deprives the new-born baby of close contact with its birth mother and…of the advantages of breastfeeding' (p.33, 131).

A more recent case where a mother and her new-born baby were separated at birth *without* a court order was also deemed by Mr Justice Munby to be unlawful even though the mother was said to have 'raised no objection' to the plan. He ruled that this was not tantamount to consent and was a breach of both the domestic law and the right to family life under Article 8 of the Human Rights Act.[2]

Further assessment following the birth

It is rare, however, that final decisions can be taken before birth: families have the potential to confound professionals' expectations. The birth of a baby may be the crisis that brings about a change for better or worse, and parenting capacity cannot be fully assessed until then. Midwives will have valuable information about the parents' relationship with their baby and their ability to provide care. Babies born to women using drugs or alcohol will need specialist monitoring by a paediatrician and may spend their first days or weeks being cared for on a special-care baby unit. Again, the staff involved will have extensive

---

1   *P, C & S* v. *United Kingdom* (No.56547/00) [2002] All ER (D) 239 (Jul).

2   *R (G)* v. *Nottingham City Council* [2008] EWHC 400 (Admin).

information about whether parents can care for the baby over a 24-hour period, whether they can tolerate the stress of their baby's withdrawal symptoms and whether there is evidence that their substance use is out of control. These are difficult issues for a social worker to assess within their more limited contact with families.

Anxiety about the vulnerability of babies, combined with a reluctance to sever the maternal bond, means that a period of assessment in a residential unit may be suggested. Such assessments have a contribution to make but it is important that they are purposeful rather than being offered as a safe place for the family to fail. Is there any point in placing a mother with a chronic psychotic illness, and who has had all her previous children removed, in a residential unit for assessment? When undertaking pre-birth assessments, professionals may conclude that no amount of further assessment is going to tell them anything different: this particular child cannot be cared for by these parents. Mr Justice Munby (2003) is right to emphasise the fact that separation must only be considered when there is compelling evidence, but this does not mean that babies should be exposed to significant harm while professionals wait to see what happens.

Conclusion

The fundamental question, when deciding whether a pre-birth assessment is required, is: will this new-born baby be safe in the care of these parents, and is there a realistic prospect of these parents being able to provide adequate care throughout childhood? Where there is reason for doubt, a pre-birth assessment is indicated. Although targeted at a small minority of families, a pre-birth assessment provides the opportunity to ensure that support and protection are available to the most vulnerable children from the start of their lives. The goal of intervention at this time is compatible with the broader political agenda of improving the outcomes for all children through *Every Child Matters* (Cm 5860 2003).

Recommended reading

Graham, H. (1980) 'Mothers' Accounts of Anger and Aggression towards their Babies.' In N. Frude (ed.) *Psychological Approaches to Child Abuse*. London: Batsford.

Hollway, W. and Featherstone, B. (eds) (1997) *Mothering and Ambivalence*. London: Routledge.

Howe, D. (2005) *Child Abuse and Neglect: Attachment, Development and Intervention*. Basingstoke: Palgrave.

Parton, N. (1998) 'Risk, advanced liberalism and child welfare: the need to rediscover uncertainty and ambiguity.' *British Journal of Social Work 28*, 1, 5–27.

References

Barker, R. (1997) 'Unborn children and child protection – legal, policy and practice issues.' *The Liverpool Law Review XIX*, 2, 219–229.

Brandon, M., Belderson, P., Warren, C., Howe, D. *et al.* (2008) *Analysing Child Deaths and Serious Injury through Abuse and Neglect: What Can We Learn? A Biennial Analysis of Serious Case Reviews 2003–2005*. Research Report DCSF-RR023. London: Department for Children, Schools and Families.

Calder, M. (2003) 'Unborn Children: A Framework for Assessment and Intervention.' In M. Calder and S. Hackett (eds) *Assessment in Child Care: Using and Developing Frameworks for Practice*. Lyme Regis: Russell House Publishing.

Cm 5860 (2003) *Every Child Matters*. Green Paper. London: The Stationery Office.

Corner, R. (1997) *Pre-birth Risk Assessment in Child Protection.* Social Work Monographs. Norwich: University of East Anglia.

Creighton, S. (1995) 'Fatal child abuse: how preventable is it?' *Child Abuse Review 4*, December, 318–328.

Datta, J. and Hart, D. (2008) *A Shared Responsibility: Safeguarding Arrangements between Hospitals and Children's Social Services.* London: National Children's Bureau. Available at www.ncb.org.uk/dotpdf/books/sres_final_web.pdf, accessed on 3 May 2009.

Department for Children, Schools and Families (2008) *Referrals, Assessments and Children and Young People who are the Subject of a Child Protection Plan: England – Year Ending 31 March 2008.* Available at www.dfes.gov.uk/rsgateway/DB/SFR/s0005000811/index.shtml, accessed on 3 May 2009.

Department of Health (2003) *Integrated Children's System: Core Assessment Record – Prebirth to Child Aged 12 Months.* Available at www.ecm.gov.uk/ics, accessed on 3 May 2009.

Department of Health and Department for Education and Skills (2004) *National Service Framework for Children, Young People and Maternity Services.* London: The Stationery Office.

Department of Health, Department for Education and Employment and Home Office (2000) *Framework for the Assessment of Children in Need and their Families.* London: The Stationery Office.

Dingwall, R. (1989) 'Predicting Child Abuse and Neglect.' In O. Stevenson (ed.) *Child Abuse: Public Policy and Professional Practice.* Hemel Hempstead: Harvester Wheatsheaf.

Dyer, C. (1994) 'Sharp Practices.' *The Guardian*, 11 January, G2, 14.

Edinburgh and the Lothians Child Protection Committee (2003) *Report of the Caleb Ness Inquiry. Edinburgh: City of Edinburgh Council.*

Featherstone, B. (2000) 'Researching into Mothers' Violence: Some Thoughts on the Process.' In B. Fawcett, B. Featherstone J. Fook and A. Rossiter (eds) *Practice and Research in Social Work: Postmodern Feminist Perspectives.* London: Routledge.

Hart, D. (2002) *The Contested Subject: Child Protection Assessment before Birth.* Unpublished PhD thesis, University of Southampton.

HM Government (2006) *Working Together to Safeguard Children: A Guide to Inter-agency Working to Safeguard and Promote the Welfare of Children.* London: The Stationery Office.

HM Government (2007) *Statutory Guidance on Making Arrangements to Safeguard and Promote the Welfare of Children under Section 11 of the Children Act 2004.* Nottingham: Department for Education and Skills.

Houston, S. and Griffiths, H. (2000) 'Reflections on risk in child protection: is it time for a shift in paradigms?' *Child and Family Social Work 5*, 1, 1–10.

Lambeth, Southwark and Lewisham Area Review Committee (1989) *The Doreen Aston Report.* London: Lambeth, Southwark and Lewisham Area Review Committee.

London Borough of Lambeth (1987) *Whose Child? The Report of the Panel Appointed to Inquire into the Death of Tyra Henry.* London: London Borough of Lambeth.

London Safeguarding Children Board (2007) *London Child Protection Procedures,* 3rd edn. Available at www.londonscb.gov.uk/files/procedures/london_cp_procedures_v.3_10.01.08.pdf, accessed on 13 July 2009.

Munby, J. (2003) *Re M (Care Proceedings: Judicial Review)* [2003] EWHC 850 (admin) 2 FLR 171.

Munro, E. (2002) *Effective Child Protection.* London: Sage Publications.

O'Hagan, K. (1997) 'The problem of engaging men in child protection work.' *British Journal of Social Work 27*, 1, 25–42.

Peters, R. and Barlow, J. (2003) 'Systematic review of instruments designed to predict child maltreatment during the antenatal and postnatal periods.' *Child Abuse Review 12*, 6, 416–439.

Reder, P. and Duncan, S. (1999) *Lost Innocents: A Follow-up Study of Fatal Child Abuse.* London: Routledge.

Rose, W. and Barnes, J. (2008) *Improving Safeguarding Practice: Study of Serious Case Reviews 2001–2003.* London: Department for Children, Schools and Families/Open University.

Seneviratne, G., Conroy, S. and Marks, M. (2003) 'Parenting assessment in a psychiatric mother and baby unit.' *British Journal of Social Work 33*, 4, 535–555.

Sinclair, R. and Bullock, R. (2002) *Learning from Past Experience: A Review of Serious Case Reviews.* London: Department of Health.

Tredinnick, A. and Fairburn, A. (1980) 'Left holding the baby.' *Community Care*, 10 April, 22–25.

United Nations (1991) *UN Convention on the Rights of the Child.* Geneva: United Nations.

White, S. (1998) 'Interdiscursivity and child welfare: the ascent and durability of psycho-legalism.' *Sociological Review 46*, 2, 264–292.

CHAPTER 15

Safeguarding and Prompting the Welfare of Children who have been Sexually Abused: The Assessment Challenges

Arnon Bentovim

It is important to emphasise that the assessment should concentrate on the harm that has occurred or is likely to occur to the child as a result of child maltreatment, in order to inform plans and the nature of services required.

(From the Framework for the Assessment of Children in Need and their Families, p.8, 1.27)

In this chapter consideration is given to:

- defining child sexual abuse

- identifying harm from possible sexual abuse

- gathering information about children who have been sexually abused and their families

- making sense of the information, using cycles of positive and harmful parenting

- factors associated with the risk of re-abuse and the prognosis for intervention

- formulating a plan of intervention

- therapeutic work in a context of safety.

Introduction

As described in Chapter 2, children who are suffering or are likely to suffer significant harm as a result of child maltreatment are children in need under section 17 of the Children Act 1989. This means that their needs should be assessed using the *Framework for the Assessment of Children in Need and their Families* (Department of Health *et al.* 2000). In cases where there are suspicions or allegations about child maltreatment the local authority is obliged to consider initiating enquiries to find out what is happening to a child and whether action should be taken to protect a child as set out in section 47 of the Children Act 1989 (Department of Health *et al.* 2000, p.7, 1.25). The procedures for this course of action are outlined in *Working Together to Safeguard Children* (HM Government 2006). In this chapter consideration is given to the assessment process within this context. Particular attention will be given to the crucial stage in the process of assessing the likelihood of the child remaining or returning to the family and the risks of re-abuse.

As can be seen from the title of this chapter the focus will be on assessing the needs of children who have been sexually abused, but the content of the chapter will also be of value to those assessing the needs of children who have been physically abused, emotionally harmed or neglected.

Sexual abuse: definition

Sexual abuse is described in *Working Together* (HM Government 2006, p.38, 1.32) as:

> forcing or enticing a child or young person to take part in sexual activities, including prostitution, whether or not the child is aware of what is happening. The activities may involve physical contact, including penetrative (e.g. rape, buggery or oral sex) or non-penetrative acts. They may include non-contact activities, such as involving children in looking at, or in the production of, sexual online images, watching sexual activities, or encouraging children to behave in sexually inappropriate ways.

Recent studies of prevalence rates of abuse in the UK, using computer-assisted safe interviewing, indicate 7 per cent of young people report severe physical abuse and 16 per cent sexual abuse (Cawson *et al.* 2000). There can be considerable biases in the recognition, reporting and registration or substantiation of cases depending on social class, ethnicity, perceived status and experience. In the late 1980s and early 1990s greater awareness of child sexual abuse led to a rapid increase in reported cases. However, there has been a recent decrease in the reported incidence of child sexual abuse in both the US and the UK of around 30 per cent. It is likely that public education and a change in public attitudes towards violence in families has had an effect in reducing the incidence of sexual abuse on children. It is important, however, that practitioners are aware that child sexual abuse does exist, has a significant detrimental effect on children and occurs in a range of different contexts. These contexts include:

- Intra-familial abuse, including abuse within the nuclear and extended family. This may include family friends, lodgers or close acquaintances with the knowledge of the family. Abuse within adoptive or foster families is also included.

- Extra-familial includes abuse with adults frequently known to the child from a variety of sources including neighbours, family, friends, school friends, parents, as well as abuse within 'sex rings', either family or stranger led.

- Institutional abuse which includes abuse occurring within schools, residential children's establishments, day nurseries, holiday camps, for example cubs, brownies, boy scouts and other organisations, both secular and religious.

- Street or stranger abuse. This includes assaults on children in public places and child abduction.

As described in Chapters 3 and 4 assessment is an ongoing process involving identification of possible concerns about the needs of a child; assessment of these needs; planning and initiating interventions to meet the needs of the child and their family; and reviewing the effectiveness of those interventions, recognising that the needs and circumstances of the child and family change. As part of this process consideration has to be given to the possibility of re-abuse. The different stages are described in Table 15.1.

Table 15.1: Stages of the process of safeguarding children where there are concerns about child sexual abuse

Stage 1	The phase of identification of harm and initial safeguarding.
Stage 2	Making a full assessment of the child's needs, parenting capacity, family and environmental factors and levels of harm.
Stage 3	Establishing the nature and level of harm and harmful effects.
Stage 4	Assessing the likelihood of response to professional intervention in the context of the level of the child's needs and the level of parenting capacity and family and environmental difficulties.
Stage 5	Developing a plan of intervention to include therapeutic work in a context of safety and protection from harm.
Stage 6	Rehabilitation of the child to the family when living separately or moving on from a context of protection and support.
Stage 7	Placement of children in new family contexts where rehabilitation is not possible.

In order to complete the process effectively practitioners should follow the guidance in the *Framework for the Assessment of Children in Need and their Families* (Department of Health *et al.* 2000) and *Working Together* (HM Government 2006). And, where appropriate, practitioners should also take account of *Achieving Best Evidence in Criminal Proceedings: Guidance on Interviewing Victims and Witnesses and Using Special Measures* (Criminal Justice System 2007).

Identifying harm from possible sexual abuse

If practitioners are to be able to identify the harm to children and young people from sexual abuse, they should be aware of the possible indicators of child sexual abuse.

Presentation of possible sexual abuse in children and young people

The initial awareness of possible child sexual abuse is likely to occur through either disclosure by the victim or the presentation of physical, psychosomatic, behavioural or social indicators as described in Table 15.2.

Table 15.2: Presentation of child sexual abuse (adapted from Vizard and Tranter in Bentovim *et al.* 1988)

1. Disclosure	By child or third party.
2. Physical indicators	Rectal or vaginal bleeding, pain on defecation Sexually transmitted disease (STD) Vulvovaginitis/vaginal discharge/'sore' Dysuria and frequency, urinary tract infections Physical abuse; note association of burns, pattern of injury, death Pregnancy.
3. Psychosomatic indicators	Recurrent abdominal pain Headache, migraine Eating disorders, bulimic variety Encopresis Secondary enuresis Total refusal syndrome.
4. Behavioural indicators	
i) Pre-school	Sexually explicit play, 'excessive' masturbation, insertion of foreign bodies (girls), self-mutilation, withdrawn, poor appetite, sleep disturbance, clingy, delayed development, aggression.
ii) Middle years	Sexualised play, sexually explicit drawing or sexual precocity, self-mutilation, anxiety, depression, anger, poor school performance, mute.
iii) Teenagers	Sexually precocious, prostitution, anxiety, anger, aggression, depression, truancy, running away, solvent/alcohol/drug abuse, self-destructive behaviour, overdoses, self-mutilation, suicide.
5. Children with learning problems or physical disability	May present with depression, disturbed – including aggressive or sexualised behaviour. Attempts at disclosure may not be understood. May be physical and psychosomatic indicators as above.
6. Social indicators	Concern by parent or third party, sibling, relative or friend of abused child. Known offender in close contact with child.

The immediate post-traumatic stress disorders associated with sexual abuse, which provide possible indicators of abuse, are as follows:

- re-experiencing, where children are observed talking about abuse or playing out abusive patterns
- flashbacks and nightmares

- indulging in inappropriate sexual activity

- memories occurring in places or with people and objects associated with the abuse and considered to be symbolic of them

- visualisation, drawing, day-dreaming their experiences

- avoidant responses associated with the avoidance of people, places and things associated with abuse.

Children may also be fearful of going into particular houses or rooms, or of people who reminded the child of the abuser. For example, the child may dislike men or older people. Associated with this is an often extreme unwillingness to talk about abuse, and evidence of dissociation – a total lack of memory, including memories earlier than the abuse itself. Children who have been sexually abused may also complain of difficulties falling or staying asleep. These are often associated with anxieties about going to sleep. Irritable, aggressive behaviour may be noted: a reversal of the passive sense of having to be involved with abuse. Distractibility, difficulty in concentrating and a degree of hyper-alertness, shown by anxiety or being easily startled, may be noted in a previously calm child.

The longer the abuse continues and the greater the number of stages that abuse continues through (for example from touching to penetrative sex), the more disturbed the child is likely to be, the more depressed and sad, and the greater their loss of self-esteem. Abuse by a number of individuals, the employment of force and being subject to penetration represent significantly traumatic events which can cause longstanding effects without adequate treatment. Children who have suffered chronic long-term sexual abuse may feel negatively about themselves and all aspects of their relationships. They may demonstrate high levels of distress, which can impact on functioning as adults. Traumatic sexualisation enlarges the traumatic effects described earlier and leads to a cycle of avoidance of anything to do with sexuality. Alternatively, sexual preoccupations and sexually inappropriate/promiscuous behaviour with other children and adults may occur.

Gender differences

Boys and girls may differ in their responses to child sexual abuse. Girls are more likely to internalise issues, blame themselves or attribute sexual abusive action to some aspect of themselves. This is often reinforced by the abuser. The most worrying responses in older girls are major depressive symptoms, poor self-esteem and self-worth, self-injurious behaviour, early pregnancy. There may be overdosing, wrist slashing, bulimic responses, re-enactment of abusive experiences, gaining relief through hurting themselves, suicidal attempts of self-starvation, 'total refusal syndromes' – withdrawal, refusal to eat, talk or walk. Self-medication with drugs and alcohol is a further risk.

Boys, in contrast, generally follow a male mode and externalise their responses, look for somebody else to blame and take over their negative self-representation. They may find someone younger to abuse who reminds them of their own powerlessness. They may develop an abusive, hostile, aggressive style of relating to others, with associated conduct disorders and alcohol and substance abuse. Boys are more likely to adopt a sexually abusive orientation if they have been physically abused as well as sexually abused in their own families; if there is violence between the parents; and if they have suffered disruptions of care and have been rejected by their family. An attitude of grievance is more likely to occur under these circumstances with the adoption of an abusive role in turn. It is, however, important to note that some girls may also follow this 'male' externalising mode response.

In both sexes a sense of betrayal and stigmatisation is felt as a result of the threats, secrecy and self-justifying attitude of the abuser. Guilt and a low opinion of oneself may lead to promiscuous seeking of redeeming relationships, early pregnancy, clinging to unstable partners. Problems of partnering and parenting may follow.

The identification process

The identification of sexual abuse can be relatively straightforward if a child makes a clear statement consistent with abuse. This is likely to occur when there are supportive physical findings and the alleged perpetrator takes responsibility for the act, providing a history which is consistent with the statement of the child. More often, however, the child's statement is contradictory, inconsistent and unclear, the physical findings are equivocal, and there is a high level of denial by the alleged perpetrator. To identify sexual abuse requires a careful and skilled approach to each of the pieces of the jigsaw. An initial assessment of a child is helpful to assess whether a traumatic process has occurred. It should include observations of the child's general behaviour; response in school; and patterns of relationships with family members and with peers. These provide key pieces of the diagnostic puzzle. It is also important to remember dissociated responses can give the appearance of a child who has not been traumatised, so that an accurate and broad-based assessment is required.

Identifying sexual abuse in children who do not have language, have a learning disability or are autistic is a highly complex process. Yet children with learning disabilities, speech and language delays are most vulnerable to being abused, as a potential perpetrator may believe that the child will not have the capacity to speak about their experience of abuse. Observations of a child's behaviour which has changed recently may alert to concerns. Unexpected sexualisation of behaviour or unexpected severe regression of a child who is making good progress are also possible indications.

Interviewing children

Interviewing children where there are concerns about child sexual abuse should be undertaken in line with *Working Together* (HM Government 2006) guidance and *Achieving Best Evidence in Criminal Proceedings: Guidance on Interviewing Victims and Witnesses and Using Special Measures* (Criminal Justice System 2007). Effective interviewing relies on approaches which are open, build on the account given by a child and are child led rather than led by the interviewer. (For further guidance see Chapter 7.) An approach which attempts to get the child to agree with the interviewer's suggestions can distort and lead to inaccuracies. Traumatic experiences also distort memories through the process of dissociation and defensive elaboration. There may also be features which are consistent with children who have been induced into false beliefs that they have been abused through the use of language which reflects adult convictions, rather than the child's experience, and without affective responses.

The use of diagrams and anatomically correct dolls has been used to allow a young child to demonstrate sexualised behaviour that he or she would not be expected to be aware of. There has been concern that such aids to identification may have a leading effect on children. However, behaviour enacted, whether with dolls or with other children and adults, may have a quality of response which is outside what would be expected for the age and stage of the child, and may be accompanied by sounds and physical responses which could not have been understood without experiences. Exposure to pornographic material may be used by some perpetrators as a way of grooming and inducing a child to take part in sexual activities. Inadvertent exposure can also be highly confusing, and can have an eroticising effect. To identify sexual abuse requires openness to the possibility that a child has been abused, despite a context which appears caring and concerned. Conclusions about abuse should not be arrived at without adequate, careful consideration and being aware that an accurate identification requires the pieces to fit together, rather than one piece providing certainty. It is also important to be aware of alternate explanations for unusual behaviour in vulnerable children.

Gathering information about children's needs, parenting capacity, family and environmental factors

The full extent of harm to a child who has been sexually abused and the impact on their health and development may not be known initially (Carlson 1998). Moreover, the presence of severe or extensive abuse of a child, for example sexual abuse associated with physical abuse and neglect, will make it more likely that there will be major difficulties associated with parenting capacity and family and environmental factors. It is for these reasons that it is important that practitioners complete a core assessment in order to identify the needs of the child and ways in which these needs can be met. As discussed in detail in Chapter 2 a range of standardised assessment tools have been developed to enable practitioners to gather information about the child and their family.

Specialist assessments

As part of the process of gathering information during the core assessment specialist assessments may be required (see Chapter 3 for more detail). For example, child mental health assessments can assist in identifying post-traumatic states. Assessments may also be necessary regarding the perpetrator's sexual offending behaviour (see Chapter 19). Such assessments have an important role in assessing the impact of harm on a child and understanding and assessing the factors associated with harm, and harmful parenting, as well as the carer's potential for change.

Constructing a comprehensive chronology

An important element of a core assessment, as discussed in Chapter 3, is the construction of a comprehensive chronology of significant information from medical, children's social care, police and educational contexts. This helps to establish the nature of risk of harm and protective factors experienced by the young person and the family. It is often a challenge to gather and analyse information about a child's history and map the interventions and outcomes in previous work with the child and family. But such information is central to establishing the harm and protective factors a child has already experienced and to assessing the potential for change. Systems for collecting and analysing information from documents are useful to ensure a full picture is obtained. For example, the Integrated Children's System (Department of Health 2003) includes a chronology for use by social workers when working with children and families. Cross-sectional research at Great Ormond Street Hospital for Children, London (Skuse *et al.* 1998), which looked at the history of young people who had displayed sexually abusive behaviour, showed that information from case notes, and so on, could be reliably analysed using descriptors. Bifulco and colleagues have demonstrated that an instrument, the CECA – *Childhood Experience of Care and Abuse* (Bifulco *et al.* 1994) – used to assess the presence of physical, sexual or emotional abuse and neglect, can be applied to chronological/historical data from case files, or elsewhere, in order to construct a chronology for a child or young person.

Making sense of the information

To make sense of information gathered following child maltreatment it is useful to focus on the identified parental strengths and difficulties and the potential resulting effects on children's functioning and the potential harm which may result. By using the Assessment Framework (Department of Health *et al.* 2000) to explore each dimension in turn, it is possible to draw out some key themes and connections between strengths and difficulties in specific dimensions of parenting capacity, and to begin to identify the impact on meeting the child's developmental needs.

Cycles of positive and harmful parenting (Bentovim et al. 2009)

In a family with parenting strengths, it is possible to map some links between the provision of positive parenting in each dimension and the predominant potential impact on the child's development and wellbeing as shown in Figure 15.1.

Figure 15.1 represents a benign developmental cycle related to positive parenting. It illustrates the way that *positive family and environmental factors* provide the background for parents to develop *adequate parenting skills*. Linking these parental capacities in a circular fashion indicates that there is an interactional process which involves each of these particular parental qualities. The positive parenting skills impact in turn on *children's development and wellbeing* resulting in the child thriving and being free from harm.

Cycles of more harmful parenting, resulting from parenting difficulties, are represented in the diagram in Figure 15.2. Here *negative family and environmental factors* are associated with *difficulties in parenting capacities*. These difficulties affect the provision of basic care and attention to health needs, parental responsiveness, protection and security, consistency of emotional warmth, stimulation and communication, providing guidance and boundaries, managing children's behaviour and maintaining stable relationships.

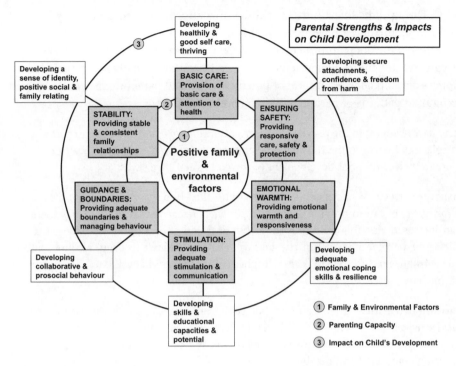

Source: Bentovim *et al.* 2009

Figure 15.1: *Cycle of positive parenting*

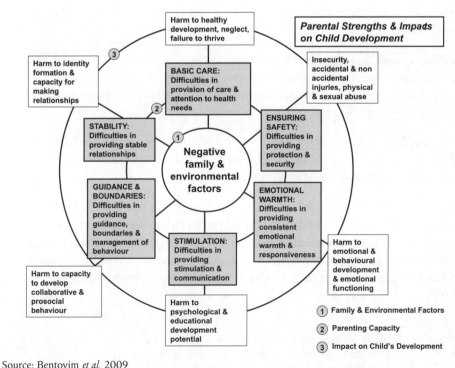

Source: Bentovim *et al.* 2009

Figure 15.2: *Cycle of harmful parenting*

In turn, parenting difficulties in each of these dimensions relate to potentially harmful impacts on children's development and wellbeing.

Representing the domains in a circular fashion indicates the interaction between these various parental difficulties which reinforce, interact and are cumulative in their impact on children's development. Each form of potentially harmful parenting may be associated with recognised patterns of harm to children and young people:

Basic care: Failures in the provision of *care and attention to health* can result in patterns of neglect and harm to the healthy development of the child with poor health care, failure to thrive and poor development of the child's self-care skills.

Ensuring safety: When parents do not ensure the child's *safety in the home and in the community* or fail to provide adequate *supervision, responsiveness and protection* there is an increased risk the child will suffer physical and sexual harm, be exposed to violence or become involved in risk-taking behaviour related to drug, alcohol and other substance misuse. There is also a higher risk of the child developing disordered attachments.

Emotional warmth: A failure to provide *consistent emotional warmth, containment and empathic responses* may result in a child having problems in managing their emotional states, having disordered expression of emotions and poor emotional coping skills and being emotionally vulnerable.

Stimulation: When parents do not provide *adequate stimulation, effective communication and attention* to a child's educational and social learning needs this can result in the child developing negative attitudes to learning and failing to achieve their educational potential.

Guidance and boundaries: Parental difficulties in providing *adequate guidance, boundaries and management of behaviour* can result in the child failing to develop prosocial and collaborative behaviour in the child with the risk of anti-social behaviour and disorders of conduct and oppositional behaviour.

Stability: Failures in providing *stable family and social relationships* can result in harm to the formation of the child's sense of identity and potential problems for them in interpersonal relationships and maintaining attachments.

To demonstrate how the concept of circles of harm works in practice, a case example is presented in Table 15.3 of a child who was subject to extensive maltreatment including neglect, exposure and experience of violence, and sexual abuse. The account provided was prepared as the first stage of creating a Trauma Life Narrative[1] to help her recovery by processing the extreme experiences to which she had been exposed and this is reflected in the style.

---

1   Trauma Life Narrative refers to the process of bringing together information about the abusive experiences a child has been exposed to during their life, so they can be processed, made sense of and transformed to lessen their negative effect on a child's emotional life.

Table 15.3: Charlotte's life experiences

1996 You were born	• You lived on an estate
1998 2 years old	• Your brother was born
1999 3 years old	• Your sister was born
2000 4 years old	• Dad, Mum and your brother and sister moved around all over the country. Dad got violent to your uncle when you were staying with him. The police arrested him. Mum was scared and left, she was too scared of Dad to take you, she had a handicap
2001 5 years old	• Dad was arrested for being drunk, he argued with your aunt and left with you and your sibs, he had a lot of trouble with anger • You all moved to another house with Dad's friends who used drugs. You went on moving, living in pubs and homeless accommodation, people touched you badly
2002 6 years old	• Dad had a gun, Dad was drinking a lot, you were filthy
2003/2004 7/8 years old	• You were living in a mess, not being fed or looked after, not going to school • After a lot of concerns by social workers you are taken into care, Dad is in prison for hitting someone badly

Source: Cox (2005).

Expressing the impact of the negative parenting which she experienced, the inner circle of the diagram in Figure 15.3 illustrates the cycle of negative parenting. The outer circle illustrates the impact on all aspects of her functioning, including the sexualisation of her behaviour and the specific impact of exposure to sexual abuse. The picture emerges of a child with evidence of harm in all areas of functioning relating to each area of parenting – poor growth and neglect, pseudo-parental behaviour, restlessness, significant failure of educational attainment, extreme difficulties in identity, clinging to her abusive father, rejecting and controlling her foster carers, oppositional and defiant behaviour, extreme emotional distress, inability to manage emotional states, extensive post-traumatic imagery. Studies on children in this age group who require fostering indicate that sexual abuse commonly occurs in a context of multiple forms of abuse and neglect (Pears *et al.* 2008).

Analysing the specific effects of harmful parenting on the child

Having identified the broad themes and connections between positive and negative patterns of parenting and their potential impact on children's developmental needs, it is helpful to take each area of parenting and consider in detail whether it is possible to relate the elements of parenting difficulties to specific harmful effects. In Tables 15.4 and 15.5, descriptions of strengths and difficulties in parenting capacity are juxtaposed with descriptions of the impact on the child's developmental needs, when needs are met adequately or when there is a risk of harm. Two examples are given – maintaining safety and

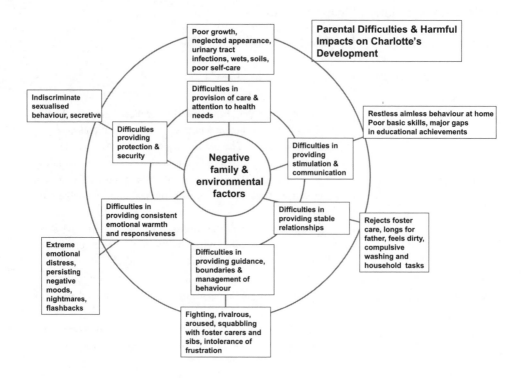

Figure 15.3*: Parental difficulties and harmful impacts on Charlotte's development*

emotional warmth, which have particular relevance to children who have been sexually abused (Bentovim *et al.* 2009).

The tables describe parental strengths and difficulties in providing emotional warmth and containment and the impact on children's emotional and behavioural development. This is the area associated with the risk of emotional abuse, and is frequently associated with sexually abusive behaviour as a way of justifying sexual activities with the child or young person. Difficulties in parenting capacities associated with potentially emotionally abusive actions include parents failing to express or respond to feelings and the presence of a predominant, critical, humiliating, rejecting tone in the relationship between parent and child. Associated with a failure of empathic, emotional understanding, parents may ignore or respond punitively to a child's expression of their emotional needs. Parents may also perceive the child's normal assertiveness as oppositional, defiant, rebellious and aggressive leading to disqualification and lack of support of the child. Passivity is also labelled as acceptance of inappropriate sexual activities.

Two major areas of potentially abusive aspects of parenting capacity in this dimension are the failure to protect children from potentially traumatically stressful events or from the extremes of inconsistent parental emotional states and distorted perceptions. This can include exposure to sexual abuse of a child or other family members. Parents may fail to

Table 15.4: Parental provision of responsiveness, safety and protection

PARENTAL PROVISION OF RESPONSIVENESS, SAFETY AND PROTECTION

Parental strengths	*Parental difficulties*
• Attuned, responsive, reliable, coherent caregiving.	• Unresponsive, unreliable, fragmented caregiving.
• Safe environment, appropriate discipline and relating.	• Unsafe environment, inappropriate punitiveness, sexualised relating, risk of physical and/or sexual abuse.
• Reasonable expectation of children's dependence or independence, self-care and care of others.	• Unreasonable expectation of children's dependence or independence, self-care and care of others.
• Adequate supervision of activities inside and outside the home.	• Inadequate supervision of activities inside and outside the home.
• Provision of safe environment, protection from physical hazards and risky individuals inside and outside the home.	• Environment unsafe, failure of protection from physical hazards and risky individuals inside and outside the home.
Impact on the child when adequate safety and protection provided	*Risk of harm – impact on the child when failure to provide adequate safety and protection*
• Developing secure primary and secondary attachment responses.	• Developing insecure, disorganised or indiscriminate attachment responses.
• Age-appropriate capacity for safe independent behaviour, care of self and others at home and in the environment.	• A lack of age-appropriate capacities for safe independent care of self – at home and in the environment – over-dependent, pseudo-mature.
• No evidence of physical or sexual harm sustained at home or in the environment.	• Evidence of physical or sexual harm sustained at home or in the environment.
• Injuries sustained consistent with age and developmental stage.	• Injuries sustained not consistent with age and developmental stage.

protect children from the impact of parental relationship conflicts of their own, including exposure to parental violence: both physical and sexual.

The responses of children to these emotionally highly stressful experiences can result in children being unable to develop normal emotional responsiveness or to regulate their emotional states. This may be demonstrated in the child by frozen emotional responses, high emotional arousal states, marked anger or oppositional responses, avoidance or a fear of closeness. A child may have a pervasive negative mood and low self-perception and be unable to cope with disappointment.

A child experiencing an absence of emotional warmth from their parents or caregivers may also have difficulty in developing a capacity for empathy and present as unfeeling, aggressive, withdrawn or distancing in response to others. There may be evidence of persistent grief, unresolved traumatic symptoms and failure of emotional adjustment, linked with persistent fear, distress, anxiety, anger and regression. Responses can include the child or young person taking on a predominately care-taking role or developing a negative self-image based on the parents' misrepresentation.

Table 15.5: Emotional warmth and containment

EMOTIONAL WARMTH AND CONTAINMENT

Parental strengths	*Parental difficulties*
• Satisfactory expression and reception of feelings, valuing, respecting, consistent.	• Failure to express or respond to feeling, critical, humiliating, rejecting, inconsistent.
• General emotional tone, warmth, calmness, humour, support, engagement.	• General emotional tone, negative, undermining, exploiting, disqualifying, coldness, lack of support, disengaged.
• Empathy, understanding of child's emotional responses and states, containment and tolerance, non-punitive responses.	• Lack of empathy, failure to understand child's emotional states, lack of containment, intolerance, punitive responses.
• Protection from current traumatic losses and stressful events and situations, mental health, parental conflict or personality issues, current and early development.	• Failure to protect from current traumatic losses, situations, stressful events, parental conflict, mental health or personality issues, current and early development.
Impact on the child when provision of emotional warmth and containment adequate	*Risk of harm – impact on the child when emotional warmth and containment inadequate*
• Child is part of a network of secure, organised attachments.	• Child is part of a network of insecure, disorganised attachments, clinging, indiscriminate, avoiding or controlling responses.
• Capacity to respond appropriately to emotional communication, emotional states well regulated.	• Lack of a capacity to respond to emotional communication, arousal, frozenness results, and emotional states poorly regulated.
• Shows basic positive emotional mood, brief appropriate responses to disappointment and change.	• Pervasive negative mood, failure to cope with disappointment and change.
• Traumatic and stressful events have been processed without lasting effects.	• Persistent fear, distress, traumatic responses, failure of processing.
• Positive emotional adjustment.	• Negative emotional adjustment, mood difficulties, anxiety states and self-harm.

Given the picture of harm which emerges from the evidence-based assessments of the strengths and difficulties in each dimension of parenting capacity, the identification of any harmful parenting and the analysis of the impact on children's developmental needs, it then becomes feasible to create a profile of harm.

Making decisions about the needs of the child and their family

In order to make decisions about the needs of the sexually abused child, practitioners should complete a functional systemic analysis of the processes which have led to the occurrence of patterns of significant harm including sexual abuse and associated forms of harm. This includes understanding the information obtained using the dimensions of the Assessment Framework and the interaction between the dimensions and domains. It also requires a consideration of the weight of negative processes which may be acting as maintaining factors and the magnitude of strengths – the weight of positive processes – which are potentially protective factors. (This is considered in detail in Chapters 4, 10 and 18.)

Second, establishing the prognosis for change, that is assessing the likelihood of achieving change within the child's time frame, using information about factors associated with the risk of re-abuse, and knowledge about the likelihood of response to intervention. This requires a consideration of each domain, an assessment of the level of difficulty in each of the dimensions, the recognition of difficulty by parents, children and young people, and the likelihood of response within the child's timescale. Based on a review of each domain, an overall assessment of prognosis can be made, and an appropriate intervention plan formulated. Central questions are:

- Do parents acknowledge the extensiveness of their child's difficulties, and need for intervention?

- Do they acknowledge responsibility for the harm they may have been responsible for?

- Is there a willingness to address individual, family and environmental issues which may be having a deleterious impact on parenting capacities?

- Is there a prospect for positive change within the young person's time frame?

On the basis of the profile drawn up, it then becomes possible to take a view as to whether the overall prognosis is *reasonably hopeful*, in that there are sufficient factors to feel that a positive outcome can be achieved within the child's time frame. For example, the perpetrator takes responsibility for abusive action and is likely to respond to therapeutic work, the caring parent believes the child's statements and puts the needs of the child first, the traumatic impact of abuse is not triggering life threatening self-harm or mental health difficulties. Alternatively, some factors make it *highly unlikely* that a safe context can be achieved for the child. For example, there is strong evidence of abuse having occurred yet the parents stand together to deny that abuse could have occurred, blaming the child or young person for making malicious allegations, or that professionals have 'induced' the child to describe abuse through the mechanism of false memories. Very frequently there is a *degree of doubt*, because there is a lack of clarity about whether an abuser can take an appropriate degree of responsibility, and there is doubt whether a caring parent can sustain belief in the child given pressure from partner and family members. This indicates the requirement for further assessments to determine whether a degree of clarity about prognosis can be achieved. (This is considered in detail in Chapter 17.)

Factors associated with the risk of re-abuse and the prognosis for intervention

Jones (1998) and Jones *et al.* (2006) summarise factors associated with re-abuse in family contexts. These factors include parental denial, antisocial personality disorders and learning disability associated with mental health problems.

Sylvester *et al.* (1995) note that a key issue associated with the prognosis for rehabilitation is the attribution of blame to children when the child is perceived by the parents as being responsible for the parent's abusive action. Relationships can be 'organised' by traumatic events. Based on this work, a 12-step process is described in Table 15.6 to determine the risk of re-abuse and the prospect for rehabilitation.

Table 15.6: 12-step process for assessing the risk of re-abuse to a child, parenting capacity and prospects of rehabilitation

Step 1: Examine the overall levels of harm, past and present, and examine the impact on the child's health and safety, educational issues, emotional life, behaviour and identity, and how the child's needs were met in the past and currently.

Step 2: Assess the level of parenting, protection and therapeutic work the child requires, considering the levels and extensiveness of harm, and factors which would act as an additional factor requiring particular parenting skills, for example learning disability.

Step 3: Establish the following: do parents acknowledge the level of harm? Can they take appropriate responsibility for harm? Do they acknowledge the need for protection and therapeutic work to ensure the child's future safety and recovery?

Step 4: Consider the level of parenting capacity in the areas of provision of basic care, ensuring safety, providing emotional warmth, stimulation, guidance and boundaries and stability.

Step 5: Establish whether parents acknowledge the nature and level of current difficulties in parenting capacity and they have the motivation to achieve change.

Step 6: Assess the parents' potential to respond to the child's needs and to develop their capacity to help children recover from abusive effects and achieve their potential.

Step 7: Identify the influence of individual and family factors on parenting capacity, considering factors from the parents' childhood, health, relationships, family organisation and family relationships, including with the wider family.

Step 8: Find out whether the parents acknowledge the role of individual and family factors and their effect on parenting and their level of motivation to change.

Step 9: Assess the potential for change in individual and family factors and to respond to intervention and improve parenting to meet the children's needs.

Step 10: Consider the role of environmental factors such as housing, employment, income and family integration and their impact on parenting, individual and family functioning and the parents' capacity to meet children's needs.

Step 11: Establish whether parents recognise the role of environmental factors and the potential for change.

Step 12: Explore the nature of family professional relationships, and establish whether there is a potential for working together and the availability of resources to achieve change within the child's time frame.

Formulating a plan of intervention – therapeutic work in a context of safety

A plan of intervention should take into account the level of harm to the child which has occurred, the risks of re-abuse and the prospects of rehabilitation if the child has been removed from parents or carers. In a study of outcomes following child sexual abuse 9 per cent of children were rehabilitated to the family, which included the abuser, 52 per cent lived with a protective parent, and 37 per cent could not live with any family members because of rejection or disbelief (Bentovim *et al.* 1988).

Meeting the needs of the sexually abused child

When a child has experienced sexual abuse it is essential to protect the child, increase social support available to the child and their family, and treat psychological symptoms and behaviours associated with abuse. In these situations interdisciplinary working to meet the many and varied needs of children and families is essential.

Learning a variety of coping strategies – relaxation, finding a safe place emotionally – is a crucial first step for children who have been sexually abused. There needs to be a focus on addressing emotional and traumatic symptoms including fear, sadness and anxiety, as well as their avoidance, anger outbursts, sexualised responses, self-harm and maladaptive anger. Jones and Ramchandani (1999) in their review of intervention for sexual abuse support the importance of psycho-education – for children and young people to understand the way in which they have been involved in sexual activities to which they could not give informed consent. Forming a 'Trauma Narrative' – drawing out an account of trauma and abuse – helps to desensitise and habituate disturbing memories. These can be shared with caring, non-abusive family members to provide a 'witness' of the child's experiences.

The child needs help to become aware of the 'false beliefs' of attribution and blame projected on to them. A protective parent needs to be able to be open to the experiences of the child, to be able to listen and share, and contain what may have been an extreme sense of terror, fear and powerlessness at the hands of the abusive parent. The development of safe family-care rituals to cope with sleeping difficulties is required, as are ways of coping with excitement, anger, sexualised behaviour, and a change of relationship style to avoid re-traumatisation.

For the child to develop a more satisfactory sense of themselves, he or she has to be helped to realise that what is defined as problematic, for example switching off, angry oppositional behaviour, fear and avoidance, are part of a survival strategy – a strength not a weakness. Family work needs to be absolutely clear about the origins of blame, to help the child understand the way in which the abuser attributes abusive action to the victim, rather than taking responsibility themselves. Where rehabilitation is a possibility, family work requires a carefully planned apology and taking of responsibility for abusive action. This must be more than the often brief acknowledgement from the abuser which is possible in the earlier phases of work. Questions the child has about what has happened to him or her can be put to the abusive parent. Responses by the abuser can be worked out with the therapists.

Alternative care

When a child cannot return home, intensive family work within a new family context, such as a foster family, is required. Sexually abused children may have a high level of sexual knowledge, may be prone to a sexual behavioural disorder, and may have an aggressive or victimising stance themselves. A protective context needs to be planned within the new family context, and careful consideration of the appropriate mode of contact with the original family. Work with the foster family or adoptive family is essential to maintain an appropriate supportive stance, and to incorporate the sexually abused child into a new family context.

There is a current emphasis on placing children within the family network before considering placements in non-family placements. Kinship placements have the strengths of maintaining the child's sense of identity, and the maintenance of established relationships. However, there may be risks of the child being exposed to significant adversity, depending on the patterns of strength and difficulty of the extended family network, and there may be risks of re-traumatisation and undermining of placement security through contact with abusive family members. Therefore, kinship placements should be carefully assessed before such a decision is made.

Summary

Sexual abuse frequently occurs in a context of family adversity, where children are neglected, emotionally abused and rejected. They are treated as objects of sexual interest, and may be groomed to be compliant, or threatened and physically harmed to adapt to the older, more powerful individual's needs. The child is silenced to prevent disclosure, so that discovery is often by chance, through the alert observer noting changes in the child's behaviour or knowledgeable professionals who appreciate the jigsaw puzzle of symptoms and signs which present. The process of assessment can be complex, because of the pervasive effect of denial and blame by the alleged perpetrator, both of the child for falsifying and the professional for imagining abuse, which does not exist. The impact of sexual abuse on the child's emotional and social life and on their relationships can be considerable, depending on the extensiveness of abuse, and the support provided for the child post discovery. Effects can be long lasting and impact on adolescent, adult life, partnering and parenting. It is essential that there is a holistic assessment using the Assessment Framework to establish the profile of harm, and the capacity of parents to provide more satisfactory care. Therapeutic work has to take place in a context of good care, safety for the child, emotional support, belief and stable relationships. The child or young person needs to be helped to cope with the traumatic emotional effects, and the 'internalising' and 'externalising' responses, before there can be an unfolding of the nature of the child's experiences, and sharing of traumatic memories. Where an abuser adult or young person within the family context can face their abusive action, a process of clarification and appropriate taking of responsibility can take place. Rehabilitation of the child with non-abusive family members is a more likely outcome than with perpetrators. The cost of taking responsibility for abusive action may be too high for some perpetrators; there is risk of long-term family breakdown and loss. Therapeutic work needs to be available at key points of the life-cycle when there is a re-awakening of traumatic memories, for example at child-birth, menstruation, first sexual relationships. There is a risk of a 'cumulative burden' in the lives of individuals who have been sexually abused (Noll *et al.* 2009). A good deal is known about effective intervention and prevention of long-term effects. This knowledge needs to be put into practice.

Recommended reading

Bentovim, A., Cox, A., Bingley Miller, L. and Pizzey, S. (2009) *Safeguarding Children Living with Trauma and Family Violence: Evidence-based Assessment and Planning Interventions.* London: Jessica Kingsley Publishers.

Bentovim, A., Elton, A., Hildebrand, J., Tranter, M. and Vizard, E. (1988) *Child Sexual Abuse within the Family.* London: Wright Butterworth Press.

Cohen, J.A., Mannarino, A.P., Berliner, L. and Deblinger, E. (2000) 'Trauma-focused cognitive behavioural therapy for children and adolescents: an empirical update.' *Journal of Interpersonal Violence 15,* 1202–1223.

Ferguson, D.M. and Mullen, P.E. (1999) 'Childhood sexual abuse: an evidence-based perspective.' *Developmental Clinical Psychology and Psychiatry 40.* Thousand Oaks, CA: Sage.

Jones, D.P.H. and Ramchandani, P. (1999) *Child Sexual Abuse: Informing Practice from Research.* Abingdon: Radcliffe.

References

Bentovim, A., Cox, A., Bingley Miller, L. and Pizzey, S. (2009) *Safeguarding Children Living with Trauma and Family Violence: Evidence-based Assessment and Planning Interventions.* London: Jessica Kingsley Publishers.

Bentovim, A., Elton, A., Hildebrand, J., Tranter, M. and Vizard, E. (1988) *Child Sexual Abuse within the Family.* London: Wright Butterworth Press.

Bifulco, A., Brown, G.W. and Harris, T.O. (1994) 'Childhood Experience of Care and Abuse (CECA) – a retrospective intervention measure.' *Journal of Child Psychology and Psychiatry 35,* 1419–1435.

Carlson, E.A. (1998) 'A prospective longitudinal study of attachment disorganisation/disorientation.' *Child Development 69,* 1107–1129.

Cawson, P., Wattam, C., Brooker, S. and Kelly, G. (2000) *Child Maltreatment in the United Kingdom.* London: NSPCC.

Cox, R. (2005) Kaleidoscope – personal communication.

Criminal Justice System (2007) *Achieving Best Evidence in Criminal Proceedings: Guidance on Interviewing Victims and Witnesses and Using Special Measures.* Available at www.cps.gov.uk/Publications/docs/Achieving_Best_Evidence_Final.pdf, accessed on 27 May 2009.

Department of Health (2003) *The Integrated Children's System.* London: Department of Health.

Department of Health, Department for Education and Employment and Home Office (2000) *Framework for the Assessment of Children in Need and their Families.* London: The Stationery Office.

HM Government (2006) *Working Together to Safeguard Children: A Guide to Inter-agency Working to Safeguard and Promote the Welfare of Children.* London: The Stationery Office.

Jones, D.P.H. (1998) 'The Effectiveness of Intervention'. In M. Adcock and R. White (eds) *Significant Harm: Its Management and Outcome.* Croydon: Significant Publications.

Jones, D.P.H. and Ramchandani, P. (1999) *Child Sexual Abuse: Informing Practice from Research.* Abingdon: Radcliffe.

Jones, D.P.H., Hindley, N. and Ramchandani, P. (2006) 'Making Plans: Assessment, Intervention and Evaluating Outcomes.' In J. Aldgate, D.P.H. Jones, W. Rose and C. Jeffery (eds) *The Developing World of the Child.* London: Jessica Kingsley Publishers.

Noll, J., Trickett, P.K., Harris, W.W. and Putnam, F. (2009) 'The cumulative burden borne by offspring whose mothers were sexually abused as children.' *Journal of Interpersonal Violence 24,* 424–449.

Pears, K., Kim, H.K. and Fisher, P.A. (2008) 'Psychosocial and cognitive functioning of children with specific profiles of maltreatment.' *Child Abuse and Neglect 32,* 958–971.

Skuse, D., Bentovim, A., Hodges, J., Stevenson, J. *et al.* (1998) 'Risk factors for development of sexually abusive behaviour in sexually victimised adolescent boys: cross sectional study.' *British Medical Journal 317,* 175–179.

Sylvester, J., Bentovim, A., Stratton, P. and Hanks, H. (1995) 'Using spoken attributions to classify abusive families.' *Child Abuse and Neglect 26,* 23–37.

CHAPTER 16

Assessing the Needs and Risk of Re-offending of Young People who Sexually Abuse

Bobbie Print, Helen Bradshaw, James Bickley and Marcus Erooga

For a small number of children the causes of concern will be serious and complex and the relationship between their needs, their parents' responses and the circumstances in which they are living is less straightforward. In these situations, further, more detailed specialist assessments will be required.

(From the Framework for the Assessment of Children in Need and their Families, p.26, 2.25)

This chapter will:

- provide a way of understanding a young person's motivation to sexually abuse

- explain why assessment tools for assessing risk of re-offending by adults are not appropriate for use with adolescents who have sexually offended

- outline the importance of a strengths-based assessment and intervention approach

- review the newly designed AIM2 assessment model

- consider how an assessment using AIM2 can contribute to a core assessment using the *Framework for the Assessment of Children in Need and their Families*.

Introduction

In this chapter the main theoretical ideas that have emerged in the literature to date are outlined in order to enable practitioners to understand the development and maintenance of sexually abusive behaviour by young people. Whilst there are no British validated assessment tools available for use in evaluating the risk of re-offending with this group, recent developments in the assessment of adolescents who sexually abuse are considered. In particular, a UK-developed tool, the AIM2 model of specialist assessment, is explored. As this chapter can only provide an overview of the relevant research and theory, a number of models are referenced for further reading purposes.

As will be discussed below, AIM2 shares the same principles as the *Framework for the Assessment of Children in Need and their Families* (Department of Health *et al.* 2000), which are described in detail in Chapter 2. They are both based on an ecological approach and have similar domains. Moreover, a key perspective underpinning AIM2 is recognising that young people who sexually abuse are children in need under section 17 of the Children Act 1989, as well as perpetrators of sexual abuse. The AIM2 model, designed to consider sexual risk issues, therefore complements and can contribute to an assessment of a child in need in this respect. In this chapter we explore ways in which an assessment using AIM2 can contribute to the core assessment using the Assessment Framework.

Why do some young people sexually abuse?

Many theories exist as to why people might engage in sexually abusive behaviour. According to Ward *et al.* (2005) the theories fall into one of three categories:

- comprehensive explanations of sexual abuse
- single factors associated with sexual abuse
- offence process descriptions.

These categories differ in the level of explanation they offer, moving from a macro level (all factors known to be associated with sexually abusive behaviour) to a micro level (offence-specific factors). However, the received view is that researchers and practitioners should attempt to integrate all three categories in order to achieve a global theory (Ward *et al.* 2005). Comprehensive explanations of sexual abuse are multi-factorial models that attempt to explain the aetiology of sexually abusive behaviour by giving a complete account of all the possible causes. For example, Finkelhor's (1984) four factor model, Marshall and Barbaree's (1990) integrated theory, or Ward and Siegert's (2002) pathways model. At the next level, single factors are highlighted which are known to be associated particularly with sexual abuse, for example deficits in empathy or cognitive distortions (Marshall *et al.* 1995). At the third level, offence process descriptions attempt to describe the 'how' of sexually abusive behaviour by focusing on the temporal factors relating to the commission of a sexual offence (for example cognition, behaviour, motivation and social factors). Examples of this include Lane's (1997) 'sexual abuse cycle' or Ward and Hudson's (1998) 'self-regulation pathway'.

Based on these different theoretical frameworks a number of plausible causes associated with sexually abusive behaviour have been put forward. These include:

- genetic predispositions
- adverse developmental experiences
- psychological dispositions/trait factors
- familial factors
- social and cultural factors
- environmental factors
- situational or precipitating factors.

However, as will be seen below, young people who sexually abuse are an extremely diverse, heterogeneous group and to date there are no clear distinguishing factors that can be reliably employed to identify this group from those young people who have not abused (Rich 2003). Moreover, those who do abuse may engage in many different types of sexually abusive behaviour at multiple levels of severity and intensity. Such behaviour can be driven by a number of different motivating factors or goals and can also be influenced by a number of individual and contextual factors that direct different young people along a variety of 'pathways'. Nonetheless, it is reasonable to seek commonalities, or 'common threads', in these pathways that allow the identification of danger signs for both the development and maintenance of sexually abusive behaviour. Whilst, therefore, there is no 'prototypical profile' of young people who sexually abuse it does seem that there are a number of identifiable individual characteristics and contextual factors that appear with a degree of regularity in this population (Rich 2003).

Pathways to sexually abusive behaviour

Whilst many theories have been developed in relation to adult sex offenders, Rich (2003) offers a more specific developmental pathway approach for young people's sexually abusive behaviour. This takes into consideration early negative life experiences, what Rich terms 'developmental vulnerabilities' or 'predisposing' factors. Such experiences include:

- attachment difficulties/discontinuity of care
- childhood maltreatment, neglect or abuse
- early exposure to domestic violence or high-stress family environment
- inadequate parenting capacity.

For some young people genetic, biological factors and early life experiences can result in them developing individual psychological characteristics or traits that increase their vulnerability to engage in sexually abusive behaviour. That is, because they have not had the opportunity to develop interpersonal, intimacy or self-regulation skills, in the context of a securely attached relationship with their caregiver, they often develop dysfunctional beliefs or strategies that impact on their ability to form appropriate relationships with others (see Chapter 11). Examples of these dispositional characteristics or 'concerns' include:

- attitudes or beliefs that are supportive of sexual abuse
- deviant or obsessive sexual interests

- poor self-concept (low self-esteem or self-efficacy)

- limited pro-social skills (for example unassertiveness, poor perspective taking or empathy)

- inadequate self-management abilities (for example impulsiveness, poor problem-solving skills).

These inappropriate interpersonal skills and interests are likely to be reinforced or maintained because of their short-term benefits (for example, gaining a sense of 'control', intimacy, or sexual satisfaction). However, they also prevent the young person from developing stable and satisfying relationships with others, and consequently maintain their poor sense of self-worth. Furthermore, their social isolation impedes the young person's ability to develop pro-social skills and the capacity to empathise with others.

It is important that 'contextual' factors are identified to help understand their influence on sexually harmful behaviour. Therefore, a young person's developmental pathway should always be considered in the context of their environment. The influence of the young person's family, peer group, wider culture and society as well as access to media may all have a role to play in both the development and maintenance of sexually abusive behaviour. Contextual factors could include exposure to pornography, lack of sexual boundaries in the family, a high-stress family environment, inadequate parenting or supervision, social isolation or negative peer associations. An additional consideration is the extent to which the young person's context provides opportunities or resources to help them achieve meaningful goals (for example relationships, education, employment).

Highlighting the importance of both individual and contextual factors can help practitioners to understand why a young person engaged in sexually abusive behaviour at a particular point in time (the 'why now?' question). Both types of factors can be identified as possible 'precipitating' events or triggers. These may include:

- acute life stressors or lifecycle transitions (for example being a victim of bullying, experiencing parental separation)

- access to a potential victim

- acute thoughts/feelings supportive of abusive behaviour (for example a sense of entitlement, sexual arousal).

Whilst reviewing the potential predisposing, precipitating and ongoing individual and contextual concerns that might help understand a young person's sexually harmful behaviour it is also important to consider 'strengths' and resilience. That is, a young person will not always commit sexual offences even if the developmental vulnerabilities and precipitating factors described above are present. It is therefore important to consider potential individual and contextual protective factors or strengths that might help a young person to refrain from sexually abusive behaviour. Individual strengths might include a young person having good cognitive abilities, an internal locus of control, positive talents or engaging in leisure activities. Contextual strengths can include the young person having good social supports, effective communication in the family and appropriate sexual boundaries. In addition, the opportunity to make a positive contribution to their society through positive education and employment can act as a contextual strength. (See Chapter 10 for more information about resilience.)

Assessment approaches and models

As described elsewhere in this book the *Framework for the Assessment of Children in Need and their Families* (Department of Health *et al.* 2000) is an ecological model that assists practitioners in identifying the developmental needs of a child, the parent or carer's capacity to meet those needs and the influence of family and environmental factors on both the child and their carer. As outlined above all of these domains are relevant when assessing the offending pathways of young people who sexually abuse. However, when assessing the needs of young people who sexually harm, a more specialist assessment is also required in order to assess the risk of re-offending. This additional assessment should be commissioned as part of an in-depth or core assessment of the needs of a young person who has sexually abused. In addition, the findings from this specialist assessment should inform the decisions that are made with regard to not only meeting the needs of the young person but recognising the potential risk of further sexual abuse and protecting others from sexual harm. It is therefore important that practitioners have an understanding of methods for assessing risk of re-offending in relation to young people who commit sexual offences.

Assessing risk of re-offending

The two most popular approaches to assessing risk of re-offending are actuarial instruments and clinical judgement-based approaches, which are discussed below.

ACTUARIAL ASSESSMENT

Actuarial assessments are based on static or historical risk factors identified in research studies undertaken with relevant offender populations. They guide not only the variables to be considered but also the precise procedure through which ratings of these variables can be translated into a risk level. Amongst the limitations of the actuarial approach are that:

- they yield a probability, not a certainty, of future recidivism
- they seek to estimate long-term risk and take no account of contextual risk factors that might indicate imminent re-offending
- they rely on large base rates of the problem behaviour to be statistically robust
- unusual factors that are relevant to the individual case are ignored
- an individual with a low actuarial risk classification may nevertheless sometimes be likely to re-offend (for example an intra-familial sex offender with continuing access to a past victim)
- they do not indicate which clinical/dispositional factors need to be addressed in treatment for risk to be reduced.

Whilst there are a number of actuarial assessment tools validated for use with male adults who sexually offend, for example Rapid Risk Assessment for Sexual Recidivism (RRASOR) (Hanson 1997), Static-99 (Hanson and Thornton 2000), Risk Matrix 2000 (Thornton *et al.* 2003) and the Sex Offence Risk Appraisal Guide (SORAG) (Quinsey *et al.* 1998), no validated actuarial tools currently exist for adolescents. As the risk factors for adolescents are not the same as for adult offenders, it is not possible to generalise the results from assessment tools based on adult offender samples to adolescents. These actuarial tools are therefore not appropriate for adolescents who sexually abuse and use of them is highly likely to give grossly misleading results, as discussed further below.

CLINICAL JUDGEMENT-BASED ASSESSMENT

The clinical judgement approach is a subjective assessment based on gathering material at interview with an offender as well as other available data – essentially relying on professional judgement. Criticisms of clinical judgement approaches are that they include:

- clinician bias
- reliance on variables that may be meaningless or without empirical support
- inconsistent administration by clinicians
- unstructured or poorly constructed methods
- unproven and inaccurate assumptions
- confusing formulation.

There are, however, some research-guided clinical judgement instruments, such as the Etiological Model of Risk (Beech and Ward 2004), that employ a set of factors informed by research and theory to direct professional assessment without being prescriptive.

Adolescent risk assessment

Whilst validated tools for assessing risk of re-offending amongst adults who sexually abuse are routinely used throughout the UK (Thornton *et al.* 2003), the limited research data available on young people who sexually abuse means that there are currently no such validated models for this group. Unfortunately this has led, in some instances, to assessment methods for adults being used with young people, without validation for an adolescent population or recognition of the very different developmental issues that are relevant to young people.

LACK OF RESEARCH

A review of the literature, regarding young people who sexually abuse, shows that re-offending rates are generally low, with most studies showing rates of between 3 per cent and 14 per cent (Worling and Långström 2003). There is a general consensus, however, that there exists a relatively small subgroup of adolescents who are at high risk of re-offending sexually or violently (Barbaree *et al.* 1993; Righthand *et al.* 2005; Worling and Långström 2003). The current paucity of research significantly restricts the ability to accurately identify who these high-risk young people are.

Whilst efforts are being made to increase the available research in relation to young people who sexually re-offend, this will remain limited until the development of a cohort of good quality long-term studies that provide better information about such individuals. In the meantime, simply transferring risk factors identified for adults to young people is likely to result in inaccurate assessments with far-reaching consequences for the individuals concerned. Calder (2001) suggests that as a result of this lack of research, practitioners have been attributing labels of low, medium or high risk to young people with little empirical evidence to support such decisions. The potential consequences of such action can lead both to ascribing false positives, where individuals are deemed high risk where there is no such risk, and false negatives, where young people are deemed low risk when they are in fact dangerous. Given the worrying implications of such judgements, both for those who are potential victims and for those who have abused, there has been a demand to develop more reliable and sophisticated means of assessing risk of re-offending in young people who sexually abuse.

A number of assessment tools for use with young people who sexually abuse have been developed and are widely respected and commonly used throughout North America and to a lesser extent Europe. These include the research-based Juvenile Sex Offender Assessment Protocol (J-SOAP) (Prentky *et al.* 2000) and the Estimate of Risk of Adolescent Sexual Offender Recidivism (ERASOR) (Worling and Curwen 2000, 2001). Both rely in part on data from research on adult sex offenders and both are from North American populations. Their transferability to UK adolescent populations therefore needs to be considered carefully. The J-SOAP is primarily concerned with assessing risk of re-offending but can also contribute towards treatment planning, whilst ERASOR has a greater emphasis on intervention recommendations and delivery. Although early research to validate these tools has shown encouraging results neither can yet claim to have predictive validity for assessing future sexual offending.

Within England and Wales one of the most commonly used assessment tools (Hackett *et al.* 2003) is the AIM initial assessment model (Print *et al.* 2001). This model has been recently updated and revised into the AIM2 model.

The AIM2 model of assessment

As there are no scientifically validated methods available to assist in these tasks, the assessment of the needs of young people who sexually abuse remains a complex task that cannot be reduced to a simple procedure and should not simply focus on risk of recidivism. There is a clear need for professionals to have a validated assessment tool that not only helps to identify whether an individual young person is likely to be amongst those that continue to commit abuse but also identifies what intervention is required to reduce such risk. The AIM2 initial assessment model (Print *et al.* 2007), whilst not scientifically validated, is an evidence-based model developed in the UK. The AIM2 model is an updated version of the original AIM model first published in 2001.

The current version incorporates changes suggested by an evaluation of the original model commissioned by the Youth Justice Board (Griffin and Beech 2003) as well as feedback from practitioners and additional relevant research. The new version includes advice on the process of conducting assessments, culturally sensitive practice, and the formulation of intervention plans. Used together with the Assessment Framework, AIM2 can assist professionals to consider both the level of supervision that is required for an individual, bearing in mind the nature of their sexual offending behaviour, their developmental needs and interventions that address both their offending behaviour and their identified developmental needs.

The AIM2 model reflects professional recognition that the factors that lead to an individual exhibiting sexually abusive behaviours are complex and broad ranging. Assessment therefore requires a holistic consideration of the individual-in-context and not merely an examination of the abuse and the young person's personal characteristics. Thus, as with the original model, AIM2 assessment includes attention to a wide range of factors represented in four domains – development; family; environment; and offence details. The factors to consider, which are included in each of the domains, are those that have an evidence base in research on recidivism. The specific areas that need to be addressed are outlined in Table 16.1.

Table 16.1: The four assessment domains

Offence specific	Developmental
• Nature of index sexual offence/abuse	• Resilience factors
• Young person and family's attitude to victim	• Health issues
• Amount and nature of offence planning	• Experiences of physical/sexual/emotional abuse or neglect
• Use of threats, violence or aggression during commission of offence/abuse	• Witnessed domestic violence
• Young person's offending and abusive behaviour history	• Quality of the young person's early life experiences
• Previous professional involvement with young person and family regarding offending/abusive behaviours	• History of behaviour problems
• Motivation to engage with professionals	• Sexual development and interests
Family/carers	**Environment**
• Level of functioning	• Young person's access to vulnerable others
• Attitudes and beliefs	• Opportunity for further offending
• Sexual boundaries	• Community attitudes to young person and family
• Parental competence	• Wider supervisory and support network

The AIM2 model also attempts to consider the developmental needs of young people by means of assessing not only their developmental history but also their family, social, environmental and cultural context. The importance of such a holistic approach is widely accepted in the literature (Rich 2003; Ryan and Associates 1999) and further supported by the multi-systemic therapy model (MST) that locates an individual's treatment goals within their community and social systems. MST has much support in the literature on intervention with general offending and anti-social youth (Hollin 1999; Rutter *et al.* 1998) and its efficacy in reducing sexual recidivism has been evidenced (Borduin *et al.* 1990; Worling and Curwen 2000).

This format connects the model explicitly with the Assessment Framework, where the focus is on the first three of the AIM2 domains, and the ASSET assessment tool (Youth Justice Board of England and Wales 2003) used in the context of youth justice, where the focus includes the fourth domain. In this way it is intended that the model can be used alongside, and is relevant to, both systems and draws on the skills of the professionals involved in each. The completion of an AIM2 can either be a stand-alone process or more commonly will be commissioned as a specialist assessment informing a core assessment using the Assessment Framework. It may also be incorporated into ASSET forms or pre-sentence reports. In this chapter the focus is on AIM2 being completed as a specialist assessment contributing to a core assessment.

GATHERING INFORMATION USING AIM2

The AIM2 model can be completed within 28 working days. The timescale fits well with the 35 working days timescale for completing core assessments. The model requires assessors to gather relevant information from a range of sources, including the young person and their family. Table 16.2 identifies the possible sources of information within each of the four domains. As is true for most assessments there is a necessity for inter-agency liaison as well as the involvement of young people and their families to assist in gathering the required information. When an AIM2 assessment is commissioned as part of the core assessment process, consideration should be given to ways in which practitioners will work together to avoid duplication in terms of gathering information from the young person, their family and other professionals.

The methods used to gather information for the assessment will usually rely on reading professional documentation and interviews with relevant professionals, family members, carers and the young person. Issues of confidentiality are an essential consideration in planning these tasks and will vary according to each situation. In all cases, however, the level of information shared with information sources about the details of the young person's sexually abusive behaviour must be carefully considered and limited to a need-to-know basis. Additionally, a clear statement regarding the level and limits of confidentiality offered to those providing information must be given.

The information gathered is used to score a number of static and dynamic items, with scores that relate to the nature of the evidence base that support the item's inclusion. Items are considered to be *evidence based* where there are at least two credible pieces of research relating the item to risk of recidivism in adolescents who sexually abuse, *evidence supported* where there is only a small research base relating the item to risk of recidivism in adolescents who sexually abuse or there is research that links recidivism to adults who sexually abuse or adolescents who commit serious non-sexual offending, or *theoretically supported* where there are not sufficient credible pieces of research but there is a strong consensus in the literature that the item is connected to recidivism in adolescents who sexually abuse.

Table 16.2: Possible sources of information for use in assessment

	Professional network	Young person	Family/carers	Community
Offence	• Records of police interview with offender, witness and victims including video-recorded interviews. • Previous professional concerns regarding offending or abusive behaviours.	• Attitudes, thoughts and feelings surrounding the victim and the offence behaviours. • Sexual knowledge, beliefs and interests. • Acceptance of responsibility. • Feelings of remorse, shame and guilt. • Motivation to accept help.	• Previous concerns regarding sexual behaviours. • Attitudes to victim. • Knowledge of young person's sexual interests and behaviours.	• Awareness of the young person's behaviour. • Response to the young person. • Possible risks to the young person.
Development	• Professional records and knowledge including health, social services, education and youth justice.	• Knowledge, feelings and understanding of personal history. • Recognition of personal skills, strengths and needs. • Relationships with significant others including peer relationships. • Personal goals and ambitions. • Religious beliefs, culture.	• Details of young person's health, social, educational and behavioural history. • Young person's strengths and difficulties. • Young person's friendships and social activities.	• Characteristics of family and young person's community. • Religious/ cultural norms, attitudes and beliefs of the family/ young person's community. • Employment record. • Community recognition of young person's skills, for example awards, sporting achievements.

Continued over page

Table 16.2: Possible sources of information for use in assessment (*cont.*)

	Professional network	Young person	Family/carers	Community
Family	• Professional records of family strengths and problems. • Family/carer's ability to support and manage the young person. • Risk to the young person. • Risk from the young person.	• Family relationships and dynamics. • Family attitudes and beliefs. • Wishes for future relationships, contact, placement, etc.	• Family composition. • Family history and functioning. • Family attitudes and beliefs about sex, sexuality and the young person's behaviour. • Family/carer's understanding of risk. • Family/carer's willingness to support young person.	• Family involvement in community. • Community attitude towards family. • Resources to support family.
Environment	• Understanding and view of family/ young person's community. • Opportunities for further abusive behaviour.	• Social activities, skills and interests. • Peer network. • Educational/ employment interests.	• Sources of support. • Recognition of risk.	• Attitude towards the young person. • Sources of support. • Social, educational, employment opportunities.

MAKING SENSE OF THE INFORMATION: INDIVIDUAL
RESILIENCE, STRENGTHS AND CONCERNS

The AIM2 model, together with other recently developed tools (Borum *et al.* 2003; Bremer 2001), reflects a growing interest in the increasing body of research regarding an individual's resilience and how protective factors can positively influence the outcomes for children and young people who are exposed to traumatic and/or difficult experiences (Katz 1997; Rasmussen 1999, 2004). Whilst there has been documented theoretical support for the inclusion of resilience factors in the assessment of adolescents who sexually abuse (Dewhurst and Nielsen 1999; Gilgun 1990, 1999a, 2006) there has been little research to support its use. However, the efficacy of the incorporation of strengths and resilience factors is supported by research that shows that these factors can have a significant impact on the likelihood of general recidivism (Carr and Vandiver 2001; Hoge and Andrews 1996). In her research on adult sex offenders Gilgun (1999b) identified that having a confidant was a significant factor in reducing recidivism and that the presence of healthy peer, family and community relationships were also positively significant. O'Callaghan (2002) described how interventions with young people who sexually abuse need to be informed by factors that promote resilience and positive outcomes. AIM2 therefore incorporates strength or resilience factors as components of the assessment, as well as deficits, and thereby helps to diminish the likelihood of negative labelling. Additionally, a focus on strengths helps to promote an 'approach goal' method of intervention that works with a young person to achieve positive goals rather than the traditional, more negative focus of diminishing negative behaviours. The use of the approach goal method is currently receiving increasing attention in a number of programmes that work with those who sexually offend (Mann 2004; Marshall *et al.* 1995; Ward and Gannon 2006).

Whilst the original AIM model based the inclusion of such strength factors on the theoretical prediction that those young people with greater strengths are more likely to be successful in dealing with and overcoming their negative behaviours, the current model utilises a small-scale follow-up study to evidence the significance of strengths. The study had a sample of 70 young men who had sexually abused during adolescence, seven of whom were identified by the Home Office as having sexually re-offended (Beech and Griffin, in press). The AIM2 model was applied to the sample and the results analysed to examine whether specific concern or strength factors could be associated with those who had sexually recidivated. The results identified a small number of concern factors that were particularly associated with those young men who had re-offended. These concern factors, however, were also identified in a number of young men who were not known to have re-offended. The two groups were differentiated by a number of strength factors that appeared to act as protective factors for those that had not re-offended.

The concerns and strengths identified by the research which should be used to indicate the level of supervision required are:

CONCERNS

- evidence of previous contact sexually abusive behaviours
- sexually abused a stranger
- used or threatened violence during sexual assault
- previous non-sexual offending
- cold, callous attitude toward sexual offending
- generally highly impulsive or compulsive
- difficulties emotionally regulating
- maintains contact with pro-criminal peers.

STRENGTHS

- healthy physical developmental history
- average/above average intelligence
- positive talents and/or leisure interests

- the most significant adults in young person's life demonstrate good protective attitudes and behaviours

- the most significant adults in young person's life demonstrate positive emotional coping strategies

- young person has at least one emotional confidant

- young person has positive evaluations from work/education staff

- young person has positive relationships with carers.

AIM2 weights these items in accordance with the level of evidence that supports their inclusion. For example, there is robust support that links 'evidence of previous contact sexually abusive behaviours' with recidivism and so that item attracts a high score.

THE OUTCOMES OF AN AIM2 ASSESSMENT

The good predictive quality that the combination of the identified concern and strength factors were shown to produce, in the research described above, permits a degree of confidence in the use of the AIM2 assessment in helping to identify the 'level of supervision required'. This measure differentiates those whose scores indicate they are most likely to commit further abuse from those who are less likely to do so. That is, the tool helps to evaluate the likelihood of re-offending but does not consider the level of harm that would be incurred as a result of any further abusive behaviours. Thus, evaluators must consider this latter element in addition to the outcomes of an AIM2 assessment. For example, if a young person commits a particularly violent act, such as rape, his level of required supervision is likely to be enhanced given the potential harm he would inflict if he were to re-offend.

The decision to identify 'the level of supervision required' as opposed to alternative terminology was based on the view that it is not helpful to label young men as being 'high risk', 'medium risk' or 'low risk', particularly, as already noted, the research base on which such outcomes are determined is not scientifically validated. The level of supervision required, whilst identifying the level of professional concern there should be about an individual, provides a more practical result in that it indicates the degree of external risk management that is likely to be necessary to prevent further abuse occurring. The 'level of supervision' terminology also places emphasis on the requirements of the professional system rather than on labelling the individual.

In addition to considering the level of supervision an individual may require, AIM2 is also designed to help practitioners evaluate what intervention is needed with regard to their offending behaviour. The model is constructed to allow an analysis of the strengths and concerns in each domain, thereby allowing assessors to reflect on the assets and needs of an individual's environment (placement), family (contact, support, etc.), developmental issues (thoughts, feelings and behaviours) and offence issues (distorted thoughts, attitudes, etc.). This information can then be used to help construct plans to support and promote strengths as well as therapeutically address needs.

The AIM2 model is designed to assist clinical judgement; it is not an empirically validated model and is intended to provide no more than guidance. Professional judgement remains an essential part of the assessment and in order for professionals to feel confident in their judgement, and not isolated or anxious, it is essential that they receive skilled professional supervision and/or consultancy and make use of multi-agency fora to share their views and seek support and challenge for their judgements.

Case example

Kevin, a 14-year-old, was accused of having intercourse with his half-sister (aged seven) and half-brother (aged six) on three separate occasions. Kevin was interviewed by the police and admitted the behaviour. He was accommodated by the local authority, placed in a residential home and an AIM2 assessment was undertaken jointly by a member of the local Youth Offending Team, who also completed ASSET and ROSH (Risk of Serious Harm) assessments, together with a member of the local Children's Social Care Services Team who also undertook a core assessment using the *Framework for the Assessment of Children in Need and their Families* (Department of Health *et al.* 2000).

The assessors collected further background information from children's social care records, his residential carers, his school, his GP and the police, and they interviewed Kevin on three occasions and his parents on two occasions.

On completing the AIM2 assessment forms it emerged that Kevin's areas of static concerns included a number of individual and contextual factors, such as experiencing attachment difficulties, domestic violence, parental separation and physical abuse. He did, however, have a number of strengths that included having had his mother as a consistent positive caregiver, an average level of intelligence and a healthy physical development.

Kevin's dynamic concerns were predominantly in his Developmental Domain and included his low self-esteem, difficulties in emotional regulation, poor social skills and a sense of loneliness. His sporting abilities and interests together with his positive attitudes towards professionals and undertaking work to address his sexually inappropriate behaviours were included as dynamic strengths.

The AIM2 assessment provides an indication of the level of supervision that the young person requires. By comparing key concern and strength factors, Kevin was viewed as requiring a medium level of supervision. This suggested that whilst Kevin could be safely managed in the community he required a moderate level of supervision and a full programme of therapeutic intervention. The AIM2 scores also identified his placement as positive and that if this was to change, for example by a return home, his required level of supervision would significantly increase.

The assessment scores were also used to help identify Kevin's needs. His high level of static concerns suggested that he required focused help in addressing some of his own traumatic experiences and the thoughts, feelings and behaviours that may be connected to these. His scores in the dynamic realm suggested that in addition to work on his sexual thoughts, feelings and behaviours, Kevin needed help to improve his self-esteem, social skills and emotional regulation. In order to promote and enhance his strengths it was considered important that Kevin be involved in pursuing his sporting interests within the safe boundaries of ongoing risk assessments. His mother's support was particularly important to Kevin but the high concern scores that the assessment identified in the Family Domain suggested that the provision of family work was also very important.

Kevin was convicted in the Crown Court of six counts of rape. The Pre-Sentence Report offered to the Court by the Youth Offending Service included the outcomes and recommendations of his AIM2 assessment. The Judge remarked that whilst he had been considering a custodial sentence for Kevin he was persuaded by the report to give a community sentence and Kevin was made the subject of a three-year Supervision Order and placed on the Sex Offender Register for five years. Kevin remained in the residential unit for two years and engaged in a programme of work designed to address his abusive behaviours. Kevin's mother also participated in work to help her support her son. The outcomes were considered to be very positive and when Kevin left the residential unit he lived independently, had regular, positive contact with his family and attended full-time college where he made a number of peer-aged friends and engaged in a range of social activities.

MANAGING THE INTERFACE: CORE ASSESSMENTS AND AIM2

To summarise, the AIM2 assessment model is a specialist tool designed to evaluate the specific needs and risks presented by an adolescent male whose behaviour is regarded as sexually harmful. AIM2 is constructed so that it can run alongside, and contribute to, a core assessment. Figure 16.1 provides an overview of how the two processes can interlink.

Important considerations

In addition to the challenges outlined above in terms of adolescent assessments of sexual offending behaviour, due to lack of research there are additional difficulties when considering the assessment of young people with a learning disability, young people from ethnic minorities and young females.

Young people with learning disabilities

Young people who have a learning disability are statistically over-represented amongst those who are known to have sexually abused. UK studies identify between one third and a half of young people who sexually abuse have a learning disability or significant educational problems (Beckett 1999; Dolan *et al.* 1996; Epps 1991; Monk and New 1996; Vizard 2000). This high proportion may be explained by a number of factors including: the repetitive and habitual nature of their offending; an increased level of impulsivity; and a relatively high level of naivety when challenged (Thompson and Brown 1998). Whilst the majority of factors commonly associated with the development of sexual aggression in young people are likely to be generally applicable to understanding this behaviour in young people with a learning disability (Lindsay *et al.* 2001; Thompson and Brown 1998). O'Callaghan (2006) identifies differential life opportunities and developmental processes which also need to be taken into account. These include a limited opportunity for social development, social isolation, limited sex education, a lack of privacy, a lack of opportunity to experience normative and appropriate sexual interactions, specific difficulties in communication, and the impact of specific genetic and medical factors. Whilst there is almost no research that has specifically addressed factors associated with risk of

1. Young person alleged to have sexually abused – referral directed to police, children's social care services or youth offending team.

↓

2. Inter-agency liaison to agree process including the necessity of a child protection conference, immediate legal actions and assessments required. If a core assessment and an AIM2 assessment are to be completed then at least one of the AIM2 assessors should be involved in completing the core assessment.

↓

3. Information relevant to both the AIM2 and core assessments is gathered by the co-assessors from all pertinent professional agencies.

↓

4. Interviews are conducted with the young person, family/carers and relevant others to gather further required information.

↓

5. The AIM2 assessment can normally be completed within 28 days and an AIM2 assessment report produced.

↓

6. The AIM2 outcomes can then be used to inform the completion of a core assessment, safeguarding and criminal justice recommendations.

Figure 16.1: Flow diagram of assessor tasks

re-offending for sexually aggressive young people with learning disabilities, the original AIM initial assessment model (Print *et al.* 2001) has been adapted for use with these young people (O'Callaghan 2001). O'Callaghan used the same framework of a strengths/ concerns continuum as the original model but sensitised it to the needs of young people with a learning disability, reflecting clinical experience and theory.

Young people from ethnic minorities

Whilst there is no doubt that race and culture are major components influencing an individual's development (Calder 2001; McGoldrick 1998) there is little reference in the literature as to how race, ethnicity and culture may impact on the development, maintenance and recurrence of sexually abusive behaviour by adolescents. Equally, whilst the experience of oppression can result in a level of mistrust, defensiveness and self-protective reactions toward professionals, there is little available to guide those who are undertaking assessments as to good practice in the particularly sensitive and complex work with those who have sexually abused. The recently published AIM2 initial assessment model (Print *et al.* 2007) has begun to address this issue by inclusion of guidance by Mir and Okotie on developing cultural sensitivity to the needs of Asian and black young people who sexually abuse.

Young females

There is a similar dearth of research regarding young females who sexually abuse. It is, however, increasingly recognised that whilst the incidence of sexual abuse by females may be less prevalent, the seriousness of the harm they inflict is equal to their male counterparts (Rosencrans 1997). Research suggests that females may account for up to 5 per cent of all sexual offences against children (Bunting 2005) but there is scant information as to how many of these females are under the age of 18 and to what extent their developmental pathways, in relation to sexual offending, vary from those of young males. There are a small number of studies that have examined the characteristics of females who sexually abuse and some apparent differences from their male counterparts have been noted. For example, there is evidence to suggest that females who abuse are more likely to have experienced multiple types of abuse, including sexual abuse (Lewis and Stanley 2000; Ray and English 1995), than males who abuse. Additionally, there is considerable discussion in the literature as to the influence of sociological factors on identifying and responding to females who sexually abuse with a predominating view that they are more likely to go unnoticed, unreported and diverted from the criminal justice system than males (Blues *et al.* 1999; Frey 2006; Mathews *et al.* 1997; Robinson 2005, 2006).

Based on the literature on female adolescent development and sexual offending, Robinson (2005) has provided assessment guidelines for young females who sexually harm. For example, she suggests that a thorough understanding of a young woman's development, strengths, vulnerabilities, any impact of trauma and socio-cultural scripts are essential components of any assessment. However, she acknowledges that due to the lack of research regarding young women who sexually harm, the development of specific assessment tools is still work in progress.

Conclusion

The reasons why young people sexually abuse are multi-factorial involving developmental, familial, environmental, social-cultural and interpersonal elements but most importantly the combinations are unique in each case. Consequently, it is essential that any assessment fully recognises the young person in his or her family and community context, as the role of the family environment and the wider social networks all have positive prognostic implications, as well as indicating possible areas which need attention in order to reduce risk of harm (Erooga and Masson 2006).

Assessments of young people who sexually abuse should therefore go beyond simply assessing risk of re-offending and adopt a more holistic approach, taking into account the developmental needs of the young person, their strengths as well as deficits. In this way, it is possible to give credence to an individual's unique characteristics and circumstances and inform issues such as the level of external controls, the supervision required, appropriateness of placements and the intervention needs of the young person and their support systems.

The AIM2 model of assessment is a UK-developed research-guided clinical judgement framework that helps practitioners collect, organise, analyse and evaluate information in order to construct recommendations for the safe and appropriate management of a young person and the intervention required to reduce future risk. Whilst it is not a validated instrument, it has the benefit of an evidence base and when carefully employed it combines efficiently with the *Framework for the Assessment of Children in Need and their Families* (Department of Health *et al.* 2000).

Recommended reading

Erooga, M. and Masson, H. (2006) *Children and Young People who Sexually Abuse Others: Current Developments and Practice Responses.* London: Routledge.

Reilly, G., Marshall, W.L., Beckett, R. and Carr, A. (eds) (2004) *Handbook of Clinical Interventions with Juvenile Sexual Offenders.* London: Routledge.

Rich, P. (2003) *Understanding, Assessing and Rehabilitating Juvenile Sexual Offenders.* New York, NY: John Wiley & Sons.

Ward, T., Polaschek, D.L. and Beech, A.R. (2005) *Theories of Sexual Offending.* Chichester: John Wiley & Sons.

References

Barbaree, H.E., Hudson, S.M. and Seto, M.C. (1993) 'Sexual Assault in Society: The Role of the Juvenile Offender.' In H.E. Barbaree, W.L. Marshall and S.M. Hudson (eds) *The Juvenile Sex Offender.* New York, NY: Guilford Press.

Beckett, R. (1999) *Young Abusers: The Hidden Crime of Children who Sexually Abuse Children.* Paper presented to Info-Log Conference, Royal Over-Seas House, Park Place, London (October).

Beech, A. and Griffin, H. (in press) *Concerns and Strengths that Differentiate Recidivism in a Sample of Adolescents who Sexually Abused.*

Beech, A. and Ward, T. (2004) 'The integration of etiology and risk in sexual offenders: a theoretical framework.' *Aggression and Violent Behaviour 10*, 1, 31–63.

Blues, A. Moffat, C. and Telford, P. (1999) 'Work with Adolescent Females who Sexually Offend.' In M. Erooga and H. Masson (eds) *Children and Young People who Sexually Abuse Others.* London: Routledge.

Borduin, C.M., Hengeller, S.W., Blaske, D.M. and Stein, R.J. (1990) 'Multisystemic treatment of adolescent sex offenders.' *International Journal of Offender Therapy and Comparative Criminology 34*, 2, 105–113.

Borum, R., Bartel, P. and Forth, A. (2003) *Manual for the Structured Assessment of Violence Risk in Youth (SAVRY).* Tampa, FL: University of South Florida.

Bremer, J.F. (2001) *The Protective Factors Scale: Assessing Youth with Sexual Concerns.* Plenary address presented at the 16th annual conference of the National Adolescent Perpetration Network, Kansas City, MO.

Bunting, L. (2005) *Females who Sexually Offend against Children: Responses of the Child Protection and Criminal Justice Systems.* London: NSPCC.

Calder, M.A. (2001) *Juveniles and Children who Sexually Abuse: Frameworks for Assessment.* Lyme Regis: Russell House Publishing.

Carr, M. and Vandiver, T. (2001) 'Risk and protective factors among youth offenders.' *Adolescence 36*, 143, 409–426.

Department of Health, Department for Education and Employment and Home Office (2000) *Framework for the Assessment of Children in Need and their Families.* London: The Stationery Office.

Dewhurst, A.M. and Nielsen, K.M. (1999) 'A resiliency-based approach to working with sexual offenders.' *Sexual Addiction and Compulsivity: The Journal of Treatment and Prevention 6*, 4, 271–279.

Dolan, M., Holloway, J., Bailey, S. and Kroll, L. (1996) 'The psychosocial characteristics of juvenile sexual offenders referred to an adolescent forensic service in the UK.' *Medicine, Science and Law 36*, 4, 343–352.

Epps, K. (1991) 'The residential treatment of adolescent sex offenders.' *Issues in Criminological and Legal Psychology 1*, 17, 58–67.

Erooga, M. and Masson, H. (2006) *Children and Young People Who Sexually Abuse Others: Current Developments and Practice Responses.* London: Routledge.

Finkelhor, D. (1984) *Child Sexual Abuse.* New York, NY: Free Press.

Frey, L.L. (2006) 'Girls Don't Do That, Do They? Adolescent Females who Sexually Abuse.' In R.E. Longo and D.S. Prescott (eds) *Current Perspectives: Working with Sexually Aggressive Youth and Youth with Sexual Behaviour Problems.* Holyoke, MA: NEARI Press.

Gilgun, J. (1990) 'Factors Mediating the Effects of Childhood Maltreatment.' In M. Hunter (ed.) *The Sexually Abused Male: Prevalence, Impact and Treatment.* Lexington, MA: Lexington Books.

Gilgun, J. (1999a) 'CASPARS: Clinical Assessment Instruments that Measure Strengths and Risks in Children and Families.' In M.C. Calder (ed.) *Working with Young People who Sexually Abuse: New Pieces of the Jigsaw Puzzle.* Lyme Regis: Russell House Publishing.

Gilgun, J. (1999b) 'Mapping Resilience as Process among Adults Maltreated in Childhood.' In H. McCubbin, E. Thompson and J. Futrell (eds) *The Dynamics of Resilient Families.* Thousand Oaks, CA: Sage.

Gilgun, J. (2006) 'Children and Adolescents with Problematic Sexual Behaviours: Lessons from Research on Resilience.' In R. Longo and D. Prescott (eds) *Current Perspectives: Working with Sexually Aggressive Youth and Youth with Sexual Behavior Problems.* Holyoke, MA: NEARI Press.

Griffin, H. and Beech, A.R. (2003) *An Evaluation of the AIM Framework for the Assessment of Adolescents who Display Sexually Harmful Behaviour.* London: Youth Justice Board.

Hackett, S., Masson, H. and Phillips, S. (2003) *Mapping and Exploring Services for Young People who have Sexually Abused Others.* Final Report. Durham: University of Durham.

Hanson, R.K. (1997) 'The development of a brief actuarial risk scale for sexual offense recidivism.' *User Report No. 1997–04.* Ottawa, ON: Department of the Solicitor General of Canada.

Hanson, R.K. and Thornton, D. (2000) 'Static-99: improving actuarial risk assessments for sex offenders.' *User Report No. 1999–02.* Ottawa, ON: Department of the Solicitor General of Canada.

Hoge, R.D. and Andrews, D.A. (1996) *Assessing the Youthful Offender: Issues and Techniques.* New York, NY: Plenum Press.

Hollin, C. (1999) 'Treatment programmes for offenders: meta-analysis, "What Works", and beyond.' *International Journal of Law and Psychiatry 22,* 3–4, 361–372.

Katz, M. (1997) *On Playing a Poor Hand Well: Insights from the Lives of Those who have Overcome Childhood Risks and Adversities.* New York, NY: W.W. Norton.

Lane, S. (1997) 'Assessment of Sexually Abusive Youth.' In G. Ryan and S. Lane (eds) *Juvenile Sexual Offending: Causes, Consequences, and Correction* (rev. edn). San Francisco, CA: Jossey-Bass.

Lewis, C.F. and Stanley, C.R. (2000) 'Women accused of sexual offences.' *Behavioral Sciences and the Law 18,* 1, 73–81.

Lindsay, W.R., Neilson, C.Q., Morrison, F. and Smith, A.H. (2001) 'A comparison of physical and sexual abuse histories of sexual and non-sexual offenders with intellectual disability.' *Child Abuse and Neglect 25,* 7, 989–995.

Mann, R.E. (2004) 'Innovations in sex offender treatment.' *Journal of Sexual Aggression 10,* 2, 141–152.

Marshall, W.L. and Barbaree, H.E. (1990) 'An Integrated Theory of the Etiology of Sexual Offending.' In W.L. Marshall, D.R. Laws and H.E. Barbaree (eds) *Handbook of Sexual Assault: Issues, Theories, and Treatment of the Offender.* New York, NY: Plenum.

Marshall, W.L., Hudson, S.M., Jones, R. and Fernandez, Y.M. (1995) 'Empathy in sex offenders.' *Clinical Psychology Review 15,* 2, 99–113.

Mathews, R., Hunter, J.A. and Vuz, J. (1997) 'Juvenile female sexual offenders: clinical characteristics and treatment issues.' *Sexual Abuse: A Journal of Research and Treatment 9,* 3, 187–199.

McGoldrick, M. (1998) *Re-visioning Family Therapy: Race, Culture, and Gender in Clinical Practice.* London: Guilford Press.

Monk, E. and New, M. (1996) *Report of a Study of Sexually Abused Children and Adolescents and of Young Perpetrators of Sexual Abuse who were Treated in Voluntary Agency Community Facilities.* London: HMSO.

O'Callaghan, D. (2001) 'A Framework for Understanding Initial Assessments of Young People with Intellectual Disabilities who Present Problematic/Harmful Sexual Behaviours.' In *AIM Assessment Intervention: Moving On, Getting Started.* Manchester: The AIM Project.

O'Callaghan, D. (2002) 'Providing a Research Informed Service for Young People who Sexually Abuse.' In M.C. Calder (ed.) *Young People who Sexually Abuse: Building the Evidence Base for Your Practice.* Lyme Regis: Russell House Publishing.

O'Callaghan, D. (2006) 'Group Treatment of Young People with Intellectual Impairment who Sexually Harm.' In R.E. Longo and D.S. Prescott (eds) *Current Perspectives: Working with Sexually Aggressive Youth and Youth with Sexual Behaviour Problems.* Holyoke, MA: NEARI Press.

Prentky, R., Harris, B., Frizzell, K. and Righthand, S. (2000) 'An actuarial procedure for assessing risk in juvenile sex offenders.' *Sexual Abuse: A Journal of Research and Treatment 12,* 2, 71–93.

Print, B., Beech, A., Quayle, J., Bradshaw, H., Henniker, J. and Morrison, T. (2007) *AIM2: An Initial Assessment Model for Young People who Display Sexually Harmful Behaviour.* Manchester: The AIM Project.

Print, B., Morrison, M. and Henniker, J. (2001) 'An Inter-agency Assessment and Framework for Young People who Sexually Abuse: Principles, Processes and Practicalities.' In M.C. Calder (ed.) *Juveniles and Children who Sexually Abuse: Framework for Assessment.* Lyme Regis: Russell House Publishing.

Quinsey, V.L., Harris, G.T., Rice, M.E. and Cormier, C.A. (1998) *Violent Offenders: Appraising and Managing Risk.* Washington, DC: American Psychological Association.

Rasmussen, L.A. (1999) 'The Trauma Outcome Process: an integrated model for guiding clinical practice with children with sexually abusive behaviour problems.' *Journal of Child Sexual Abuse 8,* 4, 3–33.

Rasmussen, L.A. (2004) 'Differentiating Youth with Sexual Behaviour Problems: Applying a Multidimensional Framework when Assessing and Treating Subtypes.' *Journal of Child Sexual Abuse 13,* 3–4, 57–82. Published simultaneously in R. Geffner, K.C. Franey, T.G. Arnold and R. Falconer (eds) *Identifying and Treating Youth who Sexually Offend: Current Approaches, Techniques, and Research.* Binghamton, NY: Haworth Trauma and Maltreatment Press.

Ray, J.A. and English, D.J. (1995) 'Comparison of female and male children with sexual behaviour problems.' *Journal of Youth and Adolescence 24,* 4, 439–451.

Rich, P. (2003) *Understanding, Assessing and Rehabilitating Juvenile Sexual Offenders.* Hoboken, NJ: John Wiley & Sons.

Righthand, S., Prentky, R.A., Knight, R., Carpenter, E., Hecker, J.E. and Nangle, D. (2005) 'Factor structure and validation of the juvenile sex offender assessment protocol (J-SOAP).' *Sexual Abuse: A Journal of Research and Treatment 17,* 13–30.

Robinson, S. (2005) 'Considerations for the Assessment of Female Sexually Abusive Youth.' In M.C. Calder (ed.) *Children and Young People who Sexually Abuse: New Theory, Research and Practice Developments.* Lyme Regis: Russell House Publishing.

Robinson, S. (2006) 'Adolescent Females with Sexual Behaviour Problems: What Constitutes Best Practice?' In R.E. Longo and D.S. Prescott (eds) *Current Perspectives: Working with Sexually Aggressive Youth and Youth with Sexual Behaviour Problems.* Holyoke, MA: NEARI Press.

Rosencrans, B. (1997) *The Last Secret: Daughters Sexually Abused by Mothers.* Orwell, VT: Safer Society Press.

Rutter, M., Hagell, A. and Giller, H. (1998) *Antisocial Behaviour by Young People.* Cambridge: Cambridge University Press.

Ryan, G. and Associates (1999) *Web of Meaning: A Developmental-Contextual Approach in Sexual Abuse Treatment.* Brandon, VT: Safer Society Press.

Thompson, D. and Brown, H. (1998) *Response-ability: Working with Men with Learning Disabilities who have Difficult or Abusive Sexual Behaviours.* Brighton: Pavilion.

Thornton, D., Mann, R., Webster, S., Blud, L. *et al.* (2003) 'Distinguishing and Combining Risks for Sexual and Violent Recidivism.' In R. Prentky, E. Janus, M. Seto and A.W. Burgess (eds) *Understanding and Managing Sexually Coercive Behaviour. Annals of the New York Academy of Sciences 989,* 225–235. New York, NY: The New York Academy of Sciences.

Vizard, E. (2000) *Characteristics of a British Sample of Sexually Abusive Children.* Keynote presentation to the BASPCAN National Congress, University of York (September).

Ward, T. and Gannon, T.A. (2006) 'Rehabilitation, etiology, and self-regulation: the comprehensive good lives model of treatment for sexual offenders.' *Aggression and Violent Behavior: A Review Journal 11,* 77–94.

Ward, T. and Hudson, S.M. (1998) 'A model of the relapse process in sexual offenders.' *Journal of Interpersonal Violence 13,* 6, 700–725.

Ward, T. and Siegert, R. (2002) 'Toward a comprehensive theory of child sexual abuse: a theory knitting perspective.' *Psychology, Crime, & Law 8,* 4, 319–351.

Ward, T., Polaschek, D. and Beech, A. (2005) *Theories of Sexual Offending.* Chichester: John Wiley & Sons.

Worling, J.R. and Curwen, T. (2000) 'Adolescent sexual offenders recidivism: success of specialized treatment and implications for risk prediction.' *Child Abuse and Neglect 24,* 7, 965–982.

Worling, J.R. and Curwen, T. (2001) 'Estimate of Risk of Adolescent Sexual Offense Recidivism (The ERASOR–Version 2.0).' In M.C. Calder (ed.) *Juveniles and Children who Sexually Abuse: Frameworks for Assessment.* Lyme Regis: Russell House Publishing.

Worling, J.R. and Långström, N. (2003) 'Assessment of criminal recidivism risk with adolescents who have offended sexually: a review.' *Trauma, Violence, & Abuse 4,* 4, 341–362.

Youth Justice Board of England and Wales (2003) *ASSET* (B108). London: HMSO.

PART III
Assessing Parenting Capacity and Parenting Issues

CHAPTER 17

Assessment of Parenting

David Jones

Critically important to a child's health and development is the ability of parents and caregivers to ensure that the child's developmental needs are being appropriately and adequately responded to, and to adapt to his or her changing needs over time.

(From the Framework for the Assessment of Children in Need and their Families, p.20, 2.9)

Chapter contents include:

- contemporary perspective on parenting:
    - some outstanding questions regarding parenting
    - summary.
- children's needs from their caregivers
- child outcomes arising from parenting difficulties and limitations
- assessment process:
    - some essential preliminary considerations
    - what is involved in assessment?
    - interviewing parents
    - interviewing children
    - observations
    - assessment of attachment status
    - standardised assessments
    - complementary sources of information.

- the value of planning
- assessing risk of maltreatment recurring
- care planning.

Introduction

Parenting can be defined as those activities and behaviours of caregiving adults that are needed by children to enable them to function successfully as adults within their culture.

Human parents aim to rear their young to be healthy individuals who will be capable of participating fully within the culture in which they will live. There is a considerable degree of similarity in how this is conceptualised and practised across different cultures. At the same time there remains significant relativity with respect to what is considered necessary for parents to do in different communities. One dimension to these differences is that which distinguishes the parenting of children within an individualist society compared with that which occurs within collectivist societies (Bornstein *et al.* 2007). For example, in Eastern cultures, such as those in south-east Asia and Japan, greater emphasis is placed upon commitment to the greater good of the group; whereas in Western democracies, particularly the USA, the emphasis is on individual attainment.

Contemporary perspective on parenting

A contemporary view of parenting goes well beyond the idea of a capacity that may or may not reside somewhere within an individual person. Instead, parenting is viewed from a multi-dimensional perspective. Parenting is seen in terms of its several elements. Jay Belsky, in 1984, put forward a model of the 'determinants of parenting' which took into account child factors and parent factors, setting these within the broad ecology within which families operated. In this way we could understand parenting in context. Similarly, relationships occur in both directions between child and parent. Parenting should not be construed as a uni-directional parent-to-child phenomenon, or a static capacity or thing residing within a person. These fundamental shifts in our understanding have been developed further over the past two decades. As a consequence, some dispense with the word 'parenting' and instead use the term 'caregiving' in order to reflect this shift of emphasis, but also to include foster and adoptive parents. Here 'parent' and 'caregiver' are used interchangeably to include all those persons in principal caregiving roles for the child.

We now understand that there are both genetic and environmental influences upon adult parents themselves, as well as upon children, all of which have the potential to affect what we see as parenting. In addition, there are interactions between genetic and environmental influences so that genes themselves can be affected by environmental factors and vice versa. These so-called 'GE interactions' are extremely important in relation to the notion of parenting (Rutter 2005).

Belsky's original proposal of multiple aspects or domains of a child's life which have the potential to affect parenting had been previously proposed by Bronfenbrenner (1977), with his notion of the different ecologies or systems of social organisation which surrounded an individual child – immediate family, extended family, neighbourhood, and broader cultural influences. These ecological perspectives on child development were further elaborated by developmental psychologists who emphasised strengths and weaknesses, or risk and resilience factors. Dante Cicchetti (1989) emphasised that not only did different factors interact with one another but they literally transformed one another in what he termed 'transactions' between factors. In this way, the eco-developmental perspective on child development has originated and this has much relevance for the notion of parenting too. Several examples of this complexity can be considered, but here we can select just a few to illustrate the main points.

The case of Attention Deficit Hyperactivity Disorder (ADHD) is a very interesting one. While there is some evidence for a link between adverse or hostile parenting in some cases of ADHD, we also know that when ADHD is subject to proper clinical treatment behaviourally, and in some cases through the use of medication, analysis of parenting shows a parallel improvement. This illustrates the poverty of adopting a uni-directional perspective on parenting.

Another example, illustrating the complexity, is that parents' capacity can be affected by the number of children that they are called upon to look after. Thus, a family may be relatively functional and its parenting very positive with two or three children, but become markedly dysfunctional with the arrival of the fifth or sixth child.

There are also developmental aspects to consider. It is a truism that the needs of infants are different from those of teenagers. They require different skills and sensitivities from caregivers.

In a similar vein, children with significant impairments may need particular skills from their carer or parent. Some carers are quite able to meet the needs of their non-impaired offspring but then find it more difficult to manage a physically or mentally impaired child (Butcher *et al.* 2008; Epstein *et al.* 2008).

It is also important to take into account family perspectives on parenting. For example, it has been noted that a parent's competence and their sensitivity to their child can be observed to be perfectly adequate and functional when in the role of primary or sole carer. However, when the dynamics are changed by the presence of another adult carer, some parents' capacity declines radically. This is most spectacular in cases involving intimate partner violence (domestic abuse). A mother who is perfectly warm, emotionally available and fully competent when caring for her child on her own may be rendered frankly neglectful when in the presence of her abusive partner. From a positive perspective the extent to which adult carers or parents can work together co-operatively in looking after their child or children has been the focus of important research in the family therapy tradition (McHale and Rasmussen 1998; McHale *et al.* 1996). The notion of co-parenting with its positive and more negative implications has been useful in understanding the complexities of parenting. It also takes us away from the idea that parenting is something which resides within a person and remains a static object. That is, parenting competencies and an individual parent's sensitivity toward their child can vary according to dynamics and circumstances within the family.

Neighbourhood influences can also affect parenting. It is extremely difficult, though not impossible, to raise a child successfully in a violent, socially deprived and impoverished neighbourhood (Garbarino 1997). There are marked differences between neighbourhoods, even when matched for the residents' economic and educational backgrounds (Korbin 2002). Some neighbourhoods are simply more conducive to raising children than others, in that they have more social support networks and a stronger ethos of mutual co-operation and support than others. This is then reflected in interesting differences in relative rates of child maltreatment, in the expected direction.

It has also been postulated that there are broader cultural influences upon parenting and caregiving. For example, rates of serious abuse and child deaths from maltreatment have been demonstrated to have a link with the extent of inter-country hostilities and where the parenting is occurring within the context of a war zone (Jenny and Isaac 2006). Rates of child maltreatment are higher in conflict zones when compared with equivalent economically deprived areas where there is less or no conflict.

As discussed in detail in Chapter 2, the *Framework for the Assessment of Children in Need and their Families* (Department of Health *et al.* 2000) draws together these factors and influences diagrammatically into a triangle with the child in the centre, and parenting on the right-hand side.

Some outstanding questions regarding parenting

There can be difficulty in deciding the relative weight that should be ascribed to each particular dimension of parenting. Is one aspect of parenting more important than another? If so, how much more important? Clearly, when faced with life-threatening absences of care, the question of weight becomes redundant, but with lesser deficits we are not able to weigh different dimensions numerically. What guidance we do have is described below. However, there are some preliminary factors to consider when thinking about the weight to be ascribed to different aspects of parenting or caregiving. In the first place, as already mentioned, transactions between different dimensions of parenting are important. One aspect of this is the relationship between positive influences and deficits or parenting problems. To what extent can we say that one cancels out the other? Richard Gelles (1993) has written persuasively that some acts are so dangerous that the question of weighing one against another should not be contemplated. For example, a significant blow to the head of an infant cannot be evenly weighted by positive observations concerning security of attachment. There are significant problems with measurement. Some parenting behaviours and activities have proved more elusive than others, in terms of ease of measurement. For example, quantifying emotional availability is much more difficult than the physical status of the home.

There are also significant variations in what we term a family. For instance, 'families' include two parents, one parent, step and re-constituted families, and shared parenting arrangements. There are also less familiar constellations, such as families containing lesbian or gay parents, and parents caring for children of the new reproductive technologies.

Summary

Two major points emerge from the foregoing discussion on our current perspective on parenting. First, it is essential to place a child's needs in centre stage, and consider parenting from that vantage point. Second, there are different aspects or dimensions of parenting, ranging from physical care to sensitive, timely responsiveness, but all centred on the individual child's needs. Therefore, a comprehensive, fair assessment of parenting demands multiple perspectives that are culturally sensitive and contextually relevant to any identified concerns. Turning to the first of these, what then do children need from their caregivers, and what are the consequences if they do not have these needs responded to appropriately and therefore met?

What children need from their caregivers

Cicchetti (1989) summarised the key stages of child development. These comprise the following:

- attachment (0 to 12 months)
- autonomy and self-development (1 to 3 years)
- establishing peer relationships (3 to 7 years)
- hierarchical integration of attachment, autonomy and peer relationships (7 to 12 years).

Cicchetti emphasises the importance of seeing each of these stages in terms of foundations for successive ones, rather than observable stages which come to the forefront and then merely fade over time while the next comes into focus. Earlier stages may be less prominent to the observer but are no less important for future competence. This approach not only emphasises the progression of development, but also the crucial requirement for integration as the child grows and achieves mastery and competence, over the life span. A good example is attachment security. Although attachment is considered a key early developmental issue, it remains centrally important throughout life. An individual's attachment status will undergo a series of important integrations into other aspects of the person's developing world. For example, during a child's school years, when social integration becomes the more prominent developmental task, attachment security is essential bedrock for the child's competence in the social arena. Lack of integration of early attachment can lead to severe, disabling difficulties during later childhood and through to adult life.

A parent's task in relation to these developmental issues is to bring the necessary elements to bear in order to maximise the child's capacity to achieve these goals. The focus is on minimum necessary parenting, rather than an idealised notion of the perfect parent. However, in placing parenting behaviour in direct proximity to the developmental challenges facing the child, it is immediately clear that what is required from a parent will change during the life span (see Aldgate *et al.* 2006 for an overview). The task of parenting in infancy is significantly different from that required during teenage years.

A basic minimum competence in each parenting dimension (Figure 17.1) is necessary throughout childhood and adolescence in order to meet the developing person's needs and to enable the child or young person to develop satisfactorily (Aldgate *et al.* 2006). Nonetheless, some parenting qualities become especially salient at different points in development in order to respond to children's evolving needs, at particular stages. For example, provision of emotional warmth in infancy revolves around attachment to the primary caregiver. During teenage years it is more likely to comprise emotional warmth and availability to listen and help the young person with his or her everyday problems, and to provide a secure base from which the young person can establish a network of friends for themselves. In the next paragraphs, key developmental tasks are briefly described, with especially salient parenting dimensions, A–F (Figure 17.1), noted in parentheses. We can see, however, that the dimensions remain applicable and necessary across developmental phases, but require changing forms of expression to meet the evolving needs of the child.

Development of a secure attachment relationship with the primary caregiver is regarded as the key developmental issue during the first year of life (see Chapter 11). This relationship becomes evident through infant and parent behaviours from age five months on, though its origins and foundations will have been laid well before this and can be evident from the first days of life [B, C, F]. The exchange of affection between parent and child, combined with recognition of and absorption with one another, and an accompanying ability on the part of the infant to cope with stress, are the hallmarks of successful negotiation at this stage [C]. If the parent is unable to meet this need in the infant, effects can be seen in terms of the infant's behaviour, the quality of relationship between infant and caregiver, and in the caregiver's own sense of satisfaction and contentment.

Between the ages of approximately one and three years the primary task of the infant is the development of an autonomous self. That is the beginnings of the development of the sense of self as a person separate from others. This differentiation is thought to depend upon the earlier consolidation of secure attachment during infancy. Key issues for parents, during this phase, include their sensitivity and ability to be flexible enough to respond to their toddler, as he or she struggles to discover the limits of personal identity and power within their world [C, E]. The parent enables the growing toddler to explore his or her environment while at the same time enabling reliance on a parent or parent figure for safety and security [C, D, E, F]. This period is also marked by the child's increasing recognition of the experience of their own emotional state and the parent is called upon to enable the developing toddler to regulate and to begin to be aware of internal feeling states [E].

This process becomes more sophisticated in the third year of life as the developing child increasingly differentiates him- or herself from others. The rapid development of language and the capacity to represent self and others and inanimate objects in play and language marks this period. The parents' sensitivity and availability, emotionally, and to the joys of language, are key parental competencies at this time [C, D]. Further emotional understanding and regulation also occurs during this period [E].

The period from three to seven years is characterised by establishing friendships and connections with other children. The ability to form friendships and to become integrated into peer groups requires the foundation of the previous stages of development.

A. Basic care

This is providing for the child's physical needs and ensuring appropriate medical and dental care. It includes provision of food, drink, warmth, shelter, clean and appropriate clothing, and adequate personal hygiene.

B. Ensuring safety

Ensuring the child is adequately protected from harm or danger. It includes protection from significant harm or danger and from contact with unsafe adults and other children, and from self-harm. It also requires recognition of hazards and danger, in the home and elsewhere.

C. Emotional warmth

Ensuring the child's emotional needs are met and giving the child a sense of being specially valued and a positive sense of their own racial and cultural identity. It includes ensuring the child's requirements for secure, stable and affectionate relationships with their caregiver(s) are met, with appropriate sensitivity and responsiveness to the child's individual needs. Meeting such needs will require appropriate physical contact, comfort and cuddling, sufficient demonstration of affection, warm regard, praise and encouragement.

D. Stimulation

Promoting the child's learning and intellectual development through encouragement in cognitive stimulation, play, and promoting social opportunities. It includes facilitating the child's cognitive development and potential through interaction, communication, talking and responding to the child's language and questions, encouraging and joining the child's play, and promoting educational opportunities. It also means enabling the child to experience success and ensuring school attendance or equivalent opportunity. It means generally helping the child to meet the challenges of life.

E. Guidance and boundaries

Enabling the child to regulate his or her own emotions and behaviour. The key parental tasks are demonstrating and modelling appropriate behaviour and control of emotions and interactions with others; guidance, which involves setting boundaries so that the child is able to develop an internal model of moral values and conscience; and social behaviour appropriate for the society in which he or she will grow up. The aim is to enable children to grow up into autonomous adults holding their own values and able to demonstrate appropriate behaviour with others, rather than having to be dependent on rules outside themselves. It involves not shielding or over-protecting children from exploratory or learning experiences. It also includes social problem-solving, anger management, consideration for others and effective discipline and shaping of behaviour.

F. Stability

Providing a sufficiently stable family environment to enable a child to develop and maintain a secure attachment to a primary caregiver in order to ensure optimal development. This includes ensuring secure attachments are not disrupted, providing consistency of emotional warmth over time, and responding in a similar manner to the same behaviour on different occasions. It also includes consistency and a predictable environment for parental control and discipline. Parental responses change and develop according to the child's developmental progress. In addition, ensuring children keep in contact with important family members and significant others.

(Adapted from Department of Health et al. 2000)

Figure 17.1: *Dimensions of parenting*

Self-regulation and the capacity to exhibit empathy and pro-social behaviour, combined with awareness of culturally relevant social mores, are key features. Parents' roles are now significantly different in terms of meeting the developmental needs of a child [D, E, F]. Nevertheless, parental sensitivities and capabilities, which proved successful when the child was younger, provide the core for positive caregiver development in a progressive and incremental manner, which mirrors the infant's development into childhood.

Between 7 and 12 years the task for the child becomes one of integration. This integration is based upon secure attachment, and a capacity to differentiate self and other, as well as extending peer relationships and social networks. Also, during this phase, the child becomes increasingly aware of his or her own intentions and preferences. The sense of right and wrong, with the development of moral ideas, becomes strong during this time, as does a child's awareness of internal thought processes and feeling states. Children's increased capacity to act individually and to assume responsibilities becomes clear to the observer. Parental guidance, boundary setting and assisting with learning, educationally and psychosocially, are very important for the child during this period [D, E].

During adolescent years these qualities are further developed, extending the process of integration and emotional development, and increasing the scope and scale of peer relationships, as well as relationships with other significant adults within the young person's world outside their family. Further progression of cognitive development occurs during adolescence. Alongside these changes, moral development is significant, intertwined with major changes in a young person's sense of self, and aspects of personal and social identity. Parents are central to how this phase of life is successfully negotiated, particularly through warmth, guidance and stability [C, E, F].

Child outcomes arising from parenting difficulties and limitations

The impact of not receiving adequate caregiving for a child or young person should be seen against a backdrop of their developmental needs. From a developmental perspective, deficits in early life would be expected to be more pervasive and severe in their effects than later parenting problems. The reason for this is because, from this perspective, developmental competencies build up over time, each one dependent and reliant upon successful negotiation of previous stages. It is for this reason that secure attachment is considered so important and fundamental for successful development. Other competencies and abilities within the child and young person are built upon these over the years. The impact of early neglect illustrates this all too clearly. Neglect during the early months of life is often seen by lay and professional alike as having less significance than later on in the child's life because the child is pre-verbal. 'Surely he won't be affected, he can't talk yet?' However, when looked at through the lens of what is required by children for adequate developmental progress, and the central importance of good quality early attachment, the severe effect of neglect during infancy makes perfect sense, perhaps all the more so for pre-verbal children. Conversely, consider the teenager who is being severely neglected, but who is seemingly robust in the face of adversity. The young person appears less damaged than expected despite suffering significant neglect, perhaps as a consequence of parental mental illness or substance misuse. In some such cases we discover that, during the young person's earlier years, they experienced good quality, warm, affectionate caregiving. In such cases sometimes the early building blocks have served to provide a degree of resilience for the young person during less fortunate times.

A simple, linear cause–effect relationship between 'parenting' and child/young person outcomes will not be forthcoming. This is partly because of the diversity of the capacities, functions and sensitivities involved in the construct of parenting/caregiving, but also because parenting is not an isolated phenomenon, but describes a set of caregiver functions set in the context of the child's needs and the surrounding family and social circumstances (O'Connor 2002). Furthermore, developmental considerations apply both to the developing child and parents themselves. Some children may be particularly resistant to 'ordinary' parenting, such as those with a deficient capacity for warmth, care and empathy and who are inherently callous towards other people (see Dadds and Rhodes 2008 for a discussion of the implications of this for their caregivers). Nonetheless, good evidence exists for links between aspects of parenting/caregiving and subsequent outcomes for children.

Various dimensions of parenting/caregiving (Figure 17.1) are associated with child health outcomes. Behavioural and emotional problems within children are associated with conflict between parents and children, inadequate parental monitoring, and lack of parental involvement with their children. Such conflict includes fighting and arguing, as well as overt dislike, hostility toward and rejection of the child (Quinton 2004). It also includes harsh punishment. These qualities have been linked with behaviour problems and later delinquency. Inadequate parental monitoring involves inadequate supervision and lack of knowledge about the children's whereabouts or activities. Lack of positive parental involvement with their children includes cognitive stimulation as well as lack of emotional support and weak parent–child attachments. Excessive parent–child conflict creates a poor model for conflict resolution, and teaches children unhelpful approaches to managing such conflict. Similarly, violence and harsh punishments set a precedent for meeting behaviour difficulties with parental violence. Additionally, inadequate parental monitoring means that opportunities to help the child with social problem solving and emotional regulation are sparse, while lack of positive involvement reduces opportunities for children to develop internal controls and to understand and manage their own emotional state and impulses. Wasserman et al. (1996) found that these three areas – conflict, inadequate monitoring and lack of positive involvement – each contributed to children's behaviour problems independently, as well as having a summative effect if all three were present.

Some groups of parents are likely to have these kinds of difficulties to a greater degree than comparison parents. They include parents with a history of childhood deprivation (Rutter 1989), particularly when they have a history of abuse and neglect which have not been assimilated or understood in a coherent way prior to becoming a parent (George 1996). On the other hand, involved and effective parenting, with consistency between caregivers (authoritative, but not authoritarian, control), is associated with fewer behaviour problems in children and adolescents (Quinton 2004). It also helps children with behaviour difficulties to overcome them during childhood.

What emerges, despite the variety of terms and constructs used, are two broad qualities of effective parenting that can be linked to children's mental health, and especially aggression and conduct problems – first, warmth and, second, control (O'Connor 2002). The various aspects of warmth are described in Figure 17.1. Parental control appears in the framework model as 'Guidance and boundaries' and under 'Stability' (see Figure 17.1), but can be usefully further analysed for our purposes. Van Aken *et al.* (2008), summarised different aspects of parental control that have been linked with outcomes for children. These authors distinguish between:

- positive discipline (noting, rewarding, advocating, requesting and encouraging good behaviour)
- psychological control (verbal punishments and withdrawing affection or interest)
- physical punishment
- structure (consistency and an organised, predictable environment for the child).

Each contributes to behaviour and especially aggression in children. The first of these four aspects of control is linked with positive behaviour outcomes for children, and the latter three with negative behaviour outcomes for the child if these control strategies are frequently used by caregivers within an unstructured context (see 'Stability', Figure 17.1). It may be noted that an inadequate structure may be characterised through being overly lax, inconsistent, unpredictable and involve parental overreaction.

Child maltreatment (the antithesis of parenting dimensions in Figure 17.1) is associated with behaviour and emotional negative outcomes. This is hardly surprising, but the links between maltreatment and particular outcomes (for example, conduct disorder, eating disorders, attempted and actual suicide, substance abuse) are so strong and specific as to be considered causal, and furthermore are known to extend to physical health (Waylen *et al.* 2008), and to persist into adult life (see Jones 2008 for a review). There are also strong associations between early infant–parent attachment difficulties, especially disorganised patterns, and poor mental health outcomes. Such attachment difficulties have emerged as central to poor outcomes in adolescence and adult life in more than one major longitudinal study (Grossmann *et al.* 2005; Sroufe *et al.* 2005). Findings concerning attachment and maltreatment underline the public health importance of safeguarding initiatives and interventions for young children, in order to have the best chance of averting poor outcomes later in childhood, and for adult health too (Hughes *et al.* 2005; Jones 2008).

Parenting capacity is also affected by a serious disharmony or violence between a child's parents, or where one or both parents suffers from mental illness of disorder (Stein *et al.* 2008), or alcohol or substance abuse (see Chapter 19). The precise mechanisms through which these forms of parental disorder affect parenting are complex and consist of multiple influences on different levels within the parent–child relationship, family and neighbourhood contexts. For example, the impact of maternal depression on parental functioning and child behaviour and emotional status is unlikely to derive from mood per se. It is much more likely that depressed mood affects other aspects of family life and social relationships, as well as the availability of social support, and possibly subsequent social isolation, and that all these factors affect parenting.

In addition, there is little research to help us unravel the various transactions between different factors which may be present in any one family, rendering it impossible to precisely unravel or weight numerically the consequences for an index child of a combination of risk and ameliorative influences (Jones *et al.* 2006). That said, available evidence can be marshalled to aid care planning (see below) and decision-making (Jones 2008). For example, some helpful information has been obtained from the study of the impact of parental mental illness on parenting and the subsequent outcome for children (Stein *et al.* 2008). Studies such as these reveal the importance of ameliorative influences, such as having a spouse or partner without mental illness who provides support for an unwell parent, as well as being able to positively parent any children. Equally, the child's temperament or inherent resilience are factors affecting the degree to which he or she is affected by parental mental disorder. However, child factors are unlikely to be as influential as parental ones for outcome (Kaufman and Zigler 1989).

Assessment process

Some essential preliminary considerations

There are major implications from the foregoing discussion for assessment by practitioners. These include the following:

- Parenting is a useful concept for practitioners, *provided* it is kept in mind that parenting is something which is embedded within the whole of the child's world. In this way, the emphasis shifts from simply looking at parenting and parent–child relationships in isolation to considering parenting within the context of co-parenting and family relationships, extended family and friendship networks, as well as the influence of the local neighbourhood on parenting capacity. Poverty is also incorporated within our perspective on parenting, as are influences of hostile environments and broader cultural influences, such as surrounding attitudes towards violence, social relationships, race, ethnicity and minorities.

- A developmental perspective on both adult caregiving and children is central and important to maintain when considering assessment of parenting.

- Adopting a child's perspective or child's-eye view on parenting helps a practitioner to maintain the child's welfare focus throughout assessment.

- It is important that parenting is firmly yoked to a child's individual needs and characteristics.

- It is necessary to consider which adults contribute to caretaking, or who else could do so, when planning an assessment.

- Multiple perspectives on parenting are required, in order to evaluate caregiving in the different settings in which it may be exercised, such as home, clinic, alone or with a partner, etc.

- It is important to emphasise both strengths and difficulties in relation to each dimension of parenting.

What is involved in assessment?

As discussed in Chapters 3 and 4, parenting assessments comprise interviews with parents/carers, children themselves, especially if older, assessment of the family, observations, and sometimes structured assessments. Normally, information will be required from other sources too, involving interviews with other professionals and obtaining reports. The final, but crucial, stage in the process is an analysis of the data gathered. The overall aim is to assess each carer's parenting with respect to each child in a family.

In this chapter we concentrate on assessment of parenting and parent–child relationships. However, as described in Chapter 2, an in-depth assessment would include such a parenting assessment alongside assessments of each child, adult carer, and a family's overall functioning in the context of their environment (Department of Health *et al.* 2000).

Interviewing parents

Figure 17.2 sets out a schema for interviewing a parent and listing primary areas to gather information upon. Chapter 6 provides advice on engaging parents in the assessment process. It is likely to require seeing them on more than one occasion, and the setting will vary from office to home or family centre, as available, and to best suit a parent and child. Interviews start with establishing the reason for the assessment, identifying confidentiality concerns and limitations, and outlining the intended process and outputs from the process. This may be difficult if parents are feeling coerced rather than voluntarily requesting help, but transparency from the start pays dividends later. A letter to confirm arrangements can be valuable, or the inclusion of a support person for the parent, particularly where there are language, cultural or developmental impairment issues (Jones 2009).

The overall approach to interviewing parents should be a combination of obtaining factual information, together with eliciting the parents' feelings and thoughts about each child at different stages of his or her development. It can be helpful to obtain a time line for this, tracing through parental feelings and views from pregnancy, through birth and the child or young person's development, and noting any changes or shifts in feelings, attitudes or perspectives as development progresses. The practitioner will be able to link any such changes elicited to any other life events or changes in the family, or broader ecology within the neighbourhood.

Feelings of close affection and the timing when these first emerged during antenatal and post-birth periods are important to evaluate. Most mothers can recall their child's first movements antenatally, particularly with their first born. Permission-giving questions are useful when assessing any delay in parental affection or warmth for a newborn baby; for example, 'Not everyone feels close to their baby immediately after birth; how long did it take you to feel close to X?'

It is useful to obtain each parent's views about any concerns that have been raised about their parenting, using the six dimensions of parenting (Figure 17.1) in the Assessment Framework. Parental perspectives on changes required will need detailed assessment. Parents are often insightful about the best outcomes for themselves and their children. Practitioners will be assessing parental motivation and preparedness to work with professionals on achieving any changes required. They will need to evaluate parental likelihood

Aims, process of assessment and confidentiality issues

Area(s) of concern or presenting problems

- each parent's perspective on caregiving
- any episodes of harm to child(ren)
- each parent's view on any changes required.*

Current health and psychological adjustment

- child(ren)
- parent(s).

Child(ren)'s personal history and development

- pregnancy
- delivery
- neo-natal period
- attachment and caretaking relationships
- milestones
- physical health
- behaviour and mental health
- parent's views on child, and his/her needs.*

Each parent's personal history and development

- childhood and adolescent years
- education
- work and training
- parental experiences of care during childhood*
- personal relationships (friendships and romantic)
- history of anti-social behaviour and/or delinquency
- substance abuse
- mental health history.

Family structure, history and functioning

- family structure and history
  - partnerships, pregnancies and births
- family relationships
  - parent/child relationships
  - parental relationship (including any violence)
  - type of communication within the family.

Family/social relationships

- friendships
- relations with wider family
- social support.

* Consider the six domains of parenting (Figure 17.1).

Figure 17.2: A schema for interviewing parents

to achieve change, particularly when the child's welfare is currently being compromised. (This is discussed in detail in Chapter 18.)

The interview concerning each child's personal history and development will often reveal the carer's views on each child and his or her individual needs. Usually attitudes towards discipline and boundary setting will have emerged during this part of the interview, but if not, it can be enquired about directly.

Each parent's account of their own history will need to be specific about experiences of care and possible maltreatment during their childhood.

Family history and assessments of family interaction are of special importance. Disharmony and inter-parental violence impact upon children directly, but also lead to a decline in an adult's parenting capacity (see Chapter 19). Social relationships are often significant and impact upon parenting. It is useful to identify who is part of each parent's social network, and exactly what type of contact, emotionally, or in terms of advice and support, may be forthcoming from each person. It is important to clarify when the person was last seen, and exactly how often contact occurs, as relationships may be idealised.

Interviewing children

An important part of a parenting assessment is the interview with the child (see Chapter 7). With younger children, this might involve a play-based session but with older children it is important that the practitioner talks directly to them, and on their own if possible (see Jones 2003 and Chapter 7). It is helpful to obtain children's views on current concerns; what they would like to happen, and what they see as the best way forward to address these. Children may well have fears about the future and being removed from home. Children's views on social and family relationships can be extremely helpful, complementing those provided by adult carers. They can surprise evaluators with their clarity about who they perceive to be supportive adults and about their feelings of security, care and safety. In addition, their views on school, and their success and relationships there, will be of importance in an overall assessment of parenting. Children's friendships are significantly and negatively affected by maltreatment experiences at home and so these will be important to evaluate too.

Observations

Observations constitute a vital part of parenting assessments (see Chapter 3 for more detail). It is useful to record observations made about each individual adult carer and each child within the family. Practitioners should note behaviour and expressed emotion, as well as speech, and in the case of children, play and activities.

Observations of family interactions also form an important part of parenting assessments, noting behaviour and emotional expression between adult carers, and between parents and their children, as well as noting the overall atmosphere within the family.

A central focus for observation is, of course, on parenting itself and parent–child relationships. Here it is useful to use the first five of the six dimensions of parenting described in the Assessment Framework: basic care, ensuring safety, emotional warmth, stimulation, and guidance and boundaries. These dimensions serve as a useful framework for recording observations made and the parenting competencies of each adult carer. It is important to record positive examples, as well as those which might raise further concern, within each dimension.

Practitioners will often need to see parents and children interacting together in different settings, and undertaking tasks relevant to parenting, in order to obtain a fair picture. Observations of parenting and parent–child interactions normally include those made within the family home or in another familiar setting if at all possible.

Practitioners will also want to make observations of the child's response to the adult carer's parenting initiatives. Records of children's emotional responsiveness and their reactions to their parents are valuable, along with observations made about their behaviour towards each parent. Observations of behaviours and expressions of emotion relevant to attachment status will also be of interest. For example, to what extent does the child use the parent as a 'secure base' from whom to venture out? Does the child show an age-appropriate level of exploration and interest in his or her surroundings? What is the child's response to separation and reunion?

Figure 17.3 lists suggested aspects of parent–child interaction that can be assessed in young children under the age of three and their parents.

Table 17.1 sets out aspects of parent and child interaction that can be observed in older children and young people, using the Assessment Framework parenting dimensions as a guide.

Assessment of attachment status

Attachment is an integral part of a parenting assessment (see Chapter 11). It is useful to consider three main aspects of attachment that may be assessed. These are: the child's attachment to an adult carer; an adult parent's caregiving; and a parent's own memory and experience of attachment during their own childhood. The main sources of information are: interviews with parents; interviews with children and young people; and observations of the parent–child interaction. Parent interviews provide information about their children's attachment behaviours, the adult's caregiving, as well as their own experiences of attachment in childhood and into their adult life (see Figure 17.2). Interviews with children and young people provide a window into their own experiences and feelings of attachment towards different adults and the care they have received. Observations of parent–child interaction include many elements relevant to the attachment system (see Figure 17.3 and Table 17.1). All these may be included within parenting assessments. Specialised assessments may utilise structured interviews and procedures and representational methods (see Chapter 11).

Parent interviews can include questions about each child's attachment and separation behaviour during the course of their development; their responses to changes such as attending nursery and school, illness and everyday traumas and injuries. Interviews can also include information about the child's response to being left with relatives or friends, and perhaps overnight stays with other children. Enquiries can be made about behaviour with different potential attachment figures, such as grandparents and other available adults. Parent interviews also provide information about adult caregiving. How did the parent

Child
- attachment behaviour
- exploratory behaviour
- emotional state
- general behaviour
- responsiveness to parent.

Parent
Psychological aspects:
- emotional expression
- responsiveness and recognition
- warmth/empathy
- cognitive stimulation/verbal interaction
- play
- behaviour management
- distance/closeness regulation
- emotional management/containment.

Physical care:
- feeding
- bathing/changing
- sleep
- safety.

Dyadic interaction
- co-operation
- reciprocity/Joint attention.

Figure 17.3: *Observations of parent–child interaction (younger child)*

feel about and respond to each child's attachment, and exploratory wishes and behaviours at different points, from prenatally and through a child's life?

Parents and children can be asked about their own experiences of care as well as maltreatment. It is useful to discover whom they have felt close to and why. There are likely to be differences between attachment figures, their feelings about them and the responses they received from them when upset, stressed or ill. Responses to separations will be important to explore, as well as their experiences of staying overnight or being away from carers. Any experiences of rejection or threat are important to elicit, as well as their feelings about being safe with particular carers. It may be possible to explore some of these thoughts and feelings through family genograms or family drawings with children and young people.

Observations about attachment and caregiving are included within several dimensions of parenting, for example emotional warmth, stimulation and stability (see Table 17.1). In younger child–carer pairs, observations of children's attachment and exploratory behaviour can be directly observed, along with caregivers' timely responsiveness

Table 17.1: Observations of parent–child interactions in children/young people

Dimension	Parent	Child
A. Basic care	Toileting, feeding, clothing and shelter.	Response to care – at ease, familiar, fearful, etc.?
B. Safety	Age-appropriate protection. Awareness of safety issues.	Reaction to checks. Ability to self-regulate.
C. Emotional warmth	Displays of affection, apparent indifference or other emotions, for example negativity or hostility. Tone of voice. Acceptance and positive regard or rejection. Is affection conditional?	Responsiveness. Expressed emotion toward each parent; warmth, fear, hostility, aggression? Seeking comfort and security?
D. Stimulation	Toys and materials, including books and drawings. Talking with child. Capacity to work with child, and be attuned to child's/young person's world. Facilitation of exploration and exposure to new experiences.	Initiate play or conversation? Response to parental ideas, questions, conversation or instruction? Ask for help or assistance? Capacity to express own views, ideas and ask questions? Exploration and investigation of surroundings?
E. Guidance/ boundaries	Managing unexpected. Clear-up of materials. Homework. Managing unwanted behaviour; or negative or aggressive behaviour. Managing teenage behaviour. Consistency of management.	Response to guidance or boundary setting by each parent. Capacity to express agreement or disagreement, and to manage such.
F. Stability	Providing continuity, or abandonment, rejection? Predictable environment. Consistent, measured responses.	Reaction and response to possible separation or alternative caretaking? Responses to parental inconsistency or unpredictability.
Child's developmental needs	Attuned to child/young person's needs? Attitude, expectations and actions toward these needs and demands. Caregiver's facilitation and response to child's attachment and exploration behaviour.	Developmental status? Behaviour and emotional state. Capacity for sustained attention. Response to greeting, reunion and separation.
Family/environment	Parental presentation, manner, mood state and general behaviour.	Interactions with siblings. Responses to strangers, and professionals, including bids for affection and care from them.

in everyday care. It is useful to observe an episode that involves stress to the attachment system, because it may only be then that attachment behaviour and responsive caregiving is witnessed, for example leaving a child at playgroup, contact sessions, behaviour during illness, hospital or clinic visits, and subsequent reunions (Aldgate and Jones 2006). Relevant observations are also made when considering a child's developmental needs (Table 17.1). Practitioners will be alert to abnormal behaviours (for example unattached behaviour, anxious, clinging or ambivalent paradoxical behaviours) as well as indications of secure links. It can be seen that attachment assessment is embedded within several aspects of the Assessment Framework.

Standardised assessments

Structured and standardised assessments can sometimes be useful to augment the practitioner's everyday or individually structured observations and assessments (Department of Health and Cox and Bentovim 2000). It is important not to over-rely upon standardised assessments. Many factors can influence their validity, including the practitioner's familiarity and experience with the instrument; family members' concern to positively impress the evaluator; or parents' attitudes and emotional reaction to the assessment process or its setting. Therefore, it is important that standardised assessments are interpreted with care and caution. They should be viewed as one piece of an assessment jigsaw. Practitioners should not over-interpret from any single source and this applies to standardised assessments as to any other means of assessment. Furthermore, there is no single 'test' of parenting. This is hardly surprising given its multifaceted nature and dependence upon context for expression. We can, however, approach the construct using multiple methods and settings. Standardised assessments have the potential advantages of encouraging objectivity, broadening the scope and reducing practitioner bias. On the other hand, they can lack flexibility unless great care is taken with selection and use.

Normally a parenting assessment would only use one or two standardised assessments, selected for a particular purpose and to address the concerns raised in an individual case. It is important to stress that an assessment of parenting is not somehow lacking merely because it does not include a standardised assessment.

Complementary sources of information

It will usually be necessary to obtain complementary sources of information, either through interview with other family members or friends of each parent, or from other professionals, or alternatively through a report from school, nursery or other services such as health visiting. Sometimes original records of a carer's past health status, educational achievement or concerning criminal activities will be necessary (Jones 2009). Also when assessing children, accounts from nursery and schools provide useful comparison with the parental account or direct observations made by the evaluator. Permission will need to be granted to interview and obtain reports from other sources, and confidentiality concerns will need to be discussed with parents. If parental consent is not forthcoming it may be necessary to obtain an order from the family court. In some situations a corroborative account is essential. For example, where parents are suspected of having a personality disorder, or where fabricated or induced illness is suspected (Jones 2009).

The value of planning

The principal issue is to plan to cover each dimension of parenting in an assessment plan (see Chapter 3). Preliminary planning will often indicate dimensions of parenting that seem particularly important for an individual child, and therefore require specific assessment. This may lead to an individualised plan, or using a standardised measure (for example maternal depression combined with alcohol use and concerns about child neglect could lead to an adult symptom checklist, alcohol use questionnaire, neglect checklist and the use of the HOME Inventory; or, focused clinical attention to each of these areas, including a home visit; or, any combination thereof). It is useful to have access to a wide range of assessments, or to be able to obtain them through specialist services, for example speech and language assessment or child mental health evaluation. Whatever choice is made, the assessment plan will aim to gather data in relevant areas of concern.

Whether or not standardised measures are utilised, it is essential that our assessments comprehensively cover all six dimensions of parenting, and allow for positive strengths as well as difficulties to emerge. Otherwise the practitioner's focus becomes prematurely constricted. Furthermore, by using a broad scheme covering all six dimensions, unforeseen strengths and difficulties may be revealed.

The next, crucial step is an analysis of the data and making sense of it (see Chapter 4 for further detail). So often data is gathered but not evaluated for its salience, or clear statements offered about child safety and welfare. In the case of parenting assessments, analysis will need to be integrated with the other two sides of the triangle and not stand-alone, as has been stressed already. Analysis will lead to an assessment of risk concerning child safety and overall welfare status and these will inform the plan for the child.

Assessing risk of maltreatment recurring

We have access to good information about what risk and protective factors lead to good and less good outcomes, enabling practitioners to approach decision-making in a structured way, while awaiting findings from further research. This is based on both narrative and systematic review of research on risk factors linked with recurrence of maltreatment (Jones 2008; Jones et al. 2006).

Table 17.2 lists, by ecological domain, factors which are more likely to be associated with future recurrence and those which appear to be protective with regard to future risk, lessening the likelihood that this will occur. Those in italics have emerged from systematic review of published studies, while other factors have emerged from other research approaches or more fine-grained studies of particular factors.

Our systematic review of studies (Hindley et al. 2006) revealed a 20 per cent recurrence rate of maltreatment for an individual child. The rate for any child within the same family to be re-abused, after one child had been protected, was 30 per cent, over a five-year period. The most risky time for recurrence were the first months following detection.

Table 17.2: Factors associated with future harm

Factors	Future significant harm more likely	Future significant harm less likely
Abuse	Severe physical abuse inc. burns/scalds *Neglect* Severe growth failure Mixed abuse *Previous maltreatment* Sexual abuse with penetration or over-long duration Fabricated/induced illness Sadistic abuse	Less severe forms of abuse If severe, yet compliance and lack of denial, success still possible
Child	Developmental delay with special needs Mental health problems Very young – requiring rapid parental change	Healthy child Attributions (in sexual abuse) Later age of onset One good corrective relationship
Parent	*Personality* • antisocial • sadism • aggressive Lack of compliance Denial of problems Learning difficulties plus *mental illness* Substance abuse *Paranoid psychosis* Abuse in childhood – not recognised as a problem	Non-abusive partner Willingness to engage with services Recognition of problem Responsibility taken Mental disorder, responsive to treatment Adaptation to childhood abuse
Parenting and parent–child interaction	Disordered attachment Lack of empathy for child Poor parenting competency Own needs before child's	Normal attachment Empathy for child Competence in some areas
Family	*Inter-parental conflict and violence* Family stress Power problems: poor negotiation, autonomy and affect expression	Absence of domestic violence Non-abusive partner Capacity for change Supportive extended family
Professional	Lack of resources Ineptitude	Therapeutic relationship with child Outreach to family Partnership with parents
Social setting	Social isolation Lack of social support Violent, unsupportive neighbourhood	Social support More local child care facilities Volunteer networks

Source: adapted from Jones *et al.* (2006).

Thereafter, the rate declined steadily. After two years, the rate levelled out and remained low over a five-year period. Factors associated with recurrence were strongest for cases involving prior maltreatment, neglect cases, those involving parental conflict and where one or both caregivers had significant mental health problems. We estimated risk recurrence, when a child had been previously maltreated prior to the most recent referral, to be raised six-fold. Furthermore, risk of recurrent maltreatment increases after each maltreatment event and the time between episodes shortens as the number of episodes increases. Other factors with a lesser effect, but nonetheless significant, included parental substance and alcohol use, family stress, lack of social support, younger children, caregivers with histories of abuse during their own childhood, and families previously involved with social services for other reasons prior to the abuse incident. Family stress was a composite measure including parental stress, perceptions of child vulnerability and high conflict families. Certain factors did not emerge from our systematic review as being significant in terms of recurrence of maltreatment. These included quality of attachment or closeness in the relationship between parent and child, or the severity of abuse. This was probably because systematic reviews tend to focus on large-scale studies with large sample sizes, which rarely reveal the kind of fine-grain level of assessment or observation necessary to bring out such factors.

These findings underline the need for multidisciplinary assessments because risk and protective factors exist in a wide variety of family, child, parental and environmental domains, which are likely to be identified by different professionals and services.

Care planning

The crucial importance to care planning of analysing, evaluating and decision-making is considered in detail in Chapter 4. We have advocated a staged approach to care planning in order to emphasise and impart structure to this phase of the work (Jones 1991; Jones *et al.* 2006). Fair and reflective assessments of caregiving by children's parents are critical to child safety and welfare.

Sometimes, parenting assessments reveal such severe deficits, and major risks to children's safety, that immediate safeguarding is necessary and even life-saving. In other situations, although risk of harm is moderately high, it is not considered an imminent risk, and so a measured trial of a care plan with adequate checks and balances is embarked upon. However, the plan may not achieve improvement, or subsequent developments lead to a reassessment of risk of harm to a child to a higher level. We have to acknowledge that some situations cannot be changed for the better, and that some families are simply untreatable (Jones 1987). Continued professional optimism may be misplaced (Dingwall *et al.* 1983), and even dangerous.

These situations are major challenges for children's social care and other services, but must be faced and responded to by front-line workers and their supervisors. These cases do not represent failure, but in fact successful professional practice, to the extent that a sustained focus on child welfare has been achieved. Nonetheless, these untreatable family situations can lead to complex emotional reactions among staff, who, after all, blend their commitment to child safeguarding with an admirable desire to encourage change among their clients. When these two powerful, professional motivators come into conflict it is critical that practitioners are assisted to allow safeguarding to 'trump' hope for change.

Summary

We have a great deal of information about what comprises parenting and how it might be assessed; and about risk and protective factors for recurrence of maltreatment when caregiving goes awry, although our knowledge base about how best to organise these into care plans is relatively less well developed. We hope the next decade will bring further clarity to these processes. In the meantime, a structured and equitable approach to the assessment of parenting, and its implications for care planning, is set out here. This approach to assessment offers a reliable basis for the care of vulnerable and maltreated children, whether or not they remain with their caregivers at the end of the process.

Recommended reading

Aldgate, J., Jones, D.P.H., Rose, W. and Jeffery, C. (2006) *The Developing World of the Child*. London: Jessica Kingsley Publishers.

Budd, K.S. (2001) 'Asssessing parenting competence in child protection cases: a clinical practice model.' *Clinical Child and Family Psychology Review 4*, 1, 1–18.

Jones, D.P.H. (2009) 'Assessment of parenting for the family court.' *Psychiatry 8*, 1, 38–42.

Scott, S. (2008) 'Parenting Programs.' In M. Rutter, D. Bishop, D. Pine, S. Scott *et al.* (eds) *Rutter's Child and Adolescent Psychiatry*. Oxford: Blackwell.

References

Aldgate, J. and Jones, D.P.H. (2006) 'The Place of Attachment in Child Development.' In J. Aldgate, D. Jones, W. Rose and C. Jeffrey (eds) *The Developing World of the Child*. London: Jessica Kingsley Publishers.

Aldgate, J., Jones, D.P.H., Rose, W. and Jeffrey, C. (2006) *The Developing World of the Child*. London: Jessica Kingsley Publishers.

Belsky, J. (1984) 'The determinants of parenting: a process model.' *Child Development 55*, 83–96.

Bornstein, M.H., Hahn, C.S., Haynes, O.M., Belsky, J. *et al.* (2007) 'Maternal personality and parenting cognitions in cross-cultural perspective.' *International Journal of Behavioral Development 31*, 3, 193–209.

Bronfenbrenner, U. (1977) 'Towards an experimental ecology of human development.' *American Psychologist 52*, 513–531.

Butcher, P.R., Wind, T. and Bouma, A. (2008) 'Parenting stress in mothers and fathers of a child with a hemiparesis: sources of stress, intervening factors and long-term expressions of stress.' *Child Care Health and Development 34*, 4, 530–541.

Cicchetti, D. (1989) 'How Research on Child Maltreatment has Informed the Study of Child Development: Perspectives from Developmental Psychopathology.' In D. Cicchetti and B. Carlson (eds) *Child Maltreatment: Theory and Research on the Causes and Consequences of Child Abuse and Neglect*. Cambridge: Cambridge University Press.

Dadds, M.R. and Rhodes, T. (2008) 'Aggression in young children with concurrent callous-unemotional traits: can the neurosciences inform progress and innovation in treatment approaches?' *Philosophical Transactions of the Royal Society 363*, 2567–2576.

Department of Health and Cox, A. and Bentovim, A. (2000) *The Family Pack of Questionnaires and Scales*. London: The Stationery Office.

Department of Health, Department for Education and Employment and Home Office (2000) *Framework for the Assessment of Children in Need and their Families*. London: The Stationery Office.

Dingwall, R., Eekelaar, J. and Murray, T. (1983) *Protection of Children: State Intervention and Family Life*. Oxford: Blackwell.

Epstein, T., Saltzman-Benaiah, J., O'Hare, A., Goll, J.C. and Tuck, S. (2008) 'Associated features of Asperger Syndrome and their relationship to parenting stress.' *Child Care, Health and Development 34*, 4, 503–511.

Garbarino, J. (1997) 'Growing Up in a Socially Toxic Environment.' In D. Cicchetti and S.L. Toth (eds) *Developmental Perspectives on Trauma: Theory, Research, and Intervention*. New York: University of Rochester Press.

Gelles, R.J. (1993) 'Family reunification/family preservation: are children really being protected?' *Journal of Interpersonal Violence 8*, 557–562.

George, C. (1996) 'A representational perspective of child abuse and intervention: internal working models of attachment and caregiving.' *Child Abuse and Neglect 20*, 411–424.

Grossmann, K.E., Grossmann, K. and Waters, E. (2005) *Attachment from Infancy to Adulthood: The Major Longitudinal Studies*. London: Guilford.

Hindley, N., Ramchandani, P. and Jones, D.P.H. (2006) 'Risk factors for recurrence of maltreatment: a systematic review.' *Archives of Disease in Childhood 91*, 9, 744–752.

Hughes, M., Earls, M.F., Odom, C.H., Dubay, K.L. *et al.* (2005) 'Preventing child maltreatment in North Carolina: new directions for supporting families and children.' *North Carolina Medical Journal 66*, 5, 343–355.

Jenny, C. and Isaac, R. (2006) 'The relation between child death and child maltreatment.' *Archives of Disease in Childhood 91*, 3, 265–269.

Jones, D.P.H. (1987) 'The untreatable family.' *Child Abuse and Neglect 11*, 409–420.

Jones, D.P.H. (1991) 'The Effectiveness of Intervention and the Significant Harm Criteria.' In M. Adcock, R. White and A. Hollows (eds) *Significant Harm*. Croydon: Significant Publications.

Jones, D.P.H. (2003) *Communicating with Vulnerable Children: A Guide for Practitioners*. London: Gaskell.

Jones, D.P.H. (2008) 'Child Maltreatment.' In M. Rutter, D. Bishop, D. Pine, S. Scott *et al.* (eds) *Rutter's Child and Adolescent Psychiatry*. Oxford: Blackwell.

Jones, D.P.H. (2009) 'Assessment of parenting for the family court.' *Psychiatry 8*, 1, 38–42.

Jones, D.P.H., Hindley, N. and Ramchandani, P. (2006) 'Making Plans: Assessment, Intervention and Evaluating Outcomes.' In J. Aldgate, D. Jones, W. Rose and C. Jeffery (eds) *The Developing World of the Child*. London: Jessica Kingsley Publishers.

Kaufman, J. and Zigler, E. (1989) 'Intergenerational Transmission of Child Abuse.' In D. Cicchetti and B. Carlson (eds) *Child Maltreatment: Theory and Research on the Causes and Consequences of Child Abuse and Neglect*. Cambridge: Cambridge University Press.

Korbin, J.E. (2002) 'Culture and child maltreatment: cultural competence and beyond.' *Child Abuse and Neglect 26*, 637–644.

McHale, J.P. and Rasmussen, J.L. (1998) 'Coparental and family group-level dynamics during infancy: early family precursors of child and family functioning during preschool years.' *Development and Psychopathology 10*, 39–59.

McHale, J.P., Kuersten, R. and Lauretti, A. (1996) 'New directions in the study of family-level dynamics during infancy and early childhood.' *New Directions for Child Development 74*, 5–26.

O'Connor, T.G. (2002) 'The effects of parenting reconsidered: findings, challenges and applications.' *Journal of Child Psychology and Psychiatry 43*, 5, 555–572.

Quinton, D. (2004) *Supporting Parents: Messages from Research*. London: Jessica Kingsley Publishers.

Rutter, M. (1989) 'Intergenerational continuities and discontinuities in serious parenting difficulties.' In D. Cicchetti and B. Carlson (eds) *Child Maltreatment: Theory and Research on the Causes and Consequences of Child Abuse and Neglect*. Cambridge: Cambridge University Press.

Rutter, M. (2005) 'How the environment affects mental health.' *British Journal of Psychiatry 186*, 4–6.

Sroufe, L.A., Egeland, B., Carlson, E.A. and Collins, W.A. (2005) *The Development of the Person: The Minnesota Study of Risk and Adaptation from Birth to Adulthood*. London: Guilford.

Stein, A., Ramchandani, P. and Murray, L. (2008) 'Impact of Parental Psychiatric Disorder and Physical Illness.' In M. Rutter, D. Bishop, D. Pine, S. Scott *et al.* (eds) *Rutter's Child and Adolescent Psychiatry*. Oxford: Blackwell.

Van Aken, C., Junger, M., Verhoeven, M., Van Aken, M.A.G. and Dekovic, M. (2008) 'The longitudinal relations between parenting and toddlers' attention problems and aggressive behaviours.' *Infant Behavior and Development 31*, 432–446.

Waylen, A., Stallard, N. and Stewart-Brown, S. (2008) 'Parenting and health in mid childhood: a longitudinal study.' *European Journal of Public Health 18*, 3, 300–305.

Wasserman, G., Miller, L., Pinner, E. and Jaramillo, B. (1996) 'Parenting predictors of early conduct problems in urban high risk boys.' *Journal of the American Academy of Child and Adolescent Psychiatry 35*, 1227–1236.

CHAPTER 18

Assessing Parental Motivation for Change

Tony Morrison

It has to be recognised that in families where a child has been maltreated there are some parents who will not be able to change sufficiently within the child's time-scales in order to ensure their children do not continue to suffer significant harm... However, most parents are capable of change and following appropriate interventions, able to provide a safe family context for their child.

(From the Framework for the Assessment of Children in Need and their Families, p.58, 4.25)

This chapter will:

- consider the reasons for assessing parental motivation
- discuss the concept of motivation and its fit with constructs of parenting
- outline Prochaska and DiClemente's Model of Change and the 7 Steps of Contemplation
- describe the concept of motivational dialogue and the impact of the assessor's interviewing style on the assessment of parental motivation.

Introduction

The chapter explores the concept of motivation in the context of assessing parental motivation to change. Two theoretical models about change and motivation are presented and discussed in terms of their application to practice. The first model is Prochaska and

DiClemente's (1982) Model of Change. The second is a motivation continuum, referred to as the 7 Steps of Contemplation (Morrison 1998), which provides a framework for analysing the level of parental motivation. Although the main context of use is to support the *Framework for the Assessment of Children in Need and their Families* (Department of Health *et al.* 2000), the principles and models presented here are applicable to a wide range of situations where change is sought, including health, education and criminal justice contexts as well as supervisory, team or organisational contexts.

The underpinning ethos of the models described is that collaborative approaches to assessment can be therapeutic by engaging service users in the early stages of a change process (Miller and Corby 2006). However, the effective use of these models relies both on an approach that is coherent, transparent, collaborative and empathic, and one that engages and motivates parents to participate openly and honestly in assessment work. The practitioner's capacity and confidence to be able to work in this manner will, in no small part, turn on the quality of practice support and guidance provided by their supervisors. As Beth *et al.* (2007) note, supervision is key to the effective use of assessment frameworks.

The chapter is in four sections: section one offers a brief review of the quality of assessment practice in relation to assessing parental motivation; section two explores the concept of motivation; section three presents the Model of Change and the 7 Steps of Contemplation; and the final section describes the motivational approach and the practice implications of these models.

Assessing parental motivation

The importance of accurate assessment of parental motivation could hardly be overstated, and is an issue of critical importance to all agencies involved in safeguarding children work. Miller and Rollnick (2002) describe motivation as the probability that someone will enter into, continue and adhere to a specific change strategy. However, many factors, both internal and external, affect the level of an individual's motivation to change. Motivation occurs in the context of an individual's relationship with their environment. Thus, a significant factor for parents is their relationship and interaction with the practitioner conducting the assessment. The practitioner's attitude becomes a significant determinant of the service user's motivational state (Miller and Rollnick 2002). As Biehal (2006) reported in her study of adolescents receiving preventative services, the combination of their own motivation, together with optimism about the worker's ability to help, were significant predictors of change.

In the context of the Assessment Framework, assessing parental motivation is a multi-disciplinary task. Indeed, without observations of how parents engage with their children and with agencies in different settings, the chances of getting a full picture of parental motivation are reduced. Parents demonstrate different aspects of their parenting strengths or difficulties in different situations, and talk about these in different ways, to different professionals. Thus, the development of shared models to understand motivation and its assessment play a potentially significant role in supporting a multidisciplinary assessment approach.

Except in the most severe cases, judgements about whether to leave a child at home, and what sort of intervention is required, hinge on the interplay of the child's needs, parental capacity, external factors, and the parent's motivation to engage with services and address problems. Misjudgements about the meaning and nature of parental motivation, both towards their child, and in relation to the need for change, have been repeatedly identified as problematic factors in child death inquiries, as Reder *et al.* (1993) have commented. More recently Brandon *et al.* (2008) expressed concern about the dangers of 'disguised compliance' where parents appear on the surface to comply with agency plans whilst in reality nothing is changing. The case of Baby Peter was a tragic example of the consequences of not spotting this process. The same authors also described the 'start again syndrome' in which repeated attempts are made to engage parents, without proper regard to extensive histories of concerns, leading to delays in planning for children. In summary, lessons from serious case reviews show the importance of distinguishing between compliance, co-operation, engagement and change.

However, since the publication of the *Framework for the Assessment of Children in Need and their Families* (Department of Health *et al.* 2000), there has been growing concern about inadequate analysis of information (Cleaver and Walker 2004); superficial assessment of parenting (Woodcock 2003); and a failure to consider how both social and psychological factors affect parenting. The result can be a narrow focus on current parenting problems and interventions that are overly focused on compliance with externally identified requirements. Howe (1996) articulated these concerns over a decade ago when he wrote:

> In task-focused and contract-orientated practices, immediate realities are negotiated, and definitions of what is and what is to be are agreed. Clients are not understood within the context of an ordered narrative... Work is short term, time-limited and brief, when the 'event' is over the case is closed... There is no requirement to explore the causes of behaviours and situations...practice does not respond to the inherent meaning of the case. (Howe 1996, pp.91–2)

Part of the problem is the absence of an empirically derived model in child welfare literature for understanding and assessing motivation to change. One consequence, for social workers in particular, who carry the burden of statutory responsibility, is that families and workers can too easily become ensnared in an adversarial dynamic. Banks (2006) has described this as the 'responsibility-avoidance syndrome' in which service user and worker each resist taking responsibility, but for different reasons. Notions of responsibility, denial, resistance and blame become hopelessly intertwined, and discussion of motivation becomes polarised between families who 'co-operate' and families who 'resist'. This view fails to take account of the ways in which motivation is fluid, changeable and context dependent.

The assessment of parental motivation needs to be situated in two related bodies of knowledge: first on parenting, and second on motivation. How a parent's motivation is perceived is linked to a practitioner's view about what constitutes reasonable parenting. As the subject of parenting is addressed elsewhere (see Chapter 17) discussion here will be brief. To date, research has tended to focus on whether social workers use a family support or a child protection model (Thoburn *et al.* 2000) rather than on how social workers (and other professionals) conceptualise parenting. A study by Woodcock (2003) revealed that whilst social workers had a *theoretical* appreciation of the impact of underlying psychological factors on parenting, in practice parenting assessment tended to focus on identifying and changing parenting behaviours. Thus:

> The assessment was of parents' ability to carry out the parenting task, rather than how other factors (for instance psychological and socio-environmental factors) may determine the quality of those skills. Social workers seemed to lack a psychologically informed strategy for responding to parenting problems…and relied on exhorting the parents to change and seeking to get them to take responsibility… (Woodcock 2003, p.98)

In her study Woodcock used the phrase 'surface-static' to describe an approach to parenting assessment that focuses on external behaviours, without seeking to locate these within either an environmental or psychological context. Thus, the interplay between the internal and external factors which influence parenting were not analysed. Parents who failed to respond to the practitioner's exhortation to change were too often labelled as 'resistant'. Of course such processes can equally be seen in the response of schools to pupil behaviour problems, by health professionals to substance misuse issues or probation officers to criminality.

However, practitioners' perceptions of parenting and parental motivation are also affected by operating in highly pressurised and often turbulent organisational environments. Faced with the pressure to complete assessments and write lengthy reports within prescribed timescales, analysis can become oversimplified, and decision-making rushed (Morrison 1996). Added to this, Parton (2008) has voiced concern that electronic formats for case recording may result in a data-based way of thinking. In sum, without well-informed conceptual models of parenting, and motivation, which combine sociological and psychological explanations for human behaviour, our ability to retain a thoughtful and collaborative approach to the assessment of parental motivation is inevitably weakened. Thus, we turn to motivation.

The concept of motivation

Our starting point is the concept of motivation per se. Maslow (1943) described motivation in relation to a hierarchy of needs in which physical safety was at the base and self-actualisation was the most advanced form of need. McAdams (1997), quoting Bakan (1966), argues that at the heart of human existence there are two core drivers which organise our wants, needs, desires and goals: *agency* and *communion*. 'Agency' refers to our need to be separate from others, and to assert, protect and expand the self. 'Communion' refers to our need to relate, belong to and identify as a social being with others in ways that are warm, close, intimate and loving. Put simply, our needs for both autonomy and connectedness, which are often in conflict, are deeply embedded in our motivational systems. Therefore, in assessing a parent's capacity to change, we should be sensitive as to what is at stake in such a process. Change affects more than behaviour; it affects a person's identity, esteem, control, confidence and sense of belonging.

In psychological terms, how the self is organised and what motivates behaviour is understood as a primarily cognitive process. Thus core beliefs are internalised through early experiences of parenting and socialisation, and it is these beliefs that help individuals to explain, predict and control their lives (Ward and Keenan 1999). Such beliefs act as drivers and filters through which desires lead to action, and form the framework within which people's behaviour is interpreted (Wellman 1990). Trait theory has argued that these underlying drivers create relatively stable personality factors such as introversion, extroversion or levels of anxiety. The stability of such features has led to the development of personality testing as a way of predicting a person's behaviour (Costa and McCrea 1986).

However, it is not only cognitions and genetics that are at work. Emotions also play a central role in human behaviour, especially in helping us make sense of the meaning of situations (Fineman 2005; Siegal 1999). From a neurological perspective, emotions are responsible for the co-ordination of behavioural, physiological, affective and cognitive responses to major adaptive problems, for instance change and the associated anxieties (Panksepp 2000). Emotions are also at the heart of attachment theory, which describes different strategies employed by the emotionally distressed mind to contain anxiety (see Chapter 11) Attachment theory states that core beliefs about comfort, closeness, safety and predictability are derived from children's early experiences of care, and form internal working models (Crittenden 2000; Howe 2005). From a motivational perspective these internal working models can be seen as core drivers to our behaviour, providing templates for how a person, such as a stressed parent, responds under conditions of threat, anxiety or danger. Experiences of abuse, neglect or emotional rejection are thought to have a particularly insidious impact resulting in internal working models that may include themes such as: 'It's not safe to be close; no one can love me; I am bad.' Identifying and understanding the influence of these core emotional beliefs offers powerful clues to the underlying meaning and function of behaviour, and can help us understand why someone has engaged in a problematic behaviour.

To recap: human behaviour can be described as purposeful in the sense that it is motivated by deeply ingrained beliefs and desires, which are shaped by the interaction of internal and external factors. Even when the outward presentation of behaviour appears disordered, self-defeating or even self-destructive, it is almost always inwardly purposeful. Understanding how a person's behaviour has meaning and purpose for them is fundamental to identifying what they are motivated for, and what is at stake when change is required. Furthermore, because core beliefs and desires are internalised so early in life, much of it before the acquisition of language, the individual can only be partially aware at best of these drivers. Thus, motivation must in part be understood as an unconscious force, especially when it is the source of non-rational behaviours. In this manner parents may be unwittingly motivated by forces of which they are unaware. For instance, a parent may persist in seeking contact with their child, whilst failing to attend contact sessions. The model for understanding motivation is presented in Figure 18.1.

This model depicts behaviour as arising from the interaction of external and internal factors. It shows how environmental supports and stressors interact with an individual's intellectual and physiological capacity, core beliefs, needs and desires. Whilst many of

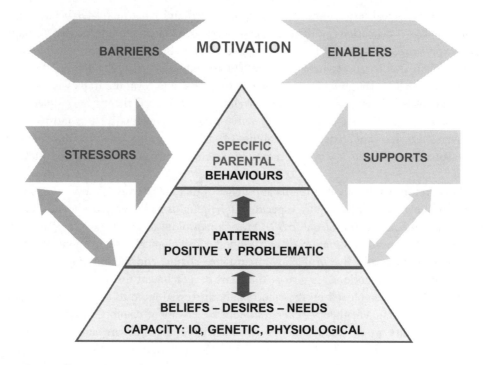

Figure 18.1: *Understanding motivation*

these factors are fluid and malleable, others, such as IQ or disability, are more fixed. These interactions in turn generate patterns of thoughts, feelings and behaviours that give rise to specific behaviours. The large diagonal arrows represent the reciprocal influence of external and internal factors on each other, in line with Rutter's (1985) ideas about the interaction of risk and protective factors. Hence, supportive environments, where there are positive family and social networks, are more likely to lead to the development of positive self-beliefs. This increases the likelihood of positive patterns of interaction with the external world that increases available external resources and social capital. This is not to suggest that adversity cannot be transformed into resilience, but rather that, to understand, and enhance, parental motivation to change, motivation needs to be located within an ecological and dynamic process.

Assessing motivation thus involves understanding the interaction between:

- an individual's beliefs, feelings and behaviour
- past, present and future expectations and goals
- the individual and significant others
- personal and environmental resources, opportunities and constraints.

The model also suggests that changing behaviour, especially when it is long-standing and embedded in underlying belief systems, is less likely to happen unless both the worker and service user have some appreciation of the underlying context and drivers for the behaviour. Senge (1990), discussing organisational behaviour, suggests that problems can be analysed at three levels: event (what happened); pattern (the wider patterns of behaviour); and structure, which can be translated into needs and cognitions (the underlying psychological drivers for behaviours). The danger occurs when attempts are made to adopt a 'quick fix' approach to complex problems. These ideas can be visually represented in the form of a pyramid showing the three levels of problem analysis and the danger of quick-fix solutions that address only the surface problem, with the risk that the problem resurfaces often in more serious form later (see Figure 18.2).

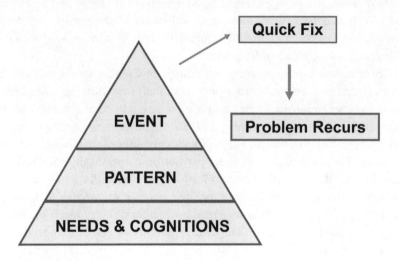

Figure 18.2: *Three levels of explanation*

Brandon *et al.*'s (2000) study of 105 significantly harmed children identified that before they received a co-ordinated response, many were subject to repeated referrals, or received one-off 'band aid' interventions. It was not until their situations deteriorated, and they became the subject of section 47 enquiries, that they received a properly co-ordinated assessment.

To recap this section: the discussion so far has stressed the need to set motivation in a broader context, recognising the parent's core beliefs. In life there are continuous motivational tensions between our desire for stability and status quo and our desire or need to change. Equally, the wish to be in control and the wish to belong are often in conflict with each other. At any point we are all more or less motivated about something, in relation to a particular context and set of relationships. Put this way, individuals cannot be said to be either 'motivated' or 'unmotivated', 'co-operative' or 'resistant'. Rather, it is more helpful to think of individuals as being continuously motivated but often beset by conflictual intentions – 'to be or not to be'. Thus, a mother's desire to protect her child from an aggressive partner may be in conflict with her need to avoid loneliness. Understanding the context, meaning, strength and flux of these conflicting motivations is essential in engaging and assessing the protective motivations of parents in such situations.

The Model of Change and the 7 Steps of Contemplation

The Model of Change

One model that can assist workers in assessing motivation and readiness for change is Prochaska and DiClemente's (1982) Model of Change. This generic model of the stages of change originated in the field of smoking cessation and has been widely used in the field of addictions treatment (Tober and Raistrick 2007). However, it has been applied in other fields including treatment of adult sex offenders (Ginsberg *et al.* 2002); group work (O'Reilly *et al.* 2001); and organisational change (Barnowski 1990; Prochaska 2000; Winett 1995). It has also been presented by Morrison (1991, 1998) and by Horwath and Morrison (2001) as a framework to assist practitioners in conceptualising processes of change in relation to work with families. Tuck (2004) used it in work on risk analysis in relation to safeguarding children from harm.

The Change Model, incorporating the 7 Steps of Contemplation, has also been extensively presented to a very wide range of professionals from different disciplines both in the UK and in other countries. It has also been presented in court reports. This extensive road testing of its relevance, acceptability and face validity by a wide range of experienced professionals operating in different fields provides an authoritative basis for its inclusion in this chapter. Thus, although the model has not been specifically validated outside of the addiction field (Corden and Somerton 2004), its credibility as a practice tool has been established through clinical experience and practice knowledge (Gilgun 2005). In addition, many professionals have commented how relevant this model is to circumstances beyond the workplace in terms of their own experiences of change. Indeed, readers are invited to consider whether they can relate the model to their own experiences of change, for instance losing weight or improving self-esteem. It is good to be reminded of how hard changing behaviours, beliefs or relationships can be.

The two models are therefore presented as practice tools based on practice knowledge designed to offer a common language about motivation for use between practitioners and service users, between different agencies or between supervisors and staff to understand and assess progress towards change.

The Change Model describes five main elements of an *intentional* change process: contemplation, decision, action, maintenance and lapse. In addition, the model describes two barriers to change: pre-contemplation and relapse. Although originally presented as a sequential 'staged' model in which individuals moved progressively through the five stages of change, the notion of 'stages' was later replaced by a more iterative or spiral idea. Change occurs more as a *two steps forward and one back* process. However, the experience of each change, even if unsuccessful, is such that we can never actually go back to 'square one', whatever it feels on a bad day. Hence, although Figure 18.3 appears to present change as a linear process, the reality is messier, the boundaries between different stages of change more diffuse, and the timescales unique to each individual.

The model's premise is that change is a matter of balance, and thus ambivalence is a key feature of the change process. Change occurs when the forces in favour of change are greater than those in favour of the status quo. Motivating people to change involves creating or increasing supports for change, whilst removing or decreasing barriers, whether

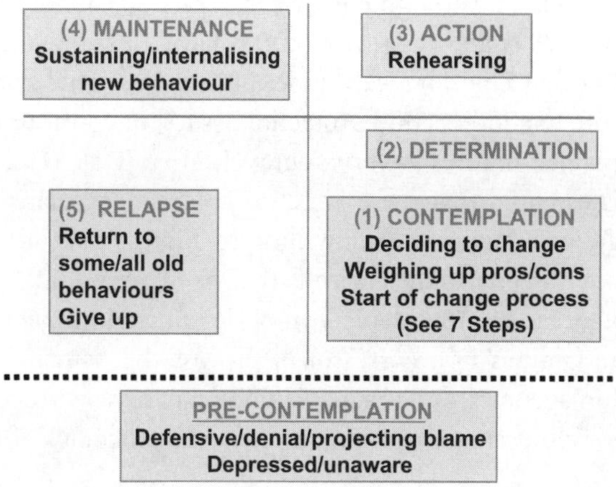

(4) MAINTENANCE **Sustaining/internalising new behaviour**	(3) ACTION **Rehearsing**
	(2) DETERMINATION
(5) RELAPSE **Return to some/all old behaviours Give up**	(1) CONTEMPLATION **Deciding to change Weighing up pros/cons Start of change process (See 7 Steps)**

PRE-CONTEMPLATION
**Defensive/denial/projecting blame
Depressed/unaware**

Figure 18.3: *Comprehensive Model of Change*

these be psychological, social or environmental. According to Miller and Rollnick (2002) people only change when they are ready, willing and able.

The model is relevant to three main practice contexts: first, where parents are requesting help with a problem and are engaged with services on a *voluntary basis*; second, where external agencies are concerned about the safety of a child and intervene on a *statutory basis*; and in addition there is a third group of cases which might be termed '*conditional voluntarism.* This third group are cases where agencies have a high degree of concern which is brought to the family's attention, in terms that make clear that statutory action might result if the family does not engage with agencies. Whilst being technically a non-statutory intervention, psychologically the dynamic of conditional voluntarism has much of the feel of an involuntary process, both for families and workers.

Examples of such *conditional voluntary* situations are cases which sit below the threshold for statutory intervention, but where there are concerns about parenting arising from factors such as substance misuse, domestic violence or parents with mental health or learning disabilities whose capacity to engage with services may be compromised or limited. Such cases might be described as *children with complex needs and compromised parenting* in which parents' responses to agencies are ambivalent and may oscillate between withdrawal, disguised compliance, and aggression (Brandon *et al.* 2008; Department of Health 2002). Child death serious case reviews have repeatedly identified these situations as being as potentially harmful to children as those cases requiring formal child protection plans. Indeed only 12 per cent of children subject to serious case reviews conducted between 2003 and 2005 were named on the child protection register at the time of the incident (Brandon *et al.* 2008). The need for a well co-ordinated multidisciplinary assessment of parental motivation and capacity to change is particularly important in such cases.

However, for practitioners, the capacity, and in some cases personal courage, required to remain focused and involved with such cases also depends on the quality of supervisory support and leadership from their agencies. The need for the practitioner's own anxieties and fears to be contained through effective supervision cannot be overstated. Reder *et al.* (1993), Morrison (1997) and Ferguson (2005) have all commented on ways that hidden fears and unexpressed emotions can undermine professional confidence and judgement leading to a failure to address child protection issues, or confront parents about suspicious events or unexplained injuries to very young children (Dale *et al.* 2002).

Finally, it is essential that there are clear contingency plans where review processes identify that parents are unable or unwilling to address risk of harm issues. An essential component to any safeguarding service is that dangerous adults are confronted and children are protected. Figure 18.4 depicts an optimum environment within which practitioners can engage families in an assessment process that is collaborative across agencies, containing within agencies, and where planning and review processes are consistent with, and outcomes for children are contingent upon, the outcomes of the assessment.

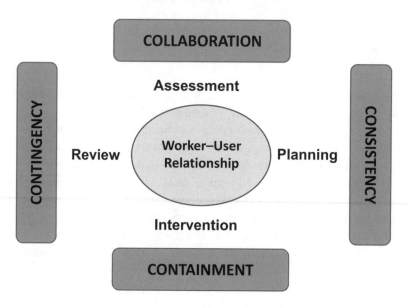

Figure 18.4: Optimum environment for engaging parents in the assessment process

PRE-CONTEMPLATION

Many of the cases falling into the statutory or conditional voluntary groups will be at this point during the initial stages of agency intervention, particularly where a statutory section 47 enquiry is required. Much is at stake for these families: fear of exposure, stigma, removal of their children or even prosecution. Fearful and anxious at the intrusion of external agencies, they may be defensive, angry and unwilling to acknowledge the reality of any difficulties. Negative previous experiences of statutory agencies may exacerbate this. Blame and responsibility may be externalised in terms of 'we were fine until you lot [agencies] arrived'.

Alternatively, Pre-contemplation may be expressed in a more passive or helpless response, where parents cannot comprehend what has happened to their child, and seemingly do not react to professionals' high levels of concern. Such responses may result from shock, depression, mental illness or learning disabilities, all of which limit the parent's capacity to understand the concerns. Equally, there may be language barriers which prevent parents understanding the nature of concerns. The result is one in which parents are neither willing, ready or able to consider change.

At this stage there may be no alternative to removing the child from the family, which is likely to further reinforce the Pre-contemplation process. In the majority of situations this will not be necessary. Either way, at the point of the initial child protection conference, agencies will be anxious to move ahead into the Action stage, whilst some parents remain in the Pre-contemplation stage. Others may agree to the plan out of fear for what may happen if they do not (conditional voluntarism), whilst lacking any real understanding or ownership of the concerns. This is not to argue that external leverage should not play a role in the change process, but as a reminder about the need to distinguish between compliance and engagement.

Central to this model is the idea that effective work to bring about change cannot occur unless workers understand the stage at which parents are, and tailor their interventions accordingly. For instance, if professionals are at the Action stage, whilst parents are barely emerging from Pre-contemplation in 'agreeing' to the child protection plan, little change will occur. Family centre staff frequently comment on the disparity between professionals' expectations of parents at this point to 'engage in an agreed plan for work', and the actual levels of parental readiness and willingness. Change cannot occur whilst agencies and parents are at different stages of the process. It can only begin once parents are enabled to move into the Contemplation stage, and assisting parents to do this is a primary task for practitioners.

Clearly, in the face of serious concerns about the safety of a child, and parents who are unable to move beyond Pre-contemplation, recourse to further statutory action may be required. The process of engaging and motivating parents cannot be extended beyond the point at which delays in planning become detrimental to the child (recall the 'start-again' syndrome in cases of neglect identified by Brandon *et al.* 2008). Finally, it should be noted that even where parents voluntarily seek assistance, they may still encounter unexpected difficulties, which they are not ready to acknowledge, that trigger a retreat into Pre-contemplation.

CONTEMPLATION

The idea that change is a matter of balance is particularly reflected in this stage. Contemplation involves thinking about and preparing for change on a range of levels. These include:

- consideration of the pros and cons of the current situation
- whether, if change occurs, things will be better or worse
- for whom any changes will be better or worse
- level of confidence about making the change
- whether any changes can be sustained.

For parents who are voluntarily seeking assistance, perhaps with child management prob-lems, this is their starting point. For other parents, for instance where their child has been made the subject of a multi-agency child protection plan, this may be the beginning of a journey in recognising and coming to terms with the existence of a problem. Parents may be genuinely unaware of a problem, for instance a child's developmental delay, or in a situation where one parent knows there is a problem but the other parent is unable or unwilling to acknowledge it.

The 7 Steps of Contemplation

Contemplation involves a number of elements which together build readiness, willingness and capacity to change, and is a crucial phase in the journey between Pre-contemplation and Action. In Spiller *et al.*'s (2007) study of the Change Model it was found that discrep-ancy, positive expectations and self-efficacy were critical elements in negotiating change. Because Contemplation is a complex stage, it has been helpful to break it down into 7 Steps of Contemplation (Horwath and Morrison 2001; Morrison 1998), in similar fashion to Martino *et al.*'s (2007) Motivation to Change Scale. The 7 Steps of Contemplation in-volve: understanding and owning a problem; facing discomfort; acknowledging the need for change; identifying ambivalence; and building confidence and self-efficacy. These are now described, taking as a practice example parents whose child is not putting on weight and who is hard to feed.

STEP 1. I ACCEPT THERE IS A PROBLEM: 'THE DOCTOR SAYS MY CHILD IS NOT GROWING'

At this earliest phase of Contemplation there may only be minimal agreement that there is a problem, with little acceptance of responsibility. Nevertheless, if a parent can acknowl-edge publicly a problem which they had previously denied, this is a step in the right direction. Although this is only a first step, it needs to be positively acknowledged, even if the parents are as yet unable to acknowledge their own contribution to the problem. The practitioner might comment positively that it can be hard for parents to acknowledge the existence of external concern about their child. Clearly, Step 1 will not be sufficient for change to occur. However, if parents can be presented with clear and evidenced concerns from agencies, shared in a respectful and thoughtful manner, this may stimulate further progress, especially when delivered in association with the provision of other support ser-vices. However, this needs to be followed quickly by the engagement of family members in a collaborative assessment process which can help parents to understand the nature and source of their difficulties, and thereby assist in their move to the second stage of Contemplation.

Facilitating progress from Step 1 to Step 2 is the most difficult phase of work. In the more difficult cases practitioners may be faced with hostility, withdrawal or surface compliance (Department of Health 2002). This may create anxiety, apprehension or even a fear for personal safety for the practitioner (Brandon *et al.* 2008). Practitioners need to be working within an effective multidisciplinary process and supported by structured and knowledgeable supervision.

Whilst there are no magic wands for engaging parents in such situations, joint visiting, as part of the assessment process, is one strategy to consider. For families who may be wary of statutory agencies, a joint visit by a health or education professional, together with a social worker, can serve to provide the combination of a supportive and authoritative presence. Such a dual presence both contains turbulent family dynamics, whilst encouraging and supporting parental engagement in the assessment process. It also boosts the confidence and focus of the practitioners, either of whom on their own might find such visits very difficult.

Additionally, approaches that emphasise strengths as well as needs and risks of harm are important, such as Turnell and Edwards' (1999) Signs of Safety. Their solution and safety-orientated approach contains a number of practice elements which are useful at any stage in the change process:

- Understanding the position of each family member in relation to the way they see the problem; for example, 'When I was brought up, you couldn't leave the table till you cleared your plate.'

- Searching for exceptions to the problem conveys the message that the practitioner believes that the problem is not occurring the whole time and that the parents have skills to address the issue; for example, 'Can you tell me what happens when your child is able to finish his meal?'

- Asking about strengths, for example; 'Tell me what good days in this family look and feel like?'

- Using scaling questions; for example, 'On a 0–10 scale, right now how confident do you feel about managing mealtimes?'

- Focusing on the positive futures and goals parents have for their children. If, for instance, their confidence level on managing mealtimes was rated very low, at say 2 out of 10, the follow-up question might be: 'What would need to be happening for your confidence to get to 3 out of 10, and what would you notice about how Julie was behaving and how you were being with her?'

These questions are motivational in their approach whilst also providing, through the parent's response, information about the parent's willingness, readiness and capacity to make changes.

STEP 2. I HAVE SOME RESPONSIBILITY FOR THE PROBLEM: 'I NEVER HAD ENOUGH TIME TO FEED HER, SHE IS SUCH A SLOW EATER'

At this stage it is not necessary, or even realistic, for total responsibility to be taken by the parent for their actions, but there has to be some willingness to recognise how the parent may have contributed to the difficulties. However, the term 'responsibility' needs to be used with care and defined in terms that appreciate the complexity and multiplicity of factors which contribute to parenting difficulties. Moreover, conveying a message that parents will have wanted to do the best for their child, however things have turned out, can do a lot to prevent the discussion of responsibility being heard as blaming. At the same time workers must be aware that acknowledging responsibility does not necessarily equate with the reduction of risk of harm; for example, 'Yes I hit him, but I was hit as a child and it never did me any harm,' or 'It's what the alcohol does to me.'

STEP 3. I HAVE SOME DISCOMFORT ABOUT THE PROBLEM: 'I AM WORRIED THAT MY CHILD IS NOT GROWING PROPERLY'

Treacher and Carpenter (1989) suggest that discomfort about the status quo is an important component of motivation, and contributes to seeking or accepting external help. Internal discomfort reveals that the individual feels that their behaviour is, at some level, in conflict with their core values and beliefs about what is appropriate parenting. Raistrick (2007) states that motivation depends on finding core beliefs that are incompatible with the individual's problematic behaviours. This increases the internal discrepancy between who I am as a parent and who I would like to be. Unfortunately, some parents have uninformed or distorted views about children, for instance believing that a baby's eating difficulties arise from the baby's wilful defiance. Understanding the nature of these beliefs is a critical element in the assessment.

Internal discomfort is, of course, different to the external discomfort created when parents experience outside agencies as 'lecturing' or 'warning' them about their inappropriate behaviours and potential consequences. Insensitive or judgemental approaches to such sensitive issues as parenting can rapidly lead to a breakdown of the working relationship with the practitioner from which it can be hard to recover (Miller and Rollnick 2002). Spratt and Callan (2004), in their research, noted how parents repeatedly returned to their experience of the first contact with the practitioner. In general, however, the presence of discomfort is a positive sign of motivation, although it is important to be mindful as to where the discomfort is focused, and that it includes an empathic concern for the child.

STEP 4. I BELIEVE THAT THINGS MUST CHANGE: 'I CAN'T GO ON HAVING THESE FIGHTS EVERY MEALTIME WITH MY CHILD'

Here there is the realisation that something must change, although this may not mean that the parent knows what this is, or how to achieve it. It is at this stage that the parent may say in desperation 'I'll do whatever you say', perhaps at the end of a fraught initial child protection conference, in which the consequences of non-compliance have been spelt out. Although willingness to acknowledge such external realities, and to co-operate, are important, they are insufficient in themselves to demonstrate readiness and ability to change. There is, therefore, a need to avoid rushing to the Action stage, without exploring the remaining three steps of Contemplation, which focus on building the parent's own sense of competence and readiness to make changes.

STEP 5. I CAN SEE THAT I CAN BE PART OF THE SOLUTION: 'I KNOW THAT I AM CAPABLE OF MAKING SOME CHANGES, HOWEVER SMALL'

Identifying and building positive expectations and encouraging the individual's sense of personal competence and self-efficacy are crucial motivational elements (Raistrick 2007). Miller and Rollnick (2002) state that the aims of motivational interviewing are to help people to make their own arguments for change, and assisting them to resolve their ambivalence about change. Practitioners' well-intentioned words of encouragement and belief in the person's capacity to change may result in overlooking a parent's underlying ambivalence or fear of change. The more positive and encouraging the practitioner sounds, the harder it may be for the parent to explore their conflicting feelings or low levels of confidence about making changes. If, instead, the focus is on helping the parent identify previous successes in dealing with problems, or positive personal beliefs and resources, this will increase their level of self-efficacy and confidence. In so doing, this will also increase their readiness for change.

STEP 6. I CAN MAKE A CHOICE: 'EVEN THOUGH I FEEL ANGRY AT THE WAY THE AGENCIES INTERVENED, I WANT TO GO TO THE FAMILY CENTRE'

The recognition of a choice point is important in clarifying within the mind of the parent that they have some power to choose, even if the range of choices is limited. This is particularly relevant in working with people in involuntary situations (Ivanoff *et al.* 1994) who have experienced others, such as courts or case conferences, making decisions about them or their family. Being an 'involuntary' service user inevitably depletes the individual's sense of personal worth and competence. For example, 'I must be, or things must be, even worse than I thought if you cannot trust me to work with you on a voluntary basis.' The response of parents under such circumstances can sometimes be to deny they can make any choice at all, as in 'there's no point, you have already decided'.

In order to reverse this loss of confidence and to increase positive engagement in choice-making, three things are necessary. First, agency processes must be procedurally fair, transparent, and maximise service users' participation. This may involve the use of advocates on behalf of parents when their relationships with agencies are difficult and conflictual. Second, this is a time, more than ever, for identifying parents' strengths. Third, it is essential to ensure that parents are receiving support services. Together these approaches will increase parents' abilities to be involved in making positive choices for their children. Finally, the logic of stages 5 and 6 suggests we must avoid, wherever possible, making premature demands on parents to make difficult choices, whilst recognising that the pace of parental change cannot be allowed to jeopardise meeting the needs of the child.

STEP 7. I CAN SEE THE NEXT STEPS TOWARD CHANGE – PREPARATION: 'I KNOW SOMETHING PRACTICAL I AM GOING TO DO NEXT WEEK TO MAKE ONE SMALL CHANGE'

This is the preparation-for-action stage. The parent has now established sufficient readiness and willingness that, together with the practitioner, they are able to plan a change strategy. The focus here will be on identifying the specific goals to be achieved; how parents and practitioner will each contribute to achieving these; and what changes and rewards will occur once these goals are met. There will also be a need to spell out any contingencies or consequences that will occur should parents fail to stick with the strategy or further concerns arise. It may well be that a series of mini-contracts are required as progress is achieved in small stages. At this point delay in service provision, or allocation of new workers, can undermine motivation, leaving parents in a state of problem-awareness without the practical and emotional support to improve things. Unfortunately, as Brandon *et al.* (2008) discovered, sometimes agencies mirrored the same ambivalent pattern as the families, by changing workers, closing cases, losing files or starting and stopping court proceedings.

ACTION

Research into intervention has shown the importance of targeting specific interventions for specific problems, in an ordered sequence. Care has to be taken that families with multiple problems are not overwhelmed with different appointments. The plan could include work with children, parent-skill classes, or family work, alongside other supportive services designed to alleviate stress or address children's needs. This model of change can thereby accommodate a range of different interventions, as long as the intervention is matched to the parent's readiness, willingness and capacity to change.

MAINTENANCE

By this stage the emphasis moves to consolidating changes already made. This may be achieved through longer-term support for families which allows them to embed the changes, whilst retaining access to continued support and advice. This is the importance of conducting regular multidisciplinary reviews, for instance in the example mentioned earlier, of the child's weight gain. Specific attention also needs to be paid to relapse prevention work, aimed at anticipating stresses and triggers that may undermine newly acquired coping skills, and devising coping strategies. Unfortunately, the pressure on resources is such that this aspect of change work is sometimes given little or no space. However, if changes have not been sufficiently integrated into daily life, new stresses may quickly overwhelm parents' fledgling confidence and skills, causing relapse. Some parents with particular difficulties, such as a learning disability, are likely to need long-term support to maintain their parenting at an acceptable level for their children (Cleaver and Nicholson 2007).

RELAPSE

One of the strengths of this model is that it allows for the reality that few people succeed first time round. Change comes from repeated efforts, re-evaluation, renewal of commitment and incremental successes. However, the model distinguishes between *lapse* and *relapse*. Lapses occur when individuals or families get themselves into high-risk situations – for instance, one parent feels angry because the child once again refuses to eat her food. At this point parents need to recognise the danger signal, and put into action whatever strategy they have agreed, for instance to ask their partner to come and take over the situation. Lapse can be considered as part of, rather than the failure, of change, as long as appropriate responses follow. In contrast a relapse occurs with a return to the unwanted behaviour, for instance locking the child in her bedroom if she refuses to eat her food. In some cases where the risks of harm associated with *relapse* to the child are sufficiently high, court orders may be required to monitor this process and to ensure that contingency plans will protect children from further harm should the need arise.

Summary

The thrust of the Change Model and the 7 Steps of Contemplation is to reassert that assessment can be therapeutic in its own right (Miller and Corby 2006). Change does not start when parents enter the Action stage; it starts when we enable an anxious, fearful or angry parent to make the first steps along the pathway of Contemplation.

Although it is presented in an ordered way for the convenience of the reader, change is messy. We go backwards and forwards, may spend years contemplating a change, before suddenly one day instigating it. Readiness is rarely predictable and may have as much to do with the synergy of events as conscious planning. Family members may well be at different stages of motivation and readiness for change. As social beings, important changes rarely happen without reference to, and the influence of, significant people and forces around us. These include family, friends and community as well as the cultural and media influences that surround us. Change may be sparked by emotions, events, internal changes, or just doing something differently. Nevertheless, if such changes are to endure there must be some integration of change with belief systems, roles and relationships. Without this, change may be short-lived. Whilst acknowledging the variations in the way change occurs, it behoves workers charged with planning and safeguarding respon-sibilities for children to be clear and transparent about the frameworks they are using in assessing parental motivation and capacity for change.

Motivational approach

Assessing parental motivation requires the practitioner to possess good interpersonal and motivational skills. Miller and Rollnick (2002) argue that the likelihood of change occur-ring is strongly influenced by interpersonal interactions. Holland's (2000) study of social workers' interactions with parents during assessments showed how significant verbal interactions were in shaping social worker's judgements about parents. She also noted that the practitioner's judgement about parental capacity and motivation relied heavily on how parents performed during assessment interviews, their level of co-operation and relationship with practitioners during assessment. Confrontational interviewing styles increase the resistance of service users to acknowledging their problems and thinking about change (Miller *et al.* 1993), which in turn may lead practitioners to interpreting such responses as resistance.

McKeown's (2000) research on change factors in family support work identified that whilst 40 per cent of the change effort was accounted for by the characteristics of the service user (IQ, history, health, socio-economic status, social support) 30 per cent of the change effort was accounted for by the quality of the practitioner's relationship with the service user. Only 15 per cent was accounted for by the method of intervention and 15 per cent by the service user's verbally expressed optimism. McKeown's research underlines the fact that the relationship skills of the practitioner, when discussing emotionally or morally laden issues such as attachment, trauma or parenting practices, play a significant role in the outcome of the assessment.

Taken together these findings call for assessment to be conducted in a collaborative spirit that motivates parents to engage in the process, and which enables them to identify their strengths whilst feeling supported to take ownership of their difficulties. This is the ethos underpinning the *Framework for the Assessment of Children in Need and their Families* (Department of Health *et al.* 2000). Tober and Raistrick (2007) use the term 'motivational dialogue' to describe such an approach. This is based on the premise that the practitioner is a significant determinant of the service user's engagement and motivation. Motivational dialogue stresses the need for an empathic style that supports the exploration of discrepancy and ambivalence whilst at the same time building the individual's sense of optimism and self-efficacy. This is most likely to occur when the practitioner's style incorporates the following approaches:

1. open-ended questions

2. using reflective statements that explore, elaborate and elicit meaning

3. affirming the validity of the parent's realities, and perceptions, whilst not necessarily agreeing with these

4. identifying core beliefs, discrepancies and sources of ambivalence

5. summarising regularly

6. emphasising choice and clarifying potential gains, losses and consequences

7. engaging in change planning.

In summary, Miller and Rollnick (2002) describe this approach as one based on four levels of change talk: identifying the disadvantage of status quo; identifying the potential advantages of change; building confidence and self-efficacy; and creating intentions, plans and strategies. To this we must add establishing contingency plans that will safeguard children in the event of parents being unable or unwilling to continue and adhere to their change strategy.

Conclusion

This chapter has presented two linked models for thinking about the processes of change and motivation, and located it within a broader view of human behaviour and functioning. The importance of having a clear and transparent framework for assessing parental motivation, in terms that can be communicated between practitioners and parents, has been stressed. The two models discussed can act as a common framework to be used between agencies, as well as between staff and their supervisors, to describe, evidence and evaluate the strength, direction and potential of parents' motivation for change. Equally, however, the responsibility and skills of practitioners to apply this model within a motivational approach is central. In the wrong hands this model, like any model, can be applied in a mechanistic and judgemental way which not only misreads the parent's motivation but potentially reduces it. Conversely, in a context in which workers are well trained, supported and supervised, not only will these models improve assessment, they will also enhance the motivation of both parents and their practitioners.

Recommended reading

Berg, I. (1994) *Family-based Services*. New York, NY: Norton.

Ivanoff, A., Blythe, B. and Tripodi, T. (1994) *Involuntary Clients in Social Work Practice*. New York, NY: Aldine de Gruyter.

Jenkins, A. (1991) *Invitations to Responsibility*. Adelaide: Dulwich Publications.

Miller, W. and Rollnick, S. (2002) *Motivational Interviewing*. London: Guilford Press.

Turnell, A. and Edwards, S. (1999) *Signs of Safety: A Solution and Safety-orientated Approach to Child Protection*. New York, NY: Norton.

References

Bakan, D. (1966) *The Duality of Human Existence: Isolation and Community in Western Man*. Boston, MA: Beacon Press.

Banks, N. (2006) 'The Responsibility-avoidance Syndrome: Unconscious Processes in Practitioners who Work Therapeutically with Children and Young People who Sexually Abuse.' In M. Erooga and H. Masson (eds) *Children and Young People who Sexually Abuse Others*, 2nd edn. London: Routledge.

Barnowski, T. (1990) 'Reciprocal determinism at the stages of behaviour change: an integration of community, personal, and behavioural perspectives.' *International Quarterly of Community Health Education 40*, 297–327.

Beth, C., Anderson, M., Orme, J. and Lister, P. (2007) 'Assessment frameworks: a critical reflection.' *British Journal of Social Work 37*, 1059–1077.

Biehal, N. (2006) 'Preventative services for adolescents: exploring the process of change.' *British Journal of Social Work 38*, 3, 441–461.

Brandon M., Belderson, P., Warren, C., Howe, D. *et al.* (2008) *Analysing Child Deaths and Serious Injuries: What Can We Learn? A Biennial Analysis of Serious Case Reviews*. Research Report DCSF-RR023. Nottingham: DCSF.

Brandon, M., Thoburn, J., Lewis, A. and Way, A. (2000) *Safeguarding Children with the Children Act 1989*. London: The Stationery Office.

Cleaver, H. and Nicholson, D. (2007) *Parental Learning Disability and Children's Needs*. London: Jessica Kingsley Publishers.

Cleaver, H. and Walker, S. (2004) 'From policy to practice: the implementation of a new framework for social work assessments of children and families.' *Child and Family Social Work 9*, 81–90.

Corden, J. and Somerton, J. (2004) 'The transtheoretical model of change: a reliable blueprint for assessment in work with children and families?' *British Journal of Social Work 34*, 1024–1044.

Costa, P. and McCrea, R. (1986) 'Personality stability and its implications for clinical psychology.' *Clinical Psychology Review 6*, 407–423.

Crittenden, P. (2000) 'A Dynamic Maturational Approach to Continuity and Change in the Pattern of Attachment.' In P. Crittenden and A. Claussen (eds) *The Organisation of Attachment Relationships*. Cambridge: Cambridge University Press.

Dale, P., Green, R. and Fellows, R. (2002) 'Serious and fatal injuries to infants with discrepant explanations: some assessment and case management issues.' *Child Abuse Review 11*, 296–312.

Department of Health (2002) *Learning from Experience: A Review of Serious Case Reviews*. London: Department of Health.

Department of Health, Department for Education and Employment and Home Office (2000) *Framework for the Assessment of Children in Need and their Families*. London: The Stationery Office.

Ferguson, H. (2005) 'Working with violence, the emotions and the psycho-social dynamics of child protection: reflections on the Victoria Climbié case.' *Social Work Education 24*, 7, 781–795.

Fineman, S. (2005) *Understanding Emotion at Work*. London: Sage.

Gilgun, J. (2005) 'The four cornerstones of evidence-based practice in social work.' *Research on Social Work Practice 15*, 1, 52–61.

Ginsberg, J., Mann, R., Rotgers, F. and Weekes, J. (2002) 'Motivational Interviewing with Criminal Justice Populations.' In W. Miller and S. Rollnick (eds) *Motivational Interviewing: Preparing People for Change*, 2nd edn. London: Guilford Press.

Holland, S. (2000) 'The assessment relationship: interactions between social workers and parents in child protection assessments.' *British Journal of Social Work 30*, 149–163.

Horwath, J. and Morrison, T. (2001) 'Assessment of Parental Motivation to Change.' In J. Horwath (ed.) *The Child's World: Assessing Children in Need*. London: Jessica Kingsley Publishers.

Howe, D. (1992) 'Theories of Helping, Empowerment and Participation.' In J. Thoburn (ed.) *Participation in Practice – Involving Families in Child Protection*. Norwich: University of East Anglia.

Howe, D. (1996) 'Surface and Depth in Social Work Practice.' In N. Parton (ed.) *Social Theory, Social Change and Social Work*. London: Routledge.

Howe, D. (2005) *Child Abuse and Neglect: Attachment, Development and Intervention*. Basingstoke: Palgrave.

Ivanoff, A., Blythe, B. and Tripodi, T. (1994) *Involuntary Clients in Social Work Practice*. New York, NY: Aldine de Gruyter.

Martino, S., Carroll, K. and Ball, S. (2007) 'Teaching, Monitoring and Evaluating Motivational Interviewing Practice.' In G. Tober and D. Raistrick (eds) *Motivational Dialogue: Preparing Addiction Professionals to Motivational Interviewing Practice*. London: Routledge.

Maslow, A. (1943) 'A theory of human motivation.' *Psychological Review 50*, 370–396.

McAdams, D. (1997) *The Stories We Live By*. New York, NY: Guilford Press.

McKeown, K. (2000) *A Guide to What Works in Family Support Services for Vulnerable Families*. Dublin: Department for Health and Children.

Miller, M. and Corby, B. (2006) 'The Framework for the Assessment of Children in Need and their Families – a basis for a "therapeutic" encounter?' *British Journal of Social Work 36*, 887–899.

Miller, W. and Rollnick, S. (2002) *Motivational Interviewing: Preparing People for Change*, 2nd edn. London: Guilford Press.

Miller, W., Benefield, R. and Tonigan, J. (1993) 'Enhancing motivation for change in problem drinking: a controlled comparison of two therapist styles.' *Journal of Consulting and Clinical Psychology 61*, 455–461.

Morrison, T. (1991) 'Change Control and the Legal Framework.' In M. Adcock and R. White (eds) *Significant Harm*. Croydon: Significant Publications.

Morrison, T. (1996) 'Partnership and collaboration: rhetoric and reality.' *Child Abuse and Neglect 20*, 2, 127–140.

Morrison, T. (1997) 'Emotionally Competent Child Protection Organisations: Fallacy, Fiction or Necessity?' In J. Bates, R. Pugh and N. Thompson (eds) *Protecting Children: Challenges and Change*. Aldershot: Arena.

Morrison, T. (1998) 'Partnership, Collaboration and Change under the Children Act 1989.' In M. Adcock and R. White (eds) *Significant Harm*, 2nd edn. Croydon: Significant Publications.

O'Reilly, G., Morrison, T., Sheerin, D. and Carr, A. (2001) 'A group-based module for adolescents to improve motivation to change sexually abusive behaviour.' *Child Abuse Review 10*, 3, 150–169.

Panksepp, J. (2000) 'Emotions as Natural Kinds within the Mammalian Brain.' In M. Lewis and J. Haviland-Jones (eds) *Handbook of Emotions*. London: Guilford Press.

Parton, N. (2008) 'Changes in the form of knowledge in social work: from the "social" to the informational.' *British Journal of Social Work 38*, 253–269.

Prochaska, J. (2000) 'A transtheoretical model for assessing organisational change: a study of family service agencies.' *The Journal of Contemporary Human Services 81*, 1, 76–84.

Prochaska, J. and DiClemente, C. (1982) 'Trans-theoretical therapy: toward a more integrative model of change.' *Psychotherapy: Theory, Research and Practice 19*, 3, 276–288.

Raistrick, D. (2007) 'Motivation and Barriers to Change.' In G. Tober and D. Raistrick (eds) *Motivational Dialogue: Preparing Addiction Professionals for Motivational Interviewing Practice*. London: Routledge.

Reder, P., Duncan, S. and Gray, S. (1993) *Beyond Blame*. London: Routledge.

Rutter, M. (1985) 'Resilience in the face of adversity.' *British Journal of Psychiatry 147*, 598–611.

Senge, P. (1990) *The Fifth Discipline*. New York, NY: Bantam Doubleday.

Siegal, D. (1999) *The Developing Mind: How Relationships and the Brain Interact to Shape Who We Are*. London: Guilford Press.

Spiller, V., Zavan, V. and Guelfi, G. (2007) 'Motivation and Change: A Three Dimension Continuum.' In G. Tober and D. Raistrick (eds) *Motivational Dialogue: Preparing Addiction Professionals for Motivational Interviewing Practice*. London: Routledge.

Spratt, T. and Callan, J. (2004) 'Parents' views on social work interventions in child welfare cases.' *British Journal of Social Work 34*, 199–224.

Thoburn, J., Wilding, J. and Watson, J. (2000) *Family Support in Cases of Emotional Maltreatment and Neglect*. London: The Stationery Office.

Tober, G. and Raistrick, D. (2007) *Motivational Dialogue: Preparing Addiction Professionals for Motivational Interviewing Practice*. London: Routledge.

Treacher, A. and Carpenter, J. (1989) *Problems and Solutions in Marriage and Family Therapy*. Oxford: Basil Blackwell.

Tuck, V. (2004) 'Analysing Risk in Child Protection: A Model for Assessment.' In V. White and J. Harris (eds) *Developing Good Practice in Children's Services*. London: Jessica Kingsley Publishers.

Turnell, A. and Edwards, S. (1999) *Signs of Safety: A Solution and Safety-orientated Approach to Child Protection*. New York, NY: Norton.

Ward, T. and Keenan, T. (1999) 'Child molesters' implicit theories.' *Journal of Interpersonal Violence 14*, 8, 821–838.

Wellman, H. (1990) *The Child's Theory of Mind*. Cambridge, MA: MIT Press.

Winett, R. (1995) 'A framework for health promotion and disease prevention programs.' *American Psychologist 50*, 341–350.

Woodcock, J. (2003) 'The social work assessment of parenting: an exploration.' *British Journal of Social Work 33*, 87–106.

CHAPTER 19

The Impact of Domestic Violence, Parental Mental Health Problems, Substance Misuse and Learning Disability on Parenting Capacity

Nicky Stanley, Hedy Cleaver and Di Hart

Parents may be experiencing their own problems which may have an impact through their behaviour on their capacity to respond to their child's needs.

(From the Framework for the Assessment of Children in Need and their Families, p.25, 2.20)

This chapter considers:

- the stigma associated with domestic violence, mental health problems, substance misuse and learning disability

- gender as a factor in parents' engagement with services

- assessing families where there is domestic violence

- assessing families where parents have mental health problems

- assessing families where parents have drug and alcohol problems

- assessing families where parents have learning disabilities

- the need for communication and collaboration between children's and adults' services.

Introduction

Understanding parenting issues

This chapter explores the way in which issues such as domestic violence, mental health problems, substance misuse and learning disability can impact on parenting capacity and considers how assessment and planning can best respond to such needs. Each issue is considered in detail in individual sections of the chapter. All these issues will be commonly encountered in assessment: Cleaver and Walker (2004) found that three-quarters of the 866 initial assessments they audited in 24 local authorities identified problems such as domestic violence, parental mental health problems or substance misuse. These factors may act to restrict parents' capacities to care and protect children and can, in some cases, expose children to significant harm. Whilst risks of harm may be higher in such families, this will not necessarily be the case and assessment should identify both the nature and extent of parenting problems and the impact they have on children. These effects can be mediated by a number of factors including:

- the severity and duration of the problem
- the co-existence of other problems
- the social support available for the family
- the child's access to other supportive adults
- the child's resilience. (Cleaver *et al.* 1999)

Rutter's (1985) research on children's resilience identified some of its main components: self-esteem, a child's belief in their own self-efficacy and ability to act to change their environment and a repertoire of problem-solving approaches. It is important that practitioners acknowledge that many children living in these families will not experience long-term harm and that, where possible, they convey optimism about both the child's and the family's strengths and how they can be developed. Such an approach is particularly called for, given that these families may already encounter high levels of stigma and, as we shall emphasise below, negative attitudes on the part of professionals can contribute to their feelings of shame and isolation.

The parenting issues discussed here can occur on their own or in combination. The association between them may be a causal one: in particular, research (Sheppard 1997; Sheppard with Kelly 2001) has identified the high levels of domestic violence experienced by depressed mothers involved with social services. A review of research (Cascardi *et al.* 1999) found that between 38 and 83 per cent of women experiencing domestic violence were classified as suffering depression and Humphreys and Thiara (2003) have identified some of the processes through which male control and violence erodes women's mental health. Moreover, those experiencing mental health problems or domestic violence may use drugs or alcohol as a form of self-medication (Humphreys 2006). Harwin and Forrester's (2002) study found high rates of domestic violence in families where substance misuse was a factor. When such problems are found in combination, one issue may act to mask another: for example, depression in a parent with learning disabilities may be difficult to identify. Practitioners assessing families must remain open to the possibility that parenting capacity may be affected by multiple rather than single problems and that one type of problem may be underpinned by another.

Hidden needs

The parental needs considered in this chapter are not always easily discernible by those undertaking assessments. Substance misuse, mental health problems and domestic violence all carry a social stigma which makes disclosure of such problems to professionals a risky process for families. In some settings, such as South Asian communities, domestic violence, substance misuse or mental health problems may be concealed, as disclosure of such issues may be seen to reflect on a family's honour (Mullender *et al.* 2002). Adults may go to considerable lengths to hide or disguise a substance misuse or mental health problem and those experiencing domestic violence may deny or seek to minimise its seriousness. Although parents may seek to conceal problems such as substance misuse or domestic violence from children, their success in doing so will probably be limited to very young children. Children are likely to share the sense of stigma and the need to maintain secrecy about such problems, and studies that have elicited children's views report their feelings of embarrassment and isolation (Aldridge and Becker 2003; Gorin 2004; McGee 2000; Somers 2007). They may develop a range of strategies to hide these problems, such as limiting their contact with other children, not inviting friends home or inventing stories to explain their parents' behaviour (Saunders *et al.* 1995; Stallard *et al.* 2004).

For parents, disclosure of such a problem carries the additional risk that they will lose the care of their children; any involvement from children's services may initially be perceived as a threat rather than as an offer of support. Women participating in Stanley *et al.*'s (2003a) study of mothers with mental health problems described how their fear of losing care of their children led them to withhold information and avoid requesting support from child care workers:

> Social services still say to this day if I end up in hospital…I'd lose the kids. So that hangs over your head – it makes you stay quiet rather than say anything at all… It's been said I don't give social services enough information on a regular basis – I've been put down as uncooperative – a nightmare where social services are concerned. (Stanley *et al.* 2003a, p.73)

McGee's study of children's and mothers' experiences of domestic violence found that, in some cases, abusive partners used the threat of social workers' involvement to control mothers:

> He was born on the Tuesday and we were home on the Friday. I'd been indoors half an hour, there was a row, I can't remember what it was about but he [my partner] threatened to call social services to say I was an unfit mother. In fact picked up the phone and pretended to dial the number, pretended he was speaking to somebody and was saying I was an unfit mother. (Judith) (McGee 2000, p.116)

Practitioners undertaking assessments should anticipate such responses and be prepared to work with initial hostility and defensiveness. Cleaver *et al.* (1998) suggest that parents can be reassured by being told that only a very small proportion of children referred to statutory services are ever removed from home. However, if separation is probable, it is usually better to acknowledge that possibility early on. It may take time and a number of visits before parents feel that they can trust a worker sufficiently to reveal the full extent of their problems. Practitioners, therefore, need to be prepared to raise the issue of domestic violence or substance misuse on more than one occasion. Approaches which avoid passing judgements on parents' behaviour, while emphasising children's needs, are required. It will usually be more productive to focus on the child's needs for routine, boundaries, support, stimulation and a safe environment than to highlight the damaging nature of parental behaviour. Practitioners should adopt attitudes to families that are sympathetic and encouraging rather than blaming or punishing. Studies which have elicited the views of parents have highlighted the importance of respectful, non-judgemental attitudes from practitioners (Cleaver and Freeman 1995; Stanley *et al.* 2003a). One mother with mental health problems in Stanley *et al.*'s (2003a) study noted the value of professionals who 'explained a lot about my illness and didn't judge me. Treated me as a human being and was very encouraging and supportive – she's got time for you…' (p.71).

Women living with domestic violence may feel particularly guilty about its impact on their children and their failure to protect children from the effects of such violence. In many cases, their abuser will have encouraged them to feel that they are responsible for the violence perpetrated. Making contact with statutory services is likely to involve additional risks for this group of parents who may expose themselves to further abuse if they are discovered to have revealed their partner's violence. Prioritising the safety of these parents is therefore essential if a trusting relationship in which they will participate in, and contribute to, the assessment process is to develop.

Gender as a factor in parents' engagement with services

There is a substantial body of evidence (Farmer and Owen 1995; Stanley 1997) which demonstrates that, regardless of where problems in parenting are located in a family system or which parent presents a risk to a child's welfare, children's services tend to focus their attention on mothers in families. This can result in mothers feeling scrutinised and, at worst, being allocated responsibility for controlling male violence. There have been attempts to shift the focus onto fathers (Featherstone 2003; Ghate *et al.* 2000; Ryan 2000). However, traditional attitudes regarding responsibility for the care of children, together with fathers' absences from the household and consequent lack of availability to children's services, can easily combine to ensure that fathers stay 'invisible'. Practitioners may also, consciously or unconsciously, seek to avoid engaging with fathers or father-figures who are perceived as less accessible to health and social care interventions and who may be experienced as threatening or obstructive (Daniel *et al.* 2005).

However, when working with families where domestic violence, mental health problems, substance misuse or learning disability is an issue, practitioners should be prepared to discriminate between parents and parenting figures whose parenting skills and capacity may differ substantially. Ryan (2000) emphasises that practitioners should 'ask and not assume' (p.38) what role fathers or father-figures play in the family. Their level of presence or absence as well as their involvement in child care should be established, and they should be involved in assessments as long as mothers' and children's safety will not be compromised by so doing. This may involve practitioners making additional efforts and arrangements to check that their presence does not constitute a risk to the safety of mothers and children, and to contact and engage with fathers. It will be important to establish which parent has a problem, the extent of the problem and the degree to which it impacts upon children in the family. In most cases of severe domestic violence, the perpetrator will be male (Walby and Allen 2004). Does one parent represent a source of support to the other or an alternative source of care for the child or children? If both parents have a learning disability or a mental health or substance misuse problem, do their needs differ or can they be met by the same services?

Asking such questions may raise further questions about the extent to which services are available and accessible to fathers. However, taking a gender-blind approach which assumes that both parents in a family have common needs and which ignores power differences and the uneven distribution of risks and strengths between parents may result in a very restricted and skewed understanding of parenting capacity.

Part 1: The impact of domestic violence on children and on parenting capacity

Domestic violence is a very widespread phenomenon with one in four women having experienced at least one incident of domestic violence since they were 16. For women who are parents the likelihood of experiencing domestic violence is nearly twice that for women without children (Walby and Allen 2004). Cawson's (2002) national prevalence study of young adults found that just over a quarter had witnessed violence between their parents and in 5 per cent of cases the violence was frequent and ongoing. In the UK, the Government has adopted a broad definition of domestic violence (Home Office 2000) that includes psychological abuse and threatening behaviour as well as physical and sexual violence. Such a definition acknowledges that the damaging effects of domestic violence extend beyond its physical consequences to its impact on victims' emotional wellbeing and mental health. When victims are parents, these effects may have consequences for their parenting capacity. While parents may understandably want to believe that children do not see or hear domestic violence, subsequent experience often highlights that children are frequently aware of the issue. Gorin (2004) notes that once women have left a violent home, they are more likely to discover and acknowledge the extent of their children's exposure to the violence.

Domestic violence can have a direct impact on children's health and wellbeing. First, and most serious, children can be injured in the context of domestic violence, either when they are caught up or intervene in violence in the home or 'in vitro' when violence occurs during pregnancy. Child abduction is associated with domestic violence (Plass *et al.* 1997) and there have also been a number of cases reported in the national press where violent men have taken their own lives and those of their children in acts of retaliation or revenge on their partners.

Second, a body of evidence has identified the harmful effects of living with domestic violence on children's mental health and development. Such effects include high rates of depression and anxiety (McClosky *et al.* 1995), trauma, particularly following exposure to severe acts of violence (Richards and Baker 2003), and behavioural problems, including anger and aggression. Children themselves describe feelings of fear, anxiety and guilt in relation to domestic violence (Mullender 2006) and they note that their education is affected in terms of their attendance, ability to concentrate and their relationships with peers (McGee 2000). These effects will be mediated by the child's developmental stage, their level of understanding, personality and circumstances as well as by the nature and extent of the violence and their exposure to it (Cleaver *et al.* 1999). Hester *et al.* (2006) note that pre-school children are more likely to show physical symptoms such as stomach-aches and bed-wetting. Primary school children may present a wide range of behavioural and emotional problems, while adolescents may leave home prematurely and become involved in drugs or early pregnancy. In response to this body of evidence, under section 31(9) of the Children Act 1989, amended by the Adoption and Children Act 2002, the meaning of harm now includes 'impairment suffered from seeing or hearing the ill treatment of another'.

When domestic violence is severe, victims are likely to be women (Walby and Allen 2004) and the effects of such violence can compromise mothers' parenting capacity. In the long term, domestic violence can undermine mothers' self-esteem and confidence in their own parenting, and their ability to be alert and responsive to their children's needs may be restricted. Family routines may be determined by the necessity to placate and forestall potential violence, and children's needs for play, stimulation and warmth may be subordinated to this objective (Mullender *et al.* 2002).

Moving out of the family home to escape domestic violence can have additional adverse effects for children who may be uprooted from familiar settings and relationships. Leaving friends, pets and belongings behind can be a particular source of anxiety for children who may also lose contact with part of the extended family. Court cases and contact visits may also be stressful for children and some will experience a sense of loss in relation to their fathers (McGee 2000).

Practice in assessing children in families where there is domestic violence

Asking about domestic violence can be difficult for practitioners who are aware of the stigma it can evoke and who may be anxious about opening a 'Pandora's Box' of difficulties which they feel unable to respond to adequately. Enquiring about domestic violence on a routine basis has been advocated, and Hester (2006) argues that doing so communicates professionals' awareness and recognition of the issue to women and facilitates disclosure. Some opening questions which might be used to raise the issue of domestic violence are shown in the box on the next page.

However, practitioners need to be confident that the setting in which they are asking the question is safe for any potential victim: while it may be appropriate to put such questions to a mother who is seen alone outside the home at an antenatal class for instance, raising the issue in the presence of her partner may expose her to further violence. Practitioners may also find it difficult to ask about domestic violence or to enquire into children's welfare if they feel intimidated or threatened by the presence of abusive partners (Littlechild and Bourke 2006). In such cases, concerns about the safety of children, women and staff need to be raised with managers in supervision and attempts should be made to find safe means of communication with the victim. Stanley and Humphreys (2006) suggest that, when domestic violence is an issue, assessments involving both parents should include two professionals. This offers protection for workers against intimidation and being drawn into collusive relationships with perpetrators.

> Initial questions to ask women about domestic violence:
> - How are things at home?
> - How are arguments settled?
> - How are decisions reached?
> - What happens when you argue or disagree?
> - What happens when your partner/husband gets angry?
> - Have you ever felt frightened of your partner/husband?
> - Have you ever felt threatened by your partner/husband?
>
> *(Adapted from Hester et al. 2006)*

It may be useful to consult with community safety officers or staff working in specialist domestic violence organisations, to ensure that safe means of communicating with victims of domestic violence are adopted. Thought will need to be given as to what information is shared with whom. This is particularly important for the safety of those who have left an abusive household, as their whereabouts can be inadvertently leaked to the abusive partner. The period when the abused parent has just moved out of the home or relationship is a time of particular vulnerability for domestic violence (Humphreys and Thiara 2003); pregnancy is another such period (Campbell *et al.* 1998; Mezey and Bewley 1997). These are times when violence may escalate and particular attention needs to be given to ensuring the safety of women and children.

Domestic violence can serve as an indicator for other forms of child harm. Farmer and Owen (1995) found evidence of domestic violence in about two-fifths of cases where the child's name was on the child protection register because of sexual abuse and in just under half of the cases of other forms of abuse included in their study. Cawson's (2002) prevalence study also found that high proportions of those reporting physical or sexual abuse, as children, had also experienced domestic violence as a child. Practitioners who are involved with families where there is concern about other forms of abuse, therefore, need to be alert to the possible presence of domestic violence.

We have noted above the importance of engaging both parents in assessments in order that the burden of involvement with statutory services does not fall on mothers alone. A gendered approach also considers the distribution of power in a family and identifies the perpetrator of harm. In relation to domestic violence, this means that practitioners must seek to avoid placing responsibility for the child's welfare on the mother while her partner's violence is unacknowledged (Farmer and Owen 1995; Stanley 1997). Similarly, threats to remove children if women do not leave violent partners fail to acknowledge the trap that such an approach can create for mothers who may be well aware of the potential for increased violence should they seek to leave. Practitioners should rather seek to identify ways in which violent men can be engaged in assessment and treatment programmes. This may be best undertaken by separate perpetrator services delivered by either the probation service or the voluntary sector as described by Radford *et al.* (2006).

Children are likely to show signs of recovery once they are living in safer environments. While living with domestic violence and afterwards, a child's relationship with a parent (usually the mother) who is experienced as 'safe' and 'caring' will be an important factor in determining his or her resilience (Mullender 2006). Humphreys *et al.* (2006) have emphasised the need for assessment and planning to focus on the damage done to the mother–child relationship by domestic violence and their book outlines interventions which can strengthen and repair this relationship.

Part 2: The impact of parental mental health problems on children and on parenting capacity

Mental health problems are widespread in the general population and have been shown to occur amongst 13 and 20 per cent of parents involved with children's safeguarding services (Gibbons *et al.* 1995; Thoburn *et al.* 1995). Similarly, it has been estimated that between 20 and 50 per cent of adults using mental health services are parents (Falkov *et al.* 1998). Mental health problems can take a range of forms and women are particularly susceptible to depression which is often associated with giving birth and becoming a parent. Depression in women has also been identified as a consequence of the stresses of parenting and of childhood abuse (Bifulco and Moran 1998). Lone mothers who experience the social and economic disadvantages attendant on single parenthood are particularly vulnerable to depression (Targosz *et al.* 2003).

Mental health problems, such as depression or schizophrenia, together with the side-effects of the medication used to treat psychotic disorders, can have the effect of inhibiting parents' capacity to respond to their children's cues and to offer consistent day-to-day care, supervision and emotional availability (Falkov *et al.* 1998). Parental over-involvement with or unrealistic expectations of children are possible outcomes of both personality disorders and psychotic disorders. All mental health problems can result in inconsistency and a lack of predictability that can provoke fear and worry for children (Gorin 2004). Somers (2007) compared a sample of Irish children living with a parent diagnosed with schizophrenia with a control group and found that the children whose parent was diagnosed with schizophrenia had higher rates of mental health problems, behavioural difficulties and problems with anger and were more likely to be absent from school.

A study by Glaser and Prior (1997) found parental mental health needs in nearly a third of the 94 children whose names were on the child protection register under the category of emotional abuse. Overviews of special case reviews (Brandon *et al.* 2008; Falkov 1996; Reder and Duncan 1999; Rose and Barnes 2008) have drawn attention to the association between mental health needs and high levels of risk of harm for children. However, the relationship between mental health needs and adverse outcomes for children is not straightforward. While the children of parents with mental health problems are more likely to develop mental health, social and behavioural needs during childhood (Leverton 2003), other factors, such as poverty and social exclusion, which are associated with parental mental health needs (Social Exclusion Unit 2004), may play a key role in contributing to such outcomes.

Research on young carers (Aldridge and Becker 2003) has identified the range of domestic responsibilities and tasks involving emotional support that children of parents with mental health problems can assume, which are discussed in detail in Chapter 13. One mother described the effects of such responsibilities on her son as follows: 'Even when he was in care he used to come home from school to see how I was. Felt responsible for me. He grew up too soon' (Stanley *et al.* 2003a, p.64). However, studies of young carers, while acknowledging the potential for children to carry disproportionate burdens of care, have found that parents who are incapacitated by severe mental health problems can retain the status of parents and that caring can strengthen the bonds between child and parent (Aldridge 2006).

Practice in assessment with families when parents have mental health problems

Identifying mental health problems in parents may be difficult. The stigma surrounding mental health problems often acts to delay disclosure until needs have reached an acute stage. Parents simply may not recognise that their tiredness or anxiety can be given a mental health label or, in the case of severe mental health problems, such insight may not be available to them. However, children's social care staff can sometimes fail to identify mental health problems appropriately. Sheppard and Kelly's (2001) study of social workers' interventions with depressed mothers found that in some cases depression went unrecognised. While knowledge of the symptoms of major mental disorders such as depression, schizophrenia and bi-polar disorders can assist in the assessment of parenting capacity, practitioners also need to maintain a focus on how a parent's mental health needs impact on their day-to-day parenting. Depression, which is the most commonly encountered mental health problem, can vary enormously in its severity and effects on an individual's functioning, so practitioners should not assume that a particular diagnosis will inevitably indicate poor parenting.

Practitioners need to remember that parental mental health problems may fluctuate over time. These fluctuations may be contained within the span of a day. For example, parents who are severely depressed may be much more able to engage with their children's needs in the evening than in the morning when they may find it particularly hard to function. In such cases, practitioners assessing parenting capacity will need to visit more than once and at different times of the day. They should also acknowledge that most mental health problems are transient and that parents may have periods when they require more or less support.

Cassell and Coleman (1995) suggest that, when assessing the risks of harm for children posed by a parent with mental health needs, practitioners should consider the following factors:

- the warmth of the parent–child relationship
- the parent's responsiveness to the child's needs

- the content of any delusional thinking
- the parent's history of anger management
- the availability of another responsible adult.

The risks of harm to children may be particularly high if they figure in any parental thoughts or delusions of violence or self-harm or if they are the targets of parental aggression or rejection (HM Government 2006a).

Most children will value explanations of what their parents are experiencing and what help and support is available, although the amount and level of information should be adjusted in accordance with the child's developmental level and needs (Stallard *et al.* 2004). Keeping children informed is particularly important at times of crisis when they may witness their parents acting in a frightening or disinhibited manner. If parents need to be admitted to a mental health unit, children will want to know what plans are being made for their own and their parent's care. They will also need support and assistance to make arrangements to visit their parent in hospital. This should be negotiated with mental health staff in the relevant unit in accordance with national guidelines (Department of Health 2008; Mental Health Act 1983; Mental Health Act 1983 Code of Practice 2008 Revision). As young carers, they may be entitled to a carer's assessment in their own right under the Carers (Recognition and Services) Act 1995 as discussed in Chapter 13.

Where parents are being treated by mental health services it is important that those professionals involved, from both children's and mental health services, establish good ongoing communication. Mental health practitioners may have useful information about the nature of parents' mental health needs, the impact of any medication they are being prescribed on their day-to-day functioning and their contact with mental health services. Children's services will be able to offer mental health practitioners information about the demands and stresses of parenting and any concerns about the risks of harm to children should be shared. Unless there is considered to be a risk of significant harm to children and parents refuse permission for such information to be shared, practitioners should always ask for parents' consent to sharing such information. If, however, they refuse consent and there is evidence or reasonable cause to believe that a child is suffering or at risk of suffering significant harm, guidance stresses that confidential information can be shared between professionals (HM Government 2008).

The majority of adult mental health problems are treated in the community where parenting can be supported by the provision of services at times when mental health needs are acute. Such support might range from practical support with child care and household tasks to providing opportunities for parents to voice feelings of anxiety, loss and depression and receive counselling or therapeutic services. In some parts of the country, voluntary organisations such as HomeStart, NewPIN and Building Bridges offer a number of such interventions; Children's Centres also provide a range of support services for families with pre-school children. Increasingly, midwives and health visitors are involved in identifying and offering support with parenting to women with postnatal depression, although antenatal depression is also a widespread phenomenon which requires a co-ordinated response (Stanley *et al.* 2006). However, it is important to take into account parents' views as to which services would be most useful for them and their children.

Part 3: The impact of substance misuse on parenting capacity

Children who grow up in a household where parents have a drug or alcohol problem are at risk of poor outcomes in all five areas identified as important within *Every Child Matters* (Cm 5860 2003). The *Hidden Harm* report (Advisory Council on the Misuse of Drugs 2003) estimated that at least 250,000 children in the UK had a parent who used drugs and highlighted the harm that could result from conception through to adulthood. A report on parental alcohol use (Turning Point 2006) raised similar concerns and suggested that as many as 1.3 million children might be affected. Both reports made a number of recommendations, including the need for services to work together to reduce the potential for harm.

Many children are the subject of multidisciplinary child protection plans or become looked after at some point in their childhood as a direct result of parental substance misuse (Forrester and Harwin 2006) and the assessment of such children and their families is a major challenge for practitioners. Because of the nature of the problem, these assessments will involve not only children's social workers but adult substance misuse workers, midwives, primary health care staff, criminal justice agencies and teachers and early years staff.

It is not inevitable that parenting capacity will be adversely affected by having a drug or alcohol problem but it certainly makes the task of parenting more difficult. This is not just a consequence of the substance use itself but of the complex range of associated social, legal and financial pressures that may ensue. These will be different according to the substances used. Alcohol use is legal but may place a strain on stretched financial resources. Problem drug use is often illegal in itself (although some prescribed medication can also be abused) and may lead to further criminality through the need to commit crimes to fund its use. The impact on behaviour, and therefore on the capacity to be a good-enough parent, will also vary according to the substance used and the level of use. This range of factors means it is difficult to make definitive statements about the impact of substance misuse on children's developmental needs: has this child been harmed by the fact that her father is a crack user, by the fact that he is in prison or by the social exclusion of her family within their neighbourhood? Another child in similar circumstances may thrive: not because her parent's substance misuse is less serious but because her grandfather is in the background providing love and support. Every child's situation is unique and must be assessed as such. Recent research has increased our understanding by drawing on the testimony of children and families with direct experience of living with substance misuse problems.

If parents are physically absent or unavailable through intoxication their ability to provide *basic care* can be compromised. A 17-year-old with an alcohol-using parent reported: 'I had to look after my brother, make sure he got up and went to school, had his tea… If I didn't, he wouldn't have' (Turning Point 2006). Corbett (2005) suggests that this risk of neglect is common to all types of substance misuse. This is confirmed by a study of young people aged between 15 and 27 who, having grown up with both drug- and alcohol-using parents, offered various accounts of receiving poor physical care (Bancroft *et al.* 2004).

This failure of parents to provide basic care may extend to an inability to keep children safe. Alcohol and stimulant use can increase the risk of violence or sexual abuse, either by parents themselves or their associates (Altshuler 2005). Young people describe the constant fear of living with an adult whose behaviour is violent or unpredictable (Barnard 2007; FRANK 2005). Parents' capacities to prevent accidental harm may also be reduced, with children being unsupervised or exposed to dangerous situations, such as taking methadone or being the victim of a house fire resulting from parental negligence. Recent analyses of serious case reviews since 2001 (Brandon *et al.* 2008, 2009; Rose and Barnes 2008) demonstrated that parental substance misuse is a significant factor in a number of child deaths or serious injury. A study of the causes of child deaths also raised concerns about the role of substance misusing adults, either because they were the source of drugs that had resulted in the child's death from overdose or because their ability to keep children safe had been impaired (Pearson 2008).

The all-consuming nature of significant substance misuse problems may mean that it becomes the user's primary attachment, distorting other relationships (Kroll 2004), including the ability to show their children *emotional warmth* and make them feel valued.

> I used to feel responsible but I realised it wasn't my fault, she didn't love me enough or she would have stopped [drinking] before. (Lou, age 12, quoted in Turning Point 2006, p.9).

This may be described by children as parents 'not being there for them' (Gorin 2005) and may, in turn, put their ability to form secure attachments in jeopardy, having long-term effects on their emotional health. It can be complicated by the fact that some young people perceive their parents as 'caring about' them whilst recognising that they were not being 'cared for' (Bancroft *et al.* 2004).

For the reasons described above, parents may not have the practical or emotional reserves to engage with their children in order to provide stimulation to support their development. Other parents may alternate between being playful and euphoric or irritable and withdrawn:

> I didn't sit and read to him at night. I didn't play with him with toys, I didn't colour with him, I didn't do any of they kinda things. (Mother quoted in Barnard 2007, p.77)

For some children, stimulation may be available from other sources but if the child is burdened by anxiety, as a result of their home circumstances, they may be unable to benefit from the opportunity.

Barnard's research offers a striking example of a young woman crying out for parental guidance and boundaries:

> you want a ma that'll just give you rules and all that... I want her to be...just be like a normal ma, if you do something wrong, you'll get shouted at or grounded or something. (Barnard 2007, p.90)

In the absence of this 'normal' parental behaviour, young people are at increased risk of harm: both from a sense that no one cares what they do and from a perception that criminality and substance misuse are acceptable (Kearney *et al.* 2005).

Substance misuse is characterised by a lack of stability for the adults concerned: it can best be understood as a chronic relapsing condition with crises followed by attempts to become drug or alcohol free. This cycle of change may be compounded by disruption caused by imprisonment or hospitalisation, or by family breakdown. Children living in these circumstances will experience constant change: of carer, accommodation and parental behaviour. As practitioners, we accept that a 'cure', and hence stability, will not be achieved overnight. A recent study revealed that this acceptance is not the same for children and young people (Harbin 2006): if a parent goes into treatment, they expect them to get better and may be bitterly disappointed if this is not the case.

The above are illustrations of the ways in which parental capacity may be impaired by substance misuse but it will also have a direct impact on the other assessment domains. A child's health may be jeopardised by a mother's drinking in pregnancy or their emotional development disrupted by a parent's erratic displays of affection. Similarly, dynamics within the extended family are likely to be complicated. Grandparents are often an important source of support, but this may be in a context of guilt and disapproval that are hurtful for the child (Barnard 2007; Kroll 2007). A model for considering the impact of parental substance misuse on each dimension of the Assessment Framework has been developed to assist practitioners, and is reproduced in Figure 19.1.

Practice in assessment with families where parents have drug/alcohol problems

Children and young people in these circumstances describe coping strategies they have developed, which reflect other literature on the development of resilience. Having goals and dreams, the escape provided by work or education, or the ability to challenge and take control are all described by interviewees in Bancroft *et al.*'s (2004) study. They were also able to identify what other people could do to help, ranging from supportive relationships to the formal intervention of statutory services. There are barriers in accessing services, however. In spite of the catalogue of harm described by the children participating in Barnard's (2007) research, many had not received any help from health or welfare agencies.

A major challenge lies in the denial, secrecy and stigma that surround substance misuse. One young person summed up the pressures: 'I just knew to keep it quiet...' (Corbett 2005). As noted above, families are often afraid that they will lose their children if the problem, or its extent, becomes known. Interestingly, there is some evidence that this avoidance may also influence practitioners (Hart and Powell 2006). The requirement to 'gatekeep' scarce resources means that those who do not actively seek help are unlikely to receive it, unless the need is both clear and serious. Hart and Powell's (2006) research found a mutually collusive pattern between parents and agencies whereby no one was willing to 'take the lid off' to explore what life was really like for the children in a substance-misusing household. Approaches that contributed to this were repeated initial assessments focused only on the presenting crisis; becoming distracted by the parents' problems at the expense of real engagement with the children; or a lack of knowledge

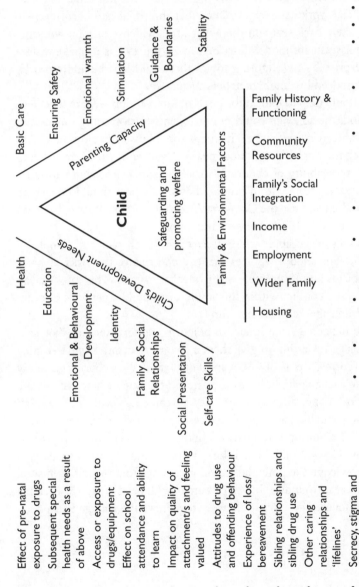

- Details of drug use and impact on parental health/behaviour/mood
- Physical availability to child and impairment of ability to provide care
- Emotional availability to child
- Strategies to protect child from impact of drugs
- Role of drugs within parental relationship/partnership
- Consistency and reliability
- Priorities – drugs or child?
- Messages to child about drug use and offending behaviour
- Previous parenting capacity

From: Adult Drug Problems, Children's Needs: Assessing the Impact of Parental Drug Use. A Toolkit for Practitioners. *Di Hart and Jane Powell* (2006) National Children's Bureau

Basic Care
Ensuring Safety
Emotional warmth
Stimulation
Guidance & Boundaries
Stability

Parenting Capacity

Health
Education
Emotional & Behavioural Development
Identity
Family & Social Relationships
Social Presentation
Self-care Skills

Child's Development Needs

Child

Safeguarding and promoting welfare

Family & Environmental Factors

Family History & Functioning
Community Resources
Family's Social Integration
Income
Employment
Wider Family
Housing

- Parental health
- Parental absences
- Past drug treatment/engagement
- Offending behaviour and convictions
- Who knows about drug use and implications for wider family relationships?
- Extended family able to act as carers
- Adequacy of material resources – money and housing
- Home is exposed to risky adults or activities
- Community attitudes and stigma
- Support network outside the home

- Effect of pre-natal exposure to drugs
- Subsequent special health needs as a result of above
- Access or exposure to drugs/equipment
- Effect on school attendance and ability to learn
- Impact on quality of attachment/s and feeling valued
- Attitudes to drug use and offending behaviour
- Experience of loss/bereavement
- Sibling relationships and sibling drug use
- Other caring relationships and 'lifelines'
- Secrecy, stigma and social exclusion
- Impact on friendships
- Level of caring responsibility for self, parents and siblings

***Figure 19.1**: Applying the Assessment Framework to families where parents have drug/alcohol problems*

and skill in assessing the impact of substance misuse. There is a real likelihood that assessments will be inadequate in these circumstances. In Hart and Powell's (2006) study, there were examples of children who had been assessed many times before becoming looked after in an emergency: they then remained in care because the true extent of their difficulties had only then become known.

An additional barrier is the sheer difficulty of multi-agency working. Although several practitioners may be involved with a family, there can be tensions in the way they perceive their respective roles and responsibilities as described in Chapter 5. Barnard (2007) describes these as 'fracture lines', with social work being set apart by other agencies because of their perceived coercive powers. This was also evident in Hart and Powell's (2006) study, with constant friction evident between children's social care and other agencies about the threshold for social work assessment. Once that threshold had been reached, other agencies tended to take a back seat and there was little evidence of joint working. One intention behind the assessment model described in Figure 19.1 is to make assessment more of a joint enterprise by highlighting topics that could best be addressed by different practitioners – or indeed by family members themselves.

A quality assessment should help to inform the goals of intervention. Where substance misuse is poorly understood, the sole aim could be for parents to stop using substances, but this may not be achievable in every family. The focus should instead be on the child's needs and the ways in which their parents' substance misuse is preventing these from being met. This is not just the responsibility of children's social care agencies: adult substance misuse workers and practitioners from within other children's services should be alert to the needs of vulnerable children and use the Common Assessment Framework (Children's Workforce Development Council 2009) to identify areas where help is needed.

Advocates of a 'risk and resilience' approach (Forrester 2004; Velleman and Templeton 2006) suggest that practitioners should work to identify and reduce the risks of harm posed by the parents' problems and to promote any protective factors. This might mean working with parents to reduce conflict within the family or to build a network of other adults who can give the child some respite – and fun.

Families in crisis have benefited from intensive practical support, such as that provided by the Option 2 project in Cardiff, to give them a chance to demonstrate that they can care for their children (Forrester et al. 2008). A specialist family drug court is currently being piloted in London to manage applications for care proceedings where parents are problem substance misusers. A specialist team attached to the court will undertake an assessment and ensure that a suitable package of services is provided to families in order to maximise their chances of retaining care of their children, and their progress will be overseen by the court (BBC News 2008). When they are given the opportunity, parents – and children – can acknowledge the potential for harm arising from substance misuse. Given the fear and stigma that surrounds it, however, parents will need proactive attempts to engage them and family-focused services, if they are to achieve the change needed.

Part 4: The impact of parental learning disability on parenting capacity

The Government is committed to promoting the safety and welfare of all children and when parents have learning disabilities this may mean providing considerable help. When children come to the attention of children's social care, practitioners should ensure that assessments, multi-agency plans and reviews address the needs of children and their parents. The findings presented in this section are drawn from research that explored these issues by focusing on the needs and outcomes of 76 children referred to children's social care, who were living with parents with learning disabilities, and a comparison group of 152 children where neither parent had a learning disability (Cleaver and Nicholson 2007). All names in the illustrative cases have been changed to ensure anonymity.

A key finding was that many parents with learning disabilities were also experiencing additional issues which affected their capacity to meet the needs of their children. For example, most parents experienced either: poor mental or physical health, domestic violence, childhood abuse, growing up in care, substance misuse, or a combination of these. The families were further disadvantaged because they frequently lived in poor housing and had little or no contact with extended family. Furthermore, many parents had the added challenge of bringing up at least one child with learning disabilities, many of whom were also physically disabled. It is the combination of learning disability with these other stressors that negatively affects parenting capacity and has long-term consequences for children's welfare (Cleaver and Nicholson 2007). Research suggests that parental learning disability in itself should not be equated with wilful neglect and abusive parenting (Tymchuck 1992).

Child's developmental needs

Social work assessments suggested that children living with parents with learning disabilities have higher levels of need, with regard to all aspects of their development (health, education, emotional and behavioural development, identity and social development, and family and social relationships), than children in the comparison group. For example, most children (80%) living with parents with learning disabilities had needs in relation to their family and social relationships (compared with 57% of the comparison group) and approximately 60 per cent had needs in relation to their health and education (compared with some 40% of the comparison group). Lynn, aged 5 years, serves as an example. The concerns at referral included a 'failure to thrive, neglect, non-school attendance, dirty clothes, frequently hungry and smelling of body odour'. It was also noted that Lynn persistently missed medical appointments and home conditions were not acceptable, being described as filthy with rotting food and dog faeces in every room.

Parenting capacity

Parents with learning disabilities were shown to be less able to meet their children's needs for basic care, safety, emotional warmth, stimulation, guidance and boundaries, and stability. For example, in over two-thirds of cases studied, parents with learning disabilities were experiencing difficulty in providing guidance and boundaries and 58 per cent in ensuring the child's safety, compared with 30 per cent and 36 per cent respectively for the comparison group.

Family and environmental factors

The pattern of greater needs for children living with parents with learning disabilities continued to apply when family and environmental factors were considered. The study found that these children were disadvantaged in relation to every dimension (family history and functioning, social resources, housing and employment). For example, although most children (89%) living with parents with learning disabilities experienced difficulties in relation to family history and functioning, this applied to less than two-thirds (64%) of the comparison group. The Tandy family (comprising four children aged 8, 7, 4 and 2 years and their parents, both of whom have a learning disability) illustrate the poor living conditions many families experience:

> Charles [father] had been drinking and the home conditions weren't improving at all. Adam [2 years] looked dirty and poorly. I asked Charles to pick up the dog excrement from the garden as the children were playing in it. (Social worker's notes recorded on the initial assessment, Cleaver and Nicholson 2007, p.32)

Outcomes for children living with parents with learning disabilities

The research also found that, during the three years following the original assessment, continuing concerns for the safety and welfare of children living with parents with learning disabilities resulted in over half the children (56%) being re-referred to children's social care and to the names of more than a third (38.5%) being placed on the child protection register. Moreover, reviews and reassessments suggest that the majority of children who remained at home continued to have needs in relation to their development, parenting capacity and family and environmental factors. Of particular concern was the finding that things had changed little for over half the children originally classified as having the greatest level of needs.

What distinguished children who remained living safely with their parents, from those who did not show satisfactory progress and those who were removed, was the day-to-day presence of another caring adult such as a partner or relative, and a willingness to engage with agencies and take advantage of proffered services. Although there was a strong trend towards continuity, when changes did occur they were generally in a positive direction. In a limited number of cases, children displayed fewer developmental needs, parenting capacity had improved, and factors within the family and environment had been addressed.

However, the research suggests that in the majority of cases children living with parents with learning disabilities continued to have developmental needs three years later. For example, in approximately 80 per cent of cases, needs endured in relation to children's education, health and emotional and behavioural development. The trend for problems to persist was also found in relation to parenting capacity. For example, in 74 per cent of cases parents continued to have difficulty in providing their children with stability and in over half the cases in providing basic care (56%) or guidance and boundaries (54%).

The following case notes illustrate continuing concerns over the safety and basic care of seven-year-old Katie:

> Mum acknowledges that she has failed to protect Katie. Katie's recent sexualised behaviours coincide with mum disclosing that Katie's step-father and grandfather have had unsupervised contact with her. When Katie has disclosed concerns regarding her grandfather mum has not believed her. Mum presents as very confused regarding her responsibility to ensure her children's safety... Mum has disclosed that on some occasions she has hurt Katie, she admitted to hitting her and kicking her. (Social worker's case notes, Cleaver and Nicholson 2007, p.92)

This pattern of continuing difficulties was also found for all the family and environmental factors. For example, difficulties continued to be present in practically every case in relation to family history and functioning and in two-thirds of cases in relation to social resources. Problems over employment and income persisted in over half the cases (56%) and housing problems continued in 44 per cent of cases.

Practice in assessment when parents have a learning disability

The research showed that in practically every case where parents had a learning disability, the assessment resulted in a child in need plan and the provision of a range of services. Although a small proportion of children were placed away from home, this decision was taken only after a substantial input of services had failed to bring about the required changes; there was no evidence to suggest that parental learning disability in itself had been the reason.

In all cases, targeted services were provided to address children's developmental needs, difficulties in parental capacity, and difficulties in relation to family and environmental factors. However, there was little evidence of contingency planning or the provision of long-term ongoing support and training to compensate for parents' learning disabilities. In most cases, the involvement of children's social care was time-limited; three years after the referral most cases were closed to children's social care and to learning disability teams within adult services. To ensure children are safe and their welfare is promoted in cases where parents with learning disabilities do not have the support of a safe partner or relative, statutory and voluntary agencies will have to continue providing regular help and support until the children are capable of looking after themselves. Short-term, targeted interventions by statutory agencies on their own are not sufficient. Children's social care should work in partnership with other statutory agencies, including adult services, and make best use of the resources within the wider family, community and voluntary agencies.

Families where parents have learning disabilities account for a small proportion of all referrals to children's services and, as a result, practitioners may not always have the necessary skills to adequately communicate and work with people with learning disabilities. Social workers who participated in the research found involving parents with learning disabilities in assessment and planning was problematic because many had difficulty in reading written information, in remembering verbal information, and keeping their attention focused on the task in hand. The challenge facing practitioners was compounded by the tendency of people with learning disabilities to respond affirmatively to whatever is asked of them and to acquiesce to those in authority. The following case illustrates the frustration and uncertainties social workers may face:

> They like attention and were quite positive... The main problem was knowing whether or not they understood what was happening and what I was saying to them. They said that they did, but I had doubts. They both tended to agree with things. (Social worker's report, Cleaver and Nicholson 2007, p.60)

However, despite the time and effort social workers took to explain to parents why an assessment was going to be carried out and what it would entail, the research suggests their efforts were not always successful; some 30 per cent of parents were unable to recall anyone explaining things to them.

The research found that successful involvement of parents with learning disabilities was supported by the following factors:

- **Accessible information.** Local authorities need to ensure that information about assessments and services is available in a format that is easily accessible to people with learning disabilities, such as Easy Read versions of leaflets, information on CD/DVD and accessible websites.

- **Additional time.** When planning assessments, sufficient time needs to be allocated for practitioners to reinforce key messages initially and during subsequent meetings, so that parents can fully understand and remember them.

- **The presence of a relative or friend.** Involving a close relative or friend can in some cases reassure parents and support communication. Care, however, must be taken to ensure they do not overprotect the parent or dominate the conversation.

- **The involvement of a known practitioner.** Involving a trusted practitioner, such as a health visitor or nursery worker, can provide the parent with support.

- **A calm setting.** When chaotic and over-stimulating home circumstances negatively affect parents' ability to concentrate, carrying out some interviews elsewhere, such as in the social work office, may help. However, this needs to be part of an overall plan, because if home conditions and interactions between parents and children are not routinely observed, the child's needs cannot be fully understood.

- **Specialist toolkits.** More use should be made of specialist toolkits and resources for working with adults with learning disabilities (CHANGE 2005; Department of Health and Department for Education and Skills 2007; Hopkins 2002; Mackinnon *et al.* 2004; McGaw *et al.* 1999; Research in Practice 2008). Greater emphasis needs to be given to ensuring training on such tools is included in future training programmes.

- **Family centres.** Family centres can provide an important service in assessing the parenting skills of adults with learning disabilities when they have the necessary expertise.

- **Regular case reviews.** Regularly reviewing the impact of services on children's needs will ensure that professionals are not unduly influenced by parents' desire to please and co-operate. Professional optimism may in some cases result in children being left in conditions that place them at risk of significant harm.

Working with adult services

This chapter has emphasised the importance of communication and collaboration between children's and adults' services when assessing children living in families where parents have complex problems. A wide range of services may be relevant here including adult social care services, learning disability services, primary health care and mental health services, Drugs and Alcohol Action Teams (DAATs), the probation service and a wide range of voluntary sector agencies including those such as Women's Aid or Refuge which provide services for families experiencing domestic violence. Cleaver *et al.* (2007) found that social work referrals to agencies providing substance misuse services or to specialist domestic violence services were not routine following an initial assessment, and such agencies were rarely involved in section 47 enquiries.

These agencies may be the first point of contact for families with complex needs and practitioners in these services need to be alert to the fact that their patients or service users may also be parents (Department of Health 2008). They need to be familiar with the Common Assessment Framework (CAF) and their roles and responsibilities in relation to it (Children's Workforce Development Council 2009) and the *Framework for the Assessment of Children in Need and their Families* (Department of Health *et al.* 2000). In some cases, such agencies will have had a long history of contact with parents and may have valuable information or knowledge of family histories which should be incorporated into an assessment. They can also bring specialist knowledge concerning the nature and extent of learning disability, mental health problems, domestic violence or substance misuse and may be able to offer particular interventions or provide access to relevant services. Pooling information and co-ordinating assessments can result in a fuller and more comprehensive picture of a child's and family's needs. Mental health services may be able to provide details of how psychotropic medication can impact on parenting capacity and how adverse effects might be ameliorated. Specialist domestic violence services can facilitate access to refuges and legal, counselling and support services for both victims and children. Substance misuse services may be able to offer structured programmes for reducing or managing substance use.

Social workers in adult social care will also be able to advise on families' entitlement to services which can support parenting. Local authority adult social care services can be allocated to support parenting roles and responsibilities if families' needs come within the Fair Access to Care criteria (Department of Health 2003). Direct payments have also proved valuable as a means of accessing additional support for families when parents have mental health needs, substance misuse problems or learning disabilities (Morris and

Wates 2006). Personal budgets are now being introduced in adult social care and, again, practitioners in adult social care will be able to advise on how these might be accessed and used to support parenting capacity.

Parents may perceive staff working in adult services, who are not associated with the possibility that children may be removed from their care, as less threatening than those working for children's social care services. Such perceptions may make it easier for professionals in adult services to develop confiding and supportive relationships with parents but they will need to retain an awareness of their duty to safeguard and promote children's welfare and ensure that they work alongside and not against children's social care staff. Likewise, children's social workers need to avoid unrealistic expectation of adult services staff. Mental health professionals working in adult services, learning disability staff or drug and alcohol workers can provide information on or assessments of an adult's needs which can inform an assessment of parenting capacity. The task of assessing children's needs and parenting capacity itself, however, should be led by a social worker in children's social care with input from all other workers (HM Government 2006).

Numerous studies (Lupton *et al.* 2001; Sinclair and Bullock 2002; Stanley *et al.* 2003a) and inquiries (Cm 5730 2003) have reported difficulties and gaps in interprofessional work in child welfare. Different professional groups regard different members of the family as their primary client (Stanley *et al.* 2003b). Needs may be conceptualised differently according to whether a medical, legal, social or community empowerment model informs professional practice. Variations in patterns of work and different service structures may act to inhibit communication: for example, social workers frequently complain about the inaccessibility of GPs. As noted earlier, services have different thresholds for intervention: these may vary considerably between universal services and targeted services. Different codes of confidentiality and conceptions of working in partnership with families are also exposed in this area of work. It is particularly important for professionals to be explicit with one another about what information can be shared with whom when families' needs are hidden and disclosure may expose them to high levels of stigma or even, as is the case with domestic violence, to further risks of harm. Practice guidance (HM Government 2008) emphasises the general principle that children and family members should be consulted about sharing confidential information or referrals to children's services. However, if consent is not given and where there is evidence or reasonable cause to believe that the child is suffering or at risk of suffering significant harm, confidential information can be shared with other professionals without the family's consent. In these circumstances, it may, however, be appropriate to inform the parents that information will be shared and with whom.

Reder and Duncan (2003) argue that interprofessional communication involves both the transfer of information and the attribution of meaning to that information. Information transfer involves a range of meta-communications: body language or facial expressions if the message is delivered face-to-face, tone of voice or intonation if communicating by telephone, and writing style or language if the message is written or sent by email. The complexity of our communications requires practitioners in health and social care to monitor the messages sent and received to ensure that we have been understood and that we have understood the message as it was intended. Paying attention to how we communicate and listen may serve to improve families' experiences of services; this is particularly so when we are communicating with practitioners who come from different professional backgrounds with different sets of expectations, different understandings of families' needs and who draw on different knowledge bases.

Conclusion

This chapter has emphasised that issues which have an impact on parenting capacity can occur singly or in combination. In some cases, a problem, such as substance misuse, can be a response to another source of pressure such as domestic violence or mental health problems. However, it is important to recognise that, while these problems in parenting can be linked to one another, their effects on parenting may differ. For example, parental learning disabilities are likely to have a sustained long-term impact on parenting while mental health problems may be more episodic so that children experience periods of normality but also less predictability. Practitioners need to be able to differentiate between parenting problems and to access knowledge and expertise relevant to a family's particular issues. While outlining the ways in which domestic violence, mental health problems, substance misuse and learning disabilities in parents can have both direct and indirect consequences for children's wellbeing, we have stressed that the research evidence shows that adverse consequences are not inevitable. The presence of another protective caring adult can be of particular value in building children's resilience, and assessments and interventions can be directed towards identifying and supporting these adults.

Some of the parenting issues described here carry a stigma and parents and children may be unwilling to disclose the extent of their problems to professionals. This means that practitioners need to reflect on their attitudes and approaches to families to ensure that they are non-judgemental and that they are distinguishing between the different roles and needs of parents in a household. Explanations of what is involved in an assessment and what the outcomes might be are important for parents and children, and parents with learning disabilities may require additional time and support to ensure that such information has been understood.

Finally, we have emphasised that effective assessment and planning for families will require communication and collaboration between professionals in children's and adults' services. Identifying and overcoming some of the barriers that can impede such work offers the opportunity for families to receive tailored packages of support that are responsive to both short-term crises and longer-term needs and which recognise the interaction between adults' and children's needs.

Recommended reading

Cleaver, H., Unell, I. and Aldgate, J. (forthcoming) *Children's Needs – Parenting Capacity. The Impact of Parental Mental Illness, Learning Disability, Problem Alcohol and Drug Use, and Domestic Violence on Children's Safety and Development.* Second Edition.

Cleaver, H. and Nicholson, D. (2007) *Parental Learning Disability and Children's Needs: Family Experiences and Effective Practice.* London: Jessica Kingsley Publishers.

Harbin, F. and Murphy, M. (2006) *Secret Lives: Growing with Substance.* Lyme Regis: Russell House Publishing.

Humphreys, C. and Stanley, N. (eds) (2006) *Domestic Violence and Child Protection: Directions for Good Practice.* London: Jessica Kingsley Publishers.

Stanley, N., Penhale, B., Riordan, D., Barbour, R.S. and Holden, S. (2003) *Child Protection and Mental Health Services: Interprofessional Responses to the Needs of Mothers.* Bristol: The Policy Press.

References

Advisory Council on the Misuse of Drugs (2003) *Hidden Harm: Responding to the Needs of Children of Problem Drug Users. The Report of an Inquiry by the Advisory Council on the Misuse of Drugs.* London: Home Office.

Aldridge, J. (2006) 'The experiences of children living with and caring for parents with mental illness.' *Child Abuse Review 15,* 2, 79–88.

Aldridge, J. and Becker, S. (2003) *Children Caring for Parents with Mental Illness: Perspectives of Young Carers, Parents and Professionals.* Bristol: The Policy Press.

Altshuler, S. (2005) 'Drug-endangered children need a collaborative community response.' *Child Welfare 84,* 2, 171–190.

Bancroft, A., Wilson, S., Cunningham-Burley, S., Backett-Milburn, K. and Masters, H. (2004) *Parental Drug and Alcohol Misuse: Resilience and Transition among Young People.* York: Joseph Rowntree Foundation.

Barnard, M. (2007) *Drug Addiction and Families.* London: Jessica Kingsley Publishers.

BBC News (2008) 'Addiction Court Hears First Case.' Available at http://news.bbc.co.uk/1/hi/uk/7212423.stm, accessed on 13 July 2009.

Bifulco, A. and Moran, P. (1998) *Wednesday's Child: Research into Women's Experiences of Neglect and Abuse in Childhood and Adult Depression.* London: Routledge.

Brandon, M., Bailey, S., Belderson, P., Gardner, R. *et al.* (2009) *Understanding Serious Case Reviews and their Impact. A Biennial Analysis of Serious Case Reviews 2005–7.* DCSF-RB129. London: Department for Children, Schools and Families. Available at www.dcsf.gov.uk/research/programmeofresearch/projectinformation.cfm?project id=15743&resultspage=1, accessed 19 August 2009.

Brandon, M., Belderson, P., Warren, C., Gardner, R. *et al.* (2008) 'The preoccupation with thresholds in cases of child death or serious injury through abuse and neglect.' *Child Abuse Review 17,* 5, 313–351.

Campbell, J., Soeken, K., McFarlane, J. and Parker, B. (1998) 'Risk Factors for Femicide among Pregnant and Non-pregnant Battered Women.' In J. Campbell (ed.) *Empowering Survivors of Abuse: Health Care for Battered Women and their Children.* Thousand Oaks, CA: Sage Publications.

Cascardi, M., O'Leary, K.D. and Schlee, K. (1999) 'Co-occurrence and correlates of posttraumatic stress disorder and major depression in physically abused women.' *Journal of Family Violence 14,* 3, 227–249.

Cassell, D. and Coleman, R. (1995) 'Parents with Psychiatric Problems.' In P. Reder and C. Lucey (eds) *Assessment of Parenting: Psychiatric and Psychological Contributions.* London: Routledge.

Cawson, P. (2002) *Child Maltreatment in the Family: The Experience of a National Sample of Young People.* London: NSPCC.

CHANGE (2005) *Report of National Gathering of Parents with Learning Disabilities.* Leeds: CHANGE.

Children's Workforce Development Council (2009) *The Common Assessment Framework for Children and Young People: A Guide for Practitioners.* Leeds: Children's Workforce Development Council.

Cleaver, H. and Freeman, P. (1995) *Parental Perspectives in Cases of Suspected Child Abuse.* London: HMSO.

Cleaver, H. and Nicholson, D. (2007) *Parental Learning Disability and Children's Needs: Family Experiences and Effective Practice.* London: Jessica Kingsley Publishers.

Cleaver, H. and Walker, S. (2004) 'From policy to practice: the implementation of a new framework for social work assessment of children and families.' *Child and Family Social Work 9,* 1, 81–90.

Cleaver, H., Nicholson, D., Tarr, S. and Cleaver, D. (2007) *Child Protection, Domestic Violence and Parental Substance Misuse.* London: Jessica Kingsley Publishers.

Cleaver, H., Unell, I. and Aldgate, J. (1999) *Children's Needs – Parenting Capacity: The Impact of Parental Mental Illness, Problem Alcohol and Drug Use and Domestic Violence on Children's Development.* London: The Stationery Office.

Cleaver, H., Wattam, C., Cawson, P. and Gordon, R. (1998) *Assessing Risk in Child Protection.* London: NSPCC.

Cm 5730 (2003) *The Victoria Climbié Inquiry: Report of an Inquiry by Lord Laming.* London: The Stationery Office.

Cm 5860 (2003) *Every Child Matters.* Green Paper. London: The Stationery Office.

Corbett, V. (2005) '"I just knew to keep it quiet…" Living with parental problematic substance use.' *Adoption and Fostering 29,* 1, 98–100.

Daniel, B., Featherstone, B., Hooper, C. and Scourfield, J. (2005) 'Why gender matters for Every Child Matters.' *British Journal of Social Work 35,* 8, 1343–1355.

Department of Health (2003) *Fair Access to Care Services Practice Guidance. Implementation Questions and Answers.* London: Department of Health.

Department of Health (2008) *Refocusing the Care Programme Approach.* London: Department of Health.

Department of Health and Department for Education and Skills (2007) *Good Practice Guidance on Working with Parents with Learning Disability.* Available at www.dh.gov.uk/en/Publicationsandstatistics/Publications/PublicationsPolicyAndGuidance/DH_075119, accessed on 20 May 2009.

Department of Health, Department for Education and Employment and Home Office (2000) *Framework for the Assessment of Children in Need and their Families.* London: The Stationery Office.

Falkov, A. (1996) *Study of Working Together 'Part 8' Reports. Fatal Child Abuse and Parental Psychiatric Disorder: An Analysis of 100 Area Child Protection Committee Case Reviews Conducted under the Terms of Part 8 Working Together under the Children Act 1989.* London: Department of Health.

Falkov, A., Mayes, K. and Diggins, M. (1998) *Crossing Bridges: Training Resources for Working with Mentally Ill Parents and their Children.* Brighton: Pavilion.

Farmer, E. and Owen, M. (1995) *Child Protection Practice: Private Risks and Public Remedies.* London: HMSO.

Featherstone, B. (2003) 'Taking fathers seriously.' *British Journal of Social Work 33,* 2, 239–254.

Forrester, D. (2004) 'Social Work Assessments with Parents who Misuse Drugs or Alcohol.' In R. Phillips (ed.) *Children Exposed to Parental Substance Misuse: Implications for Family Placement.* London: BAAF.

Forrester, D. and Harwin, J. (2006) 'Parental substance misuse and child care social work: findings from the first stage of a study of 100 families.' *Child and Family Social Work 11,* 4, 325–335.

Forrester, D., Copello, A., Waissbein, C. and Pokhrei, S. (2008) 'Evalution of an intensive family preservation service for families affected by parental substance misuse.' *Child Abuse Review 17,* 6, 410–426.

FRANK (2005) *Resources Needed to Support Children of Problematic Users of Drugs.* London: COI Communications and Home Office.

Ghate, D., Shaw, C. and Hazel, N. (2000) *Fathers and Family Centres: Engaging Fathers in Preventive Services.* London: Policy Research Bureau.

Gibbons, J., Conroy, S. and Bell, C. (1995) *Operating the Child Protection System: A Study of Child Protection Practices in English Local Authorities.* London: HMSO.

Glaser, D. and Prior, V. (1997) 'Is the term child protection applicable to emotional abuse?' *Child Abuse Review 6,* 5, 315–330.

Gorin, S. (2004) *Understanding What Children Say: Children's Experiences of Domestic Violence, Parental Substance Misuse and Parental Health Problems.* London: National Children's Bureau and NSPCC.

Gorin, S. (2005) 'The stakes are high: the impact of parental substance misuse on children.' *Childright 219,* September, 14–16.

Harbin, F. (2006) 'The Roller Coaster of Change: The Process of Parental Change from a Child's Perspective.' In F. Harbin and M. Murphy (eds) *Secret Lives: Growing with Substance.* Lyme Regis: Russell House Publishing.

Hart, D. and Powell, J. (2006) *Adult Drug Problems, Children's Needs: Assessing the Impact of Parental Drug Use. A Toolkit for Practitioners.* London: National Children's Bureau.

Harwin, J. and Forrester, D. (2002) *Parental Substance Misuse and Child Welfare, Executive Interim Report.* Prepared for Nuffield Foundation, London.

Hester, M. (2006) 'Asking about Domestic Violence: Implications for Practice.' In C. Humphreys and N. Stanley (eds) *Domestic Violence and Child Protection: Directions for Good Practice.* London: Jessica Kingsley Publishers.

Hester, M., Pearson, C. and Harwin, N. (2006) *Making an Impact: A Reader,* 2nd edn. London: Jessica Kingsley Publishers.

HM Government (2006) *Working Together to Safeguard Children: A Guide to Inter-agency Working to Safeguard and Promote the Welfare of Children.* London: Department for Education and Skills.

HM Government (2008) *Information Sharing: Guidance for Practitioners and Managers.* London: Department for Children, Schools and Families.

Home Office (2000) *Domestic Violence: Break the Chain. Multi-agency Guidance for Addressing Domestic Violence.* London: Home Office.

Hopkins, L. (2002) *Daventry Family Centre: Parenting Skills Group.* Daventry: NCH.

Humphreys, C. (2006) 'Relevant Evidence for Practice.' In C. Humphreys and N. Stanley (eds) *Domestic Violence and Child Protection: Directions for Good Practice.* London: Jessica Kingsley Publishers.

Humphreys, C. and Thiara, R. (2003) 'Domestic violence and mental health: "I call it symptoms of abuse."' *British Journal of Social Work 33,* 2, 209–226.

Humphreys, C., Mullender, A., Thiara, R. and Skamballis, A. (2006) '"Talking to My Mum": developing communication between mothers and children in the aftermath of domestic violence.' *Journal of Social Work 6,* 1, 53–63.

Kearney, J., Harbin, F., Murphy, M., Wheeler, E. and Whittle, J. (2005) *The Highs and Lows of Family Life: Familial Substance Misuse from a Child's Perspective*. Bolton: Bolton ACPC.

Kroll, B. (2004) 'Living with an elephant: growing up with parental substance misuse.' *Child and Family Social Work 9*, 2, 129–140.

Kroll, B. (2007) 'A family affair? Kinship care and parental substance misuse: some dilemmas explored.' *Child and Family Social Work 12*, 1, 84–93.

Leverton, T.J. (2003) 'Parental psychiatric illness: the implications for children.' *Current Opinion in Psychiatry 16*, 4, 395–402.

Littlechild, B. and Bourke, C. (2006) 'Men's Use of Violence and Intimidation Against Family Members and Child Protection Workers.' In C. Humphreys and N. Stanley (eds) *Domestic Violence and Child Protection: Directions for Good Practice*. London: Jessica Kingsley Publishers.

Lupton, C., North, N. and Khan, P. (2001) *Working Together or Pulling Apart? The National Health Service and Child Protection Networks*. Bristol: The Policy Press.

Mackinnon, S., Bailey, B. and Pink, L. (2004) *Understanding Learning Disabilities: A Video-based Training Resource for Trainers and Managers to Use with their Staff*. Brighton: Pavilion Publishing.

McClosky, L., Figueredo, A. and Koss, P. (1995) 'The effects of systemic family violence on children's mental health.' *Child Development 66*, 5, 1239–1261.

McGaw, S., Beckley, K., Connolly, N. and Ball, K. (1999) *Parenting Assessment Manual*. Redruth: Special Parenting Service: Cornwall and Isles of Scilly Health Authority.

McGee, C. (2000) *Childhood Experiences of Domestic Violence*. London: Jessica Kingsley Publishers.

Mezey, G. and Bewley, S. (1997) 'Domestic violence and pregnancy.' *British Journal of Obstetrics and Gynaecology 104*, 528–531.

Morris, J. and Wates, M. (2006) *Supporting Disabled Parents and Parents with Additional Support Needs: SCIE Knowledge Review 11*. Bristol: The Policy Press.

Mullender, A. (2006) 'What Children Tell Us: "He Said He Was Going to Kill Our Mum."' In C. Humphreys and N. Stanley (eds) *Domestic Violence and Child Protection: Directions for Good Practice*. London: Jessica Kingsley Publishers.

Mullender, A., Kelly, L., Hague, G., Malos, E. and Iman, U. (2002) *Children's Perspectives on Domestic Violence*. London: Routledge.

Pearson, G. (2008) *Why Children Die. A Pilot Study 2006: England (South West, North East and West Midlands), Wales and Northern Ireland*. London: CEMACH.

Plass, P., Finkelhor, D. and Hotaling, G. (1997) 'Risk factors for family abduction: demographic and family interaction characteristics.' *Journal of Family Violence 12*, 3, 333–348.

Radford, L., Blacklock, N. and Iwi, K. (2006) 'Domestic Abuse Risk Assessment and Safety Planning in Child Protection – Assessing Perpetrators.' In C. Humphreys and N. Stanley (eds) *Domestic Violence and Child Protection: Directions for Good Practice*. London: Jessica Kingsley Publishers.

Reder, P. and Duncan, S. (1999) *Lost Innocents*. London: Routledge.

Reder, P. and Duncan, S. (2003) 'Understanding communication in child protection networks.' *Child Abuse Review 12*, 2, 82–100.

Research in Practice (2008) *Positive Parenting: Supporting Parents with Learning Disabilities*. Dartington: Research in Practice.

Richards, L. and Baker, A. (2003) *Findings from the Multi-agency Domestic Violence Murder Reviews in London*. London: Association of Police Officers (ACPO).

Rose, W. and Barnes, J. (2008) *Improving Safeguarding Practice: Study of Serious Case Reviews 2001–2003*. London: Department for Children, Schools and Families.

Rutter, M. (1985) 'Resilience in the face of adversity: protective factors and resilience to psychiatric disorder.' *British Journal of Psychiatry 147*, 6, 598–611.

Ryan, M. (2000) *Working with Fathers*. Oxford: Radcliffe Medical Press and Department of Health.

Saunders, A. with Epstein, C., Keep, G. and Debbonaire, T. (1995) *It Hurts Me Too: Children's Experiences of Domestic Violence and Refuge Life*. London: WAFE, Childline and NISW.

Sinclair, R. and Bullock, R. (2002) *Learning from Past Experience: A Review of Serious Case Reviews*. London: Department of Health.

Sheppard, M. (1997) 'Double jeopardy: the link between child abuse and maternal depression in child and family social work.' *Child and Family Social Work 2*, 2, 91–107.

Sheppard, M. with Kelly, N. (2001) *Social Work Practice with Depressed Mothers in Child and Family Care*. London: The Stationery Office.

Social Exclusion Unit (2004) *Mental Health and Social Exclusion*. London: Office of the Deputy Prime Minister.

Somers, V. (2007) 'Schizophrenia: The Impact of Parental Illness on Children.' *British Journal of Social Work 37*, 8, 1319–1334.

Stallard, P., Norman, P., Huline-Dickens, S., Salter, E. and Cribb, J. (2004) 'The effects of parental mental illness upon children: a descriptive study of the views of parents and children.' *Clinical Child Psychology and Psychiatry 9*, 1, 39–52.

Stanley, N. (1997) 'Domestic violence and child abuse: developing social work practice.' *Child and Family Social Work 2*, 3, 135–146.

Stanley, N. and Humphreys, C. (2006) 'Multi-agency and Multi-disciplinary Work: Barriers and Opportunities.' In C. Humphreys and N. Stanley (eds) *Domestic Violence and Child Protection: Directions for Good Practice*. London: Jessica Kingsley Publishers.

Stanley, N., Borthwick, R. and Macleod, A. (2006) 'Antenatal depression: mothers' awareness and professional responses.' *Primary Health Care Research and Development 7*, 3, 257–268.

Stanley, N., Penhale, B., Riordan, D., Barbour, R.S. and Holden, S. (2003a) *Child Protection and Mental Health Services: Interprofessional Responses to the Needs of Mothers*. Bristol: The Policy Press.

Stanley, N., Penhale, B., Riordan, D., Barbour, R.S. and Holden, S. (2003b) 'Professional responses to families with identified mental health and child care needs.' *Health and Social Care in the Community 11*, 3, 208–218.

Targosz, S., Bebbington, P., Lewis, G., Brugha, T. *et al.* (2003) 'Lone mothers, social exclusion and depression.' *Psychological Medicine 33*, 715–722.

Thoburn, J., Lewis, A. and Shemmings, D. (1995) *Paternalism or Partnership? Family Involvement in the Child Protection Process*. London: HMSO.

Turning Point (2006) *Bottling It Up: The Effects of Alcohol Misuse on Children, Parents and Families*. London: Turning Point.

Tymchuck, A. (1992) 'Predicting adequacy of parenting by people with mental retardation.' *Child Abuse and Neglect 16*, 2, 165–178.

Velleman, R. and Templeton, L. (2006) 'Reaching Out: Promoting Resilience in the Children of Substance Misusers.' In F. Harbin and M. Murphy (eds) *Secret Lives: Growing with Substance*. Lyme Regis: Russell House Publishing.

Walby, S. and Allen, J. (2004) *Domestic Violence, Sexual Assault and Stalking: Findings from the British Crime Survey*. Home Office Research Study 276. London: Home Office Research, Development and Statistics Directorate.

PART IV
Assessing Cultural
and Socio-economic Factors

CHAPTER 20

Assessing the Needs of Black and Minority Ethnic Children and Families

Ratna Dutt and Melanie Phillips

Ensuring equality of opportunity does not mean that all children are treated the same. It does mean understanding and working sensitively and knowledgeably with diversity to identify the particular issues for a child and his/her family, taking account of experiences and family context.

(From the Framework for the Assessment of Children
in Need and their Families, p.12, 1.43)

This chapter considers:

- factors which influence children from black and minority ethnic groups achieving their potential

- working with refugee and asylum-seeking families

- the impact on assessment of making presumptions about cultures and religions

- the influence of religious beliefs and practices

- assessing children in Muslim families

- making sense of parents' past history

- engaging with male caregivers

- the role of the community
- the impact of practitioners' values and beliefs.

Introduction

On 25 February 2000 Victoria Climbié, a black African child, died in London of hypo-thermia. Victoria was found to have 128 separate injuries to her body. 'She died as a result of months of appalling ill-treatment at the hands of two individuals who were supposed to be caring for her' (Cm 5730 2003, p.15).

In January 2003, the Inquiry Report into the circumstances leading up to her death was published. It highlighted significant concerns regarding the way in which Victoria's needs were assessed by professionals in contact with Victoria and her carers. Specific concerns centred on the failure of professionals to recognise that Victoria was a member of a minority ethnic group. This led Lord Laming, the author of the report, to conclude:

> I found it hard to understand the evidence I heard from qualified social workers about what they described as a lack of clarity on how they should assess the needs of a child and its family. While the National Assessment Framework was published more recently, and welcomed, I would have expected qualified social workers at the time Victoria needed protection to be capable of completing an assessment of her needs. (Cm 5730 2003, p.67)

The Green Paper *Every Child Matters* (Cm 5860 2003) and the Children Act 2004, which followed it, were informed by Laming's recommendations and have had a significant impact on assessment practice. In addition, the 2004 Children Act and associated guid-ance have brought about significant changes to the organisational and practice contexts in which assessments of children's needs take place (see Chapter 1 for more detail). But have these changes led to improved assessment practice in relation to identifying children in need from black and minority ethnic groups? In this chapter we seek to answer this question.

Ensuring children from black and minority ethnic groups fulfil their potential: the challenges

If practitioners are to complete meaningful assessments using the *Framework for the Assessment of Children in Need and their Families* (Department of Health *et al.* 2000) they should be aware of the particular challenges for black and minority ethnic families in relation to safeguarding and promoting the welfare of their children. With this in mind we consider some of these challenges.

Health

'Health' is one of the dimensions of the child's developmental needs within the Assessment Framework. Children and adults from black and minority ethnic groups generally have poorer physical and mental health than members of other groups. For instance, the incidence of coronary heart disease and diabetes is higher than average in black and minority ethnic groups. Despite a higher incidence of poor health, members of these groups lack access to some forms of health provision, under-use health services and have lower levels of satisfaction with health provision (Department of Health 2001; Office for National Statistics 2001a; Equalities Review 2007).

However, with regard to some services, notably mental health, members of black and minority ethnic groups are over-represented. For example, black African Caribbean men are over-represented in the mental health system, which may be a result of finding themselves in situations that increase the likelihood of mental health issues, such as exclusion from schools and social deprivation (Keating 2007).

Safeguarding children

There are a number of environmental factors, such as poverty and social exclusion, that can have a negative impact on the carer's ability to keep the child safe from harm. This is a particular issue if the family is from a black or minority ethnic group. For example:

> Afro-Caribbeans and Asians are more at risk of homicide than whites. Considering too that black and minority ethnic communities are disproportionately concentrated in deprived areas, the members of those communities are more likely to experience violent crime and muggings in particular which involve a high proportion of knife usage. (Eades *et al.* 2007, p.24)

The current index of local deprivation shows that black and minority ethnic communities live in areas of high social deprivation, and most live in many of the authorities that fall within the category of 'most deprived', such as the London boroughs of Newham, Hackney, Haringey, Southwark, Lambeth and Tower Hamlets, as well as Birmingham and Manchester. Alongside the social disadvantage that this creates there are implications, as described in the above quotation, for the safety of black and minority ethnic families. (Factors practitioners should consider regarding the assessment and protection of black and minority ethnic children from abuse and neglect by carers will be explored later in the chapter.)

Education and employment

In terms of educational achievement of black and minority ethnic children, there are particular factors which need to be considered. These include recognising the following:

- In 2001/02, the highest permanent school exclusion rates were among children of mixed parentage, and children of black Caribbean origin. Unfortunately, the situation has changed very little since 2001/02 and in 2006 the Priority Review on Exclusion of black pupils undertaken by the Department for Children, Schools and Families (formerly Department for Education and Skills (DfES)) found that black pupils are three times more likely to be excluded than their white counterparts (Department for Education and Skills 2006).

• In 2001/02 people most likely to have degrees were Chinese, Indians and black Africans. Amongst men, black Caribbeans were least likely to have degrees (8%), and amongst women, Pakistanis and Bangladeshis were least likely to have degrees (7%).

• In a study of 261 care leavers (45% of whom were black and minority ethnic) Barn (2006) noted the disadvantage and discrimination faced by black and minority ethnic care leavers in a range of settings such as education, employment and training and housing.

Unemployment among young people from black and minority ethnic communities is much higher than for the white population. In 2004, black Caribbean, black African, Bangladeshi and mixed ethnic men had the highest unemployment rates; these rates were three times the rates for white English and Irish men. Amongst women, Pakistani women had the highest unemployment rates (20%) followed by black African and mixed ethnic groups (12%) (Office for National Statistics 2002, 2004).

Refugee and asylum-seeking children: the challenges to achieving potential

Experiences of refugee and asylum seekers indicate that their needs are very complex and that they are a particularly vulnerable group even in comparison to other black and minority ethnic children. They have suffered trauma, loss and separation from family members, have concerns about losing their culture and identity and they can be affected by insecure legal status (Box *et al.* 2001). Studies also show that unaccompanied young people are likely to experience difficulties in settling into a new environment and may have difficulty in making friends (Wade *et al.* 2005).

The United Nations High Commission for Refugees (UNHCR) estimated that there were 17.1 million refugees and asylum seekers in need of international protection in 2004. Of these 4.2 million were to be found in Europe. According to UNHCR estimates, the UK hosted 301,022 people needing international protection in 2003 (Patel 2005). In addition, black African children make up half the number of unaccompanied asylum-seeking young people in the care system (Thoburn *et al.* 2005).

In assessing their developmental needs, practitioners should give consideration to the impact of the child's past experiences on their current health and development, with particular emphasis on their emotional and behavioural development, identity and past and current attachments. It is also important to understand what their past experiences of parenting have been, and the implications of this in relation to meeting their current needs.

However, Wade *et al.* (2005) found that the needs of this group of children are not often assessed in the level of detail required to fully understand or plan for their individual circumstances, and that assessing the needs of asylum-seeking and refugee children posed particular difficulties to professionals. She found the process of the assessment was always challenging. Moreover, young people's initial encounters with social services were frequently marked by confusion and a degree of suspicion' (Wade *et al.* 2005). They found that core assessments in line with the Assessment Framework were rarely undertaken and in some instances assessments were based on a single interview.

Given the complexity of the circumstances of refugee and asylum-seeking children, who are often burdened with feelings of loss and separation and anxieties about their parents, siblings and other relatives, it is vital that assessments afford the time and opportunity for children to discuss their past experiences of being parented, their own attachments to parents and community and the opportunity to explore how this affects their current experience of corporate parenting. A short assessment that only focuses on practical needs will not address these emotional issues.

> Workers were often aware that these young people continued to be troubled by their pasts but felt powerless to intervene and had little choice but to focus on more practical issues in the present. Providing young people with openings to re-visit the past, however, remains important. Time brings changes. Although young people may not feel ready or be able to respond to cues at one point in time, at another they may feel the need to talk about their families or about events that have taken place. (Wade *et al.* 2005, pp.163–4)

To make a difference to the outcomes for these children, practitioners should identify opportunities for intervention in their lives that can make a positive difference to their daily experiences. This should include practical interventions which can enhance children's quality of life through increasing their resilience (see Gilligan, Chapter 10). Practitioners should also be mindful of the importance of education as a protective factor for these children. As Gilligan describes, there is widespread evidence of the importance of education in building resilience for all children but asylum-seeking children may need additional support to stay within and benefit from the educational system. For example, they are likely to experience harassment and bullying in schools (Jones 1998; King's Fund 2000).

Asylum-seeking, refugee children and unaccompanied minors represent the most vulnerable children in our community. Their inability to be completely truthful with professional agencies because of fears about their immigration status, their reliance upon adults, some of whom may be exploitative for personal gain, and their personal histories of trauma and loss leave many in vulnerable situations and beyond the reach of most statutory agencies. If every child matters, this group of children need to matter much more.

The assessment of black and minority ethnic children: factors to consider

O'Neil (2000), in her inspection of services for black and minority ethnic children and families, concluded:

> The quality of services delivered to ethnic minority families was heavily dependent on the quality of social work intervention. It is usually the case that good service delivery flows from good assessments, but we were struck by how much the burden of

responsibility to deliver ethnically sensitive services rested with individual workers. (O'Neil 2000, p.31)

She also found that, whilst the different dimensions of the three domains of the Assessment Framework were usually explored by practitioners when assessing black and minority ethnic children, practitioners failed to draw the information together to provide a holistic assessment. Brophy *et al.* (2005), in their study of care proceedings concerning black and minority ethnic children and families, sought to ascertain the views of solicitors on a variety of issues relating to care proceedings, including whether they were satisfied with the attention to race, religion, language and culture in core assessments. The study found that in relation to core assessments overall 'solicitors had not seen an improvement following the introduction of the new framework for assessments' (Brophy *et al.* 2005, p.65). This was seen less as a problem with the Assessment Framework itself, and more to do with problems in terms of resources and skills amongst staff from local authority children's social care who were undertaking assessments.

Assessing the child's developmental needs and parenting capacity: religion and culture as causation of harm

Children in need make up a small percentage of the overall population and comprise the most vulnerable children in any given area and, therefore, are not representative of all children from their community. In terms of practice with black and minority ethnic families, however, this fact is often ignored: practitioners may justify parenting practices that may be detrimental to the child by making presumptions about the particular culture or religion of the family.

Cultural explanations for abuse can obscure professionals' capacity to accurately assess the developmental needs of black and minority ethnic children. For example, Lisa Arthurworrey, Victoria Climbié's social worker in the London Borough of Haringey, gave a cultural explanation for Victoria's unusual behaviour when her aunt visited her in hospital.

> When she heard of Victoria 'standing to attention' before Kouao and Manning she 'concluded that this type of relationship was one that could be seen in many Afro-Caribbean families because respect and obedience are very important features of the Afro-Caribbean family script'. Victoria's parents, however, made it clear that she was not required to stand in this formal way when she was at home with them. (Cm 5730 2003, p.345)

Assessing children in need and their families requires a multi-dimensional approach, in which the *meaning* of culture and faith to the individual child, family and professionals involved is routinely explored in terms of the influence on the different dimensions of the three domains of the Assessment Framework. As Korbin (2007) notes:

> While knowledge of general cultural patterns provides an important starting point, each individual and family must be assessed on their merits by viewing the child

as nested in the ecological levels of the family, the community, socio-economic conditions and the larger cultural context. (Korbin 2007, pp.140–1)

Ethnicity, class, gender, disability, language and religion influence parenting styles, but even within the same family there are different patterns of parenting and approaches to child-rearing. The pivotal factors are not about difference but *difficulties and strengths*. The key question to ask is: *What sets this child and family apart from others in their community who are providing a good standard of parenting which meets the developmental needs of the child, despite the pressures of social and economic disadvantage?* When answering this question it is important that practitioners do not focus just on the difficulties in relation to parenting but also recognise parenting strengths.

Alternatively, practitioners may hold stereotypical or over-simplified views of minority ethnic culture and religion gained through books, cultural and religious awareness training or even speaking to people from the same ethnic, cultural and religious groups. For example, stereotypical views exist about 'spirit possession' and 'witchcraft' being linked to certain (predominantly black African) communities. However, maltreatment associated with these beliefs is rare and not confined to any one particular community. Moreover, not all families who believe in 'spirit possession' and 'witchcraft' abuse their children and those that do share a number of common features which are common to other abusive families, such as family stress (HM Government 2007; Stobart 2006).

The influence of religious beliefs and practices

A religious explanation, whatever its source, should never be accepted as an appropriate explanation for maltreatment. As stated in the Government practice guidance (HM Government 2007) in relation to issues of 'spirit possession' and 'witchcraft':

> Child abuse is never acceptable in any community, in any culture, in any religion, under any circumstances. This includes abuse that might arise through belief in spirit possession or other spiritual or religious beliefs. (p.3)

Whilst considerable attention has been given in recent years to the negative influences of religious beliefs and practices on family life, it is important to recognise that religion can also be a source of strength and support in relation to child rearing. For example, Jacobson (1998), in a study of Pakistani Muslim youths in London, discusses 'the ways in which Islam provides meaning in the lives of my respondents' (p.19), who 'seem to feel that Islam provides a framework within which they make sense of their lives' (p.20), partly, at least, because of the clear guidance it provides on behaviour. A study recently completed by Horwath *et al.* (2008) also found that holding religious beliefs can positively influence parenting capacity. Religious beliefs can offer parents a value system that provides a framework for positively meeting the needs of the child. Moreover, membership of a faith community can give both parents and children a support network. However, as described above, practitioners should not make presumptions that this is always the case. For example, Horwath *et al.* (2008) found that parents of disabled children did not necessarily feel supported by their faith community. Moreover, as Stewart *et al.* (2000) note it can be difficult distinguishing between religious beliefs and culture. Referring to their study of parenting variables and outcomes for adolescents in Pakistan they note, religion and culture are inextricably linked: 'Pakistan culture and its construction are moulded both by Islam and the older South Asian heritage' (p.336). Sharpe (1988) concludes that it is more important to be able to recognise religion than define it and that the only real definition is *'on the believer's part* (not the observer's)' (p.48; italics and brackets as in original).

Whilst the Assessment Framework (Department of Health *et al.* 2000) makes a number of explicit references to religion in terms of the child's sense of identity and 'places of worship', the Practice Guidance accompanying the *Framework for the Assessment of Children in Need and their Families* (Department of Health 2000) makes explicit that religion can influence all aspects of family life:

> Religion or spirituality is an issue for all families whether white or black. A family who do not practise a religion, or who are agnostic or atheists, may still have particular views about the spiritual upbringing and welfare of their children. For families where religion plays an important role in their lives, the significance of their religion will also be a vital part of their cultural traditions and beliefs. (p.49, 2.69)

Despite the significant influence that religious beliefs and practices can have on families practitioners do not appear to consider this routinely when working with children and families (Gilligan and Furness 2006; Horwath and Lees 2008; Seden 1995). For example, Cleaver and Walker (2004) found that only 29.1 per cent of referral forms to children's social care included the religion of the child even though 85 per cent of the UK population identify themselves as having a religious affiliation (Office for National Statistics 2001b).

Assessing children in Muslim families

In recent years there has been significant negative media attention focused on Islam, particularly in relation to 'terrorism', Muslim youth and 'forced marriages'. These issues have fuelled negative stereotypes of Islam and its teachings, particularly its impact on family values and parenting. An understandable professional response to negate some of the more virulent stereotypes and work more effectively with Muslim families is to gain more knowledge and information about Islam, particularly as it impacts on parenting styles. Whilst this may raise the practitioner's awareness about Islam, a difficulty with this approach is that the information received is often viewed as definitive; there is no critical analysis of the information gained and neither is there any judgement made about why a particular piece of information could be useful in the context of an assessment.

Yet it is important that practitioners recognise what being Muslim means to the child and their family. The Office for National Statistics (2002), for example, found that, for the majority of Muslim women of Bangladeshi origin living in the UK in his study, being Muslim was the most important aspect of their identity. Saeed *et al.* (1999) found that 97 per cent of a sample of 63 Scottish Pakistani youths identified themselves as Muslim – more than double those selecting a Pakistani label – whilst only 8 per cent selected the label 'I am Asian'. Saeed *et al.* argue that certain characteristics will be ascribed to Muslims by non-Muslims. This in turn can lead to presumptions being made by practitioners about what it means to be Muslim.

Disparagement of Muslims following 'terrorist attacks' in England and the USA may result in greater unity and solidarity amongst Muslims themselves. Imtiaz (2002) explored the identities of Muslim youths. He found that they defined themselves using three identity types: 'coconuts', who are successfully socially mobile but neglect cultural and religious practices; 'rude boys', who are the majority and are usually disaffected, unemployed and strong on Pakistani religious nationalism; and 'extremists', who value religious practices even when they are contrary to the dominant values in society. Jacobson (1998) also studied Muslim identities adopted by Pakistani youths. Like Imtiaz (2002) she found a range of identities from very devote individuals who practised their religion daily to those who never practised Islam but still called themselves Muslims.

Being disabled and from a minority faith might be doubly marginalising for young people. Hussain *et al.* (2002) found that religion was important to disabled young Muslims and Sikhs. These young people had a working knowledge of their religious tradition but lacked access to practice and education about religion. They concluded that services should be more sensitive to the cultural and religious values of young people from minority faiths with impairments. In respect of disabled young people Hussain *et al.* (2002) found that disabled young people valued their religious identity but had difficulties in developing their religious knowledge or engaging in religious practice, probably due to access issues. Croot (2005) also found that Asian families of disabled young people were less likely to take them to religious events within the family, like weddings, or places of worship.

Whilst there is some research and literature which examines parenting practices amongst members of South Asian communities living in the UK (see, for example, Becher and Husain 2003; Berthoud 2000; Lau 2000), much of this is related to issues such as marriage or gender roles, and even here the information can vary. For instance, Becher and Husain (2003) note: 'In traditional South Asian society, men and women are considered to have differing responsibilities. These beliefs are reflected in social and religious guidelines for the behaviour of men and women' (p.26). However, Becher and Husain (2003) also acknowledge that 'cultural' practices are not static and differ according to a number of variables including class, age, and change with time and location. They note, however, that it appears that the male–female gender roles may be changing amongst Muslim families living in Britain. They argue that this may be a result of the experience of migration, economic hardship and being a member of a minority group, leading to the traditional male Muslim roles being undermined. Zokaei and Phillips' (2000) study of Muslim communities in England confirmed that Muslim families, in what is perceived to be a largely secular society, tend to maintain strong family ties, care and respect for parents, cultural and traditional values and a sense of obligation to wider society.

Research also does not tell us how the experiences of Muslim parents vary from the experiences of parents from other religious and cultural groups. There is some basic information available, however, about Muslim communities which should be considered when completing assessments.

- Unemployment rates are higher amongst Muslims than other groups for both men and women. In 2004, Muslim men were three times more likely to be unemployed than Christian men, and Muslim women were four times more likely to be unemployed than Christian and Jewish women (Office for National Statistics 2004).

- Muslims are more likely than other groups to get married before the age of 25.

- Members of Muslim communities have the youngest age profile and tend to be members of larger families.

- Reported rates of health problems are high amongst Muslim communities. For instance, Pakistani women and Bangladeshi men are more likely to report limiting long-standing illness (Sproston and Mindell 2006).

Assessing family and environmental factors: family history and functioning

In addition to the religious backgrounds and histories of families and communities, recent evidence reinforces the importance of considering the individual histories and experiences of family members and the impact of the past on current parenting capacity. This is what is referred to by 'Family history and functioning' in the Assessment Framework. 'The psychological sensitivity and emotional availability of parents is affected by their own relationship history as well as the supports and stresses experienced in their current environment' (Brandon *et al.* 2008, p.57).

Parents' own past experiences and histories cannot predict child abuse, but they do provide a context in which current behaviour, vulnerabilities, stresses and protective factors can be more effectively analysed. However, this can only be achieved if professionals engage with parents to understand the significance of their past history in relation to their current approach to parenting. In the case of Jasmine Beckford and Sukina Hammond, who were fatally injured by their stepfather and father respectively for not being able to read, past history and attitudes to education were significant in their parenting of their children. Both men were African Caribbean, and Morris Beckford in particular had had a very abusive childhood and had educationally underachieved (Blom-Cooper 1985). Education may hold particular significance for a family within the context of concern about discrimination and educational underachievement in school for many black and minority ethnic children. Whilst this does not mean that black and minority ethnic families are more likely to abuse their children if they do not achieve educationally, the importance of understanding the *significance* of education for a parent has to be discussed and understood in order to support parents' aspirations for their children, whilst ensuring that the child is kept safe from harm.

Engaging with male caregivers

In neither of the cases described above, where children died at the hands of their fathers, was there any attempt by professionals to engage with these men to establish their views about the parenting role, education, discipline and punishment. Ironically, after Jasmine's death, Beverley Lorrington (Jasmine Beckford's mother) described in some detail her partner's parenting style and that his harsh attitude to Jasmine focused on her learning to read (Blom-Cooper 1985). It appears that racial stereotyping in respect of African Caribbean men prevented professionals undertaking assessments of these fathers out of fear of violence, and fears of allegations of racism (Bridge Child Care Consultancy 1991). In any family where professionals are too worried to speak to a parent because of fears of reprisals, serious concerns should be raised about the safety of the children who are in their care (for further discussion see Chapters 6 and 17).

The role of the community: the wider family and social integration

Family and Environmental Factors on the Assessment Triangle incorporates an ecological approach to family assessment by recognising the impact of family and community support. Many black and minority ethnic families come from communities where there is a very different relationship between the individual, the family and community from the traditional Western model of society:

> In many western societies, 'successful' families are signified by the presence of dominant cultural values of independence, autonomy, self-determination, separation, individuation, self-expression, self-sufficiency, assertiveness and competition, clear and direct verbal communication... In other societies, i.e. Eastern Europe, the East and Far East, these values would be anathema and run counter to moral and religious values. Instead, family life stresses loyalty, interdependence, harmony, co-operation and non-verbal and indirect communication through the use of symbols. (Kemp 1997, p.45)

For many black and minority ethnic families, communities provide them with practical, emotional and often spiritual support. A parent who strongly identifies with community loyalty as part of their cultural or religious beliefs may find a child's bid for 'independence' a great deal more threatening and disrespectful than a parent who sees 'individuality' as an asset to be nurtured in the developing child. Neither parental position is inherently right or wrong, but professionals can only fully appreciate the significance of the parental attitude to the child through conversations with the parent and child about the role of culture in shaping views about family history and functioning, social integration and the wider family.

Family and environmental factors: accessing community resources

Safeguarding and promoting the welfare of a child will be influenced by the child and family's ability to access services including universal and family support services. The evidence suggests that black and minority ethnic familes, including asylum-seeking ones, are not always accessing family support services and that often those services that are available are not 'culturally' appropriate (Butt and Box 1998; Statham and Biehal 2005).

The evidence shows that participation in parenting support by black and minority ethnic groups is low and, further, there is a lack of evidence on what works with them (Moran *et al.* 2004). However, there are now a number of initiatives and programmes available that are appropriate to the needs of black and minority ethnic parents and could be usefully used by practitioners. One such programme is the 'Strengthening Families, Strengthening Communities' (SFSC) parent education programme developed in the USA and adapted by the Race Equality Foundation (formerly REU) for use by parents in the

United Kingdom. The programme is based on a culturally sensitive curriculum and, according to an evaluation of the programme, has successfully reached parents with a wide variety of languages from diverse ethnic backgrounds, including recently arrived as well as more established black and minority ethnic communities (Wilding and Barton 2007).

Practitioners' values and beliefs

Professionals need to be aware of the impact of their own experiences and values about rights, responsibilities, parenting and childhood on their professional judgements: 'Professionals observe through their own cultural filters, and therefore should be attentive as to how and why they need to influence the skills of parents with whom they have become involved' (Kemp 1997, p.45).

As described in Chapters 6 and 17 it is the relationship between the social worker and the family that has a significant impact on effective practice to improve outcomes for children and their families. The specific qualities associated with positive outcomes for all children, identified by many studies, include empathy, warmth and genuineness.

> These are demonstrated when the worker is reliable, a good listener, honest, gives accurate and full information about services available and agency processes (particularly important when the formal child protecting process is involved or a child is looked after), and puts him or herself out to be available at times of stress. (Thoburn et al. 2005, p.139)

To make a difference through interventions, professionals need to form a relationship with the child and their family where the child and family feel able to explore the cultural and religious issues that are significant to them. This will facilitate a more specific understanding of the meaning of culture, faith and ethnicity to every child and family within their individual, social and community context (Horwath and Lees 2008). Moreover, by gaining this knowledge practitioners will have a greater understanding of the impact that these factors have on the needs of the child and the parents' and community's ability to meet their needs.

Summary

Despite the many legislative and policy changes that have occurred in England since the death of Victoria Climbié, the outcomes for many black and minority ethnic children and families are far from positive. There is no doubt that it is critical to establish a systems response to safeguard and promote the welfare of all children to ensure they achieve best outcomes. However, when a bureaucratic response takes centre stage, it may be done at the cost of direct engagement with children and families, as the following quote from one solicitor in the study by Brophy et al. (2005) illustrates:

> Some (assessments) are excellent and some are very poor, because there's a tick box, some rely too heavily on the tick boxes. What they do is they answer the questions but they don't pull it together at the end. So it isn't really an assessment it's a collection of information. (Brophy et al. 2005, p.66)

What is required is

> not so much the need for a set of guidelines about race or ethnicity for workers to follow, but a leap of imagination and extra sensitivity to be made in order to empathise with families. (Brandon *et al.* 1999, p.145)

Recommended reading

Horwath, J., Lees, J., Sidebotham, P., Higgins, J. and Imtiaz, A. (2008) *Religion, Beliefs and Parenting Practices: A Descriptive Study.* York: Joseph Rowntree Foundation.

Thoburn, J., Chand, A. and Procter, J. (2005) *Child Welfare for Minority Ethnic Families: The Research Reviewed.* London: Jessica Kingsley Publishers.

Wade, J., Mitchell, F. and Bayliss, G. (2005) *Unaccompanied Asylum Seeking Children: The Response of Social Work Services.* London: British Agencies for Adoption and Fostering.

References

Barn, R. (2006) 'Improving services to meet the needs of minority ethnic children and families.' Briefing paper 13. Research in Practice: Making Research Count. London: Department for Education and Skills.

Becher, H. and Husain, F. (2003) *Supporting Minority Ethnic Families. South Asian Hindus and Muslims in Britain: Developments in Family Support.* London: National Family and Parenting Institute.

Berthoud, R. (2000) *Family Formation in Multi-cultural Britain: Three Patterns of Diversity.* Working Paper of the Institute for Social and Economic Research, Paper No. 34. Colchester: ISER.

Blom-Cooper, L. (1985) *A Child in Trust: The Report of the Panel of Inquiry into the Circumstances Surrounding the Death of Jasmine Beckford.* Wembley: London Borough of Brent.

Box, L., Butt, J. and Bignall, T. (2001) 'Black and minority ethnic families policy forum.' Discussion paper 1. London: REU.

Brandon, M., Thoburn, J., Lewis, A. and Way, A. (1999) Safeguarding Children with the Children Act 1989. London: The Stationery Office.

Brandon, M., Belderson, P., Warren, C., Howard, D. *et al.* (2008) *Analysing Child Deaths and Serious Injury Through Abuse and Neglect: What Can We Learn? A Biennial Analysis of Serious Case Reviews 2003–2005.* Research Report No. DCSF-RR023. Nottingham: DCSF.

Bridge Child Care Consultancy (1991) *Sukina: An Evaluation Report of the Circumstances Leading to Her Death.* London: Bridge Child Care Consultancy.

Brophy, J., Jhutti-Johal, J. and McDonald, E. (2005) *Minority Ethnic Parents, their Solicitors and Child Protection Litigation.* London: Department for Constitutional Affairs.

Butt, J. and Box, L. (1998) *Family Centres: A Study of the Use of Family Centres by Black Families.* London: Race Equality Unit.

Cleaver, H. and Walker, S. (2004) *Assessing Children's Needs and Circumstances.* London: Jessica Kingsley Publishers.

Cm 5730 (2003) *The Victoria Climbié Inquiry Report.* London: The Stationery Office.

Cm 5860 (2003) *Every Child Matters.* Green Paper. London: The Stationery Office.

Croot, E. (2005) 'Experiencing childhood disability: parenting children with high support needs in Pakistani families in Sheffield.' Institute of General Practice and Primary Care. Sheffield: University of Sheffield.

Department for Education and Skills (2006) *Priority Review: Exclusion of Black Pupils. 'Getting It. Getting It Right.'* London: DfES.

Department of Health (2000) *Assessing Children in Need and their Families: Practice Guidance.* London: The Stationery Office.

Department of Health, Department for Education and Employment and Home Office (2000) *Framework for the Assessment of Children in Need and their Families.* London: The Stationery Office.

Department of Health (2001) *Health Survey for England 1999: The Health of Minority Ethnic Groups.* London: Department of Health.

Eades, C., Grimshaw, R., Silvestri, A. and Solomon, E. (2007) *Knife Crime: A Review of Evidence and Policy.* London: Centre for Crime and Justice Studies.

Equalities Review (2007) *Fairness and Freedom: The Final Report of the Equalities Review.* London: HMSO. Available at http://archive.cabinetoffice.gov.uk/equalitiesreview/upload/assets/www.theequalitiesreview.org.uk/equality_review.pdf, accessed 15 July 2009.

Gilligan, P. and Furness, S. (2006) 'The role of religion and spirituality in social work practice: views and experiences of social workers and students.' *British Journal of Social Work 36*, 617-637.

HM Government (2007) *Safeguarding Children from Abuse Linked to a Belief in Spirit Possession.* London: Department for Children, Schools and Families.

Horwath, J. and Lees, J. (2008) 'Assessing the influence of religious beliefs and practices on parenting capacity: the challenges for social work practitioners.' *British Journal of Social Work.* Doi: 10.1093/bjsw/bcn116. Not yet published in hard copy.

Horwath, J., Lees, J., Sidebotham, P., Higgins, J. and Imtiaz, A. (2008) *Religion, Beliefs and Parenting Practices: A Descriptive Study.* York: Joseph Rowntree Foundation.

Hussain, Y., Atkin, K. and Ahmad, W. (2002) *South Asian Young Disabled People and their Families: Findings.* York: Joseph Rowntree Foundation.

Imtiaz, S.M.A. (2002) 'Identity and the politics of representation.' Unpublished doctoral dissertation, University of London.

Jacobson, J. (1998) *Islam in Transition: Religion and Identity among British Pakistani Youth.* London: Routledge.

Jones, A. (1998) *The Child Welfare Implications of UK Immigration and Asylum Policy.* Manchester: Manchester Metropolitan University.

Keating, F. (2007) *African and Caribbean Men and Mental Health.* A Race Equality Foundation Briefing Paper. London: Race Equality Foundation.

Kemp, D. (1997) In K. Dwivedi (ed.) (2005) *Meeting the Needs of Ethnic Minority Children.* RHP.[AQ]

King's Fund (2000) *The Health and Well-being of Asylum Seekers.* London: King's Fund.

Korbin, J.E. (2007) 'Issues of Culture.' In K. Wilson and A. James (eds) *The Child Protection Handbook*, 3rd edn. Oxford: Baillière Tindall.

Lau, A. (ed.) (2000) *South Asian Children and Adolescents in Britain.* London: Whurr.

Moran, P., Ghate, D. and van der Merwe, A. (2004) *What Works in Parenting Support? A Review of the International Evidences.* Research Report RR574. London: Department for Education and Skills.

Office for National Statistics (2001a) Census 2001. Available at www.statistics.gov.uk/census2001/census2001.asp, accessed on 15 July 2009.

Office for National Statistics (2001b) *Annual Population Survey.* London: PNS.

Office for National Statistics (2002) *Annual Local Area Labour Force Survey 2001–2002.* London: ONS.

Office for National Statistics (2004) *Annual Population Survey, January 2004 to December 2004.* Available at www.esds.ac.uk/findingData/snDescription.asp?sn=5258, accessed on 13 July 2009.

O'Neil, V. (2000) *Excellence not Excuses: Inspection of Services for Ethnic Minority Children and Families.* London: Department of Health, Social Services Inspectorate.

Patel, B. (2005) *The Social Care Needs of Refugees and Asylum Seekers* Race Equality Discussion Paper. London: Social Care Institute for Excellence.

Saeed, A., Blain, N. and Forbes, D. (1999) 'New ethnic and national questions in Scotland: post-British identities among Glasgow Pakistani teenagers.' *Ethnic and Racial Studies 22*, 821–844.

Seden, J. (1995) 'Religious persuasion and the Children Act.' *Adoption and Fostering 19*, 7-15.

Sharpe, E.J. (1988) *Understanding Religion.* London: Duckworth.

Sproston, K. and Mindell, J. (eds) (2006) *Health Survey for England 2004. Vol. 1: The Health of Minority Ethnic Groups.* London: The Information Centre for Health and Social Care.

Statham, J. and Biehal, N. (2005) *Assessing the Needs of Children and Families. Briefing Paper 15, Research in Practice, Making Research Count.* London: Department for Education and Skills.

Stobart, E. (2006) *Child Abuse Linked to Accusations of 'Possession' and 'Witchcraft'.* Research Report RR750. London: Department for Education and Skills.

Stewart, S.M., Bond, M.H., Ho, L.M., Zaman, R.M., Dar, R. and Anwar, M. (2000) 'Perceptions of parents and adolescent outcomes in Pakistan.' *British Journal of Developmental Psychology 18*, 335–352.

Thoburn, J., Chand, A. and Procter, J. (2005) *Child Welfare for Minority Ethnic Families: The Research Reviewed.* London: Jessica Kingsley Publishers.

Wade, J., Mitchell, F. and Bayliss, G. (2005) *Unaccompanied Asylum Seeking Children: The Response of Social Work Services.* London: British Agencies for Adoption and Fostering.

Wilding, J. and Barton, M. (2007) *Evaluation of Strengthening Families, Strengthening Communities Programme 2004/2005.* London: Race Equality Foundation.

Zokaei, S. and Phillips, D. (2000) 'Altruism and intergenerational relations among Muslims in Britain.' *Current Sociology 28*, 4, 45–58.

CHAPTER 21

The Impact of Economic Factors on Parents or Caregivers and Children

Gordon Jack and Owen Gill

A low income over many years and parents' inability to manage on this income may mean a young adolescent being bullied at school simply because he is wearing clothes which do not have the correct designer logo.

(From the Framework for the Assessment of Children in Need and their Families, p.245, 2.19)

This chapter considers:

- the central importance of an ecological approach to the assessment of the economic circumstances of families and children
- the subjective meaning of poverty and income inequality for children and families
- those at greatest risk of experiencing poverty and the impact that it can have on their lives
- the influence of other factors, such as housing, geographical location and time of year, for families living in poverty.
- the main impacts of poverty on families and children
- from theory to practice.

Introduction

Over recent years, concerns about the number of children living in poor households in the UK, and the effects of family poverty on children's wellbeing and future life chances, have come to occupy a central position in political discourse. This was most clearly signalled in the Government's 1999 undertaking to end child poverty within 20 years, which heralded a raft of employment, tax and benefit measures aimed at achieving that goal. The Government's continuing commitment to meet this target was confirmed with the announcement in the Queen's Speech in 2008 that it planned to introduce legislation designed to ensure child poverty is eradicated by 2020.

However, although the measures taken so far have helped to lift significant numbers of children out of poverty (defined as living in a household with less than 60 per cent of the median income of the overall population), the Government failed to meet its initial target of reducing child poverty by a quarter by 2005, and the number of children living in poverty actually increased by 100,000 in 2006/07 (Department for Work and Pensions 2007). Measures announced in the 2007 and 2008 Budgets have added around £2 billion to the reduction of child poverty, but it has been estimated that the Government needs to invest an additional £2.8 billion on help for poorer families by 2010/11 if it is to meet its target of halving the level of child poverty by that date (Institute for Fiscal Studies 2008).

Against this backdrop of child poverty and other aspects of economic inequality, the purpose of this chapter is to consider the impact of economic factors on individual children and families so that effective assessments of children's needs might be made. Our starting point is that parents' or caregivers' access to financial resources is linked to a wide range of other factors which, in combination, are likely to have a profound impact on their ability to meet the needs of their children, as well as having direct effects on children's everyday lives and future life chances. In order to develop a full understanding of the combined influences of these factors on the lives of children and their families, it is necessary for practitioners undertaking assessments of children using the Common Assessment Framework (Children's Workforce Development Council 2009) and the *Framework for the Assessment of Children in Need and their Families* (Department of Health *et al.* 2000) or other more specialist assessment instruments for young offenders, for example, to use an ecological perspective (Gill and Jack 2007; Jack 1997, 2000; Jack and Gill 2003; Kane 2006).

This involves understanding the impact of the interactions between factors in different 'spheres' of children's lives on their overall development, wellbeing and future life chances. These spheres (or systems) include the child's household and wider family networks, formal institutions such as schools, neighbourhood and community settings, and the wider society and cultural contexts which shape the overall nature and expectations of childhood. Strengths in one system can support or produce strengths in others, whilst difficulties in one system are likely to exacerbate or compound those in others (Bronfenbrenner and Morris 1998). This means that children's lives will not only be affected by the financial circumstances of their families, but also by the other resources to which their families have access as a result of their financial circumstances. These include housing, community resources and the services available to them where they live.

The subjective meaning of income inequality

Carrying out assessments of a child's needs involves talking directly to parents or care-givers and children about their experiences and current circumstances. Talking about financial issues may, understandably, reveal particular sensitivities on the part of adults who are struggling to provide adequately for their children, and it may also be challenging to talk to children directly about their family's financial circumstances and how this impacts on their lives. The key to successfully engaging with both adults and children about these issues lies in the anti-discriminatory values, attitudes and explanations of practitioners undertaking assessments, conveying an understanding of the way in which economic opportunities are often unfairly structured by society, as well as the way that economic inequalities can affect a parent's or caregiver's coping capacities and a child's quality of life.

In doing this, it is important for practitioners to recognise that the subjective experience of financial hardship and economic inequality will be influenced by a range of factors, including the parent's or caregiver's history, personal characteristics and cultural expectations. Two studies of the experiences of adults and children living in poverty, in Scotland, serve to highlight the subjective, as well as the objective, impact that financial hardship can have on people's lives. In the first of these studies, Green (2007) studied the effects across Scotland of rising fuel prices. The effects on both behaviour and subjective wellbeing are illustrated by the comments of one of the adult participants:

> I now buy food and bring it home – cooked chicken and things like that, because I'm scared to use the oven because I know it costs too much money. I only use the wash-ing machine twice a week because I'm scared of what it costs. (Green 2007, p.2)

Other participants in this study described the social isolation caused by their limited fi-nancial resources and the fears associated with aggressive creditors, as well as the stresses associated with living on limited income from benefits or low-paid work:

> My husband works all night and then I'm out at college all day. All his money goes on council tax, rent and bills. We don't have a penny extra and I never see him. We'd be better off if he didn't work but he feels like he has to. (Green 2007, pp.2–3)

In the second study, conducted in four disadvantaged areas in and around Glasgow (Seaman *et al.* 2006), many parents described having to manage household expenditure very carefully, dealing with the pressures to buy fashionable items for their children as best they could:

> I'm so terrified of debt, I even budget my debt… I just budget constantly, catalogues are within my control. I mean it's not easy for a lot of folk they end up giving into their children, my children have never had a computer game or anything. If I've no got it, they don't get it and I don't go into debt for it. (Mother) (Green 2007, p.4)

The subjective experience of poverty is also influenced by the powerful imagery which abounds at cultural and community levels. In a culture focused on what one can afford to consume, and a popular media which tends to feature stories about 'fecklessness' and benefit fraud rather than the structural causes of low income, there can be a strong stigma attached to poverty. Poorer families will vary in the extent to which they incorporate such stigmatising messages into their conception of themselves, according to their understanding about who is responsible for their financial circumstances. For example, do they consider the responsibility rests with the educational and employment opportunities and income maintenance provision available to them, or do they view their financial circumstances as being the result of personal inadequacies?

Families at greater risk of experiencing poverty

Any consideration of the impact of economic factors on parents or caregivers and their children also needs to take into account that certain families are more likely to experience poverty than others. In particular, families that fall into the following categories are more likely to experience poverty:

- households in which there are no adults in paid work (Department for Work and Pensions 2005)
- households headed by a lone parent, or including a young mother (under 30 years of age), young children, or three or more children (Bradshaw 2002, 2005; Department for Work and Pensions 2005)
- children in black and minority ethnic (BME) families, particularly those of Bangladeshi, Pakistani and black African origin (Craig 2005; Marsh and Perry 2003; Platt 2007)
- asylum-seeking and refugee families (Oxfam and Refugee Council 2002; Scottish Refugee Council 2006)
- families where there is a disabled adult or child (Northway 2005; Strickland and Olsen 2005).

Since 1997, the UK Government has promoted employment as the main route out of poverty. Whilst the overall level of unemployment in Britain initially fell over this period, this was achieved on the back of increasing polarisation within the labour market, with a growth in the number of two-earner households being accompanied by rising numbers of households in which there is no working-age adult in paid employment (Department for Work and Pensions 2005). Furthermore, despite the introduction of the national minimum wage, low pay continues to be a major problem. In 2002/03, for instance, two-fifths of households living in poverty contained at least one adult in paid work (Palmer *et al.* 2004). To make matters worse, low-paid workers tend to remain low paid, and their jobs are often insecure and short term, exposing many of them to a cycle of low-paid work interspersed by periods of unemployment (Kemp *et al.* 2004). Although extra financial help is targeted at working parents, through the tax credit system, the high cost of child care in the UK can also act as a barrier to taking up paid work for many low-income families, sometimes leaving them worse off in work than on benefits (Gill and Jack 2007, p.16).

More recently, as a result of a global economic recession which has become known as the 'credit crunch', unemployment in the UK has risen again. The groups most at risk of experiencing unemployment include lone parents, people with disabilities, and BME groups, which helps to explain why these groups are all at greater risk of experiencing poverty. Often, a combination of these factors will push a family into deep poverty, as illustrated in the following case example, concerning a refugee family that is not only from a BME community, but is also very large by UK standards, and is caring for a disabled child (Barnardo's 2007).

Amira is a Somali woman, aged 46, who lives with her husband and eight of her children in temporary accommodation. Amira's husband suffers from diabetes and heart disease, and does not work. He attributes his illness to the stress of having to leave his homeland and being a refugee for a number of years. One of their children, 16-year-old Yasmine, has a physical disability which means that she is unable to walk to school.

The family are dependent on Income Support and Child Benefit, with Housing Benefit covering their housing costs. They own an old car, which they consider to be essential, especially for transporting Yasmine to school. The remainder of the family's weekly income goes on food, clothes and other essential household expenditure. Amira and her husband are committed to meeting their children's needs, but say that it is a constant struggle. Amira admits that she and her husband often go without themselves, so that the children can have some of the things they need: *We try to make the house warm for the children. It's all about giving back to children… I'm glad but I'm living under pressure.*

Amira has developed what she refers to as a 'queue' system, so that the children can take their turn at having the things they need. She describes herself as always juggling between meeting the needs of the different children: *I manage to pay for the two boys to go to sports club. The girls are missing out. We can only afford the cinema once a year – Eid day.*

At times, the family are only able to survive by borrowing money from family and friends. However, with very limited income this is often not really a solution, and Amira describes how she often has to borrow money from one friend or relative to pay back another: *I have these mixed feelings. One thing very positive I know I am borrowing for the sake of my children and my children will have good life…investing for the future. The other side I am thinking always depending on other people.*

Practitioners also need to be aware that some families are likely to be living *below* Income Support levels, often as a result of repaying debts resulting from overpayments of tax credits or loans from the Social Fund. Others might be making substantial payments to unregulated 'loan sharks' for items ranging from buying a TV licence to paying off fines, or they may be paying back regular amounts to the large organisations that provide loans at high rates of interest to people who have no other source of credit. Asylum-seeking families who are dependent on allowances from the National Asylum Support Service are likely to be experiencing particular hardship since the financial support available to them is set at only 70 per cent of the Income Support rate for adults (Oxfam and Refugee Council 2002; Scottish Refugee Council 2006).

The influence of housing, geographical location and time of year

There is now increased political recognition of the existence of a housing crisis in the UK, the underlying cause of which is the lack of decent affordable housing. This crisis impacts particularly powerfully on the most vulnerable families and their children who, as a result of their exclusion from the benefits of the property boom, have been 'left far behind with little prospect of a decent home' (Jones 2004, p.6). This trend is confirmed by a study of the amount of equity people have in their homes, which shows that 'housing wealth' now varies significantly across the UK, due to regional differences in property values. Households in the wealthiest parts of the country possessed over five times the housing wealth of those living in the poorest areas in 2003 (Thomas and Dorling 2004). Despite recent falls in the value of property in the UK, this gap is likely to continue to rise over the coming decades.

In the UK, a family's housing circumstances tend to be closely related to their overall economic situation, illustrating one of the ways in which different aspects of children's lives interact to reinforce either their advantages or disadvantages (Fitzpatrick 2004). For instance, large families, who we have already noted are at heightened risk of experiencing poverty, are also more likely to be disadvantaged in relation to housing, with overcrowding known to have a particularly negative impact on family life (Shelter 2005). In fact, there is considerable evidence about the impact of poor quality or inappropriate housing on all aspects of children's health and wellbeing (Shelter 2006). These problems affect large numbers of families and children, with over one million children in Britain estimated to be living in substandard housing, and more than half a million families living in officially overcrowded homes in 2004 (Jones 2004). The same report, by the housing charity Shelter, went on to identify the impact of poor housing on children, identifying that:

> Housing is fundamental to every part of a child's development. It is something most of us take for granted. Children need a home to feel safe, keep warm and stay healthy. Bad housing wrecks their lives, makes them sick, unhappy and under-achieve at school. (Jones 2004, p.3)

Looking at this sort of evidence in relation to *The Children's Plan* outcomes (Cm 7280 2007), the following example, which involves a lone parent talking about living with her six children in an overcrowded home, illustrates the way that poor housing can have a direct impact on, for example, children 'enjoying and achieving':

> I've got so fed up with homework and things that I've said to the school if the kids need to do homework they're going to have to stay inside at break time or dinner time. Because I can't cope with homework at home…there's no space. (Barnardo's 2008, p.11)

Homelessness and living in temporary accommodation, which typically represent the most extreme forms of housing problems, are also known to have very damaging effects on parents' or caregivers' ability to meet the needs of their children. This is graphically illustrated in the following case example, which concerns 'Sarah' and her two children, who fled domestic violence and had to live in emergency housing for a year. Sarah was particularly worried about the effect of this experience on her six-year-old daughter:

> It's been the worst for my six year old. She had to move school when we moved. I just had her first school report and she didn't do as well as I expected.
>
> When we were living in the refuge she cut her hand on razor blades. Suddenly we were living with twelve other families and there were drug addicts there. Another child made sexual remarks to her and when I complained I was just told he had some disorder. He was nine. It was terrible there. We were three in a bed. I couldn't cook for them. In the end we had to leave because of that boy. She often talks about it. She's six years old and she's depressed. She seems to be crying all the time. She's insecure. She can't be classed as normal at school. She takes it out on me. She's always asking: 'Why can't we have a house? Why haven't we got one?' I'm hoping she'll come out of it the other end but you just don't know. (Jones 2004, p.12)

Whilst a family's home conditions will have a direct impact on a child's development, the geographical location of their home is also likely to play a significant role, often serving to reinforce their financial circumstances (Department for Communities and Local Government 2008). A wide range of research demonstrates the tendency for income-deprived families to suffer further disadvantages because they live in areas characterised by high levels of other problems such as unemployment, crime, anti-social behaviour, drug and alcohol misuse, limited child care provision, and poor quality schools (Ghate and Hazel 2002; Lupton 2003; Social Exclusion Unit 1998). The impact that housing location has on the family's access to the resources of the community (and the wider family) will therefore also be an important factor when assessing their economic circumstances.

Housing location may also have other effects on the family's financial position. For example, although child poverty and other forms of deprivation may be more apparent in an urban setting, where there are higher concentrations of poorer households, individual families in rural settings can experience poverty more intensely. Not only are there liable to be few of the resources that are geared to advising families about their financial problems and supporting them in coping, but also their general living expenses may be higher. Food and services are likely to be more expensive locally, and there will be extra costs associated with accessing more distant resources. In some rural areas there will be no adequate public transport, forcing people to use taxis for everyday necessities such as buying food at the nearest supermarket, or taking children to the nearest doctor's surgery. The experience of living in poverty may be further reinforced if poor families are located in relatively affluent rural or semi-rural locations, because they are likely to routinely come into contact with others who have far higher levels of income than themselves (Gill and Jack 2007).

An in-depth assessment of the family's economic position will also necessitate exploring the amount they pay for their accommodation. Families who are buying their property may be spending a high proportion of their income on mortgage repayments leading to extreme pressure on family finances. For those dependent on welfare benefits, housing costs can also produce situations in which families are living below Income Support levels. This may be particularly the case for those families who, because of a lack of social housing, are dependent on the private rented sector, as illustrated by the following case example from a Barnardo's anti-poverty project:

> Anna is a lone mother with a ten-year-old son. She moved more than a hundred miles to her present area of residence, as a result of domestic violence and harassment. On her arrival, she was informed that she had low priority for local authority housing. She was therefore forced into the private rented sector. There has, however, been an ongoing dispute about whether Housing Benefit will cover the whole of the rent for her flat, with the result that Anna has been forced to make up the difference, amounting to £77 a month. This has had a serious impact on what she can afford to provide for her son, despite the fact that Anna often decides to 'go without' herself.

The time of year is another factor which also needs to be borne in mind when considering economic factors as part of an assessment of the child's needs. For example, many poorer carers find school holidays, especially the long summer break, to be a particularly stressful time financially, because of a combination of the extra costs of:

- providing entertainment and leisure activities for children in the summer holidays

- feeding children when they are not receiving free school meals

- preparing children for the return to school, which often involves purchasing new items of uniform, sports equipment and educational materials, especially when children are transferring from primary to secondary school, or moving schools for other reasons.

The main impacts of poverty on families and children

Parents or caregivers

It is important to recognise that most parents or caregivers living in poverty make a perfectly satisfactory job of bringing up their children. This point is made by Katz *et al.* (2007) who, on the basis of a review of the relationship between poverty and parenting, found that the majority of parents living in poverty (like those living in relative affluence) demonstrate adequate parenting capacity.

However, part of the role of the practitioner will be to assess the way in which economic factors, such as low household income and restricted access to community resources, impact on parents' or caregivers' ability to meet the needs of their children. Much research has pointed to the constant pressure experienced by those living on low incomes. For instance, in a study highlighting the significance of financial, practical and material support in addressing the root causes of marginalisation, Gillies (2006) shows how 'obtaining sufficient money and securing decent housing were consuming imperatives, shaping biographies and experiences of motherhood' (p.17).

In addition, there are likely to be significant links between the financial circumstances of parents or caregivers and their physical and mental health. They may experience feelings of depression and powerlessness, for instance, in relation to mounting debts or the stresses associated with living in inappropriate housing. These, in turn, will affect the care they are able to provide for their children. Financial stresses may also have an adverse impact on the relationships between carers, leading to disruption and tension in family life and poorer outcomes for children (Cleaver *et al.* 1999).

Transport and patterns of employment may also be significant issues. Lack of access to transport can serve to isolate parents or caregivers and their children from wider sources of support provided by family and friends, which might make the difference between coping and not coping with the demands of living in poor financial circumstances (Ghate and Hazel 2002; Gill *et al.* 2000). Hours of work can also have a major impact on family life. For example, a growing number of parents or caregivers, particularly those in lower socio-economic groups, are now forced to work at evenings and weekends. One study, using a nationally representative sample of working parents, found that, in households where parents frequently worked these 'atypical hours', family activities were more limited, with less time available for such things as reading and playing with children and helping them with their homework, as well as fewer family outings and shared family meals (La Valle *et al.* 2002). In-depth interviews with families in this study revealed that, for those in dual-parent households who worked more limited, atypical hours or who had control over the hours that they worked, their work patterns actually enabled some of them (including fathers) to spend *more* time with their children and reduce (or even eliminate) the need for non-parental child care. However, where such controls over work patterns were not present, parents (especially fathers) were less involved in family life, causing particular problems for lone parents (La Valle *et al.* 2002).

Children and young people

In addition to the influence of economic circumstances on the capacity of parents or caregivers to meet the needs of their children, it is also important to consider some of the direct effects of economic factors on children and young people themselves. This includes consideration of the impact of financial hardship on their day-to-day lives, as well as assessment of its likely longer-term impact on their development, aspirations and future life chances. The work of Ridge (2002) and Willow (2002), for example, based on children's first-hand experiences of income deprivation, highlights the pressures they were under to buy brand-name clothing and other goods, the lack of which can set them apart from their friends and peers, and result in social exclusion and bullying.

Other research has highlighted the impact on children of factors such as their parents' educational background and work patterns. For example, data emerging from the Millennium Cohort Study (MCS) indicates that, by the age of three, children of parents without educational qualifications are already a year behind children of parents with a university degree on a measure of 'school readiness', consisting of an assessment of their understanding of colours, letters, numbers, sizes and shapes (Centre for Longitudinal Studies 2007). Echoing the findings of the study by La Valle and colleagues, referred to above, the MCS also found that 5 per cent of mothers and 15 per cent of fathers considered that they did not have anything like enough time to spend with their child, usually because of long working hours (Smith 2007). The long-term effects of such work patterns when children are young have been separately investigated by Ermisch and Francesconi (2001), who found that there was a trade-off between increased family income and reduced time for parents to spend with their children. After controlling for family income, the study found that young adults whose mothers worked full time in their pre-school years were disadvantaged in both their educational attainment and employment prospects. However, part-time employment by mothers in a child's early years appeared to have few adverse effects, and the impact of fathers' employment on the outcomes studied was generally less significant than that of mothers' paid work.

Research has also shown that economic disadvantage in childhood can affect young people's aspirations for the future, with some of them effectively 'learning to be poor' (Shropshire and Middleton 1999). For example, some children and young people exclude themselves from school and social activities that they think their parents or caregivers cannot afford:

> I don't usually go on trips cos they are expensive and that… At our school they do loads of activities and they go to loads of different places… I don't bother asking. (Male, age 11) (Ridge 2002, p.77)

From theory to practice

The practice implications of the ecological perspective, believed to be of central importance in assessing the impact of economic factors on parents' or caregivers' ability to meet the needs of their children, are set out below. It is assumed that the practitioner has gained the agreement of the service users and carers involved in the assessment to gather the information suggested.

Household resources

Assessment of a family's financial circumstances will need to establish the level of household income and whether the family are receiving their full entitlement, for example, in terms of tax credits and benefits. The extent of any debts and repayments and other essential household expenditure should also be established, including accommodation and utility costs. Particular family characteristics which have an impact on their income and expenditure, such as the presence of a disabled child in the family or parental dependence on drugs or alcohol, should also be taken into account.

Wider family resources

The assessment should also consider the level of support available to the family from members of their wider family network. Some families living on very low incomes may have the impact of this lessened by financial support from relatives (particularly grandparents) whilst others, such as asylum-seeking or refugee families, may be totally without such support, even in an emergency.

Community resources

Assessments should also examine the opportunities and resources available to children and families at community and neighbourhood levels. For instance, an income-deprived family might be coping satisfactorily because they live in an area in which there are well-developed facilities for reducing the impact of household poverty, such as credit unions, free advice centres, and food co-operatives, as well as affordable child care, leisure activities and transport. In contrast, a similar family, with exactly the same level of household income, might be struggling because they are living in an area in which there are few of these opportunities and resources.

Formal institutions

Assessments should also take into account the extent to which formal institutions, such as schools, serve to either reinforce or ameliorate a family's economic circumstances. For example, state education for children in some schools can be far from free, with parents expected to contribute to the cost of things like school trips and materials for school projects. However, in others (for instance those developing 'extended' services), a range of facilities designed to alleviate some of the effects of household poverty and its impact on educational attainment may be provided, such as free (or subsidised) breakfast and after-school clubs, and access to affordable daycare, sports, leisure and ICT facilities (Department for Education and Skills 2006).

Wider society

Finally, assessments should consider some of the cultural expectations and pressures that exist within wider society. In relation to children, for example, the possession of fashionable consumer goods, including the latest mobile phones, games consoles and brand-name clothing, may be particularly important (Ridge 2002). Public attitudes towards people experiencing poverty also need to be understood, with the British Social Attitudes Survey, for example, revealing that nearly half of the general population think that poverty is a sign of laziness or lack of will power on the part of those affected (Park *et al.* 2007).

These headings are designed to remind practitioners of the importance of collecting information about a family's economic circumstances at a number of different levels of influence on families and children. However, a central component of the ecological approach to the assessment of children is the interaction between factors in different domains of the child's life. This means that economic factors at one level, such as the community resources available to residents living in a particular neighbourhood, always need to be considered alongside those that exist at other levels of influence, such as the income of individual households. For example, children and parents living in income-deprived households, trying to access leisure or educational activities during the summer holidays, may be limited both by their own relative lack of financial resources *and* by their location in a poorly resourced area which provides few activities for their children. In terms of *The Children's Plan* outcomes, this also means that a child's economic wellbeing should not be considered in isolation, but alongside all of the other outcomes (being healthy; staying safe; enjoying and achieving; and making a positive contribution), since they will all influence one another (Cm 7280 2007).

Summary

The evidence summarised in this chapter makes it clear that practitioners undertaking child and family assessments need to be aware of a wide range of issues in relation to the economic circumstances of parents or caregivers and children. These include an objective understanding of the extent of any financial hardship that they are experiencing, knowledge about the groups who are disproportionately likely to experience poverty, and awareness of the impact of poverty and associated forms of disadvantage on parents and caregivers, as well as children and young people. In doing this, the chapter has also drawn attention to the importance of considering the more subjective elements of income deprivation, and developing an understanding of how economic factors are affecting *this* family and *this* child. It has also been stressed throughout the chapter that practitioners need to engage with the overall social ecology of the child and family, taking into account interactions between their personal characteristics and the wider family and friendship support networks and community resources available to them, as well as the cultural and structural influences upon them coming from the wider society of which they are a part.

However, assessments to safeguard and promote the welfare of children are of limited use unless they also help to identify ways of improving the lives of economically disadvantaged children and their parents or caregivers. It is evident that individual practitioners will not have access to the sort of resources needed to provide comprehensive solutions to the economic problems experienced by many of the families with whom they come into contact. However, this should not result in a resigned acceptance of the *status quo*; there is a responsibility on all practitioners working in children's services to identify the consequences of economic disadvantages for children and their families, and to challenge their causes. This wider aspect of the practitioner's role should be combined with action designed to improve directly the day-to-day lives of individual parents or caregivers and their children. For example, an awareness of the financial circumstances of those dependent on welfare benefits may indicate the need for more specialist welfare rights advice. Similarly, a clear picture of the resources available within the wider family or the local community may lead to interventions designed either to help family members improve their access to potential sources of support, or to constructive action designed to increase the community resources available to families and children in their local areas.

Recommended reading

Barnardo's (2007) *It Doesn't Happen Here: The Reality of Child Poverty in the UK*. Barkingside: Barnardo's.

Ghate, D. and Hazel, N. (2002) *Parenting in Poor Environments: Stress, Support and Coping*. London: Jessica Kingsley Publishers.

Gill, O. and Jack, G. (2007) *The Child and Family in Context: Developing Ecological Practice in Disadvantaged Communities*. Lyme Regis: Russell House Publishing.

Ridge, T. (2002) *Childhood Poverty and Social Exclusion: From a Child's Perspective*. Bristol: The Policy Press.

References

Barnardo's (2007) *It Doesn't Happen Here: The Reality of Child Poverty in the UK*. Barkingside: Barnardo's.

Barnardo's (2008) *Homes Fit for Children? The Housing Crisis for Large Low Income Households in the South West*. Bristol: Barnardo's.

Bradshaw, J. (2002) 'Child poverty and child outcomes.' *Children & Society 16*, 131–140.

Bradshaw, J. (2005) 'Child Poverty in Larger Families.' In Child Poverty Action Group, *At Greatest Risk: The Children Most Likely to be Poor*. London: CPAG.

Bronfenbrenner, U. and Morris, P. (1998) 'The Ecology of Developmental Processes.' In W. Damon and R. Lerner (eds) *Handbook of Child Psychology. Vol. 1: Theoretical Methods of Human Development*, 5th edn. New York: Wiley.

Centre for Longitudinal Studies (2007) *Disadvantaged Children Up to a Year Behind by the Age of Three*. Press release, 11th June. London: Centre for Longitudinal Studies, Institute of Education, University of London.

Children's Workforce Development Council (2009) *The Common Assessment Framework for Children and Young People: A Guide for Practitioners*. Leeds: Children's Workforce Development Council.

Cleaver, H., Unell, I. and Aldgate, J. (1999) *Children's Needs – Parenting Capacity*. London: The Stationery Office.

Cm 7280 (2007) *The Children's Plan: Building Brighter Futures*. London: Department for Children, Schools and Families.

Craig, G. (2005) 'Poverty among Black and Minority Ethnic Children.' In Child Poverty Action Group, *At Greatest Risk: The Children Most Likely to be Poor*. London: CPAG.

Department for Communities and Local Government (2008) *The English Indices of Deprivation 2007*. London: Department for Communities and Local Government.

Department for Education and Skills (2006) *The Governance and Management of Extended Schools and Sure Start Children's Centres*. London: Department for Education and Skills.

Department of Health, Department for Education and Employment and Home Office (2000) *Framework for the Assessment of Children in Need and their Families*. London: The Stationery Office.

Department for Work and Pensions (2005) *Households Below Average Income 2004*. London: Office for National Statistics.

Department for Work and Pensions (2007) *Households Below Average Income 2005/06*. London: Office for National Statistics.

Ermisch, J. and Francesconi, M. (2001) *The Effects of Parents' Employment on Children's Lives*. London: Family Policy Studies Centre.

Fitzpatrick, S. (2004) *Poverty of Place*. Keynote address to the Joseph Rowntree Foundation Centenary Conference, 'Poverty and Place: Policies for Tomorrow', University of York.

Ghate, D. and Hazel, N. (2002) *Parenting in Poor Environments: Stress, Support and Coping*. London: Jessica Kingsley Publishers.

Gill, O. and Jack, G. (2007) *The Child and Family in Context: Developing Ecological Practice in Disadvantaged Communities*. Lyme Regis: Russell House Publishing.

Gill, O., Tanner, C. and Bland, L. (2000) *Family Support: Strengths and Pressures in a 'High-risk' Neighbourhood*. Barkingside: Barnardo's.

Gillies, V. (2006) *Marginalised Mothers: Exploring Working Class Experiences of Parenting*. Abingdon: Routledge.

Green, M. (2007) *Voices of People Experiencing Poverty in Scotland*. York: Joseph Rowntree Foundation.

Institute for Fiscal Studies (2008) *Poverty and Inequality in the UK: 2008*. London: IFS.

Jack, G. (1997) 'An ecological approach to social work with children and families.' *Child and Family Social Work 2*, 2, 109–120.

Jack, G. (2000) 'Ecological influences on parenting and child development.' *British Journal of Social Work 30*, 703–720.

Jack, G. and Gill, O. (2003) *The Missing Side of the Triangle: Assessing the Importance of Family and Environmental Factors in the Lives of Children*. Barkingside: Barnardo's.

Jones, S. (2004) *Toying with their Future: The Hidden Costs of the Housing Crisis*. London: Shelter.

Kane, S. (2006) *The Ecological Approach to the Assessment of Asylum Seeking and Refugee Children*. London: National Children's Bureau.

Katz, I., Corylon, J., La Placa, V. and Hunter, S. (2007) *The Relationship between Parenting and Poverty*. York: Joseph Rowntree Foundation.

Kemp, P., Bradshaw, J., Dornan, P., Finch, N. and Mayhew, E. (2004) *Routes out of Poverty: A Research Review*. York: Joseph Rowntree Foundation.

La Valle, I., Arthur, S., Millward, C. and Scott, J., with Clayden, M. (2002) *Happy Families? Atypical Work and its Influence on Family Life*. Bristol: The Policy Press.

Lupton, R. (2003) *Poverty Street: The Dynamics of Neighbourhood Decline and Renewal*. Bristol: The Policy Press.

Marsh, A. and Perry, J. (2003) 'Ethnic Minority Families: Poverty and Disadvantage.' In C. Kober (ed.) *Black and Ethnic Minority Children and Poverty: Exploring the Issues*. London: National Children's Bureau.

Northway, R. (2005) 'Disabled Children.' In Child Poverty Action Group, *At Greatest Risk: The Children Most Likely to be Poor*. London: CPAG.

Oxfam and Refugee Council (2002) *Poverty and Asylum in the UK*. London: Oxfam.

Palmer, G., Carr, J. and Kenway, P. (2004) *Monitoring Poverty and Social Exclusion*. York: Joseph Rowntree Foundation.

Park, A., Phillips, M. and Robinson, C. (2007) *Attitudes to Poverty: Findings from the British Social Attitudes Survey*. York: Joseph Rowntree Foundation.

Platt, L. (2007) *Poverty and Ethnicity in the UK*. Bristol: The Policy Press.

Ridge, T. (2002) *Childhood Poverty and Social Exclusion: From a Child's Perspective*. Bristol: The Policy Press.

Scottish Refugee Council (2006) *Poverty in Scotland*. Glasgow: Scottish Refugee Council.

Seaman, P., Turner, K., Hill, M., Stafford, A. and Walker, M. (2006) *Parenting and Children's Resilience in Disadvantaged Communities*. York: Joseph Rowntree Foundation.

Shelter (2005) *Full House: How Overcrowded Housing Affects Families*. London: Shelter.

Shelter (2006) *Chance of a Lifetime: The Impact of Bad Housing on Children's Lives*. London: Shelter.

Shropshire, J. and Middleton, S. (1999) *Small Expectations: Learning to be Poor*. York: York Publishing Services.

Smith, K. (2007) *Millennium Cohort Study Second Survey: A User's Guide to Initial Findings*. London: Centre for Longitudinal Studies, Institute of Education, University of London.

Social Exclusion Unit (1998) *Bringing Britain Together: A National Strategy for Neighbourhood Renewal*. London: Social Exclusion Unit.

Strickland, H. and Olsen, R. (2005) 'Children with Disabled Parents.' In Child Poverty Action Group, *At Greatest Risk: The Children Most Likely to be Poor*. London: CPAG.

Thomas, G. and Dorling, D. (2004) *Know Your Place: Housing Wealth and Inequality in Great Britain 1980–2003 and Beyond*. London: Shelter.

Willow, C. (2002) *Bread is Free: Children and Young People Talk about Poverty*. London: Children's Rights Alliance/Save the Children Fund.

CHAPTER 22

The Impact of Family and Community Support on Parents or Caregivers and Children

Gordon Jack and Owen Gill

The care and upbringing of children does not take place in a vacuum. All family members are influenced both positively and negatively by the wider family, the neighbourhood and social networks in which they live.

(From the Framework for the Assessment of Children in Need and their Families, p.22, 2.13)

This chapter considers:

- the importance of informal social support for parents or caregivers and children

- the role of wider family networks

- parents' or caregivers' relationships with friends and neighbours

- support from community organisations and faith communities

- the social world of the child outside the family

- from theory to practice: the strengths and pressures model.

Introduction

The purpose of this chapter is to consider the role that different types of informal support play in the lives of families and children. An ecological framework is employed to ensure that the connections between the internal (family) and external (community) components of children's lives are properly considered. In particular, ecological theory helps practitioners to examine the influence on parents or caregivers and children of the interactions between their personal and family characteristics and experiences, and the social and community environments in which they live (Bronfenbrenner 1979; Jack 2000; Jack and Gill 2003).

For the purposes of this chapter, we use the term 'community' to refer to the social relations between individuals in particular geographical areas which are external to the immediate and wider family, as well as those which exist within communities of interest or faith communities, which are not necessarily tied to particular geographical locations. The term 'informal support' is used to represent the help that is potentially available to parents or caregivers, as well as children and young people, from members of their wider family and community networks.

Evidence about the important role played by family and community support in the lives of parents or caregivers and their children has been accumulating for the past 30 years and more. For example, a body of research, initially developed in the United States, has highlighted the connections between the family and community support available to parents or caregivers, and the characteristics of their child rearing practices, including child maltreatment (for example, Belsky 1993; Garbarino and Crouter 1978; Garbarino and Sherman 1980). More recent work has confirmed the importance of different forms of social support for parenting in different locations in the UK as well (for example, Barnes 2004; Ghate and Hazel 2002). In addition, studies of the social networks of children and young people themselves have demonstrated the important influence that they have on their development and wellbeing, independent of the effects of the support available to their parents or caregivers (for example, Deater-Deckard 2001; Dunn 1993).

Although many frameworks for assessing the needs of families and children now require the influence of wider family and community factors to be taken into account (for example, Department of Health et al. 2000), for a variety of reasons most attention continues to be focused on factors internal to the family (Jack 2004; Jack and Gill 2003). Extending the scope of assessments, to include a properly integrated consideration of the influence of factors beyond the household, in the way suggested in this chapter, challenges many of the perceptions about wider family and community networks that have developed within professional child welfare work in the UK over recent decades. Moreover, in the context of widespread concerns about the dangers posed to children by paedophiles and child abuse networks over this period, a culture has developed which emphasises the protection of children against the potential dangers of communities, often at the expense of recognising their potential strengths as well (Ghate and Hazel 2002; Gill and Jack 2007; Gill et al. 2000; Jack 2006).

This means that it is important for practitioners making assessments to be able to identify the main *strengths* (as well as the potential dangers) to be found within parents' or caregivers' and children's social networks. It is also important to look at the capacity of individuals to negotiate these relationships, so that their potential strengths are brought into play and the effects of any dangers or difficulties that exist can be mitigated. In this, practitioners are assisted not only by ecological theory, which provides a framework within which to analyse the mutual influences of different factors in children's lives, but also by work that has identified the network and community factors that support the development or maintenance of resilience in children and families (for example, Gilligan 1998; Masten and Coatsworth 1998; Newman 2004).

One of the most important practice implications of this wider perspective, in the assessment of children's welfare, is the need for practitioners to listen to the voices of parents or caregivers and children. Because the qualities of social networks that extend beyond the realms of the household are often not as directly observable as internal family relationships, practitioners need to listen to children and their parents or caregivers talking about their perceptions of the particular strengths and dangers of their existing and potential sources of external support. Entering into the child's world in this way, for example, might involve talking to them about where they play and who they play with, who they walk to school with, and what experiences they have in the school playground, as well as after school and at weekends. It also involves developing some understanding of what the term 'community' means to different groups and individuals, according to factors such as their age, gender, personality, interests, abilities, religion, culture and racial background.

Wider social network and community contexts

Given the risk-focused culture that has developed in much child welfare work in the UK in recent decades, it is important to emphasise the need for practitioners to investigate the influence of social networks and other community conditions in an anti-oppressive manner, without any fixed preconceptions. Personal experiences of the support and stress emanating from wider family and community networks, as well as the services provided by welfare professionals and others, will be unique to each individual and family. The following practice example, in which a lone parent caring for her 13-year-old son with special needs is talking about the mixture of support and stress that she experiences within her local community, provides an illustration of the often complex mix of influences to be found within an individual's social ecology (from Gill and Jack 2007).

> I can remember in the beginning when Jack was diagnosed with learning difficulties and we started having all the people doing home visits and introducing themselves. I thought, at least we've got all these people coming and they're going to help... But after a little while it's wavered away and you just get left to get on with it and find things out from other mums... It's actually been the other mums in the same boat who've been the ones supporting me. I know I could get up at 2 o'clock in the morning and ring other mums and they wouldn't go, 'Oh what are you ringing me now for?' If I was at the end of my tether I wouldn't go to the professionals. Not in the slightest. Other mums of special needs children are my biggest support.
>
> The professionals I feel at a loss with really. It's like all the pouring out I've done to them over the years, it's been like a waste of time. I might as well have been talking to that wall. The difference is like someone understanding, listening to me for a few minutes. It would be more beneficial than talking to a professional for five hours. I really mean it. That's the way it is... They do just come and go. They just don't quite get it.

Talking to other mums, they have said that families and friends drop away when a special needs child comes along. I thought this was just me, but talking to other mums it's: 'My family don't bother.' My sister used to come around but now she doesn't bother. As far as people visiting me, it doesn't really happen a lot. I don't know why they don't come and see me. I always try and make them welcome. I try hard but they can't deal with it. On meeting people that live locally, I have to make more effort than they do. I do the ground-work and the hard work. I make a bigger effort on approaching people and having a chat with them. So I don't think I'm segregating myself. I'm making an effort. I overcompensate for their lack of understanding.

In the holidays Jack got up at 4 o'clock in the morning and he's very vocal and loud. And he carried on shouting all day. By about tea time I went and stood out the back by the field. I was trembling because he was shouting so much. I stood out there and a woman came down the field with her dog and said: 'Is Jack in the house on his own? Is he alright?' I was stood there and I almost burst into tears. She was more or less saying: 'Oh, you've left your son in there on his own.' She wasn't saying: 'Oh, are you alright?' I went back in but I felt bullied by the situation rather than helped.

I've taken him down the cricket club... The supporters don't say 'Hello' or anything. Just looking around and staring when they hear the noise that Jack is making, and then carrying on with their game. All the mums down there, they spread their blankets out and have a day-long picnic. They call their children away when they go too near Jack. But I find the football players and the people who support the team have a different attitude. They say: 'Oh, here comes Jack. We're going to have a good game today [Jack].' Like they have a little chat... It's like a warm glow inside. It makes me feel lovely. And now the local team's asked Jack to be their mascot when they do their cup final. And that's just made me feel like I've flown to the moon and back.

This practice example demonstrates the way that a family's social and community context typically involves a combination of factors relating to their geographical location, such as the community resources available to them in their local area (for example, child health, education and welfare services, and sports clubs), and the personal social networks and communities of interest to which they belong (for example, wider family relationships, parents or caregivers of other disabled children). Practitioners therefore need to develop an understanding of the social and community context in which particular children and families are living.

Different patterns of social support

Research has consistently found that social network relationships which provide support are associated with positive influences on parents or caregivers and children (for example, Dunst *et al.* 1997). In fact, even the *perception* that support will be available if it is needed is helpful, particularly for those who are living in disadvantaged circumstances (Hashima and Amato 1994; Sheppard 1994).

Conversely, a number of studies have found that families in which child neglect occurs are often characterised by a degree of social isolation, with the primary carers in these families generally having smaller social networks and less social interaction with adults outside of the household than other parents (Coohey 1996; Crittenden 1985; Polansky *et al.* 1985). Furthermore, where social network relationships do exist, it needs to be understood that they can just as easily be sources of stress as of support (Cochran 1993; Gibbons 1990). For example, a study comparing the social networks of single and married mothers found that, although the two groups received similar levels of support from their social networks, the single mothers also tended to experience more stress from these sources, often in the form of criticism, and that this was associated with poorer mother–child interactions (Brassard 1982). The potential for network relationships to simultaneously undermine as well as support parents or caregivers in their parenting role, as well as the tendency to have access to more restricted social networks, are both found to be problems associated with families which include a disabled child as well (Dunst *et al.* 1997).

Various studies have demonstrated that the social support available to parents or caregivers tends to influence their children's wellbeing indirectly, through more direct effects on carers' own health and wellbeing and overall family functioning (for example, Blaxter 1990). The most important functions of social support for parents' or caregivers' health and wellbeing have been shown to be practical help, information and advice, and emotional support (Cochran and Brassard 1979; Sarason *et al.* 1990). Perhaps the best known tool for assessing these different elements of social support is the 'social network map' devised by Tracey and Whittaker (1990), although other assessment instruments have been developed (see, for example, Cohen *et al.* 2000). Many practitioners will also be familiar with eco-maps, which enable the range and characteristics of the social network relationships of an individual or a family to be represented in a simple diagram (Warren 1993, pp.39–44). Eco-maps are considered in more detail in Chapter 7 by Howes.

On the basis of this sort of empirical mapping, Gardner (2003, p.47) has produced a typology of the social networks of parents living in the UK, which tend to fall into three broad groups:

Parents with extended networks

These parents have lived in the area for some time, are reasonably happy there, and maintain a full social network of friends and relatives. They also have little difficulty in approaching professionals, or in getting help to do so, if necessary.

Parents whose networks are patchy or insecure

These parents might have some strong partner or friendship relationships, but be new to the area in which they are living, or be isolated from community contacts for other reasons; alternatively, they may have work and community contacts, but be socially isolated from their family networks, either because they have recently separated from a partner, or are in conflict with members of their wider family network.

Parents whose networks are thin or poor

These parents could be described as socially excluded, in that they have very few, if any, positive and consistent relationships. They might have a history of volatile partnerships that ended in rejection (with or without violence), enmity with neighbours, 'help' perceived as intrusion from professionals, and conflict with agencies.

The practitioner assessing the social support resources of parents or caregivers (and children) therefore has to be alert not only to the number of actual (or potential) relationships within their networks, but also to a wide range of characteristics, including their strength, level and type of supportiveness or criticism, accessibility and reliability.

The role of wider family networks

Despite widespread public and media perceptions about the decline of the extended family in Britain over recent decades, there is plenty of evidence that grandparents and other adult relatives continue to be vital sources of financial, practical and emotional support for most families and children, particularly those living in disadvantaged circumstances (Ghate and Hazel 2002; Gill *et al.* 2000). The roles played by grandparents, for example, are illustrated in the findings beginning to emerge from the Millennium Cohort Study (when the children were three years of age), with an overwhelming proportion of families with a living grandparent reporting that they received financial help from them, such as gifts for the child or essentials for the household. Around a quarter of families reported receiving help with child care from grandparents as well (Hawkes and Joshi 2007). The central role played by many grandparents in modern family life in Britain has also been highlighted in a number of population surveys which have, for example, found that more than a third of grandparents regularly care for their grandchildren (Prasad 2000), most frequently to help mothers who are working part time (National Centre for Social Research 1999). Other surveys of the general population, together with more targeted research studies, have highlighted the significant levels of contact that most families have with members of their extended kin networks, as well as the central role that they play in providing a wide range of support to parents or caregivers and their children (for example, Coulthard *et al.* 2002).

Many children will be living in families where one parent is absent. In these situations it is important to assess the degree of contact that the child has with this parent, and the nature of the relationships that have evolved with the absent parent's wider family network. Depending on a number of factors, relationships between the adults and children involved in these families may range from complete breakdown or ongoing conflict at one extreme, to continuing involvement and support at the other (Gill *et al.* 2000).

What all of this serves to illustrate is that, whilst it is important for practitioners to recognise the potential support provided to parents or caregivers by grandparents and other adult members of wider family networks, it is equally important not to make assumptions about the level of help that is available from these sources. The old adage that 'you can choose your friends but not your family' is relevant here. Those with limited community social networks, who are therefore dependent on only one or two relatives for the bulk of their social support, are likely to be particularly vulnerable if that 'support' comes with large measures of criticism or unhelpful conditions attached. Others will be vulnerable because their main sources of support, within the wider family, either threaten their own or their children's health and wellbeing in some way, or are so unreliable or demanding of support themselves that they drain the energy and resources of the parent or caregiver, rather than bolstering them (Jack 1997).

It is also important to set any assessment of wider family support in the overall community context within which the child and family are living. The interplay between family and community contexts is illustrated in a study of the social support networks of families living in a disadvantaged part of Bristol undertaken by one of the authors (Gill *et al.* 2000). Although this was an area identified by child welfare agencies as producing high rates of child protection referrals, a community sample of parents with young children revealed that most of them (including the high proportion of lone parents living in the area) were well supported by grandparents and other adult relatives, a large proportion of whom lived nearby. However, opportunities for social interaction and mutual support between parents, outside of these extended family networks, were not well developed in the area. This meant that parents without access to local supportive family networks, particularly those with high levels of need who had recently moved into the area, were potentially isolated and vulnerable. Although these particular findings must be viewed as unique to this area of Bristol at the time that the study was conducted, more generally they reflect the findings of other research, such as that noted in the introduction to this chapter, which has highlighted the significant role played by informal networks of relationships in supporting (or undermining) parents or caregivers in their parenting role, both at family and community levels.

Parents' or caregivers' relationships with friends and neighbours

Besides relationships with relatives, the relationships of parents or caregivers with friends and neighbours within the community can also be important sources of support, both for themselves and their children. Research in the UK and elsewhere (for example, Ghate and Hazel 2002) has shown that, whilst relatives tend to be the most important providers of most kinds of social support to families, friends are particularly important providers of emotional support, and neighbours tend to be used for practical help with things like feeding pets, borrowing household items, and providing short-term child care in emergencies. Families who perceive themselves to be the best supported tend to be those who have access to a good balance of helpful relatives, friends and neighbours within their social networks. Conversely, families who are socially isolated, or whose social networks consist primarily of members who are not supportive, are consistently found to be the most vulnerable (Jack 1997, 2006).

It is possible to identify three broad types of relationships within communities which may be particularly stressful for parents or caregivers:

Immediate neighbours experienced as difficult and stressful

With the growth in home ownership promoted by successive governments via 'right to buy' policies over the last two decades, the public sector has increasingly come to be seen as the housing of last resort. The majority of residents living in the social rented sector nowadays, who have the personal means and aspirations to do so, tend to move out within a relatively short period of time, to be replaced by others with greater levels of need (Burrows 1997). This means that most local authority and housing association estates are characterised not only by concentrations of families and single people with significant levels of social need, but they are also subject to high levels of turnover. Some of the consequences of these processes of 'residualisation' have been highlighted by Hanley (2007), who grew up on a large public housing estate and subsequently moved to an area that went into a spiral of decline. Combining policy analysis with personal experience, she has produced a graphic portrait of the impact on families, who are all under great pressure, living alongside each other and reacting in ways which create serious difficulties for their neighbours.

Families experiencing stigmatisation in their local areas

Some families who are already burdened with problems at a number of different levels may have their difficulties compounded by the hostile attitudes of their neighbours. Frequently this is the result of either racial and cultural differences, as in the case of asylum-seeking or refugee families (see, for example, Gill and Jack 2007, pp.68–70), or standards of child care, with families ostracised because of the way in which their children are perceived to behave and the difficulties they are thought to cause in the local neighbourhood (see, for example, Gill and Jack 2007, pp.115–17).

Families put under undue pressure by others for support

As noted already in this chapter, social support can be complex and is often reciprocal in nature. Some parents or caregivers, who are themselves under great pressure, may also be regularly called upon by others to give support, which can be experienced as an additional source of stress (see, for example, Gill and Jack 2007, pp.107–8).

Once again, the balance between the supportive and stressful aspects of relationships within the community underlines the importance of the practitioner developing a clear picture of the wider social context in which families are living. Equally important is an understanding of how the parent or caregiver is able to access the support available in the community. As Horwath (2007, p.115) notes: 'parenting in a disadvantaged community requires very skilled interactions between the carer, the child and other members of the community'. The parent who is highly stressed, anxious or depressed may not have the capacity to undertake these skilled interactions.

Support from community organisations and faith or ethnic communities

In most areas of the country, including the most disadvantaged neighbourhoods, there are likely to be community organisations which have the potential to make a significant impact on the lives of families and children. In relation to the assessment of children in need, these organisations, which are typically involved in providing advice and support services and positive activities for local people, may be rich sources of information about the circumstances of particular families and children. The people involved in running these organisations are likely to have well-developed family and friendship networks in the local area themselves, as well as possibly having had experience of being parents or grandparents in the neighbourhood, enabling them to understand and empathise with the challenges faced by other local parents or caregivers.

The support available within faith and ethnic communities may be a particularly significant factor for some families. Such communities of interest, and the places of worship and community centres associated with them, can help to support and develop a wide range of social networks which can have a beneficial impact on the lives of families and children, including playing a direct role in children's education through supplementary or religious schools, and providing them with mentors and role models (Gill and Jack 2007).

Once again, however, it is important not to make the assumption that parents or caregivers who belong to particular faith communities will necessarily have links with local sources of support. Lack of accessibility, interpersonal difficulties, social isolation and recent arrival in the area can all be important reasons for parents or caregivers not benefiting from the networks of support potentially available within their faith or ethnic communities.

As indicated above, the significance of the role of local community organisations and faith communities in the lives of some children and young people raises the question of whether those involved should play any part in child welfare assessments. Whilst their contribution may potentially be highly significant, ethical practice dictates that their involvement should always be discussed with the parent or caregiver (and, if appropriate, the child) first, in the context of clear understandings about the boundaries of confidentiality.

The social world of the child outside the family

The lives of children and young people will, to a greater or lesser extent, be influenced by the quality of the relationships, support and social integration of their parents or caregivers, with difficulties in these areas likely to have a significant impact on the child. However, from the age of about two onwards, children will also be developing friendships of their own, becoming part of a progressively complex social world, which is only partly determined by the characteristics and circumstances of their parents or caregivers.

It is important to talk to children and young people directly about their social relationships outside the family. Although parents or caregivers may offer important insights into this world, it is no substitute for direct discussions or other forms of communication with the child. These discussions can helpfully be framed around the themes of support and danger, exploring the good things about the child's contact with people outside the immediate family, and any threats or difficulties associated with particular people or places. For example, are there certain times of the day or particular locations that cause difficulties for the child, such as their journeys to and from school or accessing local facilities, such as play areas or shops? Discussion of these sorts of issues will allow the practitioner to gain valuable information about the positive and negative aspects of a child's life, from the child's own perspective. Most particularly, the worker should gather information relating to issues such as the child's friendships, where they live, and any experiences of bullying and harassment that they may be experiencing.

Friendships

The importance of friendships for children's development and sense of wellbeing should not be underestimated. Children and young people consulted as part of *The Good Childhood Inquiry* conducted by the Children's Society, for example, made it clear that, along with their family, friendships were the most important thing in their lives (Children's Society 2007). Furthermore, relationships with peers, both within and outside of school, tend to become increasingly important as young people go through their teenage years and approach the transition to early adulthood. This is illustrated in a number of studies conducted in different parts of the UK (for example, MacDonald and Marsh 2005) which have demonstrated the central importance of informal social networks in most aspects of young people's lives.

Ecological theory makes it clear that the nature and extent of children's and young people's social networks is likely to be dependent on a wide range of other factors at individual, family and community levels (Jack and Gill 2003). For instance, there are some clear links between children's economic circumstances and the quality and range of their social relationships, as evidenced by a study in Scotland involving in-depth interviews with children about their everyday experiences of inequality, in which the effect of their impoverished circumstances on their social relationships was often at least as important to them as their lack of access to material resources (Backett-Milburn *et al.* 2003). Much the same point was made in a systematic review of the evidence from qualitative studies of children living in circumstances of economic disadvantage across the UK which concluded that, for many of them, life can be a struggle to avoid being set apart from friends and peers because of their material disadvantages (Attree 2006).

The influence of housing and location

Other factors, such as those linked to children's housing circumstances and geographical location, also influence their social networks. For example, children and young people whose families are facing major housing difficulties, such as periods in temporary accommodation or homelessness, are also likely to experience serious disruption to important social activities and relationships with friends, relatives, teachers and other trusted adults of the kind that are known to be important in fostering resilience (Jones 2004; Newman 2004). Other studies have revealed the influence of living in either urban or rural settings on young people's behaviour and social relationships. For example, in one study young people living in urban areas were found to be more reluctant to travel independently to visit friends or participate in social activities than their peers living in suburban or rural locations because of their perceptions about personal safety, access, and traffic danger (Jones *et al.* 2000). Perceptions of young people, about levels of safety in their local areas, are also one of the major reasons cited by them for gathering together in social groups, or 'gangs', when they are out of the house. Whilst youngsters in urban or inner-city areas tend to view gathering together in this way as essential for their self-protection, those in suburban or rural locations tend to view it as serving more of a social function (Jones *et al.* 2000; Seaman *et al.* 2006).

Bullying and harassment

One particularly negative aspect of children's social worlds that has attracted increased attention in recent years is bullying, which is linked to psychological problems later in life, for both victims and perpetrators. Whilst the full extent of this problem is still not clear, it is now recognised as a common experience in childhood (Children's Society 2007), with the central importance of safety to children's everyday lives having been recognised by the Government with the development of the *Staying Safe: Action Plan* (HM Government 2008).

In an early study, conducted in the 1990s in various settings across England and Wales, including primary and secondary schools, youth clubs and children's homes, over a third of the children and young people interviewed about difficulties in their lives said that their worst experiences had involved bullying at school. In fact, the study revealed that bullying was perceived as a 'terrifying' but almost 'natural' part of school life, as illustrated by the following quotes:

> Older kids are always pushing me around, piss-taking, laughing at me. I don't know why. I haven't done anything to them. Every day when I have to go to school, I get frightened that they're going to pick on me again today. I just try and hide and hope they don't see me. (Boy, 12)

> The bullying at school can be really nasty. Sometimes, just before break time, I start to shake in class because I'm so scared about going outside. (Girl, 13)

> (Butler and Williamson 1994, pp. 53–4)

More recent research suggests that these problems have not only been exacerbated by the development of new technology, including mobile phones and social networking sites on the internet, but also that they may be particularly prevalent in the UK. Recent international comparisons of child wellbeing, for example, have revealed that children in the UK have the poorest peer relationships in the European Union (Bradshaw *et al.* 2006; UNICEF 2007), and surveys of children's and young people's views confirm that bullying and related behaviours, such as racial harassment, are major concerns for many of them (for example, see Gill and Jack 2007, pp.65–6).

Racial harassment, which is now experienced by many children and their parents or caregivers living in the UK, including members of asylum-seeking and refugee families, can range from name calling and graffiti, to attacks on property and the person. Such harassment can have a major impact on the life of the child at many different levels. It can make the child feel less safe, less able to go outside the house and therefore less able to stay healthy or achieve his or her full potential. It can also have a significant impact on the emotional health of the child. These consequences may be further exacerbated if the child feels unsupported in the family. For instance, a dual-heritage child may be living with a white single parent who is ill equipped to effectively support the child. At a wider level, incidents of racial harassment can also have a negative impact on overall community cohesion, which can affect the life of the child because of a reduction in 'neighbourliness' and

Table 22.1: The strengths and pressures model of family and community support

STRENGTHS		PRESSURES	
Parents	Children and young people	Parents	Children and young people
Natural networks in the community			
Long-term residence of families. Non-threatening relations with immediate neighbours. Balanced community– mixed age range. Reciprocal 'helping' relationships in community.	Established and supportive social networks of children and young people. Positive contact between children and young people and significant adults from different generations in community.	High level of transience and homelessness. Culture of people 'keeping themselves to themselves'. Limited links between wider family and community networks. Social isolation. Networks produce demands rather than support.	Lack of positive contact with range of people in community. Social networks disrupted by transience. Limited links between school and community networks. Lack of access to safe meeting places.
Community norms about parenting			
Established positive community norms about parenting.	Positive sense of identity and belonging conveyed by community norms.	Lack of established positive community norms around parenting.	Community norms convey a negative sense of identity and belonging to some children and young people (for example due to poverty, BME background or disability).
The individual in the community			
Personal resources and knowledge to access available facilities. Personal resources to develop and maintain reciprocal supportive networks. Perception that local facilities are open to their family. Strong family relationships that support resilience and counter external stress.	Confidence in using available facilities and opportunities. Involved in supportive local networks with other children and young people. Perception that facilities are open to them.	Lack of personal resources or knowledge to access available facilities. Personal demands too high to develop reciprocal supportive relationships. Alienates potential sources of support. Perception that facilities are not open to their family.	Lack of personal resources to access available facilities, networks and opportunities. Alienates other children and young people. Perceptions that facilities are not open to them (for example due to poverty, BME background or disability).

other social networks, lack of safe access to public spaces, and the general heightening of neighbourhood tensions.

However, despite the increased attention that these issues have received in the media, as well as within school, social work and police anti-bullying and anti-harassment policies, many children and young people still think that not enough is being done to address the problems that some of them are experiencing on a daily basis (Awad *et al.* 2006; Children's Society 2007). Furthermore, like other aspects of children's social ecologies, bullying and racial harassment do not occur in a vacuum, and will often be linked to other factors at individual, family and community levels – once again illustrating the importance of seeing the whole child, and the way in which issues in one area of their life are likely to interact with those in others.

From theory to practice: the strengths and pressures model

In order to bring together the main points made in this chapter in the form of a practice tool that can be used in assessments, we have adapted the strengths and pressures model, put forward in an earlier publication by the authors (Jack and Gill 2003), to cover the issues relevant to assessing the impact of informal family and community support on parents or caregivers and their children (see Table 22.1).

Practitioners working within children's services who are undertaking assessments of children's needs can use the table to identify the balance between the strengths and pressures that exist within a particular family's or child's social networks, as well as considering the way that the main features are influencing one another. All of this should be openly shared with the adults and children concerned, enabling them to identify the issues that are of most significance in their lives or that require further exploration.

Summary

Exploring the social networks of parents or caregivers and children, both within their extended families and their wider communities, should not be seen by practitioners as a separate area of enquiry from the assessment of issues within the household. In the real lives of families, not only are there distinct and observable informal support processes operating at both family and community levels, but these processes also interact with each other. Strengths and pressures at a family level are likely to have an impact on how family members function at the community level, whilst those at the community level are equally likely to influence what happens within the family.

However, as suggested at the beginning of this chapter, incorporating these external aspects of the family's and child's world into assessments will often require that practitioners widen their normal perspective, which has traditionally focused on what happens *within* families. Beyond assessments, this broadening of perspective also needs to be incorporated into service responses and other interventions. It makes little sense to utilise the ecological framework discussed in this chapter to develop more holistic assessments if they have little or no impact on the subsequent actions taken to contribute to the wellbeing of children and families. Widening assessments to incorporate an understanding of how parenting and the development of children and young people are either supported or undermined by their informal social networks also means developing a form of 'ecological practice' that can effectively connect the internal and external worlds of the family (Gill and Jack 2007).

Recommended reading

Awad, A., Gill, O., Thomas, R., Hussein, Y., Noor, K. and Wiltshire, P. (2006) *Somali Children in Bristol: Achieving the Five Outcomes from Every Child Matters*. Bristol: Barnardo's.

Children's Society (2007) *Good Childhood: What You Told Us About Friends*. Available at www.childrenssociety.org.uk/resources/documents/good%20childhood/Friends%20evidence%20summary_2721_full/pdf, accessed on 13 July 2009

Ghate, D. and Hazel, N. (2002) *Parenting in Poor Environments*. London: Jessica Kingsley Publishers.

Gill, O. and Jack, G. (2007) *The Child and Family in Context: Developing Ecological Practice in Disadvantaged Communities*. Lyme Regis: Russell House Publishing.

References

Attree, P. (2006) 'The social costs of child poverty: a systematic review of the qualitative evidence.' *Children & Society 20*, 54–66.

Awad, A., Gill, O., Thomas, R., Hussein, Y., Noor, K. and Wiltshire, P. (2006) *Somali Children in Bristol: Achieving the Five Outcomes from Every Child Matters*. Bristol: Barnardo's.

Backett-Milburn, K., Cunningham-Burley, S. and Davis, J. (2003) 'Contrasting lives, contrasting views? Understandings of health inequalities from children in different social circumstances.' *Social Science and Medicine 57*, 4, 613–623.

Barnes, J. (2004) *Place and Parenting: A Study of Four Communities*. London: Institute for the Study of Children, Families and Social Issues, Birkbeck College, University of London.

Belsky, J. (1993) 'Etiology of child maltreatment: a developmental-ecological process.' *Psychological Bulletin 114*, 413–434.

Blaxter, M. (1990) *Health and Lifestyles*. London: Routledge.

Bradshaw, J., Hoelscher, P. and Richardson, D. (2006) 'An index of child well-being in the European Union.' *Social Indicators Research 80*, 1, 133–177.

Brassard, J. (1982) *Beyond Family Structure: Mother–Child Interaction and Personal Social Networks* (unpublished doctoral dissertation). Ithaca, NY: Cornell University.

Bronfenbrenner, U. (1979) *The Ecology of Human Development*. Cambridge, MA: Harvard University Press.

Burrows, R. (1997) *Contemporary Patterns of Residential Mobility in Relation to Social Housing in England*. York: Centre for Housing Policy, University of York.

Butler, I. and Williamson, H. (1994) *Children Speak: Children, Trauma and Social Work*. Harlow: Longman/NSPCC.

Children's Society (2007) *Good Childhood: What You Told Us About Friends*. Available at www.schildrenssociety.org.uk/resources/documents/good%20childhood/Friends%20evidence%20summary–2721–full.pdf, accessed on 13 July 2009.

Cochran, M. (1993) 'Parenting and Personal Social Networks.' In T. Luster and L. Okagaki (eds) *Parenting: An Ecological Perspective*. Hillsdale, NJ: Lawrence Erlbaum Associates.

Cochran, M.M. and Brassard, J.A. (1979) 'Child development and personal social networks.' *Child Development 50*, 601–615.

Cohen, S., Underwood, L.G. and Gottlieb, B.H. (2000) *Social Support Measurement and Intervention*. New York: Oxford University Press.

Coohey, C. (1996) 'Child maltreatment: testing the social isolation hypothesis.' *Child Abuse and Neglect 20*, 3, 241–254.

Coulthard, M., Walker, A. and Morgan, A. (2002) *People's Perceptions of their Neighbourhood and Community Involvement*. London: The Stationery Office.

Crittenden, P.M. (1985) 'Social networks, quality of child rearing and child development.' *Child Development 56*, 1299–1313.

Deater-Deckard, K. (2001) 'Annotation: recent research examining the role of peer relationships in the development of psychopathology.' *Journal of Child Psychology and Psychiatry 42*, 5, 565–579.

Department of Health, Department for Education and Employment and Home Office (2000) *Framework for the Assessment of Children in Need and their Families*. London: The Stationery Office.

Dunn, J. (1993) *Young Children's Close Relationships: Beyond Attachment*. Newbury Park, CA: Sage.

Dunst, C.J., Trivette, C.M. and Jodry, W. (1997) 'Influences of Social Support on Children with Disabilities and their Families.' In M.J. Guralnick (ed.) *The Effectiveness of Early Intervention*. Baltimore, MA: Paul H. Brookes.

Garbarino, J. and Crouter, A. (1978) 'Defining the community context for parent–child relations: the correlates of child maltreatment.' *Child Development 49*, 604–616.

Garbarino, J. and Sherman, D. (1980) 'High-risk neighborhoods and high-risk families: the human ecology of child maltreatment.' *Child Development 51*, 188–198.

Gardner, R. (2003) *Supporting Families: Child Protection in the Community*. Chichester: John Wiley.

Ghate, D. and Hazel, N. (2002) *Parenting in Poor Environments*. London: Jessica Kingsley Publishers.

Gibbons, J. (1990) *Family Support and Prevention: Studies in Local Areas*. London: HMSO.

Gill, O. and Jack, G. (2007) *The Child and Family in Context: Developing Ecological Practice in Disadvantaged Communities*. Lyme Regis: Russell House Publishing.

Gill, O., Tanner, C. and Bland, L. (2000) *Family Support: Strengths and Pressures in a 'High-risk' Neighbourhood*. Barkingside: Barnardo's.

Gilligan, R. (1998) 'The importance of schools and teachers in child welfare.' *Child and Family Social Work 3*, 1, 13–25.

Hanley, L. (2007) *Estates: An Intimate History*. London: Granta.

Hashima, P.Y. and Amato, P.R. (1994) 'Poverty, social support and parental behaviour.' *Child Development 65*, 394–403.

Hawkes, D. and Joshi, H. (2007) *Millennium Cohort Study Second Survey: A Guide to Initial Findings* (Ch. 4, Grandparents). London: Centre for Longitudinal Studies, Institute of Education, University of London.

HM Government (2008) *Staying Safe: Action Plan*. London: DCSF.

Horwath, J. (2007) *Child Neglect: Identification and Assessment*. Basingstoke: Palgrave Macmillan.

Jack, G. (1997) 'An ecological approach to social work with children and families.' *Child and Family Social Work 2*, 2, 109–120.

Jack, G. (2000) 'Ecological influences on parenting and child development.' *British Journal of Social Work 30*, 703–720.

Jack, G. (2004) 'Child protection at the community level.' *Child Abuse Review 13*, 368–383.

Jack, G. (2006) 'The area and community components of children's well-being.' *Children and Society 20*, 334–347.

Jack, G. and Gill, O. (2003) *The Missing Side of the Triangle: Assessing the Importance of Family and Environmental Factors in the Lives of Children*. Barkingside: Barnardo's.

Jones, L., Davis, A. and Eyers, T. (2000) 'Young people, transport and risk: Comparing access and individual mobility in urban, suburban and rural environments.' *Health Education Journal 59*, 315–328.

Jones, S. (2004) *Toying with their Future: The Hidden Costs of the Housing Crisis*. London: Shelter.

MacDonald, R. and Marsh, J. (2005) *Disconnected Youth? Growing Up in Britain's Poor Neighbourhoods*. Basingstoke: Palgrave.

Masten, A.S. and Coatsworth, J.D. (1998) 'The development of competence in favourable and unfavourable environments.' *American Psychologist 53*, 2, 205–220.

National Centre for Social Research (1999) *British Social Attitudes Survey 1999*. Abingdon: Ashgate.

Newman, T. (2004) *What Works in Building Resilience?* Barkingside: Barnardo's.

Polansky, N.A., Ammons, P.W. and Gaudin, J.M. (1985) 'Loneliness and isolation in child neglect.' *Social Casework 66*, 38–47.

Prasad, R. (2000) 'Poll reveals crucial role of grandparents.' *The Guardian*, 14th Dec.

Sarason, B.R., Sarason, I.G. and Pierce, G.R. (eds) (1990) *Social Support: An International View*. New York, NY: Wiley.

Seaman, P., Turner, K., Hill, M., Stafford, A. and Walker, M. (2006) *Parenting and Children's Resilience in Disadvantaged Communities*. London: National Children's Bureau.

Sheppard, M. (1994) 'Childcare, social support and maternal depression: A review of the evidence and application of findings.' *British Journal of Social Work 24*, 287–310.

Tracey, E.M. and Whittaker, J.K. (1990) 'The social network map: Assessing social support in clinical practice.' *Families in Society 71*, 8, 461–470.

UNICEF (2007) *An Overview of Child Well-being in Rich Countries*. Florence: UNICEF Innocenti Research Centre.

Warren, C. (1993) *Family Centres and the Children Act 1989*. Arundel: Tarrant.

The Contributors

Jo Aldridge is a lecturer in social policy in the Department of Social Sciences at Loughborough University. She is also director of the Young Carers Research Group (www.ycrg.org.uk) at Loughborough, which is known both nationally and internationally for its pioneering work on young carers.

Arnon Bentovim is a child and adolescent psychiatrist. He established the sexual abuse assessment and intervention service at Great Ormond Street Children's Hospital, and was responsible for child protection at the hospital. Since retiring he established Child and Family Training, an organisation which develops and trains practitioners in evidence-based approaches to assessment and intervention. He has written widely in the field, most recently *Safeguarding Children Living with Trauma and Family Violence* (2009).

James Bickley is a chartered consultant clinical psychologist working in the field of forensic child and adolescent mental health. He provides supervision, consultation and training to a range of organisations working with young people who sexually offend, including the Lucy Faithfull Foundation, G-Map and NSPCC. Dr Bickley is an honorary lecturer at the University of Birmingham and has presented at various international conferences.

Helen Bradshaw is a social worker who has worked extensively in delivering and developing services within the field of sexual abuse, initially with adults for the National Probation Service. More recently she has focused specifically on young people and their families whilst working for the Lucy Faithfull Foundation and the AIM Project, prior to joining G-Map as service manager in 2005.

Hedy Cleaver is an emeritus professor at Royal Holloway College, University of London. Her experience as a social worker and child psychologist has informed her research on vulnerable children and families and the impact of professional interventions. The guiding principle underpinning her work is a desire to improve the quality of life for children living in circumstances that place them at risk of abuse or neglect. Recent publications include: *Child Protection, Domestic*

Violence and Parental Substance Misuse (2007); *Parental Learning Disability and Children's Needs* (2007); *The Integrated Children's System* (2008); and *Safeguarding Children: A Shared Responsibility* (2009).

Chris Dearden is a research fellow in the Centre for Research in Social Policy in the Department of Social Sciences at Loughborough University and a member of the Young Carers Research Group.

Ratna Dutt is a qualified social worker and is presently Chief Executive of Race Equality Foundation (formerly REU), a registered charity working to improve support for black and minority ethnic communities in Britain. Ratna has written extensively on social care issues, including: a chapter in the Practice Guidance that forms part of the *Framework for the Assessment of Children in Need and their Families* entitled 'Assessing black children in need and their families'; *Letting through Light, Learning Materials on Mental Health and Black Communities* (1998); and *Meeting the Challenge: A Good Practice Guide for the Recruitment and Retention of Black and Minority Ethnic Workers* (2005). Ratna received an OBE in 2000 for her work in race equality.

Marcus Erooga is an NSPCC learning and development adviser and the professional adviser (child sexual abuse). He is a past editor and current board member of the *Journal of Sexual Aggression*. He has authored and edited some 25 publications on child protection related issues, including *Children and Young People who Sexually Abuse Others – Challenges and Responses* (2006, edited with Helen Masson). Marcus is an honorary visiting research fellow at the University of Huddersfield's Centre for Childhood Studies and is chair of the National Organisation for the Treatment of Abusers (NOTA).

Owen Gill has more than 30 years' experience as a researcher and practitioner working with the connections between children and their communities. Research for his PhD investigated the links between housing provision and patterns of adolescent delinquency, and he has worked as a practitioner with children and families in a wide range of settings, including both rural and inner-city communities. In his current post as anti-poverty co-ordinator for Barnardo's South West he manages a range of community development projects, as well as researching the various impacts of poverty on children's lives.

Robbie Gilligan is professor of social work and social policy at Trinity College Dublin, where he is also head of the School of Social Work and Social Policy, and associate director (and co-founder) of the Children's Research Centre. He has been a youth worker, social worker and foster carer. He has a wide range of publications including *Promoting Resilience* (2009) from British Agencies for Adoption and Fostering.

Danya Glaser is consultant child and adolescent psychiatrist at Great Ormond Street Children's Hospital, London. She maintains a longstanding clinical and academic involvement with all aspects of child maltreatment, including the effects of child maltreatment on the developing brain. She has recently co-authored a book on the evidence base on attachment and attachment disorders. Dr Glaser is immediate past president of ISPCAN, chair of the NICE guideline development group for When to Suspect Child Maltreatment and visiting professor at UCL.

Rosemary Gordon is an independent consultant in social care, specialising in the safeguarding of children and young people. She previously worked as head of consultancy services for the NSPCC and worked for the organisation for almost 20 years as a child protection team manager, trainer and manager of learning resources. She began her career as a probation officer. Her sector experience is wide and over the past ten years she has been working with numerous organisations in the statutory, voluntary, commercial and independent sectors. She has a strong commitment to the inclusion of disabled children in all her work.

Di Hart worked for many years as a child care social worker and manager before taking up a practice development post at the National Children's Bureau. She has a particular interest in children in secure settings. Recent work has included a review of the use of physical restraint in secure children's homes, the development of a care-planning model for looked after children who go into custody and a project aiming to improve outcomes for the children of drug-misusing parents.

Enid Hendry is director of Child Protection Training and Consultancy and Safeguarding Information Systems for the NSPCC. She is social work qualified and has extensive experience of inter-agency working and training. She was independent chair of two area child protection committees and a founder member of PIAT (Promoting Inter-Agency Training). She has published extensively on training and child protection, most recently publishing a chapter in *Safeguarding Children and Schools* (2008). Enid is on the management and steering groups for the Child Protection in Sport Unit and led the task force developing standards for safeguarding children in sport. She was also on the management board for COPCA (Catholic Office for the Protection of Children and Vulnerable Adults). Enid gave evidence to the Nolan Inquiry into abuse in the Catholic Church and to Lord Laming's Inquiry on the death of Victoria Climbié.

Sally Holland is a senior lecturer in social work in Cardiff University's School of Social Sciences. She is a former social worker in statutory and voluntary sector children's services. She has researched and published widely in the field of children's welfare, including assessment of parenting, family group conferences and participative research with looked after children. Her current research includes perceptions of children's risk and safety in neighbourhoods, evaluating the effectiveness of a substance misuse intervention for parents and life-history research with care leavers.

Jan Horwath is professor of child welfare at the University of Sheffield. She has a social work background. Jan has particular research interests in assessment practice, neglect, multidisciplinary collaboration and strategic leadership. She has contributed to the development of assessment frameworks in England, Ireland and South Africa. Jan is the author of a number of publications on child care practice; her most recent relevant book is *Child Neglect: Identification and Assessment* (2007).

David Howe is professor of social work at the University of East Anglia, Norwich. He has research interests in emotional development, adoption, developmental attachment theory, and child abuse and neglect. He is the author of many books, including most recently *Child Abuse and Neglect: Attachment, Development and Intervention* (2005), *The Emotionally Intelligent Social Worker* (2008) and *A Brief Introduction to Social Work Theory* (2009). David Howe was the founding editor of the journal *Child and Family Social Work* and is an associate editor of the journal *Attachment and Human Development*.

Norma Howes is a social worker, psychologist and psychotherapist. Norma is involved in training multi-agency staff on all aspects of childhood trauma and abuse. She has a private practice working with adults and children who have experienced severe childhood trauma. Norma was also a member of a child trauma team for 12 years assessing the therapeutic work with children who had experienced Type 1 and Type 2 trauma.

Gordon Jack is a reader in social work at Durham University and has been involved in social work education and practice with children and families for over 30 years. His research examines the links between the wellbeing of children and young people and their wider family and community circumstances, highlighting in particular the influences of poverty and other forms of inequality and disadvantage. He continues to teach and publish widely on these issues, including writing *The Child and Family in Context* with Owen Gill (2007), which considers the development of ecological practice in disadvantaged communities.

David Jones is an honorary senior lecturer and consultant child psychiatrist at the University of Oxford, Department of Psychiatry, Warneford Hospital, Oxford. He formerly led, and now consults to, a multidisciplinary child psychiatric clinical team providing services for abused children and their families. He has researched and published widely in the fields of child abuse and neglect, and consent to treatment among children.

Ruth Marchant works with very young children and children with communication impairments, usually where there are concerns about maltreatment, particularly sexual abuse. Ruth is a registered intermediary with the Ministry of Justice. Ruth has taught and published widely on these issues, including contributing to the guidance on interviewing disabled children within *Achieving Best Evidence* (Home Office), and the *Practice Guidance on Assessing Disabled Children* within the *Framework for the Assessment of Children in Need and their Families*. Ruth is a founding director of Triangle which works with children across the UK and also provides training and consultancy.

Tony Morrison is an independent child welfare trainer and consultant from Rochdale. He works both in the UK and overseas with children's services, health, criminal justice and other agencies on inter-agency collaboration, multidisciplinary leadership, supervision, assessment and practice development. He has been widely involved in development work with LSCBs and other partnerships and has recently completed a research project with Jan Horwath for the Welsh Assembly Government to benchmark LSCB performance. His published work includes papers on partnership and collaboration, and books on staff supervision, effective training and the management and treatment of young people with sexual behaviour problems. He is a visiting research fellow at the University of Huddersfield. In 1998 he was awarded an MBE for his work in promoting inter-agency co-ordination in the field of public protection.

Melanie Phillips is a social worker of Asian origin. She has 29 years' experience in children and family social work, initially as a social worker and senior practitioner in a number of London authorities, and subsequently providing independent social work, training, supervision and consultancy on child care as well as undertaking research on child protection practice. She is also an independent chair for a London Safeguarding Board and is an independent lecturer for Greenwich University's Safeguarding Children and Young People masters course. Melanie has written extensively on child protection and black and minority ethnic families, was a member of the advisory group that developed the *Framework for the Assessment of Children in Need and their Families* and co-wrote a chapter in the practice guide *Assessing the Needs of Black Children and their Families.*

Bobbie Print is a social worker and director of G-MAP Services, a therapeutic programme for young people who have sexually harmed. She is an honorary lecturer at the University of Birmingham's Department of Forensic and Family Psychology. Bobbie has worked for 20 years with young people who sexually harm and has published and trained widely on the subject during that period.

Wendy Rose is a senior research fellow at the Open University. She is a former senior civil servant advising on children's policy. She has a background in child welfare practice, policy and management. She works on national and international research and development projects, and has published widely. In England, she was involved in the development of the *Assessment Framework for Children in Need and their Families.* She is currently a professional adviser to the Scottish Government.

Peter Sidebotham is a senior lecturer in child health at the University of Warwick. He is also a practising consultant paediatrician and designated doctor for child protection in Warwickshire. Alongside his clinical work, he is actively involved in research and teaching in relation to child protection, unexpected childhood death and parenting. He has published extensively on child abuse and childhood death, and is on the editorial boards of *Child Abuse Review* and *Child Abuse and Neglect.*

Nicky Stanley is professor of social work at the University of Central Lancashire. She has a background in social work and researches and publishes widely in the areas of parents' and young people's mental health, child protection and domestic violence and interprofessional work. Recent studies include reviews of policy and professional education in relation to parental mental health and child welfare and a study of police notifications of domestic violence to children's services. She is co-editor of *Child Abuse Review.*

Harriet Ward is a professor at Loughborough University and director of the Centre for Child and Family Research. The principal function of the research centre is to carry out policy-relevant research on services for vulnerable children and adults, in particular the outcomes of services for children in need. Professor Ward led the Looking After Children programme (1993–2001) and current research projects include a prospective study of babies identified as being at risk of significant harm, studies on costs and outcomes of providing services for children in need, and transitions to adulthood of young people in care.

Mary Weeks is the designated nurse for child protection in Warwickshire. Her qualifications include midwifery and health visiting, following her initial training in London as a registered general nurse. She moved to Warwickshire initially as a community manager before moving to child protection and safeguarding children in the mid-1990s. She is an active member of the West Midlands branch of BASPCAN.

Subject Index

Author Index